70% of composition instructors indicate that the quality of the professional selections is a top consideration for their course.

I Remember Masa[1]
BY JOSÉ ANTONIO BURCIAGA

My earliest memory of *tortillas* is my *Mamá* telling me not to play with them. I had bitten eyeholes in one and was wearing it as a mask at the dinner table. As a child, I also used *tortillas* as hand warmers on cold days, and my family claims that I owe my career as an artist to my early experiments with *tortillas*. According to them, my clowning around helped me develop a strong artistic foundation. I'm not so sure, though. Sometimes I wore a *tortilla* on my head, like a *yarmulke*,[2] and yet I never had any great urge to convert from Catholicism to Judaism. But who knows? They may be right.

As you read
Think about why tortillas are so important to the author.

3   For Mexicans over the centuries, the *tortilla* has served as the spoon and the fork, the plate and the napkin. *Tortillas* originated before the Mayan civilizations, perhaps predating Europe's wheat bread. According to Mayan mythology, the great god Quetzalcoatl, realizing that the red ants knew the secret of using maize as food, transformed himself into a black ant, infiltrated the colony of red ants, and absconded with a grain of corn. (Is it any wonder that to this day, black ants and red-ants do not get along?)

> In *Patterns for a Purpose*, quality professional reading selections provide students with models of the patterns in action.

P9-CRU-802

84% of composition instructors emphasize the fundamentals of academic writing (critical reading, argument, evaluating sources).

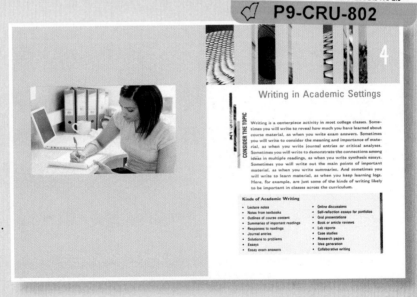

Writing in Academic Settings

CONSIDER THE TOPIC

Writing is a centerpiece activity in most college classes. Sometimes you will write to reveal how much you have learned about course material, as when you write exam answers. Sometimes you will write to consider the meaning and importance of material, as when you write journal entries or critical analyses. Sometimes you will write to demonstrate the connections among ideas in multiple readings, as when you write synthesis essays. Sometimes you will write out the main points of important material, as when you write summaries. And sometimes you will write to learn material, as when you keep learning logs. Here, for example, are just some of the kinds of writing likely to be important in classes across the curriculum.

Kinds of Academic Writing

- Lecture notes
- Notes from textbooks
- Outlines of course content
- Summaries of important readings
- Responses to readings
- Journal entries
- Solutions to problems
- Essays
- Essay exam answers
- Online discussions
- Self-reflection essays for portfolios
- Oral presentations
- Book or article reviews
- Lab reports
- Case studies
- Research papers
- Idea generation
- Collaborative writing

> The Sixth Edition of *Patterns for a Purpose* offers a new chapter, Writing In Academic Settings.

If you would like to participate in any of the McGraw-Hill research initiatives please contact us **at www.mhhe.com/faculty-research.**

Patterns for a Purpose

A RHETORICAL READER

Sixth Edition

Barbara Fine Clouse

Connect
Learn
Succeed™

For Denny, with love and admiration

The McGraw·Hill Companies

Mc Graw Hill

Connect
Learn
Succeed™

Published by McGraw-Hill, an imprint of The McGraw-Hill Companies, Inc., 1221 Avenue of the Americas, New York, NY 10020. Copyright © 2011, 2009, 2006, 2003, 1999, 1995. All rights reserved. No part of this publication may be reproduced or distributed in any form or by any means, or stored in a database or retrieval system, without the prior written consent of The McGraw-Hill Companies, Inc., including, but not limited to, in any network or other electronic storage or transmission, or broadcast for distance learning.

9 10 LCR 22 21 20

ISBN: 978-0-07-338395-8
MHID: 0-07-338395-3

Editor in Chief: *Michael Ryan*
Publisher: *David Patterson*
Director of Development: *Dawn Groundwater*
Senior Sponsoring Editor: *Christopher Bennem*
Marketing Manager: *Tierra Morgan*
Developmental Editor: *Randee Falk*
Editorial Coordinator: *Jesse Hassenger*
Production Editor: *Regina Ernst*
Manuscript Editor: *Thomas Briggs*

Design Manager: *Ashley Bedell*
Cover Designer: *Asylum Studios*
Photo Research/Manager: *Brian Pecko*
Buyer II: *Louis Swaim*
Permissions Editor: *Marty Moga*
Composition: *10/12 Palatino by Aptara®, Inc.*
Printing: *45# Pub Matte Plus, LSC Communications*

Cover: © Michael Betts/Photographer's Choice/Getty Images; © Joe Petersburger/National Geographic/Getty Images; © Comstock Images/Getty Images

Credits: The credits section for this book begins on page C-1 and is considered an extension of the copyright page.

Library of Congress Cataloging-in-Publication Data
Clouse, Barbara Fine.
  Patterns for a purpose : a rhetorical reader / Barbara Fine Clouse. — 6th ed.
    p. cm.
  Includes bibliographical references and index.
  ISBN-13: 978-0-07-338395-8 (acid-free paper)
  ISBN-10: 0-07-338395-3 (acid-free paper) 1. College readers. 2. English language—
Rhetoric—Problems, exercises, etc. 3. Report writing—Problems, exercises, etc. I. Title.
  PE1417.C6314 2011
  808'.0427—dc22

                                                           2010043884

The Internet addresses listed in the text were accurate at the time of publication. The inclusion of a Web site does not indicate an endorsement by the authors or McGraw-Hill, and McGraw-Hill does not guarantee the accuracy of the information presented at these sites.

www.mhhe.com

CHAPTER 6

Narration

CHAPTER 9

Comparison-Contrast

CHAPTER 10

Cause-and-Effect Analysis

CHAPTER 11

Classification and Division

CHAPTER 14

Combining Patterns of Development

CHAPTER 15

Locating, Evaluating, and Drawing on Sources

Language and Communication

Physical Appearance

The Law and Justice

Places with Special Meaning

Childhood, Adolescence, Adulthood, and Death

Technology

PREFACE

Patterns for a Purpose, Sixth Edition, is a rhetorical reader that helps students use the rhetorical patterns—alone and in combination—to achieve their writing purposes. In this new edition, *Patterns for a Purpose* increases its emphasis on critical thinking and analysis, adds a focus on academic writing, includes information on writing to learn, and increases coverage of using sources and avoiding plagiarism. The text retains its detailed coverage of argumentation-persuasion, an ongoing emphasis on the writing process, a rich variety of writing opportunities, and varied reading selections, both classic and contemporary.

THE FEATURES OF *PATTERNS FOR A PURPOSE*

Patterns for a Purpose offers a unique combination of features. Many of these features have been refined across the editions and shown to be effective in the classroom. The new features—suggested by users of the book—make the text more versatile.

A Connection between Patterns and Purpose

Students learn that the patterns of development offer ways to think about a topic and help them achieve their purpose for writing.

- Students learn to use each pattern to entertain, express feelings, relate experience, inform, and/or persuade. (See, especially, "Using [the Pattern] for a Purpose" in Chapters 5–12 and Chapter 14.)
- Students learn how to use each pattern outside the writing class to achieve their writing purposes across the curriculum, at work, and in their communities. (See the sections "[The Pattern] beyond the Writing Classroom" in Chapters 5–13.)
- Students have many opportunities to use the patterns to achieve a range of writing purposes. (See, for example, "Using [the Pattern] for a Purpose" assignments in Chapters 5–14.)
- Students learn how professional writers use the patterns to achieve their writing purposes. (See the headnotes before each reading selection.)

A Focus on Combining Patterns

Students learn to combine patterns to achieve their writing purposes.

- Annotated excerpts from essays illustrate how to combine patterns for a purpose. (These excerpts are included within "Combining Patterns for a Purpose" sections in Chapters 5–13.)
- Students study how professional writers combine patterns. (See, for example, "Combined Patterns and Their Purpose(s)" headnotes and "Noting Combined Patterns" questions after the reading selections.)
- Chapter 14 focuses exclusively on combining rhetorical patterns to achieve the full range of writing purposes.
- Throughout Chapters 5–13, students have many opportunities to combine patterns to achieve a range of writing purposes. (See, for example, the "Combining Patterns" assignments after the reading selections.)

An Emphasis on Critical Reading and Thinking

Critical reading and thinking are introduced at the outset and emphasized throughout the text.

- Chapter 1 teaches students the components of critical thinking and reading, strategies for critical reading, and procedures for reading visual material critically.
- "Reading Closely and Thinking Critically" questions require students to apply critical reading and thinking skills to the reading selections.
- A new chapter on academic writing requires students to use their critical reading and thinking skills for critical analysis, summarizing, and synthesizing.
- Students learn to think critically about each of the patterns of development. (See, for example, "Thinking Critically about [the Pattern]," sections in Chapters 5–13.)
- "Analyzing and Assessing" and "Connecting and Synthesizing the Readings" assignments after each reading selection emphasize critical thinking.
- Chapter 13's casebook for argumentation-persuasion calls on students to apply their critical thinking and reading skills to synthesize and evaluate multiple perspectives on controversial issues.

Extensive Coverage of Academic Writing

Patterns for a Purpose is unique among rhetorical readers for its extensive coverage of the kinds of academic writing students are most likely to encounter across the curriculum.

- Chapter 4, "Writing in Academic Settings," teaches important academic writing strategies that will serve students in many courses:
  - writing personal responses, summaries, critical analyses, and syntheses
  - paraphrasing, summarizing, and quoting responsibly

- integrating source material
- avoiding plagiarism

- A write-to-learn section in Chapter 4 shows students how to use writing as a learning tool in all their courses.
- Writing assignments after the readings give students practice with many kinds of academic writing.

Writing Process Support for Students

Explicitly introduced and explained in Chapters 2 and 3, the writing process is reinforced throughout the rhetorical-pattern chapters.

- Chapters 2 and 3 explain practical procedures for planning an essay, developing a thesis, and drafting, revising, and editing.
- The early stages and progressive drafts of a student essay in Chapters 2 and 3 illustrate the writing process.
- "Process Guidelines" give students specific strategies for using and combining patterns of development.
- "Troubleshooting Guide" boxes throughout the text help students solve common writing problems.
- A general checklist and additional revision checklists for each pattern help students revise with confidence.
- An appendix on common grammar mistakes helps students edit more successfully.

An Emphasis on Argumentation and Persuasion

Because persuasion is a writing purpose, persuasive essays appear in most chapters. In addition, Chapter 13 is devoted to argumentation-persuasion.

- Essays in almost every chapter of readings illustrate how to use the patterns of development to persuade readers.
- Chapter 13 is an in-depth study of argumentation-persuasion that includes information on induction and deduction; logos, pathos, and ethos; and the Toulmin model.
- The casebook for argumentation-persuasion in Chapter 13 offers 11 essays on three themes related to the law and society: payment to organ donors, trying juveniles as adults, and free speech on college campuses. High-interest readings, these essays also serve as departure points for writing assignments.

Extensive Coverage of Using Source Material and Avoiding Plagiarism

Students learn to use source material responsibly throughout the book.

- Chapter 4 explains how to paraphrase, summarize, quote, and integrate source material.

- Chapter 15 explains how to locate, evaluate, and document sources.
- Three student essays illustrate how to use source material.
- "Using Sources for a Purpose" sections in Chapters 5–13 illustrate how students can quote, paraphrase, and summarize material from the readings as supporting details in their own essays. These sections include "Myths about Using Sources" to address common misunderstandings about using source material.
- "Drawing on Sources" writing assignments after the reading selections give students practice using primary and secondary sources.
- Plagiarism is treated throughout the book: Chapters 4 and 15, along with Appendix C, help students understand plagiarism and learn specific strategies for avoiding intentional and unintentional plagiarism. "Avoiding Plagiarism" discussions in the "Using Sources for a Purpose" sections of rhetorical chapters help students avoid common pitfalls.

A Rich Variety of Reading Selections

Patterns for a Purpose offers a wide range of readings to serve as both models and departure points for discussion and writing.

- With 64 professional essays, 8 literary selections, 11 student essays, and 11 textbook excerpts, *Patterns for a Purpose* now offers more readings than most modes-based readers—and more instructional variety.
- A mix of classic and contemporary pieces, from a range of cultural perspectives, focuses on themes of interest to contemporary students, including classroom violence, Internet dangers, gay marriage, graphic novels, shopping malls, hoarding behavior, and pornography on campus computers.
- Eleven annotated student essays offer both instruction and realistic models.
- Annotated textbook excerpts illustrate the instructional/informative purposes of the patterns of development and suggest their potential importance to students' own academic writing.

A Generous Number and Wide Variety of Writing Opportunities

The writing prompts and assignments help students become proficient at the kinds of personal and academic writing explained in the book.

- Each professional selection is followed by
  - an online writing and discussion prompt
  - a journal prompt
  - four or more topics for writing in the pattern for a variety of purposes
  - a topic that requires combining patterns
  - a topic that requires synthesizing ideas in multiple readings
  - a critical analysis topic
  - a topic that requires using primary or secondary sources

- Twenty additional essay topics appear at the end of each rhetorical-pattern chapter.

- "Responding to an Image" topics at the end of each rhetorical chapter ask students to write in response to an image, using the pattern under consideration.

Consideration of Visual Texts

Patterns for a Purpose helps students read visual material with a critical eye and incorporate images in their own writing.

- A detailed explanation of how to read visuals critically appears in Chapter 1.

- An appendix on document design gives students guidance in incorporating visual material into their writing.

- An explanation of how to use visuals to support a thesis appears in Chapter 3.

- Three student essays illustrate the appropriate use of visuals for support.

- "Examining Visuals" sections include a variety of images to help students identify patterns and purpose in visuals.

- Visuals in the casebook for argumentation-persuasion offer another perspective on the issue under consideration.

- "Responding to an Image" topics provide the basis for writing assignments in the pattern under discussion.

- "Consider the Topic" images that open chapters prompt students to think about the chapter focus.

New to the Sixth Edition

A number of changes make the new edition more useful to both students and instructors.

- A new chapter, "Writing in Academic Settings," focuses on the kinds of writing students will use across the curriculum: personal response, summary, critical analysis, synthesis, paraphrasing, and quoting. It also explains ways to write to learn.

- A new focus on critical analysis helps students bring their critical thinking skills to their writing.

  - Chapter 4 explains how to write a critical analysis.

  - Critical analysis topics appear after each reading under the heading "Analyzing and Assessing."

  - "Thinking Critically about [the Pattern]" sections help students analyze and assess material written in each pattern of development.

- Expanded coverage of MLA style includes much more information on online sources.

- Expanded coverage of plagiarism helps students understand what constitutes plagiarism and gives specific strategies for avoiding it.

- The text has been freshened with 12 new professional selections, three new student essays, and several new images.

ALSO IN THE SIXTH EDITION

Integrated Technology Resources

Powered by *Catalyst 2.0,* the sixth edition of *Patterns for a Purpose* provides click paths that direct students to special online resources, such as interactive tutorials that help students write papers in different rhetorical patterns; tutorials on visual rhetoric; guides for avoiding plagiarism and evaluating sources; and many more tools that support students in their writing at every stage of the writing process.

SUPPLEMENTS

Online Learning Center: www.mhhe.com/patterns

Powered by *Catalyst 2.0,* the premier online tool for writing and research, the OLC offers:

- New interactive writing tutorials for different rhetorical patterns

- Tutorials on avoiding plagiarism and evaluating sources

- Over 4,500 grammar exercises with personalized feedback for each response

- Bibliomaker software for MLA, APA, Chicago, and CSE styles of documentation

And much more.

Delivered in a state-of-the-art course management system featuring online peer-review utilities, a grade book, and communications tools, *Catalyst 2.0* is available free with *Patterns for a Purpose.*

The Instructor's Resource Manual by Barbara Fine Clouse

This manual includes helpful advice for new teachers and graduate teaching assistants along with answers to the questions that follow each reading. It is available on the password-protected instructor's side of the Online Learning Center: www.mhhe.com/patterns.

ACKNOWLEDGMENTS

For this new edition, I was fortunate to work with the more-than-capable (and always cheerful) Randee Falk, who oversaw the development process with sound judgment and grace. I am grateful for all that she brought to this project. Copy editor Tom Briggs once again improved the manuscript, and I am grateful to him. I also owe much to sponsor Christopher Bennem and director of development Dawn Groundwater. Their faith in this project has meant a great deal. Photo researcher Brian Pecko made all the wonderful images in the text possible, and Regina Ernst, who oversaw the production, tended to an impossible number of details in a timely and professional manner.

The following professors gave generously of their time and expertise. Their insights, suggestions, and criticisms were invaluable. I cannot thank them enough.

Linda Barro, *East Central College*

Sarah Bruton, *Fayetteville Technical Community College*

Christy Burns, *Jacksonville State University*

Cheryl Fenno, *Urbana University*

Darren DeFrain, *Wichita State*

Maryanne Garbowsky, *Central Community College*

Beth Harper, *Ferrum College*

Connie Holloway, *Fayetteville Technical Community College*

Leigh Kolb, *East Central College*

Vickie Melograno, *Atlantic Cape Community College*

Trista Merill, *Finger Lakes Community College*

Derek Sheffield, *Wenatchee Valley College*

Finally, for his abiding patience, unfailing support, and gentle encouragement, I thank my husband and best friend, Denny. He makes it all possible; he makes it all worthwhile.

Barbara Clouse

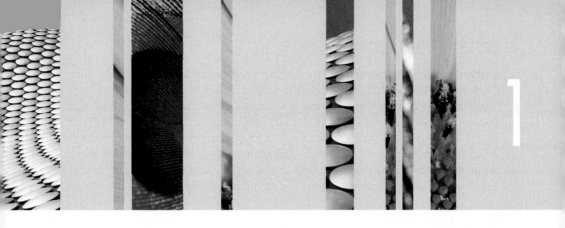

Reading Critically

When you read to relax, you can grab a well-plotted novel, put your feet up, and lose yourself in the story as the words wash over you, and the tensions of the day dissolve. Such reading is one of life's pleasures. Because your goal is to enjoy, it is okay if your mind wanders or if you feel too lazy to look up the meaning of a word.

College reading is different. It demands more of you because it requires you to stay focused on the material as you consider and evaluate it. It requires you to think of the material in light of what you already know and to judge its importance. It requires you to question, draw conclusions, make associations, develop opinions, and support those opinions. In short, college reading requires *critical reading*, the process considered in this chapter.

Critical reading skills are as important in the workplace and your personal life as they are in college classrooms. Reading done in the workplace, such as that pictured on the facing page, requires critical reading skills—think of important reports, budget analyses, contracts, and projections, for example. Even your important personal reading—gym contracts, job applications, and leases, for example—require those same skills.

Think about the importance of critical reading in your life and about opportunities for critical reading that you now have or are likely to encounter soon.

3

CRITICAL READING

Critical reading is not necessarily finding fault or "criticizing"; it is digging deep into a text to determine what the author says, how he or she says it, and what the quality, significance, and implications are. To do all that and become a critical reader, you must analyze and assess a text—whether that text is a newspaper article, a Web page, a journal article, a textbook chapter, or any other important material. *Analyzing* a text involves determining what the author is saying and how he or she is saying it; *assessing* a text involves making judgments about the quality and significance of the text.

TO ANALYZE A TEXT

- Identify the author's ideas and understand their meaning.
- Determine how the author explains or proves ideas.
- Ascertain the author's likely purpose and audience.

TO ASSESS A TEXT

- Evaluate the quality and reliability of the text.
- Draw conclusions about the significance of the ideas.
- Discover connections between the ideas and what you already know.

Critical reading is a skill you will draw on repeatedly in college as your instructors ask you to judge the significance of ideas, evaluate data, and consider theories. For example, your sociology instructor may ask you to read the latest census report and draw conclusions about the nature of the American family. Critical reading is also a skill you are likely to need on the job, as when a supervisor asks you to read a marketing analysis and evaluate a sales trend or compare the findings of two reports. Critical reading is equally important in your private life. In an election year, for example, you will read campaign literature, newspaper editorials, and magazine articles to form judgments about candidates in order to vote wisely. Or you may need to research and read opinions about treatments for a medical condition in order to decide on the best course of action.

To become a critical reader—that is, to learn how to analyze and assess a text—you must learn to distinguish facts from opinions, make inferences, synthesize information, evaluate quality, and detect errors in logic. You must also learn effective reading strategies. These matters are discussed in the next sections.

Distinguishing Facts from Opinions

People often assume that anything in print is a fact, but the words on a page or computer screen may represent only the writer's opinion. **Facts** can be or have been proved, but **opinions** are the writer's judgments, interpretations, or beliefs. For example, it is a *fact* that electricity can power automobiles, but it is an *opinion* that electrically powered cars will outnumber gasoline-powered cars in 10 years. As a critical reader, you must distinguish between facts and opinions, and when you identify opinions, determine whether they are well founded and well supported.

Sometimes people think that facts are better than opinions, but both have their place and importance. For example, scientists seeking to support a theory must be able to support it with facts. However, in thinking about the theory, scientists consider opinions. For what benefit can the theory be applied? How does the theory affect subsequent research? How should the theory influence public policy? The answers to such questions are matters of opinion but are nonetheless important, because they can guide the course of future research and the application of the theory.

Much of the reading you encounter in college will include both facts and opinions. For example, consider this paragraph from the introductory business textbook *Understanding Business* by William Nickels, James McHugh, and Susan McHugh:

> Customer-driven organizations include Nordstrom department stores (they have a very generous return policy, for example) and Disney amusement parks (the parks are kept clean and appeal to all ages). Moto Photo does its best to please customers with fast, friendly service. Such companies can successfully compete against Internet firms if they continue to offer better and friendlier service. Successful organizations must now listen more closely to customers to determine their wants and needs, then adjust the firm's products, policies, and practices to meet those demands. (19)

A fact mentioned in this paragraph is that traditional companies now have to compete with Internet companies for customers. The claim that Nordstrom, Disney, and Moto Photo are customer-driven organizations is the author's opinion, but it is based on facts, which can be checked—for example, that Nordstrom has a generous return policy or that Disney parks are kept clean. The claim that traditional companies can compete through better, friendlier service is also an opinion. Is the opinion backed up sufficiently?

Critical readers must do more than distinguish between facts and opinions. They must also evaluate the *quality* of the opinions they identify. Some opinions are more valuable than others. Valuable opinions—ones to take seriously—are offered by knowledgeable people and are backed up by solid support. Less valuable opinions—ones to be wary of—are unsupported beliefs or are offered by people with little relevant knowledge or experience.

Making Inferences

Critical readers make inferences. An **inference** is a conclusion about what a piece of writing "suggests" rather than "states." Think of making inferences as "reading between the lines." For example, consider this paragraph from "What Is Behind the Growth of Violence on College Campuses?" (page 454), an essay that examines the causes of campus violence:

> The same students who sponsor night walks to check the lighting and grounds to increase safety will hold the door open for a stranger entering their residence hall. Despite frequent warnings, students—and even faculty, administrators, and other campus personnel—act less judiciously than they would elsewhere.

In this paragraph, the author *says* that students and campus employees are not as careful on campus as they are in other places. Readers can *infer* that the author believes that this lack of caution contributes to campus crime, even though that point is not specifically made.

Making inferences is an important part of critical reading. However, your inferences must be supported by evidence. Thus, you cannot infer from the above paragraph that the author believes victims of campus crime get what they deserve because they are not sufficiently careful. As a reader, *you* might feel that way, but you cannot ascribe that idea to the author, based on the evidence in the paragraph.

Synthesizing Information

Synthesis is the process of connecting new information to what you already know. Thus, synthesis involves fitting new information into the larger scheme of your knowledge. When you read or hear a lecture, you can synthesize the information by noting how it supports, refutes, clarifies, illustrates, or calls into question other ideas, observations, or experiences. Suppose that you are reading an article that mentions the shortage of male teachers in elementary schools. If you heard an education professor comment that male elementary school teachers get little respect, you can synthesize your reading with your instructor's lecture by wondering whether there may be a cause-and-effect relationship: One reason for the shortage of male elementary school teachers might be that males do not want to teach elementary school because they do not get enough respect for doing so.

In college classes, you will synthesize by relating new ideas to information you have already learned. Your history teacher might ask you to compare some aspect of the Bill of Rights (which you just read about) with some aspect of the Magna Carta (which you studied last term). Even though in your college classes you will usually synthesize by relating new classroom learning to earlier classroom learning, do not hesitate to synthesize ideas in a more personal way as well. For example, if your education instructor lectures on bilingual education and you are an international student, you can relate your instructor's points to your own school experience using English as a second language.

Evaluating Quality

As you have learned, not everything in print or on the Internet is a fact, and not all opinions are well supported. Much material of dubious quality and questionable truth makes its way into print and onto the Internet. For this reason, critical readers evaluate the quality of their reading material. As a student, you may feel uncomfortable judging what you read. Perhaps you think that you do not know enough or are not high enough in the academic "pecking order" to make such judgments. In fact, as a student, you should practice critical reading at every opportunity. You are entitled to your opinion, as long as you back it up with evidence. Answering the following questions about reading material can help you form a reasonable judgment about its quality.

- **Are the "facts" really facts?** A point is not a fact just because a writer calls it one. The statement could be an opinion dressed up as a fact. Consider this example: "The fact that science is poorly taught in elementary school helps explain our nation's lack of scientific literacy." *Is* it a fact that science is poorly taught in elementary school? *Is* it a fact that we lack scientific literacy? No, these are opinions, and calling them facts does not make them so.

- **Are the opinions adequately supported?** Opinions backed up by sound reasoning and solid evidence are valuable; opinions offered without any support may not be. For example, an author may offer the opinion that the United States should increase spending for space exploration, but without giving reasons for doing so, the author is stating an opinion that is not worth much.

- **Is the material current?** If you are reading a biography of Abraham Lincoln, the fact that it was written 20 years ago may not be a problem (unless historians have recently made important new discoveries about Lincoln's life). However, if you are reading about population trends in rural areas, an essay with census information from 1990 will not be as relevant as a piece with census information from 2010.

- **Are the source and author trustworthy?** Consider the author's credentials and possible biases. If you are looking for a balanced view of the issues surrounding handgun control, for instance, the National Rifle Association's Web site or an essay written by the mother of a student killed in a school shooting may not be an unbiased source.

- **Is the reasoning logical?** A critical reader discounts material that contains faulty logic. The next section will help you recognize errors in logic when you read and avoid them when you write.

Detecting Errors in Logic

Be on the lookout for **errors in logic**—particular forms of faulty reasoning that can lead a person to a false conclusion. Unethical writers use errors in logic intentionally, to mislead or manipulate a reader. However, many writers do not intend to deceive; they use faulty reasoning without meaning to. In either case, as a critical reader, you should be wary of material that includes errors in logic. As a writer, you should avoid such errors in your own work. Here are some of the most common errors in logic.

1. Overgeneralizing. Very little is true all of the time, so be careful of sweeping statements.

> EXAMPLE The reason teenagers quit school is to avoid the home-work. (*This may be true for some, but not for all.*)

2. Oversimplifying. Most issues worth arguing are complex, so be wary of "quick fix" explanations or solutions.

> EXAMPLE If women would just stay home to care for their children, we would have no day care problem in this country. (*The issue is not that simple. Many women must work in order to feed their children.*)

3. Begging the question. "Begging the question" is basing an argument or conclusion on the truth of a point that has not been proved.

> EXAMPLE Because couples who live together are immature, they do not deserve spousal rights. (*Where is the proof that couples who live together are "immature"? To assume they are is to beg the question.*)

4. Name calling. Also called an *ad hominem* ("to the man") attack or mudslinging, this fallacy involves attacking the people you don't agree with instead of criticizing their ideas or sticking with issues.

> EXAMPLE People who oppose school vouchers are people who don't care about education. (*The pros and cons of school vouchers are unrelated to the people who oppose or favor them.*)

5. Either–or reasoning. With complex issues, more than two alterna-tives usually exist.

> EXAMPLE If the state does not raise taxes, we will have a fiscal cri-sis on our hands. (*What about other alternatives, such as cut-ting expenditures?*)

6. Assuming an earlier event caused a later event. This fallacy is also called *post hoc, ergo propter hoc,* which means "after this, therefore because of this." The fact that one event occurred before another does not mean that the first event caused the second.

> EXAMPLE The new mayor is really effective. He took office last month, and the crime rate is already down. (*The new mayor did not necessarily cause the drop in the crime rate.*)

7. Attacking or defending an issue on the basis of what was believed or done in the past. This kind of fallacy would have kept women from getting the vote—and almost any other change from being implemented.

EXAMPLE   If our grandparents managed without federally subsidized health care, so can we. (*Our grandparents lived in a different world.*)

8. Assuming that what is true for one person is true for everybody.

EXAMPLE   My cousin and his girlfriend live together without being married, and they are just fine. Obviously, marriage is not that important. (*What is true for the cousin may not be true for others.*)

9. Playing to general sentiments. Also called *ad populum*, which means "to the crowd," this fallacy involves winning people over by calling upon commonly held feelings such as patriotism, fear of war, and religious fervor rather than discussing issues.

EXAMPLE   I would make an excellent senator because I come from humble beginnings and know what it means to work for a living. (*This argument appeals to our respect for those who work hard to improve their circumstances. It says nothing about the speaker's political qualifications.*)

10. Falsely indicating that one point follows conclusively from another. This fallacy is also called *non sequitur*, which means "it does not follow."

EXAMPLE   Fewer minority students are attending our university this year. Apparently, minorities are losing interest in higher education. (*The conclusion does not follow from the first statement. There may be many causes for the decline in enrollment, including the fact that many minority students are attending other colleges.*)

11. Using the "as any fool can see" approach. This approach insults those who disagree. Not only is it a fallacy, but it can alienate readers.

EXAMPLE   It is apparent to everyone that deer hunting solves many wildlife problems. (*No, it is not apparent to everyone, or your essay would not be necessary.*)

12. Alluding to but not naming authorities. Careful readers distrust phrases such as "experts agree" or "research shows" because they suggest authority or evidence without naming that authority or evidence.

EXAMPLE   Studies show that most Americans distrust politicians. (*What studies?*)

STRATEGIES FOR CRITICAL READING

As you have seen, to be a critical reader, you must read thoughtfully to distinguish facts from opinions, make inferences, synthesize information, evaluate quality, and be on the lookout for errors in logic. At times, you may draw conclusions that differ from those of your classmates and other readers, but critical readers often disagree with each other. Although you need not agree with others, you must support your views with sound reasoning and evidence.

Sometimes you will be uncertain about the meaning of all or part of what you read, and that uncertainty is acceptable, too. If you are puzzled, say so. Critical reading is often an investigative process, so ask questions of other readers, and ask questions in class. Do some research, if necessary, to learn more about the text you are reading and to discover what other critical readers think. Eventually, things will become clearer to you.

Sometimes you will change your mind about a text. Yesterday you may have made one evaluation, but today you have another. Remember that reading is an ongoing process, and critical readers are willing to rethink their ideas in light of new evidence or insights. Your reactions and views can change as you continue to reflect, consider the ideas of other readers, and gain experience and knowledge that affect how you synthesize information.

The strategies explained next can help you achieve the many goals of a critical reader.

Approach Your Reading with a Reflective and Questioning Attitude

Critical readers think about what they are reading and ask questions. They consider which ideas are facts and which are opinions. They ponder the significance of points and consider the implications behind the words. They ask themselves how the author's ideas connect with what they already know. They look at whether the author is reliable and the source is current, and they evaluate the support offered for opinions. They look for errors in reasoning. In short, critical readers never automatically accept what they read; they reflect and question in order to draw their own conclusions. As you read about the critical reading strategies that follow, remember that the most important strategy is maintaining a reflective and questioning attitude—all the other strategies are based on that one.

Preview the Material

Previewing the material before you read helps you to form preliminary impressions and to create a context for your reading. It is a way to initiate your reflective and questioning attitude. To preview, do the following:

- **Consider the author and title** and what they suggest about the piece. Do you know the author's politics or usual subject matter? Is the author a newspaper columnist, a humorist, or a political commentator? Think about the title and what clues it might offer. Some titles will tell you more than others.
- **Check out the publication information.** When and where the essay first appeared will suggest how current the information is and who the intended audience was.
- **Read the headnote.** In this text, reading selections are preceded by headnotes that give the original publication information and that

tell something about the author's background and publications and the content of the selection. This information can help you evaluate the reading.

- **Read headings, charts, bold and italicized type, and lists** for clues to content.
- **Read the first paragraph or two and the first sentence of other paragraphs** to learn a little about the tone, subject matter, and organization of the piece.

Do a First Reading

After previewing the reading, you will have a first impression and some expectations about the material—an impression and expectations that may or may not be borne out as you read more closely. To begin that closer examination, read the material through in one sitting, without pausing or laboring over anything. Just relax and get a sense of the author's purpose and main points. If the piece appeals to you, enjoy it without considering exactly what techniques create the appeal. If you encounter unfamiliar words that you cannot understand from the context, circle them to look up later. If you do not understand a point, push on knowing that you will come back to it later. If the piece is too long to read in one sitting, break it into sections and do separate first readings.

Reread and Study

After your first reading, return to the piece, using your reflective and questioning attitude to look more closely and discover as much as you can. Shorter, simpler pieces may require only one rereading, but longer, more complex pieces will probably take two or more rereadings. Keep a pencil or pen in your hand so you can make notes in the margin and underline key passages. You may be accustomed to using a yellow or pink marker, although this technique is more useful for highlighting important textbook passages to study. For most other materials, critical reading goes better when you can make notes about why certain elements are significant. If you do not own the reading or prefer not to mark the text for other reasons, write your annotations on a separate sheet or in a computer file. Or use removable sticky notes, attaching them to the appropriate places. As you reread and study, the following procedures can be helpful:

- **Look up words that you circled during your first reading and any other vocabulary you are unsure of.** You can write the meanings in the margins as a study aid.
- **Identify the thesis (the central point).** If it is stated, place brackets around it or underline it. If it is implied rather than stated, write it out in your own words in the margin or at the end of the reading.
- **Identify the purpose.** Authors write for one or more purposes: to express feelings, relate experience, entertain the reader, inform the

reader, and/or convince the reader to think or act in a particular way. As you read, clues will help you identify purpose. Write out the purpose or combination of purposes in the margin or at the end of the reading. Then note how well you think the reading achieves the author's purpose. (For a discussion of a writer's purpose, see page 30.)

- **Underline major points.** As you encounter important ideas that support the thesis, underline them for special consideration. However, do not underline too much, or your underlining will not be useful. Just mark the major points; don't underline the examples, clarifying description, and other explanations unless you have a reason for doing so.

- **Make notations as you reflect and question.** Remember, as a critical reader, you need to distinguish fact from opinion, make inferences, synthesize information, and evaluate quality. For a summary of questions to ask, see the "Questions for Critical Reading" box that follows. Of course, answering questions and going back to your answers is easier to do when you have a pencil or pen in your hand and can make notes in the margins. For example, if you like a passage or strongly agree, place an exclamation point next to it. If you disagree, write "no." If a point goes unsupported, write something like "not proven." If you do not understand something, place a question mark in the margin. Note your important responses any way that is convenient for you, using notations like "clever," "reminds me of psych lecture,"and "who cares?" (For an example of a marked essay, see page 13.)

- **Reconsider any material you did not understand earlier.** If necessary, list questions to ask other readers or your instructor. Consider researching in the library or on the Internet.

- **Reconsider the reading in light of your earlier impressions.** Do you feel the same way you did during your preview and first reading? If not, how has your thinking changed and why?

By following these procedures for rereading, you will create a marked essay. You can also write your responses to the piece in a reading journal (see page 15). The box gives questions you can use in either case.

Questions for Critical Reading

- What is the source of the author's ideas: experience, observation, considered opinion, or research?
- Is the author expressing facts, opinion, or both?
- Is the author's detail adequate and convincing? Does the author support generalizations by showing and not just telling?

- What is the author's purpose, tone, intended audience, and role? (See the discussion beginning on page 30.)
- Do you agree or disagree with the author? Do you like or dislike the selection? What does it make you think of? Does it arouse any strong feelings?
- What is the significance of the selection?

A Sample Marked Essay

To see what a marked essay can look like, review the following selection marked by a student.

Americanization Is Tough on "Macho"

Rose Del Castillo Guibault

1   What is *macho*? That depends which side of the border you come from.

2   Although it's not unusual for words and expressions to lose their subtlety in translation [the negative connotations of *macho* in this country are troublesome to Hispanics.]———   *Closest thing to a stated thesis*

3   Take the newspaper descriptions of alleged mass murderer Ramon Salcido. That an insensitive, insanely jealous, hard-drinking, violent Latin male is referred to as *macho* makes Hispanics cringe.

4   "*Es muy macho*," the women in my family nod approvingly, describing a man they respect. But in the United States, when women say, "He's so macho," it's with disdain.

5   The Hispanic *macho* is manly, responsible, hardworking, a man in charge, a [patriarch.] A man who expresses strength through silence. What the Yiddish language would call a *mensch*.   *male head of family, sounds like Dad*

6   The American *macho* is a chauvinist, a brute, uncouth, selfish, loud, abrasive, capable of inflicting pain, and sexually promiscuous.   *crude*   *good description*

7   [Quintessential] *macho* models in this country are Sylvester Stallone, Arnold Schwarzenegger, and Charles Bronson. In their movies, they exude toughness, independence, masculinity. But a closer look reveals their machismo is really violence masquerading as courage, sullenness disguised as silence, and irresponsibility camouflaged as independence.   *pure*   *Interesting— never thought of this before.*

8   If the Hispanic ideal of *macho* were translated to American screen roles, they might be Jimmy Stewart, Sean Connery, and Laurence Olivier.   *needs more detail for proof*

9   In Spanish, *macho* enobles Latin males. In English, it devalues them. This pattern seems consistent with the conflicts ethnic minority males experience in this country. Typically the cultural traits other societies value don't translate as desirable characteristics in America.   *Examples from other cultures needed.*

I watched my own father struggle with these cultural ambi- 10
guities. He worked on a farm for twenty years. He laid down
miles of irrigation pipe, carefully plowed long, neat rows in

hard to handle fields, hacked away at (recalcitrant) weeds and drove tractors
through whirlpools of dust. He stoically worked twenty-hour
days during harvest season, accepting the long hours as part of
Is complaining a agricultural work. When the boss complained or upbraided
strength or a him for minor mistakes, he kept quiet, even when it was obvi-
weakness? ous the boss had erred.

He handled the most menial tasks with pride. At home he 11
was a good provider, helped out my mother's family in Mexico
without complaint, and was indulgent with me. Arguments
between my mother and him generally had to do with money,
This is my idea or with his stubborn reluctance to share his troubles. He tried
of macho — males to work them out in his own silence. He didn't want to trouble
never share my mother—a course that backfired, because the imagined is
worries & fears. always worse than the reality.

Americans regarded my father as decidedly un-*macho*. His 12
character was interpreted as nonassertive, his loyalty nonambi-
tion, and his quietness ignorance. I once overheard the boss's
son blame him for plowing crooked rows in a field. My father
merely smiled at the lie, knowing the boy had done it, but
Why unions are didn't refute it, confident his good work was well known. But
needed! the boss instead ridiculed him for being "stupid" and letting a
kid get away with a lie. Seeing my embarrassment, my father
dismissed the incident, saying, "They're the dumb ones. Imagine, me fighting with a kid."

well put I tried not to look at him with American eyes because some- 13
times the reflection hurt.

Listening to my aunts' clucks of approval, my vision focused 14
Isn't this like the on the qualities America overlooked. "He's such a hard worker.
American concept of So serious, so responsible." My aunts would secretly compli-
macho? ment my mother. The unspoken comparison was that he was
Father is meek not like some of their husbands, who drank and womanized.
but strong? My uncles represented the darker side of *macho*.

the thing to do, In a patriarchal society, few challenge their roles. If men 15
but not the drink, it's because it's the manly thing to do. If they gamble,
macho thing it's because it's how men relax. And if they fool around, well,
it's because a man simply can't hold back so much man! My
aunts didn't exactly meekly sit back, but they put up with these
transgressions because Mexican society dictated this was their
lot in life.

In the United States, I believe it was the feminist movement 16
of the early '70s that changed *macho*'s meaning. Perhaps my gen-
I don't get this. eration of Latin women was in part responsible. I recall Chicanos
complaining about the chauvinistic nature of Latin men and
the notion they wanted their women barefoot, pregnant, and in

the kitchen. The generalization that Latin men embodied chauvinistic traits led to this interesting twist of semantics. Suddenly a word that represented something positive in one culture became a negative prototype in another.

model

17   The problem with the use of *macho* today is that it's become an accepted stereotype of the Latin male. And like all stereotypes, it distorts truth.

Interesting: I wish she had explored this more.

18   The impact of language in our society is undeniable. And the misuse of *macho* hints at a deeper cultural misunderstanding that extends beyond mere word definitions.

This essay really makes me sad for all the men who show strength every day but are seen in a negative light.

Keeping a Reading Journal

You can write your responses to readings in a reading journal, which can be in either paper or electronic form. These responses can be written in addition to or instead of marking an essay during critical reading. Journal writing can enrich your reading experience in a number of ways:

- You can pursue your thinking further than you would without the benefit of writing.
- You can record thoughts that you can later use in essays.
- You can review earlier entries to see how your ideas have progressed and to discover ways to synthesize ideas.
- You can write trial drafts and experiment with ideas.
- You can summarize the reading to record the important ideas and "set" learning. (For information on writing a summary, see page 95.)

The reading journal is also a good place to record the answers to critical reading questions such as those on pages 12–13. Here, for example, are answers to these questions for "Americanization Is Tough on 'Macho,'" as they might appear in a journal.

Answers to Questions about "Americanization Is Tough on 'Macho'"

- What is the source of the author's ideas: experience, observation, considered opinion, or research? *The author's ideas came from personal experience and observation and from considered opinion based on these.*
- Is the author expressing facts, opinions, or both? *The points about the connotation of macho are facts, as are the examples about the father and other relatives. The rest is opinion.*   *(continued)*

- Is the author's detail adequate and convincing? Does the author support generalizations by showing and not just telling? *More detail is needed to prove the point in paragraph 9. At the end, the author needs to explain more about the cultural misunderstandings.*
- What are the author's purpose, tone, intended audience, and role? *Her purpose is to correct misunderstandings about the meaning of macho and the nature of Latin males. The tone is concerned, serious, and controlled. The audience is non-Hispanics. The author assumes the role of knowledgeable person, educator, and Hispanic.*
- Do you agree or disagree with the author? Do you like or dislike the selection? What does it make you think of? Does it arouse any strong feelings? *I don't have enough experience around Hispanic males to agree or disagree, but I see little evidence of the stereotyped Hispanic male in the media. I like the essay, especially the parts about the author's family, but I wish there were more details. It makes me sad for a group of men who are very strong but viewed as weak.*
- What is the significance of the selection? *The essay is important because it aims to increase understanding between cultures and dispel a common misconception. The last paragraph, in part, presents this significance.*

STRATEGIES FOR READING VISUAL MATERIAL CRITICALLY

You are accustomed to visual material in magazines and newspapers, online, and on everything from cereal boxes to buses. College reading, too, even more than in the past, has a visual component. Textbooks are making more use of graphs, charts, maps, drawings, and photographs to present and supplement essential information. In addition, instructors are making images a key component of their PowerPoint presentations, and they are directing students to the Internet for information that is often graphically displayed. Because visual material is so prevalent both in the classroom and beyond, you should learn to read it critically. The next sections can guide you.

Reading Visual Material

To read visuals critically, use the same techniques you use to read text critically. That means you should approach all visual material with a reflective and questioning attitude. Determine the purpose of the image, distinguish facts from opinions, make inferences, connect the information to what you already know, evaluate quality, and assess logic.

- **Determine the purpose of the visual.** Like texts, images are created for a purpose: They entertain, express feelings, relate experience, inform, and persuade. For example, reproductions of paintings on a museum's Web site entertain those who view the site; you sister's wedding photos posted to her blog express the love of the bride and groom; a pie chart in your economics textbook informs you about the distribution of wealth in the United States; and an advertisement in your favorite magazine persuades you to buy a particular watch. Also, like texts, images can combine purposes. For example, a political cartoon aims to both entertain and persuade.

- **Distinguish facts from opinions.** A U.S. Census Bureau bar graph comparing the number of people who live in urban areas with the number who live in rural ones conveys facts. However, an advertisement sponsored by the Seattle Chamber of Commerce that shows the fun of living and working in downtown Seattle is expressing an opinion about the qualities of that area.

- **Make inferences.** Read between the lines of both visual and textual components of the visual material. For example, a political cartoon showing a senator with a very large open mouth may be implying that the individual speaks too much or ill-advisedly. A shampoo advertisement with the text "Happiness is shiny hair" may be implying that using the shampoo will make you happier.

- **Synthesize the information in the visual.** Advertisements for weight-loss products often show an overweight "before" image and a thin "after" image of the same person. If you synthesize the images with your knowledge that computers can alter pictures, you will become skeptical of the claims in the ad.

- **Evaluate the quality.** A Web site with misspellings may not be reliable, and a 1990 graphic about global warming may be outdated, so you should be wary of these visuals. Further, do not be taken in by a beautifully executed image. Because computers can make almost anything look good, an attractive visual is not necessarily a high-quality visual.

- **Detect errors in logic.** If an advertisement for the latest computer shows a successful executive using the advertised computer and an underachieving worker without this equipment, recognize the illogical either–or reasoning that says, "Use this computer and succeed, or use something else and fail."

Reading Charts and Graphs

Charts and graphs are often used in sources such as textbooks, scholarly journals, magazines, and PowerPoint presentations. As visual representations, charts and graphs can convey a great deal of information very succinctly. Line graphs are particularly good for showing trends and changes over time; pie charts and bar graphs show how items relate to one another. The bar graph on page 18 shows the relationship of Americans' opinions about taxation to their opinions about government spending.

Not only do charts and graphs convey a lot of information, but they also allow you to analyze data and make inferences. For example, by analyzing the data in the bar graph, you can infer that Americans must want the best of both worlds on taxing and spending, as they want more spending in some areas but believe that taxes are too high. Because graphs and charts can make information easier to understand, they can also make it easier to determine how to use that information. The bar graph, for example, suggests that politicians who want to build more schools to decrease crowding must find a way to help people understand that they can't have more schools without either raising taxes or cutting services in other areas.

To read charts and graphs critically, study the data and any accompanying captions, explanations, or other text. Then be sure you can answer these questions.

Questions for Critical Reading of Charts and Graphs

- What point is the chart or graph trying to make?
- What is the source of the information—a newspaper, the government, a university, a private foundation, a corporation, an individual researcher? Is the source reliable? Does the source have a particular agenda to promote?
- What is the date of the information? Is it sufficiently current?
- Is there any attempt to mislead? For example, are important time periods or groups omitted that would detract from an author's point?
- What can you infer from the chart or graph?
- How do the data and inferences relate to the text? How do they relate to what you already know?

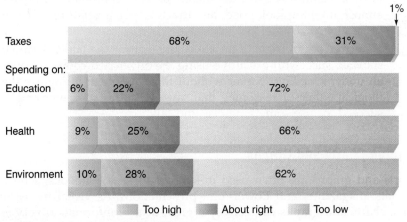

Source: National Opinion Research Center, University of Chicago.

Reading Photographs

Like charts and graphs, photographs can reveal a great deal of information and should be read accordingly. Keep in mind that photographs you encounter in the classroom have been selected by textbook authors or by your instructor for their rich insights into the subject matter.

Outside the classroom, photographs that have the purpose of persuading can ignite emotions and speed us to action. A thousand-word newspaper article about children starving in a drought-stricken nation may cause us to sigh in pity, but one photo of a starving child can lead us to send a check to a relief agency.

Consider, for example, this photograph of a young girl.

Lewis Hine, *Addie Laird, 12 Years Old. Spinner in a Cotton Mill*, North Pownal, Vermont, February 9, 1910.

Lewis Hine (1874–1940), American photographer, helped develop the photograph as social commentary. With a mission to inform complacent Americans of the nature and conditions of poverty, he photographed newly arrived immigrants, street life in the big cities, and children at work in the mines and factories of early-twentieth-century America. This photograph was taken for the National Child Labor Committee, which aimed to end child labor through federal legislation.

Study the photograph and its caption. What is the purpose of the photograph? How does Hine's choice of subject help him achieve that purpose? Look closely at the young girl. Notice her skinny arms, her soiled pinafore, and her dirty, bare feet. What can you infer from her appearance? What emotion do her face and, especially, her eyes convey? Hine posed this photograph; the young girl stands in front of the spindles she is tending and looks straight out at us. What message is she sending? How does the information in the caption help you understand the message?

To "read" a photograph, ask yourself these questions.

Questions for Critical Reading of Photographs

- Who took the photograph, and why—for what organization or cause?
- Is the photograph candid, posed, or digitally altered?
- Is the image meant to document an event, to arouse emotions, or to do both?
- What inferences can you make about the photograph? What message is it intended to convey?
- How does the caption help you understand the photograph?

Reading Advertisements

Learning to read visual material critically is an especially important skill outside the classroom because we are bombarded with images intended to influence our thinking and behavior. Television commercials and print or online advertisements are the most prominent examples. Most often such ads try to convince us to buy a particular product. Sometimes they try to convince us to have positive feelings about the company that manufactures the product or offers a service, such as an energy-company ad that showcases its concern for the environment. Either way, advertisements aim to profit those who sponsor them. The only way to avoid being manipulated by the ads is to learn to read them critically.

Consider, for example, the advertisement on page 21 featuring a photograph of a young mother. Study this advertisement, both the image and the text that accompanies it. What is State Farm's purpose in running the ad? What aspects of the photograph and text help the company achieve its purpose? Notice that the mother is wearing business clothes, which suggests that the primary audience for the ad is working mothers of young children. But the text at the top of the image implies that all moms are always working. So this ad aims to appeal also to mothers who are not paid to work outside the home. It tells women that State Farm understands their needs and can help them meet those needs.

Notice the way color is used in this ad. The only bright color is red, which is used for the company's name and logo, its slogan, and the mother's purse—where her money is kept. Notice the way motion is used in the ad: The boy in the background is on the move, and the mother is talking

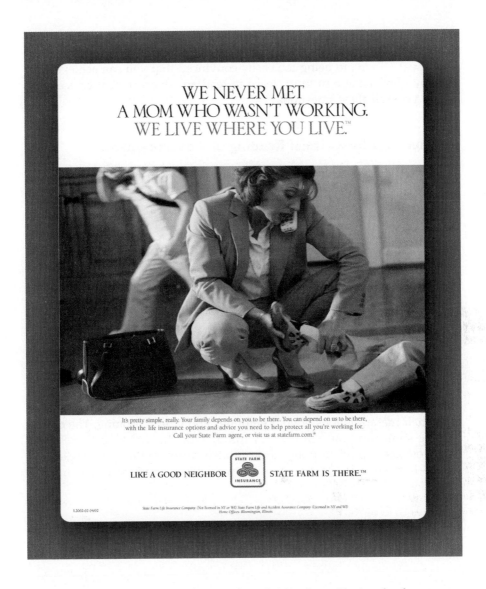

It's pretty simple, really. Your family depends on you to be there. You can depend on us to be there, with the life insurance options and advice you need to help protect all you're working for. Call your State Farm agent, or visit us at statefarm.com.®

LIKE A GOOD NEIGHBOR • STATE FARM IS THERE.™

L2002-02 04/02   State Farm Life Insurance Company (Not licensed in NY or WD) State Farm Life and Accident Assurance Company (Licensed in NY and WD) Home Offices: Bloomington, Illinois

on the phone while she puts on another child's shoe. Obviously, the woman leads a busy life, and a viewer of the ad will admire her poise as she manages to do several things at once. Does the target audience see themselves in this image? State Farm certainly hopes so.

Advertisements often work by encouraging us to identify emotionally with the individual pictured in the ad. Sometimes the appeal is to an ideal we all cherish—motherhood, in this case. Notice how this ad implies that mothers are essential, always there for their families. And the text explains that just as families depend on mothers, so mothers can depend on State Farm.

Other emotional appeals in ads are through symbols of power, pleasure, patriotism, beauty, or sex. Then the advertisement implies, "If you buy our products or services, you, too, will be a competent mother, or a powerful executive, a fun-to-be-with friend, a patriotic American, or a person with sex appeal." To avoid being too easily convinced that you can achieve your ideal by purchasing a product, learn to read an advertisement critically by asking yourself these questions.

Questions for Critical Reading of Advertisements

- What audience does the advertisement target? Are you in that audience? If not, do you respond favorably to the advertisement anyway?
- What is the purpose of the ad?
- Does the ad appeal more to reason or to emotion?
- What does the ad imply?
- How do techniques involving color, size, lighting, and so on highlight the ad's appeal?
- How does the text work with the image to achieve the ad's purpose? Are there slogans or symbols? Testimonials by celebrities? Statistics or research findings?
- Is the ad credible? Can its claims—implied or stated directly—be true? Can they be verified?

When you apply your critical reading strategies to advertisements, you are able to take *from* them what information you need without being taken *in* by their manipulations of your emotions and your reasoning. The critical reading strategies you will practice throughout *Patterns for a Purpose* will help you assess and respond appropriately to everything you read and view—in the college classroom, in the workplace, and in your community.

BACKGROUND: Born in New York City, philosopher and writer Mortimer Adler (1902–2001) taught at the University of Chicago, where he helped develop the Great Books program and where he directed the Institute for Philosophical Research. Although a high school dropout, Adler earned a Ph.D., was an editor for the *Encyclopaedia Britannica,* and wrote widely on philosophy and education. He spent much of his career popularizing the great ideas of Western civilization in works such as *Great Books of the Western World,* 54 vols. (1954, and rev. 1990). He is particularly noted for *How to Read a Book: The Art of Getting a Liberal Education* (1940). The following essay first appeared in the *Saturday Review* in 1940.

---

www.mhhe.com/clousepatterns6
Mortimer Adler

For more information on this author, go to

More resources > Chapter 1 > Mortimer Adler

READING WITH A PURPOSE: A person cannot truly own a book without writing in it, according to Mortimer Adler, for writing in a book "is not an act of mutilation but of love." Adler explains that it does not matter how many expensive volumes a person has on display. What matters is whether a person "consumes" the books with a pen or pencil in hand. Although the essay was written over 70 years ago, it still offers sound advice to readers. As you read, try to determine why this essay has remained popular for so long.

HOW TO MARK A BOOK

BY MORTIMER ADLER

YOU KNOW you have to read "between the lines" to get the most out of anything. I want to persuade you to do something equally important in the course of your reading. I want to persuade you to "write between the lines." Unless you do, you are not likely to do the most efficient kind of reading.

2   I contend, quite bluntly, that marking up a book is not an act of mutilation but of love.

3   You shouldn't mark up a book which isn't yours. Librarians (or your friends) who lend you books expect you to keep them clean, and you should. If you decide that I am right about the usefulness of marking books, you will have to buy them. Most of the world's great books are available today, in reprint editions, at less than a dollar.

> "Most of the world's great books are available today, in reprint editions, at less than a dollar."

4   There are two ways in which you can own a book. The first is the property right you establish by paying for it, just as you pay for clothes and furniture. But this act of purchase is only the prelude to possession. Full ownership comes only when you have made it a part of yourself, and the best way to make yourself a part of it is by writing in it. An illustration may make the point clear. You buy a beefsteak and transfer it from the butcher's icebox to your own. But you do not own the beefsteak in the most important sense until you consume it and get it into your

bloodstream. I am arguing that books, too, must be absorbed in your bloodstream to do you any good.

5   Confusion about what it means to *own* a book leads people to a false reverence for paper, binding, and type—a respect for the physical thing—the craft of the printer rather than the genius of the author. They forget that it is possible for a man to acquire the idea, to possess the beauty, which a great book contains, without staking his claim by pasting his bookplate inside the cover. Having a fine library doesn't prove that its owner has a mind enriched by books; it proves nothing more than that he, his father, or his wife, was rich enough to buy them.

6   There are three kinds of book owners. The first has all the standard sets and best-sellers—unread, untouched. (This deluded individual owns woodpulp and ink, not books.) The second has a great many books—a few of them read through, most of them dipped into, but all of them as clean and shiny as the day they were bought. (This person would probably like to make books his own, but is restrained by a false respect for their physical appearance.) The third has a few books or many—everyone of them dog-eared and dilapidated, shaken and loosened by continual use, marked and scribbled in from front to back. (This man owns books.)

7   Is it false respect, you may ask, to preserve intact and unblemished a beautifully printed book, an elegantly bound edition? Of course not. I'd no more scribble all over a first edition of *Paradise Lost* than I'd give my baby a set of crayons and an original Rembrandt! I wouldn't mark up a painting or a statue. Its soul, so to speak, is inseparable from its body. And the beauty of a rare edition or of a richly manufactured volume is like that of a painting or a statue.

8   But the soul of a book *can* be separated from its body. A book is more like the score of a piece of music than it is like a painting. No great musician confuses a symphony with the printed sheets of music. Arturo Toscanini reveres Brahms, but Toscanini's score of the C-minor Symphony is so thoroughly marked up that no one but the maestro himself can read it. The reason why a great conductor makes notations on his musical scores—marks them up again and again each time he returns to study them—is the reason why you should mark your books. If your respect for magnificent binding or typography gets in the way, buy yourself a cheap edition and pay your respects to the author.

"If reading is to accomplish anything more than passing time, it must be active."

9   Why is marking up a book indispensable to reading? First, it keeps you awake. (And I don't mean merely conscious; I mean wide awake.) In the second place, reading, if it is active, is thinking, and thinking tends to express itself in words, spoken or written. The marked book is usually the thought-through book. Finally, writing helps you remember the thoughts you had, or the thoughts the author expressed. Let me develop these three points.

10   If reading is to accomplish anything more than passing time, it must be active. You can't let your eyes glide across the lines of a book and come up with an understanding of what you have read. Now an ordinary piece of light fiction, like say, *Gone With the Wind*, doesn't require the most active kind of reading. The books you read for pleasure can be read in a state of relaxation, and nothing is

lost. But a great book, rich in ideas and beauty, a book that raises and tries to answer great fundamental questions, demands the most active reading of which you are capable. You don't absorb the ideas of John Dewey[1] the way you absorb the crooning of Mr. Vallee.[2]

11   If, when you've finished reading a book, the pages are filled with your notes, you know that you read actively. The most famous *active* reader of great books I know is President Hutchins, of the University of Chicago. He also has the hardest schedule of business activities of any man I know. He invariably reads with a pencil, and sometimes, when he picks up a book and pencil in the evening, he finds himself, instead of making intelligent notes, drawing what he calls "caviar factories" on the margins. When that happens, he puts the book down. He knows he's too tired to read, and he's just wasting time.

12   But, you may ask, why is writing necessary? Well, the physical act of writing, with your own hand, brings words and sentences more sharply before your mind and preserves them better in your memory. To set down your reaction to important words and sentences you have read, and the questions they have raised in your mind, is to preserve those reactions and sharpen those questions.

13   Even if you wrote on a scratch pad, and threw the paper away when you had finished writing, your grasp of the book would be surer. But you don't have to throw the paper away. The margins (top and bottom, as well as side), the endpapers, the very space between the lines, are all available. They aren't sacred. And, best of all, your marks and notes become an integral part of the book and stay there forever. You can pick up the book the following week or year, and there are all your points of agreement, disagreement, doubt, and inquiry. It's like resuming an interrupted conversation with the advantage of being able to pick up where you left off.

"The learner has to question himself and question the teacher."

14   And that is exactly what reading a book should be: a conversation between you and the author. Presumably he knows more about the subject than you do; naturally, you'll have the proper humility as you approach him. But don't let anybody tell you that a reader is supposed to be solely on the receiving end. Understanding is a two-way operation; learning doesn't consist in being an empty receptacle. The learner has to question himself and question the teacher. He even has to argue with the teacher, once he understands what the teacher is saying. And marking a book is literally an expression of your differences, or agreements of opinion, with the author.

15   There are all kinds of devices for marking a book intelligently and fruitfully. Here's the way I do it:

1.   *Underlining:* of major points, of important or forceful statements.

2.   *Vertical lines at the margin:* to emphasize a statement already underlined.

---

[1]John Dewey (1859–1952) was a philosopher and educator.
[2]Rudy Vallee (1901–1986) was a bandleader and singer.

3. *Star, asterisk, or other doo-dad at the margin:* to be used sparingly, to emphasize the ten or twenty most important statements in the book. (You may want to fold the bottom corner of each page on which you use such marks. It won't hurt the sturdy paper on which most modern books are printed, and you will be able to take the book off the shelf at any time and, by opening it at the folded-corner page, refresh your recollection of the book.)

4. *Numbers in the margin:* to indicate the sequence of points the author makes in developing a single argument.

5. *Numbers of other pages in the margin:* to indicate where else in the book the author made points relevant to the point marked; to tie up the ideas in a book, which, though they may be separated by many pages, belong together.

6. *Circling of key words or phrases.*

7. *Writing in the margin, or at the top or bottom of the page, for the sake of:* recording questions (and perhaps answers) which a passage raised in your mind; reducing a complicated discussion to a simple statement; recording the sequence of major points right through the books. I use the end-papers at the back of the book to make a personal index of the author's points in the order of their appearance.

16   The front end-papers are, to me, the most important. Some people reserve them for a fancy bookplate. I reserve them for fancy thinking. After I have finished reading the book and making my personal index on the back end-papers, I turn to the front and try to outline the book, not page by page, or point by point (I've already done that at the back), but as an integrated structure, with a basic unity and an order of parts. This outline is, to me, the measure of my understanding of the work.

17   If you're a die-hard anti-bookmarker, you may object that the margins, the space between the lines, and the end-papers don't give you room enough. All right. How about using a scratch pad slightly smaller than the page-size of the book—so that the edges of the sheets won't protrude? Make your index, outlines, and even your notes on the pad, and then insert these sheets permanently inside the front and back covers of the book.

18   Or, you may say that this business of marking books is going to slow up your reading. It probably will. That's one of the reasons for doing it. Most of us have been taken in by the notion that speed of reading is a measure of our intelligence. There is no such thing as the right speed for intelligent reading. Some things should be read quickly and effortlessly, and some should be read slowly and even laboriously. The sign of intelligence in reading is the ability to read different things differently according to their worth. In the case of good books, the point is not to see how many of them you can get through, but rather how many can get through you—how many you can make your own. A few friends are better than a thousand acquaintances. If this be your aim, as it should be, you will not be impatient if it takes more time and effort to read a great book than it does a newspaper.

"There is no such thing as the right speed for intelligent reading."

19   You may have one final objection to marking books. You can't lend them to your friends because nobody else can read them without being distracted by your notes. Furthermore, you won't want to lend them because a marked copy is a kind of intellectual diary, and lending it is almost like giving your mind away.

20   If your friend wishes to read your *Plutarch's Lives*, Shakespeare, or *The Federalist Papers*, tell him gently but firmly to buy a copy. You will lend him your car or your coat—but your books are as much a part of you as your head or your heart.

ASSIGNMENT

Reread the essay with a pencil or pen in hand, and mark the selection using the strategies for annotation found on pages 11–15. If your instructor directs, form small groups in class and compare the ways you have marked the selection. What similarities and differences do you note? What accounts for the differences?

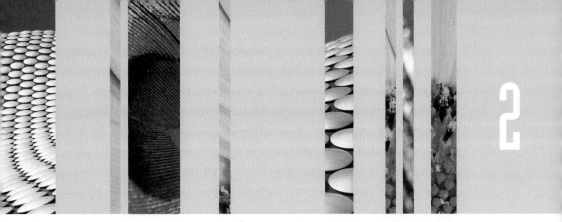

Planning an Essay and Using the Patterns of Development

To become a better tennis player, you play more tennis — but practice is not the only key to improvement. As the picture on the facing page illustrates, you must also consider what you *do* when you play tennis, so you adjust your technique, try different approach shots, experiment with different grips, and so forth. To become a better writer, you should do much the same thing by working to improve the procedures you follow when you write. You must experiment to discover the techniques that work well for you. This chapter and the next will help you with that experimentation. They explain aspects of the process that all writers must pay attention to as noted in the following chart.

Aspects of the Writing Process

- **Identifying and considering your writing context,** which is determining your purpose for writing, the audience for your writing, and your role as a writer
- **Generating ideas,** which is discovering what you have to say
- **Ordering ideas,** which is determining the progression of your ideas and their relationship to one another
- **Developing a thesis,** which is determining the central point of your writing
- **Drafting,** which is writing a preliminary version of your essay
- **Revising,** which is rewriting to improve the content, organization, and expression of ideas in your draft
- **Editing,** which is finding and correcting errors in grammar and usage

In addition to explaining aspects of the writing process, these two chapters present procedures for working through each of these aspects. Sample these procedures until you find ones that work well for you, and your writing is sure to improve. Keep in mind, however, that different writers function in different ways, and the procedures that work well for some of your classmates will not necessarily work well for you.

What do you currently do when you write? Think about your current writing process and which of your procedures you think work well and which ones need to be improved.

IDENTIFYING AND CONSIDERING YOUR WRITING CONTEXT

Successful writers do not plan their writing in a vacuum. Instead, they consider the *context* in which their writing occurs. The **writing context** includes what the reason for writing is (the writer's *purpose*), who the readers are (the *audience*), and how the writer wants to present him- or herself (the writer's *role*). Together, purpose, audience, and role affect everything the writer does — from idea generation through the final check for typos.

Purpose

Whether you are writing an e-mail to a friend, preparing a business report, or composing a college essay, you are writing for a reason — and that reason is your **purpose.** In general, these are the primary purposes for writing:

- To entertain the reader
- To express your feelings and/or to relate your experience
- To inform the reader about something interesting or important
- To persuade the reader to think or act a particular way

You encounter writing that fulfills these purposes all the time. Dave Barry's humorous books and blog *entertain;* a friend's e-mails about the frustrations of interviewing for a job *express feelings and relate experience;* the letter you receive explaining the terms of your student health insurance policy *informs* you about the nature of your coverage; and the newspaper editorial about a critical blood shortage tries to *persuade* you to donate blood to the Red Cross.

Your writing purpose influences your approach. Suppose you are a single parent who wants to write about the child care problems in this country. To entertain your reader, you can write a funny piece about what you went through the day you had to take a final, and the babysitter canceled. To express your feelings, you can describe how much you worry about whether your children get quality care while you are at school. To inform your reader, you can explain what the child care options are for a single parent of preschool children. To persuade your reader, you can argue for a federally funded child care program. Of course, you can also combine purposes. For example, you can relate your own experiences and then go on to argue that a federally funded program would make life easier for you and others. Obviously, each of these writings would have a different character because the content would be shaped by your purpose.

Because purpose influences the content and character of writing so profoundly, you should be clear about your purpose at the outset. Answering these questions can help you establish a purpose or combination of purposes.

Questions for Establishing Your Writing Purpose

- **Are you trying to entertain your readers?** Why do you want to entertain them? Do you want readers to be amused, find enjoyment, escape from reality, or something else?

- **Do you want to express your feelings and/or relate your experience?** What do you want to express or relate? How do you want readers to react to your feelings or experience?

- **Are you seeking to inform readers about something?** Why do you want readers to know this information? How do you want readers to react to this information?

- **Do you want to persuade readers to think or act a particular way?** How do you want them to think or act?

(For a reminder of the four main purposes, glance at the back inside cover of this book.)

Audience

To achieve your purpose, you need a clear sense of **audience** — that is, a clear sense of who your reader is and what that reader is like. Suppose you are writing an essay about the pollution in a local river. If the essay were written for your biology class, it might include a great deal of technical information about specific chemical pollutants. However, if the essay were for a letter to your local newspaper, such technical information might overwhelm the average reader of that paper. Now suppose that you are writing to convince your reader to support an increase in property taxes to fund school improvements. If your reader has school-age children, you could argue that the quality of their education will improve with the tax increase. However, if your reader has no children, you may do better to argue that good schools will increase the value of the reader's property.

In some writing classes, you can establish any person or group of people as your audience because your instructor will assume the role of any reader you designate, such as city council members, your house-mates, a co-worker, the head of the Environmental Protection Agency, the professors at your college, or your parents. In other writing classes, you must consider your classmates and teacher to be your audience. In either case—or in any situation in or out of the classroom—you must identify your audience and the particular characteristics and needs of that audi-ence because this information will influence your approach, your details, your word choice, and almost every other decision you make about your writing. Do you need to define a term? That depends on whether your reader is likely to know its meaning. Should you provide an example? That depends on whether your reader requires the clarification. Should you use this sophisticated word or that more common one? That depends on your reader's likely vocabulary. Which of two points will be more persuasive? That may depend on your reader's age, gender, political leanings, or economic situation.

If you need help identifying an audience for your writing, answer the following questions.

Questions for Identifying Your Audience

- **Who would enjoy reading your essay?** Who is likely to be entertained or amused? Who is likely to find reading about your topic pleasurable?

- **Whom do you want to know and understand you better?** Who would be interested in what you have to say? Who cares about your feelings and experiences?

- **Who is interested in your topic?** Who would find your topic important? Who could benefit from reading your essay?

- **Who could learn something from your essay?** Who does not currently know much about your topic? Who needs to know more about your topic?

- **Who should be convinced to think or act a particular way?** Whose viewpoint needs to be changed? Whose mind can you change? Whom can you convince to take action? Who *should* take action?

Once you have identified your audience, consider your reader's traits and needs, so you do not inadvertently bore, confuse, or annoy your audience and thereby fail to achieve your purpose. How do you assess traits and needs to avoid this outcome? Answering the following ques-tions can help.

Questions for Assessing Your Audience

- **What does your reader already know about your topic?** The answer to this question can help you decide what your reader needs to know and it can help you avoid boring your audience by providing information your reader does not need or already has. It can also help you determine the nature and number of clarifying points, such as examples and definitions, to provide.

- **How interested is your reader in what you have to say?** The answer to this question can help you decide how much of your writing should be devoted to capturing the reader's interest or convincing your reader that your topic is important.

- **Does your reader have strong feelings about your topic?** The answer to this question will help you determine whether you must overcome a reader's particular biases or respond to the reader's concerns.

- **How will your reader's age, gender, level of education, income, job, politics, or religion affect his or her reaction to your writing?** The answer to this question will help you decide on appropriate details and language.

When your audience is a diverse group — say, the readers of your local newspaper, the students on your campus, or the members of a large organization — your readers may not have much in common, so you may not be able to assess their needs and traits in a way that yields a single useful profile. In that case, you can identify one or two characteristics that are shared by many members of the group and let that information guide you. For example, if you are writing to working students on your campus, you can think of them as dealing with the stress of juggling courses, studying, and work.

Role

In addition to audience and purpose, your **role** — the way you want to present yourself — will influence the character of your writing. For example, in the role of a student writing for a teacher, you want to conform to all the terms of the assignment. In the role of an employee writing for a supervisor, you need to adopt a respectful tone and avoid saying anything that you would not want in your personnel file. In the role of a friend writing to another friend, you might include slang and abbreviations, which you would not do in the role of student writing an essay for a scholarship competition.

To appreciate the significance of the writer's role, consider how various people might report on how to select the right college. A high school counselor will provide an objective set of procedures, but a college admissions counselor may slant the detail to favor his or her school. A student may express the frustrations that are part of the process, but a parent may stress financial concerns.

If the nature of your role is not obvious, consider whether you are writing as one or more of the following.

> **Possible Roles for Student Writers**
>
> • Brother, sister, wife, husband, child, parent
> • Employer, employee
> • Student, tutor, roommate, coach
> • Neutral party, authority, interested observer, average person
> • Friend, stranger, newcomer
> • Young adult, retiree, middle-aged person

GENERATING IDEAS

Perhaps you think that writing is the product of inspiration and that it involves staring at a blank page or computer screen until a brilliant flash of insight sends your pen racing across the page or your fingers flying across the keys. If the inspiration does not strike, perhaps you assume that you cannot write, so you might as well pack it up and go play racquetball. If you think this way, you are not alone — but you are wrong.

Inspiration *does* occasionally strike writers, but most often it does not, and we must rely on other idea generation techniques. When you are not feeling inspired — and even when you are — use the idea generation techniques described in this chapter to shape writing topics and to discover ideas for developing those topics.

Shaping a Writing Topic

Many times an instructor will specify the writing topic. In that case, your first priority is to be sure you understand the assignment and its terms so you can meet your instructor's expectations. First of all, you must be sure you understand the *kind of paper* called for. Does your instructor want you to take a position and defend it? Summarize an author's ideas? Explain the meaning of a concept? Compare and contrast two essays?

Consider, for example, this assignment that could be made after students have read "Americanization Is Tough on 'Macho'" (pages 13–15):

> In what ways do movies and television influence our views of how men (or, alternatively, women) are supposed to behave?

This topic requires you to deal with only one gender; dealing with both is not called for and would result in an unwieldy paper. The topic also requires you to provide examples of specific movies and television programs in order to support your points.

Now consider this assignment based on the same reading selection:

Agree or disagree with Rose Del Castillo Guibault's claim that "the American *macho* is a chauvinist, a brute, uncouth, selfish, loud, abrasive, capable of inflicting pain, and sexually promiscuous."

This topic requires a different approach, for you must take a position and convince your reader of the validity of your position by arguing persuasively.

In addition to understanding the kind of paper required, you must also be sure you understand the *terms of the assignment:* the length; the due date; the necessary manuscript form; the need to have a teacher conference, engage in peer review, or submit an outline; and so forth. If you have questions about an assigned topic or its terms, speak to your instructor for guidance.

When you are not given a specific topic to respond to, the following idea generation techniques can help you shape a writing topic:

1. Review the marginal notes and journal entries you made during critical reading. (See Chapter 1 on critical reading.) Your comments, questions, and areas of disagreement and agreement may suggest a topic. For example, the marginal note in response to paragraph 7 of "Americanization Is Tough on 'Macho'" could prompt an essay about the image of males presented in action movies.

2. Use a provocative quotation as a topic source. For example, in paragraph 16 of "Americanization Is Tough on 'Macho,'" the author says, "I believe it was the feminist movement of the early '70s that changed *macho*'s meaning." This quotation could prompt an essay about the changing meaning of *macho*.

3. Pick a subject treated in a reading and brainstorm. To brainstorm, make a list of every idea that occurs to you on a subject and then examine your list for possible topics. For best results, do not censor yourself. Just list everything that occurs to you without evaluating the worth of the ideas. For example, one student wrote the following list to brainstorm for topics about violence in sports:

fan violence	why athletes are violent
player violence	Are athletes too violent?
causes of violence	Is it violence or aggression?
effects of violence	How can we make sports less
Is the violence justified?	violent?
violence = part of the game	Fans love it.
It's expected.	Players think it's okay.
Is society sick if it likes violence?	Are players violent off the field?
players getting hurt	fans getting hurt

The student ultimately drew his topic from the question "Are players violent off the field?" That question prompted him to write about players being violent on the playing field and nonviolent off it.

4. Freewrite for about 10 minutes on a subject found in a reading. To freewrite, write nonstop without censoring yourself. Simply record everything that occurs to you without worrying about its quality or about spelling, grammar, or neatness. Do not stop writing for any reason. If you run out of ideas, write something: the alphabet, names of family members — anything. Soon new ideas will occur to you, and you can record those. At the computer, you can try freewriting with the screen dark. Just turn off your monitor and freewrite "blindfolded." You will have many typing errors, but the freedom that comes from not seeing what you are writing can stimulate your thinking.

The following freewriting was done by a student in response to an essay arguing that female homemakers should not be financially dependent on their husbands. As you review the freewriting, notice that the author did not worry about correctness. Also notice that she allowed herself to write even silly things as she waited for better ideas to surface.

> William Raspberry says women who are homemakers shouldn't be considered as dependant on male breadwinners. Well that's true but aren't male breadwinners dependant on the homemaker too? Could they cope if the woman walked out? I bet not, theird be hell to pay. Let's see what to write, oh the guy would have to pay sommeone to come in and clean and cook and take care of the kiddies. That would be hard and expensive. Let's see what do I think now? Maybe we should pay homemakers a salary. Could that be done? Maybe, or maybe a giant PR campaign to upgrade the image of homemakers — yeah, how about some advertising? I agree with Raspberry that women shouldn't be dependant financially if they are homemakers but I know a lot of women who don't mind so I doubt anything will change.

The student's freewriting suggests at least three topics:

- The need to upgrade the image of homemakers
- Paying homemakers for the work they do
- Why some women do not mind depending on males

Your freewriting may not yield as many topics, but it likely will suggest at least one.

5. Examine the subject of a reading from different angles. Answering these questions will help:

- Does the subject make you think of something else?
- Why is the subject important?
- Do you agree or disagree with the author?
- What interests you about the subject?
- Can you give the author's ideas a broader or different application?
- Can you relate the subject to your own experience?

Narrowing Your Topic

If you have trouble working with your writing topic, perhaps that topic is too broad. A topic like "education reform" may seem perfect to you at first because you think there are so many problems with schools today. However, you may find that you have *too* much to say and don't know where to begin or how you can say it in the specified length. Try narrowing your topic by writing a tree diagram. Place your broad topic on top and "branch off" some ideas, like this:

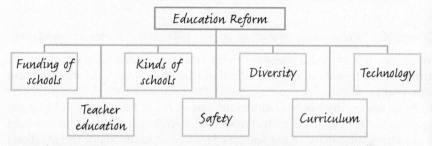

Select a branch that interests you and branch a second time, like this:

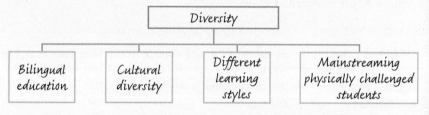

If the topics in your second branching are still too broad, branch again:

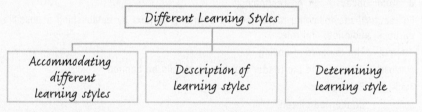

Any of these last branches could make a narrow, workable writing topic.

An Essay in Progress: Shaping a Topic and Identifying Context

To consider the different aspects of the writing process in a more concrete way, we will look at an essay as it was being written by a student writer, Jeff. Following Jeff's process can help you with your own. To shape a writing topic based on "Americanization Is Tough on 'Macho'" (pages 13–15), Jeff used brainstorming. Here is his list:

sources of American concept of "macho"
why the concept is wrong (?)

why Americans don't understand the Latin macho
nature of concept of "ideal male"
when this ideal is unreasonable
nature of concept of "ideal female"
how this ideal is unreasonable
cultural conflict over gender roles
  — world scale
  — national scale
  — local scale
need for more realistic concept of gender roles strong silence vs. aggression

Notice that Jeff placed a question mark next to an idea he was unsure of. During idea generation, use any notation that stimulates your thinking and helps you push forward.

After reviewing his brainstorming, Jeff decided his topic would be the nature of the concept of the ideal male. Jeff also decided his purpose would be to inform the reader of the source of misconceptions about the idealized male. He established his audience as the average reader and his role as that of a young adult, concerned male.

Shaping a Writing Topic and Identifying Context

1. Select two subjects from the following list, and shape a writing topic from each. For one subject, use brainstorming to shape a topic. For the other subject, use freewriting.

   a. Video games   **e.** The image of men or women in the media

   b. Education   **f.** Athletics

   c. Television   **g.** Friendship

   d. Automobiles   **h.** Technology

2. For each of the following topics, set up a writing context by establishing a possible purpose, audience, and role.

   EXAMPLE   The dangers of boxing

   PURPOSE   To persuade the reader that boxing should be banned

   AUDIENCE   Boxing fans

   ROLE   Concerned citizen.

   a. A car accident you witnessed or read about

   b. A report on the financial health of the local schools

   c. The use of pesticides on food grown in the United States

   d. The causes of the high divorce rate in the United States

3. Select one of the writing contexts you created for number 2, and change the context by altering one or more of the elements (audience, purpose, and role). How do you think the change(s) will affect the final essay?

4. Establish a writing context for the topics you generated in response to number 1. Save your work to use in a later exercise.

Discovering Ideas to Develop Your Topic

Once you have a topic, you must discover ideas for developing that topic, ideas compatible with your writing context. Some of the following idea generation techniques may help:

1. Write a discovery draft. A discovery draft is not a first draft. It is an effort to identify what you already know about your topic and what you can think of along the way. To write a discovery draft, start writing anything that comes to mind about your topic. Do not worry about anything except recording everything you can think of. If you cannot think of much, you may not know enough about your topic, or you may need to try some other idea generation techniques.

2. Review the marginal notes and journal entries you made during critical reading. They may include ideas for developing your topic. (See Chapter 1 on critical reading.)

3. Write a brainstorming list. Like brainstorming for a topic, brainstorming for ideas to develop a topic involves listing every idea that occurs to you. Remember, do not evaluate the worth of your ideas; simply write down everything you can think of. Later, you can reject anything unusable. Here is an example of a brainstorming list for one of the topics that emerged from the freewriting on page 36.

> *Topic: the need to upgrade the image of homemakers*
> *Homemakers are the backbone of the family.*
> *They work hard.*
> *They work long hours, 7 days a week.*
> *It would be very expensive to pay people to do everything that homemakers do.*
> *Homemakers make it possible for other family members to do things.*
> *They often do volunteer work that helps schools and society at large.*
> *Women would feel less like they need outside jobs for fulfillment.*
> *Nothing is more important than homemaking.*
> *We must stop assigning value according to how much money is earned.*

Because brainstorming is idea generation, its results are preliminary. You need not use everything on the list, and you can add to the list at any time.

4. Try clustering. Clustering helps you generate ideas and see how those ideas relate to one another. To cluster, first write your topic in the center of the page and draw a circle around it. As ideas to develop your topic occur to you, write them down, circle them, and draw lines attaching them to the circled ideas they relate to. Do not censor yourself. Write down everything, regardless of its quality. The following clustering was done for an essay about violence on the playing field.

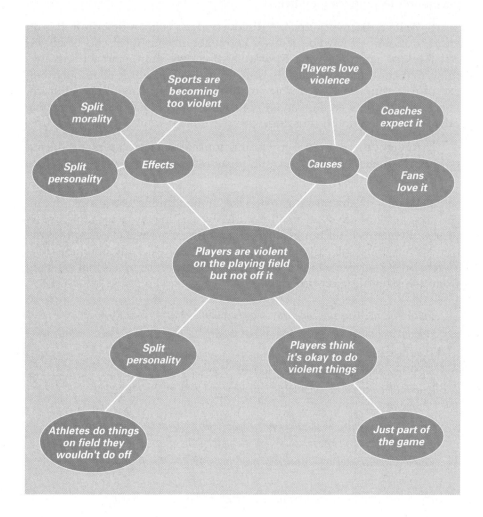

In the final version of the essay, the writer did not use all of the ideas in his clustering, and he used some ideas that do not appear in the clustering. That is fine because nothing about idea generation is set in stone. Also notice that the writer placed "split personality" in two spots on the clustering. That is also fine. If you are unsure what an idea relates to, jot it down in more than one spot and solve the problem later.

5. Talk to other people about your topic. Your classmates, in particular, can suggest ideas for developing your topic.

Using the Internet

If you have trouble generating ideas, try using the Internet.

- **Surf the Internet.** Type a subject into a search engine like one of the following, and scan the hits for possible writing topics or ideas for developing a topic.

  Alta Vista: www.altavista.com   Yahoo: www.yahoo.com

  Google: www.google.com   All the Web: www.alltheweb.com

- **Browse news sites and electronic newspapers and magazines.** Scan one of these popular sites for information on current events, health, business, and entertainment. You might get several writing ideas.

  Yahoo news: news.yahoo.com/?uReuters News Service: www.reuters.com/news.ihtm

  Google News: news.google.com

  www.refdesk.com/paper.html

  USA Today: usatoday.com

- **Browse Web sites with links to varied content.** These two sites, in particular, may give you writing ideas:

  Science and Technology Daily: scitechdaily.com

  Arts and Letters Daily: aldaily.com

---

www.mhhe.com/clousepatterns6 | Internet |

For more help with using the Internet, click on

Research > Using the Internet

---

6. **Combine techniques.** Begin by freewriting and then try clustering. Or begin with a brainstorming list and then talk to other people. Combine idea generation strategies in any way that suits you.

An Essay in Progress: Discovering Ideas to Develop Your Topic

Jeff created the cluster on page 42 as a way to discover ideas that would help him develop the topic he generated with the brainstorming list on page 38.

Discover Ideas to Develop Your Topic

1. Select three of the following topics. For each one, generate three ideas that could be used for development. Use a different idea generation technique for each topic.

    Mandatory drug testing of college athletes

    The ethical issues associated with cloning animals

    The causes of stress among college students

    The characteristics of a leader

EXERCISE 2.2

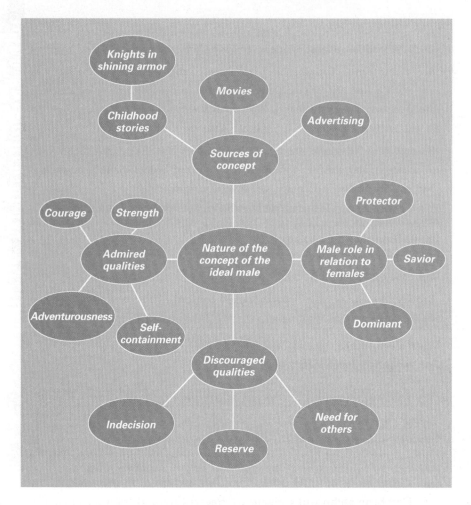

2. Using the idea generation techniques of your choice, come up with enough ideas to write a first draft on one of the topics you established a writing context for in number 4 of Exercise 2.1.

DEVELOPING A THESIS

A successful essay has a central point, a main message the writer wants to convey. This central point is the **thesis,** the idea that everything else in the essay pertains to. You can think of the thesis as the controlling idea of an essay.

Sometimes you have a good idea of what your thesis is when you first get under way. For example, if your political science instructor asks you to attack or defend the use of lobbyists by corporations and interest groups and you are opposed to them, you already have a sense of your thesis: It will express your opposition to the use of lobbyists. More often, your thesis will emerge as you generate ideas or afterward, when you study the ideas you have generated.

Your thesis should let your reader know the topic of your essay and your assertion about the topic.

TOPIC	WRITER'S ASSERTION	THESIS
MTV and children	Parents should limit their children's exposure to it.	Parents should limit their children's exposure to MTV.
People who are practical jokers	There are three kinds.	Careful observation reveals three kinds of practical jokers.
The nature of the author's father	He was a strict disciplinarian.	My father was a strict disciplinarian.

Your thesis can do more than indicate your topic and your assertion. It can also note the major points you will make in the essay:

TOPIC	MTV and children
WRITER'S ASSERTION	Parents should limit their children's exposure to it.
POINTS TO BE MADE	MTV airs sexually explicit material and demeans people.
THESIS	Parents should limit their children's exposure to MTV because the channel airs sexually explicit material and demeans people.

In scientific, technical, business, and some social science writing, thesis statements that indicate major points are fairly common. Especially when the piece of writing is long or technical, such a thesis helps the reader by indicating the main points that will follow. In papers for your writing class and many humanities courses, however, this kind of thesis can seem boring or unnecessary—particularly for a relatively brief and uncomplicated essay—so use it with caution.

Location of the Thesis

The thesis generally appears in the essay's introductory section. Often, it is at the end of that section; however, it can also be in the beginning or middle of the introduction. The following paragraphs illustrate different placements of the thesis, which is underlined as a study aid.

THESIS AT THE BEGINNING

I am always tardy, a habit that creates difficulties for my family and friends. Ever since I was a child, I have tended to get up late, show up for meals late, and leave for school late. I am not sure when I last saw the opening credits for a movie because I typically arrive 10 or 15 minutes into the film. Usually, my friends and family forgive me, but who knows how long they will tolerate my lateness when it causes them so many problems.

THESIS IN THE MIDDLE

The second Iraqi war is unlike previous wars in many ways. Chief among the differences is the fact that <u>women have proven their ability to serve in the front lines with courage and distinction.</u> As a result, the claim that woman are unsuited for combat will no longer be made.

THESIS AT THE END

Have you ever received unwanted credit cards in the mail? Did a credit card company ever offer you such a big line of credit at such a low interest rate that you could not resist the offer? Yes, accepting the cards is tempting, but they come with risks the credit card companies never mention. As a former credit card addict, <u>I can assure you that the dangers of relying on credit are very serious.</u>

In some essays, the thesis is in the last paragraph. This placement works well when all the detail in the essay builds cumulatively to a conclusion that is the essay's main point. In other essays, the thesis is not stated. Instead, it is strongly implied by the details in the essay. When the thesis is not stated, a critical reader must infer the thesis. (See page 5 on inference.)

Qualities of an Effective Thesis

An effective thesis includes the topic of the essay and the writer's assertion about that topic. In addition, try to do the following as you formulate your thesis.

1. Avoid the formal announcement.

NO	This paper will discuss the reasons the United States needs election reform.
YES	The United States would benefit from election reform.
NO	The following essay will explain how to behave during a job interview.
YES	If you want to land that dream job, follow this advice during the job interview.
NO	I want to tell you the characteristics of a nuturing family.
YES	All nurturing families share certain characteristics.

2. Present an assertion that is arguable or in need of explanation, rather than a statement of fact.

NO	Drunk drivers are a menace. (No one will disagree with this statement of fact, so why contruct an essay around it?)

YES	To make the roads safer for everyone, we should suspend the driver's license of anyone convicted of drunk driving. (This thesis presents an arguable point.)
NO	During the Depression, my grandmother raised four children by herself. (This is a statement of fact; the essay has nowhere to go from here.)
YES	I have always admired my grandmother's strength and courage during difficult times. (This thesis allows for explanation.)

3. Present a manageable topic; it should not involve more than you can cover adequately in the assigned length of your essay.

NO	Our system of education is in need of a complete overhaul. (An essay that discusses changes in every aspect of the educational system will be much longer than the standard college essay. If the essay is a reasonable length, the discussion will be superficial.)
YES	To be competitive with the rest of the world, we must require all students to take four years of high school mathematics. (This thesis presents a topic that can be treated in adequate detail in a manageable length.)

4. Use specific language; avoid vague words such as *nice, interesting, good, bad,* and *great* because they result in vague statements.

NO	Playing high school football was a great experience.
YES	Playing high school football taught me self-confidence and the importance of teamwork.

Composing Your Thesis

1. Study the ideas you generated to develop your topic. Does one idea have more points than the others? Does one idea interest you or your audience more than the others? Does one idea seem more manageable than the others? The idea that answers one or more of these questions might be a good idea to base your thesis on.

2. Engage in additional idea generation, if necessary. If you cannot formulate a thesis, you may not yet have generated enough ideas and details. Try again, this time using a different idea generation technique.

3. Consider your writing context. What do you already know or what can you determine about your audience, purpose, and role that can point you toward a thesis? Suppose you are writing about the dangers associated with the Internet. If you cannot think of a thesis, identify an audience and go from there. For example, you could establish your audience as teenagers, which could lead you to explain how teens can avoid sexual predators in chat rooms.

4. Allow your early thesis to be preliminary. Although you are learning about the qualities of an effective thesis, your first version need not have all those qualities. An imperfect thesis can be revised later. Write an announcement if doing so moves you forward. Later, you can craft a more elegant thesis.

---

www.mhhe.com/clousepatterns6 | Thesis

For help with developing a thesis, click on

Writing > Thesis/Central Idea

An Essay in Progress: Composing a Thesis

Before drafting an early version of his thesis, Jeff studied his clustering, which appears on page 42. He thought he had many good ideas, but at first he had trouble seeing how the ideas in the main circles branching off his center topic related to one another. He reflected about this and was somewhat frustrated until he considered the ideas in light of his personal dislike of the concept of the ideal male. Then he related the ideas to that dislike and found a unifying thread, which he expressed in this sentence:

The concept of the ideal male is a problem and has no basis.

He rewrote that sentence for clarity and came up with a preliminary thesis he was happy with:

The popular concept of the ideal male is unsuitable in our society.

Next, Jeff considered the thesis in light of his writing context and realized that he wanted to broaden his purpose. Rather than simply inform his reader, he also wanted to convince his audience that the concept of the ideal male is misguided.

Composing a Thesis

1. Explain what you can expect to find in an essay with each thesis. Try to determine the purpose for each essay (to entertain, express feelings, relate experience, inform, or persuade).

   EXAMPLE   The 12-month school year offers several advantages.

   EXPLANATION   The essay will mention and explain the effects of the 12-month school year, perhaps to persuade the reader that it is the best academic calendar.

   a. Professional athletes are often viewed as heroes.
   b. Karate is an excellent sport for school-age children who need to build self-esteem.
   c. To find the right job, a person needs a strategy.

EXERCISE 2.3

d. A good teacher has a sense of humor, a commitment to excellence, and the ability to be flexible.

   e. The spring drought will create economic hardships in the Midwest.

2. Indicate whether each thesis is effective or ineffective. If it is ineffective, state why and rewrite it to make it effective.

   a. Regular exercise is important to a person's physical well-being.

   b. *Seinfeld* is one of the most popular sit-coms of all time.

   c. Newspapers are a better source of information about current affairs than network news programs.

   d. The following paragraph will explain why all high school students should take four years of a foreign language.

   e. The current movie rating system is inadequate for a number of reasons.

   f. The entertainment available to Americans is of the poorest quality.

   g. Summer camp is a good experience for children.

3. Return to the idea generation material and topic you developed for number 2 of Exercise 2.2 on page 42. Study that material and develop a thesis from it. Save your work to use in a later exercise.

ORDERING IDEAS

The order in which you present your ideas is important because a reader who cannot follow the sequence will become confused and frustrated. There are many possibilities for ordering ideas. Here are three common ones, which can be used alone or in combination:

1. **Chronological order** arranges details across time. The event that occurred first is written first; the event that occurred second is written second; and so on.

2. **Spatial order** arranges details as they appear across space—front to back, near to far, top to bottom, left to right.

3. **Progressive order** arranges details from the least to the most important, compelling, interesting, representative, surprising, and so on. A progressive order allows for a big finish because the most significant point comes at the end. A variation of progressive order is to begin and end with the strongest points for a strong beginning as well as a strong ending.

Outlining

A workable outline often makes drafting go much more smoothly. However, many people resist outlining because they are familiar with only the formal outline developed with roman numerals, letters, and arabic numerals. The formal outline is very helpful, especially for long or complex essays. However, less formal and less detailed alternatives are available for simpler papers, and these are also explained in this chapter. Choose the outline that best suits your paper: The more complicated the paper, the more detailed the outline should be. Whatever type of outline you choose, you will find it helpful to begin with your preliminary statement (early version) of your thesis, as the following outline examples show.

The Scratch Outline

The scratch outline is the least detailed outline. It is simply a list of the major ideas you plan to include in your first draft, written in the order you plan to cover them. Typically, the scratch outline covers only major points and gives no details for developing those points, so it is not well suited for complicated essays or for writers who must plan in detail before drafting. As an example, here is a scratch outline based, in part, on some of the ideas generated with the clustering on page 40:

> *Preliminary thesis: Even nonviolent people are often violent on the playing field.*
> *Violence is okay because it's part of the game.*
> *A player has to be violent to compete with other players.*
> *Sports is different from the real world, so violence is justified.*
> *Fans want the violence.*

If you brainstormed on a computer, you can turn your brainstorming list into a scratch outline. First, delete ideas you do not want to use, and add any new ones that occur to you. Then, using your cut-and-paste functions, arrange the ideas in your list in the order you want to treat them in your draft.

The Informal Outline

The informal outline includes some details for developing major points, and it groups related ideas together, so you have a sense of which details will appear together in the same paragraph. Although more detailed than the scratch outline, the informal outline may still not be suitable for complex papers or for writers who need to plan in detail. An informal outline might look like this:

> *Preliminary thesis: Even nonviolent people are often violent on the playing field.*
> *Violence is okay because it's part of the game.*
>   *Use roommate as example.*
>   *Coaches play only people with killer instinct.*
> *A player has to be violent to compete with other players.*
>   *Get other guys before they get you.*
>   *If everyone else is violent, you have to be, too.*
>   *Violence is okay if you win the game.*

Sports is different from the real world, so violence is justified.
  It's only a game and not part of reality, so it's okay to be violent.
  But the injuries are real.
Fans want the violence.
  Fans cheer for violence.
  They even act violently themselves in the stands.

The Outline Tree

An outline tree, which is similar to the informal outline in degree of detail, allows a writer to see how ideas relate to each other. Many writers appreciate the visual representation the tree provides. To construct an outline tree, write your preliminary thesis at the top of a page and connect ideas with "branches," as in this example.

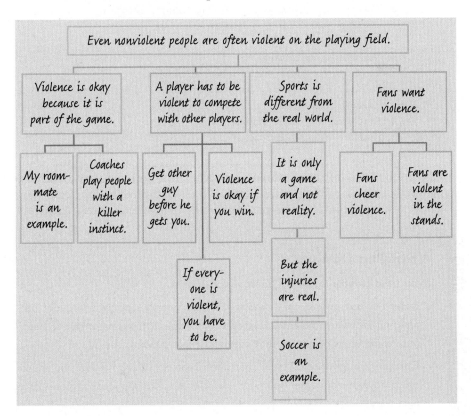

The Formal Outline

With the formal outline, you can plan your essay in considerable detail. Label your major points with roman numerals and your supporting details with capital letters. Use arabic numerals for smaller details that explain or illustrate your supporting details. You are probably familiar with formal outlines. For our student example, it might look something like this:

Preliminary thesis: Nonviolent people can be violent on the playing field.

I. *Hurting people is part of the game.*
   A. *My roommate is gentle off the basketball court and hurtful on the court.*
   B. *If he didn't hurt others, the coach would bench him.*
II. *Violence is necessary for winning.*
   A. *Players feel violence is okay if they win.*
      1. *In my soccer game, an opposing player intentionally hurt one of our players.*
      2. *He did it to win.*
   B. *Players injure others so they don't get hurt themselves.*
III. *Players think violence is okay because sports are games.*
   A. *But the violence is real.*
   B. *The injuries are lasting.*
      1. *Our soccer goalie missed a month of school.*
      2. *He still has effects from a violent play.*
IV. *Fans like violence.*
   A. *Fans encourage player violence.*
   B. *Fans are violent themselves.*

If you like to compose at the computer, check your word processing program to see if it has outlining capability. If it does, you can develop a formal outline by filling in the various levels. If it does not, develop your own outline form, using roman numerals, letters, and arabic numerals.

Writing an Outline

If you have trouble outlining, these tips can help:

- **Refer to your preliminary thesis.** Ideas that don't seem to fit in your outline may not be sufficiently related to your thesis. You may need to eliminate some ideas or adjust your thesis to accommodate them.

- **Consider your context.** Ideas that don't seem to belong may not be appropriate for your purpose, audience, or role. Adjust your ideas or context as necessary.

- **Be flexible.** The outlining process may lead you to reconsider some of your ideas or your thesis. Be ready to add and delete ideas and adjust your thesis in light of new insights.

- **Return to idea generation, if necessary.** If you cannot outline, you may not yet have enough material.

TROUBLESHOOTING GUIDE

Save the form as a file you can retrieve whenever you want to outline. To learn more about the mechanics of writing a formal outline, visit Purdue University's Online Writing Lab at http://owl.english.purdue.edu/hand-outs/general/gl_outlin.html.

| www.mhhe.com/clousepatterns6 | Outlining |

For more help with creating an outline, click on

Writing > Outlines

Writing > Outlining Tutor

An Essay in Progress: Outlining

Using his clustering as a guide (see page 42), student-writer Jeff developed the following informal outline. You will notice that Jeff did not use all the ideas from his clustering and that he included ideas that do not appear in the clustering. Writers are always free to make changes as new ideas occur to them.

Preliminary thesis: The popular concept of the ideal male is unsuitable in our society.

The sources of the ideal are ridiculous.
  movie industry
    —highly unrealistic situations
  advertising
    —deceitful industry to begin with
  folktales and childhood stories
    —originated in completely different eras and societies

The admired/discouraged qualities of the ideal are out of place.
  instinctive vs. considered action
    —increasingly complex society
  self-containment vs. need for others
    —increasingly cooperative society

The idealized male's relation to women is archaic.
  protector, savior, rescuer, dominant male
    —increasing appearance of female equality in all respects

Ordering Ideas

1. For each preliminary thesis statement, indicate whether the order of ideas is likely to be spatial, chronological, or progressive.
   a. The university should offer a study skills seminar as part of its orientation program.
   b. Once the floodwaters receded, I discovered the devastation to my apartment.
   c. The movie version of *Lord of the Rings* is better than the book version.

EXERCISE 2.4

d. I will always remember the day Julio won the state pole vault championship.

e. You can learn to change the oil in your car and save money as a result.

f. At sunset, the flower garden of Municipal Park offers a peaceful retreat.

2. Using the techniques of your choice, generate ideas for an essay with one of the following preliminary thesis statements:

> Teenagers are too materialistic.
>
> Teenagers are not too materialistic.

Then write an informal outline for the essay.

3. Using the techniques of your choice, generate ideas for an essay with one of the following preliminary thesis statements:

> Our enthusiasm for computers has gone too far.
>
> Our enthusiasm for computers has not gone too far.

Then write an outline tree for the essay.

4. Using the thesis and ideas you have from number 3 for Exercise 2.3, write either a formal outline or an outline tree. Feel free to add or delete ideas as you see fit. Save your work to use in a later exercise.

USING THE PATTERNS OF DEVELOPMENT

Patterns of development are ways to think and write about a topic. As you generate ideas, compose your thesis, and organize your draft, consider how the patterns of development can help you achieve your writing purpose, generate ideas, and find an effective order for those ideas. The following patterns of development are explained and illustrated in Chapters 5–12:

- **Description** (Chapter 5)—using words to explain what something looks, sounds, feels, smells, and/or tastes like (spatial or progressive order often used)
- **Narration** (Chapter 6)—telling a story (chronological order often used)
- **Exemplification** (Chapter 7)—providing examples (progressive order often used)
- **Process analysis** (Chapter 8)—explaining how something works or how it is made or done (chronological order often used)
- **Comparison-contrast** (Chapter 9)—explaining similarities and/or differences (block pattern or alternating pattern, explained in Chapter 9, often used)
- **Cause-and-effect analysis** (Chapter 10)—explaining the reasons for an action and/or the results of an action (progressive order often used)
- **Classification-division** (Chapter 11)—grouping items into categories and/or breaking something down into its parts (progressive order often used)
- **Definition** (Chapter 12)—explaining the meaning of a term or concept (progressive order often used)

In addition to using the strategies on pages 34 and 39, you can ask these questions related to the patterns to help shape a writing topic and generate ideas to develop that topic. (You will not be able to answer every question for every writing subject.)

Idea Generation Questions Using the Patterns

- Can you describe something related to your subject? (description)
- Can you tell a story related to your subject? (narration)
- Can you provide examples that illustrate your subject? (exemplification)
- Can you explain how your subject works or how it is made or done? (process analysis)
- What is your subject like? What is it different from? (comparison-contrast)
- What causes your subject? What are the effects of your subject (cause-and-effect analysis)
- Can you classify your subject into different categories? Can you break your subject down into parts? (classification-division)
- What is the meaning of your subject? Are there any terms or concepts you need to define? (definition)

To see how considering the patterns of development can help with idea generation and organization, consider the following chart, developed to discover ideas for an essay about the need to upgrade the image of homemakers.

The Need to Upgrade the Image of Homemakers

PATTERN	IDEA	ORDER
Description	Describe the image of the homemaker that many people have.	Although spatial order is often used to describe people and places, progressive order might be used here.
Narration	Tell the story of the time a friend felt embarrassed at a party because she was the only woman who did not work outside the home.	Chronological order is likely.
Exemplification	Give examples of advertisements that show working mothers as the ideal.	Progressive order is possible. Exemplification could be combined with classification-division, with ads for makeup discussed as one group, ads for clothing as another, and ads for electronics as a third.

PATTERN	IDEA	ORDER
Process analysis	Explain a procedure for upgrading the image of homemakers.	Chronological order could be used if the steps are performed in a specific order; progressive order could be used if steps are arranged in order of effectiveness or difficulty.
Comparison-contrast	Contrast the perception of the homemaker with the perception of the woman working outside the home.	Progressive order is possible. Using progressive order, make all the points about the homemaker first and then all the points about the working woman in what is called a *block pattern*. Alternatively, make one point about the homemaker and one about the working woman, and continue in this fashion in an *alternating pattern*.
Cause-and-effect analysis	Explain the effects the current image of the homemaker has on family life.	Progressive order is possible, with the most significant effects given last. Cause-and-effect analysis could be combined with grouping by category if effects on relationships are given together, effects on self-esteem are given together, and so on.
Classification-division	Explain the components of the image of the homemaker.	Progressive order could be used if components (personality components, physical components, and so on) are given in order of significance.
Definition	Provide a definition of a *homemaker*.	Progressive order is possible if aspects of the definition are given in order of significance.

www.mhhe.com/clousepatterns6　　　　　　　　　　　　　　　　Patterns

For more help with using the rhetorical patterns, click on
Writing > Paragraph Patterns

BACKGROUND: Born in Alabama in 1937 and raised in Asheville, North Carolina, Gail Godwin received her journalism degree from the University of North Carolina and her Ph.D. in English from the University of Iowa, where she studied with John Irving and Kurt Vonnegut. She was a journalist and an English teacher before becoming a fiction writer. She has won numerous writing awards, including the Simon Guggenheim Fellowship and the Award in Literature from the American Academy and Institute for Arts and Letters. Godwin is the author of novels, short stories, and autobiographical and literary essays. Her novels frequently appear on the *New York Times'* best-seller list. Her most recent work, *Unfinished Desires: A Novel,* was published in 2009. "The Watcher at the Gates" originally appeared in the *New York Times Book Review* in 1977.

READING WITH A PURPOSE: All writers—both student and professional— experience writer's block. In "The Watcher at the Gates," Gail Godwin looks at the cause of the block—the "inner critic" that restrains writers if it is not silenced during the early stages of writing, during idea generation and drafting. Godwin explains (and you will learn in the next chapter) that writers should hold the inner critic at bay until they are ready to revise their writing. As you read, consider your own inner critic. How much of a problem is it?

The Watcher at the Gates

BY GAIL GODWIN

I first realized I was not the only writer who had a restraining critic who lived inside me and sapped the juice from green inspirations when I was leafing through Freud's "Interpretation of Dreams" a few years ago. Ironically, it was my "inner critic" who had sent me to Freud.

I was writing a novel, and my heroine was in the middle of a dream, and then I lost faith in my own invention and rushed to "an authority" to check whether she could have such a dream. In the chapter on dream interpretation, I came upon the following passage that has helped me free myself, in some measure, from my critic and has led to many pleasant and interesting exchanges with other writers.

2 Freud quotes Schiller, who is writing a letter to a friend. The friend complains of his lack of creative power. Schiller replies with an allegory. He says it is not good if the intellect examines too closely the ideas pouring in at the gates. "In isolation, an idea may be quite insignificant, and venturesome in the extreme, but it may acquire importance from an idea which follows it . . . In the case of a creative mind, it seems to me, the intellect has withdrawn its watchers from the gates, and the ideas rush in pell-mell, and only then does it review and inspect the multitude. You are ashamed or afraid of the momentary and passing madness which is found in all real creators, the longer or shorter duration of which distinguishes the thinking artist from the dreamer . . . you reject too soon and discriminate too severely."

3 So that's what I had: a Watcher at the Gates. I decided to get to know him better. I discussed him with other writers, who told me some of the quirks and habits

of their Watchers, each of whom was as individual as his host, and all of whom seemed passionately dedicated to one goal: rejecting too soon and discriminating too severely.

4   It is amazing the lengths a Watcher will go to keep you from pursuing the flow of your imagination. Watchers are notorious pencil sharpeners, ribbon changers, plant waterers, home repairers and abhorrers of messy rooms or messy pages. They are compulsive looker-uppers. They are superstitious scaredy-cats. They cultivate self-important eccentricities they think are suitable for "writers." And they'd rather die (and kill your inspiration with them) than risk making a fool of themselves.

5   My Watcher has a wasteful penchant for 20-pound bond paper above and below the carbon of the first draft. "What's the good of writing out a whole page," he whispers begrudgingly, "if you just have to write it over again later? Get it perfect the first time!" My Watcher adores stopping in the middle of a morning's work to drive down to the library to check on the name of a flower or a World War II battle or a line of metaphysical poetry. "You can't possibly go on till you've got this right!" he admonishes. I go and get the car keys.

6   Other Watchers have informed their writers that:

7   "Whenever you get a really good sentence you should stop in the middle of it and go on tomorrow. Otherwise you might run dry."

8   "Don't try and continue with your book till your dental appointment is over. When you're worried about your teeth, you can't think about art."

9   Another Watcher makes his owner pin his finished pages to a clothesline and read them through binoculars "to see how they look from a distance." Countless other Watchers demand "bribes" for taking the day off: lethal doses of caffeine, alcoholic doses of Scotch or vodka or wine.

10   There are various ways to outsmart, pacify or coexist with your Watcher. Here are some I have tried, or my writer-friends have tried, with success:

11   Look for situations when he's likely to be off-guard. Write too fast for him in an unexpected place, at an unexpected time. (Virginia Woolf captured the "diamonds in the dustheap" by writing at a "rapid haphazard gallop" in her diary.) Write when very tired. Write in purple ink on the back of a Master Charge statement. Write whatever comes into your mind while the kettle is boiling and make the steam whistle your deadline. (Deadlines are a great way to outdistance the Watcher.)

12   Disguise what you are writing. If your Watcher refuses to let you get on with your story or novel, write a" letter" instead, telling your "correspondent" what you are going to write in your story or next chapter. Dash off a "review" of your own unfinished opus. It will stand up like a bully to your Watcher the next time he throws obstacles in your path. If you write yourself a good one.

13   Get to know your Watcher. He's yours. Do a drawing of him (or her). Pin it to the wall of your study and turn it gently to the wall when necessary. Let your Watcher feel needed. Watchers are excellent critics after inspiration has been captured; they are dependable, sharp-eyed readers of things already set down. Keep your Watcher in shape and he'll have less time to keep you from shaping. If he's really ruining your whole working day sit down, as Jung did with his personal demons, and write him

a letter. On a very bad day I once wrote my Watcher a letter. "Dear Watcher," I wrote, "What is it you're so afraid I'll do?" Then I held his pen for him, and he replied instantly with a candor that has kept me from truly despising him.

14 "Fail," he wrote back.

ASSIGNMENT

In a paragraph or two, note what Godwin says that pertains to you as a writer. If nothing pertains to you, explain why. What, if anything, did you learn from Godwin that you will apply to your own writing?

The four men in business suits who stepped off

Eastern Airlines Flight No.   from Miami to Washington

on June 16 were accustomed to traveling ~~first class.~~ *INCOGNITO,* ~~New~~

AT WASHINGTON NATIONAL AIRPORT

they rented a *black* 1972 Chrysler ~~at National Airport~~ and drove

to the Capital's fashionable Watergate Hotel, where rooms

214 and 314 had been reserved for them. They registered

at the desk under the same assumed names listed on their

plane tickets and, in their rooms, prepared for dinner.

In the candlelit Watergate Terrace Restaurant that evening

THREE OF THEM, JOINED BY ANOTHER MAN

~~they~~ dined on shish-kabob, lobster tail, filet mignon and

New York strip steak. The tab ran $44.45, plus tip~~, and~~

~~they paid with a $100 bill.~~

AND THE DINNER COMPANION

After dinner, the four men ~~were joined in Room 314~~

TWO ~~met in one~~ *men from miami at the hotel rooms(s)*

MET WITH ~~by three~~ others. In the long discussion that followed,

nats scenario

~~the~~ *the elaborate activities were* ~~maps and diagrams were consulted~~ *now reviewed* and the equipment in

orders

the room checked: lockpicks, small screwdrivers, *flashlights* pliers,

lights
screwdriver
list

walkie-talkies, two ~~85~~ 35-mm. cameras, 40 rolls of unexposed

packed with

film. Several suitcases ~~containing~~ sophisticated

were directed in military fashion

First draft of **All the President's Men** *from The Watergate Papers of Woodward & Bernstein Collection at the Harry Ransom Humanities Research Center, The University of Texas at Austin. Used with permission.*

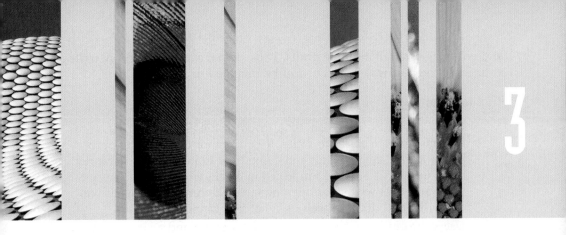

Writing and Rewriting

CONSIDER THE TOPIC

Once you have a preliminary thesis and outline, you are ready to write your **first draft,** which is your initial attempt to write your ideas in essay form. Because it is a first attempt, your first draft is supposed to be rough, which is why it is often called a *rough draft.* If you don't believe that first drafts should be rough, consider the example on the facing page, from a draft written by two Pulitzer Prize–winning journalists! On this page from Bob Woodward and Carl Bernstein's draft for their book about the Watergate investigation and cover-up, *All the President's Men,* notice all the scratchouts, additions, and rethinkings that were required because the draft was so rough. So learn from the professionals, and let your drafts be rough. You can refine them later during *revision.*

What is your current writing and revising process? Do you use a computer? Do you write multiple drafts? Do you ask other people to react to your work? Think about the steps in your current writing and revising process and about how well that process typically works.

WRITING YOUR FIRST DRAFT

Many writers expect too much of their first drafts. They think they should be able to write one draft, "fix it up" by correcting spelling and punctuation, and be done. However, this is not the way writing usually goes. For most writers, the first draft produces raw material that requires shaping and polishing through multiple drafts. Thus, do not expect perfection; write your ideas the best way you can, and be prepared to revise.

Tips for Drafting

- **If you get stuck, move on.** Skip troublesome aspects and go on to sections that are easier to write. If you cannot think of an appropriate word, leave a blank and come back to it later. If you cannot come up with a suitable introduction, begin with your first major point and deal with your opening later. Concentrate on what you *can* write, and do not dwell on what you cannot.
- **Use your outline.** Your outline can be a guide and a support system. At the same time, depart from your outline if a better strategy or idea occurs to you. Remember, inspiration is welcome no matter when it occurs.
- **Write from start to finish in one sitting.** Even if you skip parts, push through to the end to get as much raw material as possible.
- **Write the way you speak.** If you have trouble getting the words down, you may be straining for an academic style. In that case, write your draft the way you would speak it to a friend. You can polish the style later during revision.
- **Turn off your computer's AutoCorrect function.** By drafting with AutoCorrect off, you avoid being distracted by premature editing.

ESSAY STRUCTURE

Essays are typically made up of an introduction, body paragraphs, and a conclusion. Think of the introduction as the beginning of your essay, the body paragraphs as the middle, and the conclusion as the end.

The Introduction

Because first impressions are important, a successful essay begins well. In general, that beginning is a one- or two-paragraph **introduction** aimed at stimulating the reader's interest and, many times, presenting the thesis. You can approach the introduction many ways, some of which are illustrated in the examples that follow. (Notice that the thesis, underlined as a study aid in these examples, appears in different places in the introductions. Placement of the thesis is explained on page 43.)

TELL A STORY (USE NARRATION)

The new kid walked into fourth-period English with his head down. He handed a slip to Mrs. Kuhlins, who announced, "Frankie is our new student, class. I trust that you will make him welcome." With that, Frankie brushed a stray hair out of his eyes and shuffled to a seat in the back. His clothes were hopelessly out of date, and his hair was a mess. But as he passed my desk, our eyes met, and I saw something there. At that moment, I knew this new kid was special.

ESTABLISH YOURSELF AS SOMEONE KNOWLEDGEABLE ABOUT THE SUBJECT

When I was six, I joined a T-ball league and spent a glorious summer at third base. When I was ten, I began playing intramural basketball and learned the pleasures of rebounding and making foul shots. In junior high school, I began running middle distances for the track team and learned the joy of crossing the finish line in one last burst of speed. In high school, I lettered in three sports. As a result of all these years of playing team sports, I have come to realize that there are three kinds of coaches.

PROVIDE HELPFUL BACKGROUND INFORMATION

In 2001, President George W. Bush's education plan, dubbed "No Child Left Behind," created new federal guidelines for teachers, schools, and students. In particular, the plan emphasized school accountability and penalties for schools that did not help their students achieve specific standards. One of the most immediate effects of "No Child Left Behind" was an increase in testing of students and evaluation of teachers. Today, educators and politicians are divided on the success of the plan. They do, however, agree on one point: The testing program should be more flexible.

EXPLAIN WHY YOUR TOPIC IS IMPORTANT

You should know what to look for when you examine and test-drive a used automobile. Otherwise, you can make a very costly mistake and have years of aggravation.

DESCRIBE SOMETHING

I was only five minutes into seventh-grade gym, but I could tell Mr. Winnikee deserved his reputation as the gym teacher from hell. His belly swelled over his belt line and cascaded toward the bony knees that poked out between the white knee socks and navy blue polyester stretch shorts. His face was twisted into a permanent scowl, and his eyes squinted against the sun until they formed slits. To call roll, he barked each boy's name and checked it off on the clipboard that was never more than arm's reach away.

DEFINE SOMETHING

A grandmother is supposed to be a white-haired, chubby woman who rolls her stockings below the knees and spends her days knitting scarves and baking cookies for her grandchildren. However, someone forgot to tell my mother's mother all this because, believe me, she is not the typical grandmother. In fact, most people are stunned to learn that she has grandchildren.

USE AN INTERESTING OR PERTINENT QUOTATION

Last week at his press conference, the governor said, "It is with regret that I announce a 20 percent cut in subsidies for higher education. I believe, however, that this cut is the least painful way to balance the state budget." The governor is wrong: these cuts will have a catastrophic effect on the people of this state.

Note: Avoid quotations such as "The early bird gets the worm" or "Better late than never." These are clichés more likely to bore than interest a reader.

The above approaches are some common strategies. Additional approaches are given in later chapters, and you will likely come up with your own approaches. Furthermore, when you are writing in different disciplines or in the workplace, specific conventions may apply for introductions. For example, a report for your boss presenting a solution to a personnel problem would likely open with a description of the problem. In papers for science classes, you may be expected to open with a review of the relevant research on your topic. In papers for business classes, you may be expected to open with your thesis. Always learn the conventions for the field in which you are writing.

Body Paragraphs

The **body paragraphs,** which form the middle of the essay, prove or explain your thesis. They are the heart of your essay.

Each body paragraph has two parts. One part expresses the paragraph's main idea — the point the paragraph will develop to help support or explain the thesis. That part is the **topic sentence,** which can be specifically stated or strongly implied. The other part consists of the rest of your paragraph — all the points you make to support, explain, or clarify the topic sentence. Those are the **supporting details.**

The following body paragraph, taken from the final version of student-writer Jeff's essay, illustrates these two parts:

Underlined topic sentence gives the main idea of the paragraph. Supporting details back up the topic sentence by showing it is true.	Another source of deception is the advertising industry. Advertisers bombard us every day with powerful male athletes endorsing products. Men are enticed to buy the products because they are led to believe they will be similarly powerful if they do. At one time, Michael Jordan, in all his athletic, superhero grandeur, seduced us into buying Nikes. Now that torch has been passed to the latest basketball phenomenon, LeBron James. Superstars from many sports, including Lance Armstrong, Tiger Woods, and Derek Jeter, make us want the shoes with the swoosh, but even more, they make males long for their ability, acclaim, and lifestyles. We buy the shoes hoping to be more like the athletes we envy and then feel inferior because we don't achieve athletic superstardom or any of its trappings. Jason Giambi and Jeff Gordon may have sold a lot of Pepsi, but they also sold the notion that the ideal male has the strength

and physique to hit a baseball out of the park or drive a race car at 100 m.p.h. Most males can't do that, so we feel inferior, less than the ideal. Advertising sends two messages: You should buy this product because this man should be your idol, and if you want to be a "real man," you should have the athletic prowess, physique, and other characteristics of a sports star.

In a successful essay, body paragraphs have adequate supporting detail, and they have relevant supporting detail. These points are discussed next.

Providing Adequate Supporting Detail

Your reader will not believe what you say just because you say it. You must explain and prove your points convincingly. To do so, think of your thesis and each of your topic sentences as a **generalization,** a broad statement that asserts that something is true in most cases or in every case. To have *adequate* supporting detail, you must back up every generalization, including your thesis and each topic sentence, with enough detail to prove or explain it to your reader's satisfaction.

If, for instance, you write that your roommate is a practical joker, you have made a generalization. You must then prove that generalization with examples of your roommate's practical jokes. If you say that Chez Paris is the most beautiful restaurant in town, you are making a generalization and must support it with descriptive details, showing why you find it beautiful. If you say that schoolchildren should not be grouped by ability because such grouping discourages achievement, you must explain that generalization by showing how grouping by ability discourages achievement. A good way to remember the need to provide adequate detail is to remind yourself that a writer must "show and not just tell."

To appreciate the need to show and not just tell by supporting generalizations, and to see how a writer can move from the general to the specific, contrast the following two drafts. Draft A does not provide adequate supporting detail, but draft B does — by moving from the general to the specific. The specific points are underscored.

DRAFT A

Dr. Garcia is a dedicated teacher. She is concerned about students and always willing to give a struggling young scholar extra attention. In addition, she takes pains to include everyone in class discussions, even the shy students who ordinarily do not participate. Particularly impressive is the personal interest she takes in each of her students. No wonder her class is always one of the first to fill up every semester.

DRAFT B

Dr. Garcia is a dedicated teacher. She is concerned about students and always willing to give a struggling young scholar extra attention.

Last week, for example, two students were having trouble finding topics for their research papers, so Dr. Garcia met them at the library and helped them explore the possibilities. In addition, she takes pains to include everyone in class discussions, even the shy students who ordinarily do not participate. One way she does this is to ask people their opinions on subjects under discussion. That way, they do not have to worry about giving a wrong answer. Another way she brings students into discussions is to plan group work so students can talk to each other in more comfortable, smaller groups.

Particularly impressive is the personal interest Dr. Garcia takes in each of her students. Everyone writes a journal, and from the journals Dr. Garcia learns about her students' interests, successes, problems, and family life. Because she comes to know her students so well, she can talk to them about things important to them, which creates a bond between student and teacher. As a result, all her students come to understand that Dr. Garcia cares about them. No wonder her class is always one of the first to fill up every semester.

Providing Relevant Supporting Detail

Supporting details must be *relevant,* which means they must be clearly related to the thesis and to the topic sentence. Most readers will grow annoyed when details are not related to the matter at hand. If you wanted to argue for the elimination of the physical education requirement at your school, you would not mention that it would also be a good idea to eliminate the foreign language requirement. When you read the following draft, notice the distraction created by one sentence that presents irrelevant detail:

> Many universities are altering their teacher education curricula to require prospective teachers to get into the classroom as soon as possible, even in the first year. These future teachers observe, tutor, and in general get the feel of a teacher's responsibilities. The plan is a good one because students can decide early on if they are suited to teaching and change their majors if necessary. In the more traditional curriculum, an education major waits until the junior or senior year to get into the classroom, when it can be too late to change majors without serious inconvenience and expense. Many students in all programs change majors and problems are to be expected. Certainly it makes sense to move prospective teachers into the classroom as early as possible, so the plan should catch on.

You probably found the next-to-last sentence distracting because it is not related closely enough to teacher education. To avoid such irrelevant detail in your own writing, begin when you outline by making sure that all your points are related to the thesis.

The Source and Form of Supporting Details

Your supporting details can come from your own experience and observation, as well as from what you learn in the classroom and as a result of

reading, watching television, listening to the radio, or surfing the Internet. If necessary and appropriate, you can use facts, statistics, and opinions of experts, some of which you may find in this book and some of which you can research in the library and on the Internet. If you do use such material, be sure to check Chapters 4 and 15 for information on paraphrasing, quoting, and documenting source material. In addition, Chapter 4 offers advice for summarizing and synthesizing ideas from sources.

Much of this book explains various forms your supporting details can take. These forms are called *patterns of development,* and as you saw in Chapter 2, they also can help you generate and order ideas. The patterns of development are description, narration, exemplification, process analysis, comparison-contrast, cause-and-effect analysis, definition, and classification-division. You can use these patterns—alone or in combination—to organize and present your supporting details.

Each pattern of development is treated in its own chapter; however, the very last page of this book also gives a brief explanation of each pattern. Take a look now at the last page, and refer to it whenever a particular pattern is mentioned and you are unsure of its nature.

So you can see how the patterns of development can help you give the details you need to support your thesis and main points, here are examples of how each pattern could support the thesis used earlier in the chapter—that Dr. Garcia is a dedicated teacher.

DESCRIPTION	give details that show how Dr. Garcia looks and acts
NARRATION	tell a story about a time Dr. Garcia helped a student
EXEMPLIFICATION	give examples of ways Dr. Garcia shows interest in students
PROCESS ANALYSIS	explain Dr. Garcia's process for using groups to help students learn
COMPARISON-CONTRAST	compare and/or contrast Dr. Garcia with other teachers to show how good she is
CAUSE-AND-EFFECT ANALYSIS	explain the effects of one or more of Dr. Garcia's teaching methods
DEFINITION	define a "good teacher" and show how Dr. Garcia conforms to that definition
CLASSIFICATION-DIVISION	classify all the ways Dr. Garcia helps students

You would not use all these patterns in a single essay, but they do provide options to consider as you develop your supporting details.

Combining the Patterns of Development

To support your thesis, you sometimes may use a single pattern of development. Frequently, though, you may combine two or more patterns. Essays with multiple patterns are often developed by a dominant pattern with a few paragraphs organized by one or more other patterns. Sometimes, multiple

patterns are combined in roughly equal amounts. In the next chapters, you will read essays that rely primarily on a single pattern as well as ones that combine multiple patterns. In addition, Chapter 14 focuses solely on essays that combine patterns. In your own writing, your purpose, audience, and thesis will determine whether you use one or more patterns.

To see how patterns can be combined in a single paragraph, read again this excerpt from the final version of Jeff's essay, and notice the use of both exemplification and cause-and-effect analysis:

Cause-and-effect analysis: Advertisers cause males to envy sports superstars, a feeling that leads males to buy the products athletes endorse and, ultimately, to feel inferior.

Exemplification: James, Jeter, and Woods are examples of athletes who endorse products and make males feel inferior. Nike shoes and Pepsi are examples of products advertised.

Another source of deception is the advertising industry. Advertisers bombard us every day with powerful male athletes endorsing products. Men are enticed to buy the products because they are led to believe they will be similarly powerful if they do. At one time, Michael Jordan, in all his athletic, superhero grandeur, seduced us into buying Nikes. Now that torch has been passed to the latest basketball phenomenon, LeBron James. Superstars from many sports, including Lance Armstrong, Tiger Woods, and Derek Jeter, make us want the shoes with the swoosh, but even more, they make males long for their ability, acclaim, and lifestyles. We buy the shoes hoping to be more like the athletes we envy and then feel inferior because we don't achieve athletic superstardom or any of its trappings. Jason Giambi and Jeff Gordon may have sold a lot of Pepsi, but they also sold the notion that the ideal male has the strength and physique to hit a baseball out of the park or drive a race car at 100 m.p.h. Most males can't do that, so we feel inferior, less than the ideal. Advertising sends two messages: You should buy this product because this man should be your idol, and if you want to be a "real man," you should have the athletic prowess, physique, and other characteristics of a sports star.

www.mhhe.com/clousepatterns6   Patterns

For more help with writing using rhetorical patterns, click on
Writing > Paragraph Patterns

Organizing Body Paragraphs

As you have seen, each body paragraph typically focuses on one main idea, to help support or explain the thesis. (A main idea that requires considerable explanation can be the focus of more than one body paragraph.) This main idea can be expressed in a topic sentence or implied. In either case, the **topic sentence** is a generalization that must be developed with adequate, relevant supporting details.

You may find it easiest to compose body paragraphs that begin with a topic sentence and move on to the supporting details. If you were writing

an essay with the thesis "Dr. Garcia is a dedicated teacher," for example, your essay might have three body paragraphs, each beginning with a version of one of these topic sentences:

Dr. Garcia makes sure every student is relaxed in class.

Dr. Garcia is always willing to give students extra help.

Dr. Garcia takes a personal interest in each of her students.

Notice that each of these topic sentences is relevant to the thesis. Similarly, the supporting details in each body paragraph should be relevant to the topic sentence of that paragraph. Thus, the first body paragraph would include only details about helping students relax; the second, only details about providing students with extra help; and the third, only details about taking a personal interest in students.

Achieving Coherence

To have **coherence,** the supporting details in your body paragraphs, and the body paragraphs themselves, must connect to one another in ways your reader can easily understand and follow. Four strategies can help you achieve coherence: transitional words and phrases, repetition of words or ideas, synonyms, and sentences that look backward and forward.

Use Transitional Words and Phrases

Transitions are words and phrases that help you achieve coherence by signaling the relationship between ideas. The following chart lists and illustrates common transitions.

Transition Chart

RELATIONSHIP	TRANSITIONS	EXAMPLE
Addition	also, and, too, in addition, furthermore, first, further	The apartment has all the features I want. In addition, the rent is low.
Time	now, then, before, after, earlier, later, soon, finally, first, next	First, measure the flour. Then add it to the butter and eggs.
Space	near, next to, away from, beside, inside, on the left, on the right, along side, behind	Go two blocks west to the light. On the right is the park.
Comparison	similarly, likewise, in the same way, in like manner	The mayor will recommend some layoffs. Similarly, she will not approve any new hirings.
Contrast	however, in contrast, but, still, on the contrary, nevertheless, yet	The House will pass the jobs bill. However, the Senate will vote it down.

RELATIONSHIP	TRANSITIONS	EXAMPLE
Cause and effect	since, because, so, as a result, consequently, thus, therefore, hence	Because half the students are sick with the flu, school will be closed.
Emphasis	indeed, in fact, surely, certainly, without a doubt	Everyone enjoys Dr. Hill's class. In fact, it is always the first to close.
Illustration	for example, for instance, specifically, in particular	Counting fat grams is a good way to diet. Dana, for example, lost a pound a week that way.
Summary or clarification	in summary, in conclusion, in brief, in short, in other words, all in all	The president has vetoed the spending bill. In short, he will not raise taxes.

Repeat Words or Ideas

Repeating keywords or ideas can help you achieve coherence and improve the flow of your writing. Here are two examples.

REPEATING A WORD
Chronic fatigue syndrome is becoming more widely recognized in the medical community and therefore more frequently diagnosed. This syndrome is so debilitating that its sufferers often cannot work.

REPEATING AN IDEA
A group of volunteer parents is now working co-operatively with school authorities to introduce more extracurricular activities into the schools and to begin a drug awareness program. These worthy efforts will no doubt improve the quality of education in our township.

Use Synonyms

Another way to achieve coherence is to use a synonym for a word or idea mentioned earlier, as in these two sentences:

The workers expressed their dissatisfaction with management's latest wage offer. Their discontent may well lead to a strike.

Use Sentences That Look Backward and Forward

You can make an effective transition from one paragraph to another—and thereby achieve coherence—by beginning the new paragraph with a sentence that looks back to an idea in the previous paragraph and forward to an idea in this new paragraph. Suppose you have just written a paragraph about the fact that Dr. Garcia gives students extra help, and you are about to write a paragraph about how she makes students feel comfortable in class. You could write one of these sentences to connect the two paragraphs.

LOOKING BACK	LOOKING FORWARD
In addition to giving students extra help,	Dr. Garcia always makes

them feel comfortable in class.

LOOKING BACK

Dr. Garcia does more than provide extra help to those in need;

LOOKING FORWARD

she also makes sure that everyone feels comfortable in class.

---

www.mhhe.com/clousepatterns6 Coherence

For more help with paragraph coherence, click on

Writing > Coherence

Knowing When to Paragraph

Typically, writers begin a new body paragraph each time they move to a new main idea to support the thesis. However, if you have a great deal to say about one point, you can break up the discussion into two or more paragraphs. If you have a point that deserves special emphasis, you can place it in its own paragraph, or if you have an extended example or narration (a story), you can set it off by placing it in its own paragraph.

Establishing Tone

Speakers use tone of voice to help convey feelings and meaning. Similarly, writers can establish a tone for their writing. **Tone** is the writer's attitude or feelings toward the reader or the writing subject. The tone can be angry, sarcastic, serious, preachy, argumentative, conciliatory, hurtful, playful, scornful, hostile, enthusiastic, neutral, and so forth.

Most often, tone is established by the words you choose to convey supporting details. Notice, for example, how word choice creates the different tones in two sentences that are otherwise making the same point.

ANGRY AND JUDGMENTAL TONE	Many so-called citizens who are too tight-fisted to invest in the future of our children refuse to vote for the school levy.
NEUTRAL TONE	A significant number of citizens hesitate to pass the school levy and thereby increase their taxes.

Your tone should be appropriate to your writing context. The first sentence, for example, would not be appropriate for an academic writing, but the second sentence would be suitable.

---

www.mhhe.com/clousepatterns6 Word Choice

For more help with tone, click on

Editing > Word Choice

Using Visual Material for Support

You are accustomed to encountering visual material in your reading. Newspapers and magazines, textbooks, Web pages, journal articles, reports at work—much of what you read includes photos, charts, graphs, illustrations, and other images. In Chapter 1, you learned that this visual material needs to be "read" critically, in the same way you read written text.

Technological advances have made it so much easier for you to include visual material in your writing. With the Internet, you can locate and import images; with digital photography, you can insert photos into documents; and with computer programs, you can create graphs from data you supply. Before you include visual materials, however, ask your instructor whether you may use visuals and whether your instructor has guidelines for their use. In addition, keep these general guidelines in mind:

General Guidelines for Using Visuals

- **Use images *only* to help explain, illustrate, or prove a point.** Visual material should support the text, not be a substitute for it. Never use visual material to pad a piece of writing that is too short. But do use visuals if they can amplify or complement what you have written.

- **Consider your audience and purpose.** Make sure the visuals you select suit your audience and help fulfill your purpose. A complicated diagram explaining how plants turn carbon dioxide into oxygen might confuse a 10-year-old, but a simple flowchart might work perfectly. If you import visual material from another source, remember that it was developed for a different writer's purpose and audience, so evaluate it carefully. Its tone must be in keeping with your tone. A humorous cartoon may not be appropriate for a research paper examining spousal abuse, but a bar graph showing the frequency of spousal abuse by age group may be informative.

- **Consider the quality of the visual.** An image of poor quality or a graph that is difficult to decipher will detract from your writing. Select or prepare visual material that is attractive, easy to read, and easy to understand. Make sure the color, font, spacing, and other features are appropriate for your paper.

- **Write the caption carefully.** Most images require captions. Take this opportunity to guide your reader's interpretation. Provide the reader with relevant background information about the creator of the image or the purpose for which it was created. Establish the authority or reliability of the image by indicating its source and/or date. See the caption for the Lewis Hine photograph in Chapter 1 (page 19) for an example of the way caption information can guide interpretation.

- **Properly credit the source of visuals.** (Chapter 15 will help you here.)

For more on using images, see the Appendix A.

The Conclusion

The **conclusion** provides closure for your essay. It may be one or more final paragraphs or just the last sentences of your final paragraph. Your conclusion is an important part of your essay because it influences the

Selecting and Integrating Visuals in Classroom Writing

If you have trouble selecting or integrating visuals into your writing, consider this advice:

- **Select or create your visual material only after writing your first draft.** That way, you can be certain this material supplements the written text, fulfills your writing purpose, and meets the needs of your audience.

- **Place the visual as close as possible to the material it supports.** If design and layout considerations prevent that, add a cross-reference for the reader, such as "The chart on page 3 shows how different people will benefit from the tax cut."

reader's final, lasting impression. No matter how strong your introduction and body paragraphs are, if your ending is weak, your reader will come away from the essay feeling let down.

Many approaches for concluding an essay are possible. They can be used separately or in combination.

If your essay is long, with many ideas, you can summarize your main points as a helpful reminder to your reader. However, if your essay is brief and the ideas are easily remembered, summarizing is unnecessary and is more likely to bore readers than to help them.

Repeating the thesis or another important idea is an effective way to conclude your essay when the repetition provides emphasis or dramatic effect. Be careful, though. The repetition will bore a reader if it fails to provide drama or emphasis. Sometimes writers delay the thesis until the conclusion because they want to build up to it.

Another common technique is to introduce a new but related idea in the conclusion. The idea must be clearly related to the rest of your essay or your reader will be puzzled, and your conclusion ineffective.

Other approaches to the conclusion are illustrated below. In addition, the introductory sections in Chapters 5–12 suggest ways to handle conclusions.

DRAW A CONCLUSION FROM THE INFORMATION IN THE ESSAY (THIS ILLUSTRATION IS FROM AN ESSAY ABOUT THE EFFECTS OF DIVORCE.)

Recent evidence suggests that the children of divorced parents suffer a number of difficulties, regardless of their age at the time of the divorce. For this reason, parents who stay together "for the sake of the children" may be doing the right thing.

PRESENT THE FINAL, MOST IMPORTANT POINT (THIS ILLUSTRATION IS FROM AN ESSAY ARGUING AGAINST CENSORSHIP.)

The most compelling reason to oppose censorship is the threat it poses to our First Amendment rights. Once we limit free speech, we

Drafting Introductions and Conclusions

If you have trouble drafting your introduction, keep it short. Begin with your preliminary thesis and move on. During revising, you can add details to stimulate interest. Similarly, an effective conclusion can be brief, even one or two sentences. If you are stuck for a closing, end with your final point and improve the conclusion during revision, if necessary.

---

www.mhhe.com/clousepatterns6   Drafting

For more help with writing introductions and conclusions, click on

Writing > Introductions
Writing > Conclusions

---

establish a climate that permits the chipping away at our freedoms until our rights are severely curtailed.

OFFER A SOLUTION TO A PROBLEM MENTIONED IN THE ESSAY (THIS ILLUSTRATION IS FROM AN ESSAY THAT EXPLAINS PROBLEMS ASSOCIATED WITH COLLEGE ATHLETICS.)

College athletics will remain controversial until we reform the system dramatically. Perhaps the most honest thing to do is to hire the athletes to play and pay them salaries. If they want to use their paychecks to pay for tuition, fine. If not, they can just be university employees. The fans will still turn out to see the teams, regardless of whether the players are student athletes or professional athletes.

CALL YOUR READER TO ACTION (THIS ILLUSTRATION IS FROM AN ESSAY ARGUING FOR INCREASING THE SALARY OF TEACHERS.)

To improve the quality of education, we must increase teachers' salaries to make them compatible with those in business and industry. Only then will we attract the best people to the profession. Thus, we must support school levies that fund pay increases and lobby boards of education to do whatever it takes to increase teachers' salaries.

LOOK TO THE FUTURE (THIS ILLUSTRATION IS FROM AN ESSAY EXPLAINING THE EFFECTS OF THE ROUTE 8 BYPASS.)

Once the Route 8 bypass is built, our area will become a major crossroads. In ten years, our economy will be flourishing from the business and commerce that will result from our strategic location, and our tax base will broaden to the benefit of our schools and infrastructure.

LEAVE YOUR READER WITH A FINAL IMPRESSION (THIS ILLUSTRATION IS FROM AN ESSAY ON DISCRIMINATION AGAINST OVERWEIGHT PEOPLE.)

Our society discriminates against overweight people, and it's a shame. Many capable people never get a chance to show what they can do because of our narrow-mindedness.

The Title

Although the title is the first thing a reader sees, many people compose it last because a good title often suggests itself after the essay is written. There are many ways to approach the title. Sometimes a clever or funny title is a good way to pique your reader's interest. However, a clever or funny title may not be right for some essays, so it is fine to write a title that suggests the content of the essay, like "What Is Poverty?" which appears in this book. Sometimes an intriguing title like "The Watcher at the Gates," which also appears in this book, can stimulate a reader's interest. Avoid a title that presents your thesis. If your title is "Capital Punishment Is Inhumane," you will tip your hand too soon. Also, avoid very broad titles that do not suggest your content. "Television" is too broad, but "The Effects of Television Violence" is fine.

VISUALIZING AN ESSAY

The essay structure explained in this chapter is not the only one—or even the best one in all circumstances—and many of the essays in this text will illustrate departures from this structure. Nonetheless, this structure is a very serviceable one. You can use it in many writing situations. To review the structure and better visualize it, examine this graphic representation.

INTRODUCTION: The Opening Paragraph(s)
- Engages the reader's interest
- Presents the thesis (the statement of the essay's central point)

↓

BODY PARAGRAPHS: Middle Paragraphs

Each Body Paragraph
- Helps explain or prove the thesis
- Includes a topic sentence stating a main idea relevant to the thesis or implies such an idea
- Includes supporting details (the points that support, explain, or clarify the main idea)

Each Topic Sentence
- States the main idea of the paragraph
- Is relevant to the thesis

Supporting Details
- Are adequate
- Are relevant to the topic sentence
- Have coherence

↓

CONCLUSION: The Final Paragraph(s)
- Brings the essay to a satisfying close
- Leaves the reader with a positive final impression

An Essay in Progress: Drafting

Using his informal outline as a guide (see page 51), Jeff wrote the first draft that appears below. You will notice that Jeff departed from his outline at times, which is fine. Writers should always be open to new ideas and ways of organizing their material. Knowing that he would polish the draft during revision, Jeff concentrated on writing his ideas down as best he could without laboring over anything. Notice that Jeff realized some problems while drafting and wrote reminders to himself in brackets about revisions to make.

The Not-So-Ideal Ideal Male

We, the people of the United States of America, are being bullied, tricked, 1 and led astray by products of our own culture. We are being fed falsehoods, and we digest them happily, but we are being poisoned. Our own culture—our own heritage and popular society—is feeding us misinformation; we are being led to believe in an absurd concept of the ideal male. [fix intro]

The root of the inappropriateness of this idealization lies in the nature of its 2 main perpetuators—the movie and advertising industries, and folktales and child-hood stories. The most obvious of these sources is the movie industry, which produces totally unrealistic plots typically having (perhaps subtly, but still) super-human males as heroes. We watch these movies and feel that this is what our men are supposed to be like. [give examples] The cartoonish action movies are generally the most extreme, and these are targeted at the most vulnerable audience—teenage boys who are ready to become men. They see these heroes on the screen and see visions of themselves in ten years. This is tragic. An equally prevalent but less glaring source of deception is the advertising industry. They bombard use very day with quick scenes of powerful, intimidating male atheletes endorsing their products. [give examples] The message is this: you should buy this product because this man should be your idol. Physical dominance is put in the spotlight as much as the product. A third projector of this concept comes from our heritage, and that is its problem. Folktales and childhood stories are usually legends that have been passed down through generations of people. Nobody even remembers how long ago they were created. That is precisely the trouble. Triumphant men like Robin Hood originated in an entirely different society; they are heroes of the distant past, and they do not befit the present.

The problem these unsuitable sources of the ideal male present is that their 3 admired and discouraged qualities are out of place. In action movies and folktales, the hero wins the battle because his instincts are flawless. He knows just where every attacker will be in a battle, and he knows by sight which fair maiden will be faithful to him. But in the real world today, how often does a man fend off a small mob in hand-to-hand combat or choose his wife from a lineup of beautiful princesses? To apply the power of understatement—rarely. In our highly complex, and civilized, society, the considered decision is more important then the instinctive or rash one. Also, the men of advertising, movies, and legends are loners. Their great strength stems from the fact that they need no one else to help them accomplish their goals. Again, this clashes with modern society. Our world is becoming increasingly cooperative on all levels—from interpersonal to international. A realistic man knows that the help of others is esential in achieving his dream.

Finally, the men these sources give us often are deplorable in their rela- 4 tions to women. Many times the entire purpose of the movie, advertisement, or tale is for the hero to "get" the woman. He is almost invariably her protector, savior, or unrepellable lover. In a world in which possibly the characteristic of modern history is the rise of women nearer and nearer to equality, how can the ideal man have this type of relationship with women? The answer is simple: he is not the ideal man.

Drafting

EXERCISE 3.1

1. Refer to the thesis statements and supporting details you used for numbers 2 and 3 of Exercise 2.4 on page 52. For each thesis and set of supporting details, do the following:
   a. Decide on a possible approach to the introduction, and explain why the approach is a good one.
   b. Write two topic sentences that could open two body paragraphs.
   c. Decide on a possible approach to the conclusion, and explain why the approach is a good one.
2. Using the material you have from number 4 of Exercise 2.4 (and adding and deleting ideas as you wish), write a first draft.

REVISING YOUR DRAFT

Revising is improving your draft until it is ready for your reader. Most experienced writers will tell you that revising is the heart of their writing processes and that it is time consuming. Unfortunately, many inexperienced writers believe that revision involves simply changing a few words, adding a comma here and there, and checking spellings. In truth, when you revise, you should completely rethink your essay to be sure everything in it suits your purpose, audience, and role. To that end, revision requires you to consider each aspect of your draft, as shown in the following checklist, and make changes as necessary. As you can see from the checklist, revision takes in quite a bit. For this reason, you will often need to write multiple drafts before you feel satisfied that your essay is reader-ready. And because you have so much to consider, the first rule of revision is *be sure to allow plenty of time.*

Revision Checklist

FOR YOUR THESIS (see page 42), be sure:

1. _____ Your essay has a clearly stated or strongly implied thesis.

2. _____ Your thesis is not a statement of fact.

3. _____ Your thesis can be treated in a manageable length.

4. _____ Your thesis is not a formal announcement and it is expressed in specific language.

5. _____ Your thesis allows you to achieve your purpose and is geared toward your audience, and is compatible with your role.

FOR YOUR INTRODUCTION (see page 60), be sure:

1. _____ Your introduction makes a good first impression.

2. _____ Your introduction is suited to your purpose, audience, and role.

FOR YOUR BODY PARAGRAPHS (see page 62), be sure:

1. _____ All your details are suited to your purpose, audience, and role.

2. _____ Your details are in a logical order and arranged in body paragraphs.

3. _____ Each body paragraph has a topic sentence or strongly implied main idea.

4. _____ All your details are relevant to the thesis and appropriate topic sentence.

5. _____ You have enough details to support the thesis and each topic sentence.

6. _____ Transitions move the reader smoothly from idea to idea and from paragraph to paragraph.

7. _____ You avoid errors in logic (page 9).

FOR YOUR CONCLUSION (see page 70), be sure:

1. _____ Your essay comes to a satisfying finish.

2. _____ Your conclusion is appropriate to your purpose, audience, and role.

FOR EFFECTIVE EXPRESSION, be sure:

1. _____ Unnecessary words are eliminated.

2. _____ All your ideas are clearly expressed.

3. _____ Specific words are substituted for vague ones.

4. _____ Words are compatible with your tone.

5. _____ Tired expressions (clichés) such as "cold as ice" are rewritten.

6. _____ Choppy prose is eliminated.

FOR YOUR TITLE (see page 73), be sure:

1. _____ Your title suggests the content of the essay without being too broad.

2. _____ Your thesis is not given in the title.

Tips for Revising

- **Allow plenty of time** because revising is time consuming. Pace your work so you will have at least several days to revise.
- **Remember your writing context.** Every evaluation of your draft and every change you make should be done with your audience, purpose, and role in mind.
- **Revise in stages** by considering one or two of the revision concerns at a time. (Use the revision checklist to be sure you consider everything.) As an alternative, revise one or two paragraphs at a time. Be sure to take a break whenever you get tired.
- **Return to idea generation or adjust your thesis, if necessary.** If you have trouble coming up with adequate detail, try one of the idea generation techniques covered in Chapter 2 to develop more material. If that does not work, reconsider your thesis. Should you broaden it or refocus it to have enough to say?
- **Revise typed copy** at least once to catch problems you overlooked in your own handwriting or on the computer screen.
- **Think like your reader.** Identify the characteristics of your reader, and then read your draft the way someone with those characteristics would. Think about where such a reader might need more information and where he or she might lose interest. Then revise accordingly.
- **Avoid editing,** which comes later. If you deal with spelling, grammar, punctuation, and such, you will be distracted and unable to focus on revision concerns.
- **In Microsoft Word, use Track Changes.** Track Changes allows you to revise while preserving the original draft. Your changes will not become permanent until and unless you want them to, so you can easily return to and restore all or part of your earlier work.

---

www.mhhe.com/clousepatterns6 | Computers

For more help with revising using your computer, click on
Writing > Using Computers

Revising with Peer Review

Nothing can help a writer more than a reader, so ask other people to read your drafts, react, and suggest changes. In fact, your instructor may arrange for you and your classmates to exchange drafts. When you find readers on your own, be sure they are *reliable readers,* people who know the qualities of effective writing and who will not hesitate to offer constructive criticism. It makes no sense to ask a friend for help if that person has not yet taken a writing course, nor is it useful to ask people who always hesitate to tell you what they really think. Also, use more than one reader, so you have the advantage of multiple perspectives and can look for consensus. Remember, though, that you have the final say. Rather than accepting everything your readers offer, consider their reactions critically and revise accordingly.

If you have particular concerns about your draft, you can ask your readers to read and react to those concerns. Ask them to tell you what they think of your introduction, help you think of another example to support a point in paragraph 4, help you clarify an idea, and so forth. Otherwise, ask your readers to use the revision checklist on page 76 as a guide to reacting to your draft.

When readers help you, always return the favor by offering to react to *their* drafts. When it is your turn to respond, follow these guidelines.

Guidelines for Responding to Drafts

- **Comment on strengths and weaknesses.** Offering praise alone makes a writer feel good but does little to help that writer improve a draft. And offering only criticism is demoralizing.

- **Put your responses in writing.** That way, the writer has a record to refer to. (If you are given an electronic copy of a draft and you use Microsoft Word, you can insert comments using the Comment feature of the program.)

- **Be specific.** Rather than say "Paragraph 2 is unclear," write "In paragraph 2, I do not understand why you say that men experience discrimination in the workplace."

- **Offer suggestions.** When you comment on a weakness, suggest a revision strategy, like this: "If you could give an example of discrimination against males in the workplace, I would be able to accept your point more readily."

www.mhhe.com/clousepatterns6	Revising

For more help with revising, click on
Writing > Drafting and Revising

An Essay in Progress: Writing a Second Draft

Jeff knew some of the changes needed in his first draft and indicated them on the draft in brackets (see pages 74–75). Before revising to compose a second draft, Jeff reread his first draft and considered his bracketed comments. In addition, he sought responses from two classmates and his teacher. He was reassured to discover that his readers' reactions to the draft were very similar to his own. As a result, he felt confident in his ability to judge his writing accurately. The teacher's response, which helped guide Jeff's revision, follows.

Jeff,

Your draft held my interest every step of the way. I was particularly taken by the energy in your writing. You feel very strongly about your topic. Your energy and your honest emotions really propelled me forward, and I am hoping you can retain that spirit in your revision. I'd take a careful look at the introduction, though. It's a place where your emotion creates a problem. The introduction makes you seem very angry, even a bit out of control, so it is a little off-putting. Remember, you want your reader to see you as a reasonable, thoughtful person. Anger is fine, but you don't want to appear more emotional than thoughtful. You indicate that you want to work on your intro; I think softening the angry tone will help considerably.

Your thesis is very clear, and you make excellent points in paragraph 2. These points can go a long way to support your thesis, but right now you have too many main ideas in one paragraph (movies, advertising, and folktales and stories). You noted yourself that you need specific examples, and I agree. Perhaps if you give each of your main points its own body paragraph, you could more easily incorporate your examples.

You state important ideas in your last body paragraph. I was particularly intrigued by your contrast of the loner not being well adapted to today's cooperative environment—very astute. In fact, all of your points are interesting and significant.

I look forward to your revision. One last thing, though: Your last paragraph brings up your final points and is rather like a body paragraph. Do you feel the need for a separate conclusion? Frankly, I'm not sure because your final sentence provides some closure. Think about it and maybe get some other opinions.

Jeff's Second Draft

1   On the movie screen, characters played by actors like Bruce Willis, Arnold Schwarzenegger, Tom Cruise, and Daniel Craig are men of action and resolve. They depict the ideal male that men strive to be but can never achieve. However, the truth is that men are being tricked and led astray by these characterizations. We are being led to believe in an absurd image of the ideal male, not just in movies, but in advertising and childhood stories.

> The introduction is less angry. The thesis now indicates three of the main points to be discussed.

2   An obvious perpetrator of this idealization is the movie industry, which produces totally unrealistic plots typically having (perhaps subtly but still) superhuman males as heroes. We watch these movies and feel

The first body
paragraph now
discusses only one
main idea. Two
examples have been
added for support.

that this is what our men are supposed to be like. Arnold slams through walls and saves the beautiful woman from the jaws of death and The Rock does away with bad guys by singlehandedly fighting an entire compound and throwing himself through a pillar. Granted, the cartoonish action movies are generally the most extreme, but these are targeted at the most vulnerable audience—teenage boys who are ready to become men. They see these heroes on the screen and see visions of themselves in ten years. This is tragic because the boys can never be what movie action heroes are.

The second body
paragraph now
focuses on only one
main idea. Examples
have been added for
support.

An equally prevalent but less glaring source of deception is the 3 advertising industry. They bombard us every day with quick scenes of powerful, intimidating male atheletes endorsing their products. Michael Jordan who everybody worshipped in his superathlete glory made us want Nikes and now LeBron James does the same. But at the same time the image makes males want to be an athlete like them but that can never be. Sports superstars like Derek Jeter and Jason Giambi sell products, but they sell more. Physical dominance is in the spotlight as much as the product, but how likely is it that the average viewer can attain such physical dominance? Advertising sends two messages. One is to buy the product, but the more harmful one is that to be a "real man" you must look and perform like a star atkelete. Once again, the male is left feeling inadequate.

This body paragraph
now has just one
main idea. Examples
and explanation have
been added for
support.

A third projector of this concept comes from our heritage, and that 4 is the source of the problem. Folktales and childhood stories are usually legends that have been passed down through generations. Triumphant men like Robin Hood, Sir Lancelot, and Davy Crockett originated in an entirely different society; they are heroes of the distant past, and they do not befit the present. As legends, they risked their lives for the underdog, but their feats are impossible to emulate, so males exposed to these stories are made to feel inadequate.

This body paragraph
now focuses on the
idea of loners and
omits the discussion
of the hero in battle
and with women. The
Marlboro man
example has been
added.

The ideal men depicted in advertising, movies, and legends are 5 loners. Their great strength stems from the fact that they need no one else to help them accomplish their goals. For example, the Marlboro man always rides out alone; the action hero single handedly saves the day. Again, this clashes with modern society because it leads men to wall themselves off from others. Also, our world is becoming more cooperative on all levels. The loner will not succeed in the workplace where collaboration is increasingly valued.

6   Finally, the men these sources give us are often deplorable to women. Many times the entire purpose of the movie, advertisement, or tale is for the hero to "get" the woman. He is almost invariably her protector, savior, or unrepellable lover. In a world in which possibly the main characteristic of modern history is the rise of women to equality, how can the ideal man have this type of relationship with women? The answer is simple: he cannot because except in advertising, movies, and folktales, he is not the ideal male.

> Jeff chose to retain his approach to the last paragraph, although he revised to create more closure in the final sentence.

Revising the Draft

EXERCISE 3.2

1. Read the first draft that follows, and then make three suggestions you think the author should consider during revising.

IS TODAY'S ATHLETE A GOOD SPORT?

I have been playing soccer for a long time and I can see that players are playing much more violently now than they used to. Players will do anything to win, even stuff they would never consider doing off the field. I think that today's athlete is one person on the field and another person off the field.

Players think that hurting someone is okay because it's just part of the game. My roommate, for example, is a real gentle guy until he gets on the basketball court, then he's rough and ready and violent. If he didn't play that way, the coach would keep him on the bench.

Many players say they have to be violent to beat the other players. They don't feel they've done anything wrong as long as they win. In one of my soccer games, for example, an opposing player intentionally spiked the sweeper and cheated to get the goal.

A lot of times, players justify violence by saying "it's only a game" and not reality. Yes, it's a game but the injuries are real and can cause a lot of problems and pain. For example, a player on my soccer team missed a month of school as a result of an opposing player who knocked him into the goal. I'm sure the player didn't think twice about the consequences of his actions.

Unfortunately, fans love the violence. The more violence, the more cheering. They're violent in the stands, too.

The violence must stop and players should be penalized for it. Otherwise, people will get hurt more and more.

2. Revise the draft you wrote in response to number 2 of Exercise 3.1 on page 75.

EDITING YOUR DRAFT

Editing is finding and correcting mistakes in grammar, spelling, punctuation, capitalization, and usage. Finding and eliminating your errors is important because a reader can lose confidence in a writer if the essay has many errors. And if you undermine your reader's confidence, you may fail to achieve your purpose for writing. To be efficient, do most or all of your editing after you revise. Why look for errors in sentences that you ultimately strike during revision?

Tips for Editing

- **Look for the kinds of mistakes you typically make.** For example, if spelling is a problem for you, pay particular attention to spelling.

- **Learn the rules.** You cannot edit effectively if you do not know the rules. Buy a good handbook of grammar and usage at your college bookstore, consult it as needed, and learn the rules for matters that cause you problems.

- **Use computer grammar and spell checks with caution.** Be aware, however; these tools are not foolproof. For example, they will not tell you whether you have substituted *here* for *hear.*

- **Trust your instincts.** If you have a feeling that something is wrong, the odds are good that a problem exists—even if you cannot name the problem or figure out a solution at the moment.

- **Edit print copy.** You are less likely to overlook errors in print copy than on the computer screen. At the same time, be aware that computer-generated print material often looks so professional that you can be fooled into overlooking problems and mistakes.

---

www.mhhe.com/clousepatterns6　　　　　　　　　　　Editing

For more help with editing your work, click on
Editing
and select from the many subtopics available.

TROUBLESHOOTING GUIDE

Making Revising and Editing Decisions

If you have trouble knowing what to change in your draft, try the following:

- **Leave your work for at least a day** to gain some objectivity about your draft. After a break, you will be better able to identify material to revise and edit.

- **Read your work aloud** to listen for problems you have overlooked visually. Be careful to read exactly what is on the page, not what you intended to write.

- **Point to each word with a pen or pencil** and linger over it for a second or two, so you do not build the kind of speed that can lead you to overlook errors.

- **Place a ruler under each line as you edit** to block out other material and prevent it from distracting you.

PROOFREADING

After editing, make any changes necessary to put your essay into the proper form for your reader. Then, check carefully for typing errors. Read very slowly, lingering over each word and punctuation mark, so you do not build up too much speed and miss something. Type in the corrections and print a new copy.

An Essay in Progress: The Final Draft of "The Not-So-Ideal Male"

Below is the final version of the essay that Jeff wrote in response to "Americanization Is Tough on 'Macho'" (page 13). You have already viewed the idea generation (pages 37 and 41), outlining (page 51), and two of the drafts (pages 74 and 78) that preceded this final copy. Between the second draft and the final version, Jeff wrote two additional drafts in the course of revising and editing. In those drafts, he added more detail and improved his word choice.

The Not-So-Ideal Male

Jeff Caulkins

1   First there was Errol Flynn; then there was John Wayne; after him came Bruce Willis, Sylvester Stallone, Jean-Claude Van Damme, and Arnold Schwarzenegger. Now we have Daniel Craig, Tom Cruise, Hugh Jackman, Will Smith, and The Rock. These men of action and resolve are the celluloid depictions of the ideal male. They are the model that men strive for, but the goal they can never achieve. They are the men that women want but never find (off the big screen, that is). They are the reason men feel inferior. The image of these movie action heroes is one reason men feel inferior, but it is not the only reason. The truth is that we are being led to believe in an absurd image of the ideal male, and the source of this image is not just movies; it is also advertising and childhood stories.

2   An obvious contributor to the falsehood is the movie industry, which produces unrealistic plots with superhuman male heroes. Arnold (pre-governor days) slammed through brick walls and snatched the beautiful woman from the jaws of death. The Rock (before he tried to remake his image in *Race to Witch Mountain*) did away with the bad guys by single-handedly fighting an entire compound of evil-doers and throwing himself through a support pillar. Dangling on a wire, Tom Cruise breaks into an impenetrable government agency, scales mountains of heart-stopping heights, and clings to the top of a speeding train without ever losing his

Paragraph 1
The introduction engages the reader's interest by providing background information and specific examples.

The thesis presents the subject as the image of the ideal male and the writer's assertion that the image is absurd. The thesis also notes main points to be covered (movies, advertising, and childhood stories).

Paragraph 2
The topic sentence presents a general-ization about the movie industry. The examples in the paragraph provide support.

From the beginning, the tone (one of strong feeling and concern) is clear.

The author's informative and persuasive purposes are clear. His role (a concerned male) and his audience (the average, general reader, both males and females) are also becoming clear. The purpose seems to be to inform the reader about how the image of the ideal male is manipulated. The paragraph includes cause-and-effect analysis.

cool or mussing his hair. As 007, Daniel Craig stays similarly cool as he saves the world, gets the beautiful, aloof woman, and escapes from multiple near-death experiences—and that's just ten mintues after the opening credits roll. Even aging Harrison Ford performs superhuman heroics worthy of a much younger action hero, including hanging from the back of a jetliner flying at top speed in *Air Force One*. We watch these movies and feel that this is what men are supposed to be like. Granted, cartoonish action movies such as the X-Men series, featuring hunky Hugh Jackman, are generally the most extreme, but they appeal to the most vulnerable audience—teenage boys. Adolescent males see in these screen heroes visions of what they should be like when they become men. The goal is, of course, unattainable, so males feel inadequate because they do not perform remarkable deeds or look like this image of Daniel Craig in *Casino Royale*.

Image
The image illustrates the unattainable goal depicted in movies.

Daniel Craig in *Casino Royale* (2006; dir. Martin Campbell)

3   Another source of deception is the advertising industry. Advertisers bombard us every day with powerful male athletes endorsing products. Men are enticed to buy the products because they are led to believe they will be similarly powerful if they do. At one time, Michael Jordan, in all his athletic, superhero grandeur, seduced us into buying Nikes. Now that torch has been passed to the latest basketball phenomenon, LeBron James. Superstars from many sports, including Lance Armstrong, Tiger Woods, and Derek Jeter, make us want the shoes with the swoosh, but even more, they make males long for their ability, acclaim, and lifestyles. We buy the shoes hoping to be more like the athletes we envy and then feel inferior because we don't achieve athletic superstardom or any of its trappings. Jason Giambi and Jeff Gordon may have sold a lot of Pepsi, but they also sold the notion that the ideal male has the strength and physique to hit a baseball out of the park or drive a race car at 100 m.p.h. Most males can't do that, so we feel inferior, less than the ideal. Advertising sends two messages: You should buy this product because this man should be your idol, and if you want to be a "real man," you should have the athletic prowess, physique, and other characteristics of a sports star.

Paragraph 3
"Another source of deception" provides coherence by linking the paragraph to the introduction. The topic sentence is the first sentence.

Supporting details are developed with cause-and-effect analysis and examples. The paragraph would benefit from more detail on how advertisers perpetuate the false image of the ideal male.

4   A third perpetrator of the misconception is folktales and childhood stories, legends that have been passed down through generations. Triumphant men who confront danger and risk their lives for the under-dog are everywhere in our myths, and they cause males to feel inade-quate. The likes of Robin Hood, Sir Lancelot, and Davy Crockett originated in an entirely different time and society; they are heroes of the past who do not befit the present, yet their legendary (and impossible to emulate) feats shape the psyches of males. The tradition continues into more recent times, as Superman, Batman, and Spiderman fight injustice, rescue the weak, and generally contribute to the notion that real men are action figures.

Paragraph 4
The topic sentence indicates that the body paragraph will focus on folktales and childhood stories. The words "a third perpetrator of the misconception" provide coherence.

Paragraph development includes specific examples. Some readers may feel the need for more details.

5   The ideal men depicted in advertising, movies, and legends are loners. Their strength stems from the fact that they need no one to help them accomplish their goals. The Marlboro man always rides out alone; the action hero single-handedly saves the day. This fact causes problems for males who try to live up to the perceived ideal. It leads them to wall themselves off from others, depriving themselves of enjoyable, satisfying relationships. Further, our world is becoming increasingly cooperative on all levels—from interpersonal to international. A successful male knows

Paragraph 5
The first sentence presents a generalization about the depiction of men as loners. Coherence is achieved with the words "the ideal men."

Paragraph development includes cause-and-effect analysis.

that the help of others is essential to achieving his dream and that collaboration is increasingly valued in the workplace. The loner may not perform as well on the job.

Paragraph 6
The conclusion provides closure by presenting a final point and leaving the reader with a final impression. Coherence is achieved with the transition "finally."

Finally, the unfortunate image of the ideal male perpetrated by 6 advertising, movies, and myth damages relations with women. Many times the point of the movie, advertisement, or tale is that the male hero "gets" the woman. He is almost invariably her protector, savior, or unrepellable lover. In a world whose defining characteristic is the advancement of women nearer and nearer to equality, how can the ideal man have such a relationship with women? The answer is simple: He cannot. Indeed, once outside the worlds of advertising, movies, and folktales, he is not the ideal male.

Work Cited

Photograph is documented as explained in Chapter 15.

Daniel Craig in *Casino Royale*. 2006. Picture Desk, New York.

BACKGROUND: Award-winning political novelist and humorist Christopher Buckley (b. 1952) is the founding editor of *Forbes FYI* magazine. His satire and criticism have appeared in numerous publications, including the *New York Times, Washington Post, Wall Street Journal, Atlantic Monthly, Vogue,* and *Esquire.* Buckley's novels include *Thank You for Smoking* (1994), which became a critically successful movie, *No Way to Treat a First Lady* (2002), *Florence of Arabia* (2004), *Boomsday* (2007), and *Losing Mum and Pop: A Memoir* (2008). He has also published over 50 comic essays in the *New Yorker,* where "College Essay" first appeared in 2005.

READING WITH A PURPOSE: "College Essay" is a satiric piece that pokes fun at the essay high school students write as part of their college admissions application. Like all good satire, however, the piece has some truth to it. As you read, try to determine what those kernels of truth are and what Buckley is saying about admissions essays, the audience and purpose for admissions essays, and student-writers. Is this the kind of essay students often write? Is it at least a suitable first draft?

College Essay

BY CHRISTOPHER BUCKLEY

1   . . . your entrance essay must not only demonstrate your grasp of grammar and ability to write lucid, structured prose but also paint a vivid picture of your personality and character, one that compels a busy admissions officer to accept you.

—Online college-application editing service

2   It was a seventeenth-century English-person John Donne who wrote, "No man is an island." An excellent statement, but it is also true that "No woman is also an island."

3   The truth of this was brought home dramatically on September 11, 2001. Despite the fact that I was only twelve at the time, the images of that day will not soon ever be forgotten. Not by me, certainly. Though technically not a New Yorker (since I inhabit northwestern Wisconsin), I felt, as Donne would put it, "Part of the main," as I watched those buildings come down. Coincidentally, this was also the day my young sibling came down with a skin ailment that the doctors have not yet been able to determine what it is. It's not like his skin condition was a direct result of the terrorist attack, but it probably didn't help.

4   I have a personal connection to the events of that day, for some years ago my uncle by marriage's brother worked in one of the towers. He wasn't working there on 9/11, but the fact that he had been in the building only years before brought the tragedy home to Muske-lunge Township.

5   It is for this reason that I have resolved to devote my life to bringing about harmony among the nations of the world, especially in those nations who appear to dislike us enough to fly planes into our skyscrapers. With better understanding comes, I believe, the desire not to fly planes into each other's skyscrapers.

> "With better understanding comes, I believe, the desire not to fly planes into each other's skyscrapers."

6   Also, I would like to work toward finding a cure for mysterious skin ailments. Candidly, I do not know at this point if I would be a pre-med, which indeed would be a good way to begin finding the cure. But I also feel that I could contribute vitally to society even if I were a liberal-arts major, for instance majoring in writing for television.

7   Many people in the world community, indeed probably most, watch television. Therefore I feel that by writing for TV I could reach them through that powerful medium, and bring to them a higher awareness of such problems as Global Warming, Avian Flu, earthquakes in places like Pakistan, and the tsumani. Also the situation in the White House with respect to Mr. Scooter Liddy. To be precise, I believe that television could play a key role in warning people living on shorelines that they are about to be hit by one humongous wave. While it is true that in northwest Wisconsin we don't have this particular problem, it is also true that I think about it on behalf of people who do. No man is an island. To be sure.

8   Another element in my desire to devote my life to service to humanity was my parents' divorce. Because I believe that this is valuable preparation for college and, beyond, life. At college, for instance one is liable to find yourself living in a situation in which people don't get along, especially in bathrooms. Bathrooms are in that sense a microcosm of the macrocosm. Bathrooms also can be a truly dramatic crucible, as the playright Arthur Miller has demonstrated in his dramaturgical magnum opus by that title.

> "Another element in my desire to devote my life to service to humanity was my parents' divorce."

9   I am not one to say, "Omigod, like poor me," despite the fact that my dad would on numerable occasions drink an entire bottle of raspberry cordial and try to run Mamma over with the combine harvester. That is "Stinkin' Thinkin'." As the Danish composer Frederick Nietzche declared, "That which does not kill me makes me longer." This was certainly true of Mamma, especially after being run over.

10   Finally, what do I bring to the college experience? As President Kennedy observed in his second inaugural, "Ask not what your country can do to you. Ask, what can you do to your country."

11   I would bring two things, primarily. First, a positive attitude, despite all this crap I have had to deal with. Secondly, full tuition payment.

12   While Dad pretty much wiped out the money in the process of running over Mamma—she was in the house at the time—my grandparents say they can pay for my education, and even throw in a little "walking-around money" for the hard-working folks in the admissions department. Grandma says she will give up her heart and arthritis medications, and Grandpa says he will go back to work at the uranium mine in Utah despite the facts that he is eighty-two and legally blind.

13   In this way, the college won't have to give me scholarship money that could go to some even more disadvantaged applicant, assuming there is one.

ASSIGNMENT

In a paragraph or two, give the "student writer" of the piece serious advice for revision.

Writing in Academic Settings

Writing is a centerpiece activity in most college classes. Sometimes you will write to reveal how much you have learned about course material, as when you write exam answers. Sometimes you will write to consider the meaning and importance of material, as when you write journal entries or critical analyses. Sometimes you will write to demonstrate the connections among ideas in multiple readings, as when you write synthesis essays. Sometimes you will write out the main points of important material, as when you write summaries. And sometimes you will write to learn material, as when you keep learning logs. Here, for example, are just some of the kinds of writing likely to be important in classes across the curriculum.

Kinds of Academic Writing

- Lecture notes
- Notes from textbooks
- Outlines of course content
- Summaries of important readings
- Responses to readings
- Journal entries
- Solutions to problems
- Essays
- Essay exam answers

- Online discussions
- Self-reflection essays for portfolios
- Oral presentations
- Book or article reviews
- Lab reports
- Case studies
- Research papers
- Idea generation
- Collaborative writing

Consider the importance of writing in your college curriculum by thinking about how many of the writing tasks in the above box you have already completed and how many you are likely to engage in before graduation. How important is writing to your success in college?

WRITING IN RESPONSE TO READING

Much of your academic writing will be in response to required reading. In this writing, you will engage with a text in many ways — for example, by considering its meaning, judging its worth, connecting its ideas to other concepts, and determining its usefulness. This writing will also enable you to connect with other readers, by exchanging ideas, debating points, and collaboratively coming to new understandings. In your classes across the curriculum, you will be asked to engage with a text and other readers in specific ways. For example, you might evaluate an author's logic, compare and contrast the ideas in two readings, determine the significance of a proposal, define the meaning of a concept explained by an author, analyze the causes or effects of an event an author discusses, or give your opinion about a theory an author advances.

To write in response to reading, you will build on the critical reading strategies you learned in Chapter 1. When you distinguish facts from opinions, make inferences, synthesize information, evaluate the quality of a piece, and assess logic — all of which you learned to do in Chapter 1 — you draw conclusions that can be developed in academic writing. Also, the strategies you learned in Chapters 2 and 3 for planning, writing, and rewriting an essay will help you write in response to reading.

In the next sections, you will learn about some common kinds of academic writing that draw on the conclusions you reach during your critical reading. These academic writings may require that you convey to readers words and ideas from the readings. To do this, you use the following:

- **Paraphrase**—restating ideas in a reading in your own words
- **Summary**—giving the main points of a reading in your own words
- **Quotation**—restating the words in a reading

You will learn when and how to paraphrase, summarize, and quote later in this chapter.

When you paraphrase, summarize, and quote, you must give credit to the source in the following ways:

- With a *works cited entry*, a citation located on the Works Cited page at the end of the paper, which gives complete publication information on the source from which the paraphrase, summary, or quotation was taken (For an example, see page 97.)
- With a *parenthetical citation*, which is an in-text notation, given in parentheses after the paraphrase, summary, or quotation, to direct readers to a complete citation of the source on the Works Cited page (For an example, see page 100.)

Parenthetical citations and works cited entries as specified by the Modern Language Association (MLA) are explained in Chapter 15. Always check with your instructor to learn whether you should follow MLA or some other guidelines.

Writing a Personal Response

You may be asked to react to reading material on a personal level by expressing the responses and associations the reading elicits in you. Personal response essays often answer one or more of these questions:

- What does the reading make you think of? How does it make you feel?
- What similar experiences have you had?
- What have you observed that is or is not compatible with ideas in the reading?
- What did you learn from the reading?

A personal response essay is not license to write just anything and defend it by saying, "Well, that's how I feel." You must give reasons for your response, which you can do by citing the text and explaining your ideas, relating your relevant experience, and noting your pertinent observations.

Sometimes readers believe that there is one "correct" meaning buried somewhere in the text and that their job is to study the text until they unearth it. These readers tend to distrust their personal responses because they fear they don't square with that one correct meaning. In truth, any meaning, personal response, or association you have is valid and important—as long as you can back it up with evidence from the text, along with your ideas, experience, or observation.

The Purpose of a Personal Response

A personal response essay can be written for several purposes. Often your purpose is one of discovery and engagement with the text. You are enriching the reading experience by identifying what the text means to you and how it affects you. Because your personal response will include your own feelings, experience, and observation to explain your response, your purpose is often to express feelings and relate experience. A personal response essay can also inform your instructor about how you are reacting to a text and the understandings you are taking from it.

Process Guidelines: Strategies for Writing a Personal Response

When you write a personal response, follow the strategies from Chapters 1–3 that work well for you. In particular, you may find the following strategies helpful:

Step 1. If you need help deciding on the response to write about, reread the notes you made when you read and studied the text. Alternatively, answer the questions on pages 12–13.

Step 2. Follow the procedures you learned in Chapter 2 to generate ideas, develop a thesis, and order your ideas.

Step 3. Follow the procedures you learned in Chapter 3 to draft and revise your essay. To support your points, remember to cite the text and draw on your own ideas, personal experience, and observations. In addition, you can use one or more of the patterns of development:

- **Description** to give the reader a mental image of a person or place
- **Narration** to tell a story
- **Exemplification** to offer explanatory examples
- **Process analysis** to explain how something was made or done
- **Comparison-contrast** to express important similarities or differences
- **Cause-and-effect analysis** to explain why an event occurred or what the results of an event were
- **Classification-division** to categorize items or break something down into its parts
- **Definition** to explain the meaning of a concept

Step 4. If you used paraphrase, summary, or quotation, be sure you did so according to the conventions explained on pages 106–112 and that you provided parenthetical citations and a Works Cited page as explained in Chapter 15.

Sample Personal Response

"The Not-So-Ideal Male," which you read in Chapter 3 (page 83), is an example of a personal response essay; it was written by a student who had read "Americanization Is Tough on 'Macho'" (page 13). Reading the essay prompted the student to consider what it means to be "manly," and that consideration resulted in his personal response.

Take a moment to reread both "Americanization Is Tough on 'Macho'" and "The Not-So-Ideal Male" to see how the second piece is a personal response to the first. Then study the following paragraph from "The Not-So-Ideal Male" and the accompanying marginal notes to see how the points in a personal response must be backed up with evidence:

One response the student had to the reading is that the ideal man is depicted as a loner. He makes that point in the first sentence and then backs it up with a

The ideal men depicted in advertising, movies, and legends are loners. Their strength stems from the fact that they need no one to help them accomplish their goals. The Marlboro man always rides out alone; the action hero single-handedly saves the day. This fact causes problems for males who try to live up to the perceived ideal. It leads them to wall themselves off from others, depriving themselves of enjoyable, satisfying relationships. Further, our world is becoming increasingly cooperative on all levels—from interpersonal to international. A successful male knows that the help of others is essential to achieving his dream and that collaboration is increasingly valued in the workplace. The loner may not perform as well on the job.

summary of the examples given in earlier paragraphs (the Marlboro man and action heroes). He also backs up his response with an explanation of the effect of the depiction: Men are walled off and unable to work collaboratively.

Writing a Summary

When you write a **summary,** you restate the main ideas in an entire reading or a large part of that reading, using your own words and style. You must be careful to reflect faithfully the original; do not add points, alter the meaning, or interpret or evaluate. Because a summary includes only the most important points, it is much shorter than the original selection.

The Purpose of Summarizing

A summary can be a stand-alone piece of writing. In addition, summarizing has many uses in the classroom. It is a valuable study strategy because writing out the major points of a reading or a chapter gives you a study guide for that material and helps set learning. Including on examinations, your instructors may ask you to summarize reading assignments so they can check your comprehension. Finally, when you need a distillation of a selection's major points to include in one of your essays, you will again rely on summary. Later in this chapter, you will learn more about including summaries in your academic writing.

Process Guidelines: Strategies for Writing a Summary

When you write a summary, follow the strategies from Chapters 1–3 that work well for you. In addition, the following strategies, focused especially on summaries, may be helpful:

Step 1. Read the material over as many times as necessary in order to understand it. Look up unfamiliar words and get help with any passages you do not understand. (You cannot summarize material you do not understand.)

Step 2. Identify the major points and underline them in the text or list them on a piece of paper. You can omit examples, description, repetition, or explanations that support major points, unless these are necessary for clarification. Be sure to identify all the major points so your summary is complete.

Step 3. Draft an opening sentence that mentions the author's name, the title of the piece you are summarizing, and one, two, or three of the following: the author's thesis, the author's purpose, the author's point of view. Here are some examples:

AUTHOR, TITLE, AND THESIS	In "Americanization Is Tough on 'Macho,'" Rose Del Castillo Guibault explains that Americans have a negative connotation for the word *macho,* and this fact bothers Hispanics, who use the word in a positive sense.
AUTHOR, TITLE, AND PURPOSE	"Americanization Is Tough on 'Macho'" is Rose Del Castillo Guibault's attempt to inform Americans that the negative meaning they ascribe to the term macho creates cultural misunderstanding and perpetuates an inaccurate stereotype of Latin males.
AUTHOR, TITLE, POINT OF VIEW	In "Americanization Is Tough on 'Macho,'" Rose Del Castillo Guibault examines the term *macho* and the stereotype it reflects from a Mexican American's perspective.

Use present-tense verbs with the author's name because the words of the text "live on" in the present: Rose Del Castillo Guibault *explains, notes, says, expresses, examines, believes,* and so forth (not *explained, noted, said, expressed, examined, believed,* and so on).

Step 4. Following your opening statement, draft your summary by writing out the major points you underlined or listed. Be sure to express these points in your own distinctive style by using your own wording and sentence structure. If you have trouble rewording a phrase or sentence, you can use the original if you place the borrowed words in quotation marks. Just be careful to use quotations sparingly.

Step 5. To keep your summary flowing smoothly, use transitions to show how ideas relate to each other. In addition, repeat the author's name with a present-tense verb as a transitional device, like this:

Smith explains . . .

Smith further believes . . .

The author goes on to note . . .

Step 6. Check to be sure you have altered wording and style without adding or changing meaning.

Step 7. If you have quoted, be sure you followed the conventions beginning on page 108. Also, provide a parenthetical citation and a works cited entry, as explained in Chapter 15.

A Sample Summary

The following is a sample summary of "Americanization Is Tough on 'Macho,'" which appears on page 13. The annotations in the margin call your attention to some of the summary's key features. Notice that the summary is a single paragraph. Because summaries are condensed versions of readings, they are brief. However, summaries of longer selections or of selections with many ideas can be two or more paragraphs. Notice, too, that the paragraph is followed by a works cited entry acknowledging the source of the information in the summary.

Summary of "Americanization Is Tough on 'Macho'" by Rose Del Castillo Guibault

[1]In "Americanization Is Tough on 'Macho,'" Rose Del Castillo Guibault [2]explains that Americans have a negative connotation for the word *macho,* and this fact bothers Hispanics, who use the word in a positive sense. [3]While Americans use the term to refer to a man who is a [4]"chauvinist, a brute, uncouth, selfish, loud, abrasive, capable of inflicting pain, and sexually promiscuous," Hispanics use the term respectfully for a male who is [4]"responsible, hardworking, a man in charge, a patriarch." [5]Guibault [2]believes this difference in connotation reflects the fact that in the United States the traits that other cultures prize are not valued by American society. [6]She also believes that during the seventies, the rise of feminism was responsible for *macho* acquiring negative connotations. [7]More than anything, though, Guibault is concerned because Americans' sense of *macho* has become an inaccurate stereotype of the Latin man that contributes to cultural misunderstanding.

[8]Work Cited

Guibault, Rose Del Castillo. "Americanization Is Tough on 'Macho.'" *Patterns for a Purpose: A Rhetorical Reader.* Ed. Barbara Fine Clouse. 6th ed. New York: McGraw, 2011, 13–15. Print.

[1]Summary opens with a statement that gives the author, title, and thesis of material summarized.

[2]Verb is in the present tense.

[3]First major point is given.

[4]Exact words appear in quotation marks.

[5]Next major point is given. Transition is achieved through repetition of the author's name.

[6]Next major point is given. Transition is achieved with use of the pronoun and *also*.

[7]Final major point is given. Transition is achieved with repetition of the author's name and the phrase "more than anything."

[8]In your summary, the work(s) cited entry should begin on a new page. The forms for your "Work(s) Cited" page are given in Chapter 15.

Writing a Critical Analysis

In Chapter 1, you learned that critical reading requires you to analyze and assess a text. You analyze by determining what the author is saying and how he or she is saying it; you assess by judging the quality and significance of the text. A **critical analysis** reports on one or more of the conclusions you drew during your critical reading and demonstrates the soundness of your conclusion(s). To write a critical analysis, you can consider the validity of one or more ideas in the reading, or you can evaluate

Summarizing

If you have trouble expressing all or part of a passage in a different way, imagine yourself talking to a friend and explaining the ideas you just read. Then write the explanation in the words you use to summarize the passage. If necessary, you can revise the material later to make it less like speech and more like prose.

the worth of the piece, or you can judge how well the piece is written by evaluating one or more of the strategies an author uses to make his or her points. Thus, to write a critical analysis, you must use your critical reading skills to identify the author's assertion and draw conclusions about its validity and the quality of the detail put forth for support. For example, "When Children Murder: Treatment or Punishment" on page 100 is a critical analysis because it assesses an idea in an essay, judges it to be incorrect, and explains why.

When you write a critical analysis, remember that the term *critical* does not mean "giving negative comments." In this case, *critical* means "evaluating," so you will often make positive assessments about writing, when your analysis leads you to positive evaluations. To write a critical analysis, you can consider one or more of the following aspects of writing:

- **The thesis and major points.** Do you agree with the author's thesis and major points? Does the author successfully explain or prove everything? If so, how? If not, why not?
- **The supporting details.** What inferences can you make? Is the author giving facts and/or opinions? How appropriate and successful are the supporting details? For example, are the points adequately developed? Are the examples appropriate and well developed? Is the logic sound? Are important points of comparison or contrast included, or are some omitted?
- **Audience and purpose.** Does the author achieve his or her purpose with the targeted audience? If so, what strategies does he or she use to achieve that purpose? If not, why not?
- **Word choice and tone.** Does the author use an appropriate level of diction? Is the word choice appropriate or inappropriately emotional or manipulative? Fair or biased? Current or dated? What is the author's tone? For example, is it angry, frustrated, reasoned, casual,

or sarcastic? How do word choice and tone affect the writing? Do they seem appropriate for the intended audience and purpose?

No matter what analyses and assessments you make—whether positive, negative, or some of both—remember that you must back up your conclusions with specific evidence from the reading. After each reading in Chapters 5–14, writing assignments labeled "Analyzing and Assessing" will give you an opportunity to practice writing critical analyses.

The Purpose of Critical Analysis

Because a critical analysis often notes an author's ideas and characterizes a reading, it can inform about the content of a piece. Most critical analyses try to persuade readers by convincing them of the truth of an analysis or assessment. For example, suppose that for a political science class you read a journal article about why the two-party system persists in the United States. You might write a critical analysis in which you note the reasons the author gives for the endurance of the two-party system—informing your readers—and you might then go on to state that the author's reasons are no longer relevant in the twenty-first century and explain why. At this point, you would be trying to convince your reader to accept your assessment. A critical analysis can also be a component of a longer piece of writing. More than any other kind of academic writing, a critical analysis will let your instructor know how well you understand a reading and how carefully you considered the author's ideas and writing strategies. In short, a critical analysis will help your instructor judge the effectiveness of your critical reading skills.

Process Guidelines: Strategies for Writing a Critical Analysis

When you write a critical analysis, follow the strategies from Chapters 1–3 that work well for you. In addition, the following strategies, focused especially on critical analysis, may be helpful:

Step 1. As you read critically, think about which aspects of your analysis and assessment you want to consider in your written critical analysis. Answering the questions on pages 12–13 can help you decide, as can answering these questions:

- Would you recommend the reading to others? Why or why not?
- Which features help the writer achieve his or her purpose? Which do not? How do these features help or hinder?

Step 2. Identify the evidence in the reading that will support the assertion you will make in your critical analysis.

Step 3. Draft a preliminary version of your thesis and an outline to guide your draft. Draw on one or more of the patterns of development, as explained on page 52, if they can help you support your analysis or assessment.

Step 4. Check any paraphrases, summaries, and quotations to be sure you follow the conventions explained on pages 106–112. Also be sure you include parenthetical citations and a Works Cited page. (See Chapter 15.)

A Sample Critical Analysis

Here is an example of a student's brief critical analysis of an idea in "Adult Crime, Adult Time" by Linda Collier, which appears in Chapter 13. As you read, notice both the informative and the persuasive purposes. The marginal notes call your attention to some key features. (For another critical analysis, see "No Body's Perfect" on page 362.)

When Children Murder: Treatment or Punishment?

Kay Sweeney

Paragraph 1
The first two sentences of the introduction mention Sweeney's analysis of part of Collier's essay. It notes what Collier says and the source of some of her support (examples).

The thesis is the last sentence, expressed as a rhetorical question. It makes clear that the critical analysis will focus on Sweeney's assessment of the validity of Collier's belief that more juveniles should be tried and punished as adults.

In "Adult Crime, Adult Time," Linda Collier maintains that too many 1 young people who commit violent crimes are tried as juveniles rather than adults, that "too many states still treat violent offenders under 16 as juveniles who belong in the juvenile system" (609). An attorney who has represented children in court, Collier cites a number of examples to demonstrate that "the system is doing a poor job at treatment as well as punishment" (609). Frankly, I'm not sure what kind of "treatment" a child will get in an adult penal facility, but I'm quite sure the punishment will be severe enough. But is that what we want?

Paragraph 2
Most of this paragraph gives an assessment in the form of the writer's disagreement with Collier. Notice the cause-and-effect analysis to argue against Collier.

I suspect that those who want children locked away in adult prisons 2 are not looking for justice; they are after revenge. They are motivated by anger, especially when the crimes are heinous. Collier, herself, points to such crimes as evidence that we need harsher penalties for children. She cites shootings in Jonesboro, Arkansas; Paducah, Kentucky; and Daly City, California, as examples (608). And certainly there are many more. When children murder other children and adults, it is only human for us to respond with anger and a desire for revenge, but we need to move beyond these primal feelings to fix whatever is wrong in our society that such events occur with a certain frequency. Certainly locking away the shooters in horrendous adult facilities does not address the societal problems. It removes these people from our midst and makes us feel better temporarily, but there are always more juveniles who commit horrific murders and other violent crimes.

Collier also maintains that the increasing number of violent crimes 3 committed by juveniles further argues for overhauling the juvenile justice system (609). She is right. However, the needed overhaul is not trying kids as adults and locking them away with hardened adult criminals. The overhaul called for is in treatment. Let's revamp the juvenile system to provide the therapeutic interventions needed when our youngest citizens commit the worst acts. If treatment fails, then we can look at the appropriate kinds of incarceration.

Paragraph 3
This paragraph assesses Collier's belief that the juvenile justice system must be overhauled. Note the persuasive purpose of the assessment. Note also the use of comparison and contrast of the author's ideas and Collier's for support.

4   Collier's most surprising support for her assertion is her statement that "federal prosecution of juveniles is not totally unheard of" (611). In other words, she is saying that we have done it before, so it is fine to do it again. This is not the logic one expects of an attorney. Her reasoning is equivalent to saying, "If Johnny jumped off a bridge, you can too." Precedent for trying juveniles as adults does suggest that at times doing so is appropriate, and perhaps that option should be reserved for particularly special cases. That said, however, revamping the juvenile justice system to routinely try children as adults in cases of violent crime does little to solve the violence problem we have in this country.

Paragraph 4
This paragraph assesses Collier's logic and points to an error. Note the use of comparison-contrast for support. The last sentence is the conclusion.

In your critical analysis, the work cited entry is on a new page.

Work Cited

Collier, Linda J. "Adult Crime, Adult Time." *Patterns for a Purpose: A Rhetorical Reader.* Ed. Barbara Fine Clouse. 6th ed. New York: McGraw, 2011, 608–611. Print.

Writing a Synthesis

A **synthesis** integrates material from a source with your own ideas and/or with material from one or more other sources. For example, suppose you are writing on the topic of social pressure. You might write a synthesis by relating ideas from Chapter 6's "The Lottery" (about how adults pressure children) to experiences you had as a child (when you experienced pressure from a track coach). You could also write a synthesis by explaining how ideas from "The Lottery" relate to ideas in one or more other essays, perhaps arguing that the ideas in one of the essays are more valid than the ideas in the others. As you may have already figured out, critical analysis can be an important part of synthesis. This is because, to see how ideas in different readings relate to one another, or to see how they relate to your own experience and ideas, you must think about the material, draw conclusions, see relationships, make inferences, and make judgments.

The Purpose of Synthesis

In addition to completing a formal synthesis assignment, you will use synthesis in other academic writing. Synthesis is important in academic work because, in addition to helping you learn information and understand concepts, it helps you connect information and concepts and understand those connections. You will use synthesis to inform and persuade in many types of classroom writing. For example, for a paper for a child psychology class about the effects of televised violence on preschoolers, you can inform by mentioning the effects explained in several journal articles. In this way, you are connecting ideas. You can then seek to persuade by arguing that some of these effects are the most significant, and thereby show that you understand the connections. Synthesis is, of course, the basis of research papers.

Process Guidelines: Strategies for Writing a Synthesis

When you synthesize, follow the strategies from Chapters 1–3 that work well for you. In addition, some of the following strategies for drawing on multiple sources may be helpful:

Step 1. Be sure you understand everything in all the sources you are dealing with.

Step 2. Underline or list the major ideas in each source.

Step 3. Review all major ideas and determine how they relate to each other. Answering these five questions can help:

- Do the ideas in the sources confirm each other or contradict each other?
- Do the ideas in the sources suggest any cause-and-effect relationships?
- Do the ideas in one source explain or exemplify the ideas in another source?
- Do the ideas in one source pick up where the ideas in another source leave off?
- Do the sources examine the topic from different perspectives?

Step 4. Decide how you want to use the material in the sources. Answering these five questions can help:

- Can you use the information to explain something?
- Can you use the information to prove something?
- Can you show how the sources contradict one another or present different perspectives?
- Can you explain the significance of the information?
- Can you use the information to support your own experience or observation?

Step 5. Draft a preliminary version of your thesis and an outline to guide your draft. Consider how you want to organize your presentation or material from the different sources. Draw on one or more patterns of development as appropriate. (See page 52.)

Step 6. Check any paraphrases, summaries, and quotations to be sure you follow the conventions explained on pages 106–112. Also be sure you include parenthetical citations and works cited entries, as explained in Chapter 15 and illustrated in the essay in the next section.

A Sample Synthesis

This student essay synthesizes material from the following sources in Chapter 13: "Little Adult Criminals," "Should Juvenile Offenders Be Tried as Adults?" "Adult Crime, Adult Time," and "Young Voices from the Cell." The notes in the margin call your attention to some key features of the synthesis, including quotations, paraphrases, and parenthetical citations of sources. (For other examples of synthesis, see "No Body's Perfect" on page 362 and "Cast Out of Kansas" on page 589.)

Keep Juvenile Offenders in the
Juvenile Justice System
Rick David

1   Alarmingly, some of our most violent crimes are committed by children and teenagers. Until we determine why and address the causes, we are left with the problem of how to treat these juvenile offenders. Currently, we have one judicial process for adult offenders and a different judicial process for young offenders. Many people oppose that arrangement for violent juvenile offenders, believing that young people who commit murder and other violent crimes should be subject to adult laws in the adult system—"adult time for adult crime," it is called. In fact, in many states young, violent offenders are routinely tried and punished as adults. We should discontinue that practice and return young offenders to the juvenile justice system, but it should be a juvenile system that includes extensive psychiatric care.

Paragraph 1
David's ideas provide background and evaluation to lead into the synthesis.

The thesis is the last sentence.

2   First, we must ask ourselves why we put young offenders in the adult judicial system in the first place. In some cases, I fear it is a reaction to one of our baser impulses, the desire for revenge. When innocents are murdered, our first impulse is to seek revenge: We want to hurt the murderer. We want to lock the murderer up and throw away the key, so to speak. While understandable, the desire for revenge must be kept in check. We should not satisfy our appetite for revenge by taking 12-year-olds and sentencing them to hopelessly long terms in adult prisons with adult criminals.

The paragraph presents David's ideas.

Some people maintain that revenge is not the motive, that juveniles 3 who commit violent crimes should be in the adult system because the juvenile system does not serve children well. Linda J. Collier, for example, is an attorney who has worked in the juvenile courts. In "Adult Crime, Adult Time," she says that the juvenile system "is doing a poor job at treatment as well as punishment" (609). She believes the poor showing of the juvenile system is a result of the fact that it was devised to deal with "truants, vandals, and petty thieves," not the young murderers we are seeing today (610). Certainly, problems do exist in the juvenile system, very serious problems. However, the problems cannot be addressed by placing young people in the adult system where sentences are so long that prison officials see no reason to attempt rehabilitation. In "Young Voices from the Cell," Timothy Roche and Amanda Bower report this phenomenon. They cite Robert Johnson, commissioner of Mississippi's Department of Corrections, who says he makes no effort to rehabilitate prisoners who are in for life. He sees no use to it (618). Life sentences and no rehabilitation are hardly appropriate for many juvenile offenders, even those who have committed murder, because in many cases they are young enough to be treated and returned to society.

Paragraph 3
David synthesizes Collier's words and ideas with his own to counter an objection. He also synthesizes Roche and Bower's ideas with his own to support his idea that there is no rehabilitation in adult prisons. Notice the persuasive purpose.

For Laurence Steinberg, the answer lies in compromise. In "Should 4 Juvenile Offenders Be Tried as Adults?" he advocates keeping young people 12 and under in the juvenile system (605–606). Those older than 16 should be placed in the adult system, and those between 12 and 16 should be tested to determine placement (605–606). Unfortunately, this compromise will not work because neither system works well enough to meet the challenges of the violent juvenile offender.

Paragraph 4
David synthesizes Steinberg's ideas with those of the writers in paragraph 3; the last sentence is David's assessment of Steinberg's ideas. Notice the critical analysis.

The answer more logically lies with improving the juvenile system. 5 If the system does not work well enough, then legislators need to make the necessary adjustments. Courts should not move young offenders into an adult system that is even less prepared to cope effectively with them. Even Collier expresses surprise that the juvenile system has not been overhauled, especially in light of the increase in juvenile crime (611). As a first step, judges should require intensive, long-term psychiatric care for juveniles convicted of violent crimes. We can assume that juveniles who commit such crimes are emotionally disturbed. Roche and Bower report the assessment of forensic psychiatrist Park Dietz. Dietz interviewed juveniles who opened fire in schools and concludes that the shooters were depressed and angry (618)—obviously, pathologically so.

Paragraph 5
Collier's ideas support David's idea expressed in the previous sentences of the paragraph.

David's ideas are synthesized with ideas from Roche and Bower.

Psychiatrists for Jacob Davis, who shot his girlfriend's ex-lover, say that Davis was "suffering from serious depression with psychotic features" (Roche and Bower 619). If we treat the pathology, we may be able to return the juvenile to society as a productive person who does not pose a threat. Granted, the treatment can take a very long time, but the alternative is worse. Eventually, some of these juveniles will be released—as adults who may commit murder. T. J. Solomon, who is currently incarcerated in an adult prison, may be released after serving his 40-year sentence. He has flashbacks, hears screams, and hallucinates (Roche and Bower 619). He shot his classmates as a mentally ill juvenile. Do we want him on the streets as a mentally ill adult?

6   Sentencing juveniles as adults may keep young violent offenders off the streets longer, and it may satisfy our desire for revenge, but it does nothing to address the real problems—why young people kill, and how to rehabilitate the killers so they do not murder again. Neither the adult nor the juvenile justice system will address the first issue; only an overhauled juvenile system can address the second.

Paragraph 6
David concludes with a summary of the argument.

Works Cited

Collier, Linda J. "Adult Crime, Adult Time." *Patterns for a Purpose: A Rhetorical Reader.* Ed. Barbara Fine Clouse. 6th ed. New York: McGraw-Hill, 2011. 608–611. Print.

New York Times. Editorial. "Little Adult Criminals." *Patterns for a Purpose: A Rhetorical Reader.* Ed. Barbara Fine Clouse. 6th ed. New York: McGraw-Hill, 2011. 599–601. Print.

Roche, Timothy, and Amanda Bower. "Young Voices from the Cell." *Patterns for a Purpose: A Rhetorical Reader.* Ed. Barbara Fine Clouse. 6th ed. New York: McGraw-Hill, 2011. 613–619. Print.

Steinberg, Laurence. "Should Juvenile Offenders Be Tried as Adults?" *Patterns for a Purpose: A Rhetorical Reader.* Ed. Barbara Fine Clouse. 6th ed. New York: McGraw-Hill, 2011. 602–606. Print.

In your synthesis, the "works cited" entries should begin on a new page.

USING THE READINGS IN THIS BOOK AS SOURCES

In addition to using the words and ideas from the readings in your personal responses, summaries, critical analyses, and syntheses, you can use material from the readings when writing an essay on your own ideas. The readings in the book can, in this way, serve as sources for you. They provide supporting details to supplement your own ideas, as the following example illustrates. The example is a paragraph with some words and ideas taken from "Adult Crime, Adult Time," by Linda J. Collier, in Chapter 13. The material from that reading supplements the writer's own ideas in a paragraph that supports the thesis "Beginning in third grade, all schools should require students to take classes in anger management and dispute resolution."

Sentence 5 includes an idea from Collier's essay to make the point that violence among younger children is increasing. This point underscores the importance of dealing with bullying, a cause of youthful violence.

Sentence 6 includes a quotation from Collier's essay to show that the nature of the violence among youth is worsening—making the classes to address bullying even more important.

[1]Classes in anger management and dispute resolution would lessen the amount of violence in our society. [2]Consider bullying, for example. [3]Students inclined to bully people would learn more acceptable alternatives with anger management techniques, while those who become victims of bullying would learn how to defuse the situations with dispute resolution strategies. [4]Because both bullies and their victims are known to be a source of violence among young people, we must deal with that problem to reduce overall violence. [5]Further, as Linda J. Collier points out, children are committing violent acts at increasingly younger ages. [6]In fact, she notes that "where juvenile delinquency was once limited to truancy or vandalism, juveniles now are more likely to be the perpetrators of serious and deadly crimes such as arson, aggravated assault, rape and murder" (609). [7]Thus, we must address causes of violence among our youth, including bullying.

When you include words and ideas from the readings in this book, you must follow the appropriate conventions for paraphrasing, summarizing, and quoting. These are explained next. You will also need to provide parenthetical citations and works cited entries, as specified by the MLA and explained in Chapter 15. You can see all of these conventions in action in the "Using Sources for a Purpose" sections of Chapters 5–13. By using the appropriate conventions, you will avoid plagiarism, as discussed later in this chapter.

www.mhhe.com/clousepatterns6   Source Information

For more help with paraphrasing and quoting, click on
Research > Incorporating Source Information

Paraphrasing

To paraphrase, you restate another author's ideas, using your own style and wording. Paraphrasing is useful because it helps you incorporate ideas from different sources into your essays to support your own ideas. Most of the source material you incorporate into your papers should be paraphrases rather than quotes, so that your essays retain your distinctive writing style. The sample synthesis on page 103 and critical analysis on page 100 shows how to incorporate paraphrases.

When you paraphrase you should:

- Use your own wording and style, not the source's.
- Use quotation marks around keywords or phrases that are the author's distinctive expression, if these are included in the paraphrase.
- Avoid adding ideas or changing meaning.
- Provide a parenthetical citation and works cited entry according to the conventions explained in Chapter 15.

www.mhhe.com/clousepatterns6   Quotations

For more help with using quotation marks, click on

Editing > Quotation Marks

Here is an example of acceptable paraphrase and unacceptable paraphrase of part of paragraph 1 of "Fan Profanity" on page 639. Notice that the acceptable paraphrase places the author's distinctive phrasing in quotation marks. The unacceptable paraphrase fails to alter style and wording enough. It is, therefore, a type of unfair "borrowing" even though the source is credited.

SOURCE   Many free-speech controversies, especially on college campuses, are grounded in concerns for civility, politeness, and good taste. They also tend to follow the same path and end the same way. A government entity regulates speech in an effort to elevate discourse, limit the profane and protect public and personal sensitivities; courts strike down the regulations as violating the First Amendment freedom of speech; and we end up right where we started.

ACCEPTABLE PARAPHRASE   Howard M. Wasserman sees a recurring pattern to many First Amendment challenges. He says that when a college government tries to create a more mannered atmosphere by setting rules to reduce instances of profanity and "protect public and personal sensitivities," the efforts are struck down in court as a violation of free speech (639).

UNACCEPTABLE PARAPHRASE   Howard M. Wasserman says that many free-speech debates, particularly ones at colleges, are based on concerns for politeness and good taste. These debates seem to take the same course, and end the same. First a government organization controls speech to raise the level of communication. Then, the judiciary condemns the regulations for violating the Constitutional guarantee of free speech. Then we end up back at the beginning (639).

When you write your paraphrases, avoid plugging in synonyms. If you merely substitute synonyms for words in the source, the paraphrase will lack your distinctive style. Furthermore, the result is often an awkward-sounding sentence. Even worse, your paraphrase is unfair borrowing. Here is an example using "Should Juvenile Offenders Be Tried as Adults?" on page 602 as the source.

SOURCE	Few issues challenge a society's ideas about the natures of human development and justice as much as serious juvenile crime.
UNACCEPTABLE PARAPHRASE	Steinberg believes that not very many concerns confront a social order's notions about the characters of people's growth and the legal system as much as grave crime committed by young people (602).
ACCEPTABLE PARAPHRASE	Steinberg believes that of all the problems facing a society, the problem of "serious juvenile crime" is among the most difficult to grapple with (602).

Summarizing

As you saw earlier, summary can be used within essays. Like a paraphrase, a summary restates an author's ideas in your own words and style, but unlike a paraphrase, it condenses an entire piece or large part of a piece to convey only the main ideas. Summary is useful when you want to give just the highlights or gist of a piece as part of your supporting detail. For an example of a summary as part of a writer's supporting details, see "Using Sources for a Purpose" on page 132. As with paraphrasing, you may, if appropriate, include a quotation within your summary.

When you summarize, you should follow the same guidelines you follow when you paraphrase:

- Use your own wording and style.
- Use quotation marks if you include exact words.
- Avoid adding ideas or changing meaning.
- Include parenthetical citations and a works cited entry according to the conventions in Chapter 15.

Quoting

To write a **direct quotation,** reproduce the author's exact words within quotation marks. You should limit the number of quotations you use because with too many quotations, your writing may seem choppy and will lack your distinctive style. As a general guide, limit your quoting to those times when something is so well expressed that you want to preserve the original wording.

A number of conventions govern the use of quotations. The following, which are in keeping with MLA rules, are illustrated using material from "Fan Profanity" on page 639.

- **Use ellipses (three spaced periods) to indicate that something in the original text has been left out.**

SOURCE	Many free-speech controversies, especially on college campuses, are grounded in concerns for civility, politeness, and good taste.
QUOTATION	According to Howard M. Wasserman, "Many free-speech controversies . . . are grounded in concerns for civility, politeness, and good taste" (639).

- **Use brackets to add clarification or to make changes needed to work the quotation into your sentence.**

SOURCE	The Hobson's Choice that Anderson believes this creates for fans—leave the arena and stop attending games or tolerate offensive cheers—is precisely the choice people make in any public place at which expression occurs.
QUOTATION	Wasserman says, "The Hobson's Choice [a seeming choice that really is no choice] that Anderson believes this creates for fans—leave the arena and stop attending games or tolerate offensive cheers—is precisely the choice people make in any public place at which expression occurs" (641).

- **Use single quotation marks for a quotation within a quotation.**

SOURCE	The speech at issue is expression by fans related to a sporting event, to all aspects of the game and all the participants in the game—what we can call "cheering speech."
QUOTATION	Wasserman explains that "the speech at issue is expression by fans related to a sporting event, to all aspects of the game and all the participants in the game—what we can call 'cheering speech' " (640).

- **Reproduce italics that appear in the source.**

SOURCE	It is true that courts have upheld content-neutral regulations on sound and noise levels to protect captive audiences, beginning with the Supreme Court case *Kovacs v. Cooper* in 1949.
QUOTATION	One attorney explains, "It is true that courts have upheld content-neutral regulations on sound and noise levels to protect captive audiences, beginning with the Supreme Court case *Kovacs v. Cooper* in 1949" (Wasserman 640).

- **Set off long quotations (more than four lines in your paper) by indenting instead of using quotation marks.** Do not further indent the first word, even if it begins a paragraph in the source, unless you are quoting multiple paragraphs. Double-space the material and place the parenthetical citation after the final period.

SOURCE   Many free-speech controversies, especially on college
          campuses, are grounded in concerns for civility, polite-
          ness, and good taste. They also tend to follow the same
          path and end the same way. A government entity regu-
          lates speech in an effort to elevate discourse, limit the
          profane and protect public and personal sensitivities;
          courts strike down the regulations as violating the First
          Amendment freedom of speech; and we end up right
          where we started.

QUOTATION Howard Wasserman explains the cycle that free-speech
          debates often take:
              Many free-speech controversies, especially on college
              campuses, are grounded in concerns for civility, polite-
              ness, and good taste. They also tend to follow the same
              path and end the same way. A government entity reg-
              ulates speech in an effort to elevate discourse, limit the
              profane and protect public and personal sensitivities;
              courts strike down the regulations as violating the
              First Amendment freedom of speech; and we end up
              right where we started. (639)

- **Include a parenthetical citation and works cited entry** as explained
  in Chapter 15 and illustrated in "Keep Juvenile Offenders in the
  Juvenile Justice System" on page 103.

| www.mhhe.com/clousepatterns6 | Source Information |

For more help with paraphrasing and quoting, click on

Research > Incorporating Source Information

| www.mhhe.com/clousepatterns6 | Quotations |

For more help with using quotation marks, click on

Editing > Quotation Marks

Integrating Paraphrases, Summaries, and Quotations

The following strategies will help you work paraphrases, summaries, and
quotations into your paper smoothly so your writing reads well; so your
reader can tell that you are paraphrasing, summarizing, or quoting; and so
your reader understands how you are using the source material.

- **Use sources to help you fulfill your writing purpose.** Avoid
  letting your sources drive the content and organization of your
  writing, and avoid stringing together quotations and paraphrases,
  one after another. Instead, use source material for a reason, such
  as to support an argument, explain an idea, or illustrate a concept.

- **Introduce the paraphrase, summary, or quotation with the author and/or source of information.** Although most often best placed before the paraphrase, summary, or quotation, that information can also come in the middle or at the end, as shown by the italicized phrases in these examples that draw on "Adult Crime, Adult Time."

AT THE BEGINNING   *Linda J. Collier explains,* "Federal prosecution of juveniles is not totally unheard of, but it is uncommon" (611).

IN THE MIDDLE   "Federal prosecution of juveniles is not totally unheard of," *notes Collier,* "but it is uncommon" (611).

AT THE END   "Federal prosecution of juveniles is not totally unheard of, but it is uncommon," *according to Linda J. Collier* (611).

- **Vary the verbs in the present tense to work in the paraphrase, summary, or quotation.** Present tense is used because printed words—even ones written long ago—exist in the present. To avoid the monotony of repeating "Collier says," where appropriate include some other verbs, like these:

acknowledges	implies	questions
argues	insists	replies
asserts	maintains	reveals
believes	notes	suggests
contends	points out	wonders

- **Indicate the purpose of each paraphrase, summary, and quotation by choosing verbs and including language to demonstrate how the source material relates to the ideas before or after.** Here is an example using "Adult Crime, Adult Time" and "Should Juvenile Offenders Be Tried as Adults?" (602).

> Linda J. Collier believes in treating juveniles who commit violent crimes as adults because, as she states in "Adult Crime, Adult Time," the current juvenile justice system "is not appropriate for the violent juvenile offender of today" (610). *Laurence Steinberg, however, takes a less simplistic view.* In "Should Juvenile Offenders Be Tried as Adults?" Steinberg seems willing to try young people 13 and older as adults, but he expresses concern about trying children under 13 as adults because of the possibility that "children this young will not prove to be sufficiently blameworthy to warrant exposure to the harsh consequences of a criminal court adjudication" (605–606).

The reader can tell from the second sentence of the paragraph, shown in italics, that the paraphrase and quotation of Steinberg present a view that contrasts with the view expressed in the Collier quotation. Take out this clarifying language, and the reader has a more difficult time connecting the two ideas:

> Linda J. Collier believes in treating juveniles who commit violent crimes as adults because as she states in "Adult Crime, Adult Time," the current juvenile justice system "is not appropriate for the violent juvenile offender of today" (610). In "Should Juvenile Offenders Be Tried as Adults?" Steinberg seems willing to try young people 13 and older as adults, but he expresses concern about trying children under 13 as adults because of the possibility that "children this young will not prove to be sufficiently blameworthy to warrant exposure to the harsh consequences of a criminal court adjudication" (605–606).

Avoiding Plagiarism

Plagiarism, which is a serious academic offense, occurs if you download, purchase, borrow, or otherwise use someone else's work and pass it off as your own. Plagiarism can occur as a result of uncredited borrowing of as little as a few words of someone else's work, and it need not be intentional. It can occur, for example, if you do not use source material according to the established conventions. To avoid plagiarism when you paraphrase, summarize, and quote, remember the following:

- When you paraphrase and summarize, rewrite the author's ideas in your own words; do not imitate the author's style.
- Introduce your paraphrases, summaries, and quotations with a phrase that gives the author and/or source of information.
- When you paraphrase or summarize, do not add ideas or change the meaning in the source.
- When you quote, place quotation marks around the author's exact words.
- Be sure to quote accurately, using ellipses and brackets as needed.
- Include a parenthetical citation and works cited entry as explained in Chapter 15 and illustrated in "Keep Juvenile Offenders in the Juvenile Justice System" on page 103.

Plagiarism is also discussed in Chapter 15 and in Appendix C. In addition, the "Avoiding Plagiarism" and "Myths about Sources" sections of Chapters 5–13 include helpful information.

WRITING TO LEARN

Across the curriculum, writing can help you learn by helping you think about course content, understand important material, and retain information. The kinds of academic writing listed on page 91 include some of the ways writing can be used as a learning tool, and the next sections explain some of those strategies.

Keeping a Learning Log

A **learning log** is a journal in which you write about course content. It is *not* where you write your lecture notes; rather, it is a separate notebook in which you reflect on your class reading, lectures, and discussions. As you record items in your learning log, you consider course content, its significance, and your response, and thereby better understand and remember important concepts. Your learning log can include one or more of the following:

- Your reflections on course content, including your personal associations, observations, inferences, points of agreement and disagreement, and areas of uncertainty
- A list of ways the course content relates to content in other courses you are taking
- Notes on how you can use the course content in your life
- Questions you think of as you read assignments. Ask the questions in class and then write the answers into your log.

Rewriting Lecture Notes and Class Readings in New Ways

If you rewrite your lecture notes and class readings in the following ways, you can "set" your learning for better retention.

- Rewrite your lecture notes after class, while your abbreviations and jottings still make sense. Try to use paragraph formats with topic sentences, supporting details, and transitions to understand how ideas relate to one another.
- Outline your lecture notes and class readings to foreground the main ideas and most important supporting details.
- Put your lecture notes or class readings into an outline tree (explained on page 49) for a visual depiction of important points.
- Summarize sections of your notes or textbook. Placing the material in your own words will help you retain it.
- Paraphrase definitions and difficult concepts to be sure you understand them.

Using the Idea Generation Strategies

The idea generation strategies you learned in Chapter 2 can help you learn course content. Here are some possibilities:

- Examine a concept in your notes or textbook from different angles to explore its significance and to remember more about it. Questions like these can get you started: Why is the concept important? Can you relate it to your own experience? Does it have a broader application? Why is it interesting? Is it controversial? Why or why not?

- Use listing to help remember material. First, study a portion of your notes or textbook. Then look away and list all the important points. Check your list against the course material to see if you left anything out.
- Use clustering to see the relationships among ideas in your notes or textbook. Place an important concept in the center of your clustering, and then add all the points that relate to that central concept, circling points and connecting them as appropriate. This visual depiction of ideas is a powerful learning tool.
- Use freewriting to explore important ideas. Begin with one of these questions: What is the value of the idea? Why is this idea important to you? How can you use this idea in other courses?

Writing with Your Classmates

Form a group with two or three classmates, and meet regularly to engage in activities like the following:

- To prepare for an exam, write essay questions based on your lecture notes and class readings. Trade questions with a classmate and write the answers to the questions you are given. Trade back and check the responses for missing or inaccurate information.
- Write a brief reflection about an idea in your lecture notes or textbook. Give the reflection to one of your classmates, and have that person write a response to your reflection and pass it on to the next classmate, who should respond to either of the reflections. Continue until no one has anything left to write. Writing this way fosters critical thinking and retention.

Writing Explanations and Definitions for Different Audiences

To learn difficult concepts, vocabulary, and specialized terms, write explanations and definitions so different audiences will understand them. Audiences can include, say, a fifth grader, someone who does not know anything at all about the subject you are studying, and someone who has experienced frustration learning these concepts or definitions in the past.

B A C K G R O U N D : Alan Brinkley is a history professor at Columbia University, where he was also chair of the history department and is currently the provost. A talented teacher, Brinkley has won teaching awards at both Harvard and Columbia. He has written *Voices of Protest: Huey Long, Father Coughlin, and the Great Depression* (1983), which won the National Book Award. He has also written several very successful college textbooks, including *American History: A Survey* (2009), currently in its thirteenth edition, and *The Unfinished Nation: A Concise History of the American People* (2010). "The Mall" is an excerpt from *American History*.

R E A D I N G   W I T H   A   P U R P O S E : "The Mall" gives a brief history of shopping complexes in the United States and explains some of the characteristics of the different kinds of complexes. As you read, think about what this material might add to the chapter of the American history textbook that it appears in, a chapter covering the mid-1960s to the early 1990s.

The Mall

BY ALAN BRINKLEY

In the late nineteenth century, it was the department store that tried to create a magical world, attracting patrons by arousing consumer fantasies. By the late twentieth century, it was the mall that was fusing consumption, entertainment, and desire. In cities and towns in every part of America, malls became not just places for shopping, but often centers of a much-altered community life as well.

2   The modern mall is the direct descendant of an earlier retail innovation, the automobile-oriented shopping center, which strove to combine a number of different shops in a single structure, with parking for customers. The first modern shopping center, the Country Club Plaza, opened in Kansas City in 1924. By the mid-1950s, shopping centers—ranging from small "strips" to large integrated complexes—had proliferated throughout the country and were challenging traditional downtown shopping districts, which suffered from lack of parking and from the movement of middle-class residents to the suburbs.

3   In 1956, the first enclosed, climate-controlled shopping mall—the Southdale Shopping Center—opened in Minneapolis, followed quickly by similar ventures in New York, New Jersey, Illinois, North Carolina, and Tennessee. As the malls spread, they grew larger and more elaborate. They also began self-consciously to emulate some aspects of the older downtowns that they were rapidly displacing. At the same time, they tried to insulate customers from the dangers and aggravations of traditional urban shopping.

4   By the 1970s, vast "regional malls" were emerging—Tyson's Corner in Fairfax, Virginia; Roosevelt Field on Long Island; the Galleria in Houston, and many others—that drew customers from great distances and dazzled them not only with acres of varied retail space, but also with restaurants, movie theaters, skating rinks, bowling alleys, hotels, video arcades, and large public spaces with fountains, benches, trees, gardens, and concert spaces. "The more needs you fulfill, the longer people stay," one developer observed.

5   Malls had become self-contained imitations of cities—but in a setting from which many of the troubling and abrasive features of downtowns had been eliminated. Malls were insulated from the elements. They were policed by private security forces,

who (unlike real police) could and usually did keep "undesirable" customers off the premises. They were purged of bars, pornography shops, and unsavory businesses. They were off limits to beggars, vagrants, the homeless, and anyone else the managers considered unattractive to their customers. Malls set out to "perfect" urban space, recasting the city as a protected, controlled, and socially homogeneous site attractive to, and in many cases dominated by, white middle-class people.

6   Some malls also sought to become community centers in sprawling suburban areas that had few real community spaces of their own. A few malls built explicitly civic spaces—meeting halls and conference centers, where community groups could gather. Some published their own newspapers. Many staged concerts, plays, and dances. But civic activities had a difficult time competing with the principal attraction of the malls: consumption.

7   Malls were designed with women, the principal consumers in most families, mainly in mind. "I wouldn't know how to design a center for a man," one architect said of the complexes he built. They catered to the concerns of mothers about their own and their children's safety, and they offered products of particular interest to them. (Male-oriented stores—men's clothing, sporting goods, hardware stores—were much less visible in most malls than shops marketing women's and children's clothing, jewelry, lingerie, and household goods.)

8   Malls also became important to teenagers, who flocked to them in the way that earlier generations had flocked to street corners and squares in traditional downtowns. The malls were places for teenagers to meet friends, go to movies, avoid parents, hang out. They were places to buy records, clothes, or personal items. And they were places to work. Low-paying retail jobs, plentiful in malls, were typical first working experiences for many teens.

9   The proliferation of malls has dismayed many people, who see in them a threat to the sense of community in America. By insulating people from the diversity and conflict of urban life, critics argue, malls divide groups from one another and erode the bonds that make it possible for those groups to understand one another. But malls, like the suburbs they usually serve, also create a kind of community. They are homogeneous and protected, to be sure, but they are also social gathering places in many areas where the alternative is not the rich, diverse life of the downtown but the even more isolated experience of shopping in isolated strips—or through catalogs, telephone, and the Internet.

ASSIGNMENTS

- Write a one-paragraph personal response to "The Mall."
- Write a one- or two-paragraph summary of "The Mall."
- Write a brief critical analysis in response to "The Mall," using at least one paraphrase and one quotation.
- Using one or more ideas in "The Mall," along with one or more ideas in "The Snoop Next Door" (page 255) and/or "Web of Risks" (page 432), write one or two paragraphs of synthesis that could go in an essay that discusses how aspects of modern culture both bring us together and isolate us. Use at least one paraphrase and one quotation.

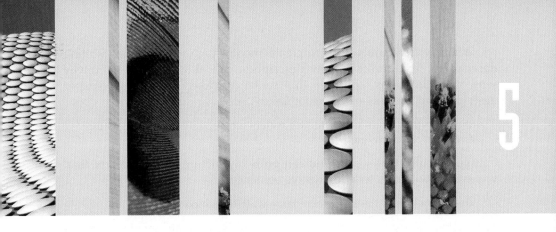

Description

Restaurant menus often include written descriptions to entice diners. For example, a chicken breast might be described as delicately sautéed with caramelized Vidalia onions, red potatoes, and roasted red peppers in a light wine tomato sauce. How would you write a menu item to describe the dish on the opposite page? How would you describe your favorite restaurant dish?

THE PATTERN

What happens when you encounter a striking landscape, hear a moving song on the radio, smell a peculiar scent in your apartment, taste a delightful dessert in a restaurant, or touch a velvety sweater in a store? Like most people, you probably want to share the experience with others, so you find yourself saying things like this:

- "Isn't that amazing!"
- "You've got to listen to this song."
- "Do you smell that?"
- "Here, you have to have a bite of this cake."
- "Oh, feel how soft this sweater is."

Writers have the same impulse. They want to share their sensory impressions, so they use words to create mental pictures that will help their readers experience a bit of what they experienced.

When writers use words to create mental pictures, they are writing **description.** To appreciate how description can allow writers to convey sensory impressions, consider this sentence, taken from a newspaper description of Tennessee's Reelfoot Lake:

> Shaggy cypress trees jut from dark waters where white waterlilies as big as dinner plates bloom.

Can you picture that scene? You can probably picture it more clearly than you would with this less descriptive sentence:

> Trees grow out of the lake where large waterlilies bloom.

The first sentence shows the power of words to create mental pictures, which is a primary purpose of description: using words to move your reader to mentally see, hear, smell, taste, and touch in a particular manner. In a similar way, writers can use words to convey how it feels to experience a situation or emotion, as in this example from "World at Dawn" (page 145), in which the author explains how it feels to be outside in complete darkness:

> On starless nights, one can feel like a lose array of limbs and purpose, and seem smaller, limited to what one can touch.

---

www.mhhe.com/clousepatterns6 | Description

For more help with description, click on
Writing > Paragraph Patterns
Writing > Writing Tutor: Description

USING DESCRIPTION FOR A PURPOSE

Description can entertain, express feelings, relate experience, inform, and persuade. When people on vacation want to share their good times, for example, they often write description on postcards to *relate their experience* and *express* to friends and relatives back home how they see and react to the beautiful scenery, local cuisine, and interesting people they encounter. Newspaper and magazine columnists often use description to *entertain* their readers, as Diane Ackerman does in her beautiful description of dawn in this chapter. On the job, people can use description to *inform* a reader. For example, the public relations director of your university might include description of your campus in your college catalog to inform prospective students about what the campus is like. Description can also be an important component of writing meant to *persuade.* Because well-written description can move a reader's emotions, it is often used to convince a reader to think or act a particular way. A travel agent trying to persuade people to take a Caribbean cruise might send an e-mail to clients describing the luxurious ship and breathtaking ports of call to get them excited about the trip and convince them to send a deposit.

Of all these purposes, description is most often expressive, helping writers share their perceptions and thus their feelings and experiences. People in general have a compelling desire to connect with other people by sharing experiences with them. Description helps us do that. In addition, because well-written description can be pleasurable to read, a secondary purpose of description is often to entertain.

Combining Patterns for a Purpose

You can combine description with other patterns if doing so helps you achieve your purpose for writing. For example, to *relate your experience* of being confined to bed for a month while you recovered from a car accident, you might add to your description of the confinement *process analysis* (an explanation of how something is done) to tell about the physical therapy sessions you endured while you were in bed. If you are describing your wedding gown to *express your feelings* about it, you can use *cause-and-effect analysis* (an explanation of the causes or effects of something) to help readers understand why you feel as you do.

To see how other patterns can be combined with description, study the following excerpt from "Struck by Lightning," an essay in this chapter in which the author describes what it was like to be struck by lightning. Notice that the author describes her awakening from unconsciousness—which she likens to being underwater—using narration.

EXCERPT FROM "STRUCK BY LIGHTNING" COMBINING DESCRIPTION AND NARRATION

Description
The highlighted description helps the writer express her feelings and relate her experience because it conveys the sensations she experienced as she gradually regained consciousness.

description of heaviness
My body is leaden, heavier than gravity. Gravity is done

description of immobility
with me. No more sinking and rising or bobbing in

description of heaviness
currents. There is a terrible feeling of oppression with no

oppressor. I try to lodge my mind against some boundary,

descriptive metaphor
some reference point, but the continent of the body

dissolves . . .

description of awakening
A single heartbeat stirs gray water. Blue trickles in,

description of awakening   description related to sound
just a tiny stream. Then a long silence.

Narration

First, the writer feels heavy. Then, she feels her heartbeat, and she starts to awaken. Next, she feels another, stronger heartbeat as she awakens further. She feels another heartbeat yet, and awakens even more. Notice how the narration structures the various descriptive details.

description related to sound and awakening

Another heartbeat. This one is louder, as if amplified.

descriptive metaphor

Sound takes a shape: it is a snowplow moving grayness

descriptive simile

aside like a heavy snowdrift. I can't tell if I'm moving,

description related to awakening   description related to awakening

but more blue water flows in. Seaweed begins to undulate,

then a whole kelp forest rises from the ocean floor.

A fish swims past and looks at me. Another heartbeat

description related to awakening

drives through dead water, and another, until I am

description related to awakening

surrounded by blue.

In addition to using description as the sole or primary pattern of development, you can use it as a secondary pattern in order to achieve your writing purpose. Because description helps readers form mental pictures, you can use it with other patterns to add interest and vividness and to *show* your readers that something is true rather than just *tell* them. For example, suppose you are writing a process analysis to explain how to make the perfect spaghetti sauce. If you tell your reader to use only the best tomatoes, you might describe how those tomatoes should look, feel, and smell, so your readers will know how to select them. If you are using narration to tell a story about the time you wrecked your uncle's classic car, you can describe what the car looked like after the wreck to help your readers appreciate how badly it was damaged.

Whether you use description as your sole pattern of development, as a primary pattern in combination with other patterns, or as a secondary pattern depends on what helps you achieve your particular writing purpose for your particular audience.

Description beyond the Writing Classroom

Description helps writers achieve their purpose in many writing situations.

IN ACADEMIC WRITING AND READING An educated person can observe closely and assess the significance of what is observed. Thus, in your college classes, you will frequently be asked to observe, describe, and evaluate. For example, in an art history course, you might be asked to describe two paintings by Van Gogh to show their similarities and differences. In a music appreciation course, you might be asked to describe a Chopin nocturne to explain the technique the performer used. In an advertising course, you might be required to describe an ad for a particular product to learn about persuasive strategies. In your history courses, you might describe conditions after a war, economic reversal, or social reform to assess its effects. In a biology lab, you might describe organs after dissection in order to understand their characteristics, and in a psychology lab, you might describe the behavior of a mouse following a particular experiment to learn about the effects of certain stimuli. In a fashion design class, you might describe classic Gucci designs, and in a dental hygiene class, you might describe the appearance of a healthy bicuspid.

You will also find description in most of your textbooks, whatever discipline you are studying. Here, for example, is description taken from an American history textbook: Notice that the description both gives readers a clear picture of what the first European settlers looked like and adds interest to the narrative.

> Europeans seemed, by the Indians' standards, grotesquely overdressed. Indeed, European fashion was ill suited to the environment between the Chesapeake and the Caribbean. Elizabethan gentlemen strutted in silk stockings attached with garters to padded, puffed knee breeches, topped by long-sleeved shirts and tight quilted jackets called "doublets." Men of lesser status wore coarse woolen hose, canvas breeches, shirts, and fitted vests known as "jerkins"; when at work, they donned aprons of dressed leather. Women wore gowns with long, full skirts, low-cut bodices, aprons, and hosiery held up by garters. Ladies went about in silk and wore hoods and mantles to ward off the sun, while the rest dressed in flannels or canvas and covered their heads with linen caps or coifs. Both sexes favored long hair, and men sported mustaches and beards. (Davidson et al., *Nation of Nations*)

Description creates a mental image of the appearance of Elizabethan men and women.

AT WORK AND IN THE COMMUNITY Description is common in workplace writing. Real estate agents describe properties in classified advertisements, and police officers describe crime scenes in crime reports. Psychologists describe their patients' demeanors in therapy notes, and scientists describe specimens before and after experiments. Nurses describe patients' appearances in medical charts, and insurance adjusters describe the condition of cars after accidents.

Description is also important in community-based writing. For instance, assume you are writing a letter to the editor of your campus newspaper to persuade students to recycle soda cans. You might describe the appearance of the campus quad littered with used aluminum cans. Or, assume you are e-mailing friends asking them to volunteer their time at a homeless shelter. You could create sympathy by describing the conditions of those forced to live on the street.

DECIDING ON A DOMINANT IMPRESSION

If you describe something small and uncomplicated, such as a chair, you can probably describe all its features. However, if you are describing something larger or more complex, including all of its features would be difficult for you and overwhelming to your reader. To keep complex descriptions manageable, settle on a **dominant impression** (one notable quality), and write only those details that express that impression.

The quality is not "dominant" because it is the most significant or noticeable feature of what you are describing. The quality is dominant because it is the characteristic your description will focus on—it is "dominant" in your essay. For example, suppose you decide to describe the house you grew up in. Do you *really* want the task of describing all aspects of that house? Probably not. You can cut the job of describing your house down to a manageable size by choosing only those details that convey some opinion you have of the house. Once you decide on that opinion, you have the dominant impression, and you can ignore details that do not convey that impression.

Let's say the house you grew up in was, among many other characteristics, run-down and cluttered, but nonetheless cheerful. You could settle on one of those characteristics for your dominant impression. If you decided to convey the impression that the house was run-down, you could describe the sagging porch and leaky roof. If you decided to convey how cluttered the house was, you could describe the collection of glass bottles that covered every tabletop. In neither case would you mention the beautiful stained-glass windows in the dining room. If you decided to convey the cheerfulness of the house, you could describe the sun flooding the front room, but not the sagging porch. You could also form a dominant impression from more than one quality—but only if doing so still gave you a manageable writing task. You could, for example, describe your house as run-down but cheerful or even as run-down and cluttered but cheerful.

SUPPORTING DETAILS

Supporting details in a descriptive essay should give your reader a clear mental image of your subject. In addition, they should convey your dominant impression of your subject and establish why you formed that impression. The strategies explained next will help you write supporting details that accomplish these goals.

Objective and Expressive Details

Objective details give a factual, impartial, unemotional account of your subject, whereas **expressive details** present a more subjective, personal, or emotional view. A bank appraiser describing a piece of property would use objective details because his or her personal opinion about the property is not relevant. However, a realtor describing the same property in an ad would use expressive detail to create an emotional appeal to persuade potential buyers to take a look. Notice the difference between objective and expressive details in these examples from readings in this chapter.

<table>
<tr>
<td>OBJECTIVE DETAILS</td>
<td>The siding [of the store] consists of rough sawn boards nailed vertically; the cracks between the boards are covered with equally rough battens. The silver steel roof is the Gendarme's most prominent feature. The raised ribs running the length of it, from the spouting to the ridge, provide a sense of purpose to the structure that is lost among the rest of its components. One small window on the side and one door in front permit a meager amount of natural light into the interior. Off to the side, a sign announcing the name of the store hangs from a pole; it is faded with age and almost hidden from view behind the branches of a small tree. ("The Gendarme," page 135)</td>
</tr>
<tr>
<td>EXPRESSIVE DETAILS</td>
<td>The earth felt like a peach that had split open in the middle; one side moved up while the other side moved down and my legs were out of rhythm. The ground rolled the way it does during an earthquake and the sky was tattered book pages waving in different directions. Was the ground liquefying under me, or had the molecular composition of my body deliquesced? ("Struck by Lightning," page 158)</td>
</tr>
</table>

Whether expressive or objective, descriptive details are **sensory details** (details that pertain to the senses: sight, sound, taste, smell, and touch). Sometimes a writer will use only one sense—typically, sight—other times a writer will appeal to several senses.

To see how writers can appeal to the five senses, consider the following sentences taken from essays in this book.

<table>
<tr>
<td>SIGHT</td>
<td>The porch is cluttered with an odd assortment of chairs and benches. An aluminum lawnchair, its nylon seat hanging in tatters, sits dejectedly next to a log bench suspended from four crooked legs of various diameters. Its top hewn flat, it appears almost as an afterthought. ("The Gendarme," page 135)</td>
</tr>
<tr>
<td>SOUND</td>
<td>"Help! Help! Help! Help! Help!" she cries. It's piercing, unvarying, insistent, like a baby bird crying for food. ("Embedded," page 167)</td>
</tr>
<tr>
<td>TASTE</td>
<td>With our fingers we pulled soft fragments of [the cooked fish] from its sides to our plates, and ate; it was delicate</td>
</tr>
</table>

fish-flesh, fresh and mild. Someone found the roe, and I ate of that too—it was fat and stronger, like egg yolk, naturally enough, and warm. ("The Deer at Providencia," page 151)

SMELL
I guess I remembered clearest of all the early mornings, when the lake was cool and motionless, remembered how the bedroom smelled of the lumber it was made of and the wet woods whose scent entered through the screen. ("Once More to the Lake," page 691)

TOUCH
To walk meant lifting each leg up by the thigh, moving it forward with my hands, setting it down. The earth felt like a peach that had split open in the middle; one side moved up while the other side moved down and my legs were out of rhythm. The ground rolled the way it does during an earthquake. ("Struck by Lightning," page 158)

Descriptive Words

Whether you are writing objective or expressive description, choose your words carefully. Most often this does *not* mean turning to the dictionary or thesaurus. In fact, while these sources can be helpful, relying on them too heavily can lead you to write an overbearing sentence like this one:

> The pulchritudinous rose imparted delightful olfactory sensations upon me.

As this sentence illustrates, when writers abandon their own natural styles and pile on words taken from the thesaurus and dictionary, their writing becomes stiff, pretentious, and unnatural.

You can always turn to a dictionary or thesaurus when you are stuck, but usually you can write effective description with words you already know. The key is to use *specific* nouns, verbs, and modifiers rather than general ones because specific words are more descriptive. *General words* give readers a broad sense of what you are referring to, while *specific words* offer them a narrower, more focused meaning. The following lists will help you see the difference between general and specific words.

GENERAL NOUNS	SPECIFIC NOUNS
sweater	cardigan
class	Physics 103
meat	filet mignon
magazine	*Newsweek*

GENERAL VERBS	SPECIFIC VERBS
walk	stroll
spoke	shouted

look	glance
went	raced

GENERAL MODIFIERS	SPECIFIC MODIFIERS
nice	elegant
awesome	overwhelming
terrible	frightening
bad	gaudy

To write effective descriptive language, expect to work through a series of refinements as you revise your drafts. Look for opportunities to use modifiers and to substitute specific nouns, verbs, and modifiers for more general ones.

Consider, for example, this sentence:

The tree moved in the wind.

The nouns are *tree* and *wind*. As a first refinement, you might make *tree* more specific:

The poplar moved in the wind.

Now you might make the verb *moved* more specific:

The poplar bent in the wind.

Next, you might add specific modifiers:

The newly planted poplar bent in the gusting wind.

Eventually, writing specific nouns, verbs, and modifiers might lead you to rewrite the entire sentence to make it more active and vivid:

The gale-force wind whipped the branches of the young poplar.

Remember that a little description can go a long way. Do not overwhelm your reader by stringing together too many modifiers, or you will create an overburdened sentence like this one:

The emaciated, spindly, waxen old man stared vacantly into the barren, colorless hallway as his bony, arthritic, pale fingers played absently with the beige fringes of the faded blue bedspread.

When you do have highly descriptive sentences, you can balance them with less descriptive ones so your reader is not overwhelmed. For example, consider this passage from "Struck by Lightning," (page 156), where a highly descriptive sentence is followed by a less descriptive one:

On the face of the mountain, a mile ahead, hard westerly gusts and sudden updrafts collided, pulling black clouds apart. Yet the storm looked harmless.

Avoiding Clichés

If you have trouble finding and eliminating **clichés** (overused expressions like "sadder but wiser" and "the last straw," which can easily creep into descriptive writing), the following suggestions may be helpful.

To identify clichés in your own writing, look for similes (see below) that are not original—ones you have heard many times before, like these:

cold as ice   **free as a bird**   **fast as lightning**   **last but not least**

To eliminate a cliché that is a simile, rewrite the simile in a new way. Here's an example from paragraph 2 of "The Gendarme" on page 135:

FIRST DRAFT   **Some sit on the railing like ducks in a row . . .**

REVISION   **Some perch like chickens on the railing . . .**

If you cannot rewrite the simile in a new way, rewrite without the simile:

FIRST DRAFT   **Some sit on the railing like ducks in a row . . .**

REVISION   **Some sit on the railing shoulder to shoulder.**

Be aware that, not all clichés are similes, and not all similes are clichés. To become more familiar with clichés, visit this Web site and browse the cliché lists: www.clichesite.com

---

www.mhhe.com/clousepatterns6   Clichés

For more help with avoiding clichés, click on

Editing > Clichés, Slang, Jargon, Colloquialisms

---

www.mhhe.com/clousepatterns6   Diction

For more help with descriptive vocabulary, click on

Editing > Adjectives and Adverbs
Learning > Links to Dictionary and Thesauri

Similes and Metaphors

Similes and metaphors can help create mental images. A **simile** uses the words *like* or *as* to compare two things that are not usually seen as similar. Here is an example of a simile taken from "Struck by Lightning" (page 156). The author uses *like* to compare being partially paralyzed in her hospital bed to being a "mummified child":

> I felt like an ancient, mummified child who had been found on a rock ledge near our ranch: bound tightly, unable to move, my dead face tipped backwards toward the moon.

A **metaphor** also compares two things not usually seen as similar, but without using *like* or *as.* In this metaphor from "Struck by Lightning," the author compares her state of semiconsciousness to being submerged in an ocean:

> Deep in an ocean. I am suspended motionless. The water is gray. . . . My arms are held out straight, cruciate, my head and legs hang limp. Nothing moves. . . . There are no shadows or sounds.

ORGANIZING DETAILS

An essay developed with description often includes a thesis that mentions both what is being described and the dominant impression. Here are two examples:

> I was always embarrassed by the run-down house I grew up in. (*The house will be described; the dominant impression is "run-down."*)

> At noon, the park comes alive with businesspeople taking a midday break from the pressures of work. (*The park at noon will be described; the dominant impression is that it is alive with the activity of businesspeople.*)

The thesis of a descriptive essay can be implied rather than stated. (See page 44 on the implied thesis.) If your thesis is implied, be sure your descriptive details create a clear sense of your dominant impression.

To order your descriptive details, you may opt for a **spatial order,** especially when you are describing a room or other contained space where it is logical to move from front to back, left to right, top to bottom, and so on. If you describe the run-down house you grew up in, for example, you can begin at the front door and move clockwise through the rooms on the first floor. Other times a **progressive order** will serve your purpose, particularly if your description is meant to persuade. A real estate agent trying to convince people to buy the house you grew up in might describe the best features last to leave the reader with the strongest possible final impression of the place. Another option is **chronological order,** in which you describe a place as if you were moving through it. To describe the house you grew up in as it was when you returned there last Thanksgiving, you could arrange the details according to what you noticed first, second, and so on as you entered and moved through the house.

VISUALIZING A DESCRIPTIVE ESSAY

The chart on the next page can help you visualize the structure for a descriptive essay. Like all good models, however, this one can be altered as needed.

INTRODUCTION

- Creates interest in what you are describing
- Can state your thesis (underlined in the example), which indicates what you are describing and your dominant impression

EXAMPLE

Before starting college, I was fortunate to travel to Israel. The beautiful mount of Masada, the Sea of Galilee, the Garden of Gethsemane are all etched into my mind forever. However, nothing assaulted my senses more than the Market Place of Old Jerusalem.

FIRST BODY PARAGRAPH

- Begins the focus on the dominant impression
- Includes objective and/or expressive details
- Includes specific words and sensory details
- May include similes and metaphors
- Arranges details in a suitable order, which may be spatial, chronological, or progressive

EXAMPLE

As I walked down the thoroughfare crowded with merchants selling their wares from stalls and makeshift counters, I was struck by delightful aromas. Fresh-baked pita breads, breadsticks, and breads laden with sesame seeds were arranged in neat rows in front of several huts, their tantalizing scents beckoning me. . . .

NEXT BODY PARAGRAPHS

- Continue until the description is complete
- Continue the focus on the dominant impression; include objective and/or expressive details, specific words and sensory details, and possibly similes and metaphors
- Arrange details in a suitable order, which may be spatial, chronological, or progressive

EXAMPLE

At high noon, the cacophony began. Calls to worship mingled with bits and pieces of conversation, loud barterings, and shouts of disagreements coming from the huts on either side of me, and . . .

CONCLUSION

- Provides a satisfying finish
- Leaves your reader with a strong final impression

EXAMPLE

As I neared the end of the long marketplace, three soldiers in combat fatigues walked toward me, creating a stark contrast to the carnival atmosphere behind me.

THINKING CRITICALLY ABOUT DESCRIPTION

As you know from Chapters 1 and 4, thinking critically about your reading and writing is an in-depth process of analysis and assessment. In addition to applying what you learned in those chapters about reading critically and writing critical analyses, ask the following questions when you read and write description:

- **Does the dominant impression misdirect the reader?** A writer might use the dominant impression "beautifully appointed" for a description of a nursing home and then describe the lovely common areas. However, if the common areas are lovely but the residents' rooms are shabby, then the writer may be selecting a dominant impression that directs the reader away from the problem of the shabby rooms.

- **Does the descriptive language manipulate readers inappropriately?** A blog entry that describes Arabs as terrorists, attorneys as ambulance chasers, or women as bimbos not only misdirects but also manipulates in support of a distorted dominant impression.

- **Is the description accurate and complete?** An advertisement on Craig's List offering a landscape painting for sale may accurately and completely describe the picture. However, if it fails to note that the frame is broken and the glass is scratched, the description could deceive a potential buyer.

- **Do the writer and reader share the same meaning for descriptive language?** For example, when a hotel describes its rooms as "deluxe accommodations," or "superior rooms," or "luxury suites," do the writer and reader have the same meaning for *deluxe, superior,* and *luxury?* To the hotel, *deluxe* may mean that the room has a view of the swimming pool, but to the reader, *deluxe* may mean "upscale."

PROCESS GUIDELINES: STRATEGIES FOR WRITING DESCRIPTION

1. **Selecting a topic.** Try to describe something you can visit and observe, such as a doctor's waiting room, a bus station, a popular campus gathering place, or a restaurant with a theme decor. When you visit the site, take notes about sensory details to make drafting easier. If you describe a subject from memory, such as a childhood haunt, your high school cafeteria, or a tree house you used to have, be sure the memory is fresh enough that you can come up with vivid, specific details.

2. **Establishing a dominant impression.** If you have trouble settling on a dominant impression, list all the emotions your subject arouses in you and all the reactions you have to your subject. Then choose one

of those feelings or reactions as your dominant impression. You need not choose your strongest reaction. You can select one you find interesting or surprising, or the one you think you can write about the best.

3. **Drafting.** Be as descriptive as you can comfortably be, but do not labor too long over individual sentences or particular words. Descriptive language does not necessarily come easily; arriving at the right specific nouns, verbs, and modifiers requires a series of revisions. In revising, you can shape your descriptive language to get it just right.

4. **Revising.** Remember to use specific words to show rather than tell. Instead of writing "The child looked tired," be specific about how the child acted: "Little Alfie rubbed his fists into his eyes and stretched his mouth into a wide yawn." Also, revise vague words like *good, nice, awful, terrible, cool, bad,* and *great.* Aim for more specific alternatives. Instead of "bad food," revise to get "overseasoned, gristly steak"; instead of "awful headache," revise to get "throbbing headache."

Checklist for Revising Description

You can use this checklist along with the one on page 76 to help you revise.

_____ 1. Details—objective and expressive—work together to create a single dominant impression.

_____ 2. The dominant impression does not misdirect your reader, and the description does not manipulate your reader.

_____ 3. The description is accurate and complete.

_____ 4. Nouns, verbs, and modifiers are specific and appeal to the appropriate senses.

_____ 5. Less descriptive sentences are balanced with highly descriptive ones.

_____ 6. Details work to fulfill your writing purpose.

_____ 7. Details are arranged in a suitable order, indicated by topic sentences and transitions, as needed.

Using Sources for a Purpose

The paragraph below, which is a body paragraph for an essay about how to improve care for people in nursing homes, illustrates how to use sources from this book in your writing. It includes a summary of six paragraphs of source material from "Embedded" on page 164. (See page 95 on how to write a summary.)

THESIS To address the crisis in nursing home care, we should provide more home care options, community-based programs, and small-group homes.

WRITING PURPOSE AND AUDIENCE To convince average, general readers that the writer's suggestions are good ones.

(continued)

The summary helps establish that nursing homes have problems, so the writer can move on to recommend the specific solutions given in the thesis.

[1]In "Embedded," Barry Corbet gives a startling firsthand account of life inside a nursing home, and the news is not good. [2]Although exceptionally independent himself, Corbet experienced a number of problems during his stay for rehabilitation following surgery. [3]He had to deal with confused residents trying to enter his room, "the ceaseless din of television sets and alarms," medication mistakes, important doctor appointments that were scheduled late by the staff, and unappealing food. [4]In addition, he observed rehabilitation patients like himself being physically or chemically restrained (164–167, 168). [5]For Corbet and others who need only temporary care, home care alternatives to institutional settings are needed. [6]Many, like Corbet, could remain at home, happier and more independent, if temporary nursing, physical therapy, and personal care service providers visited routinely. [7]Twice-weekly visits by a housekeeper, combined with regular meal delivery, could provide most of what a person needs, especially if the patient were monitored by friends and family—at a cost well below nursing home expenses. [8]Home care can benefit people who are independent enough to take advantage of it, as well as allow nursing homes to focus their resources on less independent residents.

AVOIDING PLAGIARISM

The paragraph illustrates some points about avoiding plagiarism. (For more complete information on using source material, consult Chapters 4 and 15.)

- **Introduce with the source of your summary and reintroduce as necessary.** As in sentence 1, you can introduce with the author and/or title of the work you are summarizing. As sentences 2–4 illustrate, you can repeat the author's name or use a pronoun to make clear that you are still dealing with source material.

- **Place keywords and key phrases in quotation marks.** You should summarize using your own words and style, but as sentence 3 shows, you can include some of the source's exact words if you place them in quotation marks.

MYTHS ABOUT USING SOURCES

MYTH: A summary stands on its own and does not need to be synthesized with the writer's ideas.

FACT: You must help your reader understand how the summary functions in your essay. Notice the synthesis in the sample paragraph:

- Sentence 1 synthesizes the source material by giving an overall evaluation.

- Sentence 2 synthesizes by stating a generalization the summary will support.

- Sentences 5–8 synthesize by explaining how to solve the problems given in the summary.

Using the Dictionary, Thesaurus, and OneLook Reverse Dictionary

If you have trouble finding the right descriptive word, a dictionary or thesaurus can help. But be aware of the connotations—the implied or secondary meanings—of words you take from these sources, because synonyms are not always interchangeable. While *relentless* is a synonym for *fierce*, you would not write that you encountered a relentless bear in the woods.

www.mhhe.com/clousepatterns6	Diction

For links to online dictionaries and thesauri, click on
Learning > Links to Dictionary and Thesauri

If you have a concept in mind but can't think of the word or phrase you want, use OneLook Reverse Dictionary at www.onelook.com/reverse-dictionary.shtml. You can use this site to find a word if you already know the definition, get a list of related concepts and words, and answer identification questions.

Student-author Ralph Mitchell uses expressive and objective detail to describe a one-of-a-kind store. After you read, you will have an opportunity to analyze and assess this essay.

The Gendarme
Ralph Mitchell

In an obscure corner of West Virginia, near the triangular intersection of state routes 28, 55, and 33, stands the climbing store known as The Gendarme; it is a one-of-a-kind establishment. Few of the people passing by on the nearby road are even aware of its presence. Like the mythical city of Shangri-La, it exists beyond the realm of the casual traveler; to find it takes purpose. Tucked away behind Buck Harper's General Store and the Rocks View Restaurant, its construction mimics the small barns and outbuildings of the local inhabitants. The siding consists of rough sawn boards nailed vertically; the cracks between the boards are covered with equally rough battens. The silver steel roof is The Gendarme's most prominent feature. The raised ribs running the length of it, from the spouting to the ridge, provide a sense of purpose to the structure that is lost among the rest of its components. One small window on the side and one door in front permit a meager amount of natural light into the interior. Off to the side, a sign announcing the name of the store hangs from a pole; it is faded with age and almost hidden from view behind the branches of a small tree.

The porch is cluttered with an odd assortment of chairs and benches. An aluminum lawn chair, its nylon seat hanging in tatters, sits dejectedly next to a log bench suspended from four crooked legs of various diameters. Its top hewn flat, it appears almost as an afterthought. The porch posts are tied together with a wooden railing that, judging from the amount of wear, must be used as seating also. Ashtrays, the origin of which cannot be discerned, are strewn haphazardly about. Some perch like chickens on the railing; others hunker down among the jetsam strewn about the floor, fighting for a space of their own. In the center, an old cable reel, battered, burned, carved, and stained, presides over the collection—the remnants of someone's snack still adorning its top. Pushed back against the wall to the left of the door sits a corroded

Paragraph 1
The thesis (first sentence) notes what is being described (The Gendarme) and the dominant impression (it is one of a kind). Objective description creates visual images of the store; a simile supports the dominant impression (the store is like Shangri-La).

Paragraph 2
The topic sentence (sentence 1) indicates that the paragraph's focus is the porch. Supporting details are largely objective descriptions appealing to sight. Notice the simile ("Some perch like chickens").

aluminum box about six feet long, three feet deep, and two feet high. Stenciled on the front in official looking letters are the words, "For Emergency Use Only. Stokes Litter." Covering the top of the box are bundles of firewood neatly bound and labeled "$3." A large bulletin board is handily fastened to the wall above the firewood. Covering its face are a multitude of notes, advertisements, and Park Service notices. One note reads, "To whom it may concern: Wasp nest located above the crux of Soler, use caution if climbing this route." Another offers climbing shoes for sale "cheap." A third, tattered and faded, makes a person wonder if Jennifer ever did meet Steve at the base of Old Man's route. A Park Service notice, advising of cliff closures due to the Peregrine Falcon nesting season, hangs off to the right. Immediately to the right of the notice is the door.

Paragraph 3
The topic sentence (sentence 1) indicates that the paragraph's focus will be the walls inside; it includes a transition ("Once inside") signaling a continuation of spatial order. Spatial order is also signaled with the transition "Towards the back of the store."

Once inside, a person is immediately struck by the incredible 3 amount of climbing paraphernalia clinging to the walls and counters. The sight of this immediately sets the climber salivating and probably is about as comprehensible to the nonclimber as implements used for brain surgery are to a plumber. Towards the back of the store, a collection of used and outdated equipment hangs from the wall. In any other sport, they would reside in a Hall of Fame or a museum—icons behind glass, to be revered, out of touch to all. But here they typify the innocence of the sport, where the pioneers and the legends remain accessible to even the meekest among their brethren.

Paragraph 4
The topic sentence (sentence 1) indicates that the focus will be John Markwell and includes a transition ("behind the cash register") signaling spatial order. "Holding court" is a metaphor comparing John to royalty.

Holding court behind the cash register stands John Markwell: pur- 4 veyor of fine climbing gear and finer advice. The twinkle in his eye as he talks to a customer reveals the nature of someone who truly enjoys what he is doing. A head of graying hair seems to be his only concession to the passing years, for his trim, athletic build speaks of someone years younger. He first started his business out of the back of a Volkswagen bus in the mid-60s. He was a brilliant visionary or damned lucky, as few could have foreseen the dramatic growth of the sport in the subsequent years. He lives in a fine brick home several doors back up the road, one of the seven or eight that comprise the little community of Mouth of Seneca. After living here for over 20 years, he is still regarded with suspicion by the locals. His children, however, participate fully as members of the community, after having spent their entire lives as playmates of the local children.

Towards dusk, the climbers begin filtering into the parking area across the street from Harper's General Store. Stepping gingerly over a flattened rattlesnake, they pause (no doubt wondering about the sanctity of their tents pitched nearby) then continue down the community's only alley onto the porch of The Gendarme, settling into whatever seating is still available. One climber, wearing brightly colored clothing and a rebellious haircut, stands talking animatedly. His arms gesticulate wildly, for he remains full of adrenaline from the day's climb. Another sits in a chair tipped back against the wall, hands folded across his chest, eyeing with apparent amusement the actions of the rest of the group. None is a permanent resident of the area. Most are from town and cities all over the eastern United States, and several have traveled from the West and from other countries as well. They are drawn here by the nearby climbing and the opportunity to renew old friendships and establish new ones.

5

Paragraph 5
The topic sentence (sentence 1) indicates the paragraph's focus on the store's clients. The paragraph opens with a transition ("Towards dusk") signaling chronological order.

The conversation begins as an anarchic free-for-all then gradually forms into a common subject, with everyone offering his or her own insight. The topics could include anything: from yesterday's epic climbs to tomorrow's projects, from the terminal ballistics of the newly adopted FBI 40 caliber sidearm to the amount of iguana guano produced by a pet iguana in a week. As the night turns to early morning, the group reluctantly disbands, returning to their tents to pass the remainder of the night in relative quiet.

6

Paragraph 6
The topic sentence (sentence 1) indicates that the paragraph's focus will be conversation. Mitchell emphasizes the dominant impression by noting the unique range of discussion topics.

Previous generations each laid claim to a unique edifice to serve as a focal point for their social interaction. During the 1940s, the General Store served this purpose. Later generations used the drugstore soda fountain, the drive-up root beer stand, and fast food restaurants. In today's age of the car phone, e-mail, and fax, social boundaries no longer are defined by physical limits, such as a neighborhood or a town, but by common interests and goals. The Gendarme stands as a contemporary version of a social centerpoint for one small segment of society: the climbing community.

7

Paragraph 7
The conclusion provides closure by explaining the significance of The Gendarme and by highlighting its special role.

PEER REVIEW

Responding to "The Gendarme"

Analyze and assess "The Gendarme" by responding to these questions:

1. Does the essay hold your interest? Why or why not?
2. What do you think of the thesis? Is it effective and appropriate? Why or why not?
3. Does the author use objective details well? Does he use expressive details well? Do details support the dominant impression?
4. Are the details arranged in a suitable order? Explain.
5. Are the author's word choices generally effective? Why or why not? Are there word choices you think need to be strengthened?
6. What are the chief strengths of the essay? Why do you find these features strong?
7. What one revision would you like to see? How would that revision improve the essay and help the author achieve his purpose?

EXAMINING VISUALS Description in Corporate Logos

One of the best examples of description in the corporate and organizational world is the *logo,* which is a design that a company or organization uses as a brand or symbol. If the logo is successful, consumers readily identify the design with the company or organization it represents. Two examples of very successful logos are the Nike swoosh and the Olympic rings. The Google logo is also successful, but it is unique because while its core remains the same, its details often change, as the examples here demonstrate.

- What dominant impression do each of the Google logos present?
- For what purpose do you think Google adapts its logo for different occasions or circumstances?
- How do you think Google users respond to these logos?

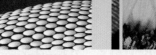

BACKGROUND: Poet, playwright, novelist, and artist N. Scott Momaday was born in Lawton, Oklahoma, in 1934. He lived at his grandparents' house on the Kiowa Indian reservation until he was a year old, when he moved to Arizona with his parents, who taught on Indian reservations. In Arizona, Momaday learned about Navajo, Apache, and Pueblo Indian traditions in addition to his own Kiowa traditions. Active in a number of activities to preserve Indian culture, Momaday is a founding trustee of the National Museum of the American Indian. His works include *House Made of Dawn* (1968), for which he won a Pulitzer; *The Way to Rainy Mountain* (1968), to which Momaday refers in paragraph 5 of the essay; *In the Presence of the Sun* (1991); *The Native Americans: Indian Country* (1993); and *Four Arrows and Magie: A Kiowa Story* (2006). "The Homestead on Rainy Mountain Creek" is an essay from *The Man Made of Words* (1997).

THE PATTERN AND ITS PURPOSES: In "The Homestead on Rainy Mountain Creek," N. Scott Momaday uses *objective description* to **relate his experience** and *share his feelings* about his childhood home and the people who were part of his formative years. Although Momaday does not use much emotional language, he still manages to convey his reverence and affection for the homestead and for Kiowa culture.

The Homestead on Rainy Mountain Creek
BY N. SCOTT MOMADAY

The house and arbor stand on a rise on the plain east of the town of Mountain View. A little to the north and west are the Washita River and Rainy Mountain Creek. A few miles to the south and west is Rainy Mountain itself, scarcely a mountain, rather a knoll or a hummock. But in a way it is a singular feature in the immediate landscape. From the top of Rainy Mountain you can see a long way in any direction. It is said that when the Kiowas camped on this ground, it inevitably rained, thus the name. At the base of the mountain is the ruin of the old Rainy Mountain School, which my grandmother, Aho, attended as a young girl. Nearby is the Rainy Mountain Baptist Church and the cemetery in which many of my forebears are buried.

As you read
Ask yourself how Momaday conveys his feelings for his homestead without using much emotional language.

2   The house was built in 1913, the year my father was born. He was in fact born while the house was under construction, in a tepee close to where the arbor now stands, on the corner closest to the well. And in that house and arbor he grew up with his sister, Clara, and his brothers, James, Lester, and Ralph.

3   My grandfather, Mammedaty, was greatly respected by all who knew him. For one thing, he was a successful farmer. The Kiowas, who migrated to the southern plains from the north, were a nomadic tribe of hunters; they never had an agrarian tradition. In my grandfather's day, when only a generation before the old roving life of the buffalo hunter had been intact, the Kiowas did not take easily to farming. Their land was fertile, but they preferred to lease it to white farmers. Mammedaty

was an exception. He worked hard, and he saw that his sons worked hard. He made a good life for himself and his family.

4 I never knew my grandfather. He died in 1933, the year before I was born. But I feel I knew him. His powerful presence was discernible in his wife and children, in the homestead on Rainy Mountain Creek, and in the countless stories I was told about him. All my life he has been an inspiration to me. His grandfather was the great chief Lone Wolf, and his grandmother was Kau-au-ointy, a Mexican captive who raised a great herd of cattle and became a prominent figure in the tribe. His mother, Keahdinekkeah, loved him above all others, I am told, and when he died she had him buried in a bronze casket, over which she placed her favorite shawl.

5 My grandmother, Aho, was the principal force in the homestead when I was a child. She was a beautiful and gracious woman, and she presided over family affairs with great generosity and goodwill. She was in her middle fifties when I was born, and she died at the age of eighty-five. About the time of her death I was writing *The Way to Rainy Mountain,* and in that writing I retraced the migration route of the Kiowas from western Montana to Oklahoma. My pilgrimage ended at my grandmother's grave. The introduction to *The Way to Rainy Mountain* is in large measure an evocation of my grandmother's spirit, and for this reason among others that book is my favorite of my works.

6 The house seems small to me now, but when I was a child it was grand and full of life. Aho and my uncle Jimmy, who never married, were always there. There were frequent reunions when my aunt Clara and my other uncles, Lester and Ralph, my cousins, and my parents and I convened to rejoice in the institution of our family. There were frequent visitors, kinsmen who brought greetings from, and news of, friends and relatives. We were always glad to see them. They would stay for days, according to the Kiowa notion of a proper visit.

7 It was not until later that I became aware of the real significance of these reunions and visitations. They were matters of ancient tradition and necessity. In the heyday of the plains culture, the tribe was composed of bands, each one going its own way. The essential integrity of the tribe was maintained by means of a kind of institutionalized visiting, whereby persons and families would venture abroad to pay visits, to keep intact a whole network of news and trade. This communion was of course a principal function of the annual Sun Dance as well.

8 The visitors I liked best, besides the children of my own age, were the old people, for they were exotic. They wore their hair in braids, both men and women, they spoke only Kiowa, and they imaged for me the bygone and infinitely exciting time of the centaurs, the warriors, and the buffalo hunters.

9 Among the visitors in my father's day was the old man Koi-khan-hodle, "Dragonfly," who to pay his respects every morning would get up before dawn, paint his face, and go out to pray aloud to the rising sun. I have stood on the red earth just east of the house where Koi-khan-hodle stood; I have seen across the plain to the edge of the world; and there I have seen the sun rise. And it was for me the deity that it was for Dragonfly. In that image is concentrated for me the great mystery of the Sun Dance, the long migration of the Kiowas to their destiny, and the tenure of my people on this continent, a tenure of many thousands of years.

10 When I was a child there was a red barn a little to the north and east of the house, near the place where Koi-khan-hodle made his prayer. I loved to play in the barn, which seemed a great cavern of possibility. There, in the dim light, lay a box of bones, the bones of a horse. The horse, called "Gudal-san," never lost a race. That its bones should be kept long after its death seems entirely appropriate in the context of the plains culture. The Kiowas owned more horses *per capita* than any other tribe on the Great Plains. There is no story of the Kiowa without the horse.

11 Off the southwest corner of the house, near the kitchen steps, was the storm cellar. On the surface it was an earthen mound supported by concrete or cement, I believe, with a large wooden trapdoor at the end nearer the house, slanted at perhaps twenty or thirty degrees. Beneath this door concrete steps led down into a small, subterranean room outfitted with a bench, and little if anything else. In the springtime, when storms raged on the plains, my mother would take me and a kerosene lamp down into that gravelike room in which the earth had a smell that I have never known elsewhere. With the wind roaring and rain—sometimes ear-splitting hail—pounding at the door, my mother would read to soothe her frayed nerves, and I would fall asleep in spite of the fury. My father, who had a Kiowa indifference to such weather, could not be bothered to join us.

12 The arbor was the center of summer. When the weather turned hot we lived in the arbor. It was a sizable frame building, open and screened on all sides, so that the air could move through it freely. It was basically one great room, though a small kitchen extended from the northwest corner. When it rained, water came in from the roof and all around. There was a large table in the middle of the red earthen floor, large enough to seat a dozen people easily. Along the south and east walls were broad wooden benches. On these we slept at night. Along the north wall were cabinets in which were kept dishes and flatware, an ice box (I loved to go with my father to Mountain View, where we bought great blocks of ice), and a shelf on which were a bucket of water and a dipper for drinking and two or three metal basins for washing. When I was old and strong enough, I drew water from the well and carried it to its place on the shelf. There was no plumbing in those days, and no electricity. We walked to the outhouse, and we lighted the nights with kerosene lamps.

13 Most of the Kiowas in the vicinity, including my grandmother, were members of the Rainy Mountain Baptist Church congregation. There were prayer meetings in the arbor on summer nights, and these were wonderful occasions. The older people came in their finery, and they brought good food in abundance. They sang hymns in Kiowa, they gave testimony to their faith in the rich oratory of the Native American oral tradition—and they visited. The children played outside in the lamplight that fell upon the grass, caught up in the sheer excitement of communion, celebration, festivity. I can still hear the singing and the laughter and the lively talk floating on the plain, reaching away to the dark river and the pecan grove, reaching perhaps to Rainy Mountain and the old school and cemetery.

14 Home. Homestead. Ancestral home. If I close my eyes, I can see Dragonfly there beyond the hedge. I can see my young parents walking toward the creek in the late afternoon, a coppery light on the path. I can hear my grandmother's voice in the rooms of the house and in the cool corners of the arbor. And these are sacred recollections of the mind and heart.

READING CLOSELY AND THINKING CRITICALLY

1. What is the primary reason the homestead on Rainy Mountain Creek is important to Momaday?
2. Why did Momaday feel that he knew his grandfather, even though he died before Momaday was born?
3. Momaday's grandfather, unlike most Kiowas at the time, was a good farmer. Why didn't the grandfather's contemporaries take to farming very readily? What does it say about Momaday's grandfather that he *did* become a good farmer? Do the answers to these questions have anything to do with assimilation and cultural persistence? Why or why not?
4. As a child, Momaday's favorite visitors included the elderly, whom he found to be "exotic" (paragraph 8). As an adult, is Momaday still likely to consider these visitors to be exotic? Why or why not?
5. When Momaday watched the sun rise across the plain, "it was for [him] the deity that it was for Dragonfly" (paragraph 9). Explain why that is the case.

EXAMINING STRUCTURE AND STRATEGY

1. In your own words, write out the thesis of the essay. Be sure to include the dominant impression.
2. Paragraphs 9–11 do more than describe aspects of Momaday's homestead. What else do they do? How do these paragraphs help the author achieve his purpose for writing?
3. Why does Momaday use so much objective description? How does it help him achieve his purpose for writing?
4. What kind of order does Momaday use for the details in paragraphs 1 and 12? Does he use this order anywhere else in the essay?
5. What words describe the tone of the essay? (See page 69 on tone.)

CONSIDERING LANGUAGE AND STYLE

1. Why does Momaday use "Homestead" rather than "Home" in the essay's title?
2. Momaday's closing paragraph begins, "Home. Homestead. Ancestral home." What progression do you notice in these sentence fragments? What point do they make?
3. Consult a dictionary if you are unsure of the meaning of any of these words: *hummock* (paragraph 1), *agrarian* (paragraph 3), *centaurs* (paragraph 8).

FOR DISCUSSION IN CLASS OR ONLINE

Does the Kiowa tradition for reunions and visits make sense for Americans today? Would it work? Does it appeal to you? Explain your views.

1. **Writing in your journal.** In a page or two, explain how connected you feel to your ancestors. If you feel a connection, explain how it is made. If you do not feel a connection, explain why not.

2. **Using description for a purpose.** The purposes in the assignments are possibilities. You may establish whatever purposes you like, within your instructor's guidelines.

   - If you recently visited a place you knew as a child—or if you can do so now—describe the place to convey your feelings upon revisiting it.

   - Momaday notes that the house seems small to him now. To express your feelings and relate your experience, describe a place that seems small to you but that seemed large when you were a child.

   - To express your feelings, relate experience, and perhaps inform, describe someone whom you consider "exotic" or once thought of as exotic.

   - To express your feelings, relate experience, and perhaps inform, describe one aspect of your childhood home (the yard, the kitchen, your bedroom, the porch, and so on) to relate the importance of your family or your cultural heritage.

3. **Combining patterns.** Use description to describe someone who is or was important to you and cause-and-effect analysis to explain why the person is or was important. (Cause-and-effect analysis is explained in Chapter 10.)

4. **Analyzing and assessing.** Although the description in "The Homestead on Rainy Mountain Creek" is largely objective, Momaday conveys emotion. Citing specific examples to support your points, explain how Momaday feels about his homestead and family. Do you think he should have used more expressive description to convey his feelings? Explain.

5. **Connecting and synthesizing the readings.** In paragraph 13, Momaday describes worship with his family. Compare and contrast that worship with the family worship in "Salvation" (page 203) and with your own family worship experience (or lack of it). What conclusions can you draw about the role of worship in family life?

6. **Drawing on sources.** Interview someone from a culture other than your own, perhaps an international student or someone else born in another country. Ask that person about some ceremony, ritual, or custom from his or her culture. You might ask about weddings, funerals, child-rearing customs, holiday celebrations, or school customs. Then write an essay describing the ritual, custom, or ceremony that you learned about.

BACKGROUND: Born in 1948 in Illinois, Diane Ackerman is a woman of many talents: journalist, children's author, poet, essayist, naturalist, and professor. Among her awards is the Academy of American Poets Prize. The *New York Times* says her well-known and well-loved *A Natural History of the Senses* (1990) "gives the reader the richest possible feeling of the worlds the senses take in." She has also written *The Zookeeper's Wife: A War Story* (2007) and over two dozen critically acclaimed works of nonfiction and fiction. She is particularly known for blending science and art in her essays and books, as you will see in "World at Dawn: The Pleasure of Life Rekindled," which was first published in *Orion* magazine in 2009.

COMBINED PATTERNS AND THEIR PURPOSES: In "World at Dawn: The Pleasure of Life Rekindled," Diane Ackerman relies heavily on expressive detail to *describe* dawn. Because she describes so beautifully, her essay **entertains**. However, you will notice that the essay also **informs** by helping us to a fresh appreciation for something familiar: sunrise. To achieve these purposes, Ackerman includes elements of *process analysis* and *definition* with her description.

WORLD AT DAWN: THE PLEASURE OF LIFE REKINDLED
BY DIANE ACKERMAN

AT DAWN, the world rises out of darkness, slowly, sense-grain by grain, as if from sleep. Life becomes visible once again. "When it is dark, it seems to me as if I were dying, and I can't think anymore," Claude Monet[1] once lamented. "More light!"

---

[1]Claude Monet (1840–1926) was a French painter and originator of the Impressionist style of painting.

Goethe[2] begged from his deathbed. Dawn is the wellspring of more light, the origin of our first to last days as we roll in space, over 6.684 billion of us in one global petri dish, shot through with sunlight, in our cells, in our minds, in our myriad metaphors of rebirth, in all the extensions to our senses that we create to enlighten our days and navigate our nights. Thanks to electricity, night doesn't last as long now, nor is it as dark as it used to be so it's hard to imagine the terror of our ancestors waiting for daybreak. On starless nights, one can feel like a loose array of limbs and purpose, and seem smaller, limited to what one can touch. In the dark, it's hard to tell friend from foe. Night-roaming predators may stalk us. Reminded of all our delectable frailties, we become vulnerable as prey. What courage it must have taken our ancestors to lie down in darkness and become helpless, invisible, and delusional for eight hours. Graceful animals stole through the forest shadows by night, but few people were awake to see them burst forth, in twilight or moonlight, forbidding, distorted, maybe even ghoulish or magical. Small wonder we personalized the night with demons. Eventually, people were willing to sacrifice anything—wealth, power, even children—to ransom the sun, immense with life, a one-eyed god[3] who fed their crops, led their travels, chased the demons from their dark, rekindled their lives.

As you read
Notice the interesting similes and metaphors in Ackerman's description.

2   Whatever else it is, dawn is always a rebirth, a fresh start, even if familiar routines and worries charge in clamoring for attention. While waking, we veer between dreamy and lucid (from the Latin *lux,* light). Crossing that threshold each morning, we step across worlds, half a mind turned inward, the other half growing aware. "I'm still a little *groggy,*" we say the eighteenth-century word for being drunk on rum. It's a time of epic uncertainly and vulnerability, as we surface from disorienting dreams and the blindness of keeping eyes shut for many hours. As the eyelids rise to flickering light and the dimly visible, it's easy to forget where we are, even what we are. Then everything shines. Paths grow easier to see, food easier to spot, jobs easier to tackle with renewed vigor. In rising light, doors and bridges become eye-catching. We may use all our other senses in the dark, but to see we need the sun spilling over the horizon, highlighting everything and pouring a thick yellow vitamin into our eyes. We're usually too hurried to savor the elemental in our lives: the reeling sun, moon, and stars; prophecy of clouds; ruckus of birdsong; moss brightly blooming; moon shadows and dew; omens of autumn in late summer; fizzy air before a storm; wind chime of leaves; fellowship of dawn and dusk. Yet we abide by forces so old we've lost the taste of their spell. It's as survivors that we greet each day.

"Whatever else it is, dawn is always a rebirth, a fresh start, even if familiar routines and worries charge in clamoring for attention."

3   When the sun fades in winter, we're instinctively driven to heights of craft and ingenuity. In the Northeast, rising humans slip from their quilted night-nests and

---

[2]Johann Wolfgang von Goethe (1749–1832) was a German poet, novelist, playwright, painter, and scientist.

[3]Perhaps a reference to Ra, the central Egyptian sun god, depicted with his head turned in profile; hence, he was a "one-eyed god."

keep warm in heat gusted by fires trapped in metal boxes. Sometimes they venture out wearing a medley of other life-forms: sap from rubber trees attached to the feet; soft belly hair from Mideastern goats wrapped around the head; pummeled cow skin fitted over the fingers; and, padding chest and torso, layers of long thick-walled plant cells that humans find indigestible but insulating and plants use to buttress their delicate tissues—that is, galoshes, wool, leather gloves, and cotton underwear. Some humans go walking, jogging, or biking—to suck more oxygen from the air—which lubricates their joints, shovels fuel into their cells, and rouses their dozy senses. Some of us migrate south like hummingbirds.

4 Right around Charleston, South Carolina, morning begins to change its mood, winter brings a chill but doesn't roll up your socks, and the sun boils over the horizon a moment sooner, because the planet's middle section begins to swell a smidgen there, just enough for pecan light at dawn, snapdragons and camellias too dew-sodden to float scent, and birds tuning their pipes, right on schedule, for a chatterbox chorale.

5 By January, the northern bird chorus has flown to *cucaracha*-ville—or, if you prefer it anglicized, palmetto-bug-ville—where swarming insects and other lowlife feed flocks of avian visitors. There they join many of the upright apes they left behind: "snow birds" who also migrate to the land of broiling noons. We may travel far in winter, but our birds travel with us.

6 Painting its own time zone, its own climate, dawn is a land of petrified forests and sleeping beauties, when dry leaves, hardened by frozen dew, become ghost hands, and deer slouch through the woods, waiting for their food to defrost. Part of the great parentheses of our lives, dawn summons us to a world alive and death-defying, when the deepest arcades of life and matter beckon. Then, as if a lamp were switched on in a dark room, nature grows crisply visible, including our own nature, ghostly hands, and fine sediment of days.

READING CLOSELY AND THINKING CRITICALLY

1. What was it like for our ancestors at night before electricity?

2. In paragraph 1, Ackerman says it is not surprising that "we personalized the night with demons." What does she mean? What cause-and-effect relationship is she referring to?

3. In paragraph 3, Ackerman says that in winter "we're instinctively driven to heights of craft and ingenuity." What does she mean? Why is winter the only season she discusses in detail?

4. Why were people "willing to sacrifice anything" to the god of the sun (paragraph 1)? Was their thinking logical? Explain.

EXAMINING STRUCTURE AND STRATEGY

1. What is Ackerman's dominant impression? Cite three examples of expressive description that convey that dominant impression. How do these descriptions help the author achieve her purpose for writing?

2. Paragraph 1 includes two quotations. Why do you think Ackerman included them?

3. Which of the senses (sight, sound, smell, taste, touch) do Ackerman's descriptions appeal to? Cite an example for each sense you mention.

4. What is the topic sentence of paragraph 3? What pattern does Ackerman use to support that topic sentence?

NOTING COMBINED PATTERNS

1. How does Ackerman use process analysis to help her achieve her writing purpose?

2. Is it possible to consider "World at Dawn" a definition essay? Why or why not?

CONSIDERING LANGUAGE AND STYLE

1. Ackerman includes many similes and metaphors (see page 128) in "World at Dawn." Cite two examples of each. What do you think of them? Why?

2. In paragraph 1, Ackerman refers to "our delectable frailties." Explain why she uses the modifier *delectable.*

3. What are "the great parentheses of our lives" (paragraph 6)? Why is the metaphor an appropriate one for the last paragraph?

4. Consult a dictionary if you are unsure of the meaning of these words: *petri dish* (paragraph 1), *myriad* (paragraph 1), *cucaracha,* (paragraph 5), *anglicized* (paragraph 5).

FOR DISCUSSION IN CLASS OR ONLINE

Ackerman says that "we abide by forces so old we've lost the taste of their spell" (paragraph 2). What else has become so familiar to us that we fail to notice it fully?

WRITING ASSIGNMENTS

1. **Writing in your journal.** In paragraph 2, Ackerman says that "we're usually too hurried to savor the elemental in our lives." What about you? In a page or so, discuss whether your life is too hurried to allow you to enjoy the "elemental."

2. **Using description for a purpose.** The purposes given in the assignments are possibilities. You may establish whatever purposes you like, within your instructor's guidelines.

   - To inform and entertain, describe what it is like to be in a city during a power outage that lasts several days.

   - To inform and entertain, describe one place at either dawn or dusk. If you choose a spot near you, try to visit it to form your dominant impression and gather details.

   - Ackerman describes a bit of what winter is like. Select a season and, to express your feelings and/or relate your experience, describe that season.

   - To entertain, describe something else that is a time of rebirth, such as New Year's Eve, your birthday, or the start of a new school year.

3. **Combining patterns.** Describe an activity you associate with a particular time of day, such as morning band practice, lunch on campus, an afternoon study session, or an

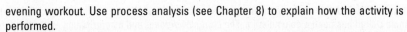

evening workout. Use process analysis (see Chapter 8) to explain how the activity is performed.

4. **Analyzing and assessing.** "World at Dawn" first appeared in *Orion* magazine. According to the magazine's Web site, "It is *Orion*'s fundamental conviction that humans are morally responsible for the world in which we live, and that the individual comes to sense this responsibility as he or she develops a personal bond with nature." Reread Ackerman's essay and discuss whether it is compatible with *Orion*'s mission. Be sure to cite specific evidence from the essay to support your assertion.

5. **Connecting and synthesizing the readings.** The authors of "World at Dawn" and "Once More to the Lake" (page 691) both describe aspects of the natural world. Look closely at both essays, and then discuss what these essays reveal about the attitudes these authors have about the natural world. Be sure to cite evidence from the essays to support your points.

6. **Drawing on sources.** Select one item powered by electricity, such as refrigerators, street lights, or television sets, and reflect on what life was like without that item, that is, before electricity. For some help, type "life before _____ [filling in the blank with the item]" into your favorite search engine.

BACKGROUND: A writer and professor emeritus at Wesleyan University in Connecticut, Annie Dillard has been a columnist for *The Living Wilderness* and a contributing editor for *Harper's* magazine. Born in 1945, Dillard won a Pulitzer Prize in 1975 for her first book of prose, *The Pilgrim at Tinker Creek,* a collection of observations about the beauty and violence of the natural world near her Virginia home. Dillard's other works include poetry; *For the Time Being* (1999), a personal narrative; *Encounters with Chinese Writers* (1984), a work about her visit to China as part of a U.S. cultural delegation; *The Writing Life* (1989), a narrative about the writing process; a book of essays, *Teaching a Stone to Talk* (1982); and the novels *The Living* (1992) and *The Maytrees* (2007). "The Deer at Providencia" is from *Teaching a Stone to Talk.*

www.mhhe.com/clousepatterns6	Annie Dillard

For more information on this author, go to

More resources > Chapter 5 > Annie Dillard

COMBINED PATTERNS AND THEIR PURPOSES: "The Deer at Providencia" is a *description* of the torment of a deer. This description is a powerful component of Dillard's *narration* (story) about the suffering of humans and animals. The weaving of the descriptive and narrative elements allows Dillard to **relate her experience** in the Ecuadorian jungle and **express her feelings** of uncertainty.

The Deer at Providencia
BY ANNIE DILLARD

There were four of us North Americans in the jungle, in the Ecuadorian jungle on the banks of the Napo River in the Amazon watershed. The other three North Americans were metropolitan men. We stayed in tents in one riverside village, and visited others. At the village called Providencia we saw a sight which moved us, and which shocked the men.

2   The first thing we saw when we climbed the riverbank to the village of Providencia was the deer. It was roped to a tree on the grass clearing near the thatch shelter where we would eat lunch.

As you read
Think about the suffering people and animals experience. How much of that suffering is avoidable?

3   The deer was small, about the size of a whitetail fawn, but apparently full-grown. It had a rope around its neck and three feet caught in the rope. Someone said that the dogs had caught it that morning and the villagers were going to cook and eat it that night.

4   This clearing lay at the edge of the little thatched-hut village. We could see the villagers going about their business, scattering feed corn for hens about their houses, and wandering down paths to the river to bathe. The village headman was our host; he stood beside us as we watched the deer struggle. Several village boys were interested in the deer; they formed part of the circle we made around it in the clearing. So also did four businessmen from Quito who were attempting to guide us around the jungle. Few of the very different

people standing in this circle had a common language. We watched the deer, and no one said much.

5   The deer lay on its side at the rope's very end, so the rope lacked slack to let it rest its head in the dust. It was "pretty," delicate of bone like all deer, and thin-skinned for the tropics. Its skin looked virtually hairless, in fact, and almost trans-lucent, like a membrane. Its neck was no thicker than my wrist; it was rubbed open on the rope, and gashed. Trying to paw itself free of the rope, the deer had scratched its own neck with its hooves. The raw underside of its neck showed red stripes and some bruises bleeding inside the muscles. Now three of its feet were hooked in the rope under its jaw. It could not stand, of course, on one leg, so it could not move to slacken the rope and ease the pull on its throat and enable it to rest its head.

6   Repeatedly the deer paused, motionless, its eyes veiled, with only its rib cage in motion, and its breaths the only sound. Then, after I would think, "It has given up; now it will die," it would heave. The rope twanged; the tree leaves clattered; the deer's free foot beat the ground. We stepped back and held our breaths. It thrashed, kicking, but only one leg moved; the other three legs tightened inside the rope's loop. Its hip jerked; its spine shook. Its eyes rolled; its tongue, thick with spittle, pushed in and out. Then it would rest again. We watched this for fifteen minutes.

7   Once three young native boys charged in, released its trapped legs, and jumped back to the circle of people. But instantly the deer scratched up its neck with its hooves and snared its forelegs in the rope again. It was easy to imagine a third and then a fourth leg soon stuck, like Brer Rabbit and the Tar Baby.

8   We watched the deer from the circle, and then we drifted on to lunch. Our palm-roofed shelter stood on a grassy promontory from which we would see the deer tied to the tree, pigs and hens walking under village houses, and black-and-white cattle standing in the river. There was even a breeze.

9   Lunch, which was the second and better lunch we had that day, was hot and fried. There was a big fish called *doncella,* a kind of catfish, dipped whole in corn flour and beaten egg, then deep fried. With our fingers we pulled soft fragments of it from its sides to our plates, and ate; it was delicate fish-flesh, fresh and mild. Someone found the roe, and I ate of that too—it was fat and stronger, like egg yolk, naturally enough, and warm.

10   There was also a stew of meat in shreds with rice and pale brown gravy. I had asked what kind of deer it was tied to the tree; Pepe had answered in Spanish, *"Gama."* Now they told us this was *gama* too, stewed. I suspect the word means merely game or venison. At any rate, I heard that the village dogs had cornered another deer just yesterday, and it was this deer which we were now eating in full sight of the whole article. It was good. I was surprised at its tenderness. But it is a fact that high levels of lactic acid, which builds up in muscle tissues during exertion, tenderizes.

11   After the fish and meat we ate bananas fried in chunks and served on a tray; they were sweet and full of flavor. I felt terrific. My shirt was wet and cool from swimming; I had had a night's sleep, two decent walks, three meals, and a swim—everything tasted good. From time to time each one of us, separately, would look beyond our shaded roof to the sunny spot where the deer was still convulsing in the dust. Our meal completed, we walked around the deer and back to the boats.

12   That night I learned that while we were watching the deer, the others were watching me.

13   We four North Americans grew close in the jungle in a way that was not the usual artificial intimacy of travelers. We liked each other. We stayed up all that night talking, murmuring, as though we rocked on hammocks slung above time. The others were from big cities: New York, Washington, Boston. They all said that I had no expression on my face when I was watching the deer—or at any rate, not the expression they expected.

14   They had looked to see how I, the only woman, and the youngest, was taking the sight of the deer's struggles. I looked detached, apparently, or hard, or calm, or focused, still. I don't know. I was thinking. I remember feeling very old and energetic. I could say like Thoreau that I have traveled widely in Roanoke, Virginia. I have thought a great deal about carnivorousness; I eat meat. These things are not issues; they are mysteries.

15   Gentlemen of the city, what surprises you? That there is suffering here, or that I know it?

16   We lay in the tent and talked. "If it had been my wife," one man said with special vigor, amazed, "she wouldn't have cared *what* was going on; she would have dropped *everything* right at that moment and gone in the village from here to there to there, she would not have *stopped* until that animal was out of its suffering one way or another. She couldn't *bear* to see a creature in agony like that."

17   I nodded.

18   Now I am home. When I wake I comb my hair before the mirror above my dresser. Every morning for the past two years I have seen in that mirror, beside my sleep-softened face, the blacked face of a burnt man. It is a wire-service photograph clipped from a newspaper and taped to my mirror. The caption reads: "Alan McDonald in Miami hospital bed." All you can see in the photograph is a smudged triangle of face from his eyelids to his lower lip; the rest is bandages. You cannot see the expression in his eyes; the bandages shade them.

19   The story, headed MAN BURNED FOR SECOND TIME, begins:

> "Why does God hate me?" Alan McDonald asked from his hospital bed.
> "When the gunpowder went off, I couldn't believe it," he said. "I just
> couldn't believe it. I said, 'No, God couldn't do this to me again.'"

He was in a burn ward in Miami, in serious condition. I do not even know if he lived. I wrote him a letter at the time, cringing.

20   He had been burned before, thirteen years previously, by flaming gasoline. For years he had been having his body restored and his face remade in dozens of operations. He had been a boy, and then a burnt boy. He had already been stunned by what could happen, by how life could veer.

21   Once I read that people who survive bad burns tend to go crazy; they have a very high suicide rate. Medicine cannot ease their pain; drugs just leak away, soaking the sheets, because there is no skin to hold them in. The people just lie there and weep. Later they kill themselves. They had not known, before they were burned, that the world included such suffering, that life could permit them personally such pain.

22   This time a bowl of gunpowder had exploded on McDonald.

"I didn't realize what had happened at first," he recounted. "And then I heard that sound from 13 years ago. I was burning. I rolled to put the fire out and I thought, 'Oh God, not again.'

"If my friend hadn't been there, I would have jumped into a canal with a rock around my neck."

His wife concludes the piece, "Man, it just isn't fair."

23   I read the whole clipping again every morning. This is the Big Time here, every minute of it. Will someone please explain to Alan McDonald in his dignity, to the deer at Providencia in his dignity, what is going on? And mail me the carbon.

24   When we walked by the deer at Providencia for the last time, I said to Pepe, with a pitying glance at the deer, *"Pobrecito"* — "poor little thing." But I was trying out Spanish. I knew at the time it was a ridiculous thing to say.

READING CLOSELY AND THINKING CRITICALLY

1. In your own words, write a sentence or two that expresses the thesis of "The Deer at Providencia."
2. Describe the way the men react to the deer. How is their reaction different from Dillard's? Why are the men surprised by Dillard's reaction to the deer?
3. Why does Dillard note (in paragraph 10) that high levels of lactic acid tenderize meat?
4. What view of women is referred to in paragraphs 15 and 16?
5. Do you agree with Dillard that *"Pobrecito"* ("poor little thing") was a ridiculous thing for her to say as she walked by the deer? Explain.
6. Why do you think Dillard kept the picture and article about Alan McDonald?

EXAMINING STRUCTURE AND STRATEGY

1. What approach does Dillard take to her introduction?
2. What do the deer at Providencia and Alan McDonald have in common? That is, how is it possible to discuss both in the same essay? How does each discussion relate to Dillard's purpose?
3. Which of the descriptive paragraphs are developed primarily with objective detail, and which with expressive detail?
4. What attitude toward the deer is Dillard's audience likely to have? How is the reader likely to react to the deer's plight? How does Dillard respond to her audience's probable reaction? How does her response further her purpose?

NOTING COMBINED PATTERNS

1. Which paragraphs are developed primarily with description?
2. Which paragraphs are developed primarily with narration (storytelling)?

1. Dillard uses descriptive language to portray the deer as fragile. Cite two examples of such language.
2. What is significant about the name of the village (Providencia)?
3. Consult a dictionary if you are unsure of the meaning of any of these words: *watershed* (paragraph 1), *thatch* (paragraph 2), *translucent* (paragraph 5), *spittle* (paragraph 6), *promontory* (paragraph 8), *carnivorousness* (paragraph 14).

FOR DISCUSSION IN CLASS OR ONLINE

With your classmates, consider this question: Do you see a difference between the suffering of the deer and the suffering of Alan McDonald? If so, explain what that difference is. If not, explain why.

WRITING ASSIGNMENTS

1. **Writing in your journal.** At one time, killing animals for food was a necessity, but many people claim that we no longer need to do so, that vegetarianism eliminates the need for animals to suffer and die for us. Attack or defend the killing of animals for food.

2. **Using description for a purpose.** The purposes given in the assignments are possibilities. You may establish whatever purposes you like, within your instructor's guidelines.

   - Like Dillard, describe an animal engaged in some activity. For example, you could describe a kitten at play, a cat washing itself, a dog chasing a ball, or fish swimming in a tank. Use expressive detail to entertain your reader (if the activity is a pleasant one), to relate the animal's experience, and to inform your reader about the animal's level of comfort.

   - If you have experienced considerable pain, describe what you went through. For example, you can describe having a broken leg, a migraine headache, or a sports injury. Your purpose can be to relate your experience, to express your feelings about it, and/or to inform your reader of what the experience was like.

   - To entertain and perhaps inform your reader, describe an animal in its natural habitat or its common surroundings. For example, you can describe a squirrel on the campus commons, a monkey in the zoo, a dog in your yard, or a cat in a pet store.

3. **Combining patterns.** Like Dillard, narrate a story that teaches something about life. Include a considerable amount of description.

4. **Analyzing and assessing.** Identify the points Dillard is making about the human condition in "The Deer at Providencia," and assess how effectively she makes those points. Be sure to cite evidence in the essay to support your ideas.

5. **Connecting and synthesizing the readings.** Do you think we do enough to reduce suffering in the world? Explain your view, drawing on your own experience and observation, the evidence in "The Deer at Providencia," and one or more of the following essays: "Embedded" (page 164), "Untouchables" (page 275), and "What Is Poverty?" (page 546).

6. **Drawing on sources.** Part of "The Deer at Providencia" focuses on the tremendous suffering endured by Alan McDonald. Many people believe that those who are

suffering and who have little or no chance to recover should be allowed to request euthanasia, sometimes called "mercy killing." Many others believe that euthanasia is wrong. To examine this controversial issue, summarize the chief arguments on both sides of the euthanasia debate. Use description to provide examples that support either or both sides. If you need a starting point, look up *euthanasia* in the *Social Sciences Index* and the *Humanities Index.* These volumes, located in your library's reference room, will direct you to articles on the subject. If you prefer to use the Internet, type in the keyword *"euthanasia"* into your favorite search engine. Your search results will lead you to a number of helpful sites.

BACKGROUND: Novelist, poet, and essayist Gretel Ehrlich was born in California in 1946 and attended Bennington College, UCLA Film School, and the New School for Social Research. She is multitalented, having been a journalist, documentary filmmaker, poet, and fiction writer. Annie Dillard, who wrote "The Deer at Providencia" (page 150), calls Ehrlich's writing "vivid, tough, and funny." Ehrlich decided to live in Wyoming after going there to make a film. She is noted for writing poetically about the vast Wyoming landscapes. Strong and capable (as the following selection reveals), Ehrlich did ranch work, sheepherding, and cattle branding. A prolific author, she has published in the *New York Times*, the *Atlantic Monthly, Time*, and *Harper's*. She has received awards from the National Endowment for the Arts and the Wyoming Council for the Arts. Ehrlich's books include *Drinking Dry Clouds: Stories from Wyoming* (1991), *A Match to the Heart: One Woman's Story of Being Struck by Lightning* (1994), *Questions of Heaven: The Chinese Journeys of an American Buddhist* (1997), *A Blizzard Year* (1999), *The Future of Ice* (2004), and *The Empire of Ice* (2010). "Struck by Lightning" is taken from *A Match to the Heart*.

www.mhhe.com/clousepatterns6 | Gretel Ehrlich

For more information on this author, go to

More resources > Chapter 5 > Gretel Ehrlich

COMBINED PATTERNS AND THEIR PURPOSES: To **express her feelings**, Gretel Ehrlich *describes* what it was like when she was struck by lightning. Although Ehrlich uses some *objective description*, she relies much more heavily on *expressive description*. Pay particular attention to the images throughout the piece, as they are among the richest and most provocative in this chapter. Notice, too, that as Ehrlich uses *narration* to **relate her experience**, she moves back and forth in time.

Struck by Lightning

BY GRETEL EHRLICH

Deep in an ocean. I am suspended motionless. The water is gray. That's all there is, and before that? My arms are held out straight, cruciate, my head and legs hang limp. Nothing moves. Brown kelp lies flat in mud and fish are buried in liquid clouds of dust. There are no shadows or sounds. Should there be? I don't know if I am alive, but if not, how do I know I am dead? My body is leaden, heavier than gravity. Gravity is done with me. No more sinking and rising or bobbing in currents. There is a terrible feeling of oppression with no oppressor. I try to lodge my mind against some boundary, some reference point, but the continent of the body dissolves . . .

As you read Try to determine why Ehrlich moves her readers back and forth in time.

2   A single heartbeat stirs gray water. Blue trickles in, just a tiny stream. Then a long silence.

3   Another heartbeat. This one is louder, as if amplified. Sound takes a shape: it is a snowplow moving grayness aside like a heavy snowdrift. I can't tell if I'm moving, but more blue water flows in. Seaweed begins to undulate, then a whole

kelp forest rises from the ocean floor. A fish swims past and looks at me. Another heartbeat drives through dead water, and another, until I am surrounded by blue.

4 Sun shines above all this. There is no pattern to the way its glint comes free and falls in long knives of light. My two beloved dogs appear. They flank me like tiny rockets, their fur pressed against my ribs. A leather harness holds us all together. The dogs climb toward light, pulling me upward at a slant from the sea.

5 I have been struck by lightning and I am alive.

6 Before electricity carved its blue path toward me, before the negative charge shot down from cloud to ground, before "streamers" jumped the positive charge back up from ground to cloud, before air expanded and contracted producing loud pressure pulses I could not hear because I was already dead, I had been walking.

7 When I started out on foot that August afternoon, the thunderstorm was blowing in fast. On the face of the mountain, a mile ahead, hard westerly gusts and sudden updrafts collided, pulling black clouds apart. Yet the storm looked harmless. When a distant thunderclap scared the dogs, I called them to my side and rubbed their ears: "Don't worry, you're okay as long as you're with me."

8 I woke in a pool of blood, lying on my stomach some distance from where I should have been, flung at an odd angle to one side of the dirt path. The whole sky had grown dark. Was it evening, and if so, which one? How many minutes or hours had elapsed since I lost consciousness, and where were the dogs? I tried to call out to them but my voice didn't work. The muscles in my throat were paralyzed and I couldn't swallow. Were the dogs dead? Everything was terribly wrong: I had trouble seeing, talking, breathing, and I couldn't move my legs or right arm. Nothing remained in my memory—no sounds, flashes, smells, no warnings of any kind. Had I been shot in the back? Had I suffered a stroke or heart attack? These thoughts were dark pools in sand.

9 The sky was black. Was this a storm in the middle of the day or was it night with a storm traveling through? When thunder exploded over me, I knew I had been hit by lightning.

10 The pain in my chest intensified and every muscle in my body ached. I was quite sure I was dying. What was it one should do or think or know? I tried to recall the Buddhist instruction regarding dying—which position to lie in, which direction to face. Did the "Lion's position" taken by the Buddha mean lying on the left or the right? And which sutra to sing? Oh yes, the Heart Sutra . . . gaté, gaté, paragaté . . . form and formlessness. Paradox and cosmic jokes. Surviving after trying to die "properly" would be truly funny, but the chances of that seemed slim.

11 Other words drifted in: how the "gateless barrier" was the gate through which one passes to reach enlightenment. Yet if there was no gate, how did one pass through? Above me, high on the hill, was the gate on the ranch that led nowhere, a gate I had mused about often. Now its presence made me smile. Even when I thought I had no aspirations for enlightenment, too much effort in that direction was being expended. How could I learn to slide, yet remain aware?

12 To be struck by lightning: what a way to get enlightened. That would be the joke if I survived. It seemed important to remember jokes. My thinking did not seem connected to the inert body that was in such terrible pain. Sweep the mind of weeds, I kept telling myself—that's what years of Buddhist practice had taught

me . . . But where were the dogs, the two precious ones I had watched being born and had raised in such intimacy and trust? I wanted them with me. I wanted them to save me again.

13   It started to rain. Every time a drop hit bare skin there was an explosion of pain. Blood crusted my left eye. I touched my good hand to my heart, which was beating wildly, erratically. My chest was numb, as if it had been sprayed with novocaine. No feeling of peace filled me. Death was a bleakness, a grayness about which it was impossible to be curious or relieved. I loved those dogs and hoped they weren't badly hurt. If I didn't die soon, how many days would pass before we were found, and when would the scavengers come? The sky was dark, or was that the way life flew out of the body, in a long tube with no light at the end? I lay on the cold ground waiting. The mountain was purple, and sage stirred against my face. I knew I had to give up all this, then my own body and all my thinking. Once more I lifted my head to look for the dogs but, unable to see them, I twisted myself until I faced east and tried to let go of all desire.

14   When my eyes opened again I knew I wasn't dead. Images from World War II movies filled my head: of wounded soldiers dragging themselves across a field, and if I could have laughed—that is, made my face work into a smile and get sounds to discharge from my throat—I would have. God, it would have been good to laugh. Instead, I considered my options: either lie there and wait for someone to find me— how many days or weeks would that take?—or somehow get back to the house. I calmly assessed what might be wrong with me—stroke, cerebral hemorrhage, gun-shot wound—but it was bigger than I could understand. The instinct to survive does not rise from particulars; a deep but general misery rollercoasted me into action. I tried to propel myself on my elbows but my right arm didn't work. The wind had swung around and was blowing in from the east. It was still a dry storm with only sputtering rain, but when I raised myself up, lightning fingered the entire sky.

15   It is not true that lightning never strikes the same place twice. I had entered a shower of sparks and furious brightness and, worried that I might be struck again, watched as lightning touched down all around me. Years before, in the high coun-try, I'd been hit by lightning: an electrical charge had rolled down an open meadow during a fearsome thunderstorm, surged up the legs of my horse, coursed through me, and bounced a big spark off the top of my head. To be struck again—and this time it was a direct hit—what did it mean?

16   The feeling had begun to come back into my legs and after many awkward attempts, I stood. To walk meant lifting each leg up by the thigh, moving it forward with my hands, setting it down. The earth felt like a peach that had split open in the middle; one side moved up while the other side moved down and my legs were out of rhythm. The ground rolled the way it does during an earthquake and the sky was tattered book pages waving in different directions. Was the ground liquefying under me, or had the molecular composition of my body deliquesced? I struggled to piece together fragments. Then it occurred to me that my brain was torn and that's where the blood had come from.

17   I walked. Sometimes my limbs held me, sometimes they didn't. I don't know how many times I fell but it didn't matter because I was making slow progress toward home.

18   Home—the ranch house—was about a quarter of a mile away. I don't remember much about getting there. My concentration went into making my legs work. The storm was strong. All the way across the basin, lightning lifted parts of mountains and sky into yellow refulgence and dropped them again, only to lift others. The inside of my eyelids turned gold and I could see the dark outlines of things through them. At the bottom of the hill I opened the door to my pickup and blew the horn with the idea that someone might hear me. No one came. My head had swollen to an indelicate shape. I tried to swallow—I was so thirsty—but the muscles in my throat were still paralyzed and I wondered when I would no longer be able to breathe.

19   Inside the house, sounds began to come out of me. I was doing crazy things, ripping my hiking boots off because the bottoms of my feet were burning, picking up the phone when I was finally able to scream. One of those times, someone happened to be on the line. I was screaming incoherently for help. My last conscious act was to dial 911.

20   Dark again. Pressing against sore ribs, my dogs pulled me out of the abyss, pulled and pulled. I smelled straw. My face was on tatami. I opened my eyes, looked up, and saw neighbors. Had they come for my funeral? The phone rang and I heard someone give directions to the ambulance driver, who was lost. A "first responder," an EMT from town who has a reputation with the girls, leaned down and asked if he could "touch me" to see if there were any broken bones. What the hell, I thought. I was going to die anyway. Let him have his feel. But his touch was gentle and professional, and I was grateful.

21   I slipped back into unconsciousness and when I woke again two EMTs were listening to my heart. I asked them to look for my dogs but they wouldn't leave me. Someone else in the room went outside and found Sam and Yaki curled up on the porch, frightened but alive. Now I could rest. I felt the medics jabbing needles into the top of my hands, trying unsuccessfully to get IVs started, then strapping me onto a backboard and carrying me out the front door of the house, down steps, into lightning and rain, into what was now a full-blown storm.

22   The ambulance rocked and slid, slamming my bruised body against the metal rails of the gurney. Every muscle was in violent spasm and there was a place on my back near the heart that burned. I heard myself yell in pain. Finally the EMTs rolled up towels and blankets and wedged them against my arms, shoulders, hips, and knees so the jolting of the vehicle wouldn't dislodge me. The ambulance slid down into ditches, struggled out, bumped from one deep rut to another. I asked to be taken to the hospital in Cody, but they said they were afraid my heart might stop again. As it was, the local hospital was thirty-five miles away, ten of them dirt, and the trip took more than an hour.

23   Our arrival seemed a portent of disaster—and an occasion for comedy. I had been struck by lightning around five in the afternoon. It was now 9:00 P.M. Nothing at the hospital worked. Their one EKG machine was nonfunctional, and jokingly the nurses blamed it on me. "Honey, you've got too much electricity in your body," one of them told me. Needles were jammed into my hand—no one had gotten an IV going yet—and the doctor on call hadn't arrived, though half an hour had elapsed. The EMTs kept assuring me: "Don't worry, we won't leave you here."

When another nurse, who was filling out an admission form, asked me how tall I was, I answered: "Too short to be struck by lightning."

24 "Electrical injury often results in ventricular fibrillation and injury to the medullary centers of the brain. Immediately after electric shock patients are usually comatose, apneic, and in circulatory collapse . . ."

25 When the doctor on call—the only doctor in town, waddled into what they called the emergency room, my aura, he said, was yellow and gray—a soul in transition. I knew that he had gone to medical school but had never completed a residency and had been barred from ER or ICU work in the hospitals of Florida, where he had lived previously. Yet I was lucky. Florida has many lightning victims, and unlike the doctors I would see later, he at least recognized the symptoms of a lightning strike. The tally sheet read this way: I had suffered a hit by lightning which caused ventricular fibrillation—cardiac arrest—though luckily my heart started beating again. Violent contractions of muscles when one is hit often cause the body to fly through the air: I was flung far and hit hard on my left side, which may have caused my heart to start again, but along with that fortuitous side effect, I sustained a concussion, broken ribs, a possible broken jaw, and lacerations above the eye. The paralysis below my waist and up through the chest and throat—called kerauno-paralysis—is common in lightning strikes and almost always temporary, but my right arm continued to be almost useless. Fernlike burns—arborescent erythema—covered my entire body. These occur when the electrical charge follows tracings of moisture on the skin—rain or sweat—thus the spidery red lines.

26 "Rapid institution of fluid and electrolyte therapy is essential with guidelines being the patient's urine output, hematocrit, osmolality, central venous pressure, and arterial blood gases . . ."

27 The nurses loaded me onto a gurney. As they wheeled me down the hall to my room, a front wheel fell off and I was slammed into the wall. Once I was in bed, the deep muscle aches continued, as did the chest pains. Later, friends came to visit. Neither doctor nor nurse had cleaned the cuts on my head, so Laura, who had herded sheep and cowboyed on all the ranches where I had lived and whose wounds I had cleaned when my saddle horse dragged her across a high mountain pasture, wiped blood and dirt from my face, arms, and hands with a cool towel and spooned yogurt into my mouth.

28 I was the only patient in the hospital. During the night, sheet lightning inlaid the walls with cool gold. I felt like an ancient, mummified child who had been found on a rock ledge near our ranch: bound tightly, unable to move, my dead face tipped backwards toward the moon.

29 In the morning, my regular doctor, Ben, called from Massachusetts, where he was vacationing, with this advice: "Get yourself out of that hospital and go somewhere else, anywhere." I was too weak to sign myself out, but Julie, the young woman who had a summer job on our ranch, retrieved me in the afternoon. She helped me get dressed in the cutoffs and torn T-shirt I had been wearing, but there were no shoes, so, barefoot, I staggered into Ben's office, where a physician's assistant kindly cleansed the gashes in my head. Then I was taken home.

30   Another thunderstorm slammed against the mountains as I limped up the path to the house. Sam and Yaki took one look at me and ran. These dogs lived with me, slept with me, understood every word I said, and I was too sick to find them, console them—even if they would have let me.

31   The next day my husband, who had just come down from the mountains where he worked in the summer, took me to another hospital. I passed out in the admissions office, was loaded onto a gurney, and taken for a CAT scan. No one bothered to find out why I had lost consciousness. Later, in the emergency unit, the doctor argued that I might not have been struck by lightning at all, as if I had imagined the incident. "Maybe a meteor hit me," I said, a suggestion he pondered seriously. After a blood panel and a brief neurological exam, which I failed—I couldn't follow his finger with my eyes or walk a straight line—he promptly released me.

32   "Patients should be monitored electrocardiographically for at least 24 hours for significant arrhythmias which often have delayed onset . . ."

33   It was difficult to know what was worse: being in a hospital where nothing worked and nobody cared, or being alone on an isolated ranch hundreds of miles from decent medical care.

34   In the morning I staggered into the kitchen. My husband, from whom I had been separated for three months, had left at 4:00 A.M. to buy cattle in another part of the state and would not be back for a month. Alone again, it was impossible to do much for myself. In the past I'd been bucked off, stiff and sore plenty of times but this felt different: I had no sense of equilibrium. My head hurt, every muscle in my body ached as if I had a triple dose of the flu, and my left eye was swollen shut and turning black and blue. Something moved in the middle of the kitchen floor. I was having difficulty seeing, but then I did see: a rattlesnake lay coiled in front of the stove. I reeled around and dove back into bed. Enough tests of character. I closed my eyes and half-slept. Later, when Julie came to the house, she found the snake and cut off its head with a shovel.

35   My only consolation was that the dogs came back. I had chest pains and all day Sam lay with his head against my heart. I cleaned a deep cut over Yaki's eye. It was half an inch deep but already healing. I couldn't tell if the dogs were sick or well, I was too miserable to know anything except that Death resided in the room: not as a human figure but as a dark fog rolling in, threatening to cover me; but the dogs stayed close and while my promise to keep them safe during a thunderstorm had proven fraudulent, their promise to keep me alive held good.

READING CLOSELY AND THINKING CRITICALLY

1.   What is Ehrlich describing in paragraphs 1–3? Should the reader take the passage literally? Why or why not?

2.   Paragraph 2 opens with "A single heartbeat stirs gray water," and paragraph 3 opens with "Another heartbeat." What is Ehrlich conveying with these sentences?

3.   What were the author's primary concerns after she regained consciousness? What do these concerns suggest about the kind of person she is?

4. In paragraph 14, Ehrlich says that when she regained consciousness at one point, "Images from World War II movies filled [her] head." Why do you think these images occurred to her?

5. Ehrlich's husband leaves her for a month shortly after she returns from the hospital. Ehrlich notes this fact without comment. What can you infer from this information?

6. Despite her dire circumstances, Ehrlich manages to have a sense of humor about her predicament. Evidence of her sense of humor appears in paragraphs 12, 20, 23, and 31. What do these humorous details reveal about the author?

EXAMINING STRUCTURE AND STRATEGY

1. Read paragraph 1 aloud, and then read paragraph 7 aloud. How do these two paragraphs differ in the way they sound? Why does Ehrlich use such different styles?

2. The movement from paragraph 7 to paragraph 8 is abrupt because it occurs without a transition or repetition. Do you think Ehrlich intended the movement between these paragraphs to jolt the reader? Explain.

3. What purpose do the quotations in paragraphs 24, 26, and 32 serve?

NOTING COMBINED PATTERNS

1. Ehrlich's descriptions fall into four main categories: descriptions of the weather, descriptions of her body after the lightning strike, descriptions of being unconscious and semiconscious, and descriptions of the hospital. Cite one description you particularly like from each category and do the following:

   a. Underline the specific words.

   b. Identify the description as objective or expressive.

   c. Explain why you like the description.

   d. Explain how the description helps Ehrlich achieve her purpose for writing.

2. Ehrlich does not begin her narration with the lightning strike and then move sequentially to the time she began to recover at home. Instead, she uses a variation of chronological order by including *flashbacks* between time periods. Explain how she uses the flashback technique. How does this technique help Ehrlich achieve her purpose?

CONSIDERING LANGUAGE AND STYLE

1. Paragraphs 1, 2, and 20 include intentional *sentence fragments* (sentence parts punctuated as sentences). How does Ehrlich use these fragments?

2. Read paragraph 6 aloud. What effect does Ehrlich create by repeating clauses that begin with *before*?

3. Explain the similes in paragraphs 16 and 35. Explain the metaphor in paragraph 16. What do these figures of speech contribute to the essay? (Similes and metaphors are explained on page 128.)

4. Consult a dictionary if you are unsure of the meaning of any of these words: *cruciate* (paragraph 1), *paradox* (paragraph 10), *deliquesced* (paragraph 16), *refulgence* (paragraph 18), *tatami* (paragraph 20), *portent* (paragraph 23), *gurney* (paragraph 27).

Did Ehrlich demonstrate courage after she was struck by lightning? Explain. Did she display more than one kind of courage? If so, what were these different kinds? With your classmates, answer these questions.

WRITING ASSIGNMENTS

1. **Writing in your journal.** Using the information in the selection, explain the kind of person you think Ehrlich is. Would you like to be more like her? Why or why not?

2. **Using description for a purpose.** The purposes given in the assignments are possibilities. You may establish whatever purposes you like, within your instructor's guidelines.

   - In paragraph 7, Ehrlich describes an approaching thunderstorm. To entertain your reader, describe the time just before or after a particular weather event: a spring shower, an ice storm, a thunderstorm, a tornado, a hurricane, a flash flood, or some other occurrence.

   - If you have been in the hospital, relate your experience and/or express your feelings by describing one room you were in.

   - Describe a doctor's or dentist's office to persuade your reader that these offices are (or are not) designed with patients in mind.

3. **Combining patterns.** Combine description and narration (see Chapter 6) to tell about a time you were ill or injured. Like Ehrlich, describe what the injury or illness felt like.

4. **Analyzing and assessing.** Explain how and why Ehrlich organizes her narration so that it moves back and forth in time. Is the technique an effective one? How does she keep readers from getting lost as the time shifts?

5. **Connecting and synthesizing the readings.** Ehrlich's relationship with her dogs is very close. In "Am I Blue?" (page 379), Alice Walker tells of her relationship with a horse. Using the information in these essays, along with your own experience and observation, discuss some aspect of the relationship between humans and animals.

6. **Drawing on sources.** Living an outdoor life in Wyoming, Ehrlich was particularly vulnerable to being hit by lightning. However, lightning strikes and other natural disasters can occur in any part of the world. Your area may be susceptible to a particular kind of natural disaster—if, for example, you live on the West Coast, you may have experienced earthquakes. What natural disasters have occurred in your area? What can you do to avoid being hurt should one occur? For ideas, try visiting the Federal Emergency Management Agency's Web site at *www.fema.gov*, and click on "Plan and Prepare." If possible, also try looking at the index or Web site for your local paper to find out about disasters that may have struck your area in the past.

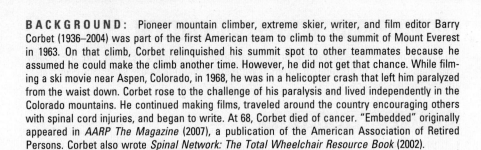

BACKGROUND: Pioneer mountain climber, extreme skier, writer, and film editor Barry Corbet (1936–2004) was part of the first American team to climb to the summit of Mount Everest in 1963. On that climb, Corbet relinquished his summit spot to other teammates because he assumed he could make the climb another time. However, he did not get that chance. While filming a ski movie near Aspen, Colorado, in 1968, he was in a helicopter crash that left him paralyzed from the waist down. Corbet rose to the challenge of his paralysis and lived independently in the Colorado mountains. He continued making films, traveled around the country encouraging others with spinal cord injuries, and began to write. At 68, Corbet died of cancer. "Embedded" originally appeared in *AARP The Magazine* (2007), a publication of the American Association of Retired Persons. Corbet also wrote *Spinal Network: The Total Wheelchair Resource Book* (2002).

COMBINED PATTERNS AND THEIR PURPOSES: To **relate his experience** and **express his feelings** about being paralyzed and spending time in a nursing home—and to **inform** readers about those experiences—Corbet combines *description* with *narration*. You will notice that the author has a **persuasive** purpose as well.

EMBEDDED

BY BARRY CORBET

IT HAPPENED SO FAST it stunned me. At the age of 67, after one week in a hospital, I found myself in a nursing home. Maybe I shouldn't have been surprised. We think nursing homes are just for old people, but that's not always true. Nursing homes also exist for people like me. Most people in nursing homes are old, but it isn't age that gets them there. It's disabilities, the kind that make us unable to get in and out of bed or get dressed or go to the bathroom on our own.

As you read Notice whether Corbet relies more on objective or expressive description, and try to determine why he opts for using more of one than the other.

2   In 1968 I was in a helicopter that crashed while I was filming a movie near Aspen, Colorado. My lower body was paralyzed, and I started using my arms and shoulders as others use their legs and hips. Now, my bones are eroded by abuse and arthritis, and muscles and tendons are long gone. For 35 years it's been slow-motion demolition. Performing everyday tasks has become so painful, my functioning so balky, that I'm ready to try a partial shoulder replacement, the only remedy medicine offers. Recovery will certainly take many months. That certainty causes real fear. So equally does the uncertainty. No one can predict how long I'll lose my physical independence. But I've done my homework and made my decision.

3   One September morning I wake up very early and hoist myself out of bed on a ceiling-mounted lift. I ride the lift to the bathroom and deal with my bags of waste, liquid and solid. Then I shower, put on jeans and a T-shirt. This is my morning routine, for years the same; what's different is how hard it is to do with ruined shoulders. In my power wheelchair, I roll out of the now empty house and into my lift-equipped van. I turn to the front, snap my chair into the driver's space, take up the hand controls, and I'm off to the hospital. It's 4:30 A.M.

* * *

4   An hour out of recovery, I wake up in a tiny hospital room. An opaque curtain separates me from my roommate, Joel, also a paraplegic. When not in the hospital,

he lives in a nursing home. Fourteen years after his injury, he's forgotten how to live in the world. We never see each other face-to-face but become buddies in a way, troubled souls living four feet apart for an entire week.

5   I pulled every string to avoid going to a nursing home after surgery. I wanted to go to a rehabilitation facility. But eventually we all get to a point where our strings aren't enough. Most people with longtime disabilities are terrified of nursing homes. Many of the young disabled arrive on one-way tickets and spend years or decades attempting to make beginnings amid people occupied with endings. Nursing homes are environments of isolation and disempowerment. They dictate when to get up, when to go to bed, when and what to eat, when to take showers and who will help, and when and if to leave.

"I pulled every string to avoid going to a nursing home after surgery."

6   The disability-rights movement resists. "Our homes," we chant, "not nursing homes." But living with a disability at home takes nerve, know-how, and resources: resources the movement is trying to build but that aren't yet adequate for most. But too many of us languish in nursing homes until the desire to live in the outside world evaporates. We become lifers, sometimes unable even to get out of bed. It's not going to happen to me, I tell myself. I'm too well informed. Too proactive.

7   I am discharged from the hospital. My daughter drives me in my van to a small town only a few miles from my home in Golden, Colorado. I am delivered to a low brick building tucked away from the highway. No sign announces its name or purpose.

8   On entering, I am met by a wall of fetid air. So many colostomies have passed this way, and here I am, bearing another. I wheel down the hall, and there's a new assault, an olfactory Doppler effect, as I pass each door. So it's true what they say, I think. Nursing homes stink. The next morning I smell nothing. Have I so quickly surrendered my senses, or is the smell really gone? On my own in my power chair, I roll outdoors. Immediately I'm overcome by the extravagance of color and warmth. I haven't realized how thoroughly my senses and my freedom have been deprived, have forgotten what fresh air and sunshine can do to a vulnerable mind. I'm embarrassed, but for two days I weep.

9   My room in the nursing home is small, but it does have a window, and it's private. This is extraordinarily lucky. Most of the rooms, just as tiny as mine, are double occupancy because that's what Medicare covers. But before I signed on with this facility, the management agreed to provide a dedicated phone line for my computer. Now it seems giving me a room with two phone connections and no roommate is the easiest way to get me online.

10   After some experimentation I conclude the new speech-recognition software doesn't work as well for me as one-handed keyboarding. It's clumsy, torture at first, but it links me to the world beyond this place. I can do some writing.

11   I'm an accidentally embedded journalist with a different kind of war to report.

* * *

12   The rehabilitation wing, where I am, is nominally separate from the long-term nursing wings, where the permanent residents are, and the secured unit, where

many of the Alzheimer's patients reside. But the borders leak. Almost every day some confused stranger wanders into my room. Negotiation seldom works, so I use my wheelchair to bar the door against intruders. Some of our crowd, too, are temporarily unhinged because of head injuries, drugs, who knows what. We are not tolerant of the people we think are crazier than we are.

13   Here, doctors are the ultimate authority of irreversible destiny. They are also rarely seen. My medical care is usually supervised by physician assistants. Medicare calls them physician extenders—an odd term—sounds like Hamburger Helper. To my pleasant surprise, the day-to-day authorities—the nurses—are good, helpful people who generally respect my 35 years of experience with spinal cord injury.

14   Every night an aide gives me a bed bath. Aides are at the bottom of the pay scale—the grunt labor, the lifters, the bathers, the meal servers, the toileters, the people who spend the most time with residents. They're the glue that holds this place together. Most are men in their late teens or 20s, people who can take the hard work and want the long shifts. Some work four 16-hour shifts a week and hold down a McJob besides. Racially and culturally they're an accurate sampling of modern America. A couple have college degrees, some are headed for nursing school or taking business courses, one has EMT[1] credentials. Some look like angels and some like hard cases, but none look as if they'd relish bathing a 67-year-old paralyzed man with Holocaust legs, bilateral toe amputations, and multiple rearrangements of his personal plumbing. Some of them look as sensitive as rocks.

15   I fear exposing myself to these men. I think how I would have hung back from such work at their age, but they show no resentment. They take the time required and attend to the task with something approaching good cheer, even tenderness. They tell me about their lives as they bathe my body, and I am touched.

* * *

16   For 35 years riding a wheelchair has been a distinguishing mark of my identity. In the group photos the wheelchair is what makes me easy to spot. Not here. Here my persona is preempted by all these stupendously old women—there are very few men in the long-term care sections—who create gridlock in the dining room and accidentally lock wheels passing one another in the halls. Practically everyone's in a wheelchair, but I'm the only one not new to wheels.

"Wheelchairs are engines of liberation to me."

17   Wheelchairs are engines of liberation to me. They enable me to go where I want when I want. This place reminds me why nondisabled people think they are tragic. In the custodial sections residents are propped up and seat-belted in their chairs, left with nothing to do but the impossible task of getting comfortable on old, unupholstered bones. Their heads hang down and they wait, their chairs no more than movable restraints.

18   Some residents still move themselves. Heading back to their rooms after meals in the big dining room, they run out of stamina and stop in their lanes, toy racecars

---

[1]EMT stands for "emergency medical technician." EMTs staff ambulances.

whose batteries have run down. For others the bid for locomotion is Sisyphean labor. Heads bent forward, they strain to gain a few yards. Then tragedy: somebody whisks them away to wherever they came from. There is usually a bright announcement of the staffer's intention, "Hi, Maria, let's go back to your room," but no request for permission.

19   The diminutives! The endearments! The idiotic *we*'s. Hello, dear how are we today? What's your name, dear? Eve? Shall we go to the dining room, Eve? Hi, hon, sorry to take so long. Don't we look nice today! You've got to eat, sweetie. Sweetie, would you take a pill for me? A little prune juice, sweetie? Chirpy singsong voices. Who thinks we want to be talked to this way?

20   The ceaseless din of television sets and alarms. So many people with so little to do. The constant pill pushing. The nighttime visits by aides: the peremptory bang on the door, the room suddenly flooded by light, like a drug raid. The unending need to educate. My safety depends on the staff's knowing the arcana of how to handle my body and its odd attachments, but each shift brings new helpers to teach.

21   The errors. I normally do my own monthly catheter change; I'm more immune to my bugs than to other people's, and the years have given me more experience than most nurses ever get. I can't do it one-handed, so I consent to a nurse's changing it. Trouble. They don't have the right size catheter. The nurse wants to install a different one, then replace it in a couple of days. Not a chance: major infection risk. Two days later the correct catheter arrives. Nurse Anita changes it efficiently and expertly. She once worked in a urologist's office. Sometimes I worry too much.

22   Or maybe not. There are repeated staff errors with my medication, even though I myself administer all my medications but one. It's easy for me to spot the errors, but what about all the residents who have no idea what they're taking?

23   The nursing home schedules any necessary doctor appointments, and I am supposed to get my sutures removed two weeks postsurgery. The day before the date specified by the surgeon, I ask a nurse if everything's arranged. "I made an appointment," she says. But she delegated the job, so she has to check. She comes back. "The appointment isn't until October 2." That's a week late. She doesn't know why it shook out that way. It's scheduled. Can't change what's scheduled. I consider accepting what is given, but instead I make my own phone call and reschedule the appointment for the next day. A small rebellion, which I am able to pull off because, with access to my own adapted van, I am not dependent on the home to get me there.

> "There are repeated staff errors with my medication."

24   That night, Squawk Lady calls for help. I've never seen her, but she's a constant aural presence with her amplified communication device. It's loud, and she can and does crank it louder. Squawk Lady is not happy with her circumstances. Now she wants to get out of her room; often it's something else she needs. "Help! Help! Help! Help! Help!" she cries. It's piercing, unvarying, insistent, like a baby bird crying for food. It's hard to ignore and hard to listen to, and it's not her fault. I feel terrible calling her Squawk Lady.

25　One day Squawk Lady falls silent. I miss her protests.

* * *

26　Overheard, a man: "Oh, for Christ's sake. I'm going home right now!" Another man: "Goddamn it! Get out of my room." Yet another, calling forlornly for his absent daughter: "Allie! Allie!" Then, scolding: "Allie!"

27　Overheard, a male aide addressing Emma, a tall, elegant woman who came into my room a day or two ago: "Oh, hi, sweetheart, let's get you back to your room."

28　"No! I'm going to get something to eat!"

29　"Come on, sweetheart, you can't be walking around like that. Let's go back to the room."

30　"I said no! No!"

31　The next morning Emma wants to walk, and she doesn't want to discuss it with the devil's instruments, the aides. Emma is wired for altitude. If she starts to stand, an ear-piercing alarm sounds and aides immediately appear. When she really wants to stand, her alarm is a constant din. "Emma, honey, you've got to sit down."

32　"I said no! Goddamn it! Get your hands off me!"

33　"Then stop hitting us."

34　Patiently: "The doctor says you can't stand up. He doesn't want you to break your hip."

35　"Bulls—!" says Emma. "Bulls—!" Emma is not cowed by medical authority.

36　She sits, but a moment later her alarm is sounding. Soon it becomes evident from her creative cursing that she has been restrained in a wheelchair. At the desk outside my door the nurses discuss Haldol. The drug is administered. Emma is quiet. At breakfast Emma and her Haldol are subjects of discussion; everybody seems to know about it. After breakfast I see her nodding in the wheelchair near the front desk. She's there all morning, for convenient watching from the desk, but it's cruel nonetheless—she's on display, visible proof that in the nursing home you can't fight city hall.

37　After lunch Emma is banging her feet on her footrest and asking to get out of her wheelchair. After lunch there is a full-court press to search the food trays. Mrs. Parker has lost her dentures. After lunch an aide tells me that on days like this, all you can do is laugh. By midafternoon Emma is screaming for someone to come to her room. "Get me out of this goddamn thing." Then, perhaps as a ploy, "I've got to go to the bathroom." She's weeping now, and it's heartbreaking. "I've got to go to the bathroom. I've got to go to the bathroom."

38　Emma's neighbor, Henry, is a usually polite, sometimes violent man who always says hello and apologizes if his wheelchair is in anyone's way. He has an alarm that sounds when he leaves the premises. He has escaped twice today, but he moves so slowly that he's easy to retrieve. A few minutes later he's trundling out the door again, answering freedom's call.

39　By now Emma has made it to the hallway in her wheelchair. The nurse recruits Bea, another resident, to visit with Emma. "Bea, would you talk to this lady while I check on another patient? Emma, this is Bea. Would you like to visit with her for a while?"

40   "I most certainly would," says Emma, her dignity restored. A perfectly rational conversation ensues and continues until dinnertime.

41   I wish today were an anomaly, but it isn't. As the days go by, there are reenactments. Emma is asleep up by the front desk almost every morning and, not surprisingly, fights with the aides who want to put her to bed right after dinner. Henry grabs an aide's arm and scares her enough that she sits sobbing at the front desk.

* * *

42   Food arrives at 8:00 A.M., noon, and 5:00 P.M. every day, each tray a study in gray, brown, and white, with accents of shocking pink—pink sugar water, pink gelatin, marshmallows bled on by other pinks. For my first ten days all meals arrive cold. The steam table isn't working. When hot food does start coming, it's manna from heaven, and it's still punishment. On a scale of bad to very bad, breakfast is the nursing home's best meal. I eat it in the small dining area near the rehab section. We're too good for the main dining room, used by the permanent residents in the long-term wings. After all, the rehab residents' median age is only about 75. We're scared to death someone will think we're old enough to actually be living here.

43   Bob, a recent amputee whose manner is far beyond sardonic, invariably claims the high ground next to the microwave. He has the place sized up, has already visited the kitchen for coffee. When I first join his group, Bob turns from his newspaper and mutters his form of welcome: "We're not very friendly." Ward, a chemist who has diabetes and a heart condition, usually sits at this table, as does Peggy, who is recovering from a fall from her roof. She has appointed herself the den mother of grumpy old men, the upholder of conversation, but it's an uphill battle. I haven't learned why Don is here.

> "We're scared to death someone will think we're old enough to actually be living here."

He has eczema, which makes him scratch his face and bat at his head with both hands like a Dick Tracy[2] villain: Fly Face! Carbuncle! Scratch! He's clearly miserable. We watch his health fail day to day.

44   We don't have much in common, but we don't need much to set ourselves apart. At the other two tables sit the older women and the people with cognitive problems. We've established a pecking order and seldom break ranks. The room is small, and we all use wheelchairs. With most of us pushed, not self-propelled, negotiating a workable seating arrangement is pure silliness and confusion. Wheelchairs are yanked and slid into place. Push rims and footrests clash. Portable oxygen tanks fall to the floor. When someone on the inside—always the inside—wants to leave, there's another round, an exaggerated version of the kid on his way to the bathroom making everyone in a theater row rise.

45   Today I sit with the ladies. It's not by choice or epiphany; some upstart has taken my place at the head table. Sitting at my new table is Phyllis, who is very old and has diabetes. "I control it," she says as she pours sugar into her coffee. "I don't eat the things I'm not supposed to." She sugars her porridge. "It doesn't give me a bit

---

[2]Dick Tracy is a detective who was the main character of a comic strip of the same name, written by Chester Gould from 1931 to 1977.

of trouble." She pockets packets of sugar to take to her room. Emma is back with us today. There's something impish about her smile that's winning. You can tell she wants to say funny things for us, and occasionally she does. She pours melted butter over her scrambled eggs, and dips her cinnamon roll in hot-pink sugar water.

46   Lana completes our foursome. She broke her hip three weeks ago. "Where are you going today?" Peggy asks Lana from the head table.

47   "I'm not going anywhere," says Lana.

48   "But you're all dressed up."

49   Lana has presence. "Well, if I do go somewhere, I'll be ready."

50   As the weeks go by, Ward goes home and our group is filled out by Tom, short for Thomasina, an energetic octogenarian who is all country talk and smart humor. Tom has a problem. She can't continue to live at her assisted-living facility, which she likes, unless she stops falling down unpredictably. If she can't find a fix, her known options are moving permanently to a nursing home, nothing else. She's brave in the face of this injustice and uncertainty, but also scared. After she joins our rehab group, our breakfast club has genuine cohesion. Everyone loves Tom.

* * *

51   Outside my room Emma dozes. Finally she starts to wheel into my room. "Emma," I say, "do you have the wrong room?" She recognizes me and backs out with the most comical "silly me" gesture imaginable. Her grace has made it a charmed communication. Sedation robs grace. Soon she's asleep in her wheelchair, then awake again, saying that her back hurts. She calls for someone to take her to her room, her voice weak and desperate. She asks a passing aide. "Not now," the aide says, with no reason, no indication of when.

52   There is coercion here, both subtle and obvious. Even in the rehab wing several people are kept in physical restraints. There are no ropes or handcuffs; for frail people in wheelchairs an immovable lap tray is restraint enough. Combined with the infernal alarms, these restraints are effective and very public. Chemical restraints (drugs) are also common. Emma's not nodding at the front desk for her health. She's there for the convenience of the staff. Henry nods right next to her.

53   In my private room I pull up the Medicare rules on the Internet. I learn that nursing home residents are guaranteed "the right to be free from seclusion and physical restraints, as well as chemical restraints with psychoactive drugs, for any reason other than the treatment of a medical condition." But what is a medical condition? Mending bones would seem to qualify. Does disorientation? Pure orneriness? As always, the devil is in the details.

> "Even in the rehab wing several people are kept in physical restraints."

54   In the broader sense, though, restraint is a constant condition for all of us here. It's not force majeure,[3] not even staff obstinacy; it's conditioning, habit, insistent reminding that this is how we do things. We know how things go smoothly. Smoothness is greatly admired here. But when smooth operation is the paramount goal, subjugation follows. It's built into the institutional model.

---

[3]Force majeure means "superior force."

55 It's time to talk discharge, says a social worker employed by the nursing home. Medicare pays for acute care, and at the moment I seem to be chronic. She proposes discharge in one week. It's up to me, not Medicare, to find some way to live—alone, with one working limb. Of course, they're not kicking me out. I am reminded that I can self-pay $150 a day and stay indefinitely. Not an option.

56 I've become increasingly functional once I'm up in my chair, but I still need help at the beginning and end of every day. I'll need a team of helpers to cover those times and to provide backup against no-shows. I don't want to end up spending the night in my wheelchair waiting for an aide who doesn't come. It is my responsibility to find these people.

57 The quest starts badly. I'm referred to Mary, a woman in her 60s who says she gives the best bed baths in the world and that both she and God love me. Mary has two partners, and she's sure I'll just love "the girls," as she calls them. I imagine myself as an imprisoned companion to these three women. God help me. The girls charge $15 an hour and want uninterrupted eight-hour shifts. Even so, I arrange to meet Mary right after church. The night before, she calls; the girls don't want to risk the steep road to my home in the foothills. I feel delivered. Other candidates want a job different from the one I have to offer. After a week of cold-calling and dead-end leads, my luck improves. Lourdes wants only a few hours a day, a few days a week. Eva wants the same.

58 Two days before I go, the Breakfast Club has changed again. Bob is walking with his new prosthesis and is itching to get out. Peggy is walking on her own and will go home two days after me. Don has been ominously absent, and Tom is losing her options. Meanwhile, the rehab wing has an influx of new residents. All these new faces, and our club's table has been usurped by perfect strangers. Pretenders! A palace putsch[4]! Yes, it's time to leave.

59 This place has given me what I needed this fall as the days grew short and the nights grew long—a safe place for the minimal therapy and substantial help needed while my shoulder heals. When I go outside, which I do several times a day, it's no hardship to come back in. After seven weeks the nursing home has lost its terrors. That's an easy statement to make knowing that I'm just about to leave.

60 The residents, myself included, are all here because we need care, temporarily or permanently. But that does not mean we need institutional care. If Medicare and Medicaid were willing to spend more on in-home help, wouldn't it keep us more active in the world, prevent unnecessary dependency, and save the taxpayers money? Since 1999's Supreme Court decision in *Olmstead v. L.C.* the law has recognized that disability services should be in the "most integrated setting." Yet the distribution of federal money continues to remain heavily biased in favor of institutional services. For many the nursing home is the only option.

61 What if I had to spend the rest of my life here? What if I had to live, as so many do, without any hope of release, without the unusual freedom of movement I have enjoyed roaming outdoors in my power chair and in cyberspace in my private room? What if I were trapped with this mindset that teaches all of us to tolerate endless cries for help, this unchanging gray existence, this total surround of

---

[4]Putsch is a sudden attempt by a group to overthrow a government.

people hoping for escape or waiting to die? If this happens, I see myself slipping away into passivity and dependency—better, I think, than cycling between obstreperousness and chemical restraint. The thought is unbearable. Utterly, unalterably unbearable. It shouldn't happen to anybody.

On Top of the World: Barry with Granddaughter Giulia and Paco the Dog in 1997.

READING CLOSELY AND THINKING CRITICALLY

1. What resources do disabled people need in order to live at home? What happens to them if they lack those resources?

2. Corbet's description of the nursing home is primarily negative, but he does include some positive aspects as well. What are the chief benefits and drawbacks for him of being in a nursing home? Do you think the benefits outweigh the drawbacks? Explain.

3. According to Corbet, nursing home residents are often restrained, either physically or chemically. Why are patients restrained? Are the restraints appropriate?

4. Corbet describes mealtime in several paragraphs. What does that description convey about life in a rehabilitation wing of a nursing home?

5. Write a list of words and phrases to describe Corbet's personality.

6. What did you learn about nursing homes and paralysis that you did not know before reading the essay?

EXAMINING STRUCTURE AND STRATEGY

1. Give examples of Corbet's use of objective description and of expressive description. Which does he use more? Why?

2. Give an example of a description that appeals to the sense of smell. Give two examples of descriptions that appeal to the sense of sound. How do these appeals to smell and sound help Corbet achieve his purpose for writing?

3. Of what is Corbet trying to convince his reader? Where does the author's persuasive purpose become apparent? Why does he wait so long to make his persuasive point?

4. Why does the author make clear, especially in paragraph 3, how independent he was prior to his shoulder surgery?

5. Cite three descriptions that you find the most informative. What do you learn from them?

NOTING COMBINED PATTERNS

1. What narration does Corbett include in his essay? How does that narration help him achieve his writing purpose?

2. Paragraphs 21, 26–37, and 38 include examples. What purpose do these examples serve?

CONSIDERING LANGUAGE AND STYLE

1. In paragraph 19, Corbet notes that the nursing home staff refers to residents with "idiotic we's" and terms such as "dear," "hon," and "sweetie." What is the significance of this language? How do you think residents react to it?

2. What similes appear in paragraphs 20 and 24? What metaphors appear in paragraphs 11, 12, and 14? (See page 128 on similes and metaphors.)

3. Consult a dictionary if you are unsure of the meaning of these words: *Sisyphean* (paragraph 18), *arcana* (paragraph 20), *anomaly* (paragraph 41), *sardonic* (paragraph 43), *epiphany* (paragraph 45).

FOR DISCUSSION IN CLASS OR ONLINE

Answer one or more of the questions raised in paragraph 61.

WRITING ASSIGNMENTS

1. **Writing in your journal.** Assume you have accepted a job as an aide in a nursing home on weekends and after school in order to help pay your college tuition. Do you think you will like the job? What do you think will be the primary challenges and rewards of the work?

2. **Using description for a purpose.** The purposes given in the assignments are possibilities. You may establish whatever purposes you like, within your instructor's guidelines.
   - In paragraph 16, Corbet says that "riding a wheelchair has been a distinguishing mark of [my] identity." To relate your experience and express your feelings, describe a distinguishing mark of your identity.
   - If you have had to use crutches or a wheelchair, or wear a brace or a cast, describe the experience to inform readers of what that experience is like. You can also argue for specific changes to accommodate those on crutches, in a wheelchair, or wearing a cast or brace.
   - If you have been in the hospital, had surgery, or experienced a difficult illness, describe your experience to inform readers of what it was like.

3. **Combining patterns.** Part of Corbet's essay discusses how he coped with his disability. If there is difficulty in your life that you must cope with, such as an illness, a learning disability, stress, or money problems, describe the difficulty and give examples of how you cope with it.

4. **Analyzing and assessing.** Identify the strategies Corbet uses to achieve his persuasive purpose, and assess how effective those strategies are. Is there anything he could have done to be more persuasive?

5. **Connecting and synthesizing the readings.** Discuss our society's perception of aging. Is the perception an appropriate one? For ideas, you can draw on portrayals of aging in the media, "Embedded," and "Once More to the Lake" (page 691.)

6. **Drawing on sources.** As the baby boomers age, our society will have more elderly than ever before. Prepare a report that explains one or more needs this aging population will have and what can be done to meet those needs. Be sure your suggestions are in compliance with *Olmstead v. L.C.* (paragraph 60), which you can learn about at the *Olmstead v. L.C.* Online Resource Center at www.bazelon.org/issues/disabilityrights/incourt/olmstead/index.htm.

BACKGROUND: Regents Professor of English at Arizona State University, Alberto Riós was born in 1952 to a Guatemalan father and an English mother. He grew up in Nogales, Arizona, on the Mexican border. The winner of many writing awards, including the prestigious Walt Whitman Award of the Academy of American Poets, the Western States Book Award, and the PEN Award, Riós received a BA from the University of Arizona in 1974 and an MFA in creative writing from the same institution in 1979. His many books include *The Lime Orchard Woman: Poems* (1988), *Pig Cookies and Other Stories* (1995), *The Curtain of Trees: Stories* (1999), *Capirotada: A Nogales Memoir* (1999), *Smallest Muscle in the Human Body* (2002), and *the Dangerous Shirt* (2009). His poetry has been set to music, and he has been featured in the documentary *Birthwrite: Growing Up Hispanic.* "The Vietnam Wall" was first published in *The Lime Orchard Woman.*

COMBINED PATTERNS AND THEIR PURPOSE: In "The Vietnam Wall," Alberto Riós *describes* the Vietnam Veterans Memorial in Washington, D.C., and **expresses** his reaction to it. As only a poet can, Riós evokes images of deceptive simplicity, creating vivid mental pictures with only a few descriptive words. You may be struck by the clarity of the images, particularly those created by Riós's similes and metaphors. As the poem approaches its conclusion, note the use of *contrast* to underscore the mood around the memorial.

Vietnam Veterans Memorial

The Vietnam Wall

BY ALBERTO RIÓS

As you read
Look at the picture on page 175, and write down your impressions of the Vietnam Veterans Memorial.

I
Have seen it
And I like it: The magic,
The way like cutting onions
It brings water out of nowhere. 5
Invisible from one side, a scar
Into the skin of the ground
From the other, a black winding
Appendix line.
    A dig. 10
    An archaeologist can explain.
The walk is slow at first Easy, a little black marble wall
Of a dollhouse,
A smoothness, a shine 15
The boys in the street want to give.
One name. And then more
Names, long lines, lines of names until
They are the shape of the U.N. building
Taller than I am: I have walked 20
Into a grave.
And everything I expect has been taken away, like that, quick:
    The names are not alphabetized.
    They are in the order of dying,
    An alphabet of—somewhere—screaming. 25
I start to walk out. I almost leave
But stop to look up names of friends,
My own name. There is somebody
Severiano Riós.
Little kids do not make the same noise 30
Here, junior high school boys don't run
Or hold each other in headlocks.
No rules, something just persists
Like pinching on St. Patrick's Day
Every year for no green. 35
    No one knows why.
Flowers are forced
Into the cracks
Between sections.
Men have cried 40
At this wall.
I have
Seen them.

CONSIDERING THE POEM

1. What magic is associated with the Vietnam Wall?
2. What effect does the wall have on children? Why does it have that effect?
3. What dominant impression does the description convey?
4. Ríos describes the wall as "a scar/Into the skin of the ground." Why do you think he uses this metaphor? What other similes and metaphors does he use?
5. What element of contrast appears in the poem? How does that contrast help Ríos achieve his purpose?

WRITING ASSIGNMENTS

1. **Writing in your journal.**
   - Record your reaction to "The Vietnam Wall." Why do you react the way you do?
   - Just to see what happens, write a draft of a poem about a place that stirs emotion in you or others.

2. **Using description for a purpose.** To relate your experience and express your feelings, describe a monument, shrine, gravesite, or tourist attraction you have visited. Your dominant impression should be the mood the place creates. If you prefer, your purpose can be to persuade readers to visit the site. The purposes in the assignment are a possibility. You may establish whatever purpose you like, within your instructor's guidelines.

3. **Drawing on sources.** Ask three people who have visited the Vietnam Veterans Memorial to read the poem and comment on their reaction to it. (If you have visited the wall, you can be one of those people.) Then ask three people who have not visited the wall to do the same. Is a reader's reaction to the poem affected by whether he or she has visited the memorial? Write your findings and any conclusions you draw from them.

WRITING DESCRIPTION

See pages 131–132 for strategies for writing description and for a revising checklist.

1. Describe a place you go to relax—a park, a spot on campus, the gym, or the zoo, for example. Try to convey why the place helps you unwind.

2. Describe a favorite nightspot, someplace people go to have fun. Try to convey the sense that people are enjoying themselves.

3. Describe a view from a window, using expressive detail to convey a dominant impression.

4. Describe a store where you frequently shop, using objective detail to convey to what extent the store's features meet the needs of its customers.

5. Describe a place where you enjoy spending leisure time—a bowling alley, the student union, a shopping mall, a porch, a theater, or a basketball court, for example. Use expressive detail to convey why the place appeals to you.

6. Describe the room you liked best in the house you grew up in. Your dominant impression will be how the room made you feel.

7. Describe a place during a holiday celebration. For example, you could describe your parents' dining room at Thanksgiving, Main Street during the Christmas season, or a city park on Independence Day.

8. Describe your favorite vacation spot, using expressive detail to convey why you enjoy this place.

9. Describe a winter scene, a fall scene, a spring scene, or a summer scene.

10. Describe one of your classrooms. Try to convey whether the room is conducive to learning.

11. Describe your bedroom. Use expressive detail to reveal what the bedroom says about you.

12. Describe a room after a party has been held there.

13. Describe the place where you work to show whether your work environment is pleasant.

14. Describe part of an amusement park.

15. Describe your favorite restaurant to persuade other people to try it.

16. Describe the neighborhood you grew up in to share a portion of your past with your reader.

17. Describe a scene at a sporting event.

18. Describe a rock concert for someone who has never been to one.

19. Describe a painting or sculpture you enjoy.

20. **Description in context:** Assume that you are a student employee in your campus admissions office. As part of the recruiting efforts, the director of admissions is putting together a large, glossy brochure that presents information about the school. You have been asked to contribute to the brochure by photographing a favorite campus spot and writing a description of it. Visit a suitable spot, decide on a dominant impression, and develop your description. Keep in mind that your purpose is to present the campus in a positive light so that potential students will want to attend your school.

RESPONDING TO AN IMAGE

You have learned that a descriptive essay often conveys a dominant impression. Visual images also convey impressions. Consider the Great Seal of the United States, which is reproduced here. What impressions of the United States does the seal convey? Is the seal a good symbol for the country? Why or why not?

Narration

Stories can be lots of fun. To have some fun, let your imagination fly, and think up a story that explains what led up to the event depicted in the picture on the opposite page.

THE PATTERN

Everyone likes a good story. We go to movies for good stories, we read stories, and we gravitate toward people who tell good stories. We read stories to our children before they go to sleep, and we tell stories to our friends when we meet them on a street corner. Another name for a story is a **narration,** and this chapter will discuss writing effective narration.

USING NARRATION FOR A PURPOSE

Obviously, narration can *entertain* because a good story can amuse readers and help them forget about themselves for a time. Romance novels and detective fiction are two popular types of stories that provide escapist entertainment. Narration can do more than entertain, however. Suppose that for many years you visited your grandfather at a retirement home, and as a result, you learned much about such facilities.

A narration of a typical day you spent with your grandfather could serve various purposes. Through such a narration, you could *express your feelings* about retirement homes and *relate your experience* with them, telling how the events of the day made you feel. You could use your narration to *inform* readers about the benefits of retirement homes, pointing out the advantages your grandfather enjoyed because he lived in the retirement home. You could *persuade* readers to volunteer at a retirement home, focusing your narration on the experiences of volunteers and the benefits to your grandfather and other residents.

Combining Patterns for a Purpose

To achieve your writing purpose, you can combine narration with one or more other patterns of development. For example, if you are narrating the story of your disastrous first day at Burger Village to *entertain* and *inform* your reader, you can *describe* your angry boss to bring him to life, or you can *describe* the confusing kitchen to put your reader at the scene. If you are narrating an account of what happened when your sister ran away *to relate experience,* you can include *cause-and-effect analysis* to note the effects of the event on your family. For a narration about the time you went skydiving, to *express feelings,* you can include a *definition* of fear.

To see how other patterns can be combined with narration, study the following excerpt from "Stripping Away Free Expression," a narrative essay in this chapter about a woman who opened a studio to teach pole dancing. Included in the narration is cause-and-effect analysis, which gives the reasons for some of the events narrated.

EXCERPT FROM "STRIPPING AWAY FREE EXPRESSION" COMBINING NARRATION AND CAUSE-AND-EFFECT ANALYSIS

This is the first event.

Narration tells the story of Babines learning pole dancing. Cause-and-effect analysis gives the reason Babines did not go to the gym.

A few years ago Babines was a senior executive at a financial services company, nary a feather boa dancing in her head, struggling with an 80-hour workweek that severely depleted her enthusiasm for the gymnasium. One night

This happened second.

Cause-and-effect analysis gives the reason Babines bought a pole.

over dinner a friend mentioned that pole dancing had become the hot new fitness trend. On a whim Babines

Cause-and-effect analysis explains what happened when Babines used the pole.

This happened third.

purchased a pole online. "I thought it would be something silly to laugh about with my friends," she says, "until I

This happened fourth.

started losing weight like crazy and fitting into cute jeans."

Cause-and-effect analysis gives the reason Babines went to Las Vegas.

With the fire of a convert burning in her rapidly

This happened fifth.

shrinking belly, Babines took a pilgrimage to the Las

Vegas studio of fitness pole dancing's grand doyen,

Fawnia Mondey, known more for her work in the instruc-

tional DVD *Strip To It: Bump n' Grind* than for her

appearances in such postapocalyptic feature films as

Cause-and-effect analysis explains what happened when Babines went to Las Vegas.

White Slave Lovers and *Forbidden Rage: White Slave Secrets.*

This happened sixth.

Babines returned home as the first Pennsylvanian to hold

one of Mondey's pole dance instructor certificates, signi-

fying mastery of more than 60 moves and routines as well

as basic first aid, should it ever be necessary to treat a cli-

ent for excessive gyration.

A brief narration, called an **anecdote,** is often a secondary pattern in essays developed primarily with patterns other than narration. For example, in an essay that gives *examples* of your mother's courage, you can include a harrowing anecdote about the time she fended off an attack by a mugger. A *comparison-contrast* that notes the differences between two mayoral candidates can include a telling anecdote about the time you met both candidates at a school board meeting. A *process analysis* that explains how to surf can tell the story of the time you broke your leg because you failed to follow a procedure given in the essay.

Remember, whether you use a pattern alone or in combination depends on what helps you achieve your particular writing purpose for your particular audience.

www.mhhe.com/clousepatterns6	Narration

For more help with narration, click on
Writing > Paragraph Patterns
Writing > Writing Tutor: Narration

Narration beyond the Writing Classroom

Narration helps writers achieve their purpose in many writing situations.

IN ACADEMIC WRITING AND READING   Narration is important in many kinds of college writing. For instance, a history paper on the events leading up to the Holocaust could tell the story of "The Night of the Broken Glass," when Jewish homes and businesses in Nazi Germany were looted and destroyed. A political science paper could narrate an account of the events and controversy following the close presidential election of 2000. In writing courses, students relate their personal experiences, and in journalism classes, students write newspaper-style accounts of current events or campus happenings.

Brief narrations, or anecdotes, are particularly useful for illustrating a point. If you write a paper for an education class that argues that people with learning disabilities do not get appropriate support in the classroom, you might tell the story of the time a learning-disabled friend was ignored in a high school algebra class. If you write a paper for a criminal justice class that argues that judges should give out harsher penalties, you could support your point by telling the story of an offender who was repeatedly released, only to commit more crimes.

Narration is a frequent component of textbooks in most disciplines. Here, for example, from an introductory psychology text is an excerpt that focuses on sleep and dreams:

The narration illustrates a kind of sleep disturbance and how serious its consequences can be.

The narration also creates interest in the discussion to come. Notice how dialogue and description help create that interest.

The crowd roared as running back Donald Dorff, age 67, took the pitch from his quarterback and accelerated smoothly across the artificial turf. As Dorff braked and pivoted to cut back over a tackle, a huge defensive lineman loomed in his path. One hundred twenty pounds of pluck, Dorff did not hesitate. But let the retired grocery merchandiser from Golden Valley, Minnesota, tell it:

"There was a 280-pound tackle waiting for me, so I decided to give him my shoulder. When I came to, I was on the floor in my bedroom. I had smashed into the dresser and knocked everything off it and broke the mirror and just made one heck of a mess. It was 1:30 A.M." (Long, 1987, p. 787)

Dorff, it turned out, was suffering from a rare condition afflicting some older men. The problem occurs when the mechanism that usually shuts down bodily movement during dreams does not function properly. People suffering from the malady have been known to hit others, smash windows, punch holes in walls — all while fast asleep. (Feldman, *Understanding Psychology*)

AT WORK AND IN THE COMMUNITY   Narration is also a component of workplace writing. For example, police officers write crime reports, and insurance investigators write accident reports, both of which narrate sequences of events. Physical therapists and nurses write narrative accounts of their patients' progress, and teachers narrate events for disciplinary reports. Supervisors write narrative accounts of employees' actions for individual personnel files, and company officials use narration to report to stockholders on the company's performance during the fiscal year.

Outside school and work, you already use narration often and will continue to do so. You may narrate events in your life in letters and e-mail to friends and in your blog or journal entries. If you are a recording secretary for an organization, you will write narrative minutes of meetings. If you write to a company to complain about a pair of shoes that wore out prematurely, you could narrate an account of what happened when you wore the shoes to work. If you are speaking at a dinner honoring a friend, you could illustrate that friend's kindness with an anecdote about the time she helped a stranger search for his lost dog.

SUPPORTING DETAILS

Your narration should make a point and have a purpose. Be sure to choose supporting details that convey your point and purpose, or you may go off on a narrative tangent, which will cause your readers to scratch their heads and wonder why they are reading your essay. Suppose you are narrating an account of being accused of shoplifting at the mall. If your point is that sales personnel accused you because you appeared to be poor, and your purpose is to inform your reader that salespeople are biased against the poor, you could emphasize aspects of your appearance that might have led the salespeople to conclude you were poor. However, if your point is that you suffered public humiliation, and your purpose is to relate an experience and express your feelings, then you may want to emphasize your appearance less and focus more on the people who stared at you when you were stopped and accused.

A narration usually includes the answers to the **journalist's questions** — *who? what? when? where? why?* and *how?* The narration explains *who* was involved, *what* happened, *when* it happened, *where* it happened, *why* it happened, and *how* it happened. Of course, you may not need to include the answers to each of these questions in every narration, but they are good starting points for generating ideas. Also, you might emphasize different answers in different narrations. In some stories, you might pay more attention to *who* was involved, but in others, you might consider *when* the event happened more significant and treat the time element in more detail. To decide which journalist's questions to emphasize, consider the point of your narration and your purpose.

www.mhhe.com/clousepatterns6	Supporting Details

For more help with supporting details, click on
Writing > Prewriting > Use Five Methods

Narration often includes descriptive detail that supports the answers being emphasized. When a person's appearance is important to the story, that person will be described; when locale or scene is important, a place will be described. For example, in "The Lottery," (page 199), Chris Abani uses description to convey detail about people and scene:

> Suddenly a lone voice screamed one word over and over: "Thief! Thief!" It was picked up slowly, as if the drizzle that afternoon had dampened the scent of blood. My aunt froze and faced the sound, nose sniffing the air like a lioness sensing prey. A man's voice, tired and breathless, tried to counter the rising chant with a feeble retort: "It's a lie! It's a lie!"

Descriptive words should be specific as discussed on page 126.

If your reader needs additional information to appreciate the story, you can provide background information or an explanation. For example, in "Salvation" (page 203), the author provides this explanation to help the reader understand why he was in church the night the story takes place:

> There was a big revival at my Auntie Reed's church. Every night for weeks there had been much preaching, singing, praying, and shouting, and some very hardened sinners had been brought to Christ, and the membership of the church had grown by leaps and bounds. Then just before the revival ended, they held a special meeting for children, "to bring the young lambs to the fold." My aunt spoke of it for days ahead. That night, I was escorted to the front row and placed on the mourner's bench with all other young sinners, who had not yet been brought to Jesus.

Writing Dialogue

Dialogue can advance the story and make it more vivid. To appreciate what dialogue can add, consider the difference between these sentences; the first one was taken from "Salvation."

> "Langston," my aunt sobbed. "Langston, why don't you come? Why don't you come and be saved? Oh, Lamb of God! Why don't you come?"

> Sobbing, my aunt repeatedly asked me why, as a Lamb of God, I wouldn't come and be saved.

The dialogue makes the first version more lively, vivid, and interesting.

When you write dialogue, follow the conventions for capitalizing and punctuating **quotations,** a speaker's or writer's exact words. Many of the conventions for punctuating quotations are illustrated here, and you can use these examples as models. (Pay particular attention to the location of quotation marks, commas, periods, question marks, and capital letters.) For other situations, consult a writing handbook.

www.mhhe.com/clousepatterns6	Quotation Marks

For more help with quotation marks, click on
Editing > Quotation Marks

When the Quotation Comes before the Speaker or Writer Is Mentioned

1. "Most people overestimate their ability to handle threatening situations," the police officer explained.
2. "How will price controls affect foreign trade?" the senator asked.

When the Quotation Comes after the Speaker or Writer Is Mentioned

1. The police officer explained, "Most people overestimate their ability to handle threatening situations."
2. The senator asked, "How will price controls affect foreign trade?"
3. Do you believe the senator asked, "How will price controls affect foreign trade"? (*The entire sentence, not just the quoted words, forms a question.*)

When the Quotation Comes Both before and after the Speaker or Writer Is Mentioned

1. "Most people," the police officer explained, "overestimate their ability to handle threatening situations." (*The words that come before the speaker or writer is mentioned* do not *form a grammatically complete sentence.*)

Paragraphing and Dialogue

If you have trouble paragraphing to identify speakers when you write dialogue, keep this convention in mind: Begin a new paragraph each time a different person speaks. The paragraph indentation signals the change in speaker, as illustrated by this passage from "Reunion" (page 284):

> "Were you clapping your hands at me?" he asked.
> "Calm down, calm down, *sommelier*," my father said. "If it isn't too much to ask of you—if it wouldn't be too much above and beyond the call of duty, we would like a couple of Beefeater Gibsons."
> "I don't like to be clapped at," the waiter said.
> "I should have brought my whistle," my father said. "I have a whistle that is audible only to the ears of old waiters. Now, take out your little pad and your little pencil and see if you can get this straight: two Beefeater Gibsons. Repeat after me: two Beefeater Gibsons."
> "I think you'd better go somewhere else," the waiter said quietly.

If one person speaks for more than a paragraph, begin that speaker's new paragraphs with quotation marks, but use closing quotation marks at the end of the quotation only, not at the end of each paragraph.

2. "Most people overestimate their ability to handle threatening situations," the police officer explained. "They mistakenly believe they can talk themselves out of danger." (*The words that come before the speaker or writer is mentioned* do *form a grammatically complete sentence.*)

3. "Should online auctions be regulated," asked Delia, "or is the business sufficiently self-regulating?" (*The words that come before and after the speaker or writer is mentioned are two parts of a compound sentence.*)

ORGANIZING DETAILS

If you've ever listened to someone tell a story and drone on and on, you know the importance of selecting narrative details to avoid boring your reader with unnecessary information. Choose carefully which *who? what? when? where? why?* and *how?* questions to answer, and be careful not to include insignificant details or overemphasize minor points. In other words, a key to a successful narration is pacing.

One way to express the point of your narration is to place it in a thesis, such as the following:

> After my recent experience with a credit card company, I realize that college students should be cautious about accepting those bank cards they get in the mail. (*The narration is about the writer's experience with a credit card company, and the point is that students should be careful about accepting the credit cards that are mailed to them.*)

If a stated thesis will disturb the flow of your story, you can imply rather than state your thesis, but be sure that your details are strong enough that your reader can infer it. Another alternative is to state the thesis at the end of the narration, so it forms the conclusion of your essay. For example, in "Salvation" (page 203), Langston Hughes tells a story about attending a revival service when he was 12. He concludes his narration with a statement of the story's significance, which reads, in part,

> I didn't believe there was a Jesus any more, since he didn't come to help me.

Arranging narrative details usually involves placing the events in **chronological order**—beginning with the first event, moving to the second, the third, and so on. For some stories, you may want to begin at the end or in the middle, then shift back to the beginning, using **flashback.**

Suppose you want to narrate an account of a car accident you were involved in. You could put the events in chronological order, in which case you might begin like this:

> A year ago, I was on my way to pick up my girlfriend, looking forward to a pleasant dinner. As I approached the intersection at Fifth and Grove, the light turned yellow, but I figured I had plenty of time to slide through.

After this opening, you could narrate an account of the accident and then go on to tell about its aftermath.

You could also begin at the end and flash back to the beginning, like this:

> Walking out of my last physical therapy session, I thought about how remarkable it is that I can walk at all. An accident nine months earlier had left me in critical condition with a smashed pelvis.

From here, you could flash back to the beginning and narrate an account of the accident and all the events leading up to the time you walked out of your last physical therapy session.

You could also begin in the middle of the chronology, like this:

> I remember waking up in the hospital with my parents and sister at my side. Mom was crying and Dad looked worried. In an instant the pain overwhelmed me and I could not remember what happened. Then all at once I remembered the accident.

From this point in the middle, you could flash back to the beginning and narrate an account of the accident. You could then move chronologically through the events until you reached the last event, walking out of your final physical therapy session.

To signal chronological order, move smoothly through your time sequence, and help your reader follow the events in your narrative, you can use *transitions* such as the following:

after	later	the next day
at first	meanwhile	then
at the same time	next	
finally	second	
in the meantime	soon	

Because a time sequence, signaled by transitions, provides your narrative with a clear structure, your reader may not need the organizational signposts of topic sentences. For this reason, you may sometimes omit topic sentences.

VISUALIZING A NARRATIVE ESSAY

The chart on the next page 190 can help you visualize the structure for a narrative essay. Like all good models, however, this one can be altered as needed.

INTRODUCTION

- Creates interest in the story
- Can state the thesis (underlined as an example), indicating the point of the story

EXAMPLE

I can still see it clearly even after all these years: a bright, cheerful fourthgrade room filled with 30 eager children of all varieties of body and mind. I can also hear the music of John Philip Sousa. <u>To that music and in that classroom, I learned the unique skill of marching.</u>

↓

FIRST BODY PARAGRAPH

- Begins the story
- Answers the appropriate journalist's questions
- May include description
- May include background information or explanation
- May include dialogue
- Arranges details in chronological order; arrangement may include flashback

EXAMPLE

She played the Sousa marches every day, that staunch old woman. Miss Thompson was more matriarch than teacher. . . .

↓

NEXT BODY PARAGRAPHS

- Continue until the story is complete
- Answer the appropriate journalist's questions; may include description, background information or explanation, and dialogue
- Arrange details in chronological order; may include flashback

EXAMPLE

Every day through the small glass window of Room 11, the students of Miss Thompson could be seen marching around the room, knees up, heads back, chests out, marching to the music of "Stars and Stripes Forever." . . .

↓

CONCLUSION

- Provides a satisfying finish
- May state the point of the story if not done elsewhere

EXAMPLE

How I learned that year. I learned to respect the grace of a woman who had midmorning tea brewed in a cup with a strange heating coil. I learned that my back did feel better if I sat erect in my chair. And I learned to march—with my knees high, my head back, and my chest out—to John Philip Sousa's classic "Stars and Stripes Forever."

THINKING CRITICALLY ABOUT NARRATION

To think critically about the narrations you read and write, use what you learned in this chapter, as well as what you learned in Chapters 1 and 4 when you studied how to read critically and how to write critical analyses. In addition, ask the following questions to analyze and assess the narrations you read and write:

- **Is the story truth or fiction?** Fictional and hypothetical stories can serve an important purpose, but they should be readily recognized as such; they should not be passed off as true accounts. Further, true stories should not be embellished with made-up details.

- **Is the purpose of the narration hurtful?** The fact that a story *can* be told does not mean that it *should* be told. For example, the story of the time a friend lost his hairpiece in a windstorm may be wildly entertaining, but if the story is being told to embarrass the friend and not just to entertain, then it is hurtful.

- **Is the narration original?** Stories get passed around—told and retold—all the time. Anyone who retells a story should credit the source. The attribution can range from a simple "As my Auntie Mim tells the story . . ." to formal documentation as explained in Chapter 15.

PROCESS GUIDELINES:
STRATEGIES FOR WRITING NARRATION

1. **Selecting a topic.** Pick a story that you want to tell for a reason: to entertain, express feelings, relate experience, inform, or persuade.
2. **Establishing the point.** Write out a statement of your narration's point. You can use a version of this statement as your thesis or imply your point through your choice of details.
3. **Generating ideas.** List the answers to the *who? what? when? where? why?* and *how?* questions. Decide which of these answers should be emphasized, based on your audience and purpose. Also, identify important features of the people and scenes of your story.
4. **Drafting.** Concentrate on getting all the events down and answering all the appropriate journalist's questions. During revision, you can look at how effectively you ordered the events and told your story.
5. **Revising.** Consider whether flashback would be effective, and consider, too, whether adding dialogue to advance your story and description to make it more vivid. Does the narration make a readily identifiable point, supported by details? Read your draft aloud; if you hear any abrupt shifts, you may need to add transitions.

Avoiding Tense Shifts

If you have trouble maintaining tense in narration, edit carefully, because tense shifts can confuse your reader by distorting the time sequence. The most common tense shifts in narration occur when the writer moves between the past and the present tenses inappropriately.

INAPPROPRIATE TENSE SHIFT FROM PAST TO PRESENT	I **walked** into the classroom and **found** a seat in the back. As soon as I **sit** down, Luis **cracks** a joke.
CORRECTION	I **walked** into the classroom and **found** a seat in the back. As soon as I **sat** down, Luis **cracked** a joke.

When you write dialogue, moving between the past tense and present tense can be appropriate.

APPROPRIATE TENSE SHIFT FROM PAST TO PRESENT	Katrina **announced**, "I **am quitting** my job and joining the Peace Corps." She **said** this yesterday, but she **is** still at work today.

---

www.mhhe.com/clousepatterns6 [Tense Shift]

For more help with verb tense, click on

Editing > Verbs and Verbals

Using Sources for a Purpose

The paragraph below, which includes source material from "Ring Leader" on page 217, illustrates how to use sources from this book in your writing. The paragraph is the introduction for an essay, and the source material helps the writer achieve a particular writing purpose.

THESIS The media promotes an impossible standard of attractiveness.

WRITING PURPOSE AND AUDIENCE To make females aware that the media are promoting a standard of attractiveness that most women cannot achieve and to convince females that they should not let the media influence their body images.

The paraphrase and quotation in sentence 9 help the writer make the point that young girls who are very thin still think they are fat.

[1]Women have poor body images largely because of the media. [2]Anorexic waifs are videotaped sashaying down runways, and the film is shown on the nightly news between the political reports and the sports. [3]Superskinny models smile out from glossy magazine ads in publications from *Time* to *Seventeen*. [4]Yes, Oprah preaches on television that we should focus less on appearance and more on fitness, but her magazine is filled with ultrathin

women airbrushed to perfection. [5]Then there are the pitifully underweight celebrities on the covers of teen magazines and all over the supermarket tabloids—celebs who are glamorized, even though their elbows could be used as fondue forks. [6]In response to this media promotion of the ultrathin feminine form, manufacturers now offer clothing in size 0—size 0, for crying out loud! [7]It's no wonder normal-size women who wear size 8, 10, 12, or even 14 feel fat and unattractive. [8]And it's not just adult women who fret over their bodies. [9]In "Ring Leader," Natalie Kusz notes a disturbing phenomenon: Young girls who are so thin that they are "wispy and hollow-cheeked" stand in front of the locker room mirror and "announce, 'My God, I disgust myself, I am *so fat*'"; buying into this wrongheadedness, their classmates reassure the girls that they are, in fact, beautiful in all of their ultrathinness (218). [10]Clearly, no matter how skinny and young, females are cursed with self-loathing because the media promotes an impossible standard of attractiveness.

AVOIDING PLAGIARISM

The paragraph above, which includes paraphrase and quotation in sentence 9, illustrates the following points about avoiding plagiarism. (For more complete information on using source material, consult Chapters 4 and 15.)

- **Introduce the source of quotations and paraphrases.** As in sentence 9, you introduce the author and/or title of your source. (Notice that the introduction is in the present tense.) When the introduction is a complete sentence, follow it with a colon, as in sentence 9. (More standard introductions, such as "she says," "the author explains," or "one researcher has found that" do not require colons.)
- **Use quotation marks correctly.** Use double quotation marks to signal where a quotation begins and ends. Use single quotation marks when a quotation appears within a quotation, as in sentence 9.
- **Reproduce italics in a quotation.** When words appear in italics in the source, duplicate those italics in your quotation, as in sentence 9.

MYTHS ABOUT USING SOURCES

MYTH: A sentence can have only 1 paraphrase or 1 quotation.

FACT: You can include multiple quotations and multiple paraphrases in a single sentence, as long as you correctly quote and document according to the conventions in Chapters 4 and 15. To illustrate, sentence 9 is reprinted below, with the quotations underscored once; and the paraphrases underscored twice.

> In "Ring Leader," Natalie Kusz notes a disturbing phenomenon: Young girls who are so thin that they are "wispy and hollow-cheeked" stand in front of the locker room mirror and "announce, 'My God, I disgust myself, I am so fat'"; buying into this wrongheadedness, their classmates reassure the girls that they are, in fact, beautiful in all of their ultrathinness (218).

Checklist for Revising Narration

You can use this checklist along with the one on page 76 to help you revise.

1. _____ The journalist's questions appropriate to your point and purpose are answered and emphasized.

2. _____ Descriptions of people and scenes are included where important.

3. _____ Dialogue is included where it can advance the narrative and make it more vivid.

4. _____ Background information or explanation required by your reader is included.

5. _____ The narration's point is easily determined, as is whether the story is fact or fiction.

6. _____ Extraneous details are deleted.

7. _____ Details are arranged in chronological order, with flashbacks if appropriate.

8. _____ Details work to fulfill your writing purpose.

9. _____ Unoriginal narrations are properly attributed to their source.

10. _____ Transitions help your reader follow the chronology.

In the following essay, student-writer Robbie Warnock shares an account of the annual family reunion and comes to see the event differently now than in the past. After you read, you will have an opportunity to evaluate this essay.

The Family Reunion, Revisited
Robbie Warnock

Once a year, with the regularity of Old Faithful, scores of people claiming to be my kin would storm my hometown. The brood did not appear gradually, but as a veritable deluge of eccentricity, and often senility. The family's elders, in their twenty-year-old gas guzzlers, circled the town like vultures, finally "nesting" at the community center. As the rusty doors squeaked open in protest, I could almost hear John Williams's "Imperial March" blasting dirgelike through my mind. It was time for the annual family reunion, and I dreaded it as much as a trip to the dentist because to a youngster like me, everyone was as old as Methuselah and as quirky as Larry, Moe, and Curly.

Every woman present was clad in a floral spring dress, each with a distinct pattern. Most of the botanical togs reeked of mothballs. This pungent aroma was the only thing that held the bees attracted by the dress at bay. The men, on the other hand, looked like reject golfers or court jesters in their mismatched clothes of many colors. After each example of Henry Ford's worst nightmare had ejected the people crammed inside, the center's double doors were opened, and the celebration commenced.

Food is a major love for my family, which explains why portliness is the status quo. At the reunion, long wooden tables, like those in Hrothgar's meadhall, were laden with all types of dishes. However, an elderly matriarch of the clan became discontented with the same old food served every year. To ease the monotony, she created the "Annual Odd Recipe Contest," the goal of which was to create the most appetizing dish from the most bizarre ingredients.

I was present at the inception of this contest, albeit reluctantly. Along with the down-home staples, fried chicken and chocolate layer cake, I sampled a curious-looking green and purple casserole. Immediately, I fell victim to Aunt Frankie's infamous "Eggplant and Kudzu Surprise." Upon

Paragraph 1
The introduction provides background and tells *what, when,* and *who.* The thesis is the last sentence. The subject is the annual reunion, and the writer's view is that he dreaded it. Note the descriptive language.

Paragraph 2
This paragraph centers on *who?,* describing the people involved. It introduces the first narrative event—arrival.

Paragraph 3
Description and specific word choice add interest and vitality.

Paragraph 4
This paragraph flashes back to the more distant past.

tasting the foul abomination, I fled to the nearest McDonald's and vowed never to consume another bite even remotely connected with the old crone.

Paragraphs 5 and 6
Each paragraph begins with a transitional phrase that establishes the chronology of the events presented. The vivid description continues.

After eating the wonderful meal of poultry and vegetation, the family would seek amusement. Refusing to simply converse the evening away, the motley crew would begin to square dance. Recovering from whatever odd recipe I had unwittingly subjected myself to, I would glance inside to view a plethora of octogenarians tramping and stomping in a futile attempt at dancing. Then the entertainment took a nosedive. Uncle Oliver produced a set a bagpipes and unleashed a sonic aberration akin to the sound produced when a few dozen cats are run over slowly by a bulldozer. 5

After the musical torture, the group underwent a schism. The men ditched their wives and each group would nestle in a separate corner and settle down enough to actually begin conversations unrelated to food. Now the talk focused on the past. At just the right moment, Uncle Oliver presented a hundred or so bags, each sealed, labeled, and containing a piece of debris from the family homeplace. As he presented these heirlooms, he recited a stentorian lecture on the "sacred domicile." Each member of the family then received a fragment of the house. 6

Paragraph 7
The conclusion presents the last event and the point of the narration (the reunion served an important purpose). The last paragraph also answers *why?*

Stomach churning, ears smarting, and bearing a Ziploc bag containing a burnt bit of shingle, I returned home at the end of the day, praising God for deliverance. Today, I see things differently, however. Rather than eccentricity, I see love and a memorial to past times. The would-be Scotsman Oliver wanted the kids to cherish their heritage. I now regret my impatience and impudence because I realize that the reunion was an annual link between the past and the present. I now realize that the past is a treasure and the key to the future. For one more chance to remember and relive those times, I would square dance, listen to bagpipes, and even choke down kudzu. 7

Responding to "The Family Reunion, Revisited"

Analyze and assess "The Family Reunion, Revisited" by responding to these questions:

1. Does the narration hold your interest? Why or why not?
2. Does the story support the writer's point? Explain.
3. What do you think of the tone of the narration? (See page 69 on tone.)
4. Does the writer use description effectively? Explain.
5. Is the word choice effective? Should the writer revise for more effective word choice?
6. Is the chronology clear? Is there anything unclear?
7. What are the chief strengths of the narration? Why do you find these features strong?
8. What is one revision you would like to see? How will that revision improve the essay and help the author achieve his purpose?

EXAMINING VISUALS   Narration in a Cartoon

Like a prose story, a cartoon tells a narrative, as the following *Curtis* cartoon illustrates. And, as with stories, a cartoon may contain a narrative within the narrative. In this cartoon, the narrative within the narrative illustrates that narration may not always be used for ethical ends.

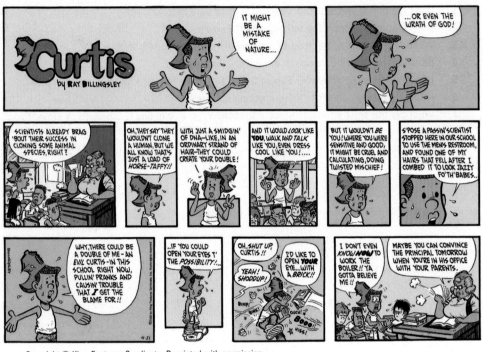

Copyright © King Features Syndicate. Reprinted with permission.

- For what purpose does Curtis tell his story?
- Is Curtis using narration to be hurtful?
- How well does Curtis assess his audience?

BACKGROUND: Born in Nigeria, award-winning poet and novelist Chris Abani teaches at The University of California, Riverside. Abani was jailed as a political prisoner three times in Nigeria for his writing and theater work. His first incarceration was in 1985, two years after his first novel was published, on the grounds that the book inspired a failed coup against the government. Abani's novels include *Masters of the Board* (1985), *Sirocco* (1987), *GraceLand* (2004), and *The Virgin of Flames* (2007). His plays are *Room at the Top* (1983) and *Song of a Broken Flute* (1990). Abani's poetry collections include *Kalakuta Republic* (2001) and *Daphne's Lot* (2003). "The Lottery" first appeared in the "Lives" section of the *New York Times Magazine* (February 2004).

THE PATTERN AND ITS PURPOSES: Abani's narration begins pleasantly enough, but it takes a chilling turn. The author *narrates* the account of justice gone awry both to **relate his experience** in Nigeria and to **inform** the reader about the nature of mob violence. It's a difficult story, but one that will grab and hold your attention.

THE LOTTERY

BY CHRIS ABANI

EVEN THOUGH IT was a wet, rainy afternoon, I was glad my aunt had taken me to the market with her. Even her religious fanaticism, which sometimes prompted her to proselytize, embarrassingly, to complete strangers, wasn't enough to deaden my good mood. The rainy season in Nigeria was my favorite even as a 10-year-old. It had something to do with the light. It was crisp, like a new bank note or a thing washed and starched. And then there was the way everything smelled.

As you read
Think about how people respond to various kinds of social pressure, particularly pressure from peers, adults, and crowds.

2   I inhaled deeply. The scent was a balanced mix of wet earth and the dry roughness of rope. There was continuity to that smell, as if it were the essence of the land itself. I closed my eyes for a moment. Other scents in the market broke through the smell of wet earth—the throat-burning sharpness of peppers, dried fish, the animal-funk of goats and chickens.

3   Suddenly, a lone voice screamed one word over and over: "Thief! Thief! Thief!" It was picked up slowly, as if the drizzle that afternoon had dampened the scent of blood. My aunt froze and faced the sound, nose sniffing the air like a lioness sensing prey. A man's voice, tired and breathless, tried to counter the rising chant with a feeble retort: "It's a lie! It's a lie!"

> "Suddenly, a lone voice screamed one word over and over: 'Thief! Thief! Thief!' "

4   I drew nearer to my aunt, confused and more than a little afraid, but she shook off my clutching hand. Her head turned like an antenna seeking a signal. The sound of a chase grew closer—desperate, pounding feet and shouts. A man with a wild expression came around a corner and nearly knocked over a stall. Young men were almost on his heels, followed some distance behind by a larger cluster. The man ran past us, and it seemed as if I could see the pores in his skin. As he pushed past, my aunt slapped him across the face. He flinched

but didn't stop; he was headed for the courtyard in the middle of the market, where the retired elders sat daily to dispense justice. I imagined the man bursting into the clearing, cries of "Sanctuary, sanctuary!" breaking from his lips. The council of elders was the highest court in my community, besides, of course, the civil system. It arbitrated on everything from murder to marital disputes, and its authority was never questioned. I felt certain the man would be safe there.

5   This was the mob justice I had read about in the newspaper editorials that my father made my homework. Rife with condemnations of the mob lynchings that were becoming the norm in the 70s, the editorials pointed out that these victims of vigilante justice received no trials and that the crimes they were accused of were never investigated. The editorials went a step further to suggest that most of those killed this way were probably innocent. But in the terror of that moment, editorials were of little use to the man running for his life and would do little to placate the angry horde. My aunt dragged me along behind the crowd that swept past us.

6   The man stood in the middle of the clearing facing the elders while the crush of people pressed around them. In the center of this sacred space, the sole elder to stand up and call for tolerance was booed and pelted with rotten fruit. He sat down quickly and turned his face away. I was sure that the man was about to be lynched. How could the crowd ignore the elder's intervention? And why didn't the other elders speak out?

"I was sure that the man was about to be lynched."

7   The mob was oddly silent; its loud breathing filled the space. The accused man began to beg, but people were too busy picking up stones and tree branches, anything that could be used as a weapon. A young man broke through the crowd carrying an old rubber tire and a metal can. He hung the tire from the accused's neck. This singular action ended the man's pleas for mercy. Resigned, he sobbed softly, mumbling inaudibly, but he didn't move as the young man emptied the contents of the can onto him. The young man smiled and talked as he went about his task: "You see why crime doesn't pay? I am doing this for you, you know. If you burn here, you won't burn in hell. God is reasonable."

8   Finishing, he held up a box of matches. The crowd roared. The elder who had tried intervening spoke again, but nobody listened. Someone called out, "Bring the children forward so that they can learn." My aunt hustled me to the front. Next to me stood a girl. Her face was impassive; I was ashamed at my fear. I never saw the match fall, but I felt the heat as the man erupted into a sheet of flame, burning like a lighthouse in the drizzly haze. "Watch," my aunt said as I tried to turn away from the writhing figure.

9   As the man burned, people began to file past him in an orderly manner like the offertory line in the Catholic church I attended. As they walked past, they spat on the incandescent figure. My aunt spat. I looked away, hand held over my nose at the smell of burning flesh, horrified that it reminded me of kebabs. "Spit," she snapped, rapping me on the head with her knuckles. I spat.

READING CLOSELY AND THINKING CRITICALLY

1. The essay's title does not prepare readers for the essay's content. Explain the significance of the title. Why do you think Abani chose it?
2. In paragraph 6, Abani asks how the crowd could disregard the elder who intervened, and he also asks why the other elders did not intervene as well. Answer these questions.
3. What point does the narration make?
4. In paragraph 1, Abani mentions that his aunt was a religious fanatic. Is that detail important? Why or why not?
5. Young Abani drew close to his aunt in fear, yet she "shook off [his] clutching hand" (paragraph 4). Why does she do this?
6. What is the significance of the fact that young Abani spat on the victim?

EXAMINING STRUCTURE AND STRATEGY

1. Does Abani answer all of the journalist's questions? Which ones does he emphasize? How does that emphasis help him achieve his writing purpose?
2. Which paragraphs provide background information? Is that information helpful? Explain.
3. What purpose does the detail in paragraph 3 serve? The detail in paragraph 7? In paragraph 8? Should Abani have included more detail in these paragraphs? Why or why not?
4. In paragraph 2, Abani focuses on the smells in the marketplace. Why is the description of smell important in this essay?
5. Abani's essay ends with the last event in the narration. Does the essay end effectively? Explain.

CONSIDERING LANGUAGE AND STYLE

1. What similes appear in paragraphs 1, 3, 4, 8, and 9? What do you think of these similes and why? (See page 128 on similes.)
2. To appreciate the brisk pacing (movement) and narrative power that derives, in part, from that pacing, read paragraphs 3 and 4 aloud. What do you notice?
3. Consult a dictionary if you are unsure of the meaning of any of these words: *proselytize* (paragraph 1), *rife* (paragraph 5), *vigilante* (paragraph 5), *offertory* (paragraph 9), *incandescent* (paragraph 9).

FOR DISCUSSION IN CLASS OR ONLINE

The time depicted in "The Lottery" was one of political unrest in Nigeria, a time of coups, revolutionaries, and extreme factionalism. Is the kind of mob pressure seen in the essay strictly a function of those circumstances, or are we all capable of succumbing to mob pressure, regardless of the political climate? Explain your view.

1. **Writing in your journal.** How did you react when you read the "The Lottery"? Why did you react that way? Would you recommend the story to a friend? Why or why not?

2. **Using narration for a purpose.** The purposes given in the assignments are possibilities. You may establish whatever purpose you like, within your instructor's guidelines.

   • To relate your experience and perhaps express your feelings, narrate an account of a time you went along with the crowd despite your better judgment. Explain why you did so and whether you would do so again in similar circumstances. If there is something to learn from your experience, your purpose can also be to inform your reader of that lesson.

   • To relate your experience and perhaps express your feelings, narrate an account of a time you pressured a person to do something against his or her will. Explain why you did so and whether you would do so again in similar circumstances. If there is something to learn from your experience, your purpose can also be to inform your reader of that lesson.

   • Narrate an account of a time justice was not served or something unfair occurred. The event might have taken place in the classroom, on the playing field, in the workplace, or in some any other environment. Your purpose can be to relate your experience or inform your reader of a lesson or of the nature of justice. You might also want to convince your reader to think or act a particular way in response to the injustice or lack of fairness.

3. **Combining patterns.** Explain the nature and effect of *peer pressure* by defining it and narrating one or more illustrative anecdotes. (See Chapter 12 for information on writing definition.)

4. **Analyzing and assessing.** Explain how the features of Abani's narration (such as his choice of details, sentence structure, word choice, organization, and pacing) make the essay so compelling.

5. **Connecting and synthesizing the readings.** In both "The Lottery" and "Salvation" (page 203), children feel coerced by adults to behave in ways that make them uncomfortable. In both cases, the adults believe they are acting in the child's best interests. Discuss to what extent adults should have the authority to impose their moral and ethical standards on young people and to what extent young people should be permitted to act in accordance with their own sense of moral and ethical beliefs.

6. **Drawing on sources.** In the 1960s, psychologist Stanley Milgram performed a now-classic experiment related to obedience. Read about the experiment in an introductory psychology textbook or by searching online for "Stanley Milgram." Then explain the nature of the experiment, its outcome, what it teaches, and how it does or does not relate to events in "The Lottery."

BACKGROUND: Born in Joplin, Missouri, Langston Hughes (1902–1967) was a prolific poet, playwright, critic, newspaper columnist, and fiction writer. He wrote 47 books, and his work has been translated into over a dozen languages, earning him an international reputation unparalleled by most other African American authors of his time. Hughes was committed to writing about racial themes, particularly the everyday life of African Americans and pride in African heritage. He also wrote about democracy and patriotism. As a newspaper columnist, Hughes created a character called "Simple," an uneducated African American who had conversations with a better educated but less sensitive African American acquaintance. His many works include *Simple Speaks His Mind* (1950), the first of four volumes of short stories; *Montage of a Dream Deferred* (1951), a collection of poetry; and *Ask Your Mamma: 12 Moods for Jazz* (1961), a collection of poetry inspired by the civil rights movement. The following selection is from Hughes's autobiographical *The Big Sea* (1940).

THE PATTERN AND ITS PURPOSES: In "Salvation," Langston Hughes employs *narration* to **relate an experience** that changed his life dramatically and to **express** the disillusionment he felt as a result of that experience. As you read, pay attention to how Hughes gives the reader background and builds tension.

Salvation

BY LANGSTON HUGHES

I was saved from sin when I was going on thirteen. But not really saved. It happened like this. There was a big revival at my Auntie Reed's church. Every night for weeks there had been much preaching, singing, praying, and shouting, and some very hardened sinners had been brought to Christ, and the membership of the church had grown by leaps and bounds. Then just before the revival ended, they held a special meeting for children, "to bring the young lambs to the fold." My aunt spoke of it for days ahead. That night, I was escorted to the front row and placed on the mourner's bench with all other young sinners, who had not yet been brought to Jesus.

As you read
Ask yourself what pressures led Hughes to take the action that he did.

2   My aunt told me that when you were saved you saw a light, and something happened to you inside! And Jesus came into your life! And God was with you from then on! She said you could see and hear and feel Jesus in your soul. I believed her. I had heard a great many old people say the same thing and it seemed to me they ought to know. So I sat there calmly in the hot, crowded church, waiting for Jesus to come to me.

3   The preacher preached a wonderful rhythmical sermon, all moans and shouts and lonely cries and dire pictures of hell, and then he sang a song about the ninety and nine safe in the fold, but one little lamb was left out in the cold. Then he said: "Won't you come? Won't you come to Jesus? Young lambs, won't you come?" and he held out his arms to all us young sinners there on the mourner's bench. And the little girls cried. And some of them jumped up and went to Jesus right away. But most of us just sat there.

4   A great many old people came and knelt around us and prayed, old women with jet-black faces and braided hair, old men with work-gnarled hands. And the

church sang a song about the lower lights are burning, some poor sinners to be saved. And the whole building rocked with prayer and song.

5   Still I kept waiting to *see* Jesus.

6   Finally all the young people had gone to the altar and were saved, but one boy and me. He was a rounder's son named Westley. Westley and I were surrounded by sisters and deacons praying. It was very hot in the church, and getting late now. Finally Westley said to me in a whisper, "God damn! I'm tired o' sitting here. Let's get up and be saved." So he got up and was saved.

7   Then I was left all alone on the mourner's bench. My aunt came and knelt at my knees and cried, while prayers and songs swirled all around me in the little church. The whole congregation prayed for me alone, in a mighty wail of moans and voices. And I kept waiting serenely for Jesus, waiting, waiting—but he didn't come. I wanted to see him, but nothing happened to me. Nothing! I wanted something to happen to me, but nothing happened.

8   I heard the songs and the minister saying, "Why don't you come? My dear child, why don't you come to Jesus? Jesus is waiting for you. He wants you. Why don't you come? Sister Reed, what is this child's name?"

9   "Langston," my aunt sobbed.

10   "Langston, why don't you come? Why don't you come and be saved? Oh, Lamb of God! Why don't you come?"

11   Now it was really getting late. I began to be ashamed of myself, holding everything up so long. I began to wonder what God thought about Westley, who certainly hadn't seen Jesus either, but who was now sitting proudly on the platform, swinging his knickerbockered legs and grinning down at me, surrounded by deacons and old women on their knees praying. God had not struck Westley dead for taking his name in vain or for lying in the temple. So I decided that maybe to save further trouble, I'd better lie, too, and say that Jesus had come, and get up and be saved.

12   So I got up.

13   Suddenly the whole room broke into a sea of shouting, as they saw me rise. Waves of rejoicing swept the place. Women leaped in the air. My aunt threw her arms around me. The minister took me by the hand and led me to the platform.

14   When things quieted down, in a hushed silence, punctuated by a few ecstatic "Amens," all the new young lambs were blessed in the name of God. Then joyous singing filled the room.

15   That night, for the last time in my life but one—for I was a big boy twelve years old—I cried. I cried, in bed alone, and couldn't stop. I buried my head under the quilts, but my aunt heard me. She woke up and told my uncle I was crying because the Holy Ghost had come into my life, and because I had seen Jesus. But I was really crying because I couldn't bear to tell her that I had lied, that I had deceived everybody in the church, that I hadn't seen Jesus, and that now I didn't believe there was a Jesus any more, since he didn't come to help me.

1. What does young Langston Hughes expect to happen at the revival? What happens instead?
2. How was Hughes affected by what happened at the revival?
3. What do you think Hughes means in the first two sentences of the narration?
4. Why does young Langston pretend to see Jesus and be saved? Do you think he was right or wrong to pretend to be saved? What would you have done in his place? Explain.
5. How do you think young Langston's aunt would have reacted if he had told her the truth about why he was crying?
6. **Situational irony** occurs when events happen in ways that are contrary to expectations. What situational irony occurs in "Salvation"?

EXAMINING STRUCTURE AND STRATEGY

1. Do the first two sentences of "Salvation" make an effective opening? Explain why or why not.
2. Where does Hughes explain the point of the narration?
3. Hughes includes description of people and events in his narration. Cite two examples of this description, and explain how it helps Hughes achieve his purpose.
4. Hughes incorporates just a bit of dialogue in the story. What purpose does that dialogue serve?
5. Which of the *who? what? when? where? why?* and *how?* questions does Hughes emphasize the most?
6. To help the reader recognize and follow the chronological order, Hughes opens several of his paragraphs with transitions that signal time order (see page 67). Which paragraphs open with transitions, and what are those transitions?
7. In addition to telling his story, Hughes offers some explanation. What is explained, and where does this explanation occur?

CONSIDERING LANGUAGE AND STYLE

1. What metaphor appears in paragraph 13? (See page 128 on metaphors.) What does this metaphor contribute to the description that appears in the essay?
2. Paragraph 12 is only four words long. Explain the effect created by this four-word paragraph. What would be lost if the four words were moved to the end of paragraph 11?
3. Consult a dictionary if you are unsure of the meaning of any of these words: *revival* (paragraph 1), *dire* (paragraph 3), *rounder* (paragraph 6), *deacons* (paragraph 6), *knickerbockered* (paragraph 11), *ecstatic* (paragraph 14).

FOR DISCUSSION IN CLASS OR ONLINE

With your classmates, consider these questions: What do you think would have happened had young Langston not pretended to see Jesus and be saved? How would his aunt have reacted? How would the other members of the congregation have reacted? How might Langston himself been differently affected?

1. **Writing in your journal.** Tell about a time you pretended to believe something. What was your motivation?

2. **Using narration for a purpose.** The purposes given in the assignments are possibilities. You may establish whatever purpose you like, within your instructor's guidelines.

   - In paragraph 2, Hughes explains that he believed his aunt when she described what it was like to be saved. However, his experience did not conform to his aunt's description. To relate your experience, express your feelings, and perhaps entertain, tell a story about a time when you were led to expect something, but it did not happen. If there is a lesson to be learned from your narration, your purpose can also be to inform.

   - Hughes says that he pretended to see Jesus "to save further trouble." To relate your experience, express your feelings, and perhaps entertain, narrate an account of a time you or someone you know did something to avoid trouble or inconvenience. Explain the outcome.

   - Hughes felt pressured to see Jesus and be saved. To relate your experience, express your feelings, and perhaps inform, narrate an account of a time you or someone you know was pressured to think or behave a particular way. Explain how you or the other person responded to the pressure.

   - The religious community and a family member pressured 12-year-old Hughes to see Jesus and be saved. Pick one organization, institution, or group—a congregation, a class, the family, the community, a peer group, and so on—and narrate a story that reveals one or more pressures it exerts. Your purpose is to convince your reader that the pressure is positive or negative.

3. **Combining patterns.** Narrate a story about a traumatic experience you had when you were young. Use cause-and-effect analysis to explain the impact the event had on you. (Cause-and-effect analysis is explained in Chapter 10.)

4. **Analyzing and assessing.** What does Hughes imply about the people in the narration? Are the adults, the young Langston Hughes, or Westley sympathetic or unsympathetic? Why or why not? How does the author create sympathy or lack of it for these characters?

5. **Connecting and synthesizing the readings.** Young people do not lead the carefree life many people think they do. Instead, they often struggle to deal with a variety of pressures from many sources. Using the information in "Salvation," "Reunion" (page 284) and, "Complexion," (page 672), along with your own experience and observation, discuss the pressures young people face.

6. **Drawing on sources.** The Harlem Renaissance was an important period in the literary history of African American literature and American literature in general. Write an essay that explains what the Harlem Renaissance was and how it affected literature, and use narration to show Langston Hughes's place in the movement. If you need a starting point, you can find articles in the *MLA International Bibliography of Books and Articles on Modern Language and Literature*. You can also find information in *Black American Literature: A Critical History*. Online, go to www.nku.edu and type "Harlem Renaissance" in the search box.

BACKGROUND: Shawn Macomber is a contributing editor to *The American Spectator*, as well as a prolific freelance writer who has written for a variety of publications, including *Decibel*, the *Los Angeles Times*, the *Weekly Standard*, the *National Review*, *Yankee magazine*, the *Wall Street Journal*, *DoubleThink* magazine, the *Journal of International Security Affairs*, and *Reason*, where "Stripping Away Free Expression" first appeared in 2009.

COMBINED PATTERNS AND THEIR PURPOSES: In "Stripping Away Free Expression," Shawn Macomber *narrates* an account of what happened in a Pennsylvania community when a woman opened an exercise studio that taught pole dancing. He also uses *cause-and-effect analysis*, and together the patterns **inform** readers of what happened and why, but Macomber may have a **persuasive** purpose in mind as well.

STRIPPING AWAY FREE EXPRESSION

BY SHAWN MACOMBER

DRESSED IN LOW-CUT PINK SHIRT, tight black booty pants, and thick, plastic platform stilettos, Stephanie Babines doesn't look the part of a political rabble-rouser. Yet an activist is exactly what Babines became when her efforts to help women shape up through fully clothed, decidedly G-rated stripper-inspired aerobics ran afoul of overzealous officials in the small western Pennsylvania town of Mars. This unyieldingly perky 31-year-old entrepreneur, standing in the small forest of steel poles that shoot up from the floor of her mirrored dance and fitness studio, has taught dance-phobic authorities an expensive lesson in federal court.

As you read
Think about appearance versus reality—the fact that things aren't always what they seem to be.

2 "It's pretty surreal to get calls from the *New York Times* and *Wall Street Journal*, never mind *Dr. Phil*, *Jerry Springer*, and *America's Got Talent*," Babines laughs, leaning back beneath a bookshelf filled with such revolutionary tomes as *The World According to Mr. Rogers* and *The Housewife's Guide to the Practical Striptease*. "It's not attention I went looking for."

> "It's pretty surreal to get calls from the *New York Times* and *Wall Street Journal*, never mind *Dr. Phil*, *Jerry Springer*, and *America's Got Talent*."

3 A few years ago Babines was a senior executive at a financial services company, nary a feather boa dancing in her head, struggling with an 80-hour workweek that severely depleted her enthusiasm for the gymnasium. One night over dinner a friend mentioned that pole dancing had become the hot new fitness trend. On a whim Babines purchased a pole online. "I thought it would be something silly to laugh about with my friends," she says, "until I started losing weight like crazy and fitting into cute jeans."

4 With the fire of a convert burning in her rapidly shrinking belly, Babines took a pilgrimage to the Las Vegas studio of fitness pole dancing's grand doyen, Fawnia Mondey, known more for her work in the instructional DVD *Strip to It: Bump n' Grind* than for her appearances in such postapocalyptic feature films as *White Slave Lovers* and *Forbidden Rage: White Slave Secrets*. Babines returned home as the first Pennsylvanian to hold one of Mondey's pole dance instructor certificates, signifying

mastery of more than 60 moves and routines as well as basic first aid, should it ever be necessary to treat a client for excessive gyration.

5 Babines printed brochures and began teaching what quickly became overflow classes three nights a week at a local dance studio. Realizing she needed a place to stake her own pole(s), Babines rented space to pursue a more expansive, vampy fitness vision, including Power Lap Dance ("challenge your core and unleash your inner vixen!"), yoga, belly dancing, Hip Hop Aerobics ("learn the art of popping, locking, crunk, & funk"), and sessions with "Pittsburgh's only certified Hoopnotica Hoop Dancing Instructor."

6 Babines sank thousands into renovating her studio. The town inspector made mostly small requests: light the exit sign, replace the furnace valve, and so on. But then she was blindsided by a subsequent letter declaring that the studio, which was christened Oh My You're Gorgeous, was an "adult business" ineligible for an occupancy permit. This was a perplexing pronouncement on a facility that forbade spectators and catered solely to fully clothed women.

7 Despite its cheeky name, the city of Mars isn't always amenable to cultural efforts perceived as alien. The "pink-and-black color scheme of Ms. Babines's website

and the high-heeled shoe in her logo" were enough, according to court documents, to convince Code Enforcement Officer Gary Peaco to protect the community from these exercise classes.

8 "I've lived here my whole life, worked hard, paid my taxes, stayed out of trouble," Babines says. "I was shocked something I worked so hard for could be taken away over a misunderstanding, no questions asked."

9 Appeals to the zoning board went nowhere. Five students, including a devoutly Christian grandmother, spoke on their instructor's behalf. No one spoke against. Babines publicly invited board members to send their wives over for a workout. "One class

with girls like me exercising in five layers of sweaty clothes, and the idea that this is an undercover strip club would have become hilarious to them," says Karen Nolan, a 25-year-old pole-exercise devotee and self-identified "ex-chunky monkey." All to no avail: Babines's two allotted appeals were denied. "Any sexual connotation, however mild, and some people suspect the worst," says another student, 47-year-old Tina Valeska. "The real story is a lot of women found an exercise program we could actually stick with. That wasn't sexy enough for their imaginations, I guess."

10   Legal bills piled up. Babines contemplated selling her house to continue the fight in state court. Desperate, she took a day off from work and drove to the Pittsburgh offices of the American Civil Liberties Union.

11   They didn't take walk-ins. It began to rain. Through tears Babines scribbled out a seven-page plea, stuffed it into the mail slot, and drove back to Mars demoralized, unaware that an ACLU lawyer would call that very afternoon or that she would soon have to warn her unsuspecting day job boss that one of his analysts was about to be outed on the A.P.[1] wire as a crusader for strip-pole rights.

12   "We don't usually take on zoning cases, but look more closely and this really is a classic ACLU case," ACLU attorney Sarah Rose says. "Government officials were using the zoning code to crack down on the First Amendment–protected teaching of an expressive art they found controversial." Last August the ACLU filed a scathing complaint in federal court, comparing authorities in Adams Township, of which Mars is a borough, unfavorably to communists ("while a repressive country like China allows dance studios to teach pole dancing, the defendants in this small Butler County town have misapplied their zoning code to deny Ms. Babines her right to teach this new combination of art and sport to interested adult women") and requesting relief from "the pall of orthodoxy imposed by defendants on the people in their town who wish to communicate unconventional ideas."

13   The township folded. Babines had her occupancy permit by October. In February she was awarded $75,000 in damages and attorney's fees. The settlement forbids "peeping booths" and nudity, up to and including "the showing of the covered male genitals in a discernibly turgid state." None of this, of course, was ever part of the program, but Babines doesn't mind codifying it. "If there's one thing I hope people take away from this, besides that they should stand up for their rights even if the situation seems hopeless," she says, "it's that women don't need to be naked in front of an audience of men to be hot or sexy or empowered."

---

[1]The Associated Press (A.P.) is a news service that provides content to newspapers.

READING CLOSELY AND THINKING CRITICALLY

1.   Is Macomber's narration meant simply to inform readers about what happened in Mars, Pennsylvania, or is he trying to convince readers of something? Explain.

2.   Which of the journalist's questions does Macomber answer? Which ones does he emphasize? Why?

3.   What point or points does the narration make? Where is that information best expressed?

EXAMINING STRUCTURE AND STRATEGY

1. Is the opening paragraph an effective beginning for the essay? Why or why not?
2. What purpose does the dialogue in paragraphs 2 and 8 serve? In paragraph 9? In paragraph 12? How does the dialogue in these paragraphs help the author achieve his purpose for writing?
3. What contrast does Macomber establish in paragraphs 1 and 2? What purpose does the contrast serve?
4. Is the title of the essay a good one? Explain.

NOTING COMBINED PATTERNS

How does the cause-and-effect analysis in the essay help the author achieve his purpose for writing? (Cause-and-effect analysis explains the causes or effects of something; see Chapter 10.)

CONSIDERING LANGUAGE AND STYLE

1. What modifiers (descriptive words) in paragraph 1 suggest which side of the issue the author is on? What side do they suggest he is on?
2. Consult a dictionary if you are unsure of the meaning of these words: *tomes* (paragraph 2), *doyen* (paragraph 4), *postapocalyptic* (paragraph 4), *vampy* (paragraph 5), *amenable* (paragraph 7).

FOR DISCUSSION IN CLASS OR ONLINE

Do you think Macomber was unduly harsh on the town of Mars? Explain.

WRITING ASSIGNMENTS

1. **Writing in your journal.** According to one of Babines's students, "'Any sexual connotation, however mild, and some people suspect the worst'" (paragraph 9). Agree or disagree with this statement, explaining and supporting your view.
2. **Using narration for a purpose.** The purposes given here are possibilities. You may establish whatever purposes you like, within your instructor's guidelines.
   - To inform and perhaps relate experience, narrate an account of a time you or someone you know opposed authority. Be sure to indicate a point or lesson to be drawn from the narration.
   - Tell a story that reveals a person or event to be something other than what he, she, or it appears to be. Your purpose can be to relate experience, inform, and/or entertain.
   - To express feelings and/or relate experience, narrate an account of a time you did something "on a whim" (paragraph 3).
   - To convince your reader that things do not always work out as they should, narrate an account of a time justice was not served.

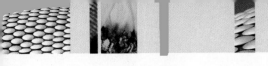

3. **Combining patterns.** Define *activist* (paragraph 1), and tell a story to illustrate that definition. (See Chapter 12 on writing definition.)

4. **Analyzing and assessing.** "Stripping Away Free Expression" first appeared in *Reason*. According to its Web site, *Reason* is a magazine of "'free minds and free markets.' It covers politics, culture, and ideas . . . [and] provides a refreshing alternative to right-wing and left-wing opinion magazines by making a principled case for liberty and individual choice in all areas of human activity." Discuss whether "Stripping Away Free Expression" is fully in line with that statement of purpose and editorial policy.

5. **Connecting and synthesizing the readings.** Do you think campus authorities should set standards for the kinds of businesses allowed on campus (such as adult book-stores and theaters, bars, and boutiques that sell drug paraphernalia) and limit access to certain Internet sites (such as pornography sites and sites with messages of hate)? Why or why not? For ideas, you can draw on your own ideas, along with "Stripping Away Free Expression" and "What Limits Should Campus Networks Place on Pornography?" (page 646).

6. **Drawing on sources.** Many freedom-of-expression issues are frequently examined and debated in communities, particularly issues such as whether art that some con-sider obscene should be displayed, whether television shows with content some find objectionable should be aired, and whether speakers with points of view some find offensive should be allowed to speak. Select one of these issues or a similar one, and discuss why that issue is significant. Your purpose is not to argue for or against censoring art, television, speakers, and so forth; it is to explain why the issue *matters*. For ideas, you can consult keywords related to your topic, such as "community stan-dards" and "censoring television," at http://news.yahoo.com/.

BACKGROUND: Former science reporter for the *Washington Post,* John Schwartz is currently the national legal correspondent for the *New York Times.* Previously, he was a science reporter for the "Science Times" section of that paper. He has written on a wide range of science-related topics, including the international space station, the problems associated with uninformed science bloggers, the publicity surrounding gay sheep, and the space shuttle. He has also written on business and financial subjects, including taxes and mutual funds, and on the post-Katrina recovery of New Orleans. The essay reprinted here is a departure for Schwartz because it is a personal piece. It first appeared in the "Education Life" supplement of the *New York Times* (2007).

COMBINED PATTERNS AND THEIR PURPOSES: In "The Poncho Bearer," John Schwartz uses *narration* to **relate the experience** of his son, who followed his own path in high school. Schwartz also uses *cause-and-effect analysis* to **inform** readers about why the boy acted as he did and what the outcome of his actions were, as well as to say something about the way we mature and define ourselves. He also **expresses his feelings** about his "own light touch as a parent."

The Poncho Bearer

BY JOHN SCHWARTZ

Sam wears a Mexican poncho to school every Friday.

2   Like a number of things about our middle child, the "why" of it is a mystery. When he started wearing it about two years ago, I guessed that he was perhaps reinterpreting the idea of casual Friday for high school. Or he might have just thought, "I will wear the poncho to school on Friday. See what happens."

As you read
Think about how high school students who fail to conform are typically treated by their peers.

3   "Thought" may be too strong a word. The poncho appeared in our home when a boy gave it to our oldest child, Elizabeth. She had no interest in it, but Sammy did. It is brightly colored, or more accurately, blinding. By all rights, he should look stupid. In a weird way, he looks good.

4   As we all know, high school for most teenagers is a time of intense pressure to conform. But at 16, Sam has become something of a quiet Joker, a subversive with a smile.

5   Sam has often found ways to stand out in situations where others try to fit in. When we first moved to our little town in New Jersey six years ago, he was entering fifth grade. After watching his new school for a while, he came home one day and told us that there were three kinds of kids: the straight-A kids, the kids who were always in trouble and the class clowns. "I think I have a shot," he said, "at class clown."

6   And so he's always made his own path. He dyed his dark blond hair Corvette red one year, got a buzz cut the next. Always changing, always distinctive, and always with that knowing smile. Then he donned the poncho. And then again. And again. Before long, he was known more as Poncho than Sam in the halls of his school.

7   A couple of his coaches didn't like it; one warned Sam that people would not take him seriously if he continued to wear it. As a compromise during football season, he threw his serape over his jersey, which players are required to wear on game days. Even he seemed to think the combination looked stupid, and ultimately he left the poncho home a couple of days in favor of the team colors.

8   Sam let us know about the coaches' displeasure—not because he wanted us to intervene, just F.Y.I.

9   Now, I am not a parent who's going to get upset if my son dresses funny. My parents taught me that lesson in the early 1970s in Galveston, Tex., when the principal of Ball High School suspended my brother Dick for having long hair.

10   My brother thought there was a First Amendment issue at stake, and my dad decided to back him up—literally, to make a federal case of it. Dick and Dad took the school district to court. It was a risky move; my father was a state senator, and it was not a popular stand. People called our home—the number was always listed—and shouted obscenities and hung up.

11   We lost the case. And I ended up thinking my father was the kind of guy who would stand up for his children no matter what.

12   So I never gave Sam any trouble about the poncho. For his part, Sam showed his coaches that he was every bit as serious about sports as he was silly in his choice of Friday attire. They've seen his determination when he pushes through the offensive line to take down an opposing quarterback. He shows the same drive on the wrestling mat and the lacrosse field.

13   With achievement came acceptance. The wrestling team gave out knit caps at the end of the season with the player's name embroidered on the back. Sam's said "Poncho." At the end of lacrosse season, one of the coaches gave a speech about all the funny things he had learned that year. The collection of inside jokes had the players rolling, but the best line was the last: "I have learned it's O.K. to wear a poncho."

14   Sammy decided to write an essay for an English class about the poncho. Many mysteries were revealed. He wrote that he started wearing it because, when he tried it on at home, it made him laugh. He also acknowledged that it has become something of an obligation.

15   "Despite the amount of fun I've had with this whole experiment, I do tire of it from time to time. I didn't know what I was getting myself into at the start, and now it's escalated to the point where if I stop more than half the school will forget that the weekend is about to come up. I feel obligated. I must fulfill my duty in this strange society of learners to remind them of the good times ahead, even if they only last a few precious days."

16   He also included a haiku:

A blur of color
I stride as poncho billows
In the strong wind gusts.

17   The essay concluded with his plan to pass his poncho along "to a predetermined underclassman who upholds all of the standards necessary to become the next Poncho Bearer" and who will "remember that the Poncho Bearer does not own the Poncho, but is merely holding onto it and taking care of it for future generations."

Sam Schwartz in His Poncho on His Way to School

18 O.K., he seems to have cribbed that from the Patek Philippe[1] ads. But it still brought a lump to my throat. The process of finding yourself only starts in high school; it goes on through the college years.

19 Defining yourself is the central question of adolescence. We ask, Am I a jock or a geek? A joker or a hippie? Am I smart? Good looking? Am I enough like everyone else? Am I distinctive? We are pulled in every direction. Sam has asked the question and, I think, begun to answer it well.

20 And so I have felt pretty good about my own light touch as a parent. That good feeling lasted about a week, until I got an instant message from my daughter at college:

21 *I got a tattoo today.*

---

[1] Patek Philippe is a brand of expensive wristwatches.

1. The poncho was originally given to Sam's sister, Elizabeth. Why do you think she had no interest in wearing it?

2. In fifth grade, Sam decided he was most suited to be a class clown, rather than one of the "straight-A kids [or] the kids who were always in trouble" (paragraph 5). Why do you think he made that choice?

3. High school students who fail to conform are often ridiculed and marginalized, but Sam was not. Why?

4. Sam planned to pass along the poncho to a student who "'upholds all of the standards necessary to become the next Poncho Bearer'" (paragraph 17). What are those standards?

5. Why did Sam feel that wearing the poncho on Fridays was "something of an obligation" (paragraph 14)?

EXAMINING STRUCTURE AND STRATEGY

1. The narration does not begin until the middle of paragraph 6. What purpose do the first five and a half paragraphs serve?

2. In paragraphs 9–11, Schwartz tells something about himself and his background. Why does he include this information? Do you think he *should* have included it?

3. Does Schwartz state or imply the point of the narration? What is that point?

4. Situational irony occurs when something happens that runs counter to what was expected. Explain the situational irony in the conclusion.

NOTING COMBINED PATTERNS

1. How does the exemplification (giving examples) in paragraphs 5 and 6 help Schwartz achieve his purpose for writing?

2. What cause-and-effect analysis appears in the essay? (Cause-and-effect analysis explains the causes or effects of something; see Chapter 10.)

3. Which paragraph includes classification? (Classification groups items into categories; see Chapter 11.)

CONSIDERING LANGUAGE AND STYLE

1. Paragraph 16 includes a haiku, which is a form of Japanese poetry made up of only 17 syllables. A haiku has three unrhymed lines. The first line is 5 syllables; the second line is 7 syllables; the third line is again 5 syllables. Write your own haiku about clothing in general or about a particular item of clothing.

2. Consult a dictionary if you are unsure of the meaning of these words: *serape* (paragraph 7), *cribbed* (paragraph 18).

FOR DISCUSSION IN CLASS OR ONLINE

Explain how the group you socialized with in high school would have responded to Sam. Would the group members have accepted him? Why or why not?

1. **Writing in your journal.** In a page or so, discuss your own experiences with clothing in high school. You might consider such issues as whether you dressed to conform or stand out, whether you were happy with the clothes you wore, and why you dressed the way you did. Did you wear clothing to achieve a special effect?

2. **Using narration for a purpose.** The purposes given in the assignments are possibilities. You may establish whatever purposes you like, within your instructor's guidelines.

   - Write a narrative account of a time you "made [your] own path" (paragraph 6) or stood out from the crowd. The narration can be humorous to entertain your reader, if you like.

   - In paragraph 13, Schwartz says that "with achievement came acceptance" for Sam. To relate experience, write a narration about a time achievement came with acceptance for you or for someone you know. Alternatively, write a narration about a time lack of achievement came with lack of acceptance.

   - To inform readers about how clothing influences our perception of people—and perhaps to convince them that we are what we wear—write a narrative account of a time clothing significantly affected how you or someone you know was perceived. Alternatively, write a narrative account of how you reacted to someone based on that person's clothes.

   - In paragraph 18, Schwartz observes that "the process of finding yourself only starts in high school; it goes on through the college years." To relate experience and express feelings, narrate an account of an event that occurred in high school or college, one that helped you find yourself.

3. **Combining patterns.** Sam classified the students where he attended fifth grade. He said that "there were three kinds of kids: the straight-A kids, the kids who were always in trouble and the class clowns" (paragraph 5). Classify the students in a school you attended, and write a narration that shows you as a member of one of the groups in the classification. (See Chapter 11 for information on classification.)

4. **Analyzing and assessing.** Included in "The Poncho Bearer" is a picture of Sam in his poncho on his way to school, an image that appeared in the original *New York Times* essay. Analyze and assess the importance of this image to the essay. Consider what it contributes and what, if anything, would be lost if the image were not included. What makes this particular image effective? Could a different image have been a better choice?

5. **Connecting and synthesizing the readings.** Both Sam in "The Poncho Bearer" and Natalie Kusz in "Ring Leader" (page 217) stand out where many others chose to blend in. Consider fitting in and standing out. When is it better to conform, and when is it better to diverge from the norm? If you like, you can choose a particular context to examine, such as the workplace, the classroom, politics, or family life.

6. **Drawing on sources.** Like Sam, many adolescents assert their individualism through their clothing. Nonetheless, an increasing number of schools are adopting school uniforms. Discuss the chief advantages and disadvantages of school uniforms. For information, you can consult *Education Index* in your library reference room or the Educator's Reference Desk site at www.eduref.org. Type in "school uniforms" in the search box.

BACKGROUND: Natalie Kusz (b. 1962) is the author of the memoir *Road Song* (1990), the story of her family's move to Alaska, and of essays published in *Harper's*, *Threepenny Review*, *McCall's*, *Allure* (where "Ring Leader" was first published in 1990), and other periodicals. Her work has earned, among others, a Whiting Writer's Award, a Pushcart Prize, and fellowships from the NEA, the Bush Foundation, and the Bunting Institute of Radcliffe College. A former faculty member of Bethel College and Harvard University, she now teaches in the MFA (master of fine arts) program at Eastern Washington University.

COMBINED PATTERNS AND THEIR PURPOSES: In "Ring Leader," Natalie Kusz **relates her experience** as an unconventional adolescent and adult and **expresses her feelings** about her physical appearance. Using *narration*, she tells something about herself, first as a high school student and then as a college teacher. Using *cause-and-effect analysis*, she explains what led her to get her nose pierced and the results of that action.

RING LEADER
BY NATALIE KUSZ

I WAS THIRTY YEARS OLD when I had my right nostril pierced, and back-home friends fell speechless at the news, lapsing into long telephone pauses of the sort that June Cleaver would employ if the Beave had ever called to report, "Mom, I'm married. His name's Eddie."[1] Not that I resemble a Cleaver or have friends who wear pearls in the shower, but people who have known me the longest would say that for me to *draw* attention to my body rather than to work all out to *repel* it is at least as out of character as the Beave's abrupt urge for his-and-his golf ensembles. A nose ring, they might tell you, would be my last choice for a fashion accessory, way down on the list with a sagenhancing specialty bra or a sign on my butt reading "Wide Load."

As you read
Notice the humor in the essay. Try to determine what purpose that humor serves.

"The fact is, I grew up ugly—no, worse than that, I grew up unusual, that unforgivable sin . . ."

2   The fact is, I grew up ugly—no, worse than that, I grew up unusual, that unforgivable sin among youth. We lived in Alaska, where, despite what you might have heard about the Rugged Individualist, teenagers still adhere to the universal rules of conformity: If Popular Patty wears contact lenses, then you will by gum get contacts too, or else pocket those glasses and pray you can distinguish the girls' bathroom door from the boys'. The bad news was that I had only one eye, having lost the other in a dog attack at age seven; so although contacts, at half the two-eyed price, were easy to talk my parents into, I was still left with an eye patch and many facial scars, signs as gaudy as neon, telling everyone, "Here is a girl who is Not Like You." And Not Like Them, remember, was equivalent to Not from This Dimension, only half (maybe one third) as interesting.

---

[1] *Leave It to Beaver* was a sit-com that ran 1957 to 1963. In its wholesome premise, the dad went to work and solved the family's minor problems, and June Cleaver, the mother, kept the perfect home. In each episode, the younger son, the Beave, always learned a lesson. Eddie was the smarmy bully on the show.

3   The rest of my anatomy did nothing to help matters. I come from a long line of famine-surviving ancestors—on my father's side, Polish and Russian, on my mother's, everything from Irish to French Canadian—and thus I have an excellent, thrifty, Ebenezer Scrooge of a metabolism. I can ingest but a single calorie, and before quitting time at the Scrooge office, my system will have spent that calorie to replace an old blood cell, to secrete a vital hormone, to send a few chemicals around the old nervous system, and still have enough left over to deposit ten fat cells in my inner thigh—a nifty little investment for the future, in case the Irish potato famine ever recurs. These metabolic wonders are delightful if you are planning a move to central Africa, but for an American kid wiggling to Jane Fonda[2] as if her life depended on it (which, in high school, it did), the luckiest people on earth seemed to be anorexics, those wispy and hollow-cheeked beings whose primary part in the locker room drama was to stand at the mirror and announce, "My God, I disgust myself, I am *so fat*." While the other girls recited their lines ("No, Samantha, don't talk like that, you're beautiful, you really *are!*"), I tried to pull on a gym shirt without removing any other shirt first, writhing inside the cloth like a cat trapped among the bedsheets.

4   Thus, if you add the oversized body to the disfigured face, and add again my family's low income and my secondhand wardrobe, you have a formula for pure, excruciating teenage angst. Hiding from public scrutiny became for me, as for many people like me, a way of life. I developed a bouncy sense of humor, the kind that makes people say, "That Natalie, she is always so *up*," and keeps them from probing for deep emotion. After teaching myself to sew, I made myself cheap versions of those Popular Patty clothes or at least the items (*never* halter tops, although this was the seventies) that a large girl could wear with any aplomb. And above all, I studied the other kids, their physical posture, their music, their methods of blow-dryer artistry, hoping one day to emerge from my body, invisible. I suppose I came as close to invisibility as my appearance would allow, for if you look at the yearbook photos from that time, you will find on my face the same "too cool to say 'cheese'" expression as on Popular Patty's eleven-man entourage.

"Hiding from public scrutiny became . . . a way of life."

5   But at age thirty, I found myself living in the (to me) incomprehensible politeness of America's Midwest, teaching at a small private college that I found suffocating, and anticipating the arrival of that all-affirming desire of college professors everywhere, that professional certification indicating you are now "one of the family": academic tenure. A first-time visitor to any college campus can easily differentiate between tenured and nontenured faculty by keeping in mind a learning institution's two main expectations: (1) that a young professor will spend her first several years on the job proving herself indispensable (sucking up), working to advance the interests of the college (sucking up), and making a name for herself in her field of study (sucking up); and (2) that a senior, tenured professor, having achieved indispensability, institutional usefulness, and fame will thereafter lend her

---

[2]Jane Fonda's exercise videos were very popular in the 1980s and early 1990s.

widely recognized name to the school's public relations office, which will use that name to attract prospective new students and faculty, who will in turn be encouraged to call on senior professors for the purpose of asking deep, scholarly questions (sucking up). Thus, a visitor touring any random campus can quickly distinguish tenured faculty persons from nontenured ones simply by noting the habitual shape and amount of chapping of their lips.

6   I anticipated a future of senior-faculty meetings with academia's own version of Popular Patty—not a nubile, cheerleading fashion plate, but a somber and scholarly denture wearer who, under the legal terms of tenure, cannot be fired except for the most grievous unprofessional behavior, such as igniting plastique under the dean's new Lexus. When that official notice landed in my In box, my sucking-up days would be over. I would have arrived. I would be family.

7   I couldn't bear it. In addition to the fact that I possessed all my own teeth, I was unsuited to Become As One with the other tenured beings because I was by nature boisterous, a collector of Elvis memorabilia, and given to not washing my car—in short, I was and always would be from Alaska.

8   Even in my leisure hours, my roots made my life of that period disorienting. Having moved to the immaculate Midwest from the far-from-immaculate wilderness, I found myself incapable of understanding, say, the nature of cul-de-sacs, those little circles of pristine homes where all the children were named Chris, and where all the parents got to vote on whether the Johnsons (they were all Johnsons) could paint their house beige. I would go to potluck suppers where the dishes were foreign to me, and twelve people at my table would take a bite, savor it with closed eyes, and say, "Ah, Tater Tot casserole. Now *that* takes me back." It got to the point where I felt defensive all the time, professing my out-of-townness whenever I was mistaken for a local, someone who understood the conversational subtexts and genteel body language of a Minnesotan. Moreover, I could never be sure what I myself said to these people with my subtextual language or my body. For all I knew, my posture during one of those impossible kaffeeklatsches proclaimed to everyone, "I am about to steal the silverware," or "I subscribe to the beliefs of Reverend Sun Myung Moon."

9   I grew depressed. Before long, I was feeling nostalgic for Alaskan eccentricities I had avoided even when I had lived there—unshaven legs and armpits, for example, and automobiles held together entirely by duct tape. I began decorating my office with absurd and nonprofessional items: velvet paintings, Mr. Potato Head, and a growing collection of snow globes from each of the fifty states. Students took to coming by to play with Legos, or to blow bubbles from those little circular wands, and a wish started to grow in my brain, a yearning for some way to transport the paraphernalia around with me, to carry it along as an indication that I was truly unconventional at heart.

"Before long, I was feeling nostalgic for Alaskan eccentricities ..."

10   So the week that I received tenure, when they could no longer fire me and when a sore nose would not get bumped during the course of any future sucking-up maneuver, I entered a little shop in the black-leather part of town and emerged within minutes with my right nostril duly pierced. The gesture was, for me, a

celebration, a visible statement that said, "Assume nothing. I might be a punk from Hennepin Avenue, or a belly dancer with brass knuckles in my purse." Polite as was the society of that region, my colleagues never referred to my nose, but I could see them looking and wondering a bit, which was exactly the thing I had wanted—a lingering question in the minds of the natives, the possibility of forces they had never fathomed.

11   After this, my comfort level changed some, and almost entirely for the better. I had warned my father, who lived with me those years, that I was thinking of piercing my nose. When I arrived home that day and the hole was through the side instead of the center—he had expected, I found out, a Maori-style bone beneath the nostrils—he looked at me, his color improved, and he asked if I wanted chicken for dinner. So that was all fine. At school, students got over their initial shock relatively quickly, having already seen the trailer-park ambience of my office, and they became less apt to question my judgment on their papers; I could hear them thinking, She looks like she must understand *something* about where I'm coming from. And my daughter—this is the best part of all—declared I was the hippest parent she knew, and decided it was O.K. to introduce me to her junior high friends; even Cool Chris—the Midwestern variety of Popular Patty—couldn't boast a body-pierced mom.

12   I have since moved away from Minnesota, and old friends (those of the afore-mentioned June Cleaver–type stunned silence) have begun to ask if I have decided to stop wearing a nose stud now that my initial reason for acquiring it has passed. And here, to me, is the interesting part: the answer, categorically, is no. Nonconfor-mity, or something like it, may have been the initial reason behind shooting a new hole through my proboscis, but a whole set of side effects, a broad and unexpected brand of liberation, has provided me a reason for keeping it. Because the one-eyed fat girl who couldn't wear Popular Patty's clothes, much less aspire to steal her boyfriends, who was long accustomed to the grocery-store stares of adults and small children ("Mommy, what happened to that fat lady's face?"), who had learned over the years to hide whenever possible, slathering her facial scars with cover stick, is now—am I dreaming?—in charge. I have now, after all, deliberately chosen a "facial flaw," a remarkable aspect of appearance. Somehow now, the glances of strangers seem less invasive, nothing to incite me to nunhood; a long look is just that—a look—and what of it? I've invited it, I've made room for it, it is no longer inflicted upon me against my will.

READING CLOSELY AND THINKING CRITICALLY

1.   Why does Kusz get her nose pierced?

2.   What were the various reactions to the author's pierced nose? Why did people react the way they did?

3.   In paragraph 2, Kusz says that among youth, looking unusual is worse than being ugly. What does she mean?

4.   Did Kusz fit in as a faculty member? Explain.

5.   Kusz felt self-conscious about her appearance, and that self-consciousness influ-enced her behavior. How did it influence her behavior as an adolescent? As an adult?

EXAMINING STRUCTURE AND STRATEGY

1. How does Kusz use flashback? How does the flashback help the author achieve her purpose?
2. What words describe the tone of the essay? (See page 69 on tone.)
3. What purpose does the humor in the essay serve? How does that purpose compare to the purpose humor served in the author's life?

NOTING COMBINED PATTERNS

1. Where does Kusz use cause-and-effect analysis? (Cause-and-effect analysis is explained in Chapter 10.)
2. Description appears throughout the essay, but particularly in paragraphs 2, 3, and 9. How does the description in those paragraphs help the author achieve her writing purpose?

CONSIDERING LANGUAGE AND STYLE

1. In paragraph 1, Kusz refers to characters from *Leave It to Beaver,* a popular television program of the late 50s and early 60s that depicted middle-class whites in an overly wholesome way. June Cleaver was the ideal wife and mother. Her son Beaver was an all-American child. Friend Eddie was a troublemaker. How does Kusz use these references?
2. Explain the word play in the title of the essay.
3. Consult a dictionary if you are unsure of the meaning of any of these words: *angst* (paragraph 4), *aplomb* (paragraph 4), *entourage* (paragraph 4), *nubile* (paragraph 6), *plastique* (paragraph 6), *cul-de-sacs* (paragraph 8), *kaffeeklatsches* (paragraph 8), *ambience* (paragraph 11), *proboscis* (paragraph 12).

FOR DISCUSSION IN CLASS OR ONLINE

Body piercing and tattooing have become popular in recent years, particularly among young people. With your classmates, discuss why you think these practices are so popular.

WRITING ASSIGNMENTS

1. **Writing in your journal.** When you were in high school, how did you feel about your appearance? To what extent did that feeling affect your behavior then, and how does it affect you now? Answer in a page or two.
2. **Using narration for a purpose.** The purposes given in the assignments are possibilities. You may establish whatever purpose you like, within your instructor's guidelines.
   - To relate your experience and perhaps express your feelings, narrate a story that reveals something about what high school was like for you.
   - In paragraph 4, Kusz refers to teenage angst. If you suffered from teenage angst, write a narration that tells about a time you experienced it. Your purpose is to express your feelings and relate your experience.

- Narrate a story in which you or someone you know is revealed as unconventional to inform your reader about this characteristic in yourself or the other person.
- Tell a story about a time you did not fit in to relate your experience and perhaps express your feelings.

3. **Combining patterns.** Kusz notes that in addition to being affected by her physical appearance, she was shaped by living in Alaska. Use narration and cause-and-effect analysis to tell a story that illustrates how you were affected by the town or neighborhood where you grew up. If you like, you can also explain why the town or neighborhood affected you the way it did. (Cause-and-effect analysis is explained in Chapter 10.)

4. **Analyzing and assessing.** Analyze the way Kusz describes people and places. You might consider her word choice, tone, and amount and kind of detail. Assess what that description contributes to the narration and to helping Kusz achieve her writing purpose.

5. **Connecting and synthesizing the readings.** Discuss the connection between our self-concepts and how we feel about our appearance. To what extent does how we think we look affect how we feel about ourselves? In addition to the ideas in "Ring Leader," the ideas in "Am I Blue?" (page 379) may be helpful.

6. **Drawing on sources.** Many people have body image problems because they look in the mirror and do not like what they see, even though they look perfectly fine. Some people speculate that the impossible standard of beauty presented in magazine and television advertisements contributes to body image problems. Study a sampling of advertisements in magazines and on television, and then agree or disagree with this speculation. You can also look in the *Social Sciences Index* under the heading "body image."

BACKGROUND: Born in 1947, award-winning author Lee K. Abbott is a distinguished professor of humanities at The Ohio State University, where he has also directed the MFA program in creative writing. He has written many collections of short stories, including *It's Only Rock and Roll: An Anthology of Rock and Roll Short Stories* (1998) and *All Things at Once* (2006). "The View of Me from Mars" was originally published in Abbott's collection *Dreams and Distant Lives* (1990). His work has appeared in *Harper's, Ploughshares, Kenyon Review,* and other publications, including *Best American Short Stories, 1984.*

COMBINED PATTERNS AND THEIR PURPOSES: In "The View of Me from Mars," Lee K. Abbott *narrates* two stories, one within the other. Look for *description,* which creates vivid scenes, and *cause-and-effect analysis,* which offers explanation and consequences of an event. Abbott himself claims that his stories are not meant to teach: "I don't write to instruct anybody about anything. I've got nothing to tell people that they didn't already know by the time they got to be fourteen." Nonetheless, you may find that in addition to **entertaining**, the story **informs** because it makes specific points about human behavior.

The View of Me from Mars

BY LEE K. ABBOTT

A week before I became a father, which now seems like the long ago and far away fairy tales happen in, I read a father-child story that went straight at the surprise one truth between children and parents is. It was called "Mirrors," and had an end, to the twenty-three-year-old would-be know-it-all I was, that literally threw me back in my chair—an end, sad somehow and wise, which held that it is now and then necessary for the child, in ways mysterious with love, to forgive the parent.

As you read
Decide what Abbott's main point is.

2   In "Mirrors" the child was a girl, though it could have been a boy just as easily, whose father—a decent man, we have to believe—takes her to the sideshow tent at a one-horse and one-elephant circus in the flatlands of Iowa or Nebraska or Kansas. She's seven or eight at this time, and—as we have all begged for toys or experiences it can be, I see now, our misfortune to receive—she begs and begs to see the snake charmer and the tattooed lady, the giant and the dwarf. He gives in, the girl decides much later, because of his decency; or he gives in, as my own father might say, because he's too much a milk-and cookies sort of fool to understand that in that smelly, ill-lit tent is knowledge it is a parent's duty often to deny or to avoid. It is a good moment, I tell you, this moment when they pay their quarters and go in, one person full of pride, the other sucking on cotton candy, the sad end of them still pages and pages away.

3   In that tent—a whole hour I think—walking from little stage to little stage, the girl is awestruck and puzzled and, well, breath-taken, full of questions about where these people, these creatures, live and what they do when they're not standing in front of a bunch of hayseeds and would it be possible to get a face, a tattoo, printed on her knee. "Can I touch?" she asks. "Do they talk?" A spotlight comes on, blue and harsh, and nearby, in a swirl of cigarette smoke and field dust, are two little people, Mr. and Mrs. Tiny, gussied up like a commodore and his society bride;

another light snaps on, yellow this time and ten paces away, and there stands a man—"A boy," the barker tells us, "only eighteen and still growing!"—who's already nine feet tall, his arms long as shovels, nothing in his face about his own parents or what he wants to be at twenty-five. These are clichés, my smart wife, Ellen Kay, tells me ("Sounds too artsy-fartsy," her exact words were when I read the thing to her), but in the story I remember, these are the exhibitions girl and man pass by—the girl Christmas Eve impatient, the man nervous—before they come to the main display, which is, in "Mirrors," a young woman, beautiful and smooth as china, who has no arms and no legs.

4   The father, complaining that he's grubby-feeling and hot, wants to get out, but his daughter, her heart hammering in her ears, can't move. As never before, she's conscious of her own hands and feet, the wonders they are. She's aware of smells—breath and oil and two-dollar cologne—and of sounds—a gasp here, a whisper there, exclamations that have in them ache and horror and fear. "C'mon," the father says, taking her elbow. But onstage, businesslike as a banker, the woman—"The Human Torso," the barker announces, "smart like the dickens"—is drinking water, the glass clamped against her neck by her shoulder; is putting on lipstick; is writing her name with a brush between her teeth; is, Lordy, about to type—with her chin maybe—a letter to a Spec 4 with the Army in Korea, her boyfriend.

5   Outside, the midway glittering and crowded with Iowans going crosswise, the girl, more fascinated than frightened (though the fright is coming), asks how that was done. The father has a Lucky Strike out now, and the narrator—seven or eight but on the verge of learning that will stay with her until seventy or eighty—realizes he's stalling. He's embarrassed, maybe sick. He says "Howdy" to a deadbeat he'd never otherwise talk to. He says he's hungry, how about a hot dog, some buttered popcorn? He's cold, he says, too cold for September. "How?" she says again, pulling at his sleeve a little and watching his face go stiff and loose in a way that has her saying to herself, "I am not scared. No, I am not." And then he says what the narrator realizes will be his answer—sometimes comic, often not—for all thereafter that astounds or baffles and will not be known: "Mirrors, it's done with mirrors."

6   There's a pause here, I remember, six sentences that tell what the weather is like and how, here and there, light bulbs are missing and what the girl's favorite subjects are in school. "What?" she thinks to ask, but doesn't. "It's an illusion," he says, his voice squeaky the way it gets when he talks about money they don't have much of. "A trick, like magic." Part of her—the part that can say the sum of two plus two, and that A is for Apple, B is for Boy—knows that mirrors have nothing to do with what she's seen; another part—the half of her that will remember this incident for ever and ever—knows that her father, now as strange to her as the giant and the dwarf, is lying.

7   His hand is working up and down, and his expression says, as lips and eyes and cheeks will, that he's sorry, he didn't mean for her to see that, she's so young. Something is trembling inside her, a muscle or a bone. One-Mississippi, she says to herself. Two-Mississippi. Over there sits a hound dog wearing a hat and somewhere a shout is going up that says somebody won a Kewpie doll or a stuffed monkey, and up ahead, creaking and clanking, the Tilt-A-Whirl is full of people spinning

round and round goggle-eyed. Her father has a smile not connected to his eyes—another lie—and his hand out to be held, and going by them is a fat lady who lives on Jefferson Street and a man with a limp who lives on Spruce. Her father seems too hairy to her now, and maybe not sharp-minded enough, with a nose too long and knobby. She tells herself what she is, which is a good dancer and smart about which side the fork goes on and who gets introduced first when strangers meet; and what she is not, which is strong enough to do pull-ups and watchful about who goes where and why. She is learning something, she thinks. There is being good, she thinks. And there is not. There is the truth, she thinks. And there is not.

8   And so, in the climax of what I read years and years ago, she says, her hands sticky and her dress white as Hollywood daylight, "Yes, mirrors, I thought so"—words that, years and years ago, said all I thought possible about lies and love and how forgiveness works.

9   In this story, which is true and only two days old and also about forgiveness, I am the father to be read about and the child is my son, Stuart Eliot Polk, Jr. (called "Pudge" in and out of the family); he's a semifat golfer—"linksman," he insists the proper term is—and honor student who will at the end of this summer go off to college and so cease to be a citizen in the sideshow tent my big house here in El Paso now clearly is. Yes, forgiveness—particularly ironic in that, since my graduation years ago from Perkins Seminary at SMU, it has been my job to say, day after day after day, the noises that are "It will get better" and "We all make mistakes" to a thousand Methodists who aim to be themselves forgiven and sent home happy. There is no "freak" here, except the ordinary one I am, and no storybook midway, except my modern kitchen and its odd come and go.

10   I am an adulterer—an old-fashioned word, sure, but the only one appropriate to the ancient sin it names; and my lover—a modern word not so full of terror and guilt and judgment as another—was, until two days ago, Terri Ann Mackey, a rich, three-times-married former Zeta Tau Alpha Texas girl who might one day make headlines for the dramatic hair she has or the way she can sing Conway Twitty tunes. In every way likable and loud and free-minded, she has, in the last four years, met me anywhere and everywhere—in the Marriott and Hilton hotels, in the Cavern of Music in Juarez, even at a preachers' retreat at the Inn of the Mountain Gods near Ruidoso in southern New Mexico's piney forests. Dressed up in this or that outfit she sent away for or got on a trip to Dallas, she has, to my delight and education, pretended to be naughty as what we imagine the Swedish are or nice as Snow White; she has pretended, in a hundred rented rooms, to be everything I thought my wife was not—daring and wicked, heedless as a tyrant. Shameful to say, it seems we have always been here, in this bright desert cowtown, now farflung and fifty percent ticky-tacky, drinking wine and fornicating and then hustling home to deceive people we were wed to. Shameful to say, it seems we have always been playing the eyes' version of footsy—her in pink and cactus yellow in a pew in the middle of St. Paul's, me in the pulpit sermonizing about parables and Jesus and what welfare we owe the lost and poor and beaten down.

11   "Yes," my wife, Ellen Kay, would answer when I told her I was at the Stanton Street Racquet Club playing handball with a UTEP management professor named

Red Walker. "Go change," she'd say, herself lovely and schoolgirl trim as that woman I'd collapsed atop a half-hour before. "I phoned," she'd say, "Mrs. Denbo said you were out." Yes, I'd tell her. I was in the choir room, hunting organ music that would inspire and not be hokey; I was in the library, looking up what the Puritan Mathers had written about witchcraft and gobbledygook we are better off without; I was taking a drive in my Volvo, the better to clear my head so I could get to the drafting of a speech for the Rotarians, or the LULAC Club of Ysleta, or the Downtown Optimists. "You work too hard," she'd say, "let's go to Acapulco this year." And I'd head to my big bedroom, the men I am, the public one amazed by his private self—the first absolutely in love with a blonde continental-history major he'd courted at the University of Texas in 1967; the second still frazzled by what, in the afternoon, is made from deceit and bednoise and indecency. And until two days ago, it was possible to believe that I knew which was which, what what.

12   "Where were you?" Ellen Kay said, making (though too violently, I think now) the tuna casserole I like enough to eat twice a year. "I called everywhere," she said. "It was as if you didn't exist." Upset, her hair spilling out of the French roll she prefers, she said more, two or three paragraphs whose theme was my peculiar behavior and the sly way I had lately and what time I was supposed to be somewhere and was not; and suddenly, taking note of the thump-thump my heart made and how one cloud in the east looked like a bell, I stood at the sink, steadily drinking glass after glass of water, trying to put some miles between me and her suspicions. Terri Ann Mackey Cruz Robinson Cross was all over me, my hands and my thighs and my face; and, a giant step away, my wife was asking where I'd been. "You were going to call," Ellen Kay said. "You had an appointment, a meeting." I had one thought, which was about the bricked-up middle of me, and another, which was about how like TV this situation was. "I talked to Bill Watson at the bank," she said. "He hasn't seen you for a week, ten days. I called—" And her wayward husband had a moment then, familiar to all cheaters and sorry folks, when he thought he'd tell the truth; a moment, before fear hit him and he got a 3-D vision of the cheap world he'd have to live in, when he thought to make plain the creature he was and the no-account stage he stood upon.

13   "I was at the golf course," I said, "watching Pudge. They have a match tomorrow." The oven was closed, the refrigerator opened. "Which course?" she said. Forks and knives had been brought out, made a pile of. "Coronado Hills," I said. "Pudge is hitting the ball pretty good." She went past me a dozen times, carrying the plates and the bread and the fruit bowl, and I tried to meet her eyes and so not give away the corrupt inside of me. I thought of several Latin words—*bellum* and *verus* and *fatum*—and the Highland Park classroom I learned them in. "All right," she said, though by the dark notes in her voice it was clear she was going to ask Pudge if he'd seen me there, by the green I'd claimed to have stood next to, applauding the expert wedge shot I'd seen with my very own eyes.

14   As in the former story of illusions and the mess they make crashing down, there is a pause here, one of two; and you are to imagine now how herky-jerky time moved in our house when Pudge drove up and came in and said howdy and washed his hands as he'd been a million times told. You are to imagine, too, the dinner we picked at and our small talk about school and American government

and what money does. While time went up and down, I thought about Pudge the way evil comic-book Martians are said to think about us: I was curious to know how I'd be affected by what, in a minute or an hour, would come from the mouth of an earthling who, so far as I knew, had never looked much beyond himself to see the insignificant dust ball he stood upon. I saw him as his own girlfriend, Traci Dixon, must: polite, fussy as a nun, soft-spoken about everything except golf and how it is, truly, a full-fledged sport.

15   Part of me—that eye and ear which would make an excellent witness at an auto wreck or similar calamity—flew up to one high corner of the room, like a ghost or an angel, and wondered what could be said about these three people who sat there and there and there. They were Democrats who, in a blue moon, liked what Reagan did; they had Allstate insurance and bank books and stacks of paper that said where they were in the world and what business they conducted with it; they played Scrabble and Clue and chose to watch the news Dan Rather read. The wife, who once upon a time could run fast enough to be useful in flag football, now used all her energy to keep mostly white-collar rednecks from using the words "nigger" and "spic" in her company; the son, who had once wanted to be an astronaut or a Houston brain surgeon, now aimed to be the only Ph.D. in computer science to win the Masters at Augusta, Georgia; and the father—well, what was there to say about a supposedly learned man for whom the spitting image of God, Who was up and yonder and everywhere, was his own father, a bent-over and gin-soaked cattle rancher in Midland, Texas? I hovered in that corner, distant and disinterested, and then Ellen Kay spoke to Pudge, and I came rushing back, dumb and helpless as anything human that falls from a great height.

16   "Daddy says you had a good round this afternoon," Ellen Kay began. "You had an especially nice wedge shot, he says." She was being sneaky, which my own sneaky self admired; and Pudge quit the work his chewing was, a little confusion in his round, smart face. He was processing, that machine between his ears crunching data that in no way could ever be, and for the fifteen seconds we made eye contact I wanted him to put aside reason and logic and algebra and see me with his guts and heart. On his lip he had a crumb that, if you didn't tell him, would stay until kingdom come; I wanted him to stop blinking and wrinkling his forehead like a first-year theater student. The air was heavy in that room, the light coming from eight directions at once, and I wanted to remind him of our trip last January to the Phoenix Open and that too-scholarly talk we'd had about the often mixed-up relations between men and women. I had a picture of me throwing a ball to him, and of him catching it. I had a picture of him learning to drive a stick shift, and of him so carefully mowing our lawn. Oddly, I thought about fishing, which I hate, and bowling, which I am silly at, and then Ellen Kay, putting detergent in the dishwasher, asked him again about events that never happened, and I took a deep breath I expected to hold until the horror stopped.

17   Here is that second pause I spoke of—that moment, before time lurches forward again, when the eye needs to look elsewhere to see what is ruined, what not. Pudge now knew I was lying. His eyes went here and there, to the clock above my shoulder, to his mother's overwatered geranium on the windowsill, to his mostly empty plate. He was learning something about me—and about himself too. Like

his made-up counterpart in "Mirrors," he was seeing that I, his father, was afraid and weak and damaged; and like the invented daddy in that story I read, a daddy whose interior life we were not permitted to see, I wanted my own child, however numbed or shocked, to forgive me for the tilt the world now stood at, to say I was not responsible for the sad magic trick our common back-and-forth really is. "Tell her," I said. I had in mind a story he could confirm—the Coke we shared in the clubhouse, a corny joke that was heard, and the help I tried to be with his short game—a story that had nowhere in it, two days ago, a father cold and alone and small.

CONSIDERING THE SHORT STORY

1. What point can be taken from "The View of Me from Mars"? Where in the story is that point expressed?

2. Both the narrator and the father in "Mirrors" tell lies. How are the lies different? Is one of the lies more justifiable than the other? Explain.

3. In paragraph 17, the narrator says his son "was learning something about me—and about himself too." What was the son learning?

4. What do you think the title of Abbott's short story means?

5. Writers use cause-and-effect analysis to explain the reasons something happens and the consequences of that event. How does Abbott use cause-and-effect analysis?

WRITING ASSIGNMENTS

1. **Writing in your journal.**
   - In a page or so, consider whether the father in "Mirrors" did the right thing in lying to his daughter.
   - Do you think the narrator's son should have lied for his father? Explain your view.

2. **Using narration for a purpose.** To relate your experience and express your feelings—or for another purpose—tell about a time you learned something positive or negative about a parent or another authority figure.

3. **Combining patterns.** Tell about a time you lied or were lied to. Explain the causes and/or effects of the lie. As an alternative, tell about a time you needed forgiveness or a time you forgave someone.

WRITING NARRATION

See pages 191–194 for strategies for writing narration and for a revision checklist.

1. Narrate an account of an event that caused you to change your view of someone or something.

2. Narrate an account of an embarrassing moment that you or someone you know suffered. If you wish, make the narration humorous.

3. Narrate an account of a childhood memory. If possible, include description and dialogue.

4. Tell the story of a time when things did not go as you expected them to. Be sure to indicate the point of the narration.

5. Tell the story of an event that marked a turning point in your life. Be sure to indicate how you were affected by this event.

6. Narrate an account of a happy birthday or holiday celebration. Try to include dialogue and description.

7. Tell the story of a time when you displayed or witnessed courage.

8. Tell the story of an athletic event in which you were involved. Be sure to indicate the point of the narration.

9. Tell the story of a disappointment someone you know experienced. Be sure to indicate the point of the narration.

10. Tell a story that shows that people can be cruel (or kind).

11. Tell a story that shows that we rely heavily on technology.

12. Tell the story of a time that you or someone you know overcame an obstacle. Be sure to indicate the point of the narration.

13. Tell the story of a time when hard work did (or did not) pay off.

14. Tell a story about a school experience you have had. Be sure to indicate the point of the narration.

15. Tell a story that reveals a personality trait of someone. For example, if you have a friend who is reckless, tell a story that illustrates that recklessness. Try to use description and dialogue.

16. Tell a story that shows that things are not always what they seem.

17. Tell a story that shows that some modern device (the car, the DVD player, the computer, or the cell phone, for example) is more trouble than it is worth. If you like, you can make the narration humorous.

18. Tell a story that shows we should be careful of what we wish for because we may get it.

19. Narrate an account of a difficult decision that you had to make. Be sure to indicate the effect the decision had on you.

20. **Narration in context.** Assume that you are contributing a piece for a "My Life" column in your campus newspaper. The piece will be a narration about a first-time experience: the first time you drove a car, a first kiss, your first day of college, your first job, your first time away from home, and so on. Your column should indicate the effect the experience had on you. If you want, you can make the narration humorous. To come up with ideas, list all the "firsts" you can think of.

The man in the car is smiling, but he probably won't be for long. Narrate an account of how he discovers where his briefcase is and what happens when he does.

Exemplification

Americans look up to many kinds of people as heroes, including firefighters like the one on the facing page. Take a minute or two to list examples of individuals we consider American heroes. Then consider your examples and think about the kinds of people we label as heroes. What qualities do these people share?

THE PATTERN

"Can you give me an example?" How many times have you asked that question? Like most people, you probably ask for examples often—and for good reason, because nothing better clarifies a point. Usually, examples clarify by making the general more specific; in this way, they also give support to your point, helping show that it is true. To understand how examples work to clarify, consider this statement:

> Living in a high-tech society has its drawbacks.

To clarify that general statement, specific examples can be added, like this:

> Living in a high-tech society has its drawbacks. For example, we give up genuine human interaction in favor of virtual relationships. We connect on Facebook rather than over lunch; we communicate through e-mail instead of on the telephone; we visit over Skype instead of in our living rooms; and we engage in fast Tweets over Twitter rather than in satisfying, extended face-to-face conversations.

233

In addition to clarifying points, specific examples can keep your writing interesting. In this chapter's "The Snoop Next Door," Jennifer Saranow notes that the Internet is being used to embarrass people publicly. The example she gives to support the point is likely to keep her audience reading because it is so interesting. See if you agree.

> Last month, Eva Burgess was eating breakfast at the Rose Cafe in Venice, Calif., when she remembered she needed to make an appointment with her eye doctor. So the New York theater director got on her cellphone and booked a date.
>
> Almost immediately, she started receiving "weird and creepy" calls directing her to a blog. There, under the posting "Eva Burgess Is Getting Glasses!" her name, cellphone number and other details mentioned in her call to the doctor's office were posted, along with the admonition, "next time, you might take your business outside." The offended blogger had been sitting next to Ms. Burgess in the cafe.

Because they support your point, examples can also help you persuade your reader. In "Untouchables," another essay in this chapter, Jonathan Kozol uses examples to convince his audience that the government treats the homeless cruelly:

> In several cities it is a crime to sleep in public; in some, armrests have been inserted in the middle of park benches to make it impossible for homeless people to lie down. In others, trash has been defined as "public property," making it a felony to forage in the rotted food.

When you use specific examples, or instances, to clarify a point, add interest, or persuade, you are using **exemplification.**

---

www.mhhe.com/clousepatterns6	Exemplification

For more help with using examples, click on

Writing > Paragraph Patterns
Writing > Writing Tutor > Exemplification

USING EXEMPLIFICATION FOR A PURPOSE

No matter what your writing purpose, examples will clarify, support, or explain a **generalization,** which is a statement of a general point you consider to be true in your own life or in a broader context. For example, to *entertain* your reader, you could give examples of your humorous mishaps on campus to support the generalization that your first week of college was a comedy of errors. You can also use examples to *express feelings* and *relate experience*. For example, in "On Being the Target of Discrimination" in this chapter, Ralph Ellison expresses the pain he felt and relates the difficulty he endured by giving examples supporting the generalization that as a child he faced racial discrimination.

By supporting generalizations, examples can also, of course, *inform* and *persuade* readers. In his essay, Jonathan Kozol gives examples of what the homeless experience in order to support the generalization that the homeless are treated unfairly and thereby inform his audience about the treatment of the homeless and persuade them that it is unfair.

Combining Patterns for a Purpose

You can combine exemplification with other patterns to achieve your purpose for writing. For example, if you want to *entertain* your readers by giving humorous examples of your blind dates gone wrong, in some of the examples, you can *describe* the outrageous appearance of your date; you can also *narrate* amusing events that occurred during some of these dates. If you want to *inform* readers by giving them examples of the best job search strategies, one example might be using a job search Web site, and you could include *process analysis* to explain how to use that Web site to best advantage.

To see how other patterns can be combined with exemplification, study the following excerpt from "Lifosuction," an essay in this chapter. Part of paragraph 4, it combines exemplification, definition, and cause-and-effect analysis.

EXCERPT FROM "LIFOSUCTION" COMBINING EXEMPLIFICATION, DEFINITION, AND CAUSE-AND-EFFECT ANALYSIS

The definition informs by explaining the meaning of a term the writer coined. Because the term is clever, the definition also entertains.

definition

But what about lifosuction—the removal from one's biography of innocuous yet somehow unsightly elements that happen to be true? It is a common procedure.

The cause-and-effect analysis informs by giving one reason people engage in lifosuction: to align the public persona and the reality.

cause-and-effect analysis and example

Musicians, for instance, have a powerful incentive to make sure that public pose and personal background are appropriately in sync.

The examples inform by giving one group of people who engage in lifosuction (musicians) and one musician in the group (Jim Morrison).

example

Jim Morrison, of The Doors, who fashioned himself into an icon of anarchy and self-destruction, never took pains to point out that he was the son of an admiral.

Because examples are so important for clarifying and supporting, adding interest, and persuading, you will use them often, even when exemplification is not your primary pattern of development. Suppose you are using cause-and-effect analysis to explain why sexually active teenagers often do not use birth control. Once you note that teens may not always understand when and how pregnancy can occur, you could support this with an example you read of a 15-year-old who became pregnant because she thought she was "safe" since it was her first sexual experience.

Whether you use exemplification alone or in combination with other patterns depends on what helps you achieve your particular writing purpose or purposes for your particular audience.

Exemplification beyond the Writing Classroom

Exemplification helps writer's achieve their purpose in many writing situations.

IN ACADEMIC WRITING AND READING   You will use exemplification in most of your academic writing, including essay examinations and required papers. Assignments that direct you to "explain and illustrate . . . ," "define and provide examples of . . . ," and "cite illustrations to show that . . ." are requiring you to use examples. In a world history class, you may be asked to explain and illustrate the role of women in ancient Egypt. In a political science class, you may argue for or against gun control legislation, and to do so, you may cite examples of murder rates in countries that either have or lack such legislation. In an education class, you might argue against proficiency exams by citing examples of problems such tests cause or fail to address. In a marketing class, you might define and illustrate target marketing, and in a biology class, you might define and illustrate natural selection.

Because examples clarify points so well, they help us understand important concepts. For that reason, you will encounter examples frequently in all your textbooks, as in this excerpt from an introduction to business textbook:

First are examples of civic institutions a business needs its employees to be involved in followed by an extended example to illustrate civic involvement and how it helps a business.

Business is perhaps the most crucial institution of civil society. For its own well-being, business depends on its employees being active in politics, law, churches, arts, charities, and so on. For example, some folks at the General Electric plastics division helped their community while developing their own team-building skills. Rather than heading to a resort hotel to participate in some isolated team-building activities, the group went into the neighborhood surrounding their offices and helped rebuild the community, barn-raising style. The result back on the job was a sense of team camaraderie that proved as lasting as the buildings that were rebuilt. (Nickels, McHugh, and McHugh, *Understanding Business*)

AT WORK AND IN THE COMMUNITY   Workplace writing also requires examples. Job application letters highlight examples of accomplishments: "As an intern in a local advertising agency, I learned a great deal about copywriting, including how to target an audience, how to assess that audience, and how to write colorfully yet succinctly." Written job descriptions state and illustrate responsibilities: "The regional sales manager supports the sales staff in any way needed. The support can include providing budget funds for travel, visiting important clients, and brainstorming for marketing ideas." Performance evaluations give examples of workplace behavior: "Lee is unreliable. He consistently arrives late, leaves early, and calls in sick."

Examples are also an important part of writing in other areas of your life. If you are writing to persuade a friend to vote for a particular candidate, you might provide examples of that person's accomplishments: "Grace Wang is a sound fiscal manager. She has been financial vice president for First Asset Mortgage Company for 12 years, and she has successfully managed the investments of Park Street Church for 10 years." When you write a condolence note to a person who lost a loved one, you can share an example of your memories of the deceased: "Whenever I talked to Juan, he always made me laugh." If you place a classified ad for a garage sale, you might give examples of your wares to attract the right customers: "Children's toys, including action figures, Hot Wheels cars, and numerous board games."

SUPPORTING DETAILS

The examples you use to support a generalization can come from a variety of sources: personal experience, observation, general knowledge, class lectures, reading research, and so forth. In "Untouchables" (page 275), for instance, Jonathan Kozol's examples of the trials of the homeless come from *research* and *observation*—he interviewed many homeless people to get his information. In "On Being the Target of Discrimination" (page 262), Ralph Ellison gives examples of encounters from his own *experience* to illustrate the nature of racial discrimination. If you wanted to illustrate how much time students spend sunbathing during spring semester, you could *observe* students on the quad over several afternoons. Or to illustrate that people lie about unimportant things, you could cite examples given during a recent psychology *class lecture* on why people lie.

Examples can take many forms. Sometimes an example is a simple fact. Jonathan Kozol makes this statement in "Untouchables":

> Several cities have devised unusual measures to assure that homeless people will learn quickly that they are not welcome.

His clarifying examples, which directly follow the statement, are simple facts:

> Several cities have devised unusual measures to assure that homeless people will learn quickly that they are not welcome. In Laramie, Wyoming, they are given one night's shelter. On the next morning, an organization called "The Good Samaritan Fund" gives them one-way tickets to another town. The college town of Lancaster, Ohio, offers homeless families one-way tickets to Columbus.

An example can also take the form of a narration. In "Untouchables," Jonathan Kozol tells the story of how a financially secure man became homeless. This narrative illustrates that even middle-class people can suffer reversals that lead to the loss of their homes.

Sometimes examples take the form of description. For example, to illustrate that people do not care about cleaning up the planet, you could describe the litter in a public park and the pollution of a local river.

You may be wondering how many examples you should use. The appropriate number should be based on audience and purpose. How much does your audience know about your topic? How difficult is the material? The less your readers know and the more challenging the material, the more examples your readers may require. Are you attempting to persuade your readers to think or act in a particular way? If so, you may need more examples than if your purpose is to entertain.

Example length can also factor into your decision about how many examples to use. If your examples are extended, you may not need to use as many as you would if they were brief. For example, in "On Being the Target of Discrimination," Ralph Ellison provides only three examples of his personal experience of racism, but each one is richly detailed. Your goal is to provide enough examples in enough detail to achieve your purpose.

Hypothetical Examples

Sometimes writers use **hypothetical examples.** These are not actual examples drawn from real life but are examples created by the writer as typical examples based on knowledge, experience, observation, and so on. To be effective, hypothetical examples must be plausible, and they must not be overused. They should also be clearly recognizable as hypothetical examples. For example, suppose you want to illustrate that advertisements make beer drinking look cool. Rather than point to specific, actual advertisements, you could say something like this:

> Beer commercials make it seem that beer drinkers have more fun. As any- one who has watched TV knows, a typical beer commercial might show

some guys on a beach having the time of their lives—and, of course, open-ing some beers—while some beautiful, scantily clad women walk by, obvi-ously hoping to join the guys with the beer.

This example, although made up, is sufficiently like real beer commercials to be effective. In other words, to be effective, a hypothetical example must be representative enough of reality that it *could* happen.

ORGANIZING DETAILS

In an exemplification essay, you might have as your thesis the generaliza-tion your examples will prove or clarify. Consider the thesis of "The Snoop Next Door," an essay in this chapter:

> Now, it's not just brutal police officers, panty-free celebrities and way-ward politicians who are being outed online. The most trivial missteps by ordinary folks are increasingly ripe for exposure as well.

Much of the rest of the essay provides examples of ordinary people who have been "outed" online; that is, it provides examples of regular folks who are being shamed online for minor social infractions, such as poor parking.

Often, in your body paragraphs, you will want to introduce your exam-ples with topic sentences, like this one from "The Snoop Next Door":

> For people singled out, the sites can represent an unsettling form of street justice, with no due process.

After this topic sentence, the author gives an example of a person singled out for online street justice—"justice" dispensed without due process.

You can often arrange your examples in a **progressive order,** from the least to the most compelling. As an effective alternative, place your two strongest examples first and last, with the others in between. Progressive order is effective for a persuasive purpose because it provides a strong final impression with its convincing example at the end.

Sometimes **chronological order** is effective. For example, to illustrate that a particular politician's record is problematic, you could give examples arranged in chronological order from the time the politician took office up to the present.

On occasion, **spatial order** is desirable. For example, to demonstrate that your campus presents obstacles for the physically disabled, you could move across the campus space (maybe north to south) giving examples of physical barriers.

VISUALIZING AN EXEMPLIFICATION ESSAY

The chart on the next page can help you visualize the structure for an exemplification essay. Like all good models, however, this one can be altered as needed.

INTRODUCTION

- Creates interest in the essay
- States the thesis (underlined in the example), which can embody the generalization that will be supported with examples

EXAMPLE

A curious phenomenon exists in America. <u>Children are told to act their age by adults who try to deny their own years.</u>

FIRST BODY PARAGRAPH

- Gives one or more examples, which can be introduced with a topic sentence and can take the form of simple fact, explanation, narration, or description
- May include brief or extended examples
- May include hypothetical examples
- Arranges details in progressive, chronological, or occasionally spatial order

EXAMPLE

Adult women (and increasingly men) alter their appearance to make it more youthful. They dye their hair to cover gray, and they get botox injections to eliminate wrinkles. . . .

NEXT BODY PARAGRAPHS

- Continue until all the examples, which may take whatever form is most appropriate, are given and developed
- Arrange details in progressive, chronological, or occasionally spatial order

EXAMPLE

Adults of a certain age don't merely try to look young; they also try to act younger than they are. They use (and mostly misuse) teenage slang, and they make themselves look ridiculous at weddings imitating the current dance crazes—almost always unsuccessfully. . . .

CONCLUSION

- Provides a satisfying finish
- Leaves your reader with a strong final impression

EXAMPLE

Maybe it's because I'm still young, but I don't understand why forty-, fifty-, and sixty-somethings can't take pleasure in the age they are rather than try to recapture their youth. Every stage has its pleasures; adults should learn that.

THINKING CRITICALLY ABOUT EXEMPLIFICATION

You learned in Chapters 1 and 4 that thinking critically about your reading and writing involves analysis and assessment. To read and write critically about exemplification, use what you learned in those chapters, and ask the following questions:

- **Are the examples real or made up?** If examples are not actual instances from the writer's experience, observation, or research, then they are made up (hypothetical). Essays can effectively use hypothetical examples, as explained on page 238. However, examples should not be made up and passed off as true. For example, a writer supporting the generalization "First-year college students experience too much stress" cannot fairly manufacture an example about a roommate who tried to commit suicide.

- **Are there enough examples in enough detail?** One or two brief examples will not likely clarify or support a generalization, so be sure that enough examples appear and that each is adequately detailed. The amount of clarification or support needed will depend on the generalization and on your audience and purpose.

PROCESS GUIDELINES: STRATEGIES FOR WRITING EXEMPLIFICATION

1. **Selecting a topic.** For a generalization to clarify with examples, fill in the blanks in one of these sentences:

   _____ is the best (worst) _____ I know.
   _____ is the most (least) _____ I know.

   You may end up with generalizations like these:

   > Television advertising is the most manipulative form of communication I know.

   > Nurses are the least appreciated professionals I know.

   > Or think of some other frames that could lead to generalizations— for example, "I've often noticed that _____."

2. **Shaping a thesis.** The generalizations you develop when you fill in the blanks may need to be shaped so that they are generalizations you can clarify and support with examples. For example, you can shape the generalization "Television advertising is the most manipulative form of communication I know" into the generalization "Television advertisements use manipulative techniques to persuade people to buy products they do not need"—a generalization that can serve as your thesis. You can then support that thesis by giving examples of manipulative advertisements for unnecessary products.

Introducing Examples in a Series

If you have trouble introducing examples in a series, including a series that begins with *such as* or *including,* follow these guidelines:

1. Use a comma before—but not after—these words. Do not use a colon.

   YES   The teacher had many innovative ideas‚ including/such as collaborative test-taking, morning yoga instruction, and self-grading.

   NO   The teacher had many innovative ideas including‚ collaborative test-taking, morning yoga instruction, and self-grading.

   NO   The teacher had many innovative ideas, such as: collaborative test-taking, morning yoga instruction, and self-grading.

2. Use a colon if the words before that colon are an independent clause (a word group that can stand alone as a sentence). Note that the independent clause would not end with *such as* or *including.*

   YES   The union had many grievances: mandatory overtime, lack of layoff procedures based on seniority, and suspension of pay raises.

   NO   The union had many grievances, such as: mandatory overtime, lack of layoff procedures based on seniority, and suspension of pay raises.

Using Sources for a Purpose

The paragraph below, which is a body paragraph for an essay about how technology undermines our privacy, illustrates how you can use sources from this book in your writing. It includes a quotation from paragraph 3 of "The Snoop Next Door" on page 255 to help the writer achieve an informational purpose.

THESIS With every technological advancement—from cell phones, to global positioning systems, to the Internet—we lose a little bit more of our privacy.

WRITING PURPOSE AND AUDIENCE To inform average, general readers that the price we pay for technology is a loss of privacy.

The quotation in sentences 5–7 gives examples of Internet sites to help support the writer's point that Internet

[1]Sometimes, two kinds of technology combine to invade our privacy, as happens when cell phones are used to take pictures and movies of us that are then posted on the Internet—without our knowledge or permission. [2]People who commit minor but embarrassing transgressions can be photographed or filmed without realizing it until the images turn up on public shaming Internet

(continued)

sites. [3]For example, able-bodied people who park in handicapped spots can unknowingly have their cars and license plates photographed and posted on a Web site. [4]From there, it's not too hard for viewers of the site to learn the transgressors' e-mail addresses and phone numbers, leading to harassing contacts of many kinds. [5]As Saranow explains:

> There is a proliferation of new sites dedicated to condemning offenses ranging from bad parking . . . and leering . . . to littering . . . and general bad behavior. . . . [6]One site documents locations where people have failed to pick up after their dogs. [7]Capturing newspaper-stealing neighbors on video is also an emerging genre. (255)

sites exist to shame people "who commit minor but embarrassing transgressions."

AVOIDING PLAGIARISM

The paragraph, which includes a quotation in sentences 5–7, illustrates these points about avoiding plagiarism. (For more complete information on using source material, consult Chapters 4 and 15.)

- **Use ellipses (...) to signal omitted words.** As sentence 5 illustrates, use three spaced periods when words are omitted from the middle of a quotation. When you omit words from the end of a sentence, add a period.

- **Use ellipses fairly.** When you use ellipses, you cannot take out words if doing so would alter the sense of the sentence. For example, in sentence 5, you cannot omit "bad" to leave "and general . . . behavior" because doing so would broaden the meaning and thereby change it.

MYTHS ABOUT USING SOURCES

MYTH: If you omit words from a quotation, you do not need to provide a parenthetical citation or works cited entry.

FACT: Quotations with omitted words should both signal the omission with ellipses and document the quotation according to the conventions in Chapter 15.

3. **Generating ideas.** To generate examples for supporting details, you can ask yourself these questions:
   a. What have you experienced that illustrates your generalization?
   b. What have you observed that illustrates your generalization?
   c. What have you read that illustrates your generalization?
   d. What have you learned in school that illustrates your generalization?
   e. What stories can you tell to illustrate your generalization?
   f. What can you describe to illustrate your generalization?

4. **Organizing details.** List all the examples you will use, and decide how you will organize them. Then number them in an order that will be effective.

5. **Drafting.** Write your draft using your numbered list as a scratch outline. Do not worry about polished prose now. You can refine later.

6. **Revising.** Ask a classmate or friend who has good judgment about writing to read your draft and evaluate whether you have enough examples and have included the right amount of detail.

Checklist for Revising Exemplification

You can use this checklist along with the one on page 76 to help you revise.

1. _____ Your generalization is clearly stated in a thesis or strongly implied.

2. _____ Examples clarify the generalization and/or support it.

3. _____ Examples are suited to your audience and purpose.

4. _____ You have enough examples developed in enough detail.

5. _____ Hypothetical examples, if you use them, are recognizable as such and are plausible.

6. _____ Examples are arranged in a progressive or other suitable order.

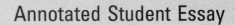

In the following essay, student-author **Shona Sequeira** uses exemplification for three purposes: to convince readers that American food qualifies as "cuisine," to inform that American food reflects American society, and to entertain. After reading, you will have an opportunity to evaluate the essay.

Food for Thought

Shona Sequeira

American cuisine? The connoisseurs of Europe scoff at the term, [1] thinking it an oxymoron. Far Eastern food snobs turn up their finely trained noses at the very idea. Americans themselves are often apologetic for what they believe to be, in the aftertaste of swank French sauces and robustly scented Thai treats, their insignificant culinary heritage. Tempting price discounts on American foods (super-size a meal for 99 cents, for example) are the most obvious manifestation of this apologetic posture, as though Americans are telling the world that if what they feed themselves cannot be labeled "cuisine," at least it can be cheap. As an Indian who was raised in the United Arab Emirates and who has traveled in parts of Europe and the Far East, I have sampled a variety of fine cuisines. However, after coming to the United States to attend college two years ago, I can tell you that American cuisine does indeed exist. It is a flavorsome force to reckon with—rich, varied, and oh-so-sinfully-good! And most significant of all, American cuisine reflects American society.

American society is diverse, unparalleled in its rich variety of people. [2] American food has its own unparalleled variety because a country with such diverse people requires an array of food choices. Contrary to popular belief, American food is not restricted to hamburgers, hot dogs, and French fries. In fact, American cuisine offers the consumer a greater and more tantalizing array of choices than most international culinary traditions have been able to cook up over centuries. For instance, ask for a Chinese fortune cookie and you will always get the same bland thing (often containing the same fortune, too). On the other hand, request an American cookie, and you can be showered with hundreds of delectable options, including oatmeal raisin, double chocolate chip, macadamia pecan delight, and coconut brownie. The same holds true for bread (white, brown, rye,

Paragraph 1
The introduction engages interest with an opening question, by noting what people who disagree with the writer believe, and with specific word choice. The thesis (given in the last three sentences) presents the generalization to be proven with examples: America does have a cuisine that is tasty and a reflection of American culture. The clever opening suggests one purpose is to entertain.

Paragraph 2
The focus of the paragraph is that American food is varied. Examples include types of cookies, bread, and pies. Notice that the first sentence helps link American cuisine to American society.

whole wheat, whole meal, speckled, low-carb), ice-cream, which comes in a palate-boggling selection of flavors, toppings, textures, fat content, and serving styles, and good old American pie (savory, fruity, cream, ice cream, double-crust, single-crust and deep dish).

Paragraph 3
The focus is on assimilation and improvement of immigrants' cuisines. Notice that one example is developed with description and contrast. Also notice the humor and that the first sentence helps link American cuisine to American society.

The United States is a land of immigrants, who not only came here 3 tired, poor, and yearning to breathe freely but with the food of their native lands. Just as the immigrants assimilated into American society, their food became a rich part of American cuisine. However, American cooks did not merely appropriate other countries' traditional delicacies but often improved these cuisines in notable ways. For instance, although it is true that pizza harbors Italian origins, the skimpy little versions they try to sell you in Rome just do not hold a candle to Domino's generous, gooey, thickly crusted, double-cheese offerings.

Paragraph 4
The topic sentence (sentence 1) includes both the focus of the paragraph and the linking of American society and American food. The examples are lists of representative foods. The word choice continues to be specific and descriptive.

Given the surplus of wealth in the United States, Americans can 4 afford many leisure activities, and they want snack food to complement that leisure. With snacks, as with so much of American culture, there is an embarrassment of riches. What other cuisine can offer such palate-pleasing choices as pretzels and peanuts, baked and fried chips, choc-olate-coated raisins and butter-drenched popcorn? All these foods are manufactured in hundreds of models (pretzels, for example, come salty, garlicky, cinnamon-sprinkled, jalapeño-flavored, chocolate-coated, sugar-covered, twisted, knotted, heart-shaped, and straight). The fact that people everywhere, from South America to Far East Asia, are now proudly munching on Pringles is testimony not only to American food's great taste and accessibility, but to its solid status as a recognized world cuisine.

Paragraph 5
The topic sentence (sentence 1) creates transition by referring to leisure, the focus of the previous paragraph. The examples are lists. Notice the humor.

Unfortunately, American leisure has, in part, created the fattest 5 citizenry on the planet, a fact that has spawned an entire American cuisine subset that includes low-fat chips, diet popcorn, reduced-fat ice cream, fat-free dessert bars, low-carb cookies, and Slim Fast shakes. Entire industries with their own food lines have sprung up to deal with American obesity. The Jenny Craig, LA Weight Loss, and Weight Watch-ers product lines include heavenly sounding entrées, tantalizing desserts, and satisfying snack items so the overweight can still enjoy their food.

Yes, even those who shouldn't eat very much have their own special cuisine because America is, after all, the land of equal opportunity where no person will be discriminated against on the basis of race, creed, or body type.

Americans enjoy gadgets and accoutrements for specific activities which explains the need for so many kinds of athletic footwear: tennis shoes, basketball shoes, baseball shoes, running shoes, cross-training shoes, aerobics shoes, and even walking shoes. This American desire for activity-specific items is also reflected in the country's cuisine. Thus, different foods are available for different pastimes. Just as snack food satisfies the cravings of the couch potato watching reruns of *The Simpsons,* the Starbucks "Frappuccino," with its frothy charms and fancy flavors, is the must-have accessory for walking around town in flip flops and khakis. Hot dogs are for ball park outings, Ramen noodles and Easy Mac provide quick meals for college students sick of cafeteria food, Cup-a-Soup feeds busy office workers lunching at their desks, trail mix is perfect for hikers needing energy on-the-go, and protein bars provide a quick nutritional boost for those engaged in any activity that won't let them stop long enough to sit down and eat.

Above all, Americans are innovators who are always looking for new ways to carry out tasks and who harbor an admirable attitude for "thinking outside the box." When it comes to cuisine, too, Americans often think outside the box, turning food for one meal into food for another. Breakfast staples are turned into substantial dinner meals, and dinner foods into breakfast fare. This explains why, even with trays of gleaming meatloaf and gravy (which is to American cuisine what curry is to Indian cuisine and sushi is to Japanese) sitting idle in the college cafeteria hot line, students still flock to the cereal counter. It's Cheerios for an entrée and Fruit Loops for dessert. If you aren't up for chicken pot pie for dinner tonight, you can always rely on a ham and cheese omelet instead, even if you had one for breakfast this morning. Or perhaps breakfast wasn't eggs at all, but the pizza (now cold) you were supposed to have eaten the previous night.

6

Paragraph 6
The topic sentence is sentence 3. The first two sentences link American cuisine to American society. Notice the specific details and that the tone remains lighthearted.

7

Paragraph 7
The topic sentence (sentence 2) presents the focus on the innovation of using the same foods for different meals. The first two sentences help link American cuisine to American society; the transition "above all" indicates that the most compelling example comes last.

Paragraph 8
The conclusion refers to the idea in the introduction (people in other countries disparage American cuisine). The writer also gets her own jab in at those who disparage American cuisine.

Although snobs in other countries may turn up their noses at the 8 notion of American cuisine, Americans should be as proud of their food as they are of their culture. After all, their food reflects their culture. If other countries find American food so repellent, then why do they welcome so many McDonalds, Pizza Huts, Burger Kings, and Taco Bells on their soil?

PEER REVIEW

Responding to "Food for Thought"

Analyze and assess "Food for Thought" by responding to these questions:

1. Does the essay hold your interest? Why or why not?
2. What do you think of the thesis? Why?
3. Do the examples clarify and support the author's generalization? Does the essay include enough examples? Are they detailed enough? Explain.
4. Are the examples arranged in a suitable order? Explain.
5. What do you think of the author's word choice? Cite examples to support your opinion.
6. What are the chief strengths of the essay? Why do you find these features strong?
7. What is one revision you would like to see? How will that revision improve the essay and help the author achieve her purpose?

The examples in this cartoon illustrate a serious generalization about education.

© Roz Chast/The New Yorker Collection/cartoonbank.com.

- What generalization do the examples of "important" books support?
- Why did the cartoonist choose these particular examples?
- Does she include enough examples to support her generalization?
- What audience is likely to find the examples funny?

BACKGROUND: A frequent writer for the *Atlantic Monthly,* Cullen Murphy (b. 1952) was its managing editor, and later its editor, until 2006, when he became an editor at *Vanity Fair.* Murphy began his magazine career in the production department of *Change,* a magazine devoted to higher education. Later, he became an editor of the *Wilson Quarterly* and wrote for *Harper's.* Murphy also writes *Prince Valiant,* the comic strip drawn by his father, which appears in newspapers around the world. Murphy's essays are on a broad range of topics, including religion, language, and social science. He often writes about popular culture and has penned essays on ventriloquism, eating habits, and the items we save. Murphy's books include *Rubbish! The Archaeology of Garbage* (1992), which he co-authored with William Rathj; *The Word According to Eve: Women and the Bible in Ancient Times and Our Own* (1998); and *Are We Rome?* (2007). "Lifosuction" first appeared in the *Atlantic Monthly* (February 2002) in Murphy's regular "Innocent Bystander" column.

THE PATTERN AND ITS PURPOSES: In "Lifosuction," Cullen Murphy uses *examples* to **inform** readers about a form of lying somewhat common among public figures, a form that may surprise you. While largely informational, the essay also aims to **entertain,** which you may not realize until the end.

LIFOSUCTION

BY CULLEN MURPHY

THOMAS M. MENINO, the mayor of Boston, is not a flashy fellow. He gets tongue-tied easily, as many of us do, and he lacks the aura of a Willie Brown or a Rudolph Giuliani.[1] But he is a tribune of the city's neighborhoods and working people, and he was elected to a third term last fall with more than 70 percent of the vote.

As you read Notice that Murphy is sometimes serious and sometimes humorous, sometimes formal and sometimes informal.

2 One of the few clouds to darken his campaign, and it was a small one, came a couple of weeks before the election, when *The Boston Globe* alleged that Menino had committed a familiar political transgression — tweaking his résumé in a manner inconsistent with the facts. Menino, the *Globe* observed, "has long cultivated an image of himself as a neighborhood kid who spurned college and made good instead by dint of hard work and shrewd politicking." The newspaper now disclosed that Menino had indeed earned a college degree — an associate's degree from Chamberlayne Junior College. The degree isn't mentioned in any of the mayor's official biographies. When a reporter asked Menino about this achievement, Menino replied, "You're just trying to dig up dirt on me."

3 We are all familiar with the more usual résumé-padding story, whereby a public figure incorporates credentials or accomplishments to which he or she has no honest claim. A recent case in point is that of the Pulitzer Prize–winning historian Joseph Ellis, whose anecdotes about military service in Vietnam, offered repeatedly in his Mount Holyoke classroom, turned out to be untrue. There have been many others. The Mayan peasant woman who is presented in the widely acclaimed and supposedly autobiographical book *I, Rigoberta Menchú* (1984) appears to have invented many of the central details of her personal history. Two years ago the civil-rights leader Paul Parks, an African-American veteran of World War II, was presented with an award

---

[1]Willie Brown was mayor of San Francisco, and Rudolph Giuliani was mayor of New York City.

by the Berlin chapter of B'nai B'rith[2] for his role in the liberation of Dachau[3]—a role, as it happens, that no one can document and that all evidence contradicts. The actress Sandra Bullock once claimed to have been voted "Girl Most Likely to Brighten Your Day" in high school, though in fact she wasn't.

4   Everyone agrees that this kind of cosmetic makeover is wrong. But what about lifosuction—the removal from one's biography of innocuous yet somehow unsightly elements that happen to be true? It is a common procedure. Musicians, for instance, have a powerful incentive to make sure that public pose and personal background are appropriately in sync. Jim Morrison, of The Doors, who fashioned himself into an icon of anarchy and self-destruction, never took pains to point out that he was the son of an admiral. During the past decade a cadre of rap musicians, black and white, have presented personal histories presumptively rooted in the violent bleakness of the streets but in truth often rooted in the bedroom communities of New York and Los Angeles. The street cred[4] of the white rapper Vanilla Ice diminished rapidly in the face of allegations involving an affluent suburban high school in Dallas and the birth name Robert Van Winkle.

5   Lifosuction is often attempted when issues of class are on the line. Bill O'Reilly, the television talk-show pugilist and the host of *The O'Reilly Factor*, has stated, "I understand working-class Americans. I'm as lower-middle-class as they come." *The Washington Post* has noted that O'Reilly grew up in not-exactly-working-class Westbury, Long Island; went to a private college without benefit of financial aid; and holds master's degrees from Boston University and Harvard. (Also, the "used car" he drives is a Lexus.) The television commentator and newspaper columnist Mike Barnicle imbues his opinions with the rough-and-tumble attitude of blue-collar Boston. He does not dateline his work "Lincoln," where he actually lives, a wealthy suburb that once made a local road into a one-way street to deter entry by people from an adjacent, working-class town.

> "Rather than discourage lifosuction, perhaps, we should encourage people to subtract even more of themselves from public view than they currently do."

6   Humble origins can be a political asset. William Henry Harrison waged the first presidential campaign with a log-cabin-to-White-House theme; Harrison's supporters ridiculed his opponent, Martin Van Buren, for wearing ruffled shirts and taking baths. In truth Harrison was himself a wealthy man, from a distinguished Virginia family. In acutely class-conscious England the pressure on Labour politicians to biovac any sign of privilege has long been intense. Harold Wilson, the Oxford-educated former Prime Minister, cultivated working-class eating habits. In public he smoked a pipe, rather than the more aristocratic cigars he preferred. In the late 1980s a Labour member of Parliament named Michael Meacher, now Tony Blair's Environment Minister, wished it to be inferred that he

---

[2]B'nai B'rith is an organization that works to promote charitable and political causes of interest to Jews.

[3]Dachau was a Nazi concentration camp.

[4]"Cred" is short for "credibility."

was a son of the soil. Then a newspaper pointed out that Meacher's father was actually an accountant who merely had retired to a farm, and suggested that Meacher came from a middle-class background. Middle class! Meacher sued the newspaper for libel. (He lost.)

7 Another person seeking identification with the rural proletariat is Subcomandante Marcos, the leader of the Zapatista National Liberation Army in the Mexican state of Chiapas. Photographs always show him wearing a ski mask. Some legends held him to be a former priest, others a veteran guerrilla fighter trained by the Cubans and the Soviets. He turned out to be the son of a prosperous Mexican furniture retailer. He studied sociology and philosophy at the National Autonomous University of Mexico and went on to earn a graduate degree and teach in a Mexican university. His ski mask is probably from Orvis.[5]

8 It's easy to raise an eyebrow at lifosuction, but hard to be censorious. We all permit ourselves some degree of cosmetic suppression, and we are ambivalent about the ethics. Philosophers and theologians send mixed signals. The Sermon on the Mount cautions against hiding your light under a bushel, and an ancient philosophical tradition warns that wrongdoing can take the form of *not* doing—there are sins of omission as well as of commission. But another long tradition, also going back to antiquity, justifies the sparing disbursement of truth—an "economy of truth," to use the artful locution—in certain circumstances. Edmund Burke once observed, "I do

---

[5]Orvis is America's oldest mail-order retailer. It specializes in clothing and gear for outdoor sports and activities.

not impute falsehood to the government, but there has been a considerable economy of truth." He characterized economies of truth as "a sort of temperance."

9   Rather than discourage lifosuction, perhaps, we should encourage people to subtract even more of themselves from public view than they currently do. Book publishers may complain about a glut of memoirs, but they continue to publish truckloads of them. Every week thousands of people place personal ads in newspapers and magazines — small masterpieces of selective revelation. Millions of people have distilled themselves into personal Web pages.

10   A case can be made, then, for turning the bio-vac up to "high." To be sure, there may be the occasional gruesome accident. With a moment's inattention the assault on unwanted ripples of biography could cause entire personas—*pfflttt*—to be suddenly sucked into oblivion. Some may see that as too great a risk. I see it as a sort of temperance.

READING CLOSELY AND THINKING CRITICALLY

1.   According to Murphy, why do people engage in lifosuction?

2.   In paragraph 8, Murphy says, "It's easy to raise an eyebrow at lifosuction, but hard to be censorious." What does he mean? How serious does Murphy think lifosuction is? How can you tell?

3.   Murphy says that lifosuction involves the removal of "innocuous" biographical elements. Do the examples he uses illustrate the removal of *harmless* elements? Explain.

4.   Why do so many of Murphy's examples deal with the removal of privilege?

5.   Menino's comment to the reporter, given at the end of paragraph 2, is surprising—even ironic. Why?

EXAMINING STRUCTURE AND STRATEGY

1.   In your own words, write out the generalization/thesis that the examples support. Where in the essay is that idea best expressed?

2.   What is the tone of the essay? Is the tone consistent throughout? (See page 69 for an explanation of tone.)

3.   How do the examples in paragraph 3 contrast with the examples in the rest of the essay? How does that contrast help the author achieve his writing purpose?

4.   In which paragraphs does Murphy introduce examples with a topic sentence? Are the topic sentences helpful to the reader? Why or why not?

5.   How does Murphy organize his examples?

CONSIDERING LANGUAGE AND STYLE

1.   *Lifosuction* is a coined word. Explain how it is made up. Do you find the term clever? Why or why not?

2.   Consult a dictionary if you are unsure of the meaning of any of these words: *tribune* (paragraph 1), *dint* (paragraph 2), *cadre* (paragraph 4), *pugilist* (paragraph 5), *proletariat* (paragraph 7).

Do you agree that Mayor Menino's omission of his college degree was only a small cloud "to darken his campaign" (paragraph 2)? Is omitting details as serious as adding them? Explain.

WRITING ASSIGNMENTS

1. **Writing in your journal.** Murphy says, "We all permit ourselves some degree of cosmetic suppression" (paragraph 8). In a page or so, tell about your own cosmetic suppressions and your reasons for them.

2. **Using exemplification for a purpose.** The purposes in the assignments are possibilities. You may establish whatever purposes you like, within your instructor's guidelines.

   * Like the public figures in "Lifosuction," we all have public personas—images of ourselves that we like to project. To inform and perhaps entertain, use examples to illustrate the ways people present and protect their public images.

   * "Lifosuction" illustrates that less is sometimes more. To inform and perhaps entertain, illustrate one or more other instances of less being more.

   * Murphy says that our society is "ambivalent about the ethics" of lifosuction (paragraph 8). State and illustrate one or more other situations about which our ethics are ambivalent. You might consider drug use among athletes; avoidance of unpleasant responsibilities, such as jury duty; or pilferage, such as taking office supplies. Argue whether or not we should be ambivalent about these situations.

   * Lifosuction is a sin of omission. To inform and perhaps entertain, explain and illustrate one or more other sins of omission. If you like, you can also argue that the sin is more (or less) serious than commonly believed.

3. **Combining patterns.** Paragraphs 4, 6, and 7 include examples of musicians and politicians who used lifosuction to help create an image. Describe the image of either musicians or politicians and give examples of people who illustrate the image. You can narrow your description to include particular kinds of musicians, such as rap singers or boy bands, or to include particular kinds of politicians, such as liberals or conservatives.

4. **Analyzing and assessing.** Murphy's tone is both serious and satiric, formal and informal. Cite examples of these contradictory tones, and explain how they help the author achieve his purpose for writing with this original audience, the readers of the *Atlantic Monthly*. Do they help him achieve his purpose with an audience of college students?

5. **Connecting and synthesizing the readings.** Both "Lifosuction" and "Salvation" (page 203) deal with dishonesty. How prevalent in our society are the kinds of dishonesty depicted in these essays? How prevalent is dishonesty in general? Does the dishonesty represent a moral decline in this country? State and defend your assertion.

6. **Drawing on sources.** Review the personal ads in your local newspaper and in any publications you subscribe to that have them, along with some personal Web pages. Analyze the words those who place these ads use to describe themselves. What might some of the words—such as "robust" or "hearty"—really mean? Then use these examples to discuss how people select words to present themselves in the best light.

BACKGROUND: Freelance writer Jennifer Saranow attended Northwestern University and Wesleyan University. She is a former staff reporter for the *Wall Street Journal* and *WSJOnline* who has also written for *The Daily Beast*. She has reported on a range of topics, including the functions added to cell phones, the design of shoes, and couples who ask guests to help pay for their weddings. Saranow has also been the *Wall Street Journal*'s automobile reporter. In that capacity, she has written about the paperwork associated with buying a car, the employee discounts for car purchases, and the automobile industry's push for consumer car leasing. "The Snoop Next Door" first appeared in the *Wall Street Journal Online* (2007).

COMBINED PATTERNS AND THEIR PURPOSE: Jennifer Saranow uses many *examples* to **inform** readers about the proliferation of public shaming sites on the Internet. These Web sites are devoted to exposing and embarrassing those who commit "trivial transgressions" of the social code—everything from talking loudly on cell phones to stealing newspapers from a neighbor. She also uses *cause-and-effect analysis* to **explain** the popularity of the sites and some of their consequences.

The Snoop Next Door

BY JENNIFER SARANOW

Last month, Eva Burgess was eating breakfast at the Rose Cafe in Venice, Calif., when she remembered she needed to make an appointment with her eye doctor. So the New York theater director got on her cellphone and booked a date.

As you read
Consider whether public shaming is an effective form of social control.

2   Almost immediately, she started receiving "weird and creepy" calls directing her to a blog. There, under the posting "Eva Burgess Is Getting Glasses!" her name, cellphone number and other details mentioned in her call to the doctor's office were posted, along with the admonition, "next time, you might take your business outside." The offended blogger had been sitting next to Ms. Burgess in the cafe.

3   It used to be the worst you could get for a petty wrong in public was a rude look. Now, it's not just brutal police officers, panty free celebrities and wayward politicians who are being outed online. The most trivial missteps by ordinary folks are increasingly ripe for exposure as well. There is a proliferation of new sites dedicated to condemning offenses ranging from bad parking (Caughtya.org) and leering (HollaBackNYC.com) to littering (LitterButt.com) and general bad behavior (RudePeople.com). One site documents locations where people have failed to pick up after their dogs. Capturing newspaper-stealing neighbors on video is also an emerging genre.

4   Helping drive the exposés are a crop of entrepreneurs who hope to sell advertising and subscriptions. One site that lets people identify bad drivers is about to offer a $5 monthly service, for people to register several of their own plate numbers and

Tim Halberg filmed a newspaper-stealing neighbor, then put the video online.

© 2007 Ann Johansson

receive notices if they are cited by other drivers. But the traffic and commercial prospects for many of the sites are so limited that clearly there is something else at work.

5   The embrace of the Web to expose trivial transgressions in part represents a return to shame as a check on social behavior, says Henry Jenkins, director of the comparative media studies program at the Massachusetts Institute of Technology. Some academics believe shame became less powerful as a control over everyday interactions with strangers in all but very small neighborhoods or social groups, as people moved to big cities or impersonal suburbs where they existed more anonymously.

6   The sites documenting minor wrongs are the flip side of an online vigilantism movement that tackles meatier social issues. Community organization Cop Watch Los Angeles encourages users to send in stories and pictures of people being brutalized or harassed by police, for posting on the Web. The governor of Texas plans to launch a site this year that will air live video of the border, in hopes that people will watch and report illegal crossings. In a trial run in November, the site received more than 14,000 emails. Tips included spottings of individuals swimming in the Rio Grande, a person wearing a large white hat and a "wild" boy at the border. In China, Web postings have become a powerful social weapon, used to rally thousands of people to hound a man who allegedly had an affair with a married woman.

AN ANONYMOUS TIP

7   For people singled out, the sites can represent an unsettling form of street justice, with no due process. Chris Roth's driving skills have been roundly criticized online by self-anointed traffic monitors. "This man needs his license revoked," wrote one poster, who accused Mr. Roth of cutting in and out. Another charged him with driving on a shoulder and having the audacity to "flip off" an old lady who wouldn't let him cut in.

8   Mr. Roth found the critiques when an anonymous writer added a comment to his MySpace profile in late November directing him to PlateWire, one of the handful

of new sites devoted to bad driving. There, a user had posted Mr. Roth's license-plate information—his vanity plate reads "IDRVFAST"—and complained about his reckless driving style. Subsequent posters found and listed his full name, cellphone number and link to his MySpace page, as well as comments like "big jerk" and "meathead." (He has no idea how they found his information.)

9   "There is no accountability. You can just go online and say whatever you want whether it's factual or not," says the 37-year-old Mr. Roth, of Raleigh, N.C., who works in technology sales. He admits he is an impatient driver and speeds, but he has no plans to change his driving style based on posts by anonymous commentators. "Who are they to decide what is safe or not?" he says.

10   If you type "ycantpark" into photo-sharing site Flickr, there are about 200 photos of bad parking jobs at Yahoo Inc.'s Sunnyvale, Calif., headquarters. The company says the posts were started anonymously around 2005 by employees disgruntled with the parking situation. During that year, Yahoo hired more than 2,100 new employees, and finding a parking space became difficult. "I don't want to have my car posted up there so I definitely think twice about how I park," says Yahoo spokeswoman Heidi Burgett.

11   The digital age allows critics to quickly find a fair amount of information about their targets. One day last November, at about 11:30 A.M., a blog focused on making New York streets more bike-friendly posted the license plate number of an SUV driver who allegedly accelerated from a dead stop to hit a bicycle blocking his way.

12   At 1:16 P.M., someone posted the registration information for the license plate, including the SUV owner's name and address. (The editor of the blog thinks the poster got the information from someone who had access to a license-plate look-up service, available to lawyers, private investigators and police.) At 1:31 P.M., another person added the owner's occupation, his business's name and his title. Ten minutes later, a user posted a link to an aerial photo of the owner's house. Within another hour, the posting also included the accused's picture and email address.

13   The SUV's owner, Ian Goldman, the chief executive of Celerant Technology Corp. in the New York City borough of Staten Island, declined to comment for this article. According to an email exchange posted on the blog, Mr. Goldman said that he had lent the vehicle in question to a relative with "an urgent medical situation" and that he was not aware of any incident. The alleged victim has decided to drop the matter since the damage to the bicycle, which he was standing next to at the time, was under $20. Last month, Aaron Naparstek, editor of the blog, says he removed Mr. Goldman's home and email addresses from the site after receiving a "lawyerly cease and desist" email asking that the whole posting be deleted.

14   Other sites have also received complaints asking that posts be removed. Most say they will remove identifying information like phone numbers or full names when it comes to their attention or if asked. Yet lawyers say alleged wrongdoers shamed online typically have little legal recourse under libel and privacy laws if the accusations in postings are true, if they are posters' opinions about behavior witnessed in a public place and if the personal information listed is available to the public. "It becomes very difficult when it comes to the shaming sites in terms of what you can do in creating a case," says Daniel Solove, an associate professor of

law at George Washington University Law School, who is working on a book about gossiping, shaming and privacy on the Internet.

15   Caughtya.org hosts pictures of cars illegally parked in handicapped spaces. (Other objects qualify, too; one photo from Plano, Texas, is called "Big Rubber Chicken parked in accessible parking spaces.") Playground snoops can log onto the five-month-old Isaw-yournanny.blogspot.com, where users have posted details about nannies committing misdeeds, like feeding children Ho Hos.

FEW POSTINGS

16   Some of the sites are attracting little attention. Caughtya.org lists fewer than 10 U.S. infractions, RudePeople.com has about six stories of rudeness and Irate-Driver.com has none.

17   Many ask for donations to cover costs, but some owners are hoping to make money. Mark Buckman launched PlateWire in May after almost getting run off the road a few months earlier by several drivers, including one who was looking in his backseat and steering with his leg. The site now lists nearly 25,000 license-plate numbers, chastised for moves like tailgating with brights on and driving too slowly in the left lane. To drum up revenue, Mr. Buckman recently added advertising and an online store with branded merchandise. Users in about 15 states can also pay $2 to have a postcard sent to an offending driver, directing the accused to the site. He plans to launch another site this year that will allow people to rate and complain about local businesses and individuals. "If I can create jobs and create an empire that would be awesome, but my main goal is to make a Web site that can actually make real world changes," Mr. Buckman says.

18   Yahoo photo site Flickr has an "I hate stupid people" group that focuses on shots of regular people parking or dressing badly, among other misdeeds. It has nearly 60 members, as does the similar "Jerks" group, for pictures of "neighbor cats pooping on your lawn" or SUVs parked in compact spots. On Google Inc.'s You-Tube, users have contributed videos of minor wrongs, like people cutting in line. On the blogs, one poster refers to this new form of revenge as "blogslapping," a word that previously just referred to when one blogger criticizes another's blog.

CAUGHT ON TAPE

19   After Tim Halberg's *Santa Barbara* [Calif.] *News-Press* didn't show up on his doorstep for six days straight last March, he grabbed his camera and launched a stakeout. He stayed up all night waiting for the newspaper to arrive. When it did, he attached a note declaring, "I'm watching you! Don't ever steal my paper again," and left it on the driveway. Then he waited with his front door open a crack to catch the thief. The robed culprit: His neighbor at the time, a man who looks to be in his 50s. Mr. Halberg captured him on video walking up to the paper, reading the note and walking away.

20   Mr. Halberg never approached the neighbor about the issue directly, but he found four of the older newspapers in front of his house the next day. The 26-year-old wedding photographer posted the video on YouTube, where it's been viewed more than 850 times.

21   Online shaming is happening across the world, with several well-publicized cases in China. Last fall, one blogger posted photos and the license plate number of a Beijing driver who got out of his car and threw aside the bicycle of a woman blocking his way. The driver was quickly identified by Internet vigilantes and soon apologized on television for his behavior. And on a popular Web site last year, after one husband accused a student of having an affair with his wife, other users posted the student's phone number and other personal details. After that, groups of people showed up at his university and parents' home, according to some reports. The student denied the affair.

22   Some suggest that public shaming could be used here as a tool for social betterment. In a paper in the November issue of the *New York University Law Review*, Lior Strahilevitz, a law professor at the University of Chicago, suggested that roads would be safer if every car had a "How's My Driving?" placard on the bumper asking other drivers to report bad behavior.

23   The neighbor-as-Big-Brother[1] approach is already being deployed offline. Since August, spectators at Cincinnati Bengals home games have been able to call 513-381-JERK to complain about rowdy fans. When a call comes in, security zooms in on the area with stadium cameras, confirms there's a problem and dispatches security. Initially, the hotline was receiving more than 100 calls a game, about 75% of which were crank calls. Reports were recently down to about 40 a game, with less than 25% being crank calls.

24   Posting a snarky message online is often safer than confronting bad behavior face to face. "You never know how people are going to react in person," says Scott Terry, 32, who works in advertising in Chicago. Last spring, he posted a photo on Flickr of a "cell phone bus yapper" who disrupted his morning commute. The caption: "Can't you use your inside voice?"

25   For others, posting can be revenge enough. In April, Grace Davis, 51, a stay-at-home mom in Santa Cruz, Calif., captured a "pushy customer" wearing a Hermès-like[2] scarf and black sunglasses while ordering around sales people at Molinari Delicatessen in San Francisco with words like "gimme." Ms. Davis posted the photo online and wrote "Not nice! No fresh Molinari raviolis for you, madam" over the woman's face. "I can just happily walk away," says Ms. Davis, "because as we say in New Age Santa Cruz, 'It's out in the universe now.'"

---

[1]Big Brother, from George Orwell's novel *Nineteen Eighty-Four* (1949), refers to someone who is always watching over others in order to maintain control.

[2]Hermès is an expensive clothing retailer based in Paris.

READING CLOSELY AND THINKING CRITICALLY

1.   Why do you think people launch or post on Web sites like the ones discussed in the essay?

2.   Mark Buckman says that he launched his public shaming site hoping to "'make real world changes'" (paragraph 17). Do you think his goal is a realistic one? Why or why not?

3. What are the primary advantages and disadvantages of public shaming sites?

4. Saranow mentions that public shaming sites exist across the world. Why does she make this point?

5. Why is public shaming often an effective form of social control?

EXAMINING STRUCTURE AND STRATEGY

1. Saranow's thesis includes a generalization that she supports with examples. What is that thesis?

2. What purpose do the first two paragraphs serve?

3. Saranow uses many examples. Would the essay have been as effective if she had used fewer examples but developed them in more detail? Explain.

4. Some of Saranow's examples are of specific Web sites. Does she give enough of these examples in enough detail? Some of her examples are of people who have been singled out for public shaming. Does she give enough of these examples in enough detail?

5. What is the source of Saranow's examples?

NOTING COMBINED PATTERNS

1. Explain how Saranow uses cause-and-effect analysis to help her achieve her purpose for writing. (Cause-and-effect analysis, which gives the causes and/or effects of something, is explained in Chapter 10.)

2. What process analysis appears in paragraphs 11–13? How does that process analysis help the author achieve her writing purpose? (Process analysis, which explains how something is made or done, is explained in Chapter 8.)

CONSIDERING LANGUAGE AND STYLE

1. Paragraphs 3 and 8 give the names of some common public shaming sites. Come up with your own name for a public shaming site, and explain why it is appropriate. Why is the name of the site important?

2. Paragraph 6 uses the term "online vigilantism" to refer to sites that shame people over "meatier social issues." Is the term a good one? Explain.

3. Consult a dictionary if you are unsure of the meaning of the word *exposé* (paragraph 4).

FOR DISCUSSION IN CLASS OR ONLINE

What do you think of public shaming sites? Are they a good idea because they are an appropriate form of social control? How would you feel if your name or picture turned up on one of these sites—even if you were guilty of the stated infraction?

WRITING ASSIGNMENTS

1. **Writing in your journal.** Tell about an incident you experienced that you could post on one of the public shaming Web sites. Would you actually be interested in posting the incident? Why or why not?

2. **Using exemplification for a purpose.** The purposes given in the assignments are possibilities. You may establish whatever purpose you like, within your instructor's guidelines.

   - Discuss and illustrate the "trivial transgressions" (paragraph 5) and "minor wrongs" (paragraph 6) that occur on your college campus—the ones that you find particularly annoying or rude. Your purpose is to persuade people to change their annoying or rude behavior.

   - To inform readers and perhaps convince people to change their behavior, discuss and illustrate annoying behavior associated with a particular activity, such as using a cell phone, driving on a freeway, shopping for groceries, or working out in a gym.

   - To inform readers, illustrate ways that "public shaming could be used . . . as a tool for social betterment" (paragraph 22).

   - "The Snoop Next Door" reveals one way that we are losing our privacy. Discuss and illustrate one or more other ways our privacy is compromised. Your purpose is to inform readers.

3. **Combining patterns.** "The Snoop Next Door" illustrates one way that technology has affected us. Use cause-and-effect analysis to explain another effect of some form of technology, such as social networking sites, instant messaging, global positioning systems, cell phones, MP3 players, or personal digital assistants. Also use exemplification to illustrate the effect.

4. **Analyzing and assessing.** Analyze the content and language of "The Snoop Next Door," and assess to what extent the essay is an example of objective reporting and to what extent it reveals the author's opinions.

5. **Connecting and synthesizing the readings.** Chris Roth, who was singled out on a public shaming site, says that a problem with such sites is that "'there is no accountability'" (paragraph 9). In "Don't Just Stand There" on page 311, Diane Cole also discusses accountability in public speech by advocating challenging those who tell hurtful jokes in public. In "Fan Profanity" on page 639, Howard M. Wasserman discusses accountability for profane speech used by college sports spectators. Drawing on "The Snoop Next Door," "Don't Just Stand There," "Fan Profanity," and your own ideas, discuss how accountable we are in our public speech. Should we be more accountable? If you like, you can limit your discussion to one context, such as television, your campus newspaper, or classroom discussions.

6. **Drawing on sources.** Examine one or more of the public shaming sites mentioned in "The Snoop Next Door." (Paragraphs 3, 10, and 17 include several sites.) Then write a critical analysis of the site suitable for your college newspaper. You might consider such features as how responsible the postings are, how safe or dangerous the site is, how difficult it is to post on and navigate the site, how clear the site's goals are, and how likely it is that those goals are achieved.

BACKGROUND: Best known for his 1952 novel *Invisible Man,* which explores racial stereotypes, Ralph Ellison (1914–1994) was born in Oklahoma. His father died in an accident when Ellison was three, forcing his mother to become an apartment house custodian—events reflected in the autobiographical essay reprinted here. Music was Ellison's first creative outlet, and his love of music is also noted in the essay. In fact, at one time Ellison hoped to become a professional musician. He studied music at Tuskegee Institute but left before graduation when confusion about his scholarship left him without sufficient tuition money. He traveled to New York City and joined the Federal Writers' Project. Among the African American authors that he met was Langston Hughes, whose work appears on page 203. After the publication of *Invisible Man,* Ellison enjoyed considerable popularity and was a sought-after speaker and teacher. He taught at a number of colleges, including New York University, Rutgers, and Yale. Ellison's essays have been collected in *Going to the Territory* (1986) and *Collected Essays* (1995). *Juneteenth,* a novel Ellison's literary executor prepared from more than 2,000 pages of drafts that Ellison wrote, was published in 1999. "On Being the Target of Discrimination" first appeared in a special *New York Times Magazine* supplement called "A World of Difference" in 1989.

www.mhhe.com/clousepatterns6

Ralph Ellison

For more information on this author, go to

More resources > Chapter 7 > Ralph Ellison

COMBINED PATTERNS AND THEIR PURPOSES: Using *exemplification,* Ralph Ellison **relates three of his experiences** with racial discrimination when he was a child growing up in Oklahoma. He also expresses the feelings he had at the time of the experiences and afterward. Each of the examples developed with *narration* and *description* also **informs** the reader about the nature of the United States during the time of the so-called separate-but-equal laws.

ON BEING THE TARGET OF DISCRIMINATION

BY RALPH ELLISON

IT GOT TO YOU FIRST at the age of six, and through your own curiosity. With kindergarten completed and the first grade ahead, you were eagerly anticipating your first day of public school. For months you had been imagining your new experience and the children, known and unknown, with whom you would study and play. But the physical framework on your imagining, an elementary school in the process of construction, lay close at hand on the block-square site across the street from your home. For over a year you had watched it rise and spread in the air to become a handsome structure of brick and stone, then seen its broad encircling grounds arrayed with seesaws, swings, and baseball diamonds. You had imagined this picture-book setting as the scene of your new experience, and when enrollment day arrived, with its grounds astir with bright colors and voices of kids like yourself, it did, indeed, become the site of your very first lesson in public schooling—though not within its classrooms, as you had imagined, but well outside its walls. For while located within a fairly mixed neighborhood this new public school was exclusively for whites.

As you read Try to determine how Ellison views race relations.

2   It was then you learned that you would attend a school located far to the south of your neighborhood, and that reaching it involved a journey which took you over, either directly or by way of a viaduct which arched head-spinning high above, a broad expanse of railroad tracks along which a constant traffic of freight-cars, switch engines, and passenger trains made it dangerous for a child to cross. And that once the tracks were safely negotiated you continued past warehouses, factories,

> "For while located within a fairly mixed neighborhood this new public school was exclusively for whites."

and loading docks, and then through a notorious red-light district where black prostitutes in brightly colored housecoats and Mary Jane shoes supplied the fantasies and needs of a white clientele. Considering the fact that you couldn't attend school with white kids this made for a confusion that was further confounded by the giggling jokes which older boys whispered about the district's peculiar form of integration. For you it was a grown-up's mystery, but streets being no less schools than routes to schools, the district would soon add a few forbidden words to your vocabulary.

3   It took a bit of time to forget the sense of incongruity aroused by your having to walk *past* a school to get *to* a school, but soon you came to like your school, your teachers, and most of your schoolmates. Indeed, you soon enjoyed the long walks and anticipated the sights you might see, the adventures you might encounter, and the many things not taught in school that could be learned along the way. Your school was not nearly so fine as that which faced your home but it had its attractions. Among them its nearness to a park, now abandoned by whites, in which you picnicked and played. And there were the two tall cylindrical fire escapes on either wing of its main building down which it was a joy to lie full-length and slide, spiraling down and around three stories to the ground—providing no outraged teacher was waiting to strap your legs once you sailed out of its chute like a shot off a fireman's shovel. Besides, in your childish way you were learning that it was better to take self-selected risks and pay the price than be denied the joy or pain of risk-taking by those who begrudged your existence.

4   Beginning when you were four or five you had known the joy of trips to the city's zoo, but one day you would ask your mother to take you there and have her sigh and explain that it was now against the law for Negro kids to view the animals. Had someone done something bad to the animals? No. Had someone tried to steal them or feed them poison? No. Could white kids still go? Yes! So why? Quit asking questions, it's the law and only because some white folks are out to turn this state into a part of the South.

5   This sudden and puzzling denial of a Saturday's pleasure was disappointing and so angered your mother that later, after the zoo was moved north of the city, she decided to do something about it. Thus one warm Saturday afternoon with you and your baby brother dressed in your best she took you on a long streetcar ride which ended at a strange lakeside park, in which you found a crowd of noisy white people. Having assumed that you were on your way to the integrated cemetery where at the age of three you had been horrified beyond all tears or forgetting when you saw your father's coffin placed in the ground, you were bewildered. But now

as your mother herded you and your brother in to the park you discovered that you'd come to the zoo and were so delighted that soon you were laughing and babbling as excitedly as the kids around you.

6   Your mother was pleased and as you moved through the crowd of white parents and children she held your brother's hand and allowed as much time for staring at the cages of rare animals as either of you desired. But once your brother began to tire she herded you out of the park and toward the streetcar line. And then it happened.

7   Just as you reached the gate through which crowds of whites were coming and going you had a memorable lesson in the strange ways of segregated-democracy as instructed by a guard in civilian clothes. He was a white man dressed in a black suit and a white straw hat, and when he looked at the fashion in which your mother was dressed, then down to you and your brother, he stiffened, turned red in the face, and stared as though at something dangerous.

8   "Girl," he shouted, "where are your *white* folks!"

9   "*White* folks," your mother said, "What white folks? I don't *have* any white folks, I'm a Negro!"

10   "Now don't you get smart with me, colored gal," the white man said, "I mean where are the white folks you come *out* here with!"

11   "But I just told you that I didn't come here with any white people," your mother said, "I came here with my boys . . ."

12   "Then what are you doing in this park," the white man said.

13   And now when your mother answered you could hear the familiar sound of anger in her voice.

14   "I'm here," she said, "because I'm a *taxpayer,* and I thought it was about time that my boys have a look at those animals. And for that I didn't *need* any *white* folks to show me the way!"

15   "Well," the white man said, "*I'm* here to tell you that you're breaking the law! So now you'll have to leave. Both you and your chillun too. The rule says no niggers is allowed in the zoo. That's the law and I'm enforcing it!"

16   "Very well," your mother said, "we've seen the animals anyway and were on our way to the streetcar line when you stopped us."

17   "That's fine," the white man said, "and when that car comes you be sure that you get on it, you hear? You and your chillun too!"

18   So it was quite a day. You had enjoyed the animals with your baby brother and had another lesson in the sudden ways good times could be turned into bad when white people looked at your color instead of *you.* But better still, you had learned something of your mother's courage and were proud that she had broken an unfair law and stood up for her right to do so. For while the white man kept staring until the streetcar arrived she ignored him and answered your brother's questions about the various animals. Then the car came with its crowd of white parents and children, and when you were entrained and rumbling home past the fine lawns and houses your mother gave way to a gale of laughter; in which, hesitantly at first, and then with assurance and pride, you joined. And from that day the incident became the source of a family joke that was sparked by accidents, faux pas, or obvious lies. Then one of you was sure to frown and say, "Well, I think you'll have

to go now, both you and your chillun too!" And the family would laugh hilariously. Discrimination teaches one to discriminate between discriminators while countering absurdity with black (Negro? Afro-American? African-American?) comedy.

19   When you were eight you would move to one of the white sections through which you often passed on the way to your father's grave and your truly last trip to the zoo. For now your mother was the custodian of several apartments located in a building which housed on its street floor a drug store, a tailor shop, a Piggly Wiggly market, and a branch post office. Built on a downward slope, the building had at its rear a long driveway which led from the side street past an empty lot to a group of garages in which the apartments' tenants stored their cars. Built at an angle with wings facing north and east, the structure supported a servant's quarters which sat above its angle like a mock watchtower atop a battlement, and it was there that you now lived.

20   Reached by a flight of outside stairs, it consisted of four small rooms, a bath, and a kitchen. Windows on three of its sides provided a view across the empty frontage to the street, of the back yards behind it, and of the back wall and windows of the building in which your mother worked. It was quite comfortable but you secretly disliked the idea of your mother living in service and missed your friends who now lived far away. Nevertheless, the neighborhood was pleasant, served by a sub-station of the street-car line, and marked by a variety of activities which challenged your curiosity. Even its affluent alleys were more exciting to explore than those of your old neighborhood, and the one white friend you were to acquire in the area lived nearby.

21   This friend was a brilliant but sickly boy who was tutored at home, and with him you shared your new interest in building radios, a hobby at which he was quite skilled. Your friendship eased your loneliness and helped dispel some of the mystery and resentment imposed by segregation. Through access to his family, headed by an important Episcopalian minister, you learned more about whites and thus about yourself. With him you could make comparisons that were not so distorted by the racial myths which obstructed your thrust toward self-perception; compare their differences in taste, discipline, and manners with those of Negro families of comparable status and income; observe variations between your friend's boyish lore and your own, and measure his intelligence, knowledge, and ambitions against your own. For you this was a most important experience and a rare privilege, because up to now the prevailing separation of the races had made it impossible to learn how you and your Negro friends compared with boys who lived on the white side of the color line. It was said by word of mouth, proclaimed in newsprint, and dramatized by acts of discriminatory law that you were inferior. You were barred from vying with them in sports and games, competing in the classroom or the world of art. Yet what you saw, heard, and smelled of them left irrepressible doubts. So you ached for objective proof, for a fair field of testing.

"It was said by word of mouth, proclaimed in newsprint, and dramatized by acts of discriminatory law that you were inferior."

22 Even your school's proud marching band was denied participation in the state-wide music contests so popular at the time, as though so airy and earth-transcending an art as music would be contaminated if performed by musicians of different races.

23 Which was especially disturbing because after the father of a friend who lived next door in your old neighborhood had taught you the beginner's techniques required to play valved instruments you had decided to become a musician. Then shortly before moving among whites your mother had given you a brass cornet, which in the isolation of the servant's quarters you practiced hours on end. But you yearned to play with other musicians and found none available. Now you lived less than a block from a white school with a famous band, but there was no one in the neighborhood with whom to explore the mysteries of the horn. You could hear the school band's music and watch their marching, but joining in making the thrilling sounds was impossible. Nor did it help that you owned the scores to a few of their marches and could play with a certain facility and fairly good tone. So there, surrounded by sounds but unable to share a sound, you went it alone. You turned yourself into a one-man band.

24 You played along as best you could with the phonograph, read the score to *The Carnival of Venice* while listening to Del Steigers executing triple-tongue variations on its themes; played the trumpet parts of your bandbook's marches while humming in your head the supporting voices of horns and reeds. And since your city was a seedbed of Southwestern jazz you played Kansas City riffs, bugle calls, and wha-wha-muted imitations of blues singers' pleas. But none of this made up for your lack of fellow musicians. And then, late one Saturday afternoon when your mother and brother were away, and when you had dozed off while reading, you awoke to the nearby sound of live music. At first you thought you were dreaming, and then that you were listening to the high school band, but that couldn't be the source because, instead of floating over building tops and bouncing off wall and windowpane, the sounds you heard rose up, somewhat muffled, from below.

25 With that you ran to a window which faced the driveway, and looking down through the high windowpane of the lighted post office you could see the metal glint of instruments. Then you were on your feet and down the stairs, keeping to the shadows as you drew close and peeped below. And there you looked down upon a room full of men and women postal workers who were playing away at a familiar march. It was like the answer to a silent prayer because you could tell by the sound that they were beginners like yourself and the covers of the thicket of bandbooks revealed that they were of the same set as yours. For a while you listened and hummed along, unseen but shaking with excitement in the dimming twilight. And then, hardly before the idea formed in your head, you were skipping up the stairs to grab your cornet, lyre, and bandbook and hurtling down again to the drive.

26 For a while you listened, hearing the music come to a pause and the sound of the conductor's voice. Then came a rap on a music stand and once again the music. And now turning to the march by the light from the window, you snapped score to lyre, raised horn to lip, and began to play; at first silently tonguing the notes through the mouthpiece and then, carried away with the thrill of stealing a part of

the music, you tensed your diaphragm and blew. And as you played, keeping time with your foot on the concrete drive, you realized that you were a better cornetist than some in the band and grew bold in the pride of your sound. Now in your mind you were marching along a downtown street to the flying of flats, the tramping of feet, and the cheering of excited crowds. For at least by an isolated act of brassy cunning you had become a member of the band.

27   Yes, but unfortunately you then let yourself become so carried away that you forgot to listen for the conductor's instructions which you were too high and hidden to see. Suddenly the music faded and you opened your ears to the fact that you were now rendering a lonely solo in the startled quietness. And before you could fully return to reality there came the sound of table legs across a floor and a rustle of movement ending in the appearance of a white startled face in the opened window. Then you heard a man's voice exclaim, "I'll be damn, it's a little nigger!" whereupon you took off like a quail at the sound of sudden shotgun fire.

28   Next thing you knew, you were up the stairs and on your bed, crying away in the dark your guilt and embarrassment. You cried and cried, asking yourself how could you have been so lacking in pride as to shame yourself and your entire race by butting in where you weren't wanted. And this just to make some amateur music. To this you had no answers but then and there you made a vow that it would never happen again. And then, slowly, slowly, as you lay in the dark, your earlier lessons in the absurd nature of racial relations came to your aid. And suddenly you found yourself laughing, both at the way you'd run away and the shock you'd caused by joining unasked in the music.

29   Then you could hear yourself intoning in your eight-year-old's imitation of a white Southern accent. "Well boy, you broke the law, so you have to go, and that means you and your chillun too!"

READING CLOSELY AND THINKING CRITICALLY

1.   In paragraph 1, Ellison says that the new school was the site of his "first lesson in public schooling." What was that lesson?

2.   What is the "peculiar form of integration" that Ellison mentions in paragraph 2? What other "peculiar form[s] of integration" can you think of?

3.   After his move to a new house, Ellison made friends with a white boy. Why was that friendship important to Ellison?

4.   Although the incident at the zoo was a painful one, it became an ongoing joke for Ellison's family. Explain why.

5.   What do you think the author means when he writes, "Discrimination teaches one to discriminate between discriminators" (paragraph 18)?

6.   Ellison has definite views on race relations and definite reactions to being the target of discrimination. What are those views and reactions?

1. Does Ellison use enough examples? Explain.

2. In what order does Ellison arrange his examples? Is this order effective? Why or why not?

3. Ellison does not directly refer to himself. Rather than use "I," he uses "you," even though the essay is autobiographical. Why do you think the author uses "you" instead of "I"?

4. How do you think an audience who has not lived during the time when segregation was legal is likely to react to the essay? How do you think Ellison wants them to react? How did *you* react?

5. The photograph on page 289 is a visual illustration of life in the United States during the time when separate-but-equal laws were considered constitutional. Are the examples in "On Being the Target of Discrimination" sufficiently vivid, or would the essay benefit from the inclusion of photos like this one? Explain.

NOTING COMBINED PATTERNS

1. In paragraph 2, Ellison offers a detailed description of the journey African American students took to their school. How does this description help the author achieve his purpose?

2. How does Ellison use narration to achieve his writing purpose?

CONSIDERING LANGUAGE AND STYLE

1. In paragraph 18, Ellison refers to "black comedy." What is "black comedy" (sometimes called "black humor")? Explain the wordplay involving the term "black comedy" at the end of the paragraph.

2. The noun *refrain* is a musical term. (If you do not know its meaning, look it up.) "On Being the Target of Discrimination" has a refrain of sorts. What is it?

3. Consult a dictionary if you are unsure of the meaning of any of these words: *viaduct* (paragraph 2), *red-light district* (paragraph 2), *Mary Jane shoes* (paragraph 2), *incongruity* (paragraph 3), *faux pas* (paragraph 18), *affluent* (paragraph 20), *irrepressible* (paragraph 21).

FOR DISCUSSION IN CLASS OR ONLINE

In paragraph 21, Ellison explains that he learned more about himself by learning more about his white friend and his family. Consider to what extent our knowledge of ourselves is a function of what we know about other people.

WRITING ASSIGNMENTS

1. **Writing in your journal.** Write about an incident of discrimination or other injustice you have experienced, witnessed, or heard about. You need not limit yourself to racial discrimination. You can discuss discrimination against or injustice toward the mentally or physically disabled, a gender, a nationality, and so forth.

2. **Using exemplification for a purpose.** The purposes in the assignments are possibilities. You may establish whatever purposes you like, within your instructor's guidelines.

   - When Ellison writes that "streets [are] no less schools than routes to schools" (paragraph 2), he is observing that much education occurs outside of schoolroom walls. Use examples to relate your own experiences outside of school to support Ellison's observation. Explain what you learned and how you learned it.
   - To relate your experience, illustrate "the sudden ways good times [can] be turned into bad" (paragraph 18).
   - Write an essay with the title "On Being _____ ." (Fill in the blank with some circumstance of your life—being tall or short, a single parent, an adult learner, an only child, a student athlete, and so forth.) To relate your experience and express your feelings, illustrate what life is or was like for you.

3. **Combining patterns.** Despite his fierce desire to do so, circumstance denied Ellison the opportunity to play in a band. Tell a story that is an example of a time you were unable to do something that you yearned to do. Use cause-and-effect analysis (explained in Chapter 10) to note how you were affected by your inability to participate.

4. **Analyzing and assessing.** Analyze the content of "On Being the Target of Discrimination," and assess its likely impact on high school students. Based on your conclusions, recommend that the essay should (or should not) appear on a reading list for high school students during Black History Month.

5. **Connecting and synthesizing the readings.** In "The Ways of Meeting Oppression" (page 492), Martin Luther King, Jr., writes that oppressed people deal with their oppression in one of three ways. Discuss the ways young Ralph Ellison and his mother deal with oppression. Do their methods fit any of King's categories? Are their methods effective?

6. **Drawing on sources.** Jim Crow laws, instituted in the 1880s and allowed to continue into the 1960s, were state laws—upheld by the U.S. Supreme Court—that created race-based segregation. The laws allowed segregated restaurants, hospitals, buses, schools, public institutions, water fountains, and other public and private facilities.

   Assume that you have been asked to contribute an essay on the Jim Crow era to a local high school newspaper in honor of Black History Month. Your audience will be young people who may not be familiar with this period of American history, and your purpose will be to bring the experience of African Americans under Jim Crow laws vividly to life. There are many Web sites rich in narratives, pictures, and historical information about Jim Crow and the fight for civil rights. An excellent place to start is the Library of Congress African American Odyssey Web site at http://memory. loc.gov/ammem/aaohtml/exhibit/aointro.html. You might also check *Africana* or *The Encyclopedia of African-American Culture and History* in your campus library, and you can interview people over 60 for their memories.

BACKGROUND: A senior editor for *Time* magazine, Jeffrey Kluger was also a staff writer for *Discover* magazine and a writer for the *New York Times Business World Magazine, Family Circle,* and *Science Digest.* For *Time,* he has written many cover stories, including pieces about the landing of the Mars Pathfinder, the *Columbia* space shuttle tragedy, and the connection between sex and health. For his cover story on global warming, Kluger won an Overseas Press Club award. His books include *Lost Moon: The Perilous Voyage of Apollo 13* (1991), which he cowrote with astronaut Jim Lovell. The book became the basis for the movie *Apollo 13,* for which he served as a technical advisor and played himself. He also wrote *Journey beyond Selene* (1999) about unmanned space exploration, *Splendid Solution: Jonas Salk and the Conquest of Polio* (2005), and *Why Simple Things Become Complex (and How Complex Things Can Be Made Simple)* (2009). "The Art of Simplexity" first appeared in *Time* in 2008.

COMBINED PATTERNS AND THEIR PURPOSES: Jeffrey Kluger combines *exemplification* with *cause-and-effect analysis* and *comparison-contrast* to **inform** about the nature of simplicity and complexity and to inform and, perhaps, **persuade** readers of the importance of understanding the difference between the two.

THE ART OF SIMPLEXITY

BY JEFFREY KLUGER

TWO OF THE SMARTEST PEOPLE YOU'LL ever meet are the guys who used to operate the M. Coy bookshop on Pine Street in Seattle. Business pressures recently forced them to shutter their shop, but for 20 years, they sold their books, and from the moment you walked into their store, they had you figured out. They noticed where your gaze would go; they noticed where you paused. They noticed what books you picked up and how long you lingered over them. They recalled earlier customers who had bought the same titles and remembered other books those shoppers bought. They flashed through their entire 20,000-book inventory and then approached you with the single most important thing they had to offer: a recommendation.

As you read Notice that the author uses a mix of brief and extended examples.

2 Across town, in the Art Deco headquarters of Amazon.com the booksellers are good at making recommendations too. Log on to their site, and you've walked into their store. There, Amazon computers also keep an eye on you. They see where you click; they see where you pause. They recall every book you've ever bought and what other customers like you have bought. They shovel through data about millions of buyers and tens of millions of sales and then, like the shopkeepers, come up with a suggestion. However, the computers don't do all this in a 1,400-g (3lb.), walnut-wrinkled mass of brain tissue but in a vast network of computers. It's easy to say that one approach is more complex than the other. It's a lot harder to say which one.

3 Of all the things that confuse human beings, perhaps nothing trips us up so much as what it means for something to be simple or complex. A houseplant, with its microhydraulics, fine-tuned metabolism and dense schematic of nucleic acids, may be more complex than a manufacturing plant. A modern army, with its thicket

of bureaucracy and static encampments, may be simpler than a nimble guerrilla group. A guppy, with its symphony of biological systems and subsystems, is vastly more complicated than a star.

4   Human beings are not wired to look at things this way. We're suckers for size, for flash, for speed, for scale; we mistake immensity for complexity and subtlety for simplicity. That has very often been our undoing. Shock and awe[1] should win a war, until an insurgency beats it back. An election should be sealed by storming Super Tuesday, until the campaign dies of a thousand little losses. The 2003 Yankees, with their $180 million payroll, should win the World Series, until the $63 million Marlins send them packing.

> "We're suckers for size, for flash, for speed, for scale."

5   These may be lessons most of us must repeat again and again, but science increasingly is learning something from them. A generation ago, the paradigm-shifting understanding of chaos theory[2] revealed the power of disorder in meteorology, marketing, plate tectonics[3] and more. Similarly, investigators across the social and scientific spectrums are today studying how systems that seem simple or complex may be just the opposite—and how that fact can expand our understanding of our world. "Ask me why I forgot my keys today, and the answer may be that something was on my mind," says neuroscientist Chris Wood of the Santa Fe Institute (SFI) in New Mexico, a multidisciplinary think tank devoted to complexity theory. "Ask me about the calcium channels in my brain that drive remembering, and you're asking a much harder question."

6   There are a lot of ways the push-pull between simplicity and complexity is being explored and explained. Consider how babies learn to speak—a job so complicated that by some measures they shouldn't be able to do it at all. By the time babies are 18 months old, they have a core vocabulary of 50 words they can pronounce and 100 more they understand. By their sixth birthday, children have a working vocabulary of 6,000 words—meaning they've learned, on average, three new words every day since birth. Mastering conversational English requires about 50,000 words. What's more, since babies can't know where they'll be born, they must start life able to learn any of the world's nearly 7,000 tongues. It's processing speed that makes all this possible.

7   At Rutgers University in Newark, N. J., neuroscientist April Benasich fits prelingual babies with caps that read electrical activity in the brain. Benasich then plays one-syllable word bits to them—da and ta sounds, for example—and watches as their brains process the difference. At first, the sounds are separated by 300 milliseconds, very fast but well within the brain's ability. She then speeds things up so that

---

[1]Shock and awe is a military strategy of using heavily dominant force to overpower an enemy quickly. The term was often used to describe the initial strategy employed when President George W. Bush ordered the military into Iraq in 2003.

[2]Chaos theory says that seemingly random events are actually predictable. In science, *chaos* does not mean "confusion"; it refers to an apparent lack of order in a system that, nonetheless, obeys particular laws.

[3]Plate tectonics is a branch of geology that studies the movement of the earth's crust.

the gap shrinks to 200 milliseconds, then 100, then 35—the point at which the length of the space is less than the length of the syllable itself. Even then the babies keep pace, getting all the way down to 10 milliseconds before the sounds run together.

8   Not all kids, however, have the same gifts. Benasich has found that some children fall out of the word-break race at about 70 milliseconds. Find the kids who later develop reading or speech disabilities, and they may also turn out to be the ones who had trouble keeping up with the sounds. "If you can't make a precise phonological map of a word," Benasich says, "you can't recognize it or reproduce it." If therapists could spot kids with such processing problems early, they could provide programs better targeted to their needs. No matter how the children's disability is corrected, it's a mark of the simple things on which speech stands or falls that the need for such retraining may turn on a few milliseconds of hearing either way.

9   Mundane matters like traffic move through simplicity choke points too. On any given day, about a million cars stream into and out of Manhattan. At any given moment, however, only about 8,000 of them are in operation in the heavily traveled midtown area. Keep those cars moving, and traffic flows smoothly all over the island. Jam them up, and gridlock can spread like ice freezing. "In fact," says urban-planning consultant Sam Schwartz, a former New York traffic commissioner who helped the city prepare for the 1980 transit strike, "in the case of true gridlock, the streets are actually 60% empty. All of the crowding is at the intersections, with nothing getting to midblock."

10   In the arts as well, simplicity and complexity may masquerade as each other. Two years ago, physicist Richard Taylor of the University of Oregon began trying to establish the authenticity of six possible Jackson Pollock[4] paintings. Taylor ultimately determined that the paintings were done by someone else, not because the materials or colors were wrong but because they lacked the microscopic fractals—repetitive patterns within patterns—that defined Pollock's abstractions. Fractals were a well-known concept in mathematics, but nobody expected to find them in a free-form splatter painting. Something in the way Pollock tossed his paint, however, allowed him not only to create fractals but also to manipulate them so that they landed only on the canvas. The floor around them? Just splatters.

11   The ability to balance on the simplicity-complexity fulcrum is producing results elsewhere too—in increasingly complex software that yields increasingly intuitive user interfaces (think the iPhone); in algorithms that show how the movements of schooling fish mirror the behavior of investors, making stock-market predictions more reliable. Murray Gell-Mann, a Nobel Prize–winning physicist and a co-founder of SFI, likes to cite the case of physicist Karl Jansky, who founded the science of radio astronomy in 1931 when he was studying the hiss of electromagnetic static that bathes the Earth—part of the same hiss you hear on a car radio. Jansky realized that the sound was caused not by atmospheric disturbances but by ancient signals streaming to us from the very center of the galaxy. What everyone else heard as noise, Gell-Mann says, Jansky heard as a "beautiful regularity." Slowly, we're all learning to listen the same way.

---

[4]Jackson Pollock (1912–1956) was an artist famous for dripping paint on canvas to create abstract art.

1. In your own words, write out the generalization that Kluger clarifies with examples. Where is that generalization best expressed? Is that sentence the thesis?

2. In paragraph 4, Kluger says that mistaking "immensity for complexity and subtlety for simplicity . . . has very often been our undoing." Explain what he means and why he believes this statement to be true.

3. Why is it important to understand "what it means for something to be simple or complex" (paragraph 3)?

4. Are you inclined to view the world around you any differently after reading "The Art of Simplexity" and to react differently to such things as current events and traffic jams? Explain.

EXAMINING STRUCTURE AND STRATEGY

1. Why do you think Kluger opens with the bookstore examples rather than with the language acquisition example?

2. Which example does Kluger give in the most detail? Why is that example developed so extensively?

3. Kluger gives examples in different categories, such as art and science. What other categories do his examples fall into? How does providing examples in these categories help him achieve his writing purpose?

4. Which paragraphs include topic sentences? What are those topic sentences, and what purpose do they serve?

NOTING COMBINED PATTERNS

1. Cite two examples developed with cause-and-effect analysis. What is the purpose of that cause-and-effect analysis?

2. How is comparison-contrast used to create an effective introduction?

CONSIDERING LANGUAGE AND STYLE

1. *Simplexity* is a coined word made by combining "simple" and "complex." Did you figure out the word's meaning before you read the first paragraph? Why or why not? After reading the essay, how would you define this coined word?

2. Consult a dictionary if you are unsure of the meaning of these words: *Art Deco* (paragraph 2), *schematic* (paragraph 3), *paradigm* (paragraph 5), *phonological* (paragraph 8), *algorithms* (paragraph 11).

FOR DISCUSSION IN CLASS OR ONLINE

Why do you think Kluger titled his essay "The Art of Simplexity" rather than "The Science of Simplexity"? Could he have used *science* just as effectively?

1. **Writing in your journal.** As a result of reading Kluger's essay, are you interested in reading his book *Why Simple Things Become Complex (and How Complex Things Can Be Made Simple)?* Why or why not?

2. **Using narration for a purpose.** The purposes in the assignments are possibilities. You may establish whatever purposes you like, within your instructor's guidelines.

    - To inform and persuade, use examples to show that we are (or are not) "suckers for size, for flash, for speed, [and/or] for scale" (paragraph 4).

    - To inform and/or persuade, use examples to show that bigger, faster, or flashier is (or is not) better.

    - To relate experience and inform, illustrate the principle of simplicity in academic life. If you like, you can consider one or more of the following: simplicity in your studies, in social interactions in or outside the classroom, during the first day of class, while taking exams, while meeting with an instructor, or while getting along with a roommate.

3. **Combining patterns.** Define "simple" or "complex" and illustrate that definition. (See Chapter 12 on writing definition.)

4. **Analyzing and assessing.** Are Kluger's examples effective ones? Consider the number of examples, their length, their order, and their content to determine how likely they are to help the author achieve his writing purpose with his original audience, the readers of *Time* magazine. If you were Kluger's editor and read the essay as a draft, would you suggest that he change the examples in any way or the use he makes of them? Be sure to back up your points with reasons.

5. **Connecting and synthesizing the readings.** What seems simple can be complex and vice versa, which is another way of saying that things are not always what they seem. Drawing on ideas in "The Art of Simplicity" and "Stripping Away Free Expression" (page 207), along with your own experience and observation, discuss the tendency of people to misjudge situations, circumstances, likely outcomes, and/or other people. What can be done to guard against this tendency?

6. **Drawing on sources.** Study several magazines aimed at different audiences—for example, a news magazine, a sports magazine, a magazine aimed at teenage girls, one aimed at technology enthusiasts, and one aimed at young adult women. Use the advertisements in these magazines to show that advertisers rely on the fact that "we're suckers for size, for flash, for speed, for scale" (paragraph 4) to sell products.

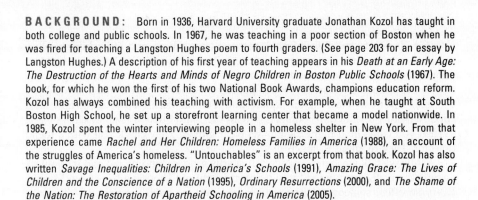

BACKGROUND: Born in 1936, Harvard University graduate Jonathan Kozol has taught in both college and public schools. In 1967, he was teaching in a poor section of Boston when he was fired for teaching a Langston Hughes poem to fourth graders. (See page 203 for an essay by Langston Hughes.) A description of his first year of teaching appears in his *Death at an Early Age: The Destruction of the Hearts and Minds of Negro Children in Boston Public Schools* (1967). The book, for which he won the first of his two National Book Awards, champions education reform. Kozol has always combined his teaching with activism. For example, when he taught at South Boston High School, he set up a storefront learning center that became a model nationwide. In 1985, Kozol spent the winter interviewing people in a homeless shelter in New York. From that experience came *Rachel and Her Children: Homeless Families in America* (1988), an account of the struggles of America's homeless. "Untouchables" is an excerpt from that book. Kozol has also written *Savage Inequalities: Children in America's Schools* (1991), *Amazing Grace: The Lives of Children and the Conscience of a Nation* (1995), *Ordinary Resurrections* (2000), and *The Shame of the Nation: The Restoration of Apartheid Schooling in America* (2005).

COMBINED PATTERNS AND THEIR PURPOSES: In "Untouchables," Jonathan Kozol combines graphic *exemplification* with an explanation of the *causes and effects* of homelessness to **inform** his reader about the plight of the homeless. In addition, Kozol works to **persuade** the reader that government policy and the general public are part of the problem.

Untouchables

BY JONATHAN KOZOL

Richard Lazarus, an educated, thirty-six-year-old Vietnam veteran I met two days after Thanksgiving in the subway underneath [New York's] Grand Central station, tells me he had never been without a job until the recent summer. In July he underwent the loss of job, children and wife, all in a single stroke. As in almost all these situations, it was the simultaneous occurrence of a number of emergencies, any of which he might sustain alone but not all at the same time, that suddenly removed him from his home.

As you read Try to determine why Kozol believes the government and the public are part of the problem of homelessness.

2   "Always, up until last summer, I have found a job that paid at least $300. Now I couldn't find a job that paid $200. When I found an opening at a department store they said that I was overqualified. If someone had asked me a year ago who are the homeless, I would not have known what to reply. Now I know the answer. They are people like myself. I went to Catholic elementary school. I had my secondary education in a private military school. I joined the service and was sent to Thailand as an airman." He has a trade. It's known as "inventory data processing." He had held a single job in data processing for seven years until last summer when the company shut down, without a warning, and moved out of state.

3   "When the company left I could find nothing. I looked everywhere. I got one job for two months in the summer. Part-time, as a security guard in one of the hotels for homeless families."

4   When I ask which one it was, he says the Martinique. "I clocked the floors for fire check. From the top floor to the lobby I swore to myself; rat infested, roach

infested, drug infested, filth infested, garbage everywhere, and little children play-ing in the stairs. Innocent people, women, children, boxed in by their misery. Most people are permitted to make more than one mistake. Not when you're poor."

5   In September he was sick. "I was guarding homeless people and I didn't have a home. I slept in Washington Square and Central Park." He's living now in a rundown hotel operated in conjunction with the Third Street Shelter on the Bowery. "When you come in at night the guards wear gloves. They check you with a metal detector. They're afraid to touch me."

6   While we talk we watch an old man nearby who is standing flat and motionless against the wall, surrounded by two dozen bright red shopping bags from Macy's. Every so often, someone stops to put a coin into his hand. I notice the care with which the people drop their coins, in order that their hands do not touch his. When I pass that spot some hours later he will still be there. I'll do the same. I'll look at his hand—the fingers worn and swollen and the nails curled in like claws—and I will drop a quarter and extract my hand and move off quickly . . .

7   Many homeless people, unable to get into shelters, frightened of disease or violence, or else intimidated by the regulations, look for refuge in such public places as train stations and church doorways.

8   Scores of people sleep in the active subway tunnels of Manhattan, inches from 600-volt live rails. Many more sleep on the ramps and station platforms. Go into the subway station under Herald Square on a December night at twelve o'clock and you will see what scarce accommodations mean at the rockbottom. Emerging from the subway, walk on Thirty-second Street to Penn station. There you will see another form of scarce accommodations: Hot-air grates in the area are highly prized. Home-less people who arrive late often find there is no vacancy, even in a cardboard box over a grate.

9   A man who's taken shelter from the wind that sweeps Fifth Avenue by sleeping beneath the outstretched arms of Jesus on the bronze doors of St. Patrick's Cathedral tells a reporter he can't sleep there anymore because shopkeepers feel that he is hurt-ing business. He moves to the south side of the church where he will be less visible.

10   Stories like these are heard in every state and city of the nation. A twenty-year-old man in Florida tells me that he ran away when he was nine years old from a juvenile detention home in Michigan. He found that he was small enough to slip his body through the deposit slot of a Good Will box. Getting in was easy, he explains, and it was warm because of the clothes and quilts and other gifts that people dropped into the box. "Getting out," he says, "was not so easy. I had to reach my arms above my head, grab hold of the metal edge, twist my body into an *S*, and pull myself out slowly through the slot. When I was fourteen I was too big to fit into the slot. I believe I am the only person in America who has lived for five years in a Good Will box."

11   Thousands of American people live in dumpsters behind restaurants, hotels, and groceries. A woman describes the unimaginable experience of being awakened in the middle of a winter's night by several late-arriving garbage trucks. She nearly drowned beneath two tons of rotting vegetables and fruit.

12   A thirty-four-year-old man in Chicago found his sanctuary in a broken trash compactor. This offered perhaps the ultimate concealment, and the rotting food

which generated heat may have protected him against the freezing weather of Chicago. One night, not knowing that the trash compactor had in his absence been repaired, he fell asleep. When the engine was turned on, he was compressed into a cube of refuse.

13   People in many cities speak of spending nights in phone booths. I have seen this only in New York. Public telephones in Grand Central Station are aligned in recessed areas outside the main concourse. On almost any night before one-thirty, visitors will see a score of people stuffed into these booths with their belongings. Even phone-booth vacancies are scarce in New York City. As in public housing, people are sometimes obliged to double up. One night I stood for an hour and observed three people—man, woman, and child—jammed into a single booth. All three were asleep.

14   Officials have tried a number of times to drive the homeless from Grand Central Station. In order to make conditions less attractive, benches have been removed throughout the terminal. One set of benches has been left there, I am told, because they have been judged "historic landmarks." The terminal's 300 lockers, used in former times by homeless people to secure their few belongings, were removed in 1986. Authorities were forced to justify this action by declaring them, in the words of the city council, "a threat to public safety." Shaving, cleaning of clothes, and other forms of hygiene are prohibited in the men's room of Grand Central. A fast-food chain that wanted to distribute unsold donuts in the terminal was denied the right to do so on the grounds that this would draw more hungry people.

15   At one-thirty every morning, homeless people are ejected from Grand Central. Many have attempted to take refuge on the ramp that leads to Forty-second Street. The ramp initially provided a degree of warmth because it was protected from the street by wooden doors. The station management responded to this challenge in two ways. First, the ramp was mopped with a strong mixture of ammonia to produce a noxious smell. When the people sleeping there brought cardboard boxes and newspapers to protect them from the fumes, the entrance doors were chained wide open. Temperatures dropped some nights to ten degrees.

16   In a case that won brief press attention in December 1985, an elderly woman who had been living in Grand Central on one of the few remaining benches was removed night after night during the weeks preceding Christmas. On Christmas Eve she became ill. No ambulance was called. At one-thirty the police compelled her to move to the ramp outside. At dawn she came inside, climbed back on bench number 9 to sleep, and died that morning of pneumonia.

17   At Penn Station, fifteen blocks away, homeless women are denied use of the bathroom. Amtrak police come by and herd them off each hour on the hour. In June of 1985, Amtrak officials issued this directive to police: "It is the policy of Amtrak to not allow the homeless and undesirables to remain . . . Officers are encouraged to eject all undesirables . . . Now is the time to train and educate them that their presence will not be tolerated as cold weather sets in." In an internal memo, according to CBS, an Amtrak official later went beyond this language and asked flatly: "Can't we get rid of this trash?"

18   In a surprising action, the union representing the police resisted this directive and brought suit against Penn Station's management in 1986. Nonetheless, as

temperatures plunged during the nights after Thanksgiving, homeless men and women were ejected from the station. At 2:00 A.M. I watched a man about my age carry his cardboard box outside the station and try to construct a barricade against the wind that tore across Eighth Avenue. The man was so cold his fingers shook and, when I spoke to him, he tried but could not answer.

19   Driving women from the toilets in a railroad station raises questions that go far beyond the issue of "deterrence." It may surprise the readers to be told that many of these women are quite young. Few are dressed in the familiar rags that are suggested by the term "bag ladies." Some are dressed so neatly and conceal their packages and bags so skillfully that one finds it hard to differentiate them from commuters waiting for a train. Given the denial of hygienic opportunities, it is difficult to know how they are able to remain presentable. The sight of clusters of police officials, mostly male, guarding a women's toilet from its use by homeless females does not speak well for the public conscience of New York.

20   Where do these women defecate? How do they bathe? What will we do when, in her physical distress, a woman finally disrobes in public and begins to urinate right on the floor? We may regard her as an animal. She may by then begin to view herself in the same way.

21   Several cities have devised unusual measures to assure that homeless people will learn quickly that they are not welcome. In Laramie, Wyoming, they are given one night's shelter. On the next morning, an organization called "The Good Samaritan Fund" gives them one-way tickets to another town. The college town of Lancaster, Ohio, offers homeless families one-way tickets to Columbus.

22   In a number of states and cities, homeless people have been murdered, knifed, or set on fire. Two high school students in California have been tried for the knife murder of a homeless man whom they found sleeping in a park. The man, an unemployed house painter, was stabbed seventeen times before his throat was slashed.

23   In Chicago a man was set ablaze while sleeping on a bench in early morning, opposite a popular restaurant. Rush-hour commuters passed him and his charred possessions for four hours before someone called police at noon. A man who watched him burning from a third-floor room above the bench refused to notify police. The purpose was "to get him out," according to a local record-store employee. A resident told reporters that the problem of the homeless was akin to that of "nuclear waste."

24   In Tucson, where police use German shepherds to hunt for the homeless in the skid-row neighborhoods, a mayor was recently elected on the promise that he'd drive the homeless out of town. "We're tired of it. Tired of feeling guilty about these people," said an anti-homeless activist in Phoenix.

25   In several cities it is a crime to sleep in public; in some, armrests have been inserted in the middle of park benches to make it impossible for homeless people to lie down. In others, trash has been defined as "public property," making it a felony to forage in the rotted food.

26   Grocers in Santa Barbara sprinkled bleach on food discarded in their dumpsters. In Portland, Oregon, owners of some shops in redeveloped Old Town have designed slow-dripping gutters (they are known as "drip lines") to prevent the homeless from attempting to take shelter underneath their awnings.

27 Harsher tactics have been recommended in Fort Lauderdale. A city council member offered a proposal to spray trash containers with rat poison to discourage foraging by homeless families. The way to "get rid of vermin," he observed, is to cut their food supply. Some of these policies have been defeated, but the inclination to sequester, punish and conceal the homeless has attracted wide support.

28 "We are the rejected waste of the society," said Lazarus. "They use us, if they think we have some use, maybe for sweeping leaves or scrubbing off graffiti in the subway stations. They don't object if we donate our blood. I've given plasma. That's one way that even worthless people can do something for democracy. We may serve another function too. Perhaps we help to scare the people who still have a home—even a place that's got no heat, that's rat infested, filthy. If they see us in the streets, maybe they are scared enough so they will learn not to complain. If they were thinking about asking for a better heater or a better stove, they're going to think twice. It's like farmers posting scarecrows in the fields. People see these terrifying figures in Penn Station and they know, with one false step, that they could be here too. They think: 'I better not complain.'

29 "The problem comes, however, when they try to find a place to hide us. So it comes to be an engineering question: waste disposal. Store owners certainly regard us in that way. We ruin business and lower the value of good buildings. People fear that we are carriers of illness. Many times we are. So they wear those plastic gloves if they are forced to touch us. It reminds me of the workers in the nuclear reactors. They have to wear protective clothing if they come in contact with the waste. Then you have state governors all over the United States refusing to allow this stuff to be deposited within their borders. Now you hear them talking about dumping toxic waste into the ocean in steel cans. Could they find an island someplace for the homeless?"

30 His question brings back a strange memory for me. In Boston, for years before the homeless were identified as a distinguishable category of the dispossessed, a de facto caste of homeless people dwelt in a vast public housing project built on a virtual island made, in part, of landfill and linked only by one access road to the United States. Columbia Point, adjacent to a camp for prisoners of war in World War II, was so crowded, violent and ugly that social workers were reluctant to pay visits there, few shop owners would operate a business, and even activists and organizers were afraid to venture there at night. From the highway to Cape Cod, one could see the distant profile of those high rise structures. A friend from California asked me if it was a prison. He told me that it looked like Alcatraz. I answered that it was a housing project. The notion of shoving these people as far out into the ocean as we can does bring to mind the way that waste-disposal problems sometimes are resolved.

31 New York has many habitable islands. One of those islands has already earned a place in history as the initial stopping point for millions of European refugees who came to the United States in search of freedom. One reason for their temporary isolation was the fear that they might carry dangerous infection. New York's permanent refugees are carriers of every possible infection; most, moreover, have no prospering relatives to vouch for them, as earlier generations sometimes did, in order to assure that they will not become a burden to the state. They are already

regarded as a burden. An island that served once as quarantine for aliens who crowded to our shore might serve this time as quarantine for those who huddle in train stations and in Herald Square.

32 Lazarus may not be paranoid in speaking of himself as human waste; he may simply read the headlines in the press. "I just can't accommodate them," says the owner of a building in midtown Manhattan. The mayor of Newark, where a number of homeless families have been sent from New York City, speaks of his fear that displaced families from New York might be "permanently dumped in Newark." He announces a deadline after which they will presumably be dumped back in New York.

33 New Yorkers, according to the *New York Times*, "are increasingly opposing [city] attempts to open jails, shelters for the homeless, garbage incinerators" in their neighborhoods. The *Times* reports the city has begun to "compensate communities" that will accept "homeless shelters and garbage-burning generating plants."

34 Do homeless children have some sense of this equation?

35 "Be not forgetful to entertain strangers," wrote Saint Paul, "for thereby some have entertained angels unawares." But the demonology that now accrues to homeless people, and the filth with which their bodies soon become encrusted, seem to reassure us that few of these strangers will turn out to have been angels in disguise.

36 When homeless infants die in New York City, some are buried not in New York itself but on an island in an unmarked grave. Homeless mothers therefore live with realistic fears that they may lose their infants to anonymous interment. Another fear is that their child may be taken from them at the hour of birth if they should be homeless at the time. Hundreds of babies taken by the state for this and other reasons—often they are very ill and sometimes drug addicted—remain in hospitals, sometimes for months or even years, before a foster home is found. Some of these "boarder babies," as they are described, have been kept so long that they have learned to walk and, for this reason, must be tethered in their cribs. Infants held in hospitals so long, physicians tell us, are likely to grow retarded. Some, even after many months, have not been given names. Like their homeless parents in the city's shelters, they remain bed numbers.

37 Many of these children do in time find homes, though most end up in dismal institutions where conditions are no better and often a great deal worse than those they would have faced had they been left with their own parents. Mayor Koch attempted in 1986 to establish a group home for six or seven of these babies in a small house on a quiet street in Queens. Unknown vandals set the house on fire. "Afraid of Babies in Queens," the *New York Times* headlined its editorial response.

38 It seems we *are* afraid of homeless children, not only in Queens but everywhere in the United States. It is hard to know exactly what it is we fear (the children themselves, the sickness they may carry, the adolescents they will soon become if they survive, or the goad to our own conscience that they represent when they are visible, nearby); but the fear is very real. Our treatment of these children reaffirms the distancing that now has taken place. They are not of us. They are "the Other."

39 What startles most observers is not simply that such tragedies persist in the United States, but that almost all have been well documented and that even the most solid documentation does not bring about corrective action. Instead of action,

a common response in New York, as elsewhere, is the forming of a "task force" to investigate. This is frequently the last we hear of it. Another substitute for action is a press event at which a city official seems to overleap immediate concerns by the unveiling of a plan to build a thousand, or a hundred thousand, homes over the course of ten or twenty years at an expense of several billion dollars. The sweep of these announcements tends to dwarf the urgency of the initial issue. When, after a year or so, we learn that little has been done and that the problem has grown worse, we tend to feel not outrage but exhaustion. Exhaustion, however, as we have seen, turns easily to a less generous reaction.

40 "I am about to be heartless," wrote a columnist in *Newsweek* in December 1986. "There are people living on the streets . . . turning sidewalks into dormitories. They are called the homeless . . . Often they are called worse. They are America's living nightmare . . . They have got to go."

41 The author notes that it is his taxes which pay for the paving and the cleaning of the streets they call their home. "That makes me their landlord. I want to evict them."

42 A senior at Boston University sees homeless people on the streets not far from where he goes to class. He complains that measures taken recently to drive them from the area have not been sufficiently aggressive: "I would very much like to see actions more severe . . ." Perhaps, he admits, it isn't possible to have them all arrested, though this notion seems to hold appeal for him; perhaps "a more suitable middle ground" may be arrived at to prevent this "nauseating . . . element" from being permitted to "run free so close to my home."

43 "Our response," says one Bostonian, "has gone from indifference to pitying . . . to hatred." I think this is coming to be true and that it marks an incremental stage in our capacity to view the frail, the ill, the disposed, the unsuccessful not as people who have certain human qualities we share but as an outcast entity. From harsh deterrence to punitive incarceration to the willful cutting off of life supports is an increasingly short journey. "I am proposing triage of a sort, triage by self-selection," writes Charles Murray[1]. "The patient always has the right to fail. Society always has the right to let him."

44 Why is it that writings which present these hardened attitudes seem to prevail so easily in public policy? It may be that kindly voices are more easily derided. Callous attitudes are never subject to the charge of being sentimental. It is a recurrent theme in *King Lear,* writes Ignatieff[2] that "there is a truth in the brutal simplicities of the merciless which the more complicated truth of the merciful is helpless to refute." A rich man, he observes, "never lacks for arguments to deny the poor his charity. 'Basest beggars' can always be found to be 'in the poorest things superfluous.'"

45 "They are a nightmare. I evict them. They will have to go."

46 So from pity we graduate to weariness; from weariness to impatience; from impatience to annoyance; from annoyance to dislike and sometimes to contempt.

---

[1]Charles Murray (b. 1943) is a political scientist who writes about social policy.

[2]Michael Ignatieff (b. 1947) is a member of the Canadian parliament, a journalist, and a novelist who has written about the homeless.

READING CLOSELY AND THINKING CRITICALLY

1. According to Kozol, what are the prevailing attitudes toward the homeless?
2. To what extent are government officials and the general public part of the problem of homelessness?
3. In paragraph 38, Kozol says that we are afraid of homeless children. What are we afraid of?
4. Are any examples particularly moving? Which ones? Why do they affect you the way they do?
5. Has your perception of the homeless changed as a result of reading "Untouchables"? Explain.

EXAMINING STRUCTURE AND STRATEGY

1. "Untouchables" lacks a stated thesis, but you can still identify the implied thesis. Write out that implied thesis.
2. In addition to the opening paragraphs, much of the essay illustrates the plight of the homeless. Cite at least five paragraphs that serve this purpose.
3. Which paragraphs illustrate government indifference to the homeless?
4. Which paragraphs illustrate the public's indifference to or fear of the homeless?

NOTING COMBINED PATTERNS

1. The opening five paragraphs are an extended example. What pattern of development is used for the example? What purposes does the example serve?
2. From paragraph 17 to the end of the essay, examples appear with cause-and-effect analysis. (Cause-and-effect analysis explains the causes or effects of something; see Chapter 10.) According to these paragraphs, what causes people to treat the homeless the way they do?

CONSIDERING LANGUAGE AND STYLE

1. The title of the essay is a reference to one aspect of India's caste system. Look up where the untouchables fit into the Indian caste system, and then explain why Kozol's reference to this caste is fitting.
2. Kozol tells the story of Richard Lazarus; however, in the introduction to his book, he notes that he has changed the names of those he writes of. Why do you think Kozol chose the name "Lazarus"? Is the name appropriate? Explain.
3. Consult a dictionary if you are unsure of the meaning of any of these words: *Bowery* (paragraph 5), *sanctuary* (paragraph 12), *refuse* (paragraph 12), *noxious* (paragraph 15), *skid-row* (paragraph 24), *foraging* (paragraph 27), *vermin* (paragraph 27), *de facto* (paragraph 30), *Alcatraz* (paragraph 30), *demonology* (paragraph 35), *interment* (paragraph 36), *goad* (paragraph 38), *triage* (paragraph 43).

What do homelessness and our reaction to the homeless say about us? Why do we fear and scorn the homeless?

WRITING ASSIGNMENTS

1. **Writing in your journal.** Lazarus says that the homeless are "'the rejected waste of the society'" (paragraph 28). In a page or so, explain what you think Lazarus means, and go on to note whether you think his assessment is correct.

2. **Using exemplification for a purpose.** The purposes in the assignments are possibilities. You may establish whatever purposes you like, within your instructor's guidelines.

   • Kozol notes that people fear the homeless. Think about someone or something that you fear. To relate your experience and express your feelings, use examples to illustrate how you react to your fear. You can also explain the cause of your fear.

   • The homeless are not the only "untouchables" in our society. Pick another group that is often feared or scorned. To inform and perhaps convince your reader to treat the group differently, give examples of our treatment of the group.

   • Were there any "untouchables" in your high school (any people feared or scorned)? If so, pick one of these groups or one of these people, and use examples to inform about how they were treated and, perhaps, why.

3. **Combining patterns.** Homelessness is a problem in society at-large. Identify a problem that currently exists in your campus society. Give examples of the problem so your reader understands its nature and seriousness. Then, using process analysis (explained in Chapter 8), explain a procedure for solving the problem or lessening its negative effects.

4. **Analyzing and assessing.** Analyze the content and language of "Untouchables" to determine how Kozol moves readers' emotions. Assess the importance of the emotional appeal to helping the author achieve his purpose for writing.

5. **Connecting and synthesizing the readings.** Using "What Is Poverty?" (page 546) and "Untouchables" to stimulate your thinking, describe our attitudes toward the poor and explain how our attitudes contribute to the problem of poverty and homelessness.

6. **Drawing on sources.** Pick a particular group of people to which you do not belong (for example, athletes, international students, adult learners, a particular minority, part-time students, or student employees). Interview at least three members of that group and then write an essay that explains what life is like for group members. Use examples to illustrate your points.

22 "I don't understand Italian," the waiter said.

23 "Oh, come off it," my father said. "You understand Italian, and you know damned well you do. *Voglimo due cooktail americani. Subito.*"

24 The waiter left us and spoke with the captain, who came over to our table and said, "I'm sorry, sir, but this table is reserved."

25 "All right," my father said. "Get us another table."

26 "All the tables are reserved," the captain said.

27 "I get it," my father said. "You don't desire our patronage. Is that it? Well, the hell with you. *Vada all' inferno.* Let's go, Charlie."

28 "I have to get my train," I said.

29 "I'm sorry, sonny," my father said. "I'm terribly sorry." He put his arm around me and pressed me against him. "I'll walk you back to the station. If there had only been time to go up to my club."

30 "That's all right, Daddy," I said.

31 "I'll get you a paper," he said. "I'll get you a paper to read on the train."

32 Then he went up to a newsstand and said, "Kind sir, will you be good enough to favor me with one of your God-damned, no-good, ten-cent afternoon papers?" The clerk turned away from him and stared at a magazine cover. "Is it asking too much, kind sir," my father said, "is it asking too much for you to sell me one of your disgusting specimens of yellow journalism?"

33 "I have to go, Daddy," I said. "It's late."

34 "Now, just wait a second, sonny," he said. "I want to get a rise out of this chap."

35 "Goodbye, Daddy," I said, and I went down the stairs and got my train, and that was the last time I saw my father.

CONSIDERING THE SHORT STORY

1. Charlie says that his father was "[his] future and [his] doom" (paragraph 1). What does he mean?

2. A great deal is left unsaid in "Reunion." What can you infer about the reason for the divorce, about why Charlie hadn't seen his father for three years, and about why he never saw his father again? What can you infer about Charlie's opinion of his father? (See page 5 on inference.)

3. Charlie barely speaks during his father's encounters with the waiters and newsstand vendor. Why doesn't Charlie speak more?

4. How many examples does Cheever include in the story? What purpose do those examples serve?

5. How does Cheever connect the conclusion of the story with the opening?

1. **Writing in your journal.** Charlie sees his father as "[his] future and [his] doom." To what extent do you think a person's parents are that person's future and doom?

2. **Using exemplification for a purpose.** To express your feelings and relate your experience, use examples to show that one or more of your parents proved to be your future and/or your doom. (The purpose in this assignment is a possibility. You may establish whatever purpose you like, within your instructor's guidelines.)

3. **Combining patterns.** Like Cheever does in "Reunion," narrate an account of a period of time you spent with someone. Also like Cheever does in the story, include examples of situations that reveal this individual's character.

WRITING EXEMPLIFICATION

See pages 241–244 for strategies for writing exemplification and for a revision checklist.

1. Use examples to show that the life of a teenager is not an easy one.
2. Use examples to prove that advertisements cause people to want things that they do not really need.
3. Use examples to show that life has its surprising moments.
4. Use examples to show that our society does (or does not) worship youth.
5. Use examples to illustrate the benefits or drawbacks of computers or some other form of technology.
6. Form a generalization about the way some group is depicted on television (women, police officers, the elderly, teenagers, or fathers, for instance), and provide examples to illustrate that generalization. Evaluate the accuracy of the depiction.
7. Provide examples to illustrate the fact that appearances can be deceiving.
8. Use examples to show that advertisements can mislead the consumer.
9. Use illustrations to persuade your reader that sometimes a lie is better than the truth.
10. Provide humorous examples to illustrate Murphy's First Law ("What *can* go wrong, *will* go wrong").
11. Provide examples to show that people are at their worst when they are behind the wheels of their cars.
12. Use examples to persuade your reader that athletics have (or have not) assumed excessive importance in this country.
13. Use examples to persuade your reader that the American family is (or is not) changing for the better.
14. Use examples to persuade your reader that some aspect of the U.S. education system should be reformed.
15. Use examples to illustrate the best characteristics of your favorite teacher.
16. Use examples to illustrate the fact that sometimes people can surprise you.
17. Use examples to illustrate some aspect of the relationship you had with your best friend when you were growing up.
18. Provide examples to illustrate the fact that jealousy (or another emotion) can be destructive.
19. Provide examples to illustrate the fact that people make their own luck.
20. **Exemplification in context:** Assume that your local Parents-Teachers Association (PTA) has asked families and schools to consider a month-long ban on television viewing for school-age children. The organization's goal is to get children away from their television sets and engaged in "more worthwhile" activities, such as reading, interacting with family members, studying, playing sports, and enjoying hobbies. A public forum is being held to look at the advantages and disadvantages of the proposal. Write a position paper to be distributed at the forum, a paper in which you support or attack the moratorium by offering illustrations to convince people that television has negative (or positive) effects on children.

In 1896, the Supreme Court ruled in *Plessy v. Ferguson* that a Louisiana law requiring whites and blacks to ride in separate railroad cars was legal. This ruling provided federal protection for the separate-but-equal laws that enabled so much segregation. In its 1954 decision in *Brown v. Board of Education of Topeka,* the Supreme Court determined that racially segregated schools were not constitutional. That decision doomed separate-but-equal laws. "On Being the Target of Discrimination" on page 262 describes and illustrates life between the *Plessy* and *Brown* decisions. If you were including that essay in a lesson for a history class about the era of segregation, why do you think it would be a good idea to also include the following photo? What does it exemplify? What would students learn from it that they might not understand in the same way from Ellison's essay by itself? Explain.

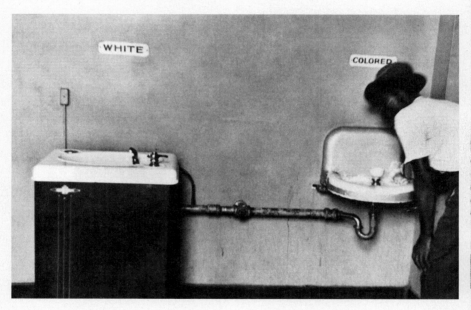

Separate but Equal?

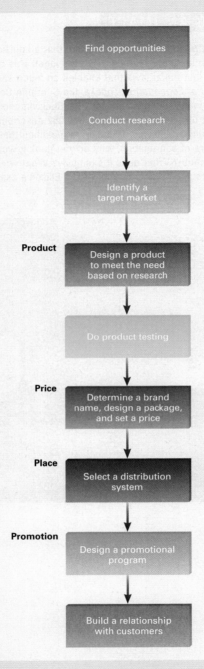

The Marketing Process with the Four Ps

Process Analysis

8

CONSIDER THE PATTERN

The chart on the opposite page, taken from a business textbook, explains the marketing process for an audience of business students. You will likely have to learn many processes on the way to your degree. Think about the processes you will have to learn for the courses you are taking this term and for your major. Why is it important to learn those processes?

THE PATTERN

A **process analysis** explains how something works, how something is made, or how something is done. There are two kinds of process analyses:

- Directional process analysis
- Explanatory process analysis

A **directional process analysis** gives the steps in a procedure the reader may want to perform. For example, when you buy a cell phone, the accompanying instruction booklet explains how to add and delete phone numbers, how to change the battery, and how to work the camera. Each of these explanations is a directional process analysis. When you consult a recipe to prepare a new dish, you are reading and following a directional process analysis. Similarly, if you apply for a scholarship, the instructions for completing the application are a directional process analysis.

An **explanatory process analysis** is a bit different. Like a directional process analysis, it tells how something works, how something is made, or how something is done, but the procedure explained will *not* be performed by the reader. Explanatory process analyses are also common. For example, a biology textbook explains how plants convert carbon dioxide to oxygen through the process of photosynthesis. Since no reader will engage in photosynthesis, the process analysis is purely explanatory, meant to increase understanding. Similarly, explanations of how an internal combustion engine works, how natural selection occurs, and how rivers become polluted are examples of explanatory process analyses.

www.mhhe.com/clousepatterns6	Process Analysis

For more help with process analysis, click on
Writing > Writing Tutor > Process Analysis

USING PROCESS ANALYSIS FOR A PURPOSE

Process analysis, whether directional or explanatory, often *informs* readers. A directional process analysis can inform a reader about how to perform a particular procedure or other process—for example, how to install a computer program. Sometimes it informs readers of a better or different way to do something. For example, you already know how to study, but a process analysis essay titled "Six Steps to More Efficient Studying" may help

TROUBLESHOOTING GUIDE

Using Imperative and Declarative Sentences

If you have trouble keeping your approach consistent in a process analysis, remember the difference between imperative and declarative sentences. An imperative sentence gives a directive. Its subject is *you*, which can be stated or unstated. A declarative sentence makes a statement. Its subject, which is stated, can be any noun or pronoun. Directional process analyses often use imperative sentences; explanatory process analyses have declarative sentences. The following examples for process analyses about bread baking illustrate the difference.

IMPERATIVE SENTENCES (FOR DIRECTIONAL PROCESS ANALYSIS) **Dissolve the yeast in the water and let it sit for 10 minutes. In a big bowl, combine the water/yeast, milk, sugar, salt, and oil.**

DECLARATIVE SENTENCES (FOR EXPLANATORY PROCESS ANALYSIS) **Yeast eats sugar, and from the sugar it creates alcohol and carbon dioxide gas. The carbon dioxide gas gives bread its texture, and the alcohol flavors the bread.**

you by showing you an even better way. An explanatory process analysis can inform a reader who desires a better understanding of how a procedure or other process works. For example, "Behind the Formaldehyde Curtain" in this chapter, which explains how a body is prepared for burial, gives readers an understanding of this process. An explanatory process analysis can also inform a reader about the beauty, difficulty, or complexity of a process so the reader can better appreciate it. For example, if you are a distance runner, you might describe a cross-country race to enable your reader to appreciate the rigor and discipline that go into running the race.

In addition to informing a reader, a process analysis can *entertain.* In "Science: It's Just Not Fair" in this chapter, for example, Dave Barry gives a humorous account of how to participate in a school science fair.

A process analysis can also *express feelings* and *relate experience.* If one of your happiest childhood memories is of your annual fishing trips with your grandfather, you could relate part of that experience by explaining how you and your grandfather prepared for the trip and interacted during the process.

Finally, a process analysis can *persuade.* To convince your reader that gun registration procedures are inadequate, you might explain the registration process and point out its flaws. To persuade your reader to use a particular computer security system, you could explain how the system works and point out its benefits.

Combining Patterns for a Purpose

You can combine process analysis with other patterns of development to achieve your writing purpose. For instance, if you are *informing* readers about the job interview process, you might mention the importance of appropriate body language and *describe* how to sit, hold your head, and make eye contact. Or you might mention the need to demonstrate knowledge of the company's goals and give *examples* of answers that would do so. If your reader is unlikely to understand a specialized term in your process analysis, you should include *definition.* For example, if you are explaining how global warming works and note that carbon dioxide absorbs infrared radiation, you could define infrared radiation.

To see how another pattern can be combined with process analysis, study the following excerpt from paragraph 4 of "In the Kitchen," an essay in this chapter explaining hair-straightening processes that African Americans followed at one time.

EXCERPT FROM "IN THE KITCHEN"
COMBINING PROCESS ANALYSIS AND DESCRIPTION

The sentences explain one step in the hair-straightening process.

describes temperature of item used in process

Mama would stroke that red-hot iron—which by this time had been in the gas fire for half an hour or more—slowly

The highlighted
description helps
clarify how a step in
the process was
performed and the
outcome of the
process.

describes motion used in process

but firmly through their hair, from scalp to strand's end. It

describes sound of step in process

made a scorching, crinkly sound, the hot iron did, as it

burned its way through the kink, leaving in its wake

describes result of process

straight strands of hair, standing long and tall but drooping

simile describes result of process

over at the ends, their shape like the top of a heavy

willow tree.

Process analysis can be a secondary pattern in essays developed primarily with other patterns. For example, if you are classifying effective ways to save energy, and you mention purchasing a hybrid car, you can briefly explain how the engines of hybrid cars work and how they save energy. If you are illustrating the effects of identity theft on consumers, you can give background information on how thieves steal an identity.

Whether you use process analysis alone or in combination with other patterns depends on what helps you achieve your writing purpose.

Process Analysis Beyond the Writing Classroom

Process analysis helps writers achieve their purpose in many writing situations.

IN ACADEMIC WRITING AND READING   Both directional and explanatory process analyses are important in your college writing. In biology, chemistry, and physics lab reports, you will write directional process analyses to explain the processes you followed to complete experiments. For a marketing class examination answer, you might write a directional process analysis to explain how to conduct an online survey. For a computer science class report, you might write a directional process analysis to explain how to develop a certain kind of computer program. For a psychology research paper, you might write an explanatory process analysis to explain how children acquire language, and for a political science class, you might write a paper that explains how the electoral college works.

Process analysis—particularly explanatory process analysis—is a common component in textbooks of all kinds. Here, for example, is an excerpt from an introductory psychology textbook. It explains the classic experiments that Russian psychologist Ivan Pavlov performed to learn about a form of learning called *classical conditioning*, which occurs when an organism is trained or "conditioned" to produce a response not ordinarily associated with a particular stimulus.

> To demonstrate and analyze classical conditioning, Pavlov conducted a series of experiments (Pavlov, 1927). In one, he attached a tube to the salivary gland of a dog, allowing him to measure precisely the amount of salivation that occurred. He then sounded a tuning fork and, just a few seconds later, presented the dog with meat powder. This pairing, carefully planned so that exactly the same amount of time elapsed between the presentation of the sound and the meat powder, occurred repeatedly. At first the dog would salivate only when the meat powder itself was presented, but soon it began to salivate at the sound of the tuning fork. In fact, even when Pavlov stopped presenting the meat powder, the dog still salivated after hearing the sound. The dog had been classically conditioned to salivate to the tone. (Feldman, *Understanding Psychology*)

This portion gives the steps in the process.

This portion tells how a step is performed.

This portion gives the effect of the process.

This process analysis helps students understand that an animal (in this case, a dog) can be conditioned to produce a response (salivating) that is normally unrelated to the stimulus (the sound of the tuning fork). It also helps students remember classical conditioning by helping them visualize the concept in action.

AT WORK AND IN THE COMMUNITY   Process analysis is an important component of workplace communications. A restaurant manager might post in the kitchen, for employees to read, an explanatory process analysis that describes how food poisoning occurs. Human resource managers send memos explaining procedures for using vacation days; physical therapists write out instructions for performing exercises; and safety officers write out procedures for emergency evacuations of buildings.

Process analysis is also important to writing you do in the community. When you write out directions to your home or another location, you are writing a directional process analysis. If you e-mail a friend about how to install a computer firewall to protect against viruses, you are also writing a directional process analysis, and if you send a letter to the editor urging people to donate blood by explaining how simple the procedure is, you are writing an explanatory process analysis.

SUPPORTING DETAILS

Because a process analysis explains how something is made, how something works, or how something is done, the primary details are usually the steps in the process. Often, in giving the steps, you will also need to explain *how* a particular step is performed. For example, in "Don't Just Stand There," an essay in this chapter, Diane Cole describes how to deal with racial, ethnic, and sexist remarks. At one point, she tells what to do when the remark occurs at a large meeting or public talk, and then she goes on to explain *how* to perform the step:

> At a large meeting or public talk, you might consider passing the speaker a note . . . You could write, "You may not realize it, but your remarks were offensive because . . ."

At times, you should explain *why* a step is performed so your reader appreciates the importance of the step. Assume you are explaining the best job application procedure, and you mention that applicants should follow every interview with a letter of thanks that also reaffirms their interest in the position. To help your reader appreciate the importance of this step, you can explain that the letter marks the applicant as a courteous person who follows through—qualities that can help a person land the job.

An example may help you clarify a step to be sure your reader understands. In this excerpt from "Don't Just Stand There," the author uses an example to clarify how the host can control the behavior of guests:

> If you, yourself, are the host, you can exercise more control; you are, after all, the one who sets the rules and the tone of behavior in your home. Once, when Professor Kahn's party guests began singing offensive, racist songs, for instance, he kicked them all out, saying "You don't sing songs like that in my house!" And, he adds, "they never did again."

If you think your reader might perform a step incorrectly or might perform an unnecessary step, you can explain what *not* to do and why. For example, in "Don't Just Stand There," the author cautions the reader not to deal with offensive remarks by embarrassing a person publicly:

> But in general, psychologists say, shaming a person in public may have the opposite effect of the one you want: The speaker may deny his offense all the more strongly in order to save face.

If a step is sometimes troublesome, you can point that out to the reader, as Jessica Mitford does in "Behind the Formaldehyde Curtain":

> Proper placement of the body requires a delicate sense of balance. It should lie as high as possible in the casket, yet not so high that the lid, when lowered, will hit the nose. On the other hand, we are cautioned, placing the body too low creates the impression that the body is in a box.

ORGANIZING DETAILS

Your thesis for a process analysis can mention the process to be explained:

> A person should take great care when choosing a personal physician. *(Thesis indicates that the essay will explain how to choose a personal physician.)*

In addition to mentioning the process, your thesis can explain why understanding the process is important:

> To avoid making a costly mistake, follow this procedure to shop for a car. *(Thesis indicates that the process is important because it can save money.)*

If you do not mention the importance of the process in your thesis, you can do so elsewhere in the essay. In "Don't Just Stand There," Diane Cole uses her fourth paragraph to explain why knowing a process for dealing with racial and ethnic insults is important:

> But left unchecked, racial slurs and offensive ethnic jokes "can poison the atmosphere," says Michael McQuillan, adviser for racial/ethnic affairs for the Brooklyn borough president's office. "Hearing these remarks conditions us to accept them; and if we accept these, we can become accepting of other acts."

If you want your reader to know why you are qualified to describe the process, you can give your credentials in your introduction. For example, if you are explaining a note-taking system you devised, you can mention that you devised and use the system; if you add that you have made the dean's list every term since you started using the system, you will also be giving evidence of the effectiveness of your process.

If the process requires particular materials, note that fact early, perhaps even in the first paragraph. If, for example, you are explaining how to build a bookcase, note the lumber, tools, and other materials needed.

When the steps in the process must be performed in a particular order, arrange details in a **chronological** (or time) **order.** To help your reader follow the chronological order, use transitions like these:

First, you must . . .
Next, be careful to . . .
Now, you can . . .
After that, try . . .
Finally, you should . . .

If you need to mention what *not* to do so your reader does not make a mistake or misunderstand a step, include this information at the point in the process when the confusion can occur. If you need to define a term, do so the first time the term is used. Finally, if you need to explain why a step is performed, do so when the step is given.

VISUALIZING A PROCESS ANALYSIS ESSAY

The chart on page 299 can help you visualize the structure for a process analysis. Like all good models, this one can be altered as needed.

THINKING CRITICALLY ABOUT PROCESS ANALYSIS

The material you learned in Chapters 1 and 4 about how to read critically and write critical analyses can help you think critically about the process analyses you read and write. Additionally, you can ask the following questions:

- **Is the process analysis responsible and ethical?** Some processes should not be explained. For example, it is not responsible or ethical to explain how to create and distribute a computer virus, how to pilfer supplies from an employer, or how to smuggle a weapon onto an airplane.
- **Is the explanation original?** Like any essay, a process analysis should be original. Internet sites like www.howstuffworks.com explain many processes. This material should never be downloaded and passed off as original, nor should explanations of a process be copied from any other source. If a process is researched and the analysis includes source material, the conventions for summarizing, quoting, paraphrasing, and documenting that are explained in Chapters 4 and 15 should be followed.

PROCESS GUIDELINES:
STRATEGIES FOR WRITING A PROCESS ANALYSIS

1. **Selecting a topic.** If possible, select a process you know well so you do not struggle for detail or present the process incompletely.
2. **Establishing a purpose.** To establish your purpose, ask these questions:
   - Are you writing a directional process analysis to inform your reader how to perform the process? Or are you writing an explanatory process analysis to inform a reader who will *not* perform the process? Do you want this reader to appreciate the beauty, difficulty, or complexity of this process?
   - Do you want to entertain your reader?
   - Do you want to relate part of your experience or express your feelings about something associated with the process?
   - Do you want to convince your reader that the process is a better way to do something? Or do you want to show the flaws in the process and suggest ways in which it might be improved?

INTRODUCTION

- Creates interest in your essay
- Can explain why you are qualified to explain the process
- Can note what materials, if any, are needed
- States the thesis (underlined in the example), which mentions the process to be explained and may note why it is important to understand the process

EXAMPLE

Lightning is the most destructive force in nature. In the United States, it kills more people than any other natural force or disaster. <u>Yet lives could be saved if people took the appropriate precautions during a thunderstorm.</u>

FIRST BODY PARAGRAPH

- Gives the first step in the process
- May explain how the step is performed, why the step is performed, and what not to do
- May clarify the step, including through examples, or point out a troublesome aspect
- May include description or definition of specialized vocabulary
- Arranges details in chronological order

EXAMPLE

People caught outside during an electrical storm must be particularly careful to protect themselves. The best action is to remain in a closed car. . . .

NEXT BODY PARAGRAPHS

- Give the remaining steps in the process
- May explain how the steps are performed, why the steps are performed, and what not to do
- May clarify the steps, including through examples, or point out troublesome aspects
- May include description or definition of specialized vocabulary
- Arrange details in chronological order

EXAMPLE

Although most lightning deaths occur outside, people inside are not out of danger and, therefore, must know what to do. Lightning can enter the house through the chimney, plumbing, wiring, or roof, so everyone should be aware of the safest spots in the house. . . .

CONCLUSION

- Provides a satisfying finish
- Leaves your reader with a strong final impression

EXAMPLE

During thunderstorm season, everyone should stay aware of the local weather forecasts and, when lightning is a threat, take precautions. It is a killer like no other.

3. **Assessing your audience.** To assess your audience, ask whether your reader appreciates the importance of the process, understands any part of the process, or would find any of the steps difficult to perform or understand. In addition, consider why your reader might be interested in the process.

4. **Generating ideas.** List every step in the process in the order it is performed. Then write a statement that explains the importance of the process.

5. **Drafting.** With your list of steps as a guide, write out the process. Visualize the process as you are describing it. Are you providing enough information? Do the steps follow a logical order? Include a statement that indicates the importance of understanding the process. If you wish, this statement can be your thesis.

6. **Revising.** Omit anything that would be obvious to the reader or that explains how to do something the reader already knows how to do. For example, to explain how to use a specialized search engine, you need not tell your reader to turn on the computer. In addition, be sure to define any specialized terms.

Avoiding Person Shifts

If you have trouble knowing when to use *you* and *your*, remember that these words refer to the reader. If you use one of these pronouns to refer to a noun or to yourself—that is, if you are *not* referring to the reader—you create a problem called *person shift*.

PERSON SHIFT	**Intelligent women often overestimate their ability to handle dangerous situations. For example, they think they can talk themselves out of a confrontation, but you should always remember that your first step should be to walk—or run—away.**
CORRECTION	**Intelligent women often overestimate their ability to handle dangerous situations. For example, they think they can talk themselves out of a confrontation, but they should always remember that their first step should be to walk—or run—away.**

For more help with pronouns, click on

Editing > Pronouns
Editing > Pronoun–Antecedent Agreement

Using Sources for a Purpose

Below is a body paragraph for an essay discussing the lack of respect we give to police officers; it illustrates how you can use sources from this book in your writing. It includes a paraphrase and a quotation from paragraph 5 of "Shoot to Kill" on page 325. The source material helps the writer support the point that police officers can be sued for doing their duty.

THESIS We are a nation of laws, and police officers enforce those laws. I find it wrong, therefore, that we fail to give our police officers the respect they deserve.

WRITING PURPOSE AND AUDIENCE To convince college students that we do not give police officers enough respect.

[1]If you don't believe that police officers in this country are unappreciated, consider the fact that in addition to risking their lives, they also risk lawsuits from an ungrateful public. [2]The aftermath of the Columbine High School shootings is an excellent example. [3]On April 20, 1999, at Columbine High School in Littleton, Colorado, two students opened fire, killing twelve students and a teacher and wounding twenty-three other students, before killing themselves. [4]Then came the lawsuits. [5]According to Timothy Harper in "Shoot to Kill," fifteen Columbine families filed lawsuits because they believed the police could have saved some lives had they entered the building more quickly (326). [6]Perhaps they could have, but the police did nothing wrong. [7]On the contrary, says Harper, "Columbine was handled by the book" (326). [8]However, even though the officers handled Columbine according to standard police procedure, they had to defend themselves in court. [9]Forcing police officers to defend their actions when they followed procedures is both unfair and demeaning.

> The paraphrase in sentence 5 illustrates the point made in sentence 1: Police officers face lawsuits. The quotation in sentence 7 proves the point made in sentence 6: The police officers did nothing wrong. Notice that sentences 4, 6, and 8 help integrate the source material.

AVOIDING PLAGIARISM

The paragraph illustrates the following points about avoiding plagiarism. (For more complete information on using source material, consult Chapters 4 and 15.)

- **Do not attribute your own ideas to sources.** Sentence 5 is a paraphrase attributed to Harper, and sentence 7 is a quotation attributed to Harper. Sentence 6, however, is the author's material meant to help synthesize sentences 5 and 7; therefore, it is not attributed to Harper.

(continued)

- **Reintroduce as necessary.** As sentence 7 illustrates, when you return to a source you used earlier in the paragraph or essay (in this case, in sentence 5), reintroduce the source so your reader understands that you have come back to it.

MYTHS ABOUT USING SOURCES

MYTH: You must document anything you use in your writing that you encounter in a source.

FACT: You need not document information that is common knowledge. Common knowledge includes dates of historical record, such as when Lincoln was born and when World War II ended in the Pacific. It also includes information that people agree on, such as the fact that the terrorist attacks of September 11, 2001, changed American air travel, and information that most people know, such as the fact that London is the capital of England. The information in sentence 3 is considered common knowledge because it is a matter of historical record. For that reason, it is not documented.

Checklist for Revising a Process Analysis

You can use this checklist along with the one on page 76 to help you revise.

_____ 1. The process you explain is ethical and your explanation is original.

_____ 2. All steps are included and are chronologically arranged.

_____ 3. Details, as necessary, explain how steps are performed and why steps are performed, provide clarifying explanations, mention what not to do, and point out troublesome aspects.

_____ 4. Terms your reader may not understand are defined.

_____ 5. The importance of understanding the process is indicated, if relevant.

_____ 6. Information your reader does not need is not included.

_____ 7. Transitions indicate sequence.

The following student essay is a process analysis that says as much about the *joy* of performing the process as it does about *how* to perform the process. After you read, you will have an opportunity to analyze and assess this essay.

A Visit to Candyland
Debi McKinney

You may have been to the supermarket around Christmastime and seen a gingerbread house kit. It probably involved graham-cracker slabs meant to be stuck together with thick white frosting and decorated with gumdrops. In my family, making gingerbread houses is a long-standing tradition, and one that involves far more than simply slapping some cookies and frosting together. Each year, in early December, we decide on a theme and go on to create an elaborate gingerbread structure that reflects the season and our interests. Our cardinal rule in gingerbread house making often comes as a surprise to the friends who visit to marvel at our creations: Absolutely everything in the gingerbread house must be edible, and not only edible, but tasty.

We begin by coming up with a concept. One year, it was a crèche scene with Mary, Joseph, the baby Jesus, and various animals, shepherds, and angels. Another year, it was a covered bridge under snow, with a horse-drawn carriage. Once we've decided on a theme, we might visit the library or go on the Internet to find visual ideas we can incorporate into our design. Then, after we've done some preliminary sketches, we make a pattern, measuring carefully with a ruler to make sure each piece will fit with the others. These pattern pieces are drawn onto thin paper and then precisely cut out with sharp scissors. We've found it helps to note on each pattern piece how many need to be made—a roof, for example, is usually made of two equal rectangles, and only one pattern piece is needed.

The next step is to make the gingerbread. We use an old family recipe that produces a sturdy but extremely tasty gingerbread cookie, flavored with molasses, cinnamon, ground cloves, and lots of ginger. In order to make a really tough cookie, many cups of flour have to be incorporated into the batter. Once all the flour has been added, the dough is so dense it's almost impossible to stir, so we hand it off to my

Paragraph 1
The introduction gives background information. The thesis is not stated, but the paragraph suggests a focus on making gingerbread houses.

Paragraph 2
The paragraph gives several steps in the process. The details include examples of the first step and information on how the last of these is performed.

Paragraph 3
The topic sentence (sentence 1) gives the next step in the process. Detail is included on why part of the step is performed.

father, whose arms are the strongest. After the dough is finished, it has to sit in the refrigerator for a time period ranging from several hours to a week. This cooling period makes the dough easier to handle and the finished cookie even tougher.

Paragraph 4
The topic sentence (sentence 1) gives the next step in the process. Detail explaining why is part of this step. Notice that two sentences begin with the transition "Once . . ."

Once the dough is ready to bake, it's time to make the pieces of 4 the house. We do this by rolling out the dough onto sheets of tinfoil. We try to avoid handling the dough too much—if it gets warm before it goes into the oven, it loses some of its resilience. We roll the dough until it's a little less than a quarter of an inch thick. Then we place the pattern pieces onto the rolled dough. Using a small knife, we cut around the pattern piece, discarding the excess dough. After we've cut out the windows on the wall pieces, we fill the holes with broken bits of hard candy. In the oven, these candy pieces will melt and harden, forming what looks like stained glass. Once that's done, we slide the tinfoil with the cookie pieces on it onto a cookie sheet and put them into the oven.

Paragraph 5
The paragraph opens with the transition "Seven to ten minutes later." The paragraph also notes a troublesome aspect related to the step discussed in the paragraph.

Seven to ten minutes later, the cookies are done, and we slide 5 them onto wire racks to cool. After they've cooled, we peel off the tinfoil backing and admire the colored light through the little stained-glass windows. Now we're ready for the hardest part of the whole process: putting the house together. Frosting is simply not tough enough for the elaborate structures we make, so instead we use melted sugar. We sprinkle regular granulated sugar into a wide, flat pan and heat it over a medium-high flame. In a few minutes it forms a glossy, dark-brown liquid. The ends of the gingerbread pieces that are to be stuck together have to be dipped very quickly into the melted sugar and then speedily and precisely joined to their intended mates. If this process is done too quickly, there may not be enough sugar to make the pieces stick, or we may stick them on at the wrong angle. If it's done too slowly, the sugar can harden, its sticking powers completely lost. When my brothers and I were little, we were not allowed to participate in the melted-sugar operation, but now we've developed the necessary manual dexterity and nerves of steel.

Paragraph 6
The topic sentence (sentence 1) gives the next step and includes a transition ("Now"). The transition "Then" joins two parts of this step.

Now the house is assembled and ready for everyone's favorite 6 stage: decoration. We make frosting out of butter, confectioner's sugar, and food coloring, and add a base coat to the parts of the house that seem to need it, like the roof. We generally leave the sides bare, because the dark brown gingerbread is such a pretty color, but we add details with frosting piped out of a wax-paper tube. Then we add decorations. In the past we've used raisins, cinnamon sticks, star anise, nuts, and, of course, many different kinds of candy. Necco wafers, broken in half, make particularly good shingles.

When we're finished, we've usually consumed a substantial quantity of decorations, spoonfuls of frosting, and cookie scraps. Naturally we make gingerbread men to live in the house, but their life spans tend to be extremely short—sometimes they don't even get frosted. We're too full to do anything but sit and admire our handiwork. A few days later, however, we host our annual holiday party, where the final part of the tradition comes into play. The youngest child at the event (apart from babies, of course) is handed an orange suspended from a red satin ribbon. This is the gingerbread wrecking ball, and it's swung at the house until total destruction has been achieved. We're always sorry to see the house ruined, but then we have the pleasure, along with our guests, of eating our annual masterpiece.

Paragraph 7
The conclusion signaled by the transition "When we're finished," provides closure by explaining what is done with the gingerbread house. It highlights a family tradition—a sort of final step introduced with "A few days later."

PEER REVIEW

Responding to "A Visit to Candyland"

Analyze and assess "A Visit to Candyland" by responding to these questions:

1. Does the essay hold your interest? Why or why not?
2. Are the introduction and conclusion effective? Explain.
3. Is the essay a directional or an explanatory process analysis? If it is the former, could you perform the process after reading the essay? If it is the latter, do you understand and appreciate the process after reading the essay?
4. Were the steps clearly ordered and sufficiently detailed?
5. What do you think of the author's word choice? Why? Cite an example to support your evaluation.
6. What are the chief strengths of the essay? Why do you find these features strong?
7. What is one revision you would like to see? How will that revision improve the essay or help the author achieve her purpose?

EXAMINING VISUALS Process Analysis in a Photograph

When a process in depicted in a photograph, we may come to appreciate the process more because we see what goes into it. For example, you may have seen a maneuver like the one shown in the photograph here many times, but perhaps it was executed so quickly that you did not realize the skill it took.

- Would you term the photograph a directional or explanatory process analysis?
- Does the photograph increase your appreciation of the process depicted?
- Does the photograph show all of the steps in the process?
- What purpose do you think the photographer had in mind for this image?

BACKGROUND: Born in 1947, author and humorist Dave Barry wrote a tremendously popular nationally syndicated column for the *Miami Herald* from 1983 to 2005. In 1988, he became the only humor writer to win the Pulitzer Prize for Distinguished Commentary. Called "the funniest man in America" by the *New York Times,* Barry has written more than 30 books, including *Dave Barry's Guide to Marriage and/or Sex* (1999), *Big Trouble* (2000), *Dave Barry Hits below the Beltway: A Vicious and Unprovoked Attack on Our Most Cherished Political Institutions* (2001), *Boogers Are My Beat* (2007), and *Dave Barry's History of the Millennium (So Far)* (2007). He has also written a series of books for young people with Ridley Pearson. "Science: It's Just Not Fair" first appeared in the *Miami Herald* in 1998 and was reprinted there in 2007.

THE PATTERN AND ITS PURPOSES: Dave Barry uses *process analysis* to take a humorous look at school science fairs and students who participate in them. Although **entertaining,** the essay also **informs** readers of some truths.

Science: It's Just Not Fair

BY DAVE BARRY

TODAY'S TOPIC FOR YOUNG PEOPLE IS: How To Do A School Science Fair Project.

2   So your school is having a science fair! Great! The science fair has long been a favorite educational tool in the American school system, and for a good reason: Your teachers hate you. Ha-ha! No, seriously, although a science fair can seem like a big "pain," it can help you understand important scientific principles, such as Newton's First Law of Inertia,[1] which states: "A body at rest will remain at rest until 8:45 P.M. the night before the science fair project is due, at which point the body will come rushing to the body's parents, who are already in their pajamas, and shout, 'I JUST REMEMBERED THE SCIENCE FAIR IS TOMORROW AND WE GOTTA GO TO THE STORE RIGHT NOW!'"

As you read
The best humor has elements of truth at its core. Look for the elements of truth in Dave Barry's humor.

3   Being driven to the store by pajama-wearing parents at the last minute is the most important part of any science fair project, because your project, to be legal, must have an Official Science Fair Display Board. This is a big white board that you fold into three sections, thus giving it the stability that it needs to collapse instantly when approached by humans. The international scientific community does not recognize any scientific discovery that does not have an Official Science Fair Display Board teetering behind it; many top scientists fail to win the Nobel Prize for exactly this reason.

4   Once you have returned home and gotten your display board folded into three sections (allow about six hours for this), it's time to start thinking about what kind of project to do. The prize-winning projects are the ones that clearly yet imaginatively demonstrate an interesting scientific principle.

---

[1]Sir Isaac Newton (1642–1727) was a mathematician and physicist whose three laws of motion (about objects in motion or at rest) transformed our understanding of the universe.

5   So you can forget about winning a prize. What you need is a project that can be done at 1 A.M. using materials found in your house. Ideally, it should also involve a minimum of property damage or death, which is why, on the advice of this newspaper's legal counsel, we are not going to discuss some of our popular project topics from previous years, such as "What Is Inside Plumbing?" and "Flame-Proofing Your Cat." Whatever topic you select, your project should be divided into three parts: (1) The Hypothesis, (2) The Part That Goes After The Hypothesis and (3) The Conclusion (this should always be the same as the Hypothesis).

6   The hypothesis—which comes from the Greek words "hypot," meaning "word," and "hesis," meaning "that I am looking up in the dictionary right now"—is defined as "an unproved theory, proposition, supposition, etc., tentatively accepted to explain certain facts." For example, a good hypothesis for your science fair project might be: "There is a lot of gravity around." You could prove this via an experiment in which you pick up various household items such as underwear, small appliances, siblings, etc., and observe what happens when you let go of them. Your conclusion would, of course, be: "There is a lot of gravity around." This would be dramatically illustrated in your science fair exhibit by the fact that your Official Science Fair Display Board was lying face down on the floor.

7   If that project sounds like too much effort, you might consider duplicating the one that my wife swears she did in the 7th grade late on the night before the science fair. It was called "Waves," and it consisted entirely of a baking pan filled with water, and a pencil. "You swished the pencil around in the water, and it made waves," my wife explained.

8   I asked her what scientific principle this project demonstrated, and, after thinking about it for a moment, she answered: "The movement of the water."

9   Impossible though it may sound, I did a project in 6th grade that was even lamer than that. It was called "Phases of the Moon," and it consisted of a small rubber ball that I had darkened half of by scribbling on it with a pen. You were supposed to rotate the ball, thus demonstrating scientifically that the phases of the moon were caused by, I don't know, ink.

10   The total elapsed time involved in conceiving of and constructing this project was maybe 10 minutes, of which at least nine were devoted to scribbling. But it still might have been a success had it not been for the fact that some of my fellow students found it amusing to snatch up the moon and throw it, so that it became sort of a gypsy exhibit, traveling around the Harold C. Crittenden Junior High School gymnasium, landing in and becoming part of other projects, helping to demonstrate magnetism, photosynthesis, etc. So my project ended up being just a sign saying "PHASES OF THE MOON" sitting on an otherwise bare naked table, the scientific implication being that the moon is a very moody celestial body that sometimes gets in a phase where it just takes off without telling anybody.

11   Of course, if you want to get a good grade, you have to do a project that will impress your teachers. Here's a proven winner:

12   "HYPOTHESIS—That (Name of Teacher) and (Name of Another Teacher) would prefer that I not distribute the photo I took of them when they were 'chaperoning' our class trip to Epcot Center and they ducked behind the cottage-cheese

exhibit in the Amazing World of Curds." Depending on the quality of your research, you might get more than a good grade from your teachers: You might get actual money! Yes, science truly can be rewarding. So why wait until the last minute to start your science fair project? Why not get started immediately on exploring the amazing world of science, without which we would not have modern technology. Television, for example.

13   Let's turn it on right now.

READING CLOSELY AND THINKING CRITICALLY

1.   Although the essay is humorous, Barry points out some truths about science fairs and students who participate in them. What are those truths?

2.   What point about science fairs is Barry making in paragraphs 3 and 4?

3.   In paragraph 5, Barry explains how to organize a science fair project. What point is he making?

4.   What does Barry's opinion of students seem to be? What gives you this impression?

EXAMINING STRUCTURE AND STRATEGY

1.   Where does Barry explain why understanding the process is important? What does he say? Is he serious? How does that explanation help him achieve his writing purpose?

2.   Where does Barry define a specialized term? How does that definition help him achieve his writing purpose?

3.   Which paragraphs include examples? What purpose do those examples serve?

4.   In what paragraphs does Barry explain the importance of a step in the process?

CONSIDERING LANGUAGE AND STYLE

1.   Barry often exaggerates for comic effect. Cite two examples of such exaggeration.

2.   Barry uses a mock serious tone—that is, he seems serious when he is not. (See page 69 on tone.) For example, in paragraph 2, he says, "The science fair has long been a favorite educational tool in the American school system." What is the purpose of this tone?

3.   Some of Barry's humor comes from surprising *juxtapositions* (side-by-side placements). For example, in paragraph 3, he follows "giving [the board] the stability that it needs" with "to collapse instantly." Cite another example of a surprising juxtaposition.

4.   Consult a dictionary if you are unsure of the meaning of *inertia* (paragraph 1).

FOR DISCUSSION IN CLASS OR ONLINE

Discuss how much of Barry's essay is accurate and how much is inaccurate, being sure to note why you believe the way you do. Do you think the author is fair to students and to science fairs?

WRITING ASSIGNMENTS

1. **Writing in your journal.** Discuss your own experience with school science fairs, either as a student or as a parent. Alternatively, discuss your experience with another school science activity, such as dissecting, using a microscope, taking a field trip, or conducting a lab experiment.

2. **Using process analysis for a purpose.** The purposes given here are possibilities. You may establish whatever purposes you like, within your instructor's guidelines.

    *   Like Barry, to entertain, write a humorous process analysis that begins, "Today's topic for young people is: How to _____." Fill in the blank with a high-school- or middle-school-related process, such as eat in the school cafeteria, dissect a frog, survive gym class, or be in the marching band. Your essay should also point to some truths.

    *   To entertain, write a process analysis that explains how to procrastinate.

    *   To entertain and perhaps persuade, write a humorous process analysis that helps new students learn to do something on campus, such as live in a residence hall, get along with a roommate, choose a major, or have a conference with a writing instructor.

    *   To inform, write a serious process analysis that explains how to complete a science fair project or other school project.

3. **Combining patterns.** Write a process analysis that explains how to perform a task—such as buy a birthday gift, clean your apartment before guests arrive, or prepare a dinner party—at the last minute. Include examples to illustrate and clarify steps.

4. **Analyzing and assessing.** Analyze what Barry is saying about education, teachers, students, and parents in "Science: It's Just Not Fair," and assess whether his points are valid educational commentary. If you completed the "For Discussion in Class or Online" activity above, you may already have some ideas for this essay.

5. **Connecting and synthesizing the readings.** Using the ideas in "Science: It's Just Not Fair" and "The Art of Simplexity" (page 270), explain to what extent participating in a science fair does—or does not—demonstrate the principle of simplexity.

6. **Drawing on sources.** Science fairs have long been common activities in many schools, so much so that some people consider them to be rites of passage. Do you think there is any pedagogical value in a science fair for students? Can the activity be improved? For ideas, you can interview science teachers, consider your own experience and observation, and examine source material. One place to start is this Web site that explains a process for designing a project that is very different from the process Barry explains: http://sciencefairproject.virtualave.net/observation.htm.

BACKGROUND: Born in Baltimore, Maryland, in 1952, Diane Cole attended Radcliffe College and Johns Hopkins University. In addition to serving as a contributing editor to *Psychology Today,* she has written for the *Wall Street Journal,* the *Washington Post,* the *New York Times, Parents, Newsweek, Ms.,* and *Glamour.* Her writing topics frequently include psychology and women's careers. Cole's books include *Hunting the Headhunters: A Woman's Guide* (1988), *After Great Pain: A New Life Emerges* (1992), and, with Scott Wetzler, *Is It You or Is It Me? How We Turn Our Emotions Inside Out and Blame Each Other* (1998). "Don't Just Stand There" was first published in 1989 in a *New York Times* supplement called *A World of Difference,* which was part of a campaign against bigotry sponsored by the Anti-Defamation League of B'nai B'rith, a Jewish fraternal order.

THE PATTERN AND ITS PURPOSES: Have you ever been unsure how to respond to a bigoted remark? If so, "Don't Just Stand There" can help because Diane Cole uses *process analysis* to **inform** her audience about how to react to bigoted comments and jokes. At the same time, she makes her readers more sensitive to the hurtful nature of such slurs and **persuades** them to take action when they hear them.

DON'T JUST STAND THERE

BY DIANE COLE

IT WAS MY OFFICE farewell party, and colleagues at the job I was about to leave were wishing me well. My mood was one of ebullience tinged with regret, and it was in this spirit that I spoke to the office neighbor to whom I had waved hello every morning for the past two years. He smiled broadly as he launched into a long, rambling story, pausing only after he delivered the punch line. It was a very long pause because, although he laughed, I did not: This joke was unmistakably anti-Semitic.

As you read Cole uses a great many quotations in the essay. Consider how they help achieve her purpose for writing.

2   I froze. Everyone in the office knew I was Jewish; what could he have possibly meant? Shaken and hurt, not knowing what else to do, I turned in stunned silence to the next well-wisher. Later, still angry, I wondered, what else should I—could I—have done?

3   Prejudice can make its presence felt in any setting, but hearing its nasty voice in this way can be particularly unnerving. We do not know what to do and often we feel another form of paralysis as well: We think, "Nothing I say or do will change this person's attitude, so why bother?"

4   But left unchecked, racial slurs and offensive ethnic jokes "can poison the atmosphere," says Michael McQuillan, adviser for racial/ethnic affairs for the Brooklyn borough president's office. "Hearing these remarks conditions us to accept them; and if we accept these, we can become accepting of other acts."

5   Speaking up may not magically change a biased attitude, but it can change a person's behavior by putting a strong message across. And the more messages there are, the more likely a person is to change that behavior, says Arnold Kahn, professor of psychology at James Madison University, Harrisonburg, Va., who makes this analogy: "You can't keep people from smoking in *their* house, but you can ask them not to smoke in *your* house."

6   At the same time, "Even if the other party ignores or discounts what you say, people always reflect on how others perceive them. Speaking up always counts," says LeNorman Strong, director of campus life at George Washington University, Washington, D.C.

" 'Speaking up always counts.' ..."

7   Finally, learning to respond effectively also helps people feel better about themselves, asserts Cherie Brown, executive director of the National Coalition Building Institute, a Boston-based training organization. "We've found that, when people felt they could at least in this small way make a difference, that made them more eager to take on other activities on a larger scale," she says. Although there is no "cook-book approach" to confronting such remarks—every situation is different, experts stress—there are some effective strategies.

8   *When the "joke" turns on who you are—as a member of an ethnic or religious group, a person of color, a woman, a gay or lesbian, an elderly person, or someone with a physical handicap—shocked paralysis is often the first response. Then, wounded and vulnerable, on some level you want to strike back.*

9   Lashing out or responding in kind is seldom the most effective response, however. "That can give you momentary satisfaction, but you also feel as if you've lowered yourself to that other person's level," Mr. McQuillan explains. Such a response may further label you in the speaker's mind as thin-skinned, someone not to be taken seriously. Or it may up the ante, making the speaker, and then you, reach for new insults—or physical blows.

10   "If you don't laugh at the joke, or fight, or respond in kind to the slur," says Mr. McQuillan, "that will take the person by surprise, and that can give you more control over the situation." Therefore, in situations like the one in which I found myself—a private conversation in which I knew the person making the remark—he suggests voicing your anger calmly but pointedly: "I don't know if you realize what that sounded like to me. If that's what you meant, it really hurt me."

11   State how *you* feel, rather than making an abstract statement like, "Not everyone who hears that joke might find it funny." Counsels Mr. Strong: "Personalize the sense of 'this is how I feel when you say this.' That makes it very concrete"—and harder to dismiss.

12   Make sure you heard the words and their intent correctly by repeating or rephrasing the statement: "This is what I heard you say. Is that what you meant?" It's important to give the other person the benefit of the doubt because, in fact, he may *not* have realized that the comment was offensive and, if you had not spoken up, would have had no idea of its impact on you.

13   For instance, Professor Kahn relates that he used to include in his exams multiple-choice questions that occasionally contained "incorrect funny answers." After one exam, a student came up to him in private and said, "I don't think you intended this, but I found a number of those jokes offensive to me as a woman." She explained why. "What she said made immediate sense to me," he says. "I apologized at the next class, and I never did it again."

14   But what if the speaker dismisses your objection, saying, "Oh, you're just being sensitive. Can't you take a joke?" In that case, you might say, "I'm not so sure about that, let's talk about that a little more." The key, Mr. Strong says, is to continue the

dialogue, hear the other person's concerns, and point out your own. "There are times when you're just going to have to admit defeat and end it," he adds, "but I have to feel that I did the best I could."

15 When the offending remark is made in the presence of others—at a staff meeting, for example—it can be even more distressing than an insult made privately.

16 "You have two options," says William Newlin, director of field services for the Community Relations division of the New York City Commission on Human Rights. "You can respond immediately at the meeting, or you can delay your response until afterward in private. But a response has to come."

17 Some remarks or actions may be so outrageous that they cannot go unnoted at the moment, regardless of the speaker or the setting. But in general, psychologists say, shaming a person in public may have the opposite effect of the one you want: The speaker will deny his offense all the more strongly in order to save face. Further, few people enjoy being put on the spot, and if the remark really was not intended to be offensive, publicly embarrassing the person who made it may cause an unnecessary rift or further misunderstanding. Finally, most people just don't react as well or thoughtfully under a public spotlight as they would in private.

18 Keeping that in mind, an excellent alternative is to take the offender aside afterward: "Could we talk for a minute in private?" Then use the strategies suggested above for calmly stating how you feel, giving the speaker the benefit of the doubt, and proceeding from there.

19 At a large meeting or public talk, you might consider passing the speaker a note, says David Wertheimer, executive director of the New York City Gay and Lesbian Anti-Violence Project: You could write, "You may not realize it, but your remarks were offensive because . . ."

20 "Think of your role as that of an educator," suggests James M. Jones, Ph.D., executive director for public interest at the American Psychological Association. "You have to be controlled."

21 Regardless of the setting or situation, speaking up always raises the risk of rocking the boat. If the person who made the offending remark is your boss, there may be an even bigger risk to consider: How will this affect my job? Several things can help minimize the risk, however. First, know what other resources you may have at work, suggests Caryl Stern, director of the A World of Difference—New York City campaign: Does your personnel office handle discrimination complaints? Are other grievance procedures in place?

22 You won't necessarily need to use any of these procedures, Ms. Stern stresses. In fact, she advises, "It's usually better to try a one-on-one approach first." But simply knowing a formal system exists can make you feel secure enough to set up that meeting.

23 You can also raise the issue with other colleagues who heard the remark: Did they feel the same way you did? The more support you have, the less alone you will feel. Your point will also carry more validity and be more difficult to shrug off. Finally, give your boss credit—and the benefit of the doubt: "I know you've worked hard for the company's affirmative action programs, so I'm sure you didn't realize what those remarks sounded like to me as well as the others at the meeting last week . . ."

24   If, even after this discussion, the problem persists, go back for another meeting, Ms. Stern advises. And if that, too, fails, you'll know what other options are available to you.

25   *It's a spirited dinner party, and everyone's having a good time, until one guest starts reciting a racist joke. Everyone at the table is white, including you. The others are still laughing, as you wonder what to say or do.*

26   No one likes being seen as a party-pooper, but before deciding that you'd prefer not to take on this role, you might remember that the person who told the offensive joke has already ruined your good time.

"The others are still laughing, as you wonder what to say or do."

27   If it's a group that you feel comfortable in—a family gathering, for instance—you will feel freer to speak up. Still, shaming the person by shouting, "You're wrong" or "That's not funny!" probably won't get your point across as effectively as other strategies. "If you interrupt people to condemn them, it just makes it harder," says Cherie Brown. She suggests trying instead to get at the resentments that lie beneath the joke by asking open-ended questions: "Grandpa, I know you always treat everyone with such respect. Why do people in our family talk that way about black people?" The key, Ms. Brown says, "is to listen to them first, so they will be more likely to listen to you."

28   If you don't know your fellow guests well, before speaking up you could turn discreetly to your neighbors (or excuse yourself to help the host or hostess in the kitchen) to get a reading on how they felt, and whether or not you'll find support for speaking up: "I know you probably didn't mean anything by that joke, Jim, but it really offended me . . ." It's important to say that *you* were offended—not state how the group that is the butt of the joke would feel. "Otherwise," LeNorman Strong says, "you risk coming off as a goody-two-shoes."

29   If you yourself are the host, you can exercise more control; you are, after all, the one who sets the rules and the tone of behavior in your home. Once, when Professor Kahn's party guests began singing offensive, racist songs, for instance, he kicked them all out, saying, "You don't sing songs like that in my house!" And, he adds, "they never did again."

30   *At school one day, a friend comes over and says, "Who do you think you are, hanging out with Joe? If you can be friends with those people, I'm through with you!"*

31   Peer pressure can weigh heavily on kids. They feel vulnerable and, because they are kids, they aren't as able to control the urge to fight. "But if you learn to handle these situations as kids, you'll be better able to handle them as an adult," William Newlin points out.

32   Begin by redefining to yourself what a friend is and examining what friendship means, advises Amy Lee, a human relations specialist at Panel of Americans, an intergroup relations training and educational organization. If that person from a different group fits your requirement for a friend, ask, "Why shouldn't I be friends with Joe? We have a lot in common." Try to get more information about whatever stereotypes or resentments lie beneath your friend's statement. Ms. Lee suggests: "What makes you think they're so different from us? Where did you get that information?" She explains: "People are learning these stereotypes from somewhere, and

they cannot be blamed for that. So examine where these ideas come from." Then talk about how your own experience rebuts them.

33 Kids, like adults, should also be aware of other resources to back them up: Does the school offer special programs for fighting prejudice? How supportive will the principal, the teachers, or other students be? If the school atmosphere is volatile, experts warn, make sure that taking a stand at that moment won't put you in physical danger. If that is the case, it's better to look for other alternatives.

34 These can include programs or organizations that bring kids from different backgrounds together. "When kids work together across race lines, that is how you break down the barriers and see that the stereotypes are not true," says Laurie Meadoff, president of CityKids Foundation, a nonprofit group whose programs attempt to do just that. Such programs can also provide what Cherie Brown calls a "safe place" to express the anger and pain that slurs and other offenses cause, whether the bigotry is directed against you or others.

35 In learning to speak up, everyone will develop a different style and a slightly different message to get across, experts agree. But it would be hard to do better than these two messages suggested by teenagers at CityKids: "Everyone on the face of the earth has the same intestines," said one. Another added, "Cross over the bridge. There's a lot of love on the streets."

READING CLOSELY AND THINKING CRITICALLY

1. According to Cole, why is it important to respond to racial, ethnic, and sexist slurs?
2. Why does Cole say it is best not to laugh at racial slurs and offensive ethnic jokes?
3. When a person makes an offensive remark, why is it best not to shame that person publicly?
4. Cole offers procedures to help children deal with bigotry. Why do you think she includes information for children?
5. Did you learn anything as a result of reading "Don't Just Stand There"? If so, explain what you learned.

EXAMINING STRUCTURE AND STRATEGY

1. Which sentence is Cole's thesis because it presents the process under consideration?
2. Cite three paragraphs that explain what not to do and why. Which paragraph presents a troublesome aspect of the process?
3. Cole includes a considerable number of quotations. What do you think these quotations contribute? Do they help the author achieve her purpose? Explain.

NOTING COMBINED PATTERNS

1. How does the narration in paragraphs 1 and 2 help Cole achieve her purpose?
2. Cole frequently uses exemplification. Cite at least three examples, and explain how they help Cole achieve her purpose.

1. Cole uses first- and second-person pronouns (*I, we, you, me, us*). Why does she use these pronouns rather than third-person pronouns (*he, she, they*)?
2. Paragraphs 8, 25, and 30 are set off with italics. Why?
3. Consult a dictionary if you are unsure of the meaning of any of these words: *ebullience* (paragraph 1), *tinged* (paragraph 1), *anti-Semitic* (paragraph 1), *rift* (paragraph 17), *volatile* (paragraph 33).

FOR DISCUSSION IN CLASS OR ONLINE

Do you think it is acceptable for people to tell jokes about their own race, gender, religion, or ethnicity? Why or why not?

WRITING ASSIGNMENTS

1. **Writing in your journal.** Write about a time when you overheard a racial, sexist, or ethnic slur. How did you respond and why did you respond that way? After reading Cole's essay, do you think you could have handled yourself differently? Explain.
2. **Using process analysis for a purpose.** The purposes in the assignments are possibilities. You may establish whatever purpose you like, within your instructor's guidelines.
   - Select a hurtful behavior (for example, classroom cheating, lying, or teenage drinking) and to inform your reader, describe a process for dealing with it.
   - Select a bothersome behavior that is not harmful (for example, talking in theaters, rudeness by salespeople, or inattentive table servers). To inform your reader, explain a process for dealing with the behavior.
   - Inform your reader and relate your experience by explaining your own procedure for dealing with ethnic, sexist, and/or racial slurs.
3. **Combining patterns.** Racial, ethnic, gender, and other forms of bias are current facts of life. Using cause-and-effect analysis (explained in Chapter 10), explain how you think bias originates in people or why people and society allow the bias to persist. Then use process analysis to explain what you think can be done to address the bias.
4. **Analyzing and assessing.** Analyze Cole's process analysis, and assess how helpful it is as a guide for showing people how to respond to racist, sexist, ethnic, and other inappropriate remarks. Are her suggestions easier said than done? If so, what should she have done differently? If not, what makes the suggestions effective?
5. **Connecting and synthesizing the readings.** Summarize the positions of Diane Cole in "Don't Just Stand There" and Cinnamon Stillwell in "Mob Rule on Campus" (page 622). Then indicate which author you agree with, and why.
6. **Drawing on sources.** Research the policy and procedure for handling discrimination and harassment at either your college or your workplace. Explain whether or not the policy and procedure are satisfactory, and why.

BACKGROUND: Born in 1950 in West Virginia, Henry Louis Gates, Jr., taught at Yale, Cornell (where he was the first African American male to hold an endowed chair), and Duke before joining the faculty of Harvard as the director of the W. E. B. Du Bois Institute for African and African American Research. His many honors and grants include a MacArthur Foundation "genius grant" (1981), and a mention as one of *Time* magazine's "25 Most Influential Americans" (1997). Gates's book of critical theory, *The Signifying Monkey: Towards a Theory of Afro-American Literary Criticism* (1989), earned him the American Book Award and brought him great public attention. Gates wrote and produced the PBS documentaries *America Beyond the Color Line* and *African American Lives*. A prolific author, Gates has written many volumes of literary criticism. He has also written *Colored People: A Memoir* (1994); *The Future of the Race* (1996); with Cornel West, *Thirteen Ways of Looking at a Black Man* (1997); *African American Lives* (2004), which he edited with Evelyn Higginbotham; and *The Annotated Uncle Tom's Cabin* (2006). "In the Kitchen" first appeared in 1994 in the *New Yorker*.

www.mhhe.com/clousepatterns6	Gates

For more information on this author, go to

More resources > Chapter 8 > Henry Louis Gates, Jr.

COMBINED PATTERNS AND THEIR PURPOSES: "In the Kitchen" is part memoir, part political statement. In the essay, Henry Louis Gates, Jr., uses *process analysis, definition,* and *description* to **inform** the reader of several processes African Americans used to straighten their hair, including the one he remembers his mother performing on her clients. At the same time, Gates asks readers to consider the political significance of *why* African Americans altered their appearance. As Gates explains the processes, he also **relates his own experience** observing his mother, and he **expresses his feelings** about what people went through to straighten their hair.

IN THE KITCHEN

BY HENRY LOUIS GATES, JR.

WE ALWAYS HAD a gas stove in the kitchen, in our house in Piedmont, West Virginia, where I grew up. Never electric, though using electric became fashionable in Piedmont in the sixties, like using Crest toothpaste rather than Colgate, or watching Huntley and Brinkley rather than Walter Cronkite.[1] But not us: gas, Colgate, and good ole Walter Cronkite, come what may. We used gas partly out of loyalty to Big Mom, Mama's Mama, because she was mostly blind and still loved to cook, and could feel her way more easily with gas than with electric. But the most important thing about our gas-equipped kitchen was that Mama used to do hair there. The "hot comb" was a fine-toothed iron instrument with a long wooden handle and a pair of iron curlers that opened and closed like scissors. Mama would put it in the gas fire until it glowed. You could smell those prongs heating up.

As you read Think about the ways things have changed—and the ways they have not— since the time of the essay.

---

[1]Chet Huntley and David Brinkley were the anchors of the *Huntley-Brinkley Report*, a nightly news program on NBC that ran from 1956 to 1970. Walter Cronkite anchored the *CBS Evening News* from 1962 to 1981.

2   I liked that smell. Not the smell so much, I guess, as what the smell meant for the shape of my day. There was an intimate warmth in the women's tones as they talked with my Mama, doing their hair. I knew what the women had been through to get their hair ready to be "done," because I would watch Mama do it to herself. How that kink could be transformed through grease and fire into that magnificent head of wavy hair was a miracle to me, and still is.

3   Mama would wash her hair over the sink, a towel wrapped around her shoulders, wearing just her slip and her white bra. (We had no shower—just a galvanized tub that we stored in the kitchen—until we moved down Rat Tail Road into Doc Wolverton's house, in 1954.) After she dried it, she would grease her scalp thoroughly with blue Bergamot hair grease, which came in a short, fat jar with a picture of a beautiful colored lady on it. It's important to grease your scalp real good, my Mama would explain, to keep from burning yourself. Of course, her hair would return to its natural kink almost as soon as the hot water and shampoo hit it. To me, it was another miracle how hair so "straight" would so quickly become kinky again the second it even approached some water.

> "It's important to grease your scalp . . . to keep from burning yourself."

4   My Mama had only a few "clients" whose heads she "did"—did, I think, because she enjoyed it, rather than for the few pennies it brought in. They would sit on one of our red plastic kitchen chairs, the kind with the shiny metal legs, and brace themselves for the process. Mama would stroke that red-hot iron—which by this time had been in the gas fire for half an hour or more—slowly but firmly through their hair, from scalp to strand's end. It made a scorching, crinkly sound, the hot iron did, as it burned its way through kink, leaving in its wake straight strands of hair, standing long and tall but drooping over at the ends, their shape like the top of a heavy willow tree. Slowly, steadily, Mama's hands would transform a round mound of Odetta kink into a darkened swamp of everglades. The Bergamot made the hair shiny; the heat of the hot iron gave it a brownish-red cast. Once all the hair was as straight as God allows kink to get, Mama would take the well-heated curling iron and twirl the straightened strands into more or less loosely wrapped curls. She claimed that she owed her skill as a hairdresser to the strength in her wrists, and as she worked her little finger would poke out, the way it did when she sipped tea. Mama was a south-paw, and wrote upside down and backward to produce the cleanest, roundest letters you've ever seen.

5   The "kitchen" she would all but remove from sight with a handheld pair of shears, bought just for this purpose. Now, the kitchen was the room in which we were sitting—the room where Mama did hair and washed clothes, and where we all took a bath in that galvanized tub. But the word has another meaning, and the kitchen that I'm speaking of is the very kinky bit of hair at the back of your head, where your neck meets your shirt collar. If there was ever a part of your African past that resisted assimilation, it was the kitchen. No matter how hot the iron, no matter how powerful the chemical, no matter how stringent the mashed-potatoes-and-lye

formula of a man's "process," neither God nor woman nor Sammy Davis, Jr.,[2] could straighten the kitchen. The kitchen was permanent, irredeemable, irresistible kink. Unassimilably African. No matter what you did, no matter how hard you tried, you couldn't de-kink a person's kitchen. So you trimmed it off as best you could.

6   When hair had begun to "turn," as they'd say — to return to its natural kinky glory — it was the kitchen that turned first (the kitchen around the back, and nappy edges at the temples). When the kitchen started creeping up the back of the neck, it was time to get your hair done again.

7   Sometimes, after dark, a man would come to have his hair done. It was Mr. Charlie Carroll. He was very light-complected and had a ruddy nose — it made me think of Edmund Gwenn, who played Kris Kringle in "Miracle on 34th Street." At first, Mama did him after my brother, Rocky, and I had gone to sleep. It was only later that we found out that he had come to our house so Mama could iron his hair — not with a hot comb or a curling iron but with our very own Proctor-Silex steam iron. For some reason I never understood, Mr. Charlie would conceal his Frederick Douglass-like[3] mane under a big white Stetson hat. I never saw him take it off except when he came to our house, at night, to have his hair pressed. (Later, Daddy would tell us about Mr. Charlie's most prized piece of knowledge, something that the man would only confide after his hair had been pressed, as a token of intimacy. "Not many people know this," he'd say, in a tone of circumspection, "but George Washington was Abraham Lincoln's daddy." Nodding solemnly, he'd add the clincher: "A white man told me." Though he was in dead earnest, this became a humorous refrain around our house — "a white man told me" — which we used to punctuate especially preposterous assertions.)

8   My mother examined my daughters' kitchens whenever we went home to visit, in the early eighties. It became a game between us. I had told her not to do it, because I didn't like the politics it suggested — the notion of "good" and "bad" hair. "Good" hair was "straight," "bad" hair kinky. Even in the late sixties, at the height of Black Power, almost nobody could bring themselves to say "bad" for good and "good" for bad. People still said that hair like white people's hair was "good," even if they encapsulated it in a disclaimer, like "what we used to call 'good.'"

9   Maggie would be seated in her high chair, throwing food this way and that, and Mama would be cooing about how cute it all was, how I used to do just like Maggie was doing, and wondering whether her flinging her food with her left hand meant that she was going to be left-handed like Mama. When my daughter was just about covered with Chef Boyardee Spaghetti-O's, Mama would seize the opportunity: wiping her clean, she would tilt Maggie's head to one side and reach down the back of her neck. Sometimes Mama would even rub a curl between her fingers, just to make sure that her bifocals had not deceived her. Then she'd sigh with satisfaction and relief: No kink . . . yet. Mama! I'd shout, pretending to be angry. Every once in a while, if no one was looking, I'd peek, too.

---

[2]Sammy Davis, Jr. (1925–1990), was an African American singer, actor, and dancer.

[3]Frederick Douglass (1818–1895), was a prominent abolitionist and writer.

10   I say "yet" because most black babies are born with soft, silken hair. But after a few months it begins to turn, as inevitably as do the seasons or the leaves on a tree. People once thought baby oil would stop it. They were wrong.

11   Everybody I knew as a child wanted to have good hair. You could be as ugly as homemade sin dipped in misery and still be thought attractive if you had good hair. "Jesus moss," the girls at Camp Lee, Virginia, had called Daddy's naturally "good" hair during the war. I know that he played that thick head of hair for all it was worth, too.

12   My own hair was "not a bad grade," as barbers would tell me when they cut it for the first time. It was like a doctor reporting the results of the first full physical he has given you. Like "You're in good shape" or "Blood pressure's kind of high—better cut down on salt."

13   I spent most of my childhood and adolescence messing with my hair. I definitely wanted straight hair. Like Pop's. When I was about three, I tried to stick a wad of Bazooka bubble gum to that straight hair of his. I suppose what fixed that memory for me is the spanking I got for doing so: he turned me upside down, holding me by my feet, the better to paddle my behind. Little *nigger*, he had shouted, walloping away. I started to laugh about it two days later, when my behind stopped hurting.

> "I definitely wanted straight hair. Like Pop's."

14   When black people say "straight," of course, they don't usually mean literally straight—they're not describing hair like, say, Peggy Lipton's (she was the white girl on "The Mod Squad"[4]), or like Mary's of Peter, Paul & Mary[5] fame; black people call that "stringy" hair. No, "straight" just means not kinky, no matter what contours the curl may take. I would have done *anything* to have straight hair—and I used to try everything, short of getting a process.

15   Of the wide variety of techniques and methods I came to master in the challenging prestidigitation of the follicle, almost all had two things in common: a heavy grease and the application of pressure. It's not an accident that some of the biggest black-owned companies in the fifties and sixties made hair products. And I tried them all, in search of that certain silken touch, the one that would leave neither the hand nor the pillow sullied by grease.

16   I always wondered what Frederick Douglass put on *his* hair, or what Phillis Wheatley[6] put on hers. Or why Wheatley has that rag on her head in the little engraving in the frontispiece of her book. One thing is for sure: you can bet that when Phillis Wheatley went to England and saw the Countess of Huntingdon she did not stop by the Queen's coiffeur on her way there. So many black people still get their hair straightened that it's a wonder we don't have a national holiday for

---

[4]A television series that ran from 1968 to 1973. Peggy Lipton, one of the stars, had long, straight, blond hair.

[5]Peter, Paul, and Mary were a folk-singing group popular in the 1960s. Member Mary Travers had long, straight, blond hair.

[6]Phillis Wheatley (1753–1784), was a poet who wrote the first book published by an African American.

Madame C. J. Walker, the woman who invented the process of straightening kinky hair. Call it Jheri-Kurled or call it "relaxed," it's still fried hair.

17   I used all the greases, from sea-blue Bergamot and creamy vanilla Duke (in its clear jar with the orange-white-and-green label) to the godfather of grease, the formidable Murray's. Now, Murray's was some *serious* grease. Whereas Bergamot was like oily Jello, and Duke was viscous and sickly sweet, Murray's was light brown and *hard.* Hard as lard and twice as greasy, Daddy used to say. Murray's came in an orange can with a press-on top. It was so hard that some people would put a match to the can, just to soften the stuff and make it more manageable. Then, in the late sixties, when Afros came into style, I used Afro Sheen. From Murray's to Duke to Afro Sheen: that was my progression in black consciousness.

18   We used to put hot towels or washrags over our Murray-coated heads, in order to melt the wax into the scalp and the follicles. Unfortunately, the wax also had the habit of running down your neck, ears, and forehead. Not to mention your pillowcase. Another problem was that if you put two palmfuls of Murray's on your head your hair turned white. (Duke did the same thing.) The challenge was to get rid of that white color. Because if you got rid of the white stuff you had a magnificent head of wavy hair. That was the beauty of it: Murray's was so hard that it froze your hair into the wavy style you brushed it into. It looked really good if you wore a part. A lot of guys had parts *cut* into their hair by a barber, either with the clippers or with a straight-edge razor. Especially if you had kinky hair—then you'd generally wear a short razor cut, or what we called a Quo Vadis.

19   We tried to be as innovative as possible. Everyone knew about using a stocking cap, because your father or your uncle wore one whenever something really big was about to happen, whether sacred or secular: a funeral or a dance, a wedding or a trip in which you confronted official white people. Any time you were trying to look really sharp, you wore a stocking cap in preparation. And if the event was really a big one, you made a new cap. You asked your mother for a pair of her hose, and cut it with scissors about six inches or so from the open end—the end with the elastic that goes up to the top of the thigh. Then you knotted the cut end, and it became a beehive-shaped hat, with an elastic band that you pulled down low on your forehead and down around your neck in the back. To work well, the cap had to fit tightly and snugly, like a press. And it had to fit that tightly because it *was* a press: it pressed your hair with the force of the hose's elastic. If you greased your hair down real good, and left the stocking cap on long enough, voilà: you got a head of pressed-against-the-scalp waves. (You also got a ring around your forehead when you woke up, but it went away.) And then you could enjoy your concrete do. Swore we were bad, too, with all that grease and those flat heads. My brother and I would brush it out a bit in the mornings, so that it looked—well, "natural." Grown men still wear stocking caps—especially older men, who generally keep their stocking caps in their top drawers, along with their cufflinks and their see-through silk socks, their "Maverick" ties, their silk handkerchiefs, and whatever else they prize the most.

20   A Murrayed-down stocking cap was the respectable version of the process, which, by contrast, was most definitely not a cool thing to have unless you were an entertainer by trade. Zeke and Keith and Poochie and a few other stars of the high-school basketball team all used to get a process once or twice a year. It was expensive, and you had

to go somewhere like Pittsburgh or D.C. or Uniontown—somewhere where there were enough colored people to support a trade. The guys would disappear, then reappear a day or two later, strutting like peacocks, their hair burned slightly red from the lye base. They'd also wear "rags"—cloths or handkerchiefs—around their heads when they slept or played basketball. Do-rags, they were called. But the result was straight hair, with just a hint of wave. No curl. Do-it-yourselfers took their chances at home with a concoction of mashed potatoes and lye.

21   The most famous process of all, however, outside of the process Malcolm X describes in his "Autobiography," and maybe the process of Sammy Davis, Jr., was Nat King Cole's[7] process. Nat King Cole had patent-leather hair. That man's got the finest process money can buy, or so Daddy said the night we saw Cole's TV show on NBC. It was November 5, 1956. I remember the date because everyone came to our house to watch it and to celebrate one of Daddy's buddies' birthdays. Yeah, Uncle Joe chimed in, they can do shit to his hair that the average Negro can't even *think* about—secret shit.

22   Nat King Cole was *clean.* I've had an ongoing argument with a Nigerian friend about Nat King Cole for twenty years now. Not about whether he could sing—any fool knows that he could—but about whether or not he was a handkerchief head for wearing that patent-leather process.

23   Sammy Davis, Jr.'s process was the one I detested. It didn't look good on him. Worse still, he liked to have a fried strand dangling down the middle of his forehead, so he could shake it out from the crown when he sang. But Nat King Cole's hair was a thing unto itself, a beautifully sculpted work of art that he and he alone had the right to wear. The only difference between a process and a stocking cap, really, was taste; but Nat King Cole, unlike, say, Michael Jackson, looked *good* in his. His head looked like Valentino's head in the twenties, and some say it was Valentino the process was imitating. But Nat King Cole wore a process because it suited his face, his demeanor, his name, his style. He was as clean as he wanted to be.

24   I had forgotten all about that patent-leather look until one day in 1971, when I was sitting in an Arab restaurant on the island of Zanzibar surrounded by men in fezzes and white caftans, trying to learn how to eat curried goat and rice with the fingers of my right hand and feeling two million miles from home. All of a sudden, an old transistor radio sitting on top of a china cupboard stopped blaring out its Swahili music and started playing "Fly Me to the Moon," by Nat King Cole. The restaurant's din was not affected at all, but in my mind's eye I saw it: the King's magnificent sleek black tiara. I managed, barely, to blink back the tears.

---

[7]Nat King Cole (1919–1965), was an African American singer and musician.

READING CLOSELY AND THINKING CRITICALLY

1.   Why is Gates so interested in the process his mother used to straighten hair? Why does he find that process and other hair-straightening processes important enough to write an essay about them?

2. Why did African Americans endure the difficult process of straightening their hair? Why have many people discontinued the practice in more recent years?

3. Why does Gates check his daughter's hair for kink? Why does he do so only when no one is looking?

4. What is the "patent-leather" look? Why did it suit Nat King Cole?

5. Why did Gates have to "blink back the tears" when he heard a Nat King Cole recording in Zanzibar?

EXAMINING STRUCTURE AND STRATEGY

1. Paragraph 18 includes information about why a step was performed and problems associated with a step. Why does Gates include this information?

2. Why do you think Gates titled his essay "In the Kitchen" rather than "Straightening Hair"?

NOTING COMBINED PATTERNS

1. Gates includes quite a bit of description in the essay. For example, paragraph 1 describes the hot comb; paragraph 4 includes description in the explanation of the hair-straightening process; paragraph 17 describes hair grease. What does the extensive use of description suggest about Gates's intended audience? How does it help the author achieve his purpose with that audience?

2. Which paragraphs include definition? How does the definition help Gates achieve his purpose?

3. Gates describes the processed hair of entertainers Nat King Cole and Sammy Davis, Jr., but he does not explain the process they used to achieve their hairstyles. Why not?

CONSIDERING LANGUAGE AND STYLE

1. Gates often uses specific product names. For example, he uses *Bergamot* (paragraph 3), *Murray's* (paragraph 17), and *Afro Sheen* (paragraph 17), rather than "hair grease" or "hair product." Why do you think he uses specific product names?

2. Gates describes Nat King Cole as "clean," but he does not explain his use of the term. Using evidence in the essay for clues, what do you think he means by "clean"?

3. Consult a dictionary if you are unsure of the meaning of any of these words: *galvanized* (paragraphs 3, 5), *southpaw* (paragraph 4), *assimilation* (paragraph 5), *circumspection* (paragraph 7), *refrain* (paragraph 7), *prestidigitation* (paragraph 15), *sullied* (paragraph 15), *viscous* (paragraph 17), *voilà* (paragraph 19).

FOR DISCUSSION IN CLASS OR ONLINE

Some employers require their employees to conform to specific standards of appearance. They may specify no facial hair, no dreadlocks, no long hair on males, no tattoos, or no body piercing. Consider whether such requirements are fair and appropriate.

1. **Writing in your journal.** To what extent have the times since Gates's childhood changed and to what extent have they stayed the same? Answer in a page or two.

2. **Using process analysis for a purpose.** The purposes in the assignments are possibilities. You may establish whatever purpose you like, within your instructor's guidelines.
   - To relate your experience, express your feelings, and perhaps entertain, explain a process you endure in order to meet society's standard of beauty: shaving, dying your hair, applying makeup, dieting, exercising, getting a permanent, wearing a hairpiece or wig, and so on.
   - To inform and perhaps persuade, explain the process whereby people decide what looks "good" and what looks "bad." If you like, consider one or more of the following: advertising, parental influence, peer influence, sports figures, the music industry, movies, or television.
   - To inform, write a directional process analysis that will help people avoid being manipulated by society's standards of beauty.
   - To relate your experience, express your feelings, and perhaps entertain, explain a process for purchasing something that affects your appearance, such as clothes, makeup, hair care products, or skin care products.

3. **Combining patterns.** Tell about a time you tried to look a particular way in order to be more like another person or group. Explain the process you followed. For example, in high school, you may have tried to look more like the cheerleaders or more like the football players, or even like a favorite rock star. At work, you may have tried to look more like your supervisor. Use cause-and-effect analysis (explained in Chapter 10) to explain what motivated you and how you were affected by your attempt.

4. **Analyzing and assessing.** Analyze the diction (word choice) in "In the Kitchen" to assess how it helps Gates inform a white audience.

5. **Connecting and synthesizing the readings.** Discuss one way people are affected by their childhood contexts. For ideas, you can draw on your own experience, along with "In the Kitchen" and "Complexion" (page 672).

6. **Drawing on sources.** Hairstyles have always changed with the times, but one thing has remained constant: For much of history, people have cut, colored, curled, straightened, and otherwise forced their hair into unnatural styles and colors. Why are people so obsessed with hair? How far will we go to alter our hair's natural look? For ideas, you can go to www.google.com and type in the keywords "history of hairstyles," or in your library's reference room, check the *Reader's Guide to Periodical Literature* or the *Encyclopedia of Popular Culture* under the heading "hairstyles."

BACKGROUND: Timothy Harper teaches at City University of New York. He is a writing coach and a prolific freelance writer who has won a number of awards. He writes on a remarkable range of subjects, including politics, economics, business, law, art, health, family, education, medicine, and technology. This variety of subjects has allowed him to publish in a surprising array of publications, including the *Atlantic Monthly, Reader's Digest, Time, Glamour, Seventeen, Delta Sky, Metropolitan Home, Cooking Light, Advertising Age, Medical Economics,* the *American Bar Association Journal,* and the *New York Times.* He has also written several books, including *Doing Good* (2001), *Your Name in Print* (2005), and *The Complete Idiot's Guide to the Constitution* (2007). From 1974 to 1984, Harper worked for the Associated Press and covered a number of important national stories. "Shoot to Kill" first appeared in the *Atlantic Monthly* in October 2000.

COMBINED PATTERNS AND THEIR PURPOSE: In "Shoot to Kill," Timothy Harper uses *process analysis* to **inform** his audience about how the 1999 shootings at Columbine High School changed the emergency response procedures of police departments around the country. As you read, notice that Harper explains more than one process. Notice, too, that he combines those process analyses with *contrast* and *cause-and-effect analysis.* You will even find an element of *description* in the piece.

SHOOT TO KILL

BY TIMOTHY HARPER

HIS EARS RINGING FROM GUNFIRE, his uniform damp with sweat, his breath labored and acrid-tasting from the gunpowder in the air, Officer Larry Layman ran heavily down a hallway toward an insistent *pop-pop-pop*. A gunman was running through a school shooting children, and Layman was chasing him. Layman rounded a corner, holding his gun in front of him with two stiff arms, and stopped dead. The gunman stood facing him, with an arm around a hostage's neck and a gun held to the hostage's head. "Drop your gun or I'll blow his head off!" the gunman screamed. Layman, a police officer for more than half his fifty years, had been trained always to drop his gun at a moment like this. Now he fired.

As you read
Decide how the author feels about police officers.

2   This was only a training exercise. But the point of this training is something radically new and different, and it is unsettling for Larry Layman, his fellow officers in Peoria, Illinois, and thousands of other law-enforcement officers across the country. Historically, the police in the United States have employed a standard response when confronted with armed suspects in schools, malls, banks, post offices, and other heavily populated buildings. The first officers to arrive never rushed in. Instead they set up perimeters and controlled the scene. They tried to contain the suspects, and called in a rigorously trained Special Weapons and Tactics (SWAT) team. The SWAT team arrived, assumed positions to keep the suspects pinned down, and negotiated with them until they surrendered. SWAT teams stormed buildings only when necessary to save lives, such as when hostages were being executed one by one.

3   Today, however, police officers are setting aside traditional tactics. They are being taught to enter a building if they are the first to arrive at the scene, to chase the gunman, and to kill or disable him as quickly as possible. This sweeping change

in police tactics—variously called rapid-response, emergency-response, or first-responder—is a direct result of the shootings that occurred at Columbine High School, in Littleton, Colorado, on April 20 of last year,[1] which was the worst in a series of shootings in schools across the United States in the 1990s. Two students armed with bombs and guns invaded Columbine and wandered through the school, firing indiscriminately. Twelve students and a teacher died, and twenty-three other students were wounded. The shooters took their own lives.

4   The first 911 call from Columbine that day came at 11:19 A.M. Nearly all the victims were shot during the next seventeen minutes, according to a reconstruction released a year later by the Jefferson County Sheriff's Department. The report noted that a deputy sheriff reached the scene at 11:23, four minutes after the call. Many more officers—eventually nearly a thousand of them—quickly converged on the school. But the first policemen to go in—a five-man SWAT team, moving cautiously—did not enter the school until 12:06, forty-three minutes after the first officers had arrived. The two shooters killed themselves at 12:08. Some of the wounded were not brought out until after 3:00 P.M. The teacher, reportedly, died from loss of blood before the paramedics reached him.

"The consensus among law-enforcement authorities across the country is that Columbine was handled by the book—but that the book should be rewritten."

5   Fifteen families of Columbine victims have filed lawsuits against Jefferson County, and several of those suits claim that lives could have been saved if the police had entered the school sooner.[2] The consensus among law-enforcement authorities across the country is that Columbine was handled by the book—but that the book

---

[1]1999.

[2]In 2001, eight of nine lawsuits were dismissed by a federal judge. The ninth, filed by the daughter of the teacher killed, argued that police did not try to save him and prevented others from doing so. The suit was settled for $1.5 million.

should be rewritten. The traditional police response was designed for dealing with trapped bank robbers, angry husbands, or disgruntled employees—not with disaffected teenagers running through a school killing as many people as possible.

6   Larry Glick, the executive director of the National Tactical Officers Association, says that Columbine almost immediately became a seminal event in the history of police training and tactics. Most of the nation's 17,000 police agencies, he says, especially the roughly 2,000 agencies with fifty or more officers, have instituted new rapid-response training programs in the past year. These programs are intended to train all police officers—not just SWAT teams—to respond swiftly and aggressively if they are among the first officers on the scene. Glick's association, with 37,000 members from 3,500 participating police agencies, teaches SWAT specialists to retrain their fellow officers, including everyday patrolmen like Larry Layman.

7   "The time line of the violence—from the time the shooting begins until it's over—is short," Glick says. "Traditional police responses just may not cut it." Typically, he says, an officer arrives on the scene within three or four minutes, but it takes thirty to sixty minutes to muster a SWAT team. Under the new training, the first four or five officers on a scene, no matter what their rank or experience, form a "contact team" and go in. "Their sole purpose is to move right to the shooter and stop him, using whatever force is necessary," Glick says. The contact team is supposed to pursue gunmen, pressure them to keep moving, and prevent them from taking over populated areas. (The Columbine killers seized the school library, where they killed ten and wounded twelve of their victims.)

8   The training simulates the horror and confusion of a Columbine-style shooting. Bombs explode. Water gushes from broken pipes and rains down from sprinkler systems. The lights go off. Trainers acting like madmen fire "simunitions"—nonlethal bullets that splatter paint on contact—at the trainees. Other trainers, acting as innocent bystanders or wounded victims, run toward the officers, pleading for help. Officers were traditionally trained to help the wounded and evacuate bystanders. Now they are taught to step over the wounded, push bystanders aside, and keep pursuing the shooters. In the past SWAT marksmen were expected to put a shooter down. Now every officer is instructed to "take the shot if you have it." Glick acknowledges that the fear of lawsuits is one factor behind the new tactics. "Do lawsuits drive training?" he says. "Absolutely. But the bottom line is that this training can save lives."

9   The day after Columbine, municipal officials and police chiefs across the nation asked their SWAT team leaders, "If it had happened here, what would have been the result?" They received answers similar to the one that Sergeant Jeff Adams, a longtime SWAT team leader and trainer in Peoria, gave: "The same thing would have happened here." Adams and other trainers for Peoria's Special Response Team (which, he says, was renamed because "SWAT" emphasizes weapons) went through their own retraining last winter. In March they began passing along the new tactics to each of Peoria's 235 active officers. "Columbine was a wakeup call," Adams says.

10   Under the Peoria Police Department's new rapid-response protocol, the first officer on the scene of a Columbine-style shooting waits until three others arrive to form a contact team. Officers in a smaller group or alone would not have

360-degree coverage, Adams says, and Rambo-style freelancing would confuse communications and increase the chances of "blue on blue" casualties: police officers shooting each other. The contact team forms a diamond, with a point, two flanks, and a rear guard handling radio communications. The team enters the building and moves through it as quickly as possible; team members maintain their relative positions so that they can see and hear each other. In a large building a second team may go in, either to help track down the shooters or to rescue bystanders and the wounded.

11 Adams says that gunmen are less likely to fire at innocent bystanders if they are shooting at pursuing police officers. "We train them to move to the sound of gunfire," he says. "Shooting scenes are very chaotic and stressful. You experience sensory overload. Every time you hear a gun-shot, assume someone has been wounded. Try to take ground, and isolate the shooter. If the shooter decides to commit suicide by police, we'll oblige. The person making the decision on how it will end is the bad guy. We're just reacting." Adams says, however, that "deadly force imperatives" have not changed for the Peoria police. "We teach that you should shoot what you know, not what you think you know. That man with a gun in his hand who steps out of a doorway may be a plainclothes police officer or a school security guard. Or maybe a teacher who brought a gun to school."

12 Neither trainees nor trainers doubt that the new tactics heighten the risks that police officers must accept in the line of duty. "Most officers fit into a rescue role better than an attack role," Adams acknowledges. His message to reluctant trainees in Peoria is grim: "You are a police officer. No one wants to do this. But you swore an oath of office. Your oath of office promises to serve and protect. Let's say it's your wife or children in there. What do you want me to do?" Adams has had to pull aside a couple of officers who were having difficulty with the training. "What you're seeing is terrible," he said to them. "That's why we've got to stop it."

> "Adams has had to pull aside a couple of officers who were having difficulty with the training."

13 To David Klinger, a former police officer who is now a professor of criminology at the University of Missouri at St. Louis, the unease caused by the new training is understandable. "It points up how most policemen don't ever think of using force, deadly force," he says. "It's not something officers contemplate. But now they have to contemplate it. It goes against the doctrines that we've been teaching officers for a long time. It's not going to be easy. The answer is to train more, and to let officers know that ninety-nine percent of the time they should still wait, but that in some circumstances waiting is wrong."

14 So far rapid-response training has encountered little public opposition, but Klinger expects that will change the first time the police kill a suspect instead of capturing him, or the first time an officer firing at a suspect hits an innocent person instead. "We're going to have to come to the conclusion in our society that in some situations the police need to shoot people," he says. "Regardless of the outcome, we have to accept that, even knowing that mistakes are possible. It's an incredibly complex situation in an incredibly dynamic environment."

15   The Peoria Police Department conducted its training in a department store that had gone out of business. Larry Layman and his fellow trainees wore and carried standard equipment, including bulletproof vests. The only special items employed in the exercise were simunitions, carried by the officers as well as by the trainers, and hockey-style helmets with clear-plastic visors. After lectures and videos explaining the new tactics, Layman and the three other officers in his contact team were sent into a "live" exercise. They were told that one or more gunmen were running rampant in a school. Layman was the team's point man when the trainer shouted "Go!"

16   "It was instant chaos," Layman recalls. He heard gunfire down the hall, and began moving quickly, almost running, toward it. A man shot him and then disappeared around a corner. Layman felt the pain in his arm, glanced at the splotch of red paint, and knew he'd have a bruise later. He kept jogging, making sure he didn't get too far ahead of his team. "The trainers told us we couldn't quit, even if we were hit," he said. "We had to keep going."

17   Layman stepped over people who were lying on the floor, playing wounded students. They moaned that they were hurt, clutched at his legs, and begged him to stop and help them. One man, playing a terrified but unhurt student, leaped from a doorway and grabbed him. Layman wrestled the man away and pushed him toward his trailing teammates, who in turn pushed the man behind them and told him to run back down the hallway to the exit. Another man leaped from a doorway, but this one fired at Layman's team. Others, with guns blazing, attacked from behind or sniped at the officers from doorways. When the contact team's blue-paint simunitions struck the attackers squarely on their vests or helmets, the gunmen stepped aside. They were out of the exercise.

18   One gunman stayed just ahead of Layman, shooting and then ducking around corners as Layman chased him and fired back. Often during his career Layman had considered switching to one of the high-powered semiautomatics that many younger officers now carry. Maybe a .45-caliber or a 9 mm, maybe a fifteen-shot rapid-fire Glock. At that moment, however, he was glad to have his old .38, the six-shooter he had been carrying for twenty-six years. Younger policemen laughed at his weapon and called it an underpowered antique, but it felt like an old friend in his hands as he fired all six shots and reloaded on the run, again and again. "In the old days, if you had to shoot your gun, they taught you to fire in a burst of two shots and then assess," Layman says. "You'd pause. Then another burst of two, and assess again. In this new training they teach you that if you are going to shoot your gun, you empty it."

19   When he came upon the suspect holding the gun to the hostage's head, Layman's initial impulse was to drop his gun. "That's what you were always taught—drop the gun, just like on the TV shows," he says. "Now they teach you to shoot. They say if you don't shoot, the hostage is probably going to die anyway." Most of the gunman's body was shielded by the hostage, but Layman did not hesitate. He took the shot. Blue paint exploded against the gunman's helmet. "Only about a quarter of this bad guy's head was visible, but I hit it," Layman says, marveling. "I surprised myself. At the end of the chase I was able to hit a target. I was able to stay focused and just keep shooting."

20   His clean head shot ended the exercise. The whole thing had taken barely three minutes, but it had seemed like three hours to Layman. He accepted muted

congratulations on his shot, and then sat with his contact team in a debriefing room. Layman was panting and exhausted. He was having trouble hearing in the aftermath of the gunfire. His muscles ached as his adrenaline level returned to normal. He was going to be sore all over, and black and blue where he'd been shot in the arms and legs. The trainers went over what Layman and his team had done well, and reviewed the instances in which they had been "killed." The trainers and the contact team talked for twenty minutes about what the officers could or should do differently in a live situation.

21   "Okay, you guys, good job," the officer overseeing the training finally said. "Now let's do it again."

22   Layman groaned. He grudgingly strapped his vest and helmet back on, and reloaded his gun. "You can't imagine the fatigue from a shoot-'em-up scenario like that," he says. A few minutes later he and his team were in a different part of the old department store, with a different layout and different shooters. This time they were the second team in, the rescue team. Their job was to follow the contact team, direct unhurt people toward a safe exit, and get the wounded out. "Triage is a big part of it," Layman says. "You have to make immediate decisions about who to take out, who to stop and help. It's tragic, but if several people are down, you go to the first one, and if that person is going to die, you go on to the next one."

23   A couple of nights later, nursing his aches and pains with a light beer and a cheap cigar, Layman confessed that the training unnerved him. "It's so different from what we've always been taught. It's contrary to what's become almost instinct for us," he told me. He said he's also uncertain whether all police officers can or should be put into rapid-response situations. "The first cops running into that building are going to be beat cops. If it's a school or an office building, it's probably going to be daytime during the week. The cops with the most seniority work days—the old cops, like me. A lot of older cops are just putting in their time until retirement. They don't sit around talking about police tactics. They talk about where they're going to live in Florida, or the fishing trips they're going to take in Wisconsin. I let myself get out of shape over the years, and there are other fat old doughnut-eating cops who are worse than me. I wouldn't want to go into a situation like Columbine with those guys, and I wouldn't blame another cop for not wanting to go in with me. It scares me."

24   At the same time, he says, he's glad he had the training. "Even the thought of it is terrifying, but as long as the nuts are out there, we have to prepare for them," he says. He would welcome more training, but doubts that his department, or any other, can adequately train every single police officer for a Columbine-style shooting. "The new training doesn't come close to what would be needed," he says. "To be really prepared for some thing like that, we would need to be trained almost weekly."

25   Two months after that rapid-response training session, Layman told me that it had helped motivate him to get into better shape. He began working out more, and went on a diet. He managed to lose twenty-five pounds. "The whole experience has been a real reminder of what cops are supposed to be able to do," he says. "I pray to God I'm never in a situation like that, but if I am, I want to be able to do my part."

READING CLOSELY AND THINKING CRITICALLY

1. Why did some families of Columbine victims sue Jefferson County?
2. Why have rapid-response police procedures changed as a result of the Columbine shootings?
3. How have rapid-response police procedures changed since the Columbine shootings?
4. What aspect of the new rapid-response procedures do some police officers find troubling? Why?
5. How does the author feel about police officers? How can you tell?

EXAMINING STRUCTURE AND STRATEGY

1. The original audience of "Shoot to Kill" was the readers of the *Atlantic Monthly,* a magazine of literature, reviews of the arts, political commentary, and in-depth reporting. Readers are likely to share the magazine's politically liberal viewpoint. Are the title and opening paragraph likely to engage the interest of the readers of that magazine? Explain.
2. Harper uses many direct quotations. How do these quotations help the author achieve his purpose?
3. Harper does not specifically state the importance of the processes he explains. Does he need to? Why or why not?

NOTING COMBINED PATTERNS

1. Harper uses several patterns of development in "Shoot to Kill." Where does process analysis appear? Where do you find contrast? Where is cause-and-effect analysis used?
2. Paragraph 8 includes description. What does the description add to the essay, and how does it help Harper achieve his purpose?

CONSIDERING LANGUAGE AND STYLE

1. Read the first sentence of the essay aloud. Why is the sentence so effective?
2. In paragraph 10, Harper refers to "Rambo-style freelancing." What does the phrase mean? Explain the reference to "Rambo."
3. Consult a dictionary if you are unsure of the meaning of these words: *converged* (paragraph 4), *disaffected* (paragraph 5), *seminal* (paragraph 6), *muster* (paragraph 7), *protocol* (paragraph 10), *rampant* (paragraph 15), *triage* (paragraph 22).

FOR DISCUSSION IN CLASS OR ONLINE

What kind of person would make a good police officer in today's society? Specifically, what traits should the person have? What traits should he or she *not* have?

WRITING ASSIGNMENTS

1. **Writing in your journal.** Do you think the families of the Columbine victims should sue Jefferson County? Give the reasons for your view in a page or so.

2. **Using process analysis for a purpose.** The purposes in the assignments are possibilities. You may establish whatever purpose you like, within your instructor's guidelines.
   - If you have ever done anything with some risk associated with it (white-water rafting, rock climbing, or putting shingles on a roof, for example), explain the process to relate your experience, express your feelings, and perhaps inform. Be sure to communicate the danger associated with the process.
   - To relate your experience, express your feelings, and perhaps inform, explain a process you perform with some reluctance (for example, administering your own insulin shots, washing the dog, firing an employee, or disciplining a child).
   - Schoolchildren face a number of risks other than from shootings. For example, they can be at risk from students who push drugs, gangs who encourage violence, kidnappers on the way to school, and peer groups that party with alcohol. To inform, explain a process that will help schoolchildren deal with one of the risks they face.

3. **Combining patterns.** Use process analysis to tell about something you do differently now than you did in the past. Contrast (explained in Chapter 9) the current and previous processes. Consider, for example, past and present holiday celebrations, college and high school study techniques, or communication you handled by e-mail that you now handle on Facebook.

4. **Analyzing and assessing.** Does Harper make a convincing case for the new, post-Columbine rapid-response tactics? If so, how does he make his case so convincing? If not, why not? To respond, consider the author's detail, word choice, organization, and any other features you wish.

5. **Connecting and synthesizing the readings.** Discuss one or more reasons for violent incidents that occur in our schools (including colleges if you wish), or discuss one or more effects of that violence, or discuss one or more ways to reduce the violence. In addition to your own ideas, you can draw on "Shoot to Kill" and "What Is Behind the Growth of Violence on College Campuses?" (page 454).

6. **Drawing on sources.** One theory advanced to explain why young people shoot their classmates and teachers suggests that the shooters suffer from the effects of being bullied in school. Consider what schools can do to deal effectively with bullying. For ideas, you can look up "bullying" in *Education Index* in your library. On the Internet, type the keyword "bullying" in your favorite search engine.

BACKGROUND: One of six daughters, Jessica Mitford (1917–1996) was born in England to aristocratic parents, but she never took to the aristocratic way of life. Eventually, she moved to California, became a U.S. citizen, joined the Communist Party, and held a number of jobs, including working as executive secretary for the Civil Rights Congress and teaching sociology at San Jose State University. After resigning from the Communist Party in 1958, Mitford devoted her time to writing, achieving fame as an investigative journalist who exposed corruption and excess in such American institutions as the funeral, television, prison, and diet industries. For her efforts, *Time* magazine dubbed her the "Queen of the Muckrakers." (A *muckraker* searches out and exposes misconduct.) Mitford's works include *Kind and Unusual Punishment: The Prison Business* (1979); *Poison Penmanship* (1979), a collection of her articles from the *Atlantic Monthly, Harper's,* and other magazines; and two volumes of autobiography. "Behind the Formaldehyde Curtain" is taken from Mitford's first investigative study, the 1963 exposé of the funeral business, *The American Way of Death.* Denounced by the funeral industry, the book was very successful and formed the basis of a television documentary.

www.mhhe.com/clousepatterns6	Jessica Mitford

For more information on this author, go to

More resources > Chapter 8 > Jessica Mitford

COMBINED PATTERNS AND THEIR PURPOSES: In "Behind the Form-aldehyde Curtain," Jessica Mitford **argues** that the funeral industry extracts money for unneces-sary services. At the same time, she **informs** the reader, by explaining the *process* of embalming. The excerpt also includes graphic *description* that is sometimes shocking.

Behind the Formaldehyde Curtain
BY JESSICA MITFORD

The drama begins to unfold with the arrival of the corpse at the mortuary.

2   Alas, poor Yorick.[1] How surprised he would be to see how his counterpart of today is whisked off to a funeral parlor and is in short order sprayed, sliced, pierced, pickled, trussed, trimmed, creamed, waxed, painted, rouged, and neatly dressed—transformed from a common corpse into a Beautiful Memory Picture. This process is known in the trade as embalming and restor-ative art, and is so universally employed in the United States and Canada that the funeral director does it routinely, without consulting corpse or kin.[2] He regards as eccentric those few who are hardy enough to suggest that it might be dispensed with. Yet no law requires embalm-ing, no religious doctrine commends it, nor is it dictated by considerations of health, sanitation, or even of personal daintiness. In no part of the world but in Northern

As you read Think about how Mitford reveals her attitude toward her subject.

---

[1]The reference is to Hamlet's graveyard speech to Horatio about Yorick, who was buried but not embalmed.

[2]The Federal Trade Commission now requires that families be informed that embalming is optional.

America is it widely used. The purpose of embalming is to make the corpse presentable for viewing in a suitably costly container; and here too the funeral director routinely, without first consulting the family, prepares the body for public display.

3   Is all this legal? The processes to which a dead body may be subjected are after all to some extent circumscribed by law. In most states, for instance, the signature of next of kin must be obtained before an autopsy may be performed, before the deceased may be cremated, before the body may be turned over to a medical school for research purposes; or such provision must be made in the decedent's will. In the case of embalming, no such permission is required nor is it ever sought. A textbook, *The Principles and Practices of Embalming*, comments on this: "There is some question regarding the legality of much that is done within the preparation room." The author points out that it would be most unusual for a responsible member of a bereaved family to instruct the mortician, in so many words, to "embalm" the body of a deceased relative. The very term *embalming* is so seldom used that the mortician must rely upon custom in the matter. The author concludes that unless the family specifies otherwise, the act of entrusting the body to the care of a funeral establishment carries with it an implied permission to go ahead and embalm.

4   Embalming is indeed a most extraordinary procedure, and one must wonder at the docility of Americans who each year pay hundreds of millions of dollars for its perpetuation, blissfully ignorant of what it is all about, what is done, how it is done. Not one in ten thousand has any idea of what actually takes place. Books on the subject are extremely hard to come by. They are not to be found in most libraries or bookshops.

5   In an era when huge television audiences watch surgical operations in the comfort of their living rooms, when, thanks to the animated cartoon, the geography of the digestive system has become familiar territory even to the nursery school set, in a land where the satisfaction of curiosity about almost all matters is a national pastime, the secrecy surrounding embalming can, surely, hardly be attributed to the inherent gruesomeness of the subject. Custom in this regard has within this century suffered a complete reversal. In the early days of American embalming, when it was performed in the home of the deceased, it was almost mandatory for some relative to stay by the embalmer's side and witness the procedure. Today, family members who might wish to be in attendance would certainly be dissuaded by the funeral director. All others, except apprentices, are excluded by law from the preparation room.

6   A close look at what does actually take place may explain in large measure the undertaker's intractable reticence concerning a procedure that has become his major *raison d'être*.[3] Is it possible he fears that public information about embalming might lead patrons to wonder if they really want this service? If the funeral men are loath to discuss the subject outside the trade, the reader may, understandably, be equally loath to go on reading at this point. For those who have the stomach for it, let us part the formaldehyde curtain . . .

7   The body is first laid out in the undertaker's morgue—or rather, Mr. Jones is reposing in the preparation room—to be readied to bid the world farewell.

---

[3]French phrase meaning "reason for existence."

8   The preparation room in any of the better funeral establishments has the tiled and sterile look of a surgery, and indeed the embalmer-restorative artist who does his chores there is beginning to adopt the term *dermasurgeon* (appropriately corrupted by some mortician-writers as "demi-surgeon") to describe his calling. His equipment, consisting of scalpels, scissors, augers, forceps, clamps, needles, pumps, tubes, bowls, and basins, is crudely imitative of the surgeon's, as is his technique, acquired in a nine- or twelve-month post-high-school course in an embalming school. He is supplied by an advanced chemical industry with a bewildering array of fluids, sprays, pastes, oils, powders, creams, to fix or soften tissue, shrink or distend it as needed, dry it here, restore the moisture there. There are cosmetics, waxes, and paints to fill and cover features, even plaster of Paris to replace entire limbs. There are ingenious aids to prop and stabilize the cadaver: a Vari-Pose Head Rest, the Edwards Arm and Hand Positioner, the Repose Block (to support the shoulders during the embalming), and the Throop Foot Positioner, which resembles an old-fashioned stocks.

9   Mr. John H. Eckels, president of the Eckels College of Mortuary Science, thus describes the first part of the embalming procedure: "In the hands of a skilled practitioner, this work may be done in a comparatively short time and without mutilating the body other than by slight incision—so slight that it scarcely would cause serious inconvenience if made upon a living person. It is necessary to remove the blood, and doing this not only helps in the disinfecting, but removes the principal cause of disfigurements due to discoloration."

10   Another textbook discusses the all-important time element: "The earlier this is done, the better, for every hour that elapses between death and embalming will add to the problems and complications encountered . . ." Just how soon should one get going on the embalming? The author tells us, "On the basis of such scanty information made available to this profession through its rudimentary and haphazard system of technical research, we must conclude that the best results are to be obtained if the subject is embalmed before life is completely extinct—that is, before cellular death has occurred. In the average case, this would mean within an hour after somatic death." For those who feel that there is something a little rudimentary, not to say haphazard, about this advice, a comforting thought is offered by another writer. Speaking of fears entertained in early days of premature burial, he points out, "One of the effects of embalming by chemical injection, however, has been to dispel fears of live burial." How true; once the blood is removed, chances of live burial are indeed remote.

11   To return to Mr. Jones, the blood is drained out through the veins and replaced by embalming fluid pumped in through the arteries. As noted in *The Principles and Practices of Embalming*, "every operator has a favorite injection and drainage point—a fact which becomes a handicap only if he fails or refuses to forsake his favorites when conditions demand it." Typical favorites are the carotid artery, femoral artery, jugular vein, subclavian vein. There are various choices of embalming fluid. If Flextone is used, it will produce a "mild, flexibility rigidity. The skin retains a velvety softness, the tissues are rubbery and pliable. Ideal for women and children." It may be blended with B. and G. Products Company's Lyf-Lyk tint, which is guaranteed to reproduce "nature's own skin texture . . . the velvety appearance of

living tissue." Suntone comes in three separate tints: Suntan; Special Cosmetic Tint, a pink shade "especially indicated for female subjects"; and Regular Cosmetic Tint, moderately pink.

12   About three to six gallons of a dyed and perfumed solution of formaldehyde, glycerin, borax, phenol, alcohol, and water is soon circulated through Mr. Jones, whose mouth has been sewn together with a "needle directed upward between the upper lip and gum and brought out through the left nostril," with the corners raised slightly "for a more pleasant expression." If he should be bucktoothed, his teeth are cleaned with Bon Ami and coated with colorless nail polish. His eyes, meanwhile, are closed with flesh-tinted eye caps and eye cement.

13   The next step is to have at Mr. Jones with a thing called a trocar. This is a long, hollow needle attached to a tube. It is jabbed into the abdomen, poked around the entrails and chest cavity, the contents of which are pumped out and replaced with "cavity fluid." This done, and the hole in the abdomen sewn up, Mr. Jones's face is heavily creamed (to protect the skin from burns which may be caused by leakage of the chemicals), and he is covered with a sheet and left unmolested for a while. But not for long—there is more, much more, in store for him. He has been embalmed, but not yet restored, and the best time to start the restorative work is eight to ten hours after embalming, when the tissues have become firm and dry.

14   The object of all this attention to the corpse, it must be remembered, is to make it presentable for viewing in an attitude of healthy repose. "Our customs require the presentation of our dead in the semblance of normality . . . unmarred by the ravages of illness, disease, or mutilation," says Mr. J. Sheridan Mayer in his *Restorative Art*. This is rather a large order since few people die in the full bloom of health, unravaged by illness and unmarked by some disfigurement. The funeral industry is equal to the challenge: "In some cases the gruesome appearance of a mutilated or disease-ridden subject may be quite discouraging. The task of restoration may seem impossible and shake the confidence of the embalmer. This is the time for intestinal fortitude and determination. Once the formative work is begun and affected tissues *are* cleaned or removed, all doubts of success vanish. It is surprising and gratifying to discover the results which may be obtained."

15   The embalmer, having allowed an appropriate interval to elapse, returns to the attack, but now he brings into play the skill and equipment of sculptor and cosmetician. Is a hand missing? Casting one in plaster of Paris is a simple matter. "For replacement purposes, only a cast of the back of the hand is necessary; this is within the ability of the average operator and is quite adequate." If a lip or two, a nose, or an ear should be missing, the embalmer has at hand a variety of restorative waxes with which to model replacements. Pores and skin textures are simulated by stippling with a little brush, and over this cosmetics are laid on. Head off? Decapitation cases are rather routinely handled. Ragged edges are trimmed, and head joined to torso with a series of splints, wires, and sutures. It is a good idea to have a little something at the neck—a scarf or a high collar—when time for viewing comes. Swollen mouth? Cut out tissue as needed from inside the lips. If too much is removed, the surface contour can easily be restored by padding with cotton. Swollen necks and cheeks are reduced by removing tissue through vertical incisions made down each side of the neck. "When the deceased is casketed, the pillow will

hide the suture incisions . . . as an extra precaution against leakage, the suture may be painted with liquid sealer."

16 The opposite condition is more likely to present itself — that of emaciation. His hypodermic syringe now loaded with massage cream, the embalmer seeks out and fills the hollowed and sunken areas by injection. In this procedure the backs of the hands and fingers and the under-chin area should not be neglected.

17 Positioning the lips is a problem that recurrently challenges the ingenuity of the embalmer. Closed too tightly, they tend to give a stern, even disapproving expression. Ideally, embalmers feel, the lips should give the impression of being ever so slightly parted, the upper lip protruding slightly for a more youthful appearance. This takes some engineering, however, as the lips tend to drift apart. Lip drift can sometimes be remedied by pushing one or two straight pins through the inner margin of the lower lip and then inserting them between the two front upper teeth. If Mr. Jones happens to have no teeth, the pins can just as easily be anchored in his Armstrong Face Former and Denture Replacer. Another method to maintain lip closure is to dislocate the lower jaw, which is then held in its new position by a wire run through holes which have been drilled through the upper and lower jaws at the midline. As the French are fond of saying, *il faut souffrir pour être belle.*[4]

18 If Mr. Jones has died of jaundice, the embalming fluid will very likely turn him green. Does this deter the embalmer? Not if he has intestinal fortitude. Masking pastes and cosmetics are heavily laid on, burial garments and casket interiors are color-correlated with particular care, and Jones is displayed beneath rose-colored lights. Friends will say "How *well* he looks." Death by carbon monoxide, on the other hand, can be rather a good thing from the embalmer's viewpoint: "One advantage is the fact that this type of discoloration is an exaggerated form of a natural pink coloration." This is nice because the healthy glow is already present and needs but little attention.

19 The patching and filling completed, Mr. Jones is now shaved, washed, and dressed. Cream-based cosmetic, available in pink, flesh, suntan, brunette, and blond, is applied to his hands and face, his hair is shampooed and combed (and, in the case of Mrs. Jones, set), his hands manicured. For the horny-handed son of toil special care must be taken; cream should be applied to remove ingrained grime, and the nails cleaned. "If he were not in the habit of having them manicured in life, trimming and shaping is advised for better appearance — never questioned by kin."

20 Jones is now ready for casketing (this is the present participle of the verb "to casket"). In this operation his right shoulder should be depressed slightly "to turn the body a bit to the right and soften the appearance of lying flat on the back." Positioning the hands is a matter of importance, and special rubber positioning blocks may be used. The hands should be cupped slightly for a more lifelike, relaxed appearance. Proper placement of the body requires a delicate sense of balance. It should lie as high as possible in the casket, yet not so high that the lid, when lowered, will hit the nose. On the other hand, we are cautioned, placing the body too low "creates the impression that the body is in a box."

---

[4] "You have to suffer to be beautiful."

21   Jones is next wheeled into the appointed slumber room where a few last touches may be added—his favorite pipe placed in his hand or, if he was a great reader, a book propped into position. (In the case of little Master Jones a Teddy bear may be clutched.) Here he will hold open house for a few days, visiting hours 10 A.M. to 9 P.M.

22   All now being in readiness, the funeral director calls a staff conference to make sure that each assistant knows his precise duties. Mr. Wilber Kriege writes: "This makes your staff feel that they are a part of the team, with a definite assignment that must be properly carried out if the whole plan is to succeed. You never heard of a football coach who failed to talk to his entire team before they go on the field. They have drilled on the plays they are to execute for hours and days, and yet the successful coach knows the importance of making even the bench-warming third-string substitute feel that he is important if the game is to be won." The winning of *this* game is predicated upon glass-smooth handling of the logistics. The funeral director has notified the pallbearers whose names were furnished by the family, has arranged for the presence of clergyman, organist, and soloist, has provided transportation for everybody, has organized and listed the flowers sent by friends. In *Psychology of Funeral Service* Mr. Edward A. Martin points out, "He may not always do as much as the family thinks he is doing, but it is his helpful guidance that they appreciate in knowing they are proceeding as they should . . . The important thing is how well his services can be used to make the family believe they are giving unlimited expression to their own sentiment."

23   The religious service may be held in a church or in a chapel of the funeral home; the funeral director vastly prefers the latter arrangement, for not only is it more convenient for him but it affords him the opportunity to show off his beautiful facilities to the gathered mourners. After the clergyman has had his say, the mourners queue up to file past the casket for a last look at the deceased. The family is *never* asked whether they want an open-casket ceremony; in the absence of their instruction to the contrary, this is taken for granted. Consequently well over 90 percent of all American funerals feature the open casket—a custom unknown in other parts of the world. Foreigners are astonished by it. An English woman living in San Francisco described her reaction in a letter to the writer:

> I myself have attended only one funeral here—that of an elderly fellow
> worker of mine. After the service I could not understand why everyone
> was walking towards the coffin (sorry, I mean casket), but thought I had
> better follow the crowd. It shook me rigid to get there and find the casket
> open and poor old Oscar lying there in his brown tweed suit, wearing a
> suntan makeup and just the wrong shade of lipstick. If I had not been
> extremely fond of the old boy, I have a horrible feeling that I might have
> giggled. Then and there I decided that I could never face another American
> funeral—even dead.

24   The casket (which has been resting throughout the service on a Classic Beauty Ultra Metal Casket Bier) is now transferred by a hydraulically operated device called Porto-Life to a balloon-tired, Glide Easy casket carriage which will wheel it to yet another conveyance, the Cadillac Funeral Coach. This may be lavender,

cream, light green—anything but black. Interiors, of course, are color-correlated, "for the man who cannot stop short of perfection."

25 At graveside, the casket is lowered into the earth. This office, once the prerogative of friends of the deceased, is now performed by a patented mechanical lowering device. A "Lifetime Green" artificial grass mat is at the ready to conceal the sere earth, and overhead, to conceal the sky, is a portable Steril Chapel Tent ("resists the intense heat and humidity of summer and the terrific storms of winter . . . available in Silver Gray, Rose, or Evergreen"). Now is the time for the ritual scattering of earth over the coffin, as the solemn words "earth to earth, ashes to ashes, dust to dust" are pronounced by the officiating cleric. This can today be accomplished "with a mere flick of the wrist with the Gordon Leak-Proof Earth Dispenser. No grasping of a handful of dirt, no soiled fingers. Simple, dignified, beautiful, reverent! The modern way!" The Gordon Earth Dispenser (at $5) is of nickel-plated brass construction. It is not only "attractive to the eye and long wearing"; it is also "one of the 'tools' for building better public relations" if presented as "an appropriate non-commercial gift" to the clergyman. It is shaped something like a saltshaker.

26 Untouched by human hand, the coffin and the earth are now united.

27 It is in the function of directing the participants through this maze of gadgetry that the funeral director has assigned to himself his relatively new role of "grief therapist." He has relieved the family of every detail, he has revamped the corpse to look like a living doll, he has arranged for it to nap for a few days in a slumber room, he has put on a well-oiled performance in which the concept of *death* has played no part whatsoever—unless it was inconsiderately mentioned by the clergyman who conducted the religious service. He has done everything in his power to make the funeral a real pleasure for everybody concerned. He and his team have given their all to score an upset victory over death.

READING CLOSELY AND THINKING CRITICALLY

1. In paragraph 6, Mitford says that her essay will "part the formaldehyde curtain." What do you think she means? Is the phrase effective? Explain.

2. According to Mitford, what is the real purpose of embalming? What is the ostensible (for appearances) purpose?

3. What are the steps in the embalming process?

4. Why do you think Mitford names the corpse "Mr. Jones"?

5. How would you describe Mitford's attitude toward the mortuary business?

6. Who would you judge to be the original, intended audience for Mitford's exposé? Why?

7. According to Mitford, why do morticians keep the embalming process secret?

EXAMINING STRUCTURE AND STRATEGY

1. What is the thesis of "Behind the Formaldehyde Curtain"?

2. What process does Mitford explain?

3. Mitford begins her explanation of a process in paragraph 7. What is the purpose of the first six paragraphs?
4. Mitford employs a considerable amount of **verbal irony** (saying one thing but suggesting another). For example, in paragraph 2, she refers to the casket as "a suitably costly container," but she does not really think the cost appropriate. Cite two or three other examples of verbal irony. What purpose does the irony serve? How does it reveal the author's attitude toward her subject?

NOTING COMBINED PATTERNS

The description in "Behind the Formaldehyde Curtain" is graphic and, at times, shocking. How does this graphic description help Mitford achieve her persuasive purpose?

CONSIDERING LANGUAGE AND STYLE

1. How would you describe the tone of "Behind the Formaldehyde Curtain"? (See page 76 on tone.) Cite examples to support your view.
2. Mitford opens with a reference to burial and its preparation as "drama." In what ways is the metaphor of the drama sustained in the essay? (See page 128 on metaphors.)
3. Consult a dictionary if you are unsure of the meaning of any of these words: *bereaved* (paragraph 3), *docility* (paragraph 4), *perpetuation* (paragraph 4), *intractable* (paragraph 6), *augers* (paragraph 8), *entrails* (paragraph 13), *stippling* (paragraph 15), *queue* (paragraph 23), *hydraulically* (paragraph 24).

FOR DISCUSSION IN CLASS OR ONLINE

A **euphemism** is a polite or indirect substitute for an unpleasant expression. Mitford notes a number of euphemisms common in the funeral industry. For example, in paragraph 7, she refers to a body "reposing in the preparation room" rather than "dead on a slab in the embalming chamber." With some classmates, cite other euphemisms that appear. Explain what effect these euphemisms have on perceptions of death and burial.

WRITING ASSIGNMENTS

1. **Writing in your journal.** What did you think of the funeral industry before reading the selection? Have your views of death and the funeral industry changed after reading it? Were your views influenced at all by the graphic description in the essay? Explain in a page or two.
2. **Using process analysis for a purpose.** The purposes in the assignments are possibilities. You may establish whatever purpose you like, within your instructor's guidelines.
   - Select a process that you think is unnecessary or faulty, and to inform your reader, explain how that process works. Like Mitford, use verbal irony and description to convey your attitude toward the process.
   - To inform and perhaps relate your experience, write a graphic description of a grisly or unpleasant process (for example, baiting a fishhook, cleaning a fish, or dissecting a frog).

- To convince your reader that there is a better way, devise and describe a funeral-and-burial process that you think is superior to anything you are currently aware of. As you explain the steps in the process, note why they are superior to existing rituals.

3. **Combining patterns.** If you have experienced the ritual associated with death because someone you know died, use process analysis and description to explain and describe the ritual and cause-and-effect analysis (explained in Chapter 10) to give your reaction to the ritual. Note whether you found the ritual comforting, depressing, confusing, frightening, and so on—and why. In addition, use description to give the reaction of other people who experienced the ritual.

4. **Analyzing and assessing.** Mitford attacks the funeral industry—and by extension the people involved in the industry. Analyze how she uses language and details to make the attack, and assess how fair and effective that attack is.

5. **Connecting and synthesizing the readings.** A euphemism tries to make a harsh reality less distressing by substituting a more pleasant expression for an unpleasant one. Consider the euphemisms in the selection and any others you can think of. (For example, a *waiting room* in a doctor's office is a *reception area;* a dentist does not *pull* a tooth but *performs an extraction;* and a patient experiences *discomfort,* never *pain.*) Then, decide whether Sissela Bok should add the category of euphemisms to her classification of white lies in "White Lies" on page 000. Explain why or why not.

6. **Drawing on sources.** Explain one or more of the funeral customs of a culture you are unfamiliar with. To find this information, check "funeral rites and ceremonies" in the *Social Sciences Index* in your library, or on the Internet, type the key phrase "funeral customs" into your favorite search engine.

BACKGROUND: Award-winning poet, essayist, short story writer, children's author, and teacher Naomi Shihab Nye was born in 1952 to an American mother and a Palestinian father. She grew up in St. Louis, Jerusalem, and San Antonio. She has traveled to the Middle East and Asia for the United States Information Agency promoting international goodwill through the arts. Drawing on her Palestinian American heritage and her extensive travels, Nye often writes about the shared humanity of diverse people. Her work has appeared in publications throughout North America, Europe, and the Middle and Far East. Nye's collections of poems include *Red Suitcase* (1994), *Fuel* (1998), *Is This Forever, or What? Poems and Paintings from Texas* (2004), and *You and Yours* (2006). "The Traveling Onion" is from Nye's 1986 collection *Yellow Glove*.

COMBINED PATTERNS AND THEIR PURPOSES: In "The Traveling Onion," Naomi Shihab Nye uses *process analysis* and *description* to **inform** readers of how an onion makes its way into a stew. At the same time, Nye is helping the reader to a fresh appreciation of something so familiar it is taken for granted. As is often true of poetry, the artistry of the piece **entertains** the reader.

The Traveling Onion

BY NAOMI SHIHAB NYE

It is believed that the onion originally came from India. In Egypt it was an object of worship—why I haven't been able to find out. From Egypt the onion entered Greece and on to Italy, thence into all of Europe.

—*Better Living Cookbook*

As you read
The poem notes two processes. Try to identify both of them.

When I think how far the onion has traveled
just to enter my stew today, I could kneel and praise
all small forgotten miracles,
crackly paper peeling on the drainboard,
pearly layers in smooth agreement,
the way knife enters onion, straight   5
and onion falls apart on the chopping block,
a history revealed.
And I would never scold the onion
for causing tears.
It is right that tears fall   10
for something small and forgotten.
How at meal, we sit to eat,
commenting on texture of meat or herbal aroma
but never on the translucence of onion,
now limp, now divided,   15
or its traditionally honorable career:
For the sake of others,
disappear.

CONSIDERING THE POEM

1. What two processes does the poem refer to?
2. What are the "small forgotten miracles" to which the speaker refers?
3. What is it about the onion that is "honorable"? Would the same trait in a human being be honorable? Why or why not?
4. An excerpt from *Better Living Cookbook* appears before the poem. What purpose does that excerpt serve?

NOTING COMBINED PATTERNS

1. How does Nye use description in "The Traveling Onion"?
2. Does the description help the author achieve her purpose for writing? Explain.

WRITING ASSIGNMENTS

1. **Writing in your journal.**
   - Write a list of other "small forgotten miracles." Do the items in your list have anything in common?
   - Nye shows an ordinary item—the onion—in a new perspective. Where do new perspectives come from? Tell about a time you received—or achieved—a new perspective.
2. **Using process analysis for a purpose.** To inform and perhaps entertain, explain a process for preparing a fruit or vegetable. Do so in a way likely to increase your audience's appreciation for the food. The purpose in the assignment is a possibility. You may establish whatever purpose you like, within your instructor's guidelines.
3. **Combining patterns.** Describe an item commonly taken for granted and a process associated with that item. For example, you can describe your running shoes and how they help a runner perform or the toolbar at the top of your computer screen and how it helps you work efficiently.
4. **Connecting and synthesizing the readings.** Discuss the role of food in family life. For ideas, you can draw on your own experience, "The Traveling Onion," and "A Visit to Candyland" (page 303).

WRITING PROCESS ANALYSIS

See pages 298 and 302 for strategies for writing a process analysis and for a revising checklist.

1. Explain a process you know that other people should know so they can cope with an emergency—for instance, how to administer CPR, how to administer first aid to someone badly cut, what to do if a tornado strikes, what to do if fire breaks out in the home, or how to rescue a drowning person. Your purpose is to inform your reader.

2. Select a process you perform well (for example, making pizza, wrapping gifts, throwing a surprise party, or planting a garden), and describe it so that your reader can learn how to do it. Your essay should discuss why it is important or even simply pleasurable to learn this process.

3. Explain a process that was an important part of your childhood: catching fireflies, preparing for Halloween, decorating the Christmas tree, planting a garden with your parents, and so forth.

4. Explain a process that will help your reader save money, such as how to buy a used car, how to save money on groceries, how to buy clothes at a thrift shop, how to find bargains at flea markets, or how to buy presents for less.

5. If you have a hobby, such as collecting baseball cards or keeping exotic fish, explain some process associated with that process: evaluating the worth of a baseball card or putting together a tropical fish tank, and so on. Let your pleasure at performing the process show.

6. If you play a sport well, explain some process associated with that sport: shooting a foul shot, hitting a fastball, and so on. Let your pleasure at performing the process show.

7. Rewrite "A Visit to Candyland" as a series of instructions. What do you think of the revision? Why?

8. To entertain your reader, write a humorous explanation of a process: how to flunk a test, how to make a bad impression on a date, how to irritate a teacher, how to make a bad impression on a job interview, or how to be a slob. Use verbal irony, if appropriate.

9. Explain how some mechanical device works: a DVD player, a cell phone, a compact disk, a computer, and so on.

10. To inform your reader, explain how something common—such as paper, decaffeinated coffee, or a baseball—is made. If necessary, do some research to learn about the process. (Consult Chapters 4 and 15 on how to handle material taken from sources.) Also explain why the item is important.

11. To convince your reader that people suffer unfairly to conform to society's concept of beauty, explain a process they go through.

12. Explain the wedding ritual for the religious, ethnic, or cultural group you belong to. Your purpose is to relate your experience and inform your reader. Try to use description to make aspects of the process as vivid as possible. As an alternative, explain the ritual for some other life cycle event.

13. Explain some process for improving relationships between people: how to fight fairly, how to communicate better, how to respect differences, how to offer constructive criticism, and so on.

14. To entertain your reader, write a humorous explanation of how to procrastinate.

15. To help a student who is away from home for the first time, explain how to do laundry. Use examples and keep the tone lighthearted.

16. Explain a way to perform a process to convince your reader that your procedures are better. For example, you can explain a better way to study, a better way to clean a room, a better way to shop, or a better way to plan a party.

17. To inform college students, explain a process for coping with stress.

18. To entertain your reader, explain how to survive adolescence. You may write from a parent's or child's point of view.

19. Explain how to relax.

20. **Process analysis in context:** Assume that your college is putting together a handbook for first-year students to help them adjust to school and be successful. As an experienced student, you have been asked to contribute to the handbook by describing an important academic survival skill: taking notes, taking an exam, getting along with a difficult roommate, reading a textbook, studying for finals, and so on. Be sure your process analysis is written in such a way that it is genuinely useful to a new student.

The following page, from the instruction manual for a computer printer, explains how to complete the first step in operating the printer: loading the paper. Explain how the images and words come together to help users perform the process. You might consider some of these questions: What purpose do the pictures serve? What purpose do the words serve? How important are each of these elements? Could you perform the process if the instructions included only the words? What if they included only the pictures?

Step One: Load the paper

You can load up to 100 sheets of paper (depending on thickness).

1 Place the paper against the right side of the sheet feeder, with the print side facing you.

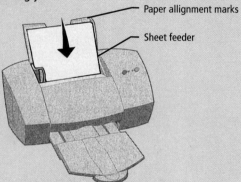

Paper allignment marks

Sheet feeder

2 Squeeze the release tab and the paper guide together and slide the paper guide to the edge of the paper.

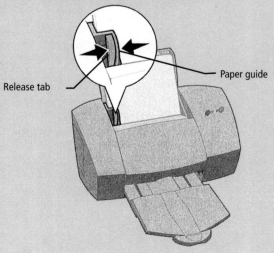

Paper guide

Release tab

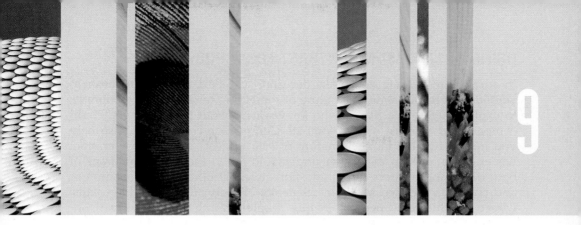

Comparison-Contrast

CONSIDER THE PATTERN

The picture on the facing page shows a laptop computer and an electric typewriter. In its day, the electric typewriter was state-of-the-art technology for preparing documents. Consider how the electric typewriter and laptop are alike and how they are different. Alternatively, compare and contrast another older form of technology with a current one—perhaps a landline phone with a cell phone.

THE PATTERN

Comparison points out similarities and **contrast** points out differences, so **comparison-contrast** points out both similarities and differences. Because comparison-contrast allows us to examine the features of two or more subjects, it is an important component of decision making. Should you buy a laptop computer or upgrade your current desktop? Is this political candidate better for the country or is that one? Will the job in Seattle make you happier than the one in Houston? Will the anthropology course be more interesting than the psychology course? To decide, you compare and contrast the merits of the two computers, the two candidates, the two jobs, and the two courses.

www.mhhe.com/clousepatterns6	Comparison-Contrast

For more help with comparison-contrast, click on

Writing > Paragraph Patterns
Writing > Writing Tutor: Comparison/Contrast

USING COMPARISON-CONTRAST FOR A PURPOSE

In addition to helping you make decisions, comparison-contrast can help you *inform* a reader about the nature of something unfamiliar. For example, to explain rugby to a reader who knows little about the sport, you could compare and contrast it with football. Comparison-contrast can also help you inform by clarifying the nature of *both* subjects under consideration. For example, to help the reader understand the virtues and limitations of both direct and indirect communication styles, Deborah Tannen compares and contrasts the two styles in "Squeaky Wheels and Protruding Nails: Direct and Indirect Speech," in this chapter. Another way comparison-contrast can inform is by providing new insight into something already familiar. In this case, the comparison-contrast serves to sharpen the reader's awareness or appreciation. For example, you already know a fair amount about both horses and people, but after reading Alice Walker's comparison-contrast in "Am I Blue?" in this chapter, you are likely to have fresh insight into the nature of both.

In addition to informing, comparison-contrast can help you to *express feelings* and *relate experience*. To relate the effects of your parents' divorce and express your feelings about it, for example, you could contrast your life before and after the divorce.

By showing that one subject is superior to the other, comparison-contrast can also work to *persuade* a reader to think or act a particular way. For instance, to convince a reader to vote for a particular candidate, you could contrast that candidate with the opposition to show that your choice is better.

If you write an amusing comparison-contrast, you can *entertain* readers. For example, a funny contrast of your two roommates—one obsessively neat and the other incredibly sloppy—can entertain at the same time it expresses your feelings about living with these extreme types.

Combining Patterns for a Purpose

To achieve your writing purpose, you can combine comparison-contrast with other patterns of development. For example, to compare and contrast the techniques of two artists to *inform* your classmates in Introduction to Art, you can *describe* how each one uses color. To compare and contrast two political candidates to *persuade* voters to support the one who favors progressive legislation, you can give the *example* that your candidate sponsored a bill to provide tax credits for working parents with children in day care centers and that the opposing candidate lobbied against it. Or to compare and contrast the styles of two baseball coaches to *increase appreciation* for what coaches do, you can *explain the process* each follows to motivate players.

To see how other patterns can be combined with comparison-contrast, study the following excerpt from "The New Trophy Wife," an essay in this chapter. The excerpt, which is part of paragraph 3 and all of paragraph 4, combines comparison-contrast and exemplification.

EXCERPT FROM "THE NEW TROPHY WIFE" COMBINING COMPARISON-CONTRAST AND EXEMPLIFICATION

The first two sentences give a contrast. At one time, successful men sought wives who were attractive, well bred, and good cooks; now they seek women of accomplishment.

In previous generations, *contrast* successful doctors, lawyers, and bankers sought wives who looked good, were well-bred and made a mean Stroganoff to boot. Now, more and more alpha males are looking for something else from the A-list: accomplishment.

According to a recent Match.com poll, 48 percent of men (and an equal percentage of women) report dating partners who draw the same income they do. Twenty percent of men report dating women who earn more. Jim

Jim Pak and Kristin Ketner are an example of a couple that illustrates the contrast to clarify it and show that it is true.

Pak, 34, *example* was introduced to Kristin Ketner, 38, a Harvard MBA and a hedge fund manager, through a mutual friend, who warned him not to be intimidated by her credentials. She was a research analyst for Goldman Sachs; he was unemployed and playing a lot of golf. "In certain regards, she outshines me," says Pak of his wife. "She's more accomplished academically. People may be more impressed with her than with me." (Pak is now chief financial officer at an electronic stock trading services group.)

You may often use comparison-contrast even when another pattern is your primary method of development. For example, if you are explaining a process for allocating donor organs to transplant recipients, and you want to convince your reader that the process is a good one, you might compare it to an alternative process to demonstrate that yours is superior.

Whether you use comparison-contrast alone or in combination with other patterns depends on what helps you achieve your particular writing purpose for your particular audience.

Comparison-Contrast beyond the Writing Classroom

Comparison-contrast helps writers achieve their purpose in many writing situations.

IN ACADEMIC WRITING AND READING   You will often use comparison-contrast in the classroom to clarify and evaluate the nature of two subjects. In a political science class, you might compare and contrast two political ideologies such as socialism and communism. In a music appreciation class, you might compare and contrast the techniques of two composers; in a literature class, you might compare and contrast the symbolism in two poems; and in a cultural anthropology class, you might compare and contrast the marriage rituals in two cultures.

You will also likely use comparison-contrast to show the superiority of one of the subjects. For example, in a clinical psychology class, you might compare and contrast two treatments for depression to show which one is better; in an advertising class, you might compare and contrast two advertising campaigns to determine which one is more effective; and in a history class, you might compare and contrast two World War II generals to determine who was the better strategist.

Because comparison-contrast clarifies ideas and concepts by showing how they are similar to and different from other ideas and concepts, textbook authors use it often. Here is an example from a passage in an American history textbook, on European reaction to Native American clothing. Two European views are compared and contrasted to each other and then to the reality.

The contrast between two European interpretations of Native American dress shows how divergent they were.

Europeans interpreted the simplicity of Indian dress in two different ways. Some saw the lack of clothing as evidence of "barbarism." André Thevet, a shocked French visitor to Brazil in 1557, voiced this point of view when he attributed nakedness to simple lust. If the Indians could weave hammocks, he sniffed, why not shirts? But other Europeans viewed unashamed nakedness as the Indians' badge of innocence. As remnants of a bygone "golden age," they believed, Indians needed clothing no more than government, laws, regular employment, or other corruptions of civilization.

The contrast with the reality

In fact, Indians were no more "naked" than they were without trade, politics, employment, or religion. While the simplest tribes of the Caribbean and Brazil wore little, the members of more advanced Indian cultures in Central and North America clothed themselves with animal pelts sewn into mantles and robes, breechclouts, leggings, and moccasins. They wrought bird feathers into headdresses and ear decorations and fashioned reptile skins into belts and pouches. Even more formidably clad were the Eskimos of the far North, who dressed head to foot in sealskin suits with waterproofed seams, turning the furry side inward for warmth in the winter and outward in the summer. (Davidson et al., *Nation of Nations*)

clarifies how wrong both views were.

The textbook authors could have described Native American dress without including the contrast between European opinions and actual Native American cultural practice, but including the contrast makes the point that Europeans misunderstood the people and cultures in the New World.

AT WORK AND IN THE COMMUNITY   Comparison-contrast is often a component of workplace writing. For example, professionals write reports that compare and contrast computer systems or phone systems to recommend a particular purchase. Similarly, a construction manager compares and contrasts two bid proposals from general contractors to determine which company will receive a building project.

Outside the classroom and workplace, you will use comparison-contrast as part of your decision-making process. For a difficult choice such as which job to take, a written comparison-contrast can not only stimulate your thinking and lead you to new ideas but also give you something concrete to mull over. As a member of an organization, you might use comparison-contrast in a committee report evaluating different fund-raising projects or membership campaigns. If you move to a new city and want to describe your new neighborhood to a friend in your former town, comparing it to your old neighborhood can help your friend better visualize where you live now.

CHOOSING SUBJECTS

Your subjects should allow you to make comparisons and contrasts that go beyond trivial points. The bicycle and automobile, for example, might not be ideal subjects for comparison-contrast. The obvious points to compare and contrast—the number of wheels and speed of travel—are trivial. However, these subjects could work if you have a fresh approach, perhaps comparing and contrasting the lifestyles associated with using each vehicle as a principal mode of transportation.

In general, your subjects should be from the same category or general type of thing or idea. Thus, you can compare and contrast two kinds of computers, two weight-loss programs, two poems, two mayors, and so forth. If your purpose is to entertain, however, you may be able to compare and contrast subjects from different categories. A political satirist, for example, might compare a former president of the United States to Ronald McDonald, and a campus humor columnist might compare studying for exams and preparing for war.

The comparison of subjects from different categories is an **analogy.** An analogy should shed light on one or both subjects. For example, a comparison of the human brain with a computer—two subjects from different categories—based on some similarities in functioning can help the reader better understand how both work. Similarly, the human eye can be compared to a camera, or an ant colony to New York City.

SUPPORTING DETAILS

Mentioning every possible point of comparison and contrast is usually undesirable—if not impossible—so you must select your details with your writing purpose in mind. Suppose you are comparing and contrasting public and private schools. If your purpose is to convince your reader that public schools are better, then you might mention that the ethnic diversity often found in these schools can teach students more about people and their cultural heritage. To relate your experiences in these schools, you can tell which school you were happier in and why. To inform, you might discuss the academic programs in each kind of school so parents can make up their own minds about which is better for their children. To entertain, you can give humorous portraits of the students and teachers in each kind of school.

Your audience will also determine the points you choose to compare and contrast. Suppose you are contrasting public and private schools to persuade your reader to increase support of public schools. If your audience includes politicians, and you do not want them to support legislation increasing funding to private schools, you can contrast enrollments in the two kinds of schools to show that more voters send children to public schools than to private ones. However, if your audience includes parents, and you want them to send their children to public rather than private schools, you can compare and contrast extracurricular activities to show that students have more options in public schools.

Most times, any point you make about one of your subjects should also be made about the other subject. Thus, if you are comparing and contrasting public and private schools, and you discuss the teachers in public school, you should also discuss the teachers in private school; if you discuss course offerings in public school, you should also discuss course offerings in private school; and so on. You may notice that the writers in this chapter do not always adhere strictly to this principle of balance. However, you need to maintain enough balance so that your essay does not become a random collection of points about the subjects rather than a comparison-contrast.

When you discuss the same points about each of your subjects, you need not do so in equal detail. You can discuss a point in more detail for one subject than for the other. For example, if you are contrasting online and traditional classrooms, you can make the point that in traditional classrooms teachers can read facial expressions and body language to determine whether students understand a point. Then you can give examples of expressions and posture that signal understanding and those that signal confusion. When you discuss the same point for online classrooms, you can simply write that online instructors do not have the opportunity to read expressions and body language.

Finally, avoid stating the obvious, or you will bore and alienate your reader. If, for example, you are contrasting online and traditional classrooms, you need not mention that students in online classrooms require computer access but students in traditional classrooms do not.

ORGANIZING DETAILS

The thesis for a comparison-contrast essay can present the subjects under consideration and indicate whether the focus will be on their similarities, on their differences, or both. Consider, for example, this thesis:

> Sloppy roommates are more fun than neat roommates.

This thesis indicates that the subjects are sloppy roommates and neat roommates, and also that the focus will be on differences. Now consider these two thesis statements:

> Islam and Christianity have more in common than most people realize.
>
> Smith and Jones have different political philosophies, but they have similar styles, so important differences between the men are not readily apparent.

The first thesis indicates that the essay will focus on similarities between Islam and Christianity. Notice that the thesis also makes clear the informational purpose. The second thesis indicates that the essay will look at both similarities and differences between politicians Smith and Jones, and the informational and persuasive purposes are apparent— the essay will argue that similarities between the two politicians mask their differences.

One way to order detail in a comparison-contrast is the **block pattern,** whereby all the points about one subject are made (in a block) and then all the points about the other subject are made (in a second block). To appreciate how block arrangement works, look at the following outline for the contrast portion of an essay comparing and contrasting Smith and Jones. Notice that balance is achieved by discussing the same points for both subjects. Also notice that the points are discussed in the same order for both subjects.

    I. Smith
        A. Believes in states funding their own health care plans
        B. Believes in supporting education with a state income tax
        C. Wants to form a task force to study lake pollution
    II. Jones
        A. Believes the federal government should fund health care
        B. Believes in supporting education with a property tax
        C. Believes lake pollution is not a priority

A second possible arrangement is the **alternating pattern,** whereby a point is made for one subject and then made for the other before proceeding on to the next point. The alternating pattern between subjects continues until all the points have been made. An outline for the contrast portion of an essay comparing and contrasting Smith and Jones with an alternating pattern could look like this:

I. View on financing health care
   A. Smith believes states should fund their own plans
   B. Jones believes the federal government should fund a plan
II. View on financing education
   A. Smith believes in a state income tax
   B. Jones believes in a property tax
III. View on lake pollution
   A. Smith wants to form a task force to study pollution
   B. Jones believes pollution is not a priority

Although comparison-contrast can be arranged using a block or an alternating pattern, the two strategies are not interchangeable. In general, the block method works better for essays with fewer points that are not extensively developed. When you have many points or very detailed points to discuss, your reader can easily lose track with a block pattern if forced to remember many points about the first subject while reading about the second. An alternating pattern is a better choice for such essays because readers can keep track of the ideas more easily. However, the points must be well developed, or you risk creating a "ping-pong" effect as you switch back and forth between subjects.

If you are focusing on similarities and differences, you can organize by treating similarities first and differences next. Or you can reverse this order.

VISUALIZING A COMPARISON-CONTRAST ESSAY

The following chart can help you visualize either the block or the alternating structure for a comparison-contrast essay. Like all good models, however, this one can be altered as needed.

INTRODUCTION
- Creates interest in your essay
- States your thesis (underlined in the example), which mentions the subjects you are considering and may indicate whether the focus will be on similarities, differences, or both

EXAMPLE

In the late 1930s, a small company in the fledgling comic book business introduced something new: the superhero. Two of the first superheroes were opposites. One had the powers of a god; the other was only a man. <u>Despite their differences, Superman and Batman became the iconic creations that set the stage for all superheroes thereafter.</u>

- In a block pattern, make and explain all the points about the first subject
- In an alternating pattern, make and explain a point about the first subject and then about the second subject
- May include any other patterns of development

EXAMPLE

While both superheroes fight crime, their motivation is vastly different. Superman is an idealist, who fights for "truth, justice, and the American way." Batman is out for vengeance. . . .

NEXT BODY PARAGRAPH(S)

- In a block pattern, make and explain all the points about the second subject
- In an alternating pattern, make and explain the next point about the first subject and then about the second subject, continuing this way until all points are made
- May include any other patterns of development

EXAMPLE

Another important difference is seen in the way criminals react to the two superheroes. Villains fear Superman's powers, but not the man, who can be trusted to behave in honorable ways. Because Batman has a dark side, criminals fear him and his lack of predictability. . . .

CONCLUSION

- Provides a satisfying finish
- Leaves your reader with a strong final impression.

EXAMPLE

Superman and Batman are as different as their alter egos Clark Kent and Bruce Wayne. Still, both superheroes have an enduring appeal, Superman for his purity and Batman for his darkness.

THINKING CRITICALLY ABOUT COMPARISON-CONTRAST

Chapters 1 and 4 explained that thinking critically about your reading and writing requires analysis and assessment. To read and write critically about comparison-contrast, use what you learned in those chapters, and ask the following questions:

- **Is the comparison-contrast worthwhile?** Many items can be compared and contrasted, but comparing and contrasting them is not necessarily worthwhile. Grapes and raisins can be compared and contrasted—but, unless you can find a special angle, who cares?
- **Are the comparisons and contrasts manipulative or biased?** A candidate for public office who compares a political rival to a Nazi is triggering strong negative emotions rather than making logical comparisons.

Using Transitions in Comparison-Contrast

If you have trouble moving smoothly from point to point or subject to subject, use transitions.

TO SHOW
SIMILARITY
similarly, likewise, in similar fashion, in like manner, in the same way

Smith believes in tax reform. Similarly, Jones wants to close tax loopholes.

TO SHOW
CONTRAST
however, on the other hand, conversely, in contrast

Smith favors tax reform. However, Jones believes current tax laws are adequate.

Repetition of keywords, particularly when combined with transitions, can also help you move smoothly between points and maintain coherence.

Smith believes in tax reform. Similarly, tax reform is important to Jones, who wants to close tax loopholes.

Smith favors tax reform. Such reform is not a priority for Jones, however, because he believes current tax laws are adequate.

- **Are all the important points of comparison or contrast included and explained in enough detail?** Omission of points or insufficient detail on points can also be manipulative or can distort the comparison-contrast. For example, in an advertising campaign, a satellite dish company might advertise its rates as lower than a rival cable company's rates. However, that comparison might be omitting the detail that the satellite dish company requires a costly activation fee that the cable company does not require. This negative point could be mentioned and dealt with as follows: "Although the satellite dish company requires a $100 start-up fee, the yearly cost is still 20 percent less than the cable company's premium service."

PROCESS GUIDELINES:
STRATEGIES FOR WRITING COMPARISON-CONTRAST

1. **Selecting a topic.** Try explaining the similarities between two things usually considered different or the differences between two things thought of as being alike. For example, you could discuss the similarities between madness and genius or the differences between getting a degree and getting an education. Be sure to select subjects from the same category.

2. **Establishing a purpose.** To establish your purpose, answer these questions:
   - Do you want to inform readers about the nature of something not well understood?

- Do you want to clarify the nature of one or both subjects?
- Do you want to offer a new insight into something familiar?
- Do you want to convince your reader that one subject is better than the other?
- Do you want to express feelings or relate experience?
- Do you want to entertain your reader?

3. **Assessing your audience.** Determine how much your reader knows about your subjects and how interested your reader is likely to be in them.

4. **Writing a thesis.** Write a preliminary thesis that names your subjects; indicates whether you will focus on similarities, differences, or both; and, possibly, suggests your purpose.

5. **Generating ideas.** Try these techniques if you need help:
   - List every similarity and or every difference you can think of. Study the list and eliminate ideas not suited to your audience and purpose.
   - Ask yourself these questions about the points on your list: Should I describe anything? Tell a story? Explain a process? Provide examples?

Using Modifiers in Comparison-Contrast

If you have trouble using modifiers (adjectives and adverbs) correctly to compare and contrast, this explanation may be helpful.

Modifiers have *comparative forms* and *superlative forms*. Use the comparative form to compare or contrast two items and the superlative form to compare and contrast more than two items.

BASE FORM	COMPARATIVE FORM	SUPERLATIVE FORM
fast	faster	fastest
unusual	more unusual	most unusual
good	better	best
bad	worse	worst

NO	Both cities have low unemployment rates, but Charleston has the best average income.
YES	Both cities have low unemployment rates, but Charleston has a better average income. (*only two cities*)
NO	Of all the tutors observed, the writing center tutors were friendlier.
YES	Of all the tutors observed, the writing center tutors were friendliest. (*more than two tutors*)

6. **Organizing.** Comparison-contrast requires careful planning, so even if you do not ordinarily write detailed outlines, write one for this essay, using a block or an alternating pattern. An outline can help you confirm that you are choosing the right pattern.

7. **Revising.** Ask a friend with good judgment about writing to read your draft and note anything that is unclear and any places where you are not moving smoothly from point to point or from subject to subject.

Using Sources for a Purpose

Below is an introductory paragraph for an essay about the traits of women who are considered successful and desirable; it illustrates how you can use sources from this book in your writing. It includes both a summary of paragraphs 1 and 2 of "Squeaky Wheels and Protruding Nails: Direct and Indirect Speech" on page 393 and a paraphrase with quotation from paragraph 5 of "The New Trophy Wife" on page 385. The source material helps the writer support the idea that women must be like men in order to be considered successful.

THESIS To be judged successful, women are too often forced to adopt traditional male values and behaviors.

WRITING PURPOSE AND AUDIENCE To inform adult men and women that women are considered successful only if they adopt male behaviors and attitudes and to persuade them not to buy into this thinking themselves.

The summary and paraphrase in sentence 4 help support the thesis assertion that successful women are expected to be assertive like men. Sentence 4 also illustrates that multiple sources can be combined in a single sentence to help make a point.

[1]To be judged successful, woman are too often forced to adopt traditional male values and behaviors. [2]That is, they must be aggressive, career oriented, and in highly paid jobs in business and industry, which means they must downplay their nurturing, collaborative spirits and family-centered impulses. [3]Rarely does our society ascribe status to or financially reward traditional female endeavors, such as being full-time mothers, volunteers, teachers, or employees in the helping and social service professions. [4]So when a respected linguist reports that a board of trustees member chided a female college president for not being sufficiently assertive and directive with her secretary (Tannen 393), and when a national consultant on women's issues notes that men are now attracted to "professionally achieving mates" (Siegel 385), we should be concerned. [5]We should be concerned because when women *do* achieve at the highest levels in the workplace, they are expected to behave like men; we should be concerned because when women choose volunteerism or one of the helping professions, they may be judged less successful and may be less desirable to men.

(continued)

AVOIDING PLAGIARISM

The paragraph illustrates the following points about avoiding plagiarism. (For more complete information on using source material, consult Chapters 4 and 15.)

• **Introduce your source material.** Sentence 4 illustrates that introductions are important because they help readers separate your own ideas from those of others, and they help readers separate the ideas of one source from those of another. Note that you need not always introduce with the author's name or the title of the source you are using, since your parenthetical citation can point readers to the source. Sentence 4 also gives the authors' credentials. Sometimes giving the credentials lends extra credibility to the source material.

• **Place keywords and key phrases in quotation marks.** Paraphrase using your own words and style, but, as sentence 4 shows, you can include some of the source's exact words if you place them in quotation marks.

MYTHS ABOUT USING SOURCES

MYTH: The parenthetical citation must always come at the end of the sentence.

FACT: Sentence 4 shows that when the source material appears in the middle of a sentence, the parenthetical citation is also placed in the middle, so it is at the end of the paraphrase, quotation, or summary.

Checklist for Revising Comparison-Contrast

You can use this checklist along with the one on page 76 to help you revise.

1. _____ Your subjects are from the same category and are worthwhile to compare.

2. _____ Your thesis presents your subjects and indicates whether the focus will be on their similarities and/or differences.

3. _____ Your details are appropriate for your audience and purpose. Points of comparison and contrast are not manipulative or biased.

4. _____ You discuss the same points for both subjects, or you have enough balance between them.

5. _____ You avoid stating obvious comparisons and contrasts, but you include all the important points of comparison and contrast.

6. _____ You use a block or alternating pattern to best advantage.

7. _____ You use transitions and repetition to move from point to point and subject to subject.

Annotated Student Essay

The following comparison-contrast, written by a student, has as its subject two pieces of literature that are on the same theme. This comparison-contrast essay includes critical analysis of the two pieces of literature and synthesizes these sources and another source. You will notice that the author draws on source material to support her assertion and that she emphasizes the similarities more than the differences. After you read, you will have an opportunity to evaluate this essay.

No Body's Perfect: Female Self-Image in Two Narratives
Angie Carmillo

Paragraph 1
The introduction gives helpful background information about prose and graphic literature and some general ways they are similar and different. The last sentence (the thesis) gives the subjects and indicates that similarities and differences will be discussed, with emphasis on similarities.

All literature, regardless of its form, consists of various elements, [1] such as character, plot, setting, and theme. Unlike prose narratives, graphic narratives use cells or frames to convey these elements visually. However, some prose narratives, like short-short stories, resemble graphic narratives in the way they use sparse language and vivid imagery to develop characters and to depict scenes. Two examples of narratives that take different forms but explore similar themes are Bonnie Jo Campbell's short-short story "Sleepover" and Marjane Satrapi's graphic novel *Persepolis 2*. Despite their contrasts, both "Sleepover" and *Persepolis 2* portray the common insecurities teenage girls struggle with as they confront their self-image.

Paragraph 2
The topic sentence (sentence 1) indicates the similarity to be discussed. The details, which include information from sources, give evidence of that similarity.

Both stories depict the awkwardness of female adolescence. As [2] these narratives clearly and humorously show, this awkwardness stems from sudden emotional and physical changes that propel the teenage girls into a state of confusion and self-doubt. Bonnie Jo Campbell's "Sleepover" begins with a scene in the teenage narrator's house, where she and her friend, Pammy, are "making out" with two teenage brothers while the narrator's mother is gone (26). The narrator explains that Pammy "wanted to be in the dark because her face was broke out" (Campbell 26). She then calls out her own sense of insecurity: Ed tells her as he kisses her that he and his brother "'were wishing your head could be on Pammy's body. . . . You two together would make the perfect girl,'" an announcement that gladdens the narrator since "unlike Pammy I was flat chested" (Campbell 26). Similarly, in the chapter titled "The Vegetable" in Marjane Satrapi's *Persepolis 2*, the teenage narrator walks the reader through each of her physical changes, which, she explains, culminate in an overall "ugly stage seemingly without end" (35). In both stories, the narrators condemn their physical flaws, suggesting that such imperfections mar their identities.

Images of body parts abound in both narratives. For example, 3 sprinkled throughout "Sleepover" are the words "face," "head," "body," "mouth," "throat," "collarbone," "pelvis," "eyeball," "tongue," "ear," "hands," "knees," "eyes," "hair," and "feet" (26). Likewise, "The Vegetable" in *Persepolis 2* shows, frame by frame, each of the narrator's body parts that change as she goes through puberty. Both narratives focus on individual body parts to emphasize the girls' fixation on their appearance as well as the stories' overarching theme of self-fragmentation. This bodily imagery suggests that the girls' physical characteristics (and what they perceive as their imperfections) define who they are: flawed and fragmented.

Paragraph 3
The topic sentence (sentence 1) gives the second similarity. Supporting details include examples from the source. Note the inference drawn in the last two sentences.

In fact, as both narratives imply, the self-criticism that accompa- 4 nies female adolescence quickly becomes inflated, creating an illusion that such physical changes are actually grotesque, unnatural, and even inhuman. Both stories use imagery of monsters to convey the awkwardness that the teenage girls feel. "Sleepover" concludes with a scene in which, after the boys are gone, the two girls watch a video of *Frankenstein.* Pammy drifts off, leaving the narrator alone to observe how "the men from the town band together to kill the monster" (Campbell 26). The story positions the narrator in opposition to the boy who insults her in the beginning and, in the end, implicitly compares the narrator to a monster being hunted by men. Similarly, "The Vegetable" in *Persepolis 2* opens with the cell shown on the next page that depicts the narrator as a brute. This image shows an exaggerated caricature of the narrator, who appears as a hulking monster bursting through her clothes with gripped fists. Her snarling expression and hair on end, coupled with the wavy motion lines surrounding her, contribute to a sense of monstrous fury. The grotesque imagery in both stories conveys the intense feelings of isolation and weirdness that the narrators share.

Paragraph 4
The comparison continues with support from sources, including an image from the graphic novel. Note the critical analysis of and inferences about both stories.

Despite their similarities, Campbell's short-short story and Satrapi's 5 graphic novel use their different forms to create a different literary effect. As opposed to the subtler prose depiction in "Sleepover," the visual

Paragraph 5
The contrast begins; note the transition "despite their similarities." Supporting details are drawn from sources. Note synthesis of a third source, used to help explain the significance of the contrast.

MY MENTAL TRANSFORMATION WAS FOLLOWED BY MY PHYSICAL METAMORPHOSIS.

Marjane Satrapi, *Persepolis 2* (New York: Pantheon-Random, 2004; print; 35).

language of *Persepolis 2* more explicitly conveys the narrator's acute awareness of her body image. Candida Rifkind argues in "Drawn from Memory: Comics, Artists, and Intergenerational Auto/biography" that graphic narratives let authors explore self-image in ways not possible through text alone: "A single frame may contain multiple selves, just as, over the sequence of frames, that self may mutate. The cartoonist, unlike the prose writer, works in a medium the very syntax of which demands that the subject always be split and frequently be multiple" (403). Although both stories share a theme of self-fragmentation, the cells of "The Vegetable" in *Persepolis 2* visually portray female adolescence in all its upclose awkwardness and incongruence. As Rifkind suggests, the visual language of graphic narratives allows them to create intricate character sketches that fundamentally differ from their prose counterparts.

Although important contrasts distinguish prose narratives from graphic narratives, both "Sleepover" and *Persepolis 2* efficiently and vibrantly convey the rich complexity of female adolescence. In compact spaces, both stories explore in delightfully vivid and humorous ways the emotional and physical changes that teenage girls experience.

Paragraph 6
The conclusion restates that the two pieces have similarities and differences, but the similarities are the emphasis.

Works Cited

Campbell, Bonnie Jo. "Sleepover." *Southeast Review* 22.2 (2003): 26. Print.

Rifkind, Candida. "Drawn from Memory: Comics, Artists, and Intergenerational Auto/biography." *Canadian Review of American Studies* 38.3 (2008): 399–427. Web. 18 Dec. 2009.

Satrapi, Marjane. *Persepolis 2*. New York: Pantheon-Random, 2004. Print.

PEER REVIEW

Responding to "No Body's Perfect: Female Self-Image in Two Narratives"

Analyze and assess "No Body's Perfect: Female Self-Image in Two Narratives" by responding to these questions:

1. Does the essay hold your interest? Why or why not?
2. Are the introduction and conclusion effective? Why or why not?
3. Do the supporting details adequately develop the thesis? Are they well balanced between subjects? Explain.
4. Is the use of source material effective? Explain.
5. Is the organizational pattern that was chosen appropriate? Why or why not?
6. Is the word choice effective? Explain.
7. What do you like best about the essay?
8. What one revision would you advise the writer to make? How would that revision improve the essay or help the author achieve her purpose?

EXAMINING VISUALS Comparison-Contrast in a Photograph

In the *Spider-Man* movies, Tobey Maguire stars as both the action hero, Spider-Man, and his alter ego, the shy and studious Peter Parker. The picture here is a still from the first *Spider-Man* movie (2002). When you study it, you may be surprised by the extent to which it incorporates comparisons and contrasts of two aspects of one individual.

- What comparison or comparisons are implied by this movie still?
- What contrast or contrasts are implied?
- Do the comparisons and contrasts you noted help explain the popularity of the Spider-Man character? The *Spider-Man* movies?

BACKGROUND: Born in Michigan and educated at Oberlin College until World War I interrupted his studies, historian Bruce Catton—pronounced "Cayton"—(1899–1978) was an authority on the Civil War. He became fascinated by the subject as a child when he heard the stories of the war veterans living in his community. He published extensively on the Civil War, including the Pulitzer Prize–winning book *A Stillness at Appomattox* (1953). Before turning to full-time literary work, Catton was a newspaper reporter in Boston and Cleveland and a public official. His work with the War Production Board during World War II led to his first major book, *The War Lords of Washington* (1948). In 1954, Catton became the editor of *American Heritage* magazine, a position he held until his death. Catton's books on the military history of the Civil War include *Mr. Lincoln's Army* (1951), *Glory Road* (1952), *This Hallowed Ground* (1956), *Grant Moves South* (1960), *Grant Takes Command* (1969), *The Centennial History of the Civil War* (3 vols., 1961–65), and *Prefaces to History* (1970). For his achievements, President Gerald Ford awarded Catton the Medal of Freedom. "Grant and Lee: A Study in Contrasts" was first published in *The American Story* (1956), a collection of essays by historians.

www.mhhe.com/clousepatterns6   Bruce Catton

For more information on this author, go to

More resources > Chapter 9 > Bruce Catton

THE PATTERN AND ITS PURPOSE: In "Grant and Lee: A Study in Contrasts," Bruce Catton *compares and contrasts* the Civil War's most important military officers to **inform** the reader that each man's personality reflected the side he represented. However, Catton does more than inform; he makes history come alive for the reader.

Grant and Lee: A Study in Contrasts
BY BRUCE CATTON

When Ulysses S. Grant and Robert E. Lee met in the parlor of a modest house at Appomattox Court House, Virginia, on April 9, 1865, to work out the terms for the surrender of Lee's Army of Northern Virginia, a great chapter in American life came to a close, and a great new chapter began.

As you read
Determine how Catton makes history come alive for the reader.

2   These men were bringing the Civil War to its virtual finish. To be sure, other armies had yet to surrender, and for a few days the fugitive Confederate government would struggle desperately and vainly, trying to find some way to go on living now that its chief support was gone. But in effect it was all over when Grant and Lee signed the papers. And the little room where they wrote out the terms was the scene of one of the poignant, dramatic contrasts in American history.

3   They were two strong men, these oddly different generals, and they represented the strengths of two conflicting currents that, through them, had come into final collision.

4   Back of Robert E. Lee was the notion that the old aristocratic concept might somehow survive and be dominant in American life.

Generals Robert E. Lee (left) and Ulysses S. Grant (right)

5   Lee was tidewater Virginia, and in his background were family, culture, and tradition . . . the age of chivalry transplanted to a New World which was making its own legends and its own myths. He embodied a way of life that had come down through the age of knighthood and the English country squire. America was a land that was beginning all over again, dedicated to nothing much more complicated than the rather hazy belief that all men had equal rights and should have an equal chance in the world. In such a land Lee stood for the feeling that it was somehow of advantage to human society to have a pronounced inequality in the social structure. There should be a leisure class, backed by ownership of land; in turn, society itself should be keyed to the land as the chief source of wealth and influence. It would bring forth (according to this ideal) a class of men with a strong sense of obligation to the community; men who lived not to gain advantage for themselves, but to meet the solemn obligations which had been laid on them by the very fact that they were privileged. From them the country would get its leadership; to them it could look for the higher values—of thought, of conduct, of personal deportment— to give it strength and virtue.

6   Lee embodied the noblest elements of this aristocratic ideal. Through him, the landed nobility justified itself. For four years, the Southern states had fought a

desperate war to uphold the ideals for which Lee stood. In the end, it almost seemed as if the Confederacy fought for Lee; as if he himself was the Confederacy . . . the best thing that the way of life for which the Confederacy stood could ever have to offer. He had passed into legend before Appomattox. Thousands of tired, underfed, poorly clothed Confederate soldiers, long since past the simple enthusiasm of the early days of the struggle, somehow considered Lee the symbol of everything for which they had been willing to die. But they could not quite put this feeling into words. If the Lost Cause, sanctified by so much heroism and so many deaths, had a living justification, its justification was General Lee.

7   Grant, the son of a tanner on the Western frontier, was everything Lee was not. He had come up the hard way and embodied nothing in particular except the eternal toughness and sinewy fiber of the men who grew up beyond the mountains. He was one of a body of men who owed reverence and obeisance to no one, who were self-reliant to a fault, who cared hardly anything for the past but who had a sharp eye for the future.

8   These frontier men were the precise opposite of the tidewater aristocrats. Back of them, in the great surge that had taken people over the Alleghenies and into the opening Western country, there was a deep, implicit dissatisfaction with a past that had settled into grooves. They stood for democracy, not from any reasoned conclusion about the proper ordering of human society, but simply because they had grown up in the middle of democracy and knew how it worked. Their society might have privileges, but they would be privileges each man had won for himself. Forms and patterns meant nothing. No man was born to anything, except perhaps to a chance to show how far he could rise. Life was competition.

9   Yet along with this feeling had come a deep sense of belonging to a national community. The Westerner who developed a farm, opened a shop, or set up in business as a trader, could hope to prosper only as his own community prospered— and his community ran from the Atlantic to the Pacific and from Canada down to Mexico. If the land was settled, with towns and highways and accessible markets, he could better himself. He saw his fate in terms of the nation's own destiny. As its horizons expanded, so did his. He had, in other words, an acute dollars-and-cents stake in the continued growth and development of his country.

10   And that, perhaps, is where the contrast between Grant and Lee becomes most striking. The Virginia aristocrat, inevitably, saw himself in relation to his own region. He lived in a static society which could endure almost anything except change. Instinctively, his first loyalty would go to the locality in which that society existed. He would fight to the limit of endurance to defend it, because in defending it he was defending everything that gave his own life its deepest meaning.

11   The Westerner, on the other hand, would fight with an equal tenacity for the broader concept of society. He fought so because everything he lived by was tied to growth, expansion, and a constantly widening horizon. What he lived by would survive or fall with the nation itself. He could not possibly stand by unmoved in the face of an attempt to destroy the Union. He would combat it with everything he had, because he could only see it as an effort to cut the ground out from under his feet.

12   So Grant and Lee were in complete contrast, representing two diametrically opposed elements in American life. Grant was the modern man emerging; beyond

him, ready to come on the stage, was the great age of steel and machinery, of crowded cities and a restless burgeoning vitality. Lee might have ridden down from the old age of chivalry, lance in hand, silken banner fluttering over his head. Each man was the perfect champion of his cause, drawing both his strengths and his weaknesses from the people he led.

13   Yet it was not all contrast, after all. Different as they were—in background, in personality, in underlying aspiration—these two great soldiers had much in common. Under everything else, they were marvelous fighters. Furthermore, their fighting qualities were really very much alike.

14   Each man had, to begin with, the great virtue of utter tenacity and fidelity. Grant fought his way down the Mississippi Valley in spite of acute personal discouragement and profound military handicaps. Lee hung on in the trenches of Petersburg after hope itself had died. In each man there was an indomitable quality . . . the born fighter's refusal to give up as long as he can still remain on his feet and lift his two fists.

15   Daring and resourcefulness they had, too; the ability to think faster and move faster than the enemy. These were the qualities which gave Lee the dazzling campaigns of Second Manassas and Chancellorsville and won Vicksburg for Grant.

16   Lastly, and perhaps greatest of all, there was the ability, at the end, to turn quickly from war to peace once the fighting was over. Out of the way these two men behaved at Appomattox came the possibility of a peace of reconciliation. It was a possibility not wholly realized, in the years to come, but which did, in the end, help the two sections to become one nation again . . . after a war whose bitterness might have seemed to make such a reunion wholly impossible. No part of either man's life became him more than the part he played in their brief meeting in the McLean house at Appomattox. Their behavior there put all succeeding generations of Americans in their debt. Two great Americans, Grant and Lee—very different, yet under everything very much alike. Their encounter at Appomattox was one of the great moments of American history.

READING CLOSELY AND THINKING CRITICALLY

1. According to Catton, how were Grant and Lee different and how were they similar? What is the most significant point of contrast between the generals? What is the most significant point of similarity?

2. According to Catton, why do Americans owe a debt to Grant and Lee?

3. Catton says that Grant and Lee represented conflicting forces in American society. What were those forces?

4. What do you think Catton's attitude toward the generals is? Does he admire one more than the other? Explain.

5. Why doesn't Catton contrast the two generals' conflicting views on slavery? Do you think he should have? Explain.

EXAMINING STRUCTURE AND STRATEGY

1. Bruce Catton was a historian. Do you think his essay was written for an audience of historians or for a different audience? How do you know?
2. Which sentence states Catton's thesis? What words in the thesis indicate that Catton will compare and contrast his subjects?
3. Catton organizes details with both block and alternating patterns. Which paragraphs include the block pattern, and which include the alternating pattern?
4. Why does Catton discuss the differences between Grant and Lee before he discusses the similarities?
5. How does Catton use description to make history come alive for the reader?

CONSIDERING LANGUAGE AND STYLE

1. What metaphor appears in paragraph 1? (See page 128 on metaphors.) Why is that metaphor appropriate? Explain.
2. Catton uses transitions effectively. Cite three examples of transitions in the essay, and explain how they contribute to the coherence of the essay.
3. Consult a dictionary if you are unsure of the meaning of any of these words: *poignant* (paragraph 2), *tidewater* (paragraph 5), *chivalry* (paragraph 5), *squire* (paragraph 5), *deportment* (paragraph 5), *sinewy* (paragraph 7), *obeisance* (paragraph 7), *static* (paragraph 10), *diametrically* (paragraph 12), *burgeoning* (paragraph 12), *tenacity* (paragraph 14), *fidelity* (paragraph 14), *indomitable* (paragraph 14).

FOR DISCUSSION IN CLASS OR ONLINE

Catton closes by saying that Grant and Lee's "encounter at Appomattox was one of the great moments of American history." What do you think Catton means by "great"? According to that definition, what other moments in American history do you consider great? Why?

WRITING ASSIGNMENTS

1. **Writing in your journal.** In a page or so, write what you learned about Grant, Lee, and the Civil War as a result of reading "Grant and Lee: A Study in Contrasts." Would you like to learn more? Why or why not?
2. **Using comparison-contrast for a purpose.** The purposes in the assignments are possibilities. You may establish whatever purpose you like, within your instructor's guidelines.
   - To inform, compare and contrast (or simply contrast) two people who do the same thing, such as two teachers, two coaches, two rock musicians, two baseball players, or two actors.
   - To inform and perhaps persuade, compare and contrast (or simply contrast) two people who represent two value systems or philosophies of life. You might consider

a coach who believes that winning is everything and a coach who does not, a liberal politician and a conservative politician, or a micromanager and someone who delegates.

- To entertain and perhaps inform, compare and contrast (or simply contrast) the way men and women do something. You might consider the way men and women communicate, argue, diet, work out, or watch football.

3. **Combining patterns.** Are Grant and Lee heroes? Answer this question by defining a hero and comparing or contrasting a hero with Grant and Lee. (Definition is discussed in Chapter 12.)

4. **Analyzing and assessing.** "Grant and Lee: A Study in Contrasts" is a classic essay that has for many years been frequently reprinted in college anthologies like this one. Why do you think it has been reprinted so often? Does the essay deserve to be considered a classic? Be sure to support your points with evidence from the essay.

5. **Connecting and synthesizing the readings.** Consider to what extent contrasting value systems, like those represented in "Grant and Lee: A Study in Contrasts," are responsible for human suffering. In addition to your own thinking, you can draw on ideas in Catton's essay as well as those in "On Being the Target of Discrimination" (page 262) and "Untouchables" (page 275).

6. **Drawing on sources.** Grant and Lee each represented a force in American society. Pick someone who represents a force in contemporary society (for example, Bono, Oprah Winfrey, Rush Limbaugh, or Al Gore), and explain what the force is and how the person's behavior represents the force. For help, use the search engine of your choice and type in the person's name as keywords, or look up the person's name in your library in the *New York Times Index, Proquest,* or the *Reader's Guide to Periodical Literature.*

BACKGROUND: Writer and teacher Anne Fadiman has been an editor of *Life, Civilization,* and *The American Scholar,* the literary magazine published by the Phi Beta Kappa Society. She has written for many publications, including *Harper's,* the *New Yorker,* the *New York Times,* and the *Washington Post.* While writing for *Life,* she won a National Magazine Award for Reporting for her account of suicide among the elderly. Her books include *The Spirit Catches You and You Fall Down: A Hmong Child, Her American Doctors, and the Collision of Two Cultures* (1997), which chronicles the experiences of an epileptic child and for which she won the National Book Critics Circle Award. She also wrote *Ex Libris: Confessions of a Common Reader* (1998), which is about buying, reading, and handling books. "Never Do That to a Book" is from *Ex Libris.*

COMBINED PATTERNS AND THEIR PURPOSES: In "Never Do That to a Book," an **entertaining** essay, Anne Fadiman *contrasts* two kinds of readers using *exemplification* to help make her points and to help her **express her feelings** and **relate her experience.**

Never Do That to a Book

BY ANNE FADIMAN

When I was eleven and my brother was thirteen, our parents took us to Europe. At the Hôtel d'Angleterre in Copenhagen, as he had done virtually every night of his literate life, Kim left a book face down on the bedside table. The next afternoon, he returned to find the book closed, a piece of paper inserted to mark the page, and the following note, signed by the chambermaid, resting on its cover:

SIR, YOU MUST NEVER DO THAT TO A BOOK.

2   My brother was stunned. How could it have come to pass that he—a reader so devoted that he'd sneaked a book and flashlight under the covers at his boarding school every night after lights-out, a crime punishable by a swat with a wooden paddle—had been branded as *someone who didn't love books?* I shared his mortification. I could not imagine a more bibliolatrous family than the Fadimans. Yet, with the exception of my mother, in the eyes of the young Danish maid we would all have been found guilty of rampant book abuse.

As you read
Decide whether Fadiman means everything she says, or whether she is merely going for laughs in some instances.

3   During the next thirty years I came to realize that just as there is more than one way to love a person, so is there more than one way to love a book. The chambermaid believed in courtly love. A book's physical self was sacrosanct to her, its form inseparable from its content; her duty as a lover was Platonic adoration, a noble but doomed attempt to conserve forever the state of perfect chastity in which it had left the bookseller. The Fadiman family believed in carnal love. To us, book's *words* were holy, but the paper, cloth, cardboard, glue, thread, and ink that contained them were a mere vessel, and it was no sacrilege to treat them as wantonly as desire and pragmatism dictated. Hard use was a sign not of disrespect but of intimacy.

4   Hilaire Belloc,[1] a courtly lover, once wrote:

Child do not throw this book about;
Refrain from the unholy pleasure
Of cutting all the pictures out!
Preserve it as your chiefest treasure.

5   What would Belloc have thought of my father, who, in order to reduce the weight of the paperbacks he read on airplanes, tore off the chapters he had completed and threw them in the trash? What would he have thought of my husband, who reads in the sauna, where heat-fissioned pages drop like petals in a storm? What would he have thought (here I am making a brazen attempt to upgrade my family by association) of Thomas Jefferson, who chopped up a priceless 1572 first edition of Plutarch's[2] works in Greek in order to interleave its pages with an English translation? Or of my old editor Byron Dobell, who, when he was researching an article on the Grand Tour,[3] once stayed up all night reading six volumes of Boswell's[4] journals and, as he puts it, "sucked them like a giant mongoose"? Byron told me, "I didn't give a damn about the condition of those volumes. In order to get where I had to go, I underlined them, wrote in them, shredded them, dropped them, tore them to pieces, and did things to them that we can't discuss in public."

6   Byron loves books. Really, he does. So does my husband, an incorrigible book-splayer whose roommate once informed him, "George, if you ever break the spine of one of my books, I want you to know you might as well be breaking *my own spine*." So does Kim, who reports that despite his experience in Copenhagen, his bedside table currently supports three spreadeagled volumes. "They are ready in an instant to let me pick them up," he explains. "To use an electronics analogy, closing a book on a bookmark is like pressing the Stop button, whereas when you leave the book facedown, you've only pressed Pause." I confess to marking my place promiscuously, sometimes splaying, sometimes committing the even more grievous sin of dog-earing the page. (Here I manage to be simultaneously abusive and compulsive: I turn down the upper corner for page-marking and the lower corner to identify passages I want to xerox for my commonplace book.)

7   All courtly lovers press Stop. My Aunt Carol—who will probably claim she's no relation once she finds out how I treat my books—places reproductions of Audubon paintings horizontally to mark the exact paragraph where she left off. If the colored side is up, she was reading the left-hand page; if it's down, the right-hand page. A college classmate of mine, a lawyer, uses his business cards, spurning his wife's silver Tiffany bookmarks because they are a few microns too thick and might leave vestigial stigmata. Another classmate, an art historian, favors Paris Métro tickets or "those inkjet-printed credit card receipts—but only in books of art criticism

---

[1]Hilaire Belloc (1870–1953) was a poet who was born in France but lived in England.
[2]Plutarch of Chaeronea (c.46–c.122) was a Greek philosopher and author.
[3]Wealthy young Englishmen of the seventeenth and eighteenth centuries often traveled around Europe for two or more years to broaden their horizons.
[4]James Boswell (1740–1795) was a Scottish essayist and diarist.

whose pretentiousness I wish to desecrate with something really crass and financial. I would never use those in fiction or poetry, which really *are* sacred."

8   Courtly lovers always remove their bookmarks when the assignation is over; carnal lovers are likely to leave romantic mementos, often three-dimensional and messy. *Birds of Yosemite and the East Slope,* a volume belonging to a science writer friend, harbors an owl feather and the tip of a squirrel's tail, evidence of a crime scene near Tioga Pass. A book critic I know took *The Collected Stories and Poems of Edgar Allan Poe* on a backpacking trip through the Yucatán, and whenever an interesting bug landed in it, she clapped the covers shut. She amassed such a bulging insectarium that she feared Poe might not make it through customs. (He did.)

9   The most permanent, and thus to the courtly lover the most terrible, thing one can leave in a book is one's own words. Even I would never write in an encyclopedia (except perhaps with a No. 3 pencil, which I'd later erase). But I've been annotating novels and poems—transforming monologues into dialogues—ever since I learned to read. Byron Dobell says that his most beloved books, such as *The Essays of Montaigne,* have been written on so many times, in so many different periods of his life, in so many colors of ink, that they have become palimpsests. I would far rather read Byron's copy of Montaigne than a virginal one from the bookstore, just as I would rather read John Adams's copy of Mary Wollstonecraft's *French Revolution,* in whose margins he argued so vehemently with the dead author ("Heavenly times!" "A barbarous theory." "Did this lady think three months time enough to form a free constitution for twenty-five millions of Frenchmen?") that, two hundred years later, his handwriting still looks angry.

10   Just think what courtly lovers miss by believing that the only thing they are permitted to do with books is *read* them! What do they use for shims, doorstops, glueing weights, and rug-flatteners? When my friend the art historian was a teenager, his cherished copy of *D'Aulaire's Book of Greek Myths* served as a drum pad on which he practiced percussion riffs from Led Zeppelin. A philosophy professor at my college, whose baby became enamored of the portrait of David Hume on a Penguin paperback, had the cover laminated in plastic so her daughter could cut her teeth on the great thinker. Menelik II, the emperor of Ethiopia at the turn of the century, liked to chew pages from his Bible. Unfortunately, he died after consuming the complete Book of Kings. I do not consider Menelik's fate an argument for keeping our hands and teeth off our books; the lesson to be drawn, clearly, is that he, too, should have laminated his pages in plastic.

11   "How beautiful to a genuine lover of reading are the sullied leaves, and worn-out appearance . . . of an old 'Circulating Library' Tom Jones, or Vicar of Wakefield!" wrote Charles Lamb.[5] "How they speak of the thousand thumbs that have turned over their pages with delight! . . . Who would have them a whit less soiled? What better condition could we desire to see them in?" Absolutely none. Thus, a landscape architect I know savors the very smell of the dirt embedded in his botany texts; it is the alluvium of his life's work. Thus, my friend the science writer considers her *Mammals of the World* to have been enhanced by the excremental splotches left by

---

[5]Charles Lamb (1775–1834) was an English essayist and critic.

Bertrand Russell, an orphaned band-tailed pigeon who perched on it when he was learning to fly. And thus, even though I own a clear plastic cookbook holder, I never use it. What a pleasure it will be, thirty years hence, to open *The Joy of Cooking* to page 581 and behold part of the *actual egg yolk* that my daughter glopped into her very first batch of blueberry muffins at age twenty-two months! The courtly mode simply doesn't work with small children. I hope I am not deluding myself when I imagine that even the Danish chambermaid, if she is now a mother, might be able to appreciate a really grungy copy of *Pat the Bunny*—a book that *invites* the reader to act like a Dobellian giant mongoose—in which Mummy's ring has been fractured and Daddy's scratchy face has been rubbed as smooth as the Blarney Stone.

12 The trouble with the carnal approach is that we love our books to pieces. My brother keeps his disintegrating *Golden Guide to Birds* in a Ziploc bag. "It consists of dozens of separate fascicles," says Kim, "and it's impossible to read. When I pick it up, the egrets fall out. But if I replaced it, the note I wrote when I saw my first trumpeter swan wouldn't be there. Also, I don't want to admit that so many species names have changed. If I bought a new edition, I'd feel I was being unfaithful to my old friend the yellow-bellied sapsucker, which has been split into three different species."

13 My friend Clark's eight thousand books, mostly works of philosophy, will never suffer the same fate as *The Golden Guide to Birds*. In fact, just *hearing* about Kim's book might trigger a nervous collapse. Clark, an investment analyst, won't let his wife raise the blinds until sundown, lest the bindings fade. He buys at least two copies of his favorite books, so that only one need be subjected to the stress of having its pages turned. When his visiting mother-in-law made the mistake of taking a book off the shelf, Clark shadowed her around the apartment to make sure she didn't do anything unspeakable to it—such as placing it facedown on a table.

14 I know these facts about Clark because when George was over there last week, he talked to Clark's wife and made some notes on the back fly-leaf of Herman Wouk's *Don't Stop the Carnival*, which he happened to be carrying in his backpack. He ripped out the page and gave it to me.

READING CLOSELY AND THINKING CRITICALLY

1. Fadiman contrasts carnal readers and courtly readers. In just a few sentences, explain the difference between the courtly and the carnal reader.

2. Fadiman thinks one kind of reader is superior to the other. Which one? How can you tell?

3. In addition to discussing differences between carnal readers and courtly readers, Fadiman compares the love of books with the love of people. What is the purpose of that comparison?

4. Why does Fadiman mention that Thomas Jefferson (paragraph 5) and John Adams (paragraph 9) were carnal readers?

EXAMINING STRUCTURE AND STRATEGY

1. Does Fadiman rely more on a block pattern or on an alternating pattern?
2. In paragraph 5, Fadiman uses a number of *rhetorical questions* (questions for which no answers are expected, often because they are obvious). What purpose do these rhetorical questions serve?
3. Does Fadiman achieve balance by treating the same points about both of her subjects? If so, what are those points? If not, is the lack of balance a problem? Explain.
4. At times, Fadiman includes exaggeration. For example, in paragraph 5, she reports Byron Dobell saying that he does things to books he "'can't discuss in public.'" Cite another example of exaggeration and explain the purpose it serves.

NOTING COMBINED PATTERNS

1. Fadiman uses a considerable number of examples. Cite three paragraphs that are developed with examples. How do the examples help her achieve her purpose for writing?
2. Fadiman opens with a brief narration or **anecdote.** Does the anecdote create an effective introduction? Explain.

CONSIDERING LANGUAGE AND STYLE

1. Fadiman's contrast is built upon her analogy of kinds of readers to kinds of lovers. How does that analogy affect the tone of the essay? (Tone is discussed on page 69.)
2. What similes appear in paragraphs 5 and 6? (See page 128 on similes.) How do the similes help Fadiman achieve her writing purpose?
3. Consult a dictionary if you are unsure of the meaning of these words: *bibliolatrous* (paragraph 2), *sacrosanct* (paragraph 3), *vestigial* (paragraph 7), *stigmata* (paragraph 7), *assignation* (paragraph 8), *palimpsests* (paragraph 9), *shim* (paragraph 10), *alluvium* (paragraph 11), *fascicles* (paragraph 12).

FOR DISCUSSION IN CLASS OR ONLINE

Are people who read online or with electronic reading devices different kinds of readers from those who read traditional print materials?

WRITING ASSIGNMENTS

1. **Writing in your journal.** In a page or two, discuss what kind of reader you are. If you like, you can answer one or more of the following questions: Do you think your reading skills are strong enough? Have your reading skills been adequate for your work in and outside of college? If you want to improve your skills, how can you do that?
2. **Using comparison-contrast for a purpose.** The purposes given here are possibilities. You may establish whatever purpose you like, within your instructor's guidelines.
   - Fadiman says there are two ways to love a person: in a courtly fashion and in a carnal fashion. Contrast two other ways to love a person romantically. Alternatively,

contrast two ways to love a person as a friend. Your purpose can be to inform, to relate experience, and/or to entertain.

- To entertain, compare and/or contrast readers in a way different from the way Fadiman does.

- To entertain, express feelings, and/or relate experience, contrast two kinds of writers.

- To entertain and perhaps inform, contrast two kinds of people who regularly use computers.

3. **Combining patterns.** Contrast two kinds of behavior other than reading that can be considered courtly or carnal. To clarify your points, use many examples, as Fadiman does.

4. **Analyzing and assessing.** Decide what kind of reader Fadiman is targeting, and determine what strategies she employs to achieve her purpose with that audience. Consider one or more of the following: her choice of examples and other details, her diction, and her tone. Be sure to cite specific evidence from the essay to support your points.

5. **Connecting and synthesizing the readings.** Sometimes people think that essays meant to entertain are not serious enough and don't make enough important points to be substantial like other essays. Drawing on "Never Do That to a Book," "Science: It's Just Not Fair" (page 307), and any other writing you care to cite, agree or disagree with that point of view.

6. **Drawing on sources.** A number of references in "Never Do That to a Book" may be unfamiliar to some average, general readers—references such as "Platonic adoration" in paragraph 3, "Grand Tour" in paragraph 5, and "Montaigne" in paragraph 9. Some of these references are footnoted, but not in much detail. Go through the essay and, using Internet and/or campus library resources, write a one-paragraph explanation for every reference you think might be unfamiliar to general readers. Avoid Wikipedia, which may be unreliable, but you might use your favorite search engine, refdesk.com, online dictionaries, and print encyclopedias.

BACKGROUND: Born to sharecroppers in Georgia in 1944, Alice Walker is the youngest of eight children. Walker's great-great-great-grandmother was a slave forced to walk from Virginia to Georgia with a baby in each arm, and her mother's grandmother was mostly Cherokee Indian. Walker began her formal education in rural schools. When she graduated from high school and prepared to leave for Spelman College, which she attended until transferring to Sarah Lawrence on a scholarship, Walker's mother gave her a sewing machine for self-sufficiency, a suitcase for independence, and a typewriter for creativity. Active in the civil rights movement, in 1962 Walker was invited to the home of Dr. Martin Luther King, Jr., and in 1963 she participated in the March on Washington, where she heard King's famous "I Have a Dream" speech. Walker also registered voters in Georgia, taught in the Head Start program in Mississippi, and worked in the welfare department in New York City. She won the Pulitzer Prize and the American Book Award for her most famous novel *The Color Purple* (1982). Walker's many books include *Possessing the Secret of Joy* (1992), *By the Light of My Father's Smile* (1998), *Letters of Love and Hope: The Story of the Cuban Five* (2005), and *Now Is the Time to Open Your Heart* (2005). Her poetry collections include *Once* (1968), *Horses Make a Landscape Look More Beautiful* (1985), and *Absolute Trust in the Goodness of the Earth* (2003). "Am I Blue?" first appeared in 1986 in *Ms* magazine.

---

www.mhhe.com/clousepatterns6　　　　　　　　Alice Walker

For more information on this author, go to

More resources > Chapter 9 > Alice Walker

COMBINED PATTERNS AND THEIR PURPOSES: In "Am I Blue?" Walker *narrates* a story that includes both *description* and *comparison-contrast* to **inform** readers about the oneness of animals and humans and to **persuade** readers to treat animals well and, perhaps, become a vegetarian. Her story also allows her to **express her feelings** and **relate her experience.** The title of the piece is the same as a great old blues song.

AM I BLUE?

BY ALICE WALKER

"Ain't these tears in these eyes tellin' you?"[1]

FOR ABOUT THREE YEARS my companion and I rented a small house in the country that stood on the edge of a large meadow that appeared to run from the end of our deck straight into the mountains. The mountains, however, were quite far away, and between us and them there was, in fact, a town. It was one of the many pleasant aspects of the house that you never really were aware of this.

As you read
Ask yourself
why the title is
so appropriate.

2　　It was a house of many windows, low, wide, nearly floor to ceiling in the living room, which faced the meadow, and it was from one of these that I first saw our closest neighbor, a large white horse, cropping grass, flipping its mane, and ambling about—not over the entire meadow, which stretched

[1]From "Am I Blue?" by Grant Clarke and Harry Akst. Copyright 1929 Warner Bros. Inc. (renewed).

well out of sight of the house, but over the five or so fenced-in acres that were next to the twenty-odd that we had rented. I soon learned that the horse, whose name was Blue, belonged to a man who lived in another town, but was boarded by our neighbors next door. Occasionally, one of the children, usually a stocky teenager, but sometimes a much younger girl or boy, could be seen riding Blue. They would appear in the meadow, climb up on his back, ride furiously for ten or fifteen minutes, then get off, slap Blue on the flanks, and not be seen again for a month or more.

3   There were many apple trees in our yard, and one by the fence that Blue could almost reach. We were soon in the habit of feeding him apples, which he relished, especially because by the middle of summer the meadow grasses—so green and succulent since January—had dried out from lack of rain, and Blue stumbled about munching the dried stalks halfheartedly. Sometimes he would stand very still just by the apple tree, and when one of us came out he would whinny, snort loudly, or stamp the ground. This meant, of course: I want an apple.

> "Sometimes he would stand very still just by the apple tree, and when one of us came out he would whinny, snort loudly, or stamp the ground."

4   It was quite wonderful to pick a few apples, or collect those that had fallen to the ground overnight, and patiently hold them, one by one, up to his large, toothy mouth. I remained as thrilled as a child by his flexible dark lips, huge, cubelike teeth that crunched the apples, core and all, with such finality, and his high, broad-breasted *enormity* beside which, I felt small indeed. When I was a child, I used to ride horses, and was especially friendly with one named Nan until the day I was riding and my brother deliberately spooked her and I was thrown, head first, against the trunk of a tree. When I came to, I was in bed and my mother was bending worriedly over me; we silently agreed that perhaps horseback riding was not the safest sport for me. Since then I have walked, and prefer walking to horseback riding—but I had forgotten the depth of feeling one could see in horses' eyes.

5   I was therefore unprepared for the expression in Blue's. Blue was lonely. Blue was horribly lonely and bored. I was not shocked that this should be the case; five acres to tramp by yourself, endlessly, even in the most beautiful of meadows—and his was—cannot provide many interesting events, and once rainy season turned to dry that was about it. No, I was shocked that I had forgotten that human animals and non-human animals can communicate quite well; if we are brought up around animals as children we take this for granted. By the time we are adults we no longer remember. However, the animals have not changed. They are in fact *completed* creations (at least they seem to be, so much more than we) who are not likely *to* change; it is their nature to express themselves. What else are they going to express? And they do. And, generally speaking, they are ignored.

6   After giving Blue the apples, I would wander back to the house, aware that he was observing me. Were more apples not forthcoming then? Was that to be his sole entertainment for the day? My partner's small son had decided he

wanted to learn how to piece a quilt; we worked in silence on our respective squares as I thought . . .

7   Well, about slavery: about white children, who were raised by black people, who knew their first all-accepting love from black women, and then, when they were twelve or so, were told they must "forget" the deep levels of communication between themselves and "mammy" that they knew. Later they would be able to relate quite calmly, "My old mammy was sold to another good family." "My old mammy was _____." Fill in the blank. Many more years later a white woman would say: "I can't understand these Negroes, these blacks. What do they want? They're so different from us."

8   And about the Indians, considered to be "like animals" by the "settlers" (a very benign euphemism for what they actually were), who did not understand their description as a compliment.

9   And about the thousands of American men who marry Japanese, Korean, Filipina, and other non-English-speaking women and of how happy they report they are, *"blissfully,"* until their brides learn to speak English, at which point the marriages tend to fall apart. What then did the men see, when they looked into the eyes of the women they married, before they could speak English? Apparently only their own reflections.

10   I thought of society's impatience with the young. "Why are they playing the music so loud?" Perhaps the children have listened to much of the music of oppressed people their parents danced to before they were born, with its passionate but soft cries for acceptance and love, and they have wondered why their parents failed to hear.

11   I do not know how long Blue had inhabited his five beautiful, boring acres before we moved into our house; a year after we had arrived—and had also traveled to other valleys, other cities, other worlds—he was still there.

12   But then, in our second year at the house, something happened in Blue's life. One morning, looking out the window at the fog that lay like a ribbon over the meadow, I saw another horse, a brown one, at the other end of Blue's field. Blue appeared to be afraid of it, and for several days made no attempt to go near. We went away for a week. When we returned, Blue had decided to make friends and the two horses ambled or galloped along together, and Blue did not come nearly as often to the fence underneath the apple tree.

> "I saw another horse, a brown one, at the end of Blue's field."

13   When he did, bringing his new friend with him, there was a different look in his eyes. A look of independence, of self-possession, of inalienable *horse*ness. His friend eventually became pregnant. For months and months there was, it seemed to me, a mutual feeling between me and the horses of justice, of peace. I fed apples to them both. The look in Blue's eyes was one of unabashed "this is *it*ness."

14   It did not, however, last forever. One day, after a visit to the city, I went out to give Blue some apples. He stood waiting, or so I thought, though not beneath the tree. When I shook the tree and jumped back from the shower of apples, he made no move. I carried some over to him. He managed to half-crunch one. The rest he

let fall to the ground. I dreaded looking into his eyes—because I had of course noticed that Brown, his partner, had gone—but I did look. If I had been born into slavery, and my partner had been sold or killed, my eyes would have looked like that. The children next door explained that Blue's partner had been "put with him" (the same expression that old people used, I had noticed, when speaking of an ancestor during slavery who had been impregnated by her owner) so that they would mate and she conceive. Since that was accomplished, she had been taken back by her owner, who lived somewhere else.

15   Will she be back? I asked.

16   They didn't know.

17   Blue was like a crazed person. Blue *was,* to me, a crazed person. He galloped furiously, as if he were being ridden, around and around his five beautiful acres. He whinnied until he couldn't. He tore at the ground with his hooves. He butted himself against his single shade tree. He looked always and always toward the road down which his partner had gone. And then, occasionally, when he came up for apples, or I took apples to him, he looked at me. It was a look so piercing, so full of grief, a look so *human,* I almost laughed (I felt too sad to cry) to think there are people who do not know that animals suffer. People like me who have forgotten, and daily forget, all that animals try to tell us. "Every-thing you do to us will happen to you; we are your teachers, as you are ours. We are one lesson" is essentially it, I think. There are those who never once have even considered animals' rights: those who have been taught that animals actually want to be used and abused by us, as small children "love" to be frightened, or women "love" to be mutilated and raped . . . They are the great-grandchildren of those who honestly thought, because someone taught them this: "Women can't think," and "niggers can't faint." But most disturbing of all, in Blue's large brown eyes was a new look, more pain-ful than the look of despair: the look of disgust with human beings, with life; the look of hatred. And it was odd what the look of hatred did. It gave him, for the first time, the look of a beast. And what that meant was that he had put up a bar-rier within to protect himself from further violence; all the apples in the world wouldn't change that fact.

> "He looked always and always toward the road down which his partner had gone."

18   And so Blue remained, a beautiful part of our landscape, very peaceful to look at from the window, white against the grass. Once a friend came to visit and said, looking out on the soothing view: "And it *would* have to be a *white* horse; the very image of freedom." And I thought, yes, the animals are forced to become for us merely "images" of what they once so beautifully expressed. And we are used to drinking milk from containers showing "contented" cows, whose real lives we want to hear nothing about, eating eggs and drumsticks from "happy" hens, and munching hamburgers advertised by bulls of integrity who seem to command their fate.

19   As we talked of freedom and justice one day for all, we sat down to steaks. I am eating misery, I thought, as I took the first bite. And spit it out.

READING CLOSELY AND THINKING CRITICALLY

1. Walker compares Blue to a human being. In what ways are the horse and a person similar?

2. In paragraphs 7–10, Blue's relationship with people is compared to a number of other human relationships. What are those relationships? What is the common element in each of these comparisons?

3. Specifically, what messages do you think Walker is trying to communicate to her reader?

4. Blue is given human qualities throughout most of the essay. However, in paragraph 17, he becomes a "beast." Why? When he becomes beastlike, is he less like a human and more like an animal? Explain.

5. Walker says that Blue has feelings and the ability to communicate those feelings. Do you agree? Explain.

EXAMINING STRUCTURE AND STRATEGY

1. Which paragraph best presents Walker's focus and the ideas she wants to convey to her reader? Why does she wait so long to present her focus?

2. Do you think Walker's title is a good one? Why or why not?

3. "Am I Blue?" appeared in *Ms.* in 1986. What kind of audience was Walker reaching? Is the essay suited to that kind of audience? Explain.

NOTING COMBINED PATTERNS

1. Which paragraphs include description? How does the description help Walker achieve her purpose?

2. To what extent is "Am I Blue?" a narrative essay (an essay that tells a story)?

CONSIDERING LANGUAGE AND STYLE

1. **Verbal irony** occurs when a speaker or writer says one thing but clearly means the opposite or nearly the opposite. Explain the irony of the images of "'contented' cows," "'happy' hens," and bulls "who seem to command their fate" (paragraph 18).

2. Walker opens paragraph 17 with this simile: "Blue was like a crazed person." (Similes are explained on page 128.) Then she follows with the more literal "Blue *was*, to me, a crazed person." Explain this movement from a simile to a more literal statement.

3. Consult a dictionary if you are unsure of the meaning of either of these words: *inalienable* (paragraph 15) and *unabashed* (paragraph 13).

FOR DISCUSSION IN CLASS OR ONLINE

In paragraph 17, Walker notes that animals say to people, "'Everything you do to us will happen to you; we are your teachers, as you are ours. We are one lesson.'" Discuss what this quote means and indicate whether you agree or disagree with it.

WRITING ASSIGNMENTS

1. **Writing in your journal.** Should people show respect for animals by not eating meat? What about wearing leather and fur? Should people wear only material not made from animals? Explore your feelings on these matters.

2. **Using comparison-contrast for a purpose.** The purposes in the assignments are possibilities. You may establish whatever purpose you like, within your instructor's guidelines.

    *   In paragraph 9, Walker refers to "the thousands of American men who marry Japanese, Korean, Filipina, and other non-English-speaking women" who are happy "until their brides learn to speak English, at which point the marriages tend to fall apart." The marriages may have fallen apart because once the wives could express themselves, conflict ensued. To relate your experience and express your feelings, compare and contrast some aspect of your life before and after you spoke up about something and created conflict.

    *   Blue's existence changed dramatically after the other horse entered his life. To relate experience, express feelings, and perhaps inform, compare and contrast your life before and after someone entered it.

    *   Blue's existence changed dramatically again after the other horse was taken away. To relate experience, express feelings, and perhaps inform, compare and contrast your life before and after someone left it.

3. **Combining patterns.** Walker compares Blue to a human being because he can feel and express emotions. If you have a pet and believe that the pet has something in common with humans, compare the pet and a human being. Use description (explained in Chapter 5) and narration (explained in Chapter 6) to help make your points. Be careful to avoid obvious comparisons, such as "My cat, like people, must eat and drink daily."

4. **Analyzing and assessing.** Walker makes a number of points about people and animals. What are those points? How well does she convince you of their truth? Explain.

5. **Connecting and synthesizing the readings.** In paragraphs 17 and 18, Walker makes a case for vegetarianism. Explain her view, and drawing on the essay "The Deer at Providencia" (page 150), and your own ideas, agree or disagree with her.

6. **Drawing on sources.** State and defend your view on one or more of these questions: Are our food production techniques cruel to animals? If they are, can anything be done to eliminate that cruelty? Is the cruelty an unfortunate but necessary component of food production? If you need ideas, check the *Social Sciences Index* under the heading "Animals, treatment of." You can also type in the phrase "animal rights" at www.yahoo.com.

BACKGROUND: A writer who specializes in women's issues, Deborah Siegel also consults with organizations such as the National Council for Research on Women, the National Women's Studies Association, the Council on Contemporary Families, and the Woodhull Institute for Ethical Leadership in order to link research on women to media and policy. She was a research scholar at Barnard College's Barnard Center for Research on Women, where she helped launch the Web journal *The Scholar & Feminist Online.* Her articles on families, women, sex, and popular culture have appeared in *Psychology Today, The Progressive,* and a number of academic journals. Siegel has written *Sisterhood, Interrupted: From Radical Women to Girls Gone Wild* (2007) and co-edited the literary anthology *Only Child: Writers on the Singular Joys and Solitary Sorrows of Growing Up Solo* (2007). "The New Trophy Wife" first appeared in *Psychology Today* in 2004.

COMBINED PATTERNS AND THEIR PURPOSE: Deborah Siegel uses *comparison-contrast* and a bit of *exemplification* to **inform** readers that many men now value wives who are bright and accomplished more than ones who are merely beautiful. She also uses *cause-and-effect analysis* to **explain** the reasons for this phenomenon.

THE NEW TROPHY WIFE

BY DEBORAH SIEGEL

PETE BEEMAN, a 36-year-old sculptor, met Page Fortna, 34, on New Year's Eve 1997, while she was studying for a doctorate in political science. "I was totally impressed that she was getting a Ph.D.," recalls Beeman. "She has a powerhouse background that speaks of personal drive and dedication. It was attractive, not in a sexual way, but in a necessary way. I'm not interested in someone who doesn't have as much to offer me as I have to offer her."

2   Massimo Tassan-Solet met Karin Dauch at an Internet merger party in 2000. She introduced herself to the derivatives trader, now 36, by announcing, "Hi, I'm Karin, and I have to go now." "She was strong and unconventional in her approach, but she did it with humor," recalls Tassan-Solet of Dauch, who at age 29 owns doubleKappa, a Web design and branding company. "I don't look at people as a list of what they've done," says Tassan-Solet. "But what she's done is remarkable."

3   Beeman and Tassan-Solet aren't the only newlyweds who are proud of their wives' CVs.[1] New trends in the mating game—marrying someone like yourself—plus an unstable economy breathe new life into the term "peer marriage." In previous generations, successful doctors, lawyers and bankers sought wives who looked good, were well-bred and made a mean Stroganoff to boot. Now, more and more alpha males[2] are looking for something else from the A-list: accomplishment.

4   According to a recent Match.com poll, 48 percent of men (and an equal percentage of women) report dating partners who draw the same income they do. Twenty percent of men report dating women who earn more. Jim Pak, 34, was

As you read Think about whether the new preference Siegel explains marks a significant shift in preference or merely one kind of trophy being replaced for another.

---

[1]*CV* is short for "curriculum vitae." More detailed than a résumé, a curriculum vitae gives education, work experience, and skills for a person looking for a job in a college or university.

[2]An alpha male or an alpha female is the dominant member of a group.

introduced to Kristin Ketner, 38, a Harvard MBA and a hedge fund manager, through a mutual friend, who warned him not to be intimidated by her credentials. She was a research analyst for Goldman Sachs;[3] he was unemployed and playing a lot of golf. "In certain regards, she outshines me," says Pak of his wife. "She's more accomplished academically. People may be more impressed with her than with me." (Pak is now chief financial officer at an electronic stock trading services group.)

5   Men's attraction to professionally achieving mates is one piece of a much larger story. "We're experiencing a historic change in the things people want out of marriage, the reasons they enter into it and stay in it," says historian Stephanie Coontz of Evergreen State College in Olympia, Washington. Men in their 20s and 30s embarking on first marriages are relieved to no longer be the sole breadwinner and decision-maker, a burden many watched their fathers shoulder. "These men are truly redefining masculinity," says Terrence Real, a psychologist and author of *How Can I Get Through to You? Closing the Intimacy Gap Between Men and Women.* And the pursuit of a high-achiever is not solely the province of youth. Status-conscious tycoons want to have second marriages—and affairs—with alpha women. "Older men now want the most impressive achiever in the office. In the eyes of a man's peers, the woman with the career and degrees counts for more than Miss America," says Frank Pittman, psychiatrist to Atlanta's elite. "Status is attached to a woman who is successful, not to a woman with a perfectly pear-shaped ass."

> "Men's attraction to professionally achieving mates is one piece of a much larger story."

6   Common wisdom holds that men are socially programmed and biologically compelled to select women based on beauty and youth, physical traits that signal reproductive health. But many men today date "across" and, increasingly, "up" the axes of education and achievement, with less regard for age, or for the notorious "arm candy" factor.

7   "There's a higher degree of parity today between marital partners," observes Pak. "Men want a wife who reflects well in every aspect." In some circles, more eyebrows are raised when a guy marries a woman who doesn't match him in education or professional status. Says David, a single 33-year-old assistant professor at a prestigious university who routinely filters online dating ads using the criterion of education: "If I were with someone who wasn't of comparable intelligence, energy and drive, there'd be those who thought I'd wimped out and chosen a relationship where I could call the shots and be the all-powerful center."

8   "Showing up with a stacked bubblehead is like conspicuous consumption," agrees Real. "It's embarrassing to flag yourself as not interested in a real relationship." But is a woman's success sexy?

9   "Absolutely," says David. "And the absence of an attempt to do something interesting or difficult is a turnoff." Henry Kissinger may have been right: Power is the ultimate aphrodisiac.

---

[3]Goldman Sachs is an investment banking firm.

RISE OF THE POWER BRIDE

10　When Scott South, a sociologist at the University at Albany, State University of New York, examined the characteristics most desirable to black and white men ages 19 to 35, he found that a woman's ability to hold a steady job mattered more than her age, previous marriages, maternal status, religion or race. Men were more willing to marry women with more, rather than less, education than they themselves had. A wise move, since women today eclipse men in the rates at which they attain bachelor's and master's degrees, and the number of women pursuing higher education continues to steadily climb.

11　Many of today's grooms believe that through positive or negative example, their own moms set the stage for a high-octane wife. After his parents separated when he was 12, Jim Pak watched his mother raise three kids while pursuing an advanced degree in art history. "That kind of role model helps you not be intimidated by highly motivated, successful women," he says. Others view their mothers' lives as cautionary tales. "My mom was very unhappy that she had little energy for anything other than raising her four kids," says a groom who recently married a woman who works in finance. "I wouldn't want to marry someone who felt that unfulfilled."

12　"Our generation is highly cognizant of the divorce rate," adds Pak. "We learned from our parents' mistakes."

13　But it's not always easy. Charting a marital course markedly different from that of one's parents means there's no role model to consult. And today's alpha woman expects more of a domestic partnership—and an emotional connection—than her husband may have seen growing up. "Women are demanding more emotionally because logistically they don't have to get married," says Real. "They want guys to be articulate and open about their feelings." The trouble, finds Real, is that "most men today are not trained to do those things."

14　A solution to this impasse, says Barry McCarthy, a psychologist in Washington, D.C., who works with many high-achieving couples, is for spouses to communicate their expectations from the get-go: "It's great that the man is no longer the success object and the woman is no longer the sex object. But when people organize their lives differently from their cultures or families of origin, they have to make it work practically and emotionally. You have to negotiate before [marriage] how you're going to deal with the core issues of sex, money and kids."

THE UNROMANTIC BOTTOM LINE

15　There's another pragmatic reason men prize new high-earning brides. Our romantic ideals are always grounded in economic realities, from the Victorian marriage model to the 1980s masters of the universe for whom a standard-issue trophy wife was a badge of honor. Today's bearish market calls for couples to act as an economic unit. Families with two breadwinners have been in the majority since 1998, and single twentysomethings' and thirtysomethings' desire for a two-income merger has intensified in the shadow of the recession. Women still earn less than men (78 cents to the male dollar) and seriously lag in the highest-paying sectors, like engineering, investment banking and high tech. But wives have been catching up to or surpassing their husbands since the 1980s, particularly among the well-off. (Of wives who earn more than $100,000, one in three is now married to a husband earning less.)

16   "It used to be that men were a good catch because they were high earners. It now looks like this applies to women, too," says University of Wisconsin economist Maria Cancian, who recently teamed up with Megan Sweeney, a University of California, Los Angeles sociologist, to study the increased importance of wives' wages.

17   How openly embraced is the prospect of a female breadwinner? According to Pak, a 30-year-old today is much less likely than his father to correlate his self-worth with his ability to provide for a family. Pak's wife, Ketner, believes that men who are comfortable with themselves will factor a potential bride's income into the marital calculus, as women have long done. Says Page Fortna, "Men think, 'If we combined our two incomes, how would we do?' But I wouldn't say it's flipped [to the point where] men say, 'I won't have to work, I'll just live off her.'"

> "How openly embraced is the prospect of a female breadwinner?"

18   Real is more emphatic: "Men aren't just OK with it. They're relieved." Men have long considered traditional marital roles "anemic and constricting," according to Real, and no longer being the sole breadwinner is a loosening of the straitjacket. Not to mention the improved standard of living. "These guys aren't worried about their male ego in relation to their wife's income," says Real. "They just want to plan a nice vacation together."

19   If financial straits make alpha women hot commodities for younger men, then financial and social status make these same women desirable to older men seeking a mistress or second wife. "Men have always chosen women who make them feel heroic," states Pittman. "It used to be sufficient to be the hero in your wife's and children's eyes. But when narcissistic men feel they've undermarried and their kids are grown, the real audience becomes your peers, the guys who are eating their hearts out because you've just married a former stripper turned circuit court judge."

20   Powerful men seek powerful wives, and in an era in which power is increasingly equated with intellectual capital, that translates into wives who match or perhaps even exceed their husbands in educational and professional status. (Think Candace Carpenter, founder of iVillage and second wife of Random House president and CEO Peter Olson.)

21   If men in first marriages are relieved to be outearned by spouse or partner, some older men are positively "proud" of this fact, finds Pittman, who also notes a spike in the number of thirtysomething and fortysomething men pursuing older, successful women. But when it comes to second wives, some things never change. Whether she's a 27-year-old secretary or a 47-year-old corporate vice president, the second wife will likely not be as beneficial a partner as was the first, says Pittman. "The woman who has seen a man get started and develop is more useful than the woman for whom he always has to perform, who may bring out the worst in him."

22   Alpha-alpha first and second marriages make sense against the backdrop of a shifting pecking order in the nation's governing class. As author David Brooks has

noted, changes in the prestige factor among couples whose wedding announce-ments make *The New York Times* bear this out. "Pedigreed elite used to be based on noble birth and breeding," writes Brooks in *Bobos in Paradise: The New Upper Class and How They Got There*. "Now it's genius that enables you to join the elect."

A CONFIDENCE GAP

23   If high-aiming women are more marriage-eligible than ever, why don't they seem to know it? When a Match.com poll asked marriage-minded men whether they were reluctant to seek out career women as partners, 62 percent said no. But 74 percent of the women surveyed think men are intimidated by women with high-powered careers. "Women have an asset they perceive as a liability," says Pepper Schwartz, author of *Love Between Equals: How Peer Marriage Really Works* and professor of sociol-ogy at the University of Washington. "Young men see these women growing up: She's your doctor, your teacher, your professor. These models can be quite erotic."

24   So why, then, the confidence gap? Men may be more intimidated by high-powered women than they're willing to admit. And high-achieving women, who tend to marry later, are used to being told that success causes their marrying and childbearing stock to plummet. Sylvia Ann Hewlett, author of *Creating a Life: Profes-sional Women and the Quest for Children,* made headlines in 2002 by recycling the claim that the more a woman achieves in the workplace, the less likely she is to marry or to have kids. The book triggered a panic reminiscent of *Newsweek*'s highly publicized 1986 report that a 40-year-old woman was more likely to be attacked by terrorists than to marry. That "finding" turned out to be a tale as tall as the heels on single icon Carrie Bradshaw's Manolo Blahniks,[4] and Hewlett's conclusions, based on a small sample of highly elite women, are equally suspect when applied to professionally ambitious women at large.

25   When Heather Boushey of the Center for Economic Policy Research in Wash-ington, D.C., crunched numbers on 33.6 million American women (gleaned from the 2000 and 2001 Current Population Survey), she found that women between the ages of 28 and 35 who work full time and earn more than $55,000 per year or have a graduate or professional degree are just as likely to be successfully married as other women who work full time. They're just finding love slightly later. While American women marry on average at age 25, college graduates marry at 27. Those with masters or professional degrees wed on average at age 30.

26   Pop-psych punditry about fragile male egos may cloud the real problem inher-ent in many alpha-alpha marriages. Psychologists agree that difficulties most often arise not because a man feels emasculated by his wife's star power ("No one can emasculate you except you," avows Pak), but because the woman grows disap-pointed with her partner.

27   "If a woman is powerful, smart and ambitious, her expectations for her hus-band, and for the relationship, rise," says Nando Pelusi, a New York City psy-chologist who has counseled plenty of alpha-alpha pairings. McCarthy says it's the

---

[4]Carrie, a character on the television program *Sex and the City* (1998–2004), often wore expensive Manolo Blahnik designer shoes.

primary reason that middle-class marriages fail in the first five years: The woman feels her spouse is not keeping his end of the pact.

28   And when women feel that their husbands aren't reaching their earning or emoting potential, men may decide they've gotten more than they bargained for. "Men truly want brighter, more articulate, aggressive women. They want to be seen in the world with them. But they also want these women to leave some of it at the doorstep," says Real. "These guys love their wives. They just haven't figured out what to do when that strength is channeled toward them."

"'Men truly want brighter, more articulate, aggressive women.'"

29   Real is quick to add that most wouldn't have it any other way. "I must have said it a thousand times," he quips: "'Mr. Jones, you wouldn't be happy with the kind of woman who would put up with you.'"

30   True to form, most alpha males take pride in the bumps. "If I can sustain a relationship with a real, serious, powerful, happening gal, it means that I'm more real, serious and happening," says Beeman.

31   "Being involved with these women is like driving a Ferrari," says Pelusi. "It can be uncomfortable and dangerous, but it's ultimately more rewarding than owning a Ford Taurus, which is safe but boring."

READING CLOSELY AND THINKING CRITICALLY

1.   Siegel contrasts the kind of wife men seek now and the kind they sought in the past. What is that contrast?

2.   Why are men seeking a different kind of wife?

3.   What stress occurs when an alpha male marries an alpha female?

4.   If so many men are valuing intellect and accomplishment more than appearance in women, why do you think so many women are still concerned about how they look?

5.   Explain the irony of the essay's title and the fact that many men now prefer bright, accomplished women.

EXAMINING STRUCTURE AND STRATEGY

1.   Where does Siegel state her thesis? Which words convey the subjects, and which indicate that contrast will occur?

2.   Does Siegel maintain balance between the discussions of the trophy wife of today and the trophy wife of past generations?

3.   Siegel uses many direct quotations. How do they help her make her contrasts and achieve her writing purpose?

4.   Siegel includes statistics and other data in paragraphs 4, 15, 23, and 25. How do these statistics and data help her achieve her writing purpose?

5.   The topic sentence of paragraph 17 is a question. Is using a question an effective way to express the topic sentence? Why or why not?

NOTING COMBINED PATTERNS

1. What cause-and-effect analysis (explained in Chapter 10) appears in the essay?
2. Siegel does more than contrast the kinds of women men marry today and those they married in past generations. In paragraph 15, she contrasts the earnings of men and women; in paragraph 21, she contrasts first and second wives; in paragraph 23, she contrasts the attitudes of men and women; and in paragraph 25, she compares and contrasts women of different ages and incomes. Why does she include this information?
3. What purpose do the examples in paragraphs 1 and 2 serve?

CONSIDERING LANGUAGE AND STYLE

1. Explain the meaning of the term *trophy wife.* Is the term apt? Does it have positive or negative connotations?
2. What simile appears in the last paragraph? What do you think of this simile? (Similes are explained on page 128.)
3. Consult a dictionary if you are unsure of the meaning of these words: *province* (paragraph 5), *parity* (paragraph 7), *cognizant* (paragraph 12), *pragmatic* (paragraph 15), *punditry* (paragraph 26).

FOR DISCUSSION IN CLASS OR ONLINE

Discuss what college students seek in a boyfriend or girlfriend. Are they after trophies? Alpha types? Why do college students seek certain traits in a boyfriend or girlfriend?

WRITING ASSIGNMENTS

1. **Writing in your journal.** In a page or two, describe your ideal spouse. Why do you value the characteristics you note?
2. **Using comparison-contrast for a purpose.** The purposes given in the assignments are possibilities. You may establish whatever purpose you like, within your instructor's guidelines.
    *   To inform, compare and/or contrast today's trophy husband with the trophy husband of some time in the past.
    *   In paragraph 6, Siegel notes a "common wisdom" that is not very true today: that men are socially and biologically "programmed" to choose beautiful, youthful women because such women are likely to have good reproductive health. Cite another common piece of wisdom that is not borne out by experience and observation, and to inform readers, contrast it with the reality. For example, you can contrast the common belief that women are not good at math with the evidence that many women excel at math; or you might contrast the common notion that student athletes are "dumb jocks" with the fact that many student athletes are very smart. Use examples to support your contrasts.

- In paragraph 13, Siegel notes the difficulty of charting a course "markedly different from that of one's parents." To relate experience and express feelings, compare and contrast something you have done that marks a departure from your parents' course.

3. **Combining patterns.** Contrast something other than trophy spouses, something that is different today from in the past. You might contrast schoolteachers, situation comedies, baseball, parenthood, etiquette, dating practices, or popular music, for example. Illustrate the change with examples, and use cause-and-effect analysis to explain the reasons for the change.

4. **Analyzing and assessing.** "The New Trophy Wife" has a scholarly quality. What features give it that quality? Despite its scholarly quality, is the essay still accessible and interesting to average readers? Why or why not?

5. **Connecting and synthesizing the readings.** Families have changed greatly in recent years. Drawing on the ideas in "The New Trophy Wife," and "Why the *M* Word Matters to Me" (page 428), along with your own ideas, discuss one or more ways that families have changed.

6. **Drawing on sources.** Ask at least 10 male college students to name the top three traits they seek in an ideal wife. Then, using your survey results for support, write an essay that explains to what extent students do and do not seek the kind of trophy wife Siegel describes. What do your responses suggest about the current state of marriage?

BACKGROUND: Born in 1945 and raised in Brooklyn, New York, linguist Deborah Tannen is a professor at Georgetown University. An authority on communication between the genders, Tannen has reported her research findings in many scholarly publications and in numerous news-paper and magazine articles. She has appeared on television programs such as *Today, Good Morning, America, CBS News, ABC World News Tonight, Oprah,* and *Larry King Live.* Tannen has lectured all over the world to audiences that have included corporations such as Corning, Chevron, Motorola, and Delta Air Lines. Her lectures often include videotaped footage of office interaction to help audiences understand what happens in conversations both in the workplace and at home. Tannen's books include *You Just Don't Understand: Men and Women in Conversation* (1990), which was on the *New York Times* best-seller list for almost four years; *Gender and Discourse* (1994); *I Only Say This Because I Love You: Talking to Your Parents, Partner, Sibs, and Kids When You're All Adults* (2001); *You're Wearing ***THAT?*** Understanding Mothers and Daughters in Con-versation* (2006), and *You Were Always Mom's Favorite: Sisters in Conversation throughout Their Lives* (2009). She has also published poetry, short stories, and personal essays. This essay first appeared in the *New York Times Magazine* in August 1994.

---

www.mhhe.com/clousepatterns6 | Deborah Tannen

For more information on this author, go to

More resources > Chapter 9 > Deborah Tannen

COMBINED PATTERNS AND THEIR PURPOSES: In "Squeaky Wheels and Protruding Nails: Direct and Indirect Speech," Deborah Tannen *defines* and *contrasts* direct and indirect forms of speech in order to **inform** readers about the nature of each communication style and to **persuade** readers that despite what they may think, one style is not better than the other. Tannen's conclusions are not just opinion, however; they are rooted in research findings, some of which appear in the essay.

SQUEAKY WHEELS AND PROTRUDING NAILS: DIRECT AND INDIRECT SPEECH BY DEBORAH TANNEN

A UNIVERSITY PRESIDENT was expecting a visit from a member of the board of trustees. When her secretary buzzed to tell her that the board member had arrived, she left her office and entered the reception area to greet him. Before ushering him into her office, she handed her secretary a sheet of paper and said: "I've just finished drafting this letter. Do you think you could type it right away? I'd like to get it out before lunch. And would you please do me a favor and hold all calls while I'm meeting with Mr. Smith?"

As you read Think about how the re-search findings given in the es-say are likely to affect readers.

2   When they sat down behind the closed door of her office, Mr. Smith began by telling her that he thought she had spoken inappropri-ately to her secretary. "Don't forget," he said. "*You're* the president!"

3   Putting aside the question of the appropriateness of his admonishing the president on her way of speaking, it is revealing—and representative of many

Americans' assumptions—that the indirect way in which the university president told her secretary what to do struck him as self-deprecating. He took it as evidence that she didn't think she had the right to make demands of her secretary. He probably thought he was giving her a needed pep talk, bolstering her self-confidence.

4   I challenge the assumption that talking in an indirect way necessarily reveals powerlessness, lack of self-confidence or anything else about the character of the speaker. Indirectness is a fundamental element in human communication. It is also one of the elements that varies most from one culture to another, and one that can cause confusion and misunderstanding when speakers have different habits with regard to using it. I also want to dispel the assumption that American women tend to be more indirect than American men. Women and men are both indirect, but in addition to differences associated with their backgrounds—regional, ethnic and class—they tend to be indirect in different situations and in different ways.

5   At work, we need to get others to do things, and we all have different ways of accomplishing this. Any individual's ways will vary depending on who is being addressed—a boss, a peer or a subordinate. At one extreme are bald commands. At the other are requests so indirect that they don't sound like requests at all, but are just a statement of need or a description of a situation. People with direct styles of asking others to do things perceive indirect requests—if they perceive them as requests at all—as manipulative. But this is often just a way of blaming others for our discomfort with their styles.

6   The indirect style is no more manipulative than making a telephone call, asking "Is Rachel there?" and expecting whoever answers the phone to put Rachel on. Only a child is likely to answer "Yes" and continue holding the phone—not out of orneriness but because of inexperience with the conventional meaning of the question. (A mischievous adult might do it to tease.) Those who feel that indirect orders are illogical or manipulative do not recognize the conventional nature of indirect requests.

7   Issuing orders indirectly can be the prerogative of those in power. Imagine, for example, a master who says "It's cold in here" and expects a servant to make a move to close a window, while a servant who says the same thing is not likely to see his employer rise to correct the situation and make him more comfortable. Indeed, a Frenchman raised in Brittany tells me that his family never gave bald commands to their servants but always communicated orders in indirect and highly polite ways. This pattern renders less surprising the finding of David Bellinger and Jean Berko Gleason that fathers' speech to their young children had a higher incidence than mothers' of both direct imperatives like "Turn the bolt with the wrench" *and* indirect orders like "The wheel is going to fall off."

8   The use of indirectness can hardly be understood without the cross-cultural perspective. Many Americans find it self-evident that directness is logical and aligned with power while indirectness is akin to dishonesty and reflects subservience. But for speakers raised in most of the world's cultures, varieties of indirectness are the norm in communication. This is the pattern found by a Japanese sociolinguist, Kunihiko Harada, in his analysis of a conversation he recorded between a Japanese boss and a subordinate.

9   The markers of superior status were clear. One speaker was a Japanese man in his late 40's who managed the local branch of a Japanese private school in the United States. His conversational partner was a Japanese-American woman in her early 20's who worked at the school. By virtue of his job, his age and his native fluency in the language being taught, the man was in the superior position. Yet when he addressed the woman, he frequently used polite language and almost always used indirectness. For example, he had tried and failed to find a photography store that would make a black-and-white print from a color negative for a brochure they were producing. He let her know that he wanted her to take over the task by stating the situation and allowed her to volunteer to do it: (This is a translation of the Japanese conversation.)

> On this matter, that, that, on the leaflet? This photo, I'm thinking of changing it to black-and-white and making it clearer . . . I went to a photo shop and asked them. They said they didn't do black-and-white. I asked if they knew any place that did. They said they didn't know. They weren't very helpful, but anyway, a place must be found, the negative brought to it, the picture developed.

10   Harada observes, "Given the fact that there are some duties to be performed and that there are two parties present, the subordinate is supposed to assume that those are his or her obligation." It was precisely because of his higher status that the boss was free to choose whether to speak formally or informally, to assert his power or to play it down and build rapport—an option not available to the subordinate, who would have seemed cheeky if she had chosen a style that enhanced friendliness and closeness.

11   The same pattern was found by a Chinese sociolinguist, Yuling Pan, in a meeting of officials involved in a neighborhood youth program. All spoke in ways that reflected their place in the hierarchy. A subordinate addressing a superior always spoke in a deferential way, but a superior addressing a subordinate could either be authoritarian, demonstrating his power, or friendly, establishing rapport. The ones in power had the option of choosing which style to use. In this spirit, I have been told by people who prefer their bosses to give orders indirectly that those who issue bald commands must be pretty insecure; otherwise why would they have to bolster their egos by throwing their weight around?

12   I am not inclined to accept that those who give orders directly are really insecure and powerless, any more than I want to accept that judgment of those who give indirect orders. The conclusion to be drawn is that ways of talking should not be taken as obvious evidence of inner psychological states like insecurity or lack of confidence. Considering the many influences on conversational style, individuals have a wide range of ways of getting things done and expressing their emotional states. Personality characteristics like insecurity cannot be linked to ways of speaking in an automatic, self-evident way.

13   Those who expect orders to be given indirectly are offended when they come unadorned. One woman said that when her boss gives her instructions, she feels she should click her heels, salute, and say "Yes, boss!" His directions strike her as so imperious as to border on the militaristic. Yet I received a letter from a man

telling me that indirect orders were a fundamental part of his military training. He wrote:

> Many years ago, when I was in the Navy, I was training to be a radio technician. One class I was in was taught by a chief radioman, a regular Navy man who had been to sea, and who was then in his third hitch. The students, about 20 of us, were fresh out of boot camp, with no sea duty and little knowledge of real Navy life. One day in class the chief said it was hot in the room. The students didn't react, except perhaps to nod in agreement. The chief repeated himself: "It's hot in this room." Again there was no reaction from the students.
>
> Then the chief explained. He wasn't looking for agreement or discussion from us. When he said that the room was hot, he expected us to do something about it—like opening the window. He tried it one more time, and this time all of us left our workbenches and headed for the windows. We had learned. And we had many opportunities to apply what we had learned.

14 This letter especially intrigued me because "It's cold in here" is the standard sentence used by linguists to illustrate an indirect way of getting someone to do something—as I used it earlier. In this example, it is the very obviousness and rigidity of the military hierarchy that makes the statement of a problem sufficient to trigger corrective action on the part of subordinates.

15 A man who had worked at the Pentagon reinforced the view that the burden of interpretation is on subordinates in the military—and he noticed the difference when he moved to a position in the private sector. He was frustrated when he'd say to his new secretary, for example, "Do we have a list of invitees?" and be told, "I don't know; we probably do" rather than "I'll get it for you." Indeed, he explained, at the Pentagon, such a question would likely be heard as a reproach that the list was not already on his desk.

16 The suggestion that indirectness is associated with the military must come as a surprise to many. But everyone is indirect, meaning more than is put into words and deriving meaning from words that are never actually said. It's a matter of where, when and how we each tend to be indirect and look for hidden meanings. But indirectness has a built-in liability. There is a risk that the other will either miss or choose to ignore your meaning.

17 On January 13, 1982, a freezing cold, snowy day in Washington, Air Florida Flight 90 took off from National Airport, but could not get the lift it needed to keep climbing. It crashed into a bridge linking Washington to the state of Virginia and plunged into the Potomac. Of the 79 people on board, all but 5 perished, many floundering and drowning in the icy water while horror-stricken bystanders watched helplessly from the river's edge and millions more watched, aghast, on their television screens. Experts later concluded that the plane had waited too long after deicing to take off. Fresh buildup of ice on the wings and engine brought the plane down. How could the pilot and co-pilot have made such a blunder? Didn't at least one of them realize it was dangerous to take off under these conditions?

18 Charlotte Linde, a linguist at the Institute for Research on Learning in Palo Alto, Calif., has studied the "black box" recordings of cockpit conversations that

preceded crashes as well as tape recordings of conversations that took place among crews during flight simulations in which problems were presented. Among the black box conversations she studied was the one between the pilot and co-pilot just before the Air Florida crash. The pilot, it turned out, had little experience flying in icy weather. The co-pilot had a bit more, and it became heartbreakingly clear on analysis that he had tried to warn the pilot, but he did so indirectly.

19   The co-pilot repeatedly called attention to the bad weather and to ice building up on other planes:

> *Co-pilot:*   Look how the ice is just hanging on his, ah, back, back there, see that? . . .
>
> *Co-pilot:*   See all those icicles on the back there and everything?
>
> *Captain:*   Yeah.

20   He expressed concern early on about the long waiting time between deicing:

> *Co-pilot:*   Boy, this is a, this is a losing battle here on trying to de-ice those things, it [gives] you a false feeling of security, that's all that does.

21   Shortly after they were given clearance to take off, he again expressed concern:

> *Co-pilot:*   Let's check these tops again since we been setting here awhile.
>
> *Captain:*   I think we get to go here in a minute.

22   When they were about to take off, the co-pilot called attention to the engine instrument readings, which were not normal:

> *Co-pilot:*   That don't seem right, does it? [three-second pause] Ah, that's not right . . .
>
> *Captain:*   Yes, it is, there's 80.
>
> *Co-pilot:*   Naw, I don't think that's right. [seven-second pause] Ah, maybe it is.
>
> *Captain:*   Hundred and twenty.
>
> *Co-pilot:*   I don't know.

23   The takeoff proceeded, and 37 seconds later the pilot and co-pilot exchanged their last words.

24   The co-pilot had repeatedly called the pilot's attention to dangerous conditions but did not directly suggest they abort the takeoff. In Linde's judgment, he was expressing his concern indirectly, and the captain didn't pick up on it—with tragic results.

25   That the co-pilot was trying to warn the captain indirectly is supported by evidence from another airline accident—a relatively minor one—investigated by Linde that also involved the unsuccessful use of indirectness.

26   On July 9, 1978, Allegheny Airlines Flight 453 was landing at Monroe County Airport in Rochester, when it overran the runway by 728 feet. Everyone survived. This meant that the captain and co-pilot could be interviewed. It turned out that the plane had been flying too fast for a safe landing. The captain should have realized

this and flown around a second time, decreasing his speed before trying to land. The captain said he simply had not been aware that he was going too fast. But the co-pilot told interviewers that he "tried to warn the captain in subtle ways, like mentioning the possibility of a tail wind and the slowness of flap extension." His exact words were recorded in the black box. The crosshatches indicate words deleted by the National Transportation Safety Board and were probably expletives:

Co-pilot:	Yeah, it looks like you got a tail wind here.
Captain:	Yeah. [?]: Yeah [it] moves awfully # slow.
Co-pilot:	Yeah the # flaps are slower than a #.
Captain:	We'll make it, gonna have to add power.
Co-pilot:	I know.

27   The co-pilot thought the captain would understand that if there was a tail wind, it would result in the plane going too fast, and if the flaps were slow, they would be inadequate to break the speed sufficiently for a safe landing. He thought the captain would then correct for the error by not trying to land. But the captain said he didn't interpret the co-pilot's remarks to mean they were going too fast.

28   Linde believes it is not a coincidence that the people being indirect in these conversations were the co-pilots. In her analyses of flight-crew conversations she found it was typical for the speech of subordinates to be more mitigated—polite, tentative or indirect. She also found that topics broached in a mitigated way were more likely to fail, and that captains were more likely to ignore hints from their crew members than the other way around. These findings are evidence that not only can indirectness and other forms of mitigation be misunderstood, but they are also easier to ignore.

29   In the Air Florida case, it is doubtful that the captain did not realize what the co-pilot was suggesting when he said, "Let's check these tops again since we been setting here awhile" (though it seems safe to assume he did not realize the gravity of the co-pilot's concern). But the indirectness of the co-pilot's phrasing certainly made it easier for the pilot to ignore it. In this sense, the captain's response, "I think we get to go here in a minute," was an indirect way of saying, "I'd rather not." In view of these patterns, the flight crews of some airlines are now given training to express their concerns, even to superiors, in more direct ways.

30   The conclusion that people should learn to express themselves more directly has a ring of truth to it—especially for Americans. But direct communication is not necessarily always preferable. If more direct expression is better communication, then the most direct-speaking crews should be the best ones. Linde was surprised to find in her research that crews that used the most mitigated speech were often judged the best crews. As part of the study of talk among cockpit crews in flight simulations, the trainers observed and rated the performances of the simulation crews. The crews they rated top in performance had a higher rate of mitigation than crews they judged to be poor.

31   This finding seems at odds with the role played by indirectness in the examples of crashes that we just saw. Linde concluded that since every utterance functions on two levels—the referential (what it says) and the relational (what it implies about

the speaker's relationships)—crews that attend to the relational level will be better crews. A similar explanation was suggested by Kunihiko Harada. He believes that the secret of successful communication lies not in teaching subordinates to be more direct, but in teaching higher-ups to be more sensitive to indirect meaning. In other words, the crashes resulted not only because the co-pilots tried to alert the captains to danger indirectly but also because the captains were not attuned to the co-pilots' hints. What made for successful performance among the best crews might have been the ability—or willingness—of listeners to pick up on hints, just as members of families or long-standing couples come to understand each other's meaning without anyone being particularly explicit.

32   It is not surprising that a Japanese sociolinguist came up with this explanation; what he described is the Japanese system, by which good communication is believed to take place when meaning is gleaned without being stated directly—or at all.

33   While Americans believe that "the squeaky wheel gets the grease" (so it's best to speak up), the Japanese say, "The nail that sticks out gets hammered back in" (so it's best to remain silent if you don't want to be hit on the head). Many Japanese scholars writing in English have tried to explain to bewildered Americans the ethics of a culture in which silence is often given greater value than speech, and ideas are believed to be best communicated without being explicitly stated. Key concepts in Japanese give a flavor of the attitudes toward language that they reveal—and set in relief the strategies that Americans encounter at work when talking to other Americans.

34   Takie Sugiyama Lebra, a Japanese-born anthropologist, explains that one of the most basic values in Japanese culture is *omoiyari,* which she translates as "empathy." Because of *omoiyari,* it should not be necessary to state one's meaning explicitly; people should be able to sense each other's meaning intuitively. Lebra explains that it is typical for a Japanese speaker to let sentences trail off rather than complete them because expressing ideas before knowing how they will be received seems intrusive. "Only an insensitive, uncouth person needs a direct, verbal, complete message," Lebra says.

35   *Sasshi,* the anticipation of another's message through insightful guesswork, is considered an indication of maturity.

36   Considering the value placed on direct communication by Americans in general, and especially by American business people, it is easy to imagine that many American readers may scoff at such conversational habits. But the success of Japanese businesses makes it impossible to continue to maintain that there is anything inherently inefficient about such conversational conventions. With indirectness, as with all aspects of conversational style, our own habitual style seems to make sense—seems polite, right and good. The light cast by the habits and assumptions of another culture can help us see our way to the flexibility and respect for other styles that is the only best way of speaking.

1. Why did the male board member criticize the female university president? Was his criticism either appropriate or helpful? Explain.
2. What determines whether an individual uses direct or indirect speech?
3. What problems are associated with indirect speech? With direct speech?
4. Explain why indirect speech is suited to spoken communication in the military.
5. Explain the communication problems that contributed to the airplane accidents mentioned in the essay. What problem with indirect communication do the accidents highlight? How can that problem be addressed?

EXAMINING STRUCTURE AND STRATEGY

1. Tannen opens her essay with an **anecdote** (a brief story). How does the anecdote help her achieve her purpose?
2. Tannen contrasts direct and indirect communication, but she also contrasts the cultural orientations of Americans and some Asians. Why does she include the latter contrast?
3. Throughout the essay, Tannen cites the research findings of others (in paragraphs 7, 9, and 10, for example). What do these citations contribute to the essay?

NOTING COMBINED PATTERNS

1. How does Tannen use cause-and-effect analysis and exemplification to achieve her purpose?
2. How does Tannen use definition in the essay?

CONSIDERING LANGUAGE AND STYLE

1. Although Tannen is a professor, a linguist, a scholar, and a researcher, she keeps her essay accessible and interesting for the typical reader of the *New York Times Magazine,* where the essay first appeared. Explain how Tannen's word choice helps make the essay accessible to a broad audience.
2. Why do linguists use "It's cold in here" as a standard sentence for illustrating indirect communication?
3. Consult a dictionary if you are unsure of the meaning of any of these words: *admonishing* (paragraph 3), *self-deprecating* (paragraph 3), *prerogative* (paragraph 7), *rapport* (paragraph 10), *cheeky* (paragraph 10), *imperious* (paragraph 13), *mitigated* (paragraph 28), *broached* (paragraph 28), *relief* (paragraph 33).

FOR DISCUSSION IN CLASS OR ONLINE

Explain the meaning of the last sentence of the essay. Do you agree with the statement? Why or why not?

1. **Writing in your journal.** Do you typically use direct or indirect speech when you make a request? Will you alter your style as a result of reading "Squeaky Wheels and Protruding Nails"? Why or why not?

2. **Using comparison-contrast for a purpose.** The purposes in the assignments are possibilities. You may establish whatever purpose you like, within your instructor's guidelines.

    - To inform and perhaps persuade that one style is better than the other, contrast the communication styles of two people in similar positions, such as two friends, two teachers, two supervisors, two coaches, or two talk show hosts.

    - To inform and perhaps persuade that one style is better than the other, contrast the communication styles of two different groups, such as physicians and patients, teachers and students, parents and teenagers, or East and West Coast residents.

    - For several days, observe the communication styles of men and women as you go about your routine. Take note of any similarities and differences you observe. Then to inform your reader, compare and contrast the way men and women talk.

3. **Combining patterns.** Consider your communication with people you interact with—teachers, bosses, coaches, friends, family, co-workers, and classmates, for example. Give examples of the direct and indirect speech you were part of, and using comparison-contrast, explain whether your experiences with direct and indirect speech conform to the principles explained in Tannen's essay. Using cause-and-effect analysis (explained in Chapter 10), tell how you reacted to the examples of direct and indirect speech you cite. Were there any misunderstandings?

4. **Analyzing and assessing.** Tannen's examples are from the workplace and the military. Analyze these examples and assess whether the points they illustrate also hold true for interpersonal relationships in other contexts.

5. **Connecting and synthesizing the readings.** Point out examples of direct and indirect speech in one or more of these essays: "On Being the Target of Discrimination" (page 262), "Reunion" (page 284), and "Don't Just Stand There" (page 311). Then using the information in "Squeaky Wheels and Protruding Nails," along with your own ideas, discuss whether the examples illustrate effective or ineffective communication. Be sure to explain why.

6. **Drawing on sources.** Because the world is a global community, we must gain a greater understanding of the communication styles in different cultures. For example, businesspeople traveling in Japan must understand the subtleties of indirect communication that Tannen touches on. Because much communication is nonverbal, we must also understand the gestures used in different cultures. In Mexico, for instance, a person might finger the lapel of another's suit as a sign of friendliness. Explain the importance of understanding the gestures used in other cultures by citing examples of those gestures, their meaning, and what could happen if that meaning were misunderstood. To research, you can check the *Social Sciences Index* under the heading "nonverbal communication." On the Internet, go to the Internet Public Library at www.ipl.org and type in the phrase "body language" or the keyword "gestures."

BACKGROUND: Arthur L. Campa (1905–1978), born in Mexico to American missionary parents, studied at the University of New Mexico and Columbia University. He was the chair of the Department of Modern Languages at the University of Denver, the director of the Center of Latin American Studies, and a cultural attaché at several U.S. embassies. Considered an authority on Hispanic American culture, Campa wrote a number of books on the subject, including *Treasure of the Sangre de Cristos* (1963), *Hispanic Folklore Studies of Arthur L. Campa* (1976), and *Hispanic Culture in the Southwest* (1978). "Anglo vs. Chicano: Why?" was first published in *Western Review* in 1972.

COMBINED PATTERNS AND THEIR PURPOSE: In "Anglo vs. Chicano: Why?" Arthur L. Campa uses *contrast* to **inform** the readers of several differences between two cultures that meet—and sometimes conflict—in the southwestern United States. In addition, he uses *cause-and-effect analysis* to **inform** by explaining the origins of these differences.

ANGLO VS. CHICANO: WHY?

BY ARTHUR L. CAMPA

THE CULTURAL DIFFERENCES between Hispanic and Anglo-American people have been dwelt upon by so many writers that we should all be well informed about the values of both. But audiences are usually of the same persuasion as the speakers, and those who consult published works are for the most part specialists looking for affirmation of what they believe. So, let us consider the same subject, exploring briefly some of the basic cultural differences that cause conflict in the Southwest, where Hispanic and Anglo-American cultures meet.

As you read Notice that Campa provides considerable historical background. Ask yourself how that background helps him achieve his purpose.

2 Cultural differences are implicit in the conceptual content of the languages of these two civilizations, and their value systems stem from a long series of historical circumstances. Therefore, it may be well to consider some of the English and Spanish cultural configurations before these Europeans set foot on American soil. English culture was basically insular, geographically and ideologically; was more integrated on the whole, except for some strong theological differences; and was particularly zealous of its racial purity. Spanish culture was peninsular, a geographical circumstance that made it a catchall of Mediterranean, central European and north African peoples. The composite nature of the population produced a marked regionalism that prevented close integration, except for religion, and led to a strong sense of individualism. These differences were reflected in the colonizing enterprise of the two cultures. The English isolated themselves from the Indians physically and culturally; the Spanish, who had strong notions about *pureza de sangre* [purity of blood] among the nobility, were not collectively averse to adding one more strain to their racial cocktail. Cortés led the way by siring the first *mestizo*[1] in

"The ultimate products of these two orientations meet today in the Southwest."

---

[1] A person of mixed blood; specifically, a person of mixed European and Native American ancestry.

North America, and the rest of the conquistadores followed suit. The ultimate products of these two orientations meet today in the Southwest.

3   Anglo-American culture was absolutist at the onset; that is, all the dominant values were considered identical for all, regardless of time and place. Such values as justice, charity, honesty were considered the superior social order for all men and were later embodied in the American Constitution. The Spaniard brought with him a relativistic viewpoint and saw fewer moral implications in man's actions. Values were looked upon as the result of social and economic conditions.

4   The motives that brought Spaniards and Englishmen to America also differed. The former came on an enterprise of discovery, searching for a new route to India initially, and later for new lands to conquer, the fountain of youth, minerals, the Seven Cities of Cibola and, in the case of the missionaries, new souls to win for the Kingdom of Heaven. The English came to escape religious persecution, and once having found a haven, they settled down to cultivate the soil and establish their homes. Since the Spaniards were not seeking a refuge or running away from anything, they continued their explorations and circled the globe 25 years after the discovery of the New World.

5   This peripatetic tendency of the Spaniard may be accounted for in part by the fact that he was the product of an equestrian culture. Men on foot do not venture far into the unknown. It was almost a century after the landing on Plymouth Rock that Governor Alexander Spotswood of Virginia crossed the Blue Ridge Mountains, and it was not until the nineteenth century that the Anglo-Americans began to move west of the Mississippi.

6   The Spaniard's equestrian role meant that he was not close to the soil, as was the Anglo-American pioneer, who tilled the land and built the greatest agricultural industry in history. The Spaniard cultivated the land only when he had Indians available to do it for him. The uses to which the horse was put also varied. The Spanish horse was essentially a mount, while the more robust English horse was used in cultivating the soil. It is therefore not surprising that the viewpoints of these two cultures should differ when we consider that the pioneer is looking at the world at the level of his eyes while the *caballero* [horseman] is looking beyond and down at the rest of the world.

> "The Spaniard cultivated the land only when he had Indians available to do it for him."

7   One of the most commonly quoted, and often misinterpreted, characteristics of Hispanic peoples is the deeply ingrained individualism in all walks of life. Hispanic individualism is a revolt against the incursion of collectivity, strongly asserted when it is felt that the ego is being fenced in. This attitude leads to a deficiency in those social qualities based on collective standards, an attitude that Hispanos do not consider negative because it manifests a measure of resistance to standardization in order to achieve a measure of individual freedom. Naturally, such an attitude has no *reglas fijas* [fixed rules].

8   Anglo-Americans who achieve a measure of success and security through institutional guidance not only do not mind a few fixed rules but demand them. The lack of a concerted plan of action, whether in business or in politics, appears unreasonable to Anglo-Americans. They have a sense of individualism, but they achieve it through

action and self-determination. Spanish individualism is based on feeling, on something that is the result not of rules and collective standards but of a person's momentary, emotional reaction. And it is subject to change when the mood changes. In contrast to Spanish emotional individualism, the Anglo-American strives for objectivity when choosing a course of action or making a decision.

9   The Southwestern Hispanos voiced strong objections to the lack of courtesy of the Anglo-Americans when they first met them in the early days of the Santa Fe trade. The same accusation is leveled at the *Americanos* today in many quarters of the Hispanic world. Some of this results from their different conceptions of polite behavior. Here too one can say that the Spanish have no *reglas fijas* because for them courtesy is simply an expression of the way one person feels toward another. To some they extend the hand, to some they bow and for the more *intimos* there is the well-known *abrazo*.[2] The concepts of "good or bad" or "right and wrong" in polite behavior are moral considerations of an absolutist culture.

10   Another cultural contrast appears in the way both cultures share part of their material substance with others. The pragmatic Anglo-American contributes regularly to such institutions as the Red Cross, the United Fund and a myriad of associations. He also establishes foundations and quite often leaves millions to such institutions. The Hispano prefers to give his contribution directly to the recipient so he can see the person he is helping.

> "Another cultural contrast appears in the way both cultures share part of their material substance with others."

11   A century of association has inevitably acculturated both Hispanos and Anglo-Americans to some extent, but there still persist a number of culture traits that neither group has relinquished altogether. Nothing is more disquieting to an Anglo-American who believes that time is money than the time perspective of Hispanos. They usually refer to this attitude as the "*mañana*[3] psychology." Actually, it is more of a "today psychology," because Hispanos cultivate the present to the exclusion of the future; because the latter has not arrived yet, it is not a reality. They are reluctant to relinquish the present, so they hold on to it until it becomes the past. To an Hispano, nine is nine until it is ten, so when he arrives at nine-thirty, he jubilantly exclaims: "*¡Justo!*" [right on time]. This may be why the clock is slowed down to a walk in Spanish while in English it runs. In the United States, our future-oriented civilization plans our lives so far in advance the present loses its meaning. January magazine issues are out in December; 1973 cars have been out since October; cemetery plots and even funeral arrangements are bought on the installment plan. To a person engrossed in living today the very idea of planning his funeral sounds like the tolling of the bells.

12   It is a natural corollary that a person who is present oriented should be compensated by being good at improvising. An Anglo-American is told in advance to prepare for an "impromptu speech," but an Hispano usually can improvise a speech because "*Nosotros la improvisamos todo*" [we improvise everything].

---

[2]Hug.
[3]Tomorrow.

13   Another source of cultural conflict arises from the difference between *being* and *doing.* Even when trying to be individualistic, the Anglo-American achieves it by what he does. Today's young generation decided to be themselves, to get away from standardization, so they let their hair grow, wore ragged clothes and even went barefoot in order to be different from the Establishment. As a result they all ended up doing the same things and created another stereotype. The freedom enjoyed by the individuality of *being* makes it unnecessary for Hispanos to strive to be different.

14   In 1963 a team of psychologists from the University of Guadalajara in Mexico and the University of Michigan compared 74 upper-middle-class students from each university. Individualism and personalism were found to be central values for the Mexican students. This was explained by saying that a Mexican's value as a person lies in his *being* rather than, as is the case of the Anglo-Americans, in concrete accomplishments. Efficiency and accomplishments are derived characteristics that do not affect worthiness in the Mexican, whereas in the American it is equated with success, a value of highest priority in American culture. Hispanic people disassociate themselves from material things or from actions that may impugn a person's sense of being, but the Anglo-American shows great concern for material things and assumes responsibility for his actions. This is expressed in the language of each culture. In Spanish one says, *"Se me cayó la taza"* [the cup fell away from me] instead of "I dropped the cup."

15   In English, one speaks of money, cash and all related transactions with frankness because material things of this high order do not trouble Anglo-Americans. In Spanish such materialistic concepts are circumvented by referring to cash as *efectivo* [effective] and when buying or selling as something *al contado* [counted out], and when without it by saying *No tengo fondos* [I have no funds]. This disassociation from material things is what produces *sobriedad* [sobriety] in the Spaniard according to Miguel de Unamuno, but in the Southwest the disassociation from materialism leads to *dejadez* [lassitude] and *desprendimiento* [disinterestedness]. A man may lose his life defending his honor but is unconcerned about the lack of material things. *Desprendimiento* causes a man to spend his last cent on a friend, which when added to lack of concern for the future may mean that tomorrow he will eat beans as a result of today's binge.

16   The implicit differences in words that appear to be identical in meaning are astonishing. Versatile is a compliment in English and an insult in Spanish. An Hispano student who is told to apologize cannot do it, because the word doesn't exist in Spanish. *Apología* means words in praise of a person. The Anglo-American either apologizes, which is a form of retraction abhorrent in Spanish, or compromises, another concept foreign to Hispanic culture. *Compromiso* means a date, not a compromise. In colonial Mexico City, two hidalgos once entered a narrow street from opposite sides, and when they could not go around, they sat in their coaches for three days until the viceroy ordered them to back out. All this because they could not work out a compromise.

"Versatile is a compliment in English and an insult in Spanish."

17   It was that way then and to some extent now. Many of today's conflicts in the Southwest have their roots in polarized cultural differences, which need not be irreconcilable when approached with mutual respect and understanding.

READING CLOSELY AND THINKING CRITICALLY

1. In your own words, write out the thesis of the essay.
2. Campa says that ideologically the English were insular, while the Spanish were peninsular. Explain what Campa means. What are the effects of the different orientations?
3. Explain a possible relationship between Hispanic individualism and the Spaniard's equestrian role (paragraph 6). How did the horse contribute to the cultural differences between Chicanos and Anglo-Americans?
4. Explain the different views of courtesy held by Hispanics and Anglo-Americans. How does the view of courtesy relate to concepts of individualism?
5. According to Campa, what values are important to Hispanics? To Anglo-Americans?

EXAMINING STRUCTURE AND STRATEGY

1. In what pattern does Campa arrange his contrasts, alternating or block?
2. If you were to pick an audience for the essay, what would it be like? How is the essay suited to that audience?
3. Does Campa maintain balance among his supporting details? Explain.
4. A number of times, Campa discusses historical backgrounds. How does the historical information help Campa fulfill his purpose?
5. What approach does Campa take to his conclusion? What do you think of his conclusion?

NOTING COMBINED PATTERNS

What cause-and-effect analysis is used in the essay? (Cause-and-effect is explained in Chapter 10.) What purpose does the cause-and-effect analysis serve?

CONSIDERING LANGUAGE AND STYLE

1. What can you learn about the relationship between language and culture from "Anglo vs. Chicano: Why?"
2. In paragraph 9, Campa calls Anglo culture "absolutist." What does he mean?
3. Consult a dictionary if you are unsure of the meaning of any of these words: *implicit* (paragraphs 2, 16), *configurations* (paragraph 2), *insular* (paragraph 2), *equestrian* (paragraph 5), *incursion* (paragraph 7), *pragmatic* (paragraph 10), *myriad* (paragraph 10), *acculturated* (paragraph 11), *impugn* (paragraph 14).

FOR DISCUSSION IN CLASS OR ONLINE

Campa concludes by saying that cultural differences "need not be irreconcilable when approached with mutual respect and understanding" (paragraph 17). Discuss one or more ways people can resolve conflict through increased understanding.

1. **Writing in your journal.** Campa explains that Anglo-Americans are future-oriented, while Chicanos are now-oriented. Do you agree? Discuss the advantages and disadvantages of each orientation.

2. **Using comparison-contrast for a purpose.** The purposes in the assignments are possibilities. You may establish whatever purpose you like, within your instructor's guidelines.

    *   To inform and perhaps relate experience and express feelings, contrast your values or beliefs with those of someone else you know. Try to explain the differences by examining your ethnic background, family situation, religious upbringing, schooling, or other relevant factors.

    *   To inform and perhaps persuade that one style is better than the other, contrast your view of money and spending practices with that of a friend, relative, or acquaintance. Try to explain the reasons for the differences.

    *   If you and someone you know behave differently because one of you is future oriented and one of you is focused on the present, contrast your different behaviors and attitudes. Your purpose can be to relate experience, express feelings, inform, and perhaps convince your reader that one approach is better than the other. If you want to use humor, your essay can also entertain.

3. **Combining patterns.** Select one of the following pairs: the control freak and the collaborator, the optimist and the pessimist, the dominant person and the submissive person, the noncompetitive person and the competitive person, the courteous person and the rude person. Use definition (explained in Chapter 12) as part of a comparison-contrast of the types of people. You can also use narration and exemplification to support your points.

4. **Analyzing and assessing.** Analyze some or all of the points that Campa makes, and assess how important they are, being sure to give reasons for your assertions. You might consider what applications his points have in various contexts, such as school, work, and social situations.

5. **Connecting and synthesizing the readings.** Conflict between two groups of people is discussed in "On Being the Target of Discrimination" (page 262) and "Grant and Lee: A Study in Contrasts" (page 367). Using any of the ideas in those essays, along with ideas from "Anglo vs. Chicano: Why?" and your own thinking, explain why so much conflict exists. If you like, you can also note something that can be done to lessen that conflict.

6. **Drawing on sources.** Devise a grade school, middle school, or high school program that could help foster respect and understanding for different cultures. For help with ideas, search "multicultural education" at www.google.com or look up "multicultural education" in *Education Index*.

BACKGROUND: Three-time Pulitzer Prize winner Robert Frost (1874–1963) is an important twentieth-century poet whose works are among the most frequently read American poems. By the time he was 40, Frost had tried a variety of jobs, attempted and abandoned college twice, and buried two children. Grief-stricken and discouraged, Frost turned his full attention to writing poetry and enjoyed considerable success. Although associated with New England culture and experience, Frost's poems consider universal ideas. They are deceptively simple, however, for they often include complex images and symbolism. First published in 1932, "Fire and Ice" is one of Frost's most frequently reprinted poems.

THE PATTERN AND ITS PURPOSE: In "Fire and Ice," Robert Frost uses *comparison-contrast* to **inform** and warn the reader about the dangers of desire and hate. Like many of Frost's poems, "Fire and Ice" is more complex than it may at first appear.

Fire and Ice

BY ROBERT FROST

As you read
Determine what
fire and ice
represent.

Some say the world will end in fire;
Some say in ice.
From what I've tasted of desire
I hold with those who favor fire.
But if it had to perish twice,   5
I think I know enough of hate
To know that for destruction ice
Is also great
And would suffice.

CONSIDERING THE POEM

1. In the poem, what does fire represent, and what does ice represent?
2. How are fire and ice—and the things fire and ice represent—similar, and how are they different?
3. In a sentence or two, tell what point Frost is making.
4. Why is desire like fire, and why is hate like ice?
5. How can desire and hate end the world?

WRITING ASSIGNMENTS

1. **Writing in your journal.** In a page or two, discuss whether you like the poem, being sure to explain why you react the way you do.
2. **Using comparison-contrast for a purpose.** To inform and perhaps convince your reader that one sentiment or movement is superior, compare and contrast two sentiments or

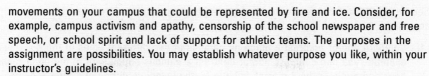

movements on your campus that could be represented by fire and ice. Consider, for example, campus activism and apathy, censorship of the school newspaper and free speech, or school spirit and lack of support for athletic teams. The purposes in the assignment are possibilities. You may establish whatever purpose you like, within your instructor's guidelines.

3. **Connecting the readings.** Is Frost correct about the destructive potential of desire and of hate? To respond, consider Frost's poem "The Lottery" (page 199) and Ellison's essay "On Being the Target of Discrimination" (page 262), along with your ideas.

WRITING COMPARISON-CONTRAST

See pages 358 and 361 for strategies for writing comparison-contrast and for a revising checklist.

1. Compare and/or contrast a place on campus at two different times of the day. For example, you can compare and/or contrast a campus eating spot at the noon rush hour and again at the 3 o'clock lull, the football stadium during and after a game, or the library before and after finals week. Use description for vividness.

2. Compare and/or contrast two close friends, illustrating their traits with example or narration.

3. Compare and/or contrast two similar television shows, such as two reality shows, two sit-coms, two news broadcasts, or two police dramas, to persuade your reader that one is better than the other.

4. Contrast two celebrations of the same holiday, such as Christmas before and after children, Independence Day as a child and as an adult, or Thanksgiving at different grandparents' houses.

5. Contrast the way a group of people (for example, mothers, police officers, fathers, or teens) is portrayed on television with the way the group is in real life.

6. Consider your circumstances before and after some change in your life, such as getting married, having children, going to college, getting a job, or joining an athletic team. If you wish, make your details humorous and entertain your reader.

7. In your campus library, look up advertisements in *Life* and *Look* magazines from the 1950s and compare and contrast one or two of these ads with ads for similar products in contemporary magazines to inform your reader of the changes. Use cause-and-effect analysis to explain the cause and/or the effects of the changes. (See Chapter 10.)

8. Contrast the right and wrong ways to do something, such as choose a major, study for an exam, write an essay, select an advisor, buy a car, or plan a first date. Make your details humorous and entertain your reader.

9. Compare and contrast the styles of two comedians, actors, or musicians to inform your reader about the characteristics of each one.

10. Compare and contrast the chief arguments on both sides of a controversial issue (for example, abortion, capital punishment, euthanasia, animal rights, sex education in schools, or cloning) to inform your reader of the thinking on both sides. If necessary, research the issue in your campus library or on the Internet.

11. Compare and/or contrast the toys of your youth with those that are popular today. Explain what those similarities and/or differences mean.

12. If you have lived in more than one place, compare and contrast life in two of those places.

13. If you or someone close to you has lived with chronic illness, contrast life as a healthy person and as a sick person to heighten your reader's awareness of what it is like to be ill.

14. Contrast your view of an event at two different times in your life. For example, you could contrast your view of Christmas before and after becoming a parent or your view of yoga classes before and after enrolling in one.

15. Using vivid description, compare and/or contrast your current view of a particular place and the view you held as a child. For example, you could compare and/or contrast your views of your elementary school, a family vacation spot, your old bedroom, or your old neighborhood.

16. Compare and/or contrast the attitudes of youth and maturity. Use examples to clarify your points. Also indicate which of the attitudes is better and why.

17. Contrast your view of a parent or other caregiver now with your view at some point in the past.

18. Compare and/or contrast your life today with what you once thought your life would be like. If there are striking contrasts, try to explain what accounts for those contrasts.

19. Compare and/or contrast the ways men are portrayed on television with the ways women are portrayed. Use specific examples from shows and commercials to clarify and support your points. If possible, explain the effects these portrayals have on the viewer.

20. **Comparison-contrast in context.** For a humor column for your student newspaper, compare and contrast the food in your campus dining halls or other campus eatery and the food you grew up eating.

RESPONDING TO AN IMAGE

The first photo below shows tennis champion Helen Wills Moody shaking hands with Elizabeth Ryan after Moody won Wimbledon in 1930. The second photo shows Venus and Serena Williams at Wimbledon in 2002. Study the photographs, and then write about the similarities and differences in clothing styles. Explain what the clothing styles suggest about the culture and values of the times. Consider what the styles say about women's tennis and what they say about women and society in general.

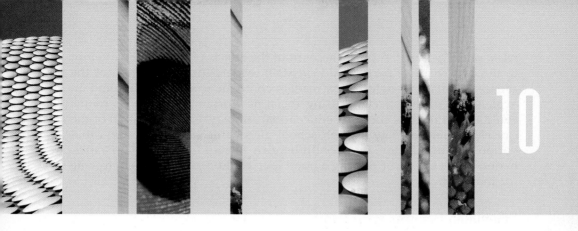

Cause-and-Effect Analysis

CONSIDER THE PATTERN

Movie studios create movie posters like the one on the facing page to generate interest in a film, but the poster alone does not get most people into the theater. What causes you and others to see a particular movie?

THE PATTERN

As human beings, we need to make sense of the world by understanding why events occur and how they might impact us. Thus, we examine the causes of earthquakes, try to determine how a presidential candidate's victory will change the economy, work to figure out why the car does not get the gas mileage it should, struggle to understand why our best friend suddenly seems distant, and so on. Understanding causes and effects is important to our sense of security and our need to deal with forces in our environment. Thus, we often use **cause-and-effect analysis** to examine causes, effects, or both. When you explore causes, you identify the reasons for an event; when you explore effects, you identify the results of an event.

USING CAUSE-AND-EFFECT ANALYSIS FOR A PURPOSE

Cause-and-effect analysis can be written for any purpose. For example, an explanation of the causes and effects of your decision to move to another state can allow you to *express your feelings* about the move and *relate your experience.* A funny account of the effects of your failed attempt to throw a surprise party could *entertain* readers. An explanation of the causes of inflation could *inform* readers about an economic force, and an explanation of the effects of using social networking sites in classrooms could *inform* readers about an educational strategy. An explanation of the causes of math anxiety in high school girls could *persuade* readers that various cultural factors may condition girls to avoid math, and an explanation of the effects of passing a bond levy could *persuade* readers to vote for that levy.

Combining Patterns for a Purpose

You can combine cause-and-effect analysis with other patterns to achieve your purpose for writing. For an essay *explaining* the reasons people graduate from high school without being able to read, you might cite social promotions as one reason and then *narrate* the story of Stella, a nonreader you know who was frequently promoted because she was a troublemaker whom teachers did not want to deal with. To *inform* readers of the effects of global warming, you could describe climate change scenarios. To explain the effects of tax reduction, you could *analyze the process* whereby lowering taxes creates more disposable income, which leads to increased spending, which spurs manufacturing, which creates jobs.

To see how other patterns can be combined with cause-and-effect analysis, study the following excerpt from the last paragraph of "Just Walk On By: A Black Man Ponders His Power to Alter Public Space," an essay in this chapter. In the essay, the author combines cause-and-effect analysis with description to explain how he is affected by other people's perception of him as threatening.

EXCERPT FROM "JUST WALK ON BY"
COMBINING CAUSE-AND-EFFECT ANALYSIS AND DESCRIPTION

The highlighted description helps readers appreciate the cause-and-effect relationship: His whistling cheery tunes while walking at night on quiet streets causes pedestrians (whose body language suggests fearfulness) to relax because they realize that he is not a mugger.

describes scene

And on late-evening constitutionals along streets less traveled by, I employ what has proved to be an excellent tension-reducing measure: I whistle melodies from Beethoven and Vivaldi and the more popular classical

describes people

composers. Even steely New Yorkers hunching toward night-time destinations seem to relax, and occasionally they even join in the tune. Virtually everybody seems to sense that a mugger wouldn't be warbling bright,

describes sound

sunny↓ selections from Vivaldi's *Four Seasons*. It is my

equivalent of the cowbell that hikers wear when they

know they are in bear country.

Cause-and-effect analysis is a common component of essays developed primarily with other patterns. For example, if you write a process analysis to inform readers about how a computer program works, you might begin or end by explaining the beneficial effects of using the program. Similarly, if you are relating experience by narrating the story of getting cut from your high school basketball team, you can include cause-and-effect analysis to explain why you were cut and how you were affected by being cut.

Whether you use cause-and-effect analysis alone or in combination with other patterns depends on what helps you achieve your particular writing purpose for your particular audience.

---

www.mhhe.com/clousepatterns6   Cause-and-Effect

For more help with cause-and-effect analysis, click on
Writing > Paragraph Patterns
Writing > Writing Tutor > Causal Analysis

Cause-and-Effect Analysis beyond the Writing Classroom

Cause-and-effect analysis helps writers achieve their purpose in many writing situations.

IN ACADEMIC WRITING AND READING   You will use cause-and-effect analysis in many college classes. In history and political science classes, you will be asked to explain the causes and effects of events or trends. For example, you could be asked on an essay exam to explain the causes of the Teapot Dome scandal, or you could be asked to write a report evaluating the causes and effects of low voter turnout. In a sociology class, you might be asked to explain the effects of the AIDS crisis on dating practices, and in a physics, chemistry, or biology class you will be asked to write lab reports explaining the effects of experiments. In an education class, you could detail the causes of teacher burnout, and in a marketing class, you could write a paper on the effects of caller-identification technology on telemarketing.

Cause-and-effect analysis is one of the most frequently occurring patterns in college textbooks. The following excerpt is from a business textbook that explains a reason for loss of American manufacturing jobs:

This is the reason some countries produce high-quality goods for low prices.

Today manufacturers in countries such as China, India, South Korea, and Mexico can produce high-quality goods at low prices because their workers are paid less money than U.S. workers and they've learned quality concepts from Japanese, German, and U.S. producers. (Nickels, McHugh, and McHugh, *Understanding Business*)

Here is another paragraph from the textbook. This one explains some specific effects of the North American Free Trade Agreement (NAFTA):

These are positive effects.

These are negative effects.

Since its approval, NAFTA has experienced both success and difficulties. On the positive side, U.S. exports to the NAFTA partners increased approximately 85 percent since the agreement was signed. Mexico has fared even better; it has experienced a 225 percent increase in trade flows and has replaced Japan as America's number two trading partner (behind Canada). On the downside, the devaluation of the Mexican peso in 1995 forced the United States to commit $30 billion in aid to Mexico. Also, it's estimated that the United States has lost almost 1 million jobs since the signing of NAFTA. (Nickels, McHugh, and McHugh, *Understanding Business*)

The explanation of the specific effects of NAFTA will help students understand that the treaty has had both positive and negative effects.

AT WORK AND IN THE COMMUNITY On the job, people frequently use cause-and-effect analysis. Educational administrators write explanations of the causes of declining test scores. Marketing managers write reports noting the reasons for a decline in sales, and dieticians give their clients a written explanation of the effects of sugar on insulin production. A police officer will fill out a report explaining the causes of an accident, and an official with the Environmental Protection Agency may write a study of the effects of a dam on river ecology.

Cause-and-effect analysis will also be an important component of your writing outside the classroom and workplace. For example, when you write a letter of complaint to a company about a faulty product, you will describe what went wrong with the product and what damage resulted. If you ever deliver a eulogy or write a condolence note, you can explain the positive ways the deceased affected you and others.

SUPPORTING DETAILS

Events typically have more than one cause and more than one effect. Suppose you are looking at the causes and effects of an enrollment decline at your college. Causes might include a weak economy, so that fewer people

Using *Affect* and *Effect* Correctly

If you have trouble understanding the difference between *affect* and *effect*, remember the following:

- *Affect* is most often a verb meaning "to influence," as in "Explain how football affects American culture."

- *Effect* is most often a noun meaning "result," as in "Explain the effects of football on American culture."

have the money to go to college; the two new colleges in the area; inadequate recruitment; and less financial aid available for prospective students. Effects might include loss of revenue, loss of prestige, low employee morale, and fewer course offerings. When an event has multiple causes and effects, do not omit any significant ones, or you will give your reader an incomplete picture. However, rather than develop them all in the same detail, focus on those of particular significance. For example, if the primary reasons for the enrollment decline are the weak economy and the two new colleges, you should discuss those causes in more detail than the reduced financial aid and lack of recruitment.

You may need to include not only *immediate* causes but also *remote* causes. Suppose you are explaining why AIDS has reached epidemic proportions. You may cite as one immediate cause laws prohibiting notification of those exposed to the disease through their HIV-positive partners without the consent of those partners. To explain these laws, you might mention that gay and HIV-positive activists successfully lobbied against such notification because they feared discrimination against those publicly identified as gay and/or infected. Their lobbying efforts would be a remote cause of the increase in AIDS.

Sometimes cause-and-effect details take the form of causal chains. In **causal chains,** a cause has an effect, that effect becomes the cause of another effect, that effect then becomes a cause, and so on. For example, to explain the effects of being very tall, you might reproduce this causal chain: Being tall made you feel awkward (effect); feeling awkward (cause) reduced your self-confidence (effect); your reduced self-confidence (cause) made it hard for you to date (effect); not dating (cause) made you depressed (effect).

Sometimes you will want to point out that something is *not*, contrary to popular belief, a cause or an effect of something else. This strategy is effective if you need to correct your reader's understanding. For example, assume that you are explaining the effects of sex education in the schools, and you think your reader mistakenly believes that sex education leads to increased sexual activity. You can note that increased sexual activity has not been proven to be an effect of sex education.

To identify causes and effects, ask yourself "why?" and "then what?" as you develop your details. For example, say you are explaining the causes of your shyness, and you have as one of your reasons the fact that you do not feel comfortable around people. If you ask yourself why you do not feel comfortable, you may remember that your family moved so frequently that you never got to know anyone very well. A new cause for inclusion in your essay, then, is those frequent moves. In a different essay, you might explain the effects that your parents' divorce had on you and have as one effect that you saw less of your father. Ask "then what?" and you might answer that you and your father drifted apart, so you never got to know him well—another effect you can write about.

ORGANIZING DETAILS

Your thesis can indicate your topic and whether your focus will be causes, effects, or both. In addition, in noting the point you will make, you can suggest your purpose. Here is an example.

> THESIS   It is certainly wrong for athletes to use drugs, but the reasons they do so are understandable.

This thesis indicates that the essay will explain the causes of drug use among athletes and that the purpose is to inform and persuade the reader that, while drug use is wrong, its causes are understandable.

For a clear organization, use topic sentences to introduce your discussion of each cause or effect. Here are the sample thesis and some topic sentences that could appear in an essay about the causes of drug abuse among athletes.

THESIS	It is certainly wrong for athletes to use drugs, but the reasons they do so are understandable.
TOPIC SENTENCE	The pressure for professional athletes to justify their huge salaries is so great that they often see performance-enhancing drugs as the answer. (*Topic sentence presents the first cause: pressure on professional athletes.*)
TOPIC SENTENCE	Furthermore, athletes may feel that they must take the drugs in order to be competitive, since so many other athletes are taking them. (*Topic sentence presents the second cause: Others take drugs.*)
TOPIC SENTENCE	Finally, some athletes get hooked on drugs because their coaches and trainers administer them. (*Topic sentence presents the third reason: Coaches and trainers give out the drugs.*)

If your purpose is persuasive, you may want a progressive order to save your most dramatic, compelling, or significant cause or effect for the end. If you are reproducing causal chains, use a chronological order, to cite the causes and effects in the order they occur. Chronological order is also called for when you are discussing causes and effects as they occurred over time. For example, a discussion of the effects of your musical talent could begin with your first music lessons, then discuss increasing commitment to practicing as you grew up, and conclude with your decision to become a music teacher. At times you will arrange your details in categories. If, for example, you are explaining the effects of the passage of a school levy, you can discuss together all the effects on teachers, then the effects on students, and finally the effects on curriculum.

Transitions can help you signal cause-and-effect relationships. Transitions signaling that one thing is the effect of another include *as a result, consequently, thus, hence, therefore,* and *for this reason.* Here are two examples:

> The midterm grades were very low. <u>For this reason</u>, Professor Werner reviewed the material with the class.
>
> The storm damage was extensive. <u>As a result</u>, the tourist trade in the coastal town declined.

Because and *since* are transitions signaling cause (*Because* [*Since*] his grades were low, he reviewed the material).

Transitions of addition (*also, in addition, additionally, furthermore,* and *another*) can be used to signal movement from one cause or effect to another, as in the following examples:

> <u>Another</u> effect of MTV is . . .
>
> <u>In addition</u>, stress fractures can be caused by . . .

VISUALIZING A CAUSE-AND-EFFECT ANALYSIS

The chart on page 420 can help you visualize the structure for a cause-and-effect analysis. Like all good models, however, this one can be altered as needed.

THINKING CRITICALLY ABOUT CAUSE-AND-EFFECT ANALYSIS

You learned in Chapters 1 and 4 that thinking critically about your reading and writing is an in-depth process of analysis and assessment. In addition to using what you learned in those chapters, when you read and write cause-and-effect analysis, ask the following questions:

- **Have any of the causes or effects been exaggerated?** Events have many causes, and effects can be difficult to calculate. Deliberate exaggeration can cause real harm, as when a manufacturer hypes its food supplement by exaggerating how much it prevents bone loss for older women, or an advertiser hypes a cereal by overstating how much it reduces cholesterol.
- **Have any important causes or effects been omitted?** Writers should not leave out important causes or effects to further their

INTRODUCTION

- Creates interest in your essay
- States your thesis (underlined below), which indicates your topic and can include whether you will focus on causes and/or effects, as well as the point you will make

  EXAMPLE

  Thanks to politicians who have made political hay from the steady decline of our schools, we now test our children repeatedly to be sure that no child is left behind. <u>Unfortunately, the testing is not working. In fact, it is creating more problems in our already troubled educational system.</u>

FIRST BODY PARAGRAPH

- Gives the first cause or effect, which can be stated in a topic sentence
- Can be developed with any pattern of development
- May include a causal chain
- May include remote as well as immediate causes
- May indicate that something is not a cause or effect
- May arrange details in a progressive or chronological order

  EXAMPLE

  Because the tests are so high-stakes—determining whether students get promoted and even graduate—we have classrooms full of stressed-out students. No wonder more children than ever before are on antidepressants and anti-anxiety medications. . . .

NEXT BODY PARAGRAPHS

- Continue until all the significant causes and/or effects are given
- Can be developed with any patterns of development
- May include a causal chain
- May include remote as well as immediate causes
- May indicate that something is not a cause or effect
- May arrange details in a progressive or chronological order

  EXAMPLE

  Students aren't the only ones affected by the testing. Teachers are harmed as well. Frequently evaluated according to how well their students score on the tests, teachers are pressured to "teach to the tests," a dangerous practice. . . .

CONCLUSION

- Provides a satisfying finish
- Leaves your reader with a strong final impression

  EXAMPLE

  Few people deny that our schools are in a state of crisis. However, far from addressing the problem, frequent high-stakes testing contributes to the problem.

writing purpose. Suppose you want to convince readers to stop using antibacterial products. You can state that bacteria are evolving to be resistant to some antibiotics as a result of the proliferation of antibacterial products, but you should not omit the point that antibacterial products such as hand sanitizer may prevent the spread of the flu. Instead, you can mention and counter that point: "Although some antibacterial soaps and lotions may prevent the spread of infections, washing with soap and water, covering coughs and sneezes, and staying home when sick can achieve the same end."

- **Has the cause-and-effect relationship been oversimplified?** Failure to consider important causes or effects may be the result of *oversimplifying* the cause-and-effect relationship. For example, presenting violence against women as solely the result of pornography ignores other factors that contribute to the problem.
- **Is an event treated as an effect of another event simply because it occurred later?** This error in logic is called *post hoc, ergo propter hoc*, which means "after this, therefore because of this." You would be making that error if you argued, for example, that television was responsible for an increase in violent crimes because crime rates increased in the decades after television was introduced.

PROCESS GUIDELINES: STRATEGIES FOR WRITING CAUSE-AND-EFFECT ANALYSIS

1. **Selecting a topic.** Consider writing about the causes and/or effects of some aspect of your life or personality, such as shyness, math anxiety, birth order, fear of heights, your parents' divorce, or living on a farm.
2. **Generating ideas.** To generate ideas and decide on which to include, use the following strategies:
   - List every cause and/or effect of your topic that you can think of, without pausing to evaluate how good your ideas are.
   - Ask "why?" and/or "then what?" of every item on your list to explore additional causes and effects. Include remote causes as well as immediate ones.
   - Consider whether you can tell a story, provide an example, describe, or explain a process to clarify any of the points on your list.
   - Consider whether your audience needs to be told that something is actually *not* a cause or an effect.
   - Review your list of ideas. Based on your audience and purpose, which should you cross off?
3. **Organizing.** Once you have a list of ideas you want to include, number these ideas in the order you will treat them in your first draft. Consider causal chains.

Avoiding "The Reason Is Because"

Avoid writing "the reason is because." This expression is redundant because "the reason" means "because." Two alternatives are *the reason is that* and *because.*

NO	**Economic development on the west side has lagged behind other areas of the city. The reason is because the Route 7 connector bridge has not been completed.**
YES	**Economic development on the west side has lagged behind other areas of the city. The reason is that the Route 7 connector bridge has not been completed.**
YES	**Economic development on the west side has lagged behind other areas of the city because the Route 7 connector bridge has not been completed.**

Using Sources for a Purpose

The paragraph below, which is a body paragraph for an essay arguing that gay marriage should be legalized, illustrates how you can use sources from this book in your writing. It includes a paraphrase of source material from paragraph 5 of "Why the *M* Word Matters to Me," on page 428.

THESIS Gay partners deserve the opportunity to enter into legal marriages affording them the same rights and protections that heterosexual couples enjoy.

WRITING PURPOSE AND AUDIENCE To convince college students to support legislation that enables gay couples to marry.

The paraphrase in sentences 3–5 counters a common objection to gay marriage. Sentences 2 and 3 integrate the paraphrase by giving its significance, and sentence 6 integrates it by interpreting it.

¹Some people object to gay marriage on religious grounds, believing that same-sex unions violate religious tenets and are, therefore, immoral. ²However, this argument is beside the point. ³As Andrew Sullivan points out in "Why the *M* Word Matters to Me," gay marriage is not a religious issue. ⁴It is a legal and civil one. ⁵Religious organizations that want to forbid gay unions are completely free to do so, explains the author, in the same way the Catholic Church forbids divorce (429). ⁶In other words, those who oppose gay marriage on religious grounds are really imposing their religious beliefs on others, and that is a clear violation of the religious freedoms this country prides itself on.

Checklist for Revising Cause-and-Effect Analysis

You can use this checklist along with the one on page 76 to help you revise.

1. _____ Your thesis indicates whether you are focusing on causes and/or effects and perhaps your purpose in making your point.

2. _____ If needed, topic sentences introduce the discussion of each cause and effect.

3. _____ You have noted all significant causes and effects—both immediate and remote—and have not exaggerated any.

4. _____ You have clarified all causes and effects; using explanation, description, narration, examples, and/or process analysis as appropriate.

5. _____ You have reproduced causal chains where appropriate.

6. _____ You have avoided oversimplifying, and *post hoc, ergo propter hoc* errors in logic.

7. _____ You have arranged details in progressive, chronological, or other appropriate order and used transitions as needed.

AVOIDING PLAGIARISM

The paragraph illustrates the following points about avoiding plagiarism when you paraphrase. (For more complete information on using source material, consult Chapters 4 and 15.)

- **Restate the author's ideas accurately.** Compare the paraphrase in sentences 3–5 to paragraph 5 of Sullivan's essay to see that the writer of the paraphrase does not add any meaning that is not in Sullivan's sentences and does not change Sullivan's meaning in any way.

- **Use your own words and style.** Compare the paraphrase in sentences 3–5 to paragraph 5 of Sullivan's essay to see that the writer does not copy Sullivan's wording or style.

- **Reintroduce as necessary.** As sentence 5 illustrates, when your paraphrase spans several sentences, reintroduce the source strategically, so readers know you are still using outside material.

MYTHS ABOUT USING SOURCES

MYTH: Only quotations have to be documented; paraphrases can be used without citation.

FACT: You must document all material that comes from sources with a parenthetical citation and an entry on a Works Cited page. The only exception is material that is common knowledge or a matter of historical or public record. Thus, you do not have to document the idea that burning fossil fuels releases carbon dioxide (common knowledge) or the fact that Germany invaded Poland in 1939 (a matter of historical record).

Annotated Student Essay

Student-writer Carl Benedict informs his reader by explaining the causes of steroid use among athletes. As you read, notice how carefully each cause is presented and explained. After you read, you will have an opportunity to evaluate this essay.

Why Athletes Use Steroids
Carl Benedict

Paragraph 1
The introduction gives background information. The thesis (the last sentence) indicates that the subject is steroid use and the essay will present causes.

One of the most heated controversies in athletics centers on the use of anabolic steroids. Behind the dispute is the evidence that steroids pose a health hazard. They are linked to cardiovascular disease, liver disorders, and cancerous tumors. In addition, there is evidence that they cause personality aberrations. Still, an alarming number of athletes are willing to risk their health for the enhanced performance steroids provide—and it is not hard to understand why.

Paragraph 2
Sentence 1 is the topic sentence. It begins with a transition to introduce the first cause under consideration.

First of all, many athletes are so blinded by the obvious benefits of steroid use that they fail to note their adverse effects. They are so focused on the increased strength, stamina, and size that result from steroid use they may overlook the abuse their bodies are sustaining—often until it is too late. That is, athletes who are delighting in turning in the best performance of their lives are not likely to think about future deleterious effects. This is the same psychology that keeps the nicotine addict smoking three packs a day, until the X ray shows the lung cancer is so advanced that nothing can be done.

Paragraph 3
The second cause is presented in the first two sentences. The paragraph also presents an effect: Contact sports become more dangerous.

Some athletes rationalize steroid use another way. They claim that anabolic steroids pose no greater health hazard than participation in such contact sports as football, boxing, and wrestling. However, these athletes fail to understand that in addition to harming the body, steroids also heighten the danger of contact sports by making the participants larger and stronger, thereby increasing their momentum and impact.

Paragraph 4
This paragraph explains something that is not a cause, then goes on to give a real cause. Note the transition *instead*.

Some people think steroid use continues despite the life-threatening effects because athletes are just "dumb jocks" who are not smart enough to appreciate the risks. I don't accept that explanation. Instead, I suspect that steroid use continues partly because most athletes are young, and young people never feel threatened. Part of being young is feeling invulnerable. That is why young people drive too fast, drink too much, and bungee jump. They just do not believe that anything can happen to them. The same psychology is at work with athletes. They are young people who feel they will live forever.

In addition, athletes assume that their bodies are so physically conditioned they can withstand more punishment than the average person, so they feel even less at risk by steroid use. They think, "The average person should not do this, but I can because my body is finely tuned."

Perhaps the biggest reason athletes use steroids can be explained by the spirit that lies at the heart of all athletes: competition. Once a handful of athletes enhance their performance artificially, then others follow in order to stay competitive. Eventually, steroid users dominate a sport, and anyone who wants to compete at the highest levels is forced to use steroids or lose out. This fact explains why unscrupulous coaches and trainers who want to win at any cost have contributed to the problem by offering steroids to their players and urging them to use them. Sadly, this practice has even filtered down to the high school level in some cases.

Competition for the thrill of winning is only part of the explanation, however. Big-time athletics means big-time money. As the financial rewards rise in a given sport, so does the pressure to win at any cost. Huge salaries, enormous purses, big bonuses, and incredibly lucrative commercial endorsements all tempt athletes to enhance their performances any way they can.

Despite drug testing before competition and dissemination of information about the dangers of anabolic steroids, athletes still use steroids because the pressures to do so are so compelling. The truth is, too many athletes think steroids hurt only the other person, or else they think using steroids is worth the risk.

Paragraph 5
The first sentence is the topic sentence. It begins with a transition and presents the next cause.

Paragraph 6
The first sentence is the topic sentence. "The biggest reason" notes that detail is in a progressive order. The paragraph presents a causal chain.

Paragraph 7
This paragraph presents a cause that is an extension of the one given in the previous paragraph.

Paragraph 8
The conclusion summarizes the main causes.

PEER REVIEW

Responding to "Why Athletes Use Steroids"

Analyze and assess "Why Athletes Use Steroids" by responding to these questions:

1. Does the essay hold your interest? Why or why not?
2. Are the introduction and conclusion effective? Why or why not?
3. Are causes and effects explained in sufficient detail? Explain.
4. Has the author accounted for both immediate and remote causes? If not, is that a problem? Explain.
5. Are there any errors in logic?
6. What do you like best about the essay?
7. What one revision would make the essay better? How will that revision improve the essay?

EXAMINING VISUALS
Cause-and-Effect Analysis in an Advertisement

Advertisements often include cause-and-effect analysis to show the beneficial effects of products. The following public service ad uses cause-and-effect analysis in a dramatically different way.

- What cause-and-effect relationship does the advertisement express?
- For what purpose is the cause-and-effect relationship depicted?
- Who is the target audience?
- How do the words and image work together to achieve the advertisement's purpose?

BACKGROUND: A native of England (b. 1963), Andrew Sullivan earned a Ph.D. in political science from Harvard's John F. Kennedy School of Government. A political and social commentator, Sullivan was a regular columnist for *Time* magazine and is currently a columnist for the *Sunday Times of London*. He was also the editor in chief of the *New Republic* magazine—the youngest editor in its history. In 2007, Sullivan became a senior editor of the *Atlantic Monthly*. A frequent lecturer on college campuses, Sullivan has also appeared on a number of radio and television programs, including *Nightline, CBS Evening News, Larry King Live,* and National Public Radio's *Fresh Air.* His books include *Virtually Normal: An Argument about Homosexuality* (1996), *Love Undetectable: Notes on Friendship, Sex, and Survival* (1998), *Same-Sex Marriage, Pro and Con: A Reader* (2004), and *The Conservative Soul: How We Lost It, How to Get It Back* (2006). Sullivan also writes the popular blog "The Daily Dish." "Why the *M* Word Matters to Me" first appeared in *Time* in 2004.

www.mhhe.com/clousepatterns6	Andrew Sullivan

For more information on this author, go to

More resources > Chapter 10 > Andrew Sullivan

THE PATTERN AND ITS PURPOSES: Andrew Sullivan uses *cause-and-effect analysis* for multiple purposes: He **relates his experience** as a gay man and **expresses his feelings** about the importance of gay marriage in order to **persuade** readers that such unions should be allowed.

WHY THE *M* WORD MATTERS TO ME

BY ANDREW SULLIVAN

AS A CHILD, I had no idea what homosexuality was. I grew up in a traditional home—Catholic, conservative, middle class. Life was relatively simple: education, work, family. I was raised to aim high in life, even though my parents hadn't gone to college. But one thing was instilled in me. What mattered was not how far you went in life, how much money you earned, how big a name you made for yourself. What really mattered was family and the love you had for one another. The most important day of your life was not graduation from college or your first day at work or a raise or even your first house. The most important day of your life was when you got married. It was on that day that all your friends and all your family got together to celebrate the most important thing in life: your happiness—your ability to make a new home, to form a new but connected family, to find love that put everything else into perspective.

> **As you read**
> Pay attention to the way Sullivan uses both reason and emotion.

> "The most important day of your life was when you got married."

2   But as I grew older, I found that this was somehow not available to me. I didn't feel the things for girls that my peers did. All the emotions and social rituals and bonding of teenage heterosexual life eluded me. I didn't know why. No one explained it. My emotional bonds to other boys were one-sided; each time I felt

myself falling in love, they sensed it, pushed it away. I didn't and couldn't blame them. I got along fine with my buds in a nonemotional context, but something was awry, something not right. I came to know almost instinctively that I would never be a part of my family the way my siblings might one day be. The love I had inside me was unmentionable, anathema. I remember writing in my teenage journal one day, "I'm a professional human being. But what do I do in my private life?"

3   I never discussed my real life. I couldn't date girls and so immersed myself in schoolwork, the debate team, school plays, anything to give me an excuse not to confront reality. When I looked toward the years ahead, I couldn't see a future. There was just a void. Was I going to be alone my whole life? Would I ever have a most important day in my life? It seemed impossible, a negation, an undoing. To be a full part of my family, I had to somehow not be me. So, like many other gay teens, I withdrew, became neurotic, depressed, at times

> "To be a full part of my family, I had to somehow not be me."

close to suicidal. I shut myself in my room with my books night after night while my peers developed the skills needed to form real relationships and loves. In wounded pride, I even voiced a rejection of family and marriage. It was the only way I could explain my isolation.

4   It took years for me to realize that I was gay, years more to tell others and more time yet to form any kind of stable emotional bond with another man. Because my sexuality had emerged in solitude—and without any link to the idea of an actual relationship—it was hard later to reconnect sex to love and self-esteem. It still is. But I persevered, each relationship slowly growing longer than the last, learning in my 20s and 30s what my straight friends had found out in their teens. But even then my parents and friends never asked the question they would have asked automatically if I were straight: So, when are you going to get married? When will we be able to celebrate it and affirm it and support it? In fact, no one—no one—has yet asked me that question.

5   When people talk about gay marriage, they miss the point. This isn't about gay marriage. It's about marriage. It's about family. It's about love. It isn't about religion. It's about *civil* marriage licenses. Churches can and should have the right to say no to marriage for gays in their congregations, just as Catholics say no to divorce, but divorce is still a civil option. These family values are not options for a happy and stable life. They are necessities. Putting gay relationships in some other category—civil unions, domestic partnerships, whatever—may alleviate real human needs, but by their very euphemism, by their very separateness, they actually build a wall

> "This isn't about gay marriage. It's about marriage."

between gay people and their families. They put back the barrier many of us have spent a lifetime trying to erase.

6   It's too late for me to undo my past. But I want above everything else to remember a young kid out there who may even be reading this now. I want to let him know that he doesn't have to choose between himself and his family anymore. I want him to know that his love has dignity, that he does indeed have a future as a full and equal part of the human race. Only marriage will do that. Only marriage can bring him home.

1. Why does Sullivan believe that gays should be allowed to marry?
2. Why is it significant that Sullivan grew up "in a traditional home—Catholic, conservative, middle class" (paragraph 1)?
3. Those who favor gay marriage often point to the fact that unless couples are legally married, they are denied many rights and benefits. For example, unmarried partners cannot refuse to testify against each other in court; one partner is not always covered under the other partner's insurance policy; and partners who bequeath estates to each other can have the wills contested by family members. Why didn't Sullivan make this point? Should he have?
4. Is the essay convincing? Do you think it is likely to change readers' minds? Explain.

EXAMINING STRUCTURE AND STRATEGY

1. In paragraph 1, Sullivan describes his childhood background. Why does he begin the essay with this information? How does the first paragraph help Sullivan achieve his writing purpose?
2. Sullivan relates a painful part of his personal experience as a teenager and young man. What purpose does sharing personal experience serve?
3. What cause-and-effect relationship does the essay explain?
4. Which paragraphs are intended to move readers' emotions? Which paragraphs are intended to appeal to readers' intellect? Does Sullivan rely more on appeals to readers' emotions or appeals to their intellect? Why?

CONSIDERING LANGUAGE AND STYLE

1. In the title, why does Sullivan use "the *M* word" rather than "marriage"?
2. In paragraph 5, Sullivan repeats the phrases "It isn't about" and "It's about." What does he achieve with that repetition?
3. Consult a dictionary if you do not know the meaning of these words: *anathema* (paragraph 2), *euphemism* (paragraph 5).

FOR DISCUSSION IN CLASS OR ONLINE

Gay marriage is an issue that arouses strong reactions—both for and against. Why is gay marriage such a "hot button" topic?

WRITING ASSIGNMENTS

1. **Writing in your journal.** In a page or two, describe how society reacts to homosexuals.
2. **Using cause-and-effect analysis for a purpose.** The purposes in the assignments are possibilities. You may establish whatever purpose you like, within your instructor's guidelines.

- As a gay teenager, Sullivan did not feel like he fit in. To inform your reader, explain what else causes young people to feel like they do not fit in.
- For a variety of reasons, many high school students feel like they don't fit in. To inform your readers and perhaps convince them to take action, explain the effects of not fitting in high school.
- If you have ever felt different—like you did not fit in—explain the causes and effects of the feeling in order to relate your experience and express your feelings.
- To inform readers and perhaps convince them that legalizing gay marriage is either a good or a bad idea, explain what would happen if gay marriage were legalized across the country. If you like, you can focus on the family values mentioned in paragraph 5.

3. **Combining patterns.** In the last paragraph, Sullivan says, "Only marriage can bring [a young gay male] home." Define *home* (see Chapter 12 on definition), and use cause-and-effect analysis to explain how marriage can cause a person to be home.

4. **Analyzing and assessing.** Assess whether Sullivan likely achieved his persuasive purpose with his original audience of *Time* magazine readers. To make your determination, you can analyze the author's use of emotion, reason, details, and any other features of the essay.

5. **Connecting and synthesizing the readings.** Sullivan notes that his adolescence was a difficult, troubled time, as adolescence is for most people. Discuss one or more of the factors that cause teenage angst (anguish, anxiety). You can also discuss what can be done to make adolescence a less difficult time. For ideas, you can draw on your own experience and observation as well as on one or more of these readings: "The Poncho Bearer" (page 212) and "Complexion" (page 672).

6. **Drawing on sources.** Read the arguments of those who favor and of those who oppose gay marriage by typing "gay marriage" into your favorite search engine or by looking up "gay marriage" in *ProQuest* or *Reader's Guide to Periodical Literature* (both located in your campus library's reference room). Then write a summary of the chief arguments for and against gay marriage.

BACKGROUND: Technology correspondent for the *New York Times,* Brad Stone was a general assignment reporter and later the technology reporter for *Newsweek* for many years. He started at *Newsweek* as a college sophomore, working for the syndicated radio show *Newsweek on Air,* and later worked in the San Francisco bureau, writing about technology and the Internet. Stone has also written for *Wired* magazine and the *Sunday Telegraph* of London. In addition to writing general business articles, Stone has reported on the ups and downs of the technology economy, the increase in spam, eBay's decision to leave China, Netflix, and the Microsoft antitrust suit. He also wrote *Gearheads: The Turbulent Rise of Robotic Sports* (2003), which the *San Francisco Chronicle* named one of best books of 2003. "Web of Risks" first appeared in *Newsweek* in 2006.

COMBINED PATTERNS AND THEIR PURPOSES: Using *cause-and-effect analysis* combined with *exemplification*, Brad Stone **informs** readers — particularly students — about privacy risks associated with the popular social-networking sites like Facebook and MySpace. He is also writing to **persuade** students to be careful about how they use social-networking sites because of their potentially troublesome *effects*. If you use one of these sites and are not aware of the risks, read carefully.

WEB OF RISKS

BY BRAD STONE

CAMERON WALKER LEARNED the hard way that sharing information online can have unintended consequences. In 2005, the sophomore at Fisher College in Boston organized a student petition dedicated to getting a campus police guard fired and posted it on the popular college social network Facebook.com. Walker wrote that the guard "loves to antagonize students . . . and needs to be eliminated." It was a poor choice of words. Another student informed school officials, who logged on and interpreted the comments as threatening. Though Walker claimed he was trying only to expose the guard's demeanor, he was expelled. He's now enrolled at another college and admits he made a serious mistake. "I was a naive 21-year-old," he says.

As you read Be sure to notice the positive effects of social-networking sites and not just the potentially troubling ones.

2   Creating a page on a social-networking site is now a cherished form of self-expression at universities around the world. Students use ad-supported services like Facebook, MySpace, TagWorld and Bebo to make friends, plan their social lives and project their personalities. The most popular site among college students is Facebook, with more than 8 million members. A student's personal Facebook page is usually a revealing, dynamic chronicle of campus life — one clearly not meant for the eyes of parents, teachers or anyone else older than 25.

3   But adults are taking notice. Sites like Facebook are accessible to nearly anyone willing to spend the time to gain access: teachers, school administrators, even potential employers and the police. Such online services can create the illusion of privacy where none actually exists. Facebook, in particular, was designed to emphasize privacy and intimacy. Only other users at your school (with the same college e-mail domain name), and those in networks you join, can see your home page. But determined off-campus visitors can persuade a student or alumnus to help them access the student's page.

BACKGROUND: One-time professor of American history at Yale, James Surowiecki (b. 1967) is the financial columnist for the *New Yorker* and a regular contributor to other publications, including the *Wall Street Journal, Salon,* and *New York* magazine. He has written on a variety of financial and business topics, including bank mergers, the stock market, and the music industry. He has also edited *Best Crime Writing of the Year* (2002) and written *The Wisdom of Crowds: Why the Many Are Smarter Than the Few and How Collective Wisdom Shapes Business, Economies, Societies, and Nations* (2004). "Paying to Play" first appeared in the *New Yorker* (2004).

COMBINED PATTERNS AND THEIR PURPOSES: Hundreds of CDs come out each week, and radio stations cannot possibly play them all. Using *cause-and-effect analysis* and *exemplification,* James Surowiecki **informs** the reader about one way stations decide what to play: Music publishers buy airtime for their recordings. Surowiecki also has a **persuasive** purpose, as he aims to convince the reader (in part, with *comparison-contrast*) that pay-for-play is a flawed system.

PAYING TO PLAY

BY JAMES SUROWIECKI

POP MUSIC THRIVES on repetition. You know a song's a hit when you've heard it so often that you'll be happy never to hear it again. Even by Top 40 standards, though, the playlist adopted a few weeks ago by the Nashville radio station WQZQ was extreme. On May 23rd, *Billboard*[1] reported, the station played "Don't Tell Me," the new single by Avril Lavigne, three times an hour, every hour, between midnight and 6 A.M. This didn't have much to do with the tastes of WQZQ's d.j.s or listeners. Instead, an independent promoter working for Lavigne's record label had effectively paid the station to play the song. "Don't Tell Me" had been hovering just outside *Billboard*'s list of the country's ten most frequently played songs, which radio programmers use to decide what singles get airtime. The extra spins the promoter bought—sometimes called "spot buys," because what's really being bought are blocks of ad time, as with an infomercial—were meant to bump "Don't Tell Me" up the list. By early June, Lavigne had a Top 10 hit.

As you read
Pay attention to how the author achieves coherence in the essay.

> "By early June, Lavigne had a Top 10 hit. She also had a lot of angry music fans to contend with."

2   She also had a lot of angry music fans to contend with. Spot buys may be legal, but to most people they're the "new payola," a modern-day equivalent of Alan Freed's[2] taking money under the table to play rock-and-roll records. (Freed called

---

[1] *Billboard* is an international news weekly about the music industry. Among its features are charts of music sales and airplay.

[2] Alan Freed (1922–1965) was a disc jockey and rock-and-roll promoter. In 1962, he pleaded guilty to accepting money to play records. Some say he was a scapegoat, punished because he played records by black artists for white audiences.

the payments "consulting fees.") It's an obvious comparison, but a misplaced one. Spot buys aren't the same as old-fashioned payola. They're worse.

3   "Payola" became a household word in the fifties, when a host of d.j.s were found to be playing songs in exchange for favors and money, but the practice is as old as pop music itself. A century ago, song writers routinely paid vaudeville singers to perform their tunes, hoping to goose demand for sheet music. In the thirties, music publishers paid off radio bandleaders. And although some forms of payola were outlawed after the midcentury scandals, various loopholes allowed other incarnations to thrive, under the guise of independent promotion. With money from the record companies, promoters used oblique tactics — subsidies, gifts, "research funds" — to encourage radio stations to add new singles to their playlists. By 2000, tens of millions of dollars a year were being spent on what you might call legal payola, and although bad publicity has severely curtailed the promotion business, paying to play is still integral to the way radio works.

4   Despite its sleazy reputation, payola has a certain rationale. In a typical year, upward of seven or eight hundred CDs are issued each week. Not even the most dedicated program director can hope to sift through all the new songs. So stations need a way to filter the possible hits from the certain bombs. Pay-for-play schemes provide one rough-and-ready way to do this, because they involve what economists call signalling. By putting money behind a record, a label signals its belief that the record has a chance to be a hit; no company will spend a lot of money trying to sell something it doesn't have high hopes for. And hits, of course, are the only thing that radio cares about.

> "And hits, of course, are the only thing that radio cares about."

5   You can see the same process at work in many other businesses, too. Supermarkets and drugstores accept billions of dollars a year in "slotting fees" to position products at the end of an aisle or at eye level. Book chains sell space on the tables at the front of their stores. And record stores accept advertising dollars from labels to push certain albums. Here, too, being willing to shell out for a good space on the shelf is a statement about how much you think people will want your product.

6   This is, at best, a flawed way to find hits. Unless a record label has a good sense of what people want to hear, it could be buying airtime for flops. And labels that don't have the cash to promote their records are out of luck. But the surprising truth is that, historically speaking, payola has often fostered musical diversity, rather than squelching it. In the fifties, the music industry was dominated by a few giant labels, much as it is today; because of payola (and payola-takers, like Alan Freed), the smaller labels that revolutionized the industry—including Atlantic, Chess, and King Records—were able to get their music on the air. In retail, too, paying for space hasn't necessarily hindered innovation. Even as slotting fees have become more common in supermarkets, for instance, the number of new products that reach the shelves each year has exploded. And the same is true with books. We tend to assume that payola favors the big players because they are the ones with the big money. But the big players also have big sales forces, big brand names,

and big connections. They'd win without having to ante up to get in on the action. Paying to play, then, creates a rough marketplace democracy: if you can come up with the cash, you get a shot. But that's all. Labels can buy themselves exposure; they can't buy themselves a hit. If people don't want to hear a record, radio stations won't keep playing it of their own accord.

7   And that's where spot buys come in. Unlike conventional pay-for-play deals, spot buys like the one that propelled Avril Lavigne into the Top 10 aren't meant to introduce listeners to songs; they're meant to game the playlist system. It's a salient feature of modern media that being thought to be popular can make you more popular. Best-selling books and records are discounted more than slow-selling ones and are positioned more prominently. Songs in *Billboard*'s Top 10 automatically end up being spun more. And if you invest lots of money in creating an illusion of popularity—by, say, buying hours of airplay on the radio—you may end up making yourself more popular. In the process, what real listeners want matters less than it ever did. In "Payola Blues," Neil Young[3] sang to Alan Freed, "The things they're doing today/Will make a saint out of you." He didn't know the half of it.

———

[3]Neil Young is an influential singer-songwriter who was particularly prominent during the 1970s and 1980s.

READING CLOSELY AND THINKING CRITICALLY

1. What is the thesis of the essay?
2. Why does Surowiecki believe that spot buys are worse than payola? Do you agree? Why or why not?
3. What are the negative effects of pay-for-play?
4. Do you think sales of music, including downloads, would decline if more people knew about pay-for-play? Why or why not?

EXAMINING STRUCTURE AND STRATEGY

1. What approach does Surowiecki use for his introduction? Why does he use this approach?
2. In paragraph 3, Surowiecki gives the history of pay-for-play. Why does he include this information? How does it help him achieve his purpose for writing?
3. Which paragraphs have topic sentences that introduce a discussion of a cause or effect of pay-for-play?
4. How does Surowiecki achieve coherence between paragraphs 1 and 2? Between paragraphs 2 and 3? Between paragraphs 3 and 4? Between paragraphs 4 and 5? (See page 67 on coherence.)
5. How does the repetition of *Avril Lavigne* in the conclusion help achieve coherence?

NOTING COMBINED PATTERNS

1. How does Surowiecki use comparison-contrast to help achieve his writing purpose?
2. Why does Surowiecki compare spot buying of radio time to paying slotting fees in retail stores?
3. The opening paragraph includes an extended example, and examples appear in paragraphs 3, 5, and 6. How does this exemplification help the author achieve his writing purpose?

CONSIDERING LANGUAGE AND STYLE

1. In paragraph 6, Surowiecki says that paying to play creates a "marketplace democracy." In your opinion, is this phrase accurate? Why or why not?
2. Surowiecki uses informal language, including "goose" (paragraph 3), "shell out" (paragraph 5), and "game the playlist" (paragraph 7). What effect does this informal usage create? Is the informal usage appropriate? Explain.
3. Consult a dictionary if you do not know the meaning of any of these words: *under the table* (paragraph 2), *incarnations* (paragraph 3), *guise* (paragraph 3), *salient* (paragraph 7).

FOR DISCUSSION IN CLASS OR ONLINE

Is "signalling" (paragraph 4) a valid way to filter "possible hits from the certain bombs"? Why or why not? Can you think of a better alternative to signalling and pay-for-play?

WRITING ASSIGNMENTS

1. **Writing in your journal.** What do you think of the manipulation of the marketplace revealed in the essay? In what other ways are consumers' choices and preferences manipulated? Who benefits, and how does that make you feel? Answer one or more of these questions in a page or so.
2. **Using cause-and-effect analysis for a purpose.** The purposes in the assignments are possibilities. You may establish whatever purpose you like, within your instructor's guidelines.
   - To express your feelings and inform, explain what causes you to like one of the following: a song, a movie, a television show, a video game, a music video, or a book. How much of the title's appeal is the result of how often you see or hear it?
   - Explain why you buy particular items in the grocery store, pharmacy, or bookstore, or from a Web site. Are you influenced by the location of the product in the store or on the Web site? Your purpose can be to inform and perhaps persuade that positioning does or does not influence buyers.
   - To inform and perhaps relate experience, explain the causes and effects of the illusions we create. You can consider such illusions as those we create in chat rooms, on résumés, and in the classroom with such artifices as posturing, lying, makeup, hair dye, wigs, and plastic surgery.

3. **Combining patterns.** In paragraph 7, Surowiecki says that "if you invest lots of money in creating an illusion of popularity . . . you may end up making yourself more popular." Use definition (explained in Chapter 12) to explain what popularity is in a particular context, such as high school, politics, media, or athletics. In addition, use cause-and-effect analysis to explain how money can create the "illusion of popularity" in that context. You can also use process analysis (explained in Chapter 8) to track the process whereby popularity is achieved.

4. **Analyzing and assessing.** Spend some time in a chain bookstore, a supermarket, and a chain drugstore analyzing the products on display. Then assess how the merchandise in these stores does or does not support Surowiecki's explanation in paragraph 5 of how businesses control the amount of choice consumers have. What do you conclude about the significance of Surowiecki's points for consumers?

5. **Connecting and synthesizing the readings.** Surowiecki says that "being thought to be popular can make you more popular" (paragraph 7). Explain what he means and whether or not you agree with him. For ideas, you can draw on your own experience and observation as well as "The Poncho Bearer" (page 212) or "Lifosuction" (page 250).

6. **Drawing on sources.** Research the payola scandal of the 1950s and Alan Freed's alleged role in it. Then write a brief summary of what happened. For information, you can type "Alan Freed payola" into your favorite search engine or look up "Alan Freed" and "payola" in *Infotrac* or *Social Sciences Index*.

BACKGROUND: Educated at the University of Michigan and Columbia, where she earned her M.A. in journalism, Carlin Flora is a staff writer for *Psychology Today,* where she has also been a features editor. She has written on many topics, including ice skaters, being happy, making good first impressions, passive-aggression, and the neuroscience of chess mastery. "The Beguiling Truth about Beauty" first appeared in *Psychology Today* in 2006.

COMBINED PATTERNS AND THEIR PURPOSE: Using *cause-and-effect analysis,* along with *exemplification* and *comparison-contrast,* Carlin Flora **informs** readers about what prompts us to think of ourselves as attractive or unattractive. Do we really see ourselves as others see us? The answer may surprise you.

THE BEGUILING TRUTH ABOUT BEAUTY

BY CARLIN FLORA

Don't hate yourself for wanting to be beautiful. Good-looking people get special treatment from strangers, employers and even their own mothers. The comely reap real social and economic gains in life, from broader romantic proposals to lighter punishment in criminal courts. The rest of us curse the advantages of beauty because we can never claim membership in the knockout club.

As you read
Think about how other people influence the way you perceive how attractive you are.

2   Or can we? We're not even close to objective when it comes to judging our own looks. Other people see the whole package. But when we look in the mirror, we're liable to zero in on the imperfections. That bump on your friend's nose? It's her trademark! It gives her character! But to you, that thing on *your* nose is downright disfiguring. Our opinion of our own looks is also capricious.

> "Don't hate yourself for wanting to be beautiful."

We can feel like the belle of the ball at one party, but downright shabby at the next, all on the same night.

3   So if we can't trust our own self-appraisal, or the reassurances of friends and family, we're left to the cool judgment of strangers to satisfy our curiosity about our appearance. The Web site "Hot or Not," which lets people anonymously submit their photos for others to rate on a 10-point scale, had nearly 2 million daily page views within a week of launching in 2000. Not exactly the best way to bolster your self-image.

4   The good news: You're almost certainly hotter than you think. It's partly a matter of limited attention—everyone else is too fixated on his or her own appearance to be critical of yours. If you are particularly attentive to your body (as women tend to be), or if you feel uncomfortable in public, you are almost *definitely* hotter than you think. And we all have the innate ability to change how other people perceive us, without a physical transformation of any kind. When you're convinced you look good, others see you in a more favorable light. Call it an internal makeover: Understanding your own powerful self-perceptions can help you stop obsessing over your appearance—and look better.

5   Why is it that our self-judgments shift like weather on a spring day? Even a stroll down a street can change the way you think about your looks. Our brains have a built-in hot-or-not meter that never stops gathering data.

6   Psychologists call it the "contrast effect": You feel prettier around ugly people and uglier around pretty people. These social comparisons happen not only when you deliberately scrutinize passersby, but constantly and automatically. In one study, people given a subliminal glimpse of an attractive female face subsequently rated themselves as less attractive than those who saw a homely one, though no one remembered having seen the images at all. Our self-concepts are built on thousands of these comparisons.

7   "I'm five feet tall and I'm curvy. I feel good about how I look," says Deanna Melluso, a New York City–based makeup artist who dolls up models for magazine shoots and runway shows. "But when I'm around tall, thin women all day, I start to feel fat. As soon as I walk outside, I feel normal again—I see that I've been in a fake world."

8   Perhaps because their social status is often contingent upon their faces and bodies, women are particularly susceptible to this effect. "When women evaluate their physical attractiveness, they compare themselves with an idealized standard of beauty, such as a fashion model," says Richard Robins, professor of psychology at the University of California, Davis. "In contrast, when both men and women evaluate their intelligence, they do not compare themselves to Einstein, but rather to a more mundane standard."

9   In a study where people were asked to solve math problems, there was no difference in how well men and women scored—when everyone was fully dressed. But when subjects were required to perform the calculations in their bathing suits, the women suddenly fared worse than their male counterparts. They were too busy wondering how they looked to crunch numbers correctly.

10   Everyone judges his or her own appearance more critically when self-aware, as when giving a presentation to coworkers. But people who score high on measures of a personality trait called "public self-consciousness" feel that way all the time. We all know someone like this—a friend who never runs out of the house to grab coffee without fixing herself up first. Strangers generally consider such people to be more physically attractive than average, says William Thornton, professor of psychology at the University of Maine. But that extra personal care doesn't correct their internal funhouse mirrors: They tend to compare themselves exclusively with very good-looking people—and feel especially down after doing so.

11   As our faces and figures evolve during childhood and adolescence, we create a picture of ourselves that is hard to get out of our minds in adulthood, however outdated or wrong it may be. Not all people who grow up disliking their appearance were ugly children, says James Rosen, emeritus professor of psychology at the University of Vermont. Some were perfectly cute as kids, but had an exceptional trait, like being very tall or heavily freckled, which drew comments and stares.

12   Our "internal mirrors" are often shaped by our parents, contends psychoanalyst Vivian Diller. A child whose parents tell him he's ugly will have to overcome that perception, but that's uncommon. More subtle is the effect of "the gleam in their eye," says Diller—whether parents sincerely light up at the sight of us and appreciate our individual charms.

13   While parental love can bolster self-esteem for some, there's no direct line between childhood experiences and adult self-image. Ugly ducklings sometimes

turn into swans—or find their looks suddenly validated by committee. Donelle Ruwe, now an English professor at Northern Arizona University, grew up terribly gawky, a teen with glasses, a back brace and, yes, even headgear. But she played piano very well. At the age of 19, she'd recently shed the brace, and a pageant scout looking to improve the talent quotient in a beauty competition suggested she sign up. She did, and was crowned Miss Meridian, Iowa, of 1985.

14 "For the first time, I felt that I was attractive," she says. That new confidence in her looks actually made her feel freer to develop her intellect—she was quicker to assert her opinions in class and debate with others. "I think that when you are self-conscious about your body, too much of your mind and emotions are focused on it," she says. "But once you let go of that self-consciousness, you can interact without it getting in the way."

15 But those who are gorgeous from the get-go face their own set of potential problems. Very attractive kids may grow up to be insecure adults, especially if they were praised solely for their appearance. They may develop a particularly harsh way of assessing themselves—what Heather Patrick, a researcher at Baylor College of Medicine, calls "contingent self-esteem." They may feel good about their looks only if they meet a specific, and usually very high, expectation, such as weighing in at a certain number. Self-satisfaction is not on a spectrum for such people: If they don't meet their standard, they feel absolutely ugly.

> "But those who are gorgeous from the get-go face their own set of potential problems."

16 Carol Alt, the former *Sports Illustrated* cover girl, fell victim to this phenomenon in 1995, when a fashion photographer declared her too jiggly for her bikini. After he spent a day on location attempting to hide her extra ounces of flesh behind rocks, he fired her and sent her back to Los Angeles, where she slipped into a weeks-long, Nyquil-soaked depression. "I'd feel fat and guilty anytime I ate," she says now. "I didn't feel I had control over my body, and that fragility was frustrating and even terrifying."

17 With looks, as in other domains of life, we relish recognition more and recover better from failure when we believe that good results come from effort and not just from what God gave us. If you are born lovely, you have only your parents' genetic contributions to thank. But if you become more attractive because you've invested energy in taking good care of yourself, the credit is all yours.

18 Alt says she feels better-looking now, in her mid-forties, than she ever has. The author of *Eating in the Raw* says that overhauling her diet made the difference. "Now I'm more complimented when someone comments on something I've worked for, such as keeping myself healthy, than when someone says, 'You're beautiful.'"

19 Ultimately, good looks aren't just a question of a lucky birth. In real life—outside the artificial bounds of lab tests and "hot or not" snapshots—our physical appearance is always evaluated alongside our body language, voice and temperament. Charm *can* trump beauty. In one study, psychologists videotaped people as they entered a room and introduced themselves to two people. They then asked strangers to rate the videotaped subjects on physical attractiveness, emotional

expressiveness and social skills. All three qualities contributed to the subjects' over-all likeability—but attractiveness was the least important factor.

20   The easiest way to influence how others view you is to demonstrate that you like them, say Ann Demarais and Valerie White, psychologists and authors of *First Impressions: What You Don't Know about How Others See You.* If you express interest in what others say, or smile and lightly touch their arm, they will likely feel flattered, comfortable around you and even more attracted to you. A person who finds you likeable will probably never notice your imperfections—besides, no one is as interested in your bald head or fleshy thighs as you are. Demarais and White tell of a client who suffered from the "spotlight illusion"—he imagined that people were homing in on his crooked teeth, which were his least favorite feature. Realizing that other people didn't really care about his teeth was freeing. "He experimented with smiling broadly when he met new people," they write. "When no one reacted in horror, and in fact responded positively, he began to feel at ease with his smile. When he seemed more comfortable in his own skin, he became more appealing to others."

21   Most of us have had the mysterious experience of watching a loved one become increasingly beautiful with time, as the relationship grows deeper. Imagine that generous gaze is upon you all the time, and you'll soon see a better reflection in others' eyes. You may not be able to turn off your inner hot-or-not meter, but you can spend less time fretting in the mirror and more time engaging with the world.

READING CLOSELY AND THINKING CRITICALLY

1.   What inference is contained in the first sentence of the essay? Is the inference a valid one? Explain. (See page 5 on inferences.)

2.   According to the essay, what are some factors that cause people to see themselves as attractive or unattractive?

3.   In your own words, explain the cause-and-effect relationship involved in the "contrast effect" explained in paragraph 6.

4.   Do you think the contrast effect is applicable to traits other than attractiveness? Explain.

5.   Paragraph 4 says that the effect of stopping our obsession with our own looks is that we end up looking better. How is that possible?

EXAMINING STRUCTURE AND STRATEGY

1.   Is there a sentence that best expresses the thesis of "The Beguiling Truth about Beauty"? If so, which one? If not, state the thesis in your own words.

2.   What approach does Flora take to her introduction in order to stimulate interest in the essay? Is the approach effective? Explain.

3.   Paragraphs 19–20 move away from a discussion of why we feel attractive or unattractive to a discussion of the causes of likability and the effects of the "'spotlight illusion.'" Why? Is the discussion of likability relevant?

4. What causal chain is established in paragraphs 13–14? How does that causal chain help Flora achieve her writing purpose?

5. What approach does Flora take to the conclusion? Is the conclusion effective? Explain.

NOTING COMBINED PATTERNS

1. What pattern of development (other than cause-and-effect analysis) is used in paragraphs 2, 8, and 9? How does that pattern help Flora achieve her purpose for writing?

2. Paragraphs 7, 13–14, and 16–18 all include examples that feature women. Why does Flora focus on women rather than men? Paragraph 20 includes an example about a man. Should the author have included more examples that feature men?

CONSIDERING LANGUAGE AND STYLE

1. Paragraph 3 includes an intentional sentence fragment. What purpose does that fragment serve?

2. Consult a dictionary if you do not know the meaning of these words: *capricious* (paragraph 2), *subliminal* (paragraph 6).

FOR DISCUSSION IN CLASS OR ONLINE

Why would people post their pictures for evaluation on the Hot or Not Web site? Do men and women do it for the same reasons?

WRITING ASSIGNMENTS

1. **Writing in your journal.** In paragraph 5, Flora says, "Our brains have a built-in hot-or-not meter that never stops gathering data." Is this statement true for you? Explain.

2. **Using cause-and-effect analysis for a purpose.** The purposes given here are possibilities. You may establish whatever purpose you like, within your instructor's guidelines.

   • To inform, write a cause-and-effect analysis of how students form their views of themselves as students. If you like, you can also include one or more of the effects of their self-perception.

   • People sometimes form opinions of others based on their appearance. To inform and/or relate experience, discuss the causes and/or effects of judging people based on their appearance.

   • Paragraph 6 refers to "social comparisons." Discuss the causes or effects of social comparisons in the workplace, on an athletic team, or at a party.

3. **Combining patterns.** In paragraph 1, Flora says, "Good-looking people get special treatment." Suggest some causes for this phenomenon and, illustrating with examples, suggest some effects.

4. **Analyzing and assessing.** Summarize Flora's main points, and assess how effectively she supports and develops them. Consider the number and quality of the examples, as well as how well those examples and the statements of cause and effect are developed and supported.

5. **Connecting and synthesizing the readings.** Drawing on the ideas in "The Beguiling Truth about Beauty," "Ring Leader" (page 217), and "In the Kitchen" (page 317), along with your own experience and observation, explain how our concepts of attractiveness affect our behavior.

6. **Drawing on sources.** Visit the Hot or Not Web site at http://www.hotornot.com, and study its contents. Then write an essay that describes the site, explains its purpose, and speculates about why people post their pictures on the site. Finally, discuss the effects of the rating system on our perceptions of attractiveness and our self-images.

BACKGROUND: Born in 1951 in Chester, Pennsylvania, Brent Staples was the oldest of nine children. He grew up in poverty and never dreamed of going to college, until a black college professor helped him take a college preparatory course. A college scholarship rescued him from a life on the streets. One of his brothers, a cocaine dealer, was killed at age 22. Staples ultimately earned his Ph.D. in psychology from the University of Chicago. A member of the *New York Times* editorial board, he writes on education, politics, and culture for the newspaper. Before joining the *Times,* he was a reporter for the *Chicago Sun-Times.* He has also written for the *New York Times Magazine, Harper's,* and *New York Woman.* His memoir, *Parallel Time: Growing Up in Black and White* (1994), recalls his childhood in Chester and the death of his younger brother. It was a finalist for the *Los Angeles Times* Book Award. "Just Walk On By" appeared in *Ms.* in 1986 and in a revised form in *Harper's* (1987) as "Black Men and Public Space."

www.mhhe.com/clousepatterns6	Brent Staples

For more information on this author, go to

More resources > Chapter 10 > Brent Staples

COMBINED PATTERNS AND THEIR PURPOSES: In "Just Walk On By," Brent Staples uses *cause-and-effect analysis* to **inform** readers that black men are at risk because they are "perceived as dangerous." To illustrate the point, he includes *narration.* He also **shares his feelings** on this issue and **relates his experience** as a black man viewed as threatening.

JUST WALK ON BY: A BLACK MAN PONDERS HIS POWER TO ALTER PUBLIC SPACE

BY BRENT STAPLES

MY FIRST VICTIM was a woman—white, well dressed, probably in her early twenties. I came upon her late one evening on a deserted street in Hyde Park, a relatively affluent neighborhood in an otherwise mean, impoverished section of Chicago. As I swung onto the avenue behind her, there seemed to be a discreet uninflammatory distance between us. Not so. She cast back a worried glance. To her, the youngish black man—a broad six feet two inches with a beard and billowing hair, both hands shoved into the pockets of a bulky military jacket—seemed menacingly close. After a few more quick glimpses, she picked up her pace and was soon running in earnest. Within seconds she disappeared into a cross street.

As you read
Think about how you react to people on the basis of their appearance.

"After a few more quick glimpses, she picked up her pace and was soon running in earnest."

2   That was more than a decade ago. I was 22 years old, a graduate student newly arrived at the University of Chicago. It was in the echo of that terrified woman's footfalls that I first began to know the unwieldy inheritance I'd come into—the ability to alter public space in ugly ways. It was clear that she thought herself the

quarry of a mugger, a rapist, or worse. Suffering a bout of insomnia, however, I was stalking sleep, not defenseless wayfarers. As a softy who is scarcely able to take a knife to a raw chicken—let alone hold it to a person's throat—I was surprised, embarrassed, and dismayed all at once. Her flight made me feel like an accomplice in tyranny. It also made it clear that I was indistinguishable from the muggers who occasionally seeped into the area from the surrounding ghetto. That first encounter, and those that followed, signified that a vast, unnerving gulf lay between nighttime pedestrians — particularly women—and me. And I soon gathered that being perceived as dangerous is a hazard in itself. I only needed to turn a corner into a dicey situation, or crowd some frightened, armed person in a foyer somewhere, or make an errant move after being pulled over by a policeman. Where fear and weapons meet—and they often do in urban America—there is always the possibility of death.

3   In that first year, my first away from my hometown, I was to become thoroughly familiar with the language of fear. At dark, shadowy intersections in Chicago, I could cross in front of a car stopped at a traffic light and elicit the *thunk, thunk, thunk, thunk* of the driver—black, white, male, or female—hammering down the door locks. On less traveled streets after dark, I grew accustomed to but never comfortable with people who crossed to the other side of the street rather than pass me. Then there were the standard unpleasantries with police, doormen, bouncers, cab drivers, and others whose business it is to screen out troublesome individuals *before* there is any nastiness.

4   I moved to New York nearly two years ago and I have remained an avid night walker. In central Manhattan, the near-constant crowd cover minimizes tense one-on-one street encounters. Elsewhere—visiting friends in SoHo, where sidewalks are narrow and tightly spaced buildings shut out the sky—things can get very taut indeed.

5   Black men have a firm place in New York mugging literature. Norman Podhoretz in his famed (or infamous) 1963 essay, "My Negro Problem—And Ours," recalls growing up in terror of black males; they "were tougher than we were, more ruthless," he writes—and as an adult on the Upper West Side of Manhattan, he continues, he cannot constrain his nervousness when he meets black men on certain streets. Similarly, a decade later, the essayist and novelist Edward Hoagland extols a New York where once "Negro bitterness bore down mainly on other Negroes." Where some see mere panhandlers, Hoagland sees "a mugger who is clearly screwing up his nerve to do more than just *ask* for money." But Hoagland has "the New Yorker's quick-hunch posture for broken-field maneuvering," and the bad guy swerves away.

> "Black men have a firm place in New York mugging literature."

6   I often witness that "hunch posture," from women after dark on the warrenlike streets of Brooklyn where I live. They seem to set their faces on neutral and, with their purse straps strung across their chests bandolier style, they forge ahead as though bracing themselves against being tackled. I understand, of course, that the danger they perceive is not a hallucination. Women are particularly vulnerable to street violence, and young black males are drastically overrepresented among the

perpetrators of that violence. Yet these truths are no solace against the kind of alienation that comes of being ever the suspect, against being set apart, a fearsome entity with whom pedestrians avoid making eye contact.

7   It is not altogether clear to me how I reached the ripe old age of 22 without being conscious of the lethality nighttime pedestrians attributed to me. Perhaps it was because in Chester, Pennsylvania, the small angry industrial town where I came of age in the 1960s, I was scarcely noticeable against a backdrop of gang warfare, street knifings, and murders. I grew up one of the good boys, had perhaps a half-dozen fist fights. In retrospect, my shyness of combat has clear sources.

8   Many things go into the making of a young thug. One of those things is the consummation of the male romance with the power to intimidate. An infant discovers that random flailings send the baby bottle flying out of the crib and crashing to the floor. Delighted, the joyful babe repeats those motions again and again, seeking to duplicate the feat. Just so, I recall the points at which some of my boyhood friends were finally seduced by the perception of themselves as tough guys. When a mark cowered and surrendered his money without resistance, myth and reality merged—and paid off. It is, after all, only manly to embrace the power to frighten and intimidate. We, as men, are not supposed to give an inch of our lane on the highway; we are to seize the fighter's edge in work and in play and even in love; we are to be valiant in the face of hostile forces.

9   Unfortunately, poor and powerless young men seem to take all this nonsense literally. As a boy, I saw countless tough guys locked away; I have since buried several, too. They were babies, really—a teenage cousin, a brother of 22, a childhood friend in his mid-twenties—all gone down in episodes of bravado played out in the streets. I came to doubt the virtues of intimidation early on. I chose, perhaps even unconsciously, to remain a shadow—timid, but a survivor.

10   The fearsomeness mistakenly attributed to me in public places often has a perilous flavor. The most frightening of these confusions occurred in the late 1970s and early 1980s when I worked as a journalist in Chicago. One day, rushing into the office of a magazine I was writing for with a deadline story in hand, I was mistaken for a burglar. The office manager called security and, with an ad hoc posse, pursued me through the labyrinthine halls, nearly to my editor's door. I had no way of proving who I was. I could only move briskly toward the company of someone who knew me.

> "I had no way of proving who I was."

11   Another time I was on assignment for a local paper and killing time before an interview. I entered a jewelry store on the city's affluent Near North Side. The proprietor excused herself and returned with an enormous red Doberman pinscher straining at the end of a leash. She stood, the dog extended toward me, silent to my questions, her eyes bulging nearly out of her head. I took a cursory look around, nodded, and bade her good night. Relatively speaking, however, I never fared as badly as another black male journalist. He went to nearby Waukegan, Illinois, a couple of summers ago to work on a story about a murderer who was born there. Mistaking the reporter for the killer, police hauled him from his car at gunpoint and but for his press credentials would probably have tried to book him. Such episodes are not uncommon. Black men trade tales like this all the time.

12   In "My Negro Problem—And Ours," Podhoretz writes that the hatred he feels for blacks makes itself known to him through a variety of avenues—one being his discomfort with that "special brand of paranoid touchiness" to which he says blacks are prone. No doubt he is speaking here of black men. In time, I learned to smother the rage I felt at so often being taken for a criminal. Not to do so would surely have led to madness—via that special "paranoid touchiness" that so annoyed Podhoretz at the time he wrote the essay.

13   I began to take precautions to make myself less threatening. I move about with care, particularly late in the evening. I give a wide berth to nervous people on subway platforms during the wee hours, particularly when I have exchanged business clothes for jeans. If I happen to be entering a building behind some people who appear skittish, I may walk by, letting them clear the lobby before I return, so as not to seem to be following them. I have been calm and extremely congenial on those rare occasions when I've been pulled over by the police.

14   And on late-evening constitutionals along streets less traveled by, I employ what has proved to be an excellent tension-reducing measure: I whistle melodies from Beethoven and Vivaldi and the more popular classical composers. Even steely New Yorkers hunching toward night-time destinations seem to relax, and occasionally they even join in the tune. Virtually everybody seems to sense that a mugger wouldn't be warbling bright, sunny selections from Vivaldi's *Four Seasons*. It is my equivalent of the cowbell that hikers wear when they know they are in bear country.

READING CLOSELY AND THINKING CRITICALLY

1. When Staples walks at night, what effect does he have on people? What do people do when they see him?

2. Although Staples is often viewed as a threat, he is the one at risk. Why?

3. Staples explains that his effect on people—particularly women—is understandable. Why does he think so?

4. According to Staples, what causes a young man to become a thug? What do you think prompts a black male to become a thug? How did Staples escape becoming a thug?

5. In paragraphs 5 and 12, Staples refers to essays by Norman Podhoretz and Edward Hoagland. What point do you think Staples is trying to make with these references?

6. Staple's essay first appeared in *Ms.* and *Harper's*. *Ms.* is a magazine about women's issues and takes a politically progressive stand; *Harper's* is one of the oldest and most prestigious American magazines, publishing literature, commentary, arts reviews, and in-depth reporting with a liberal viewpoint. Do the readers of these magazines make the best audience for the piece? Explain.

EXAMINING STRUCTURE AND STRATEGY

1. What approach does Staples take to his introduction? Does the introduction engage your interest? Explain.
2. The essay is not about what the opening sentences lead you to believe it will be about. Is that a problem? Explain.
3. In your own words, write out the thesis of "Just Walk On By." Which sentence in the essay comes closest to expressing that idea?
4. What approach does Staples take to his conclusion? Do you think the conclusion brings the essay to a satisfying close? Why or why not?

NOTING COMBINED PATTERNS

1. Staples discusses both causes and effects in his essay. What causes and effects are explained?
2. Which paragraphs include brief narrations? How do they help Staples achieve his writing purpose?

CONSIDERING LANGUAGE AND STYLE

1. What is "public space"? What does it mean to possess the power to alter public space? Name groups of people that have the power to alter public space.
2. Consult a dictionary if you are unsure of the meaning of any of these words: *quarry* (paragraph 2), *wayfarers* (paragraph 2), *errant* (paragraph 2), *extols* (paragraph 5), *warrenlike* (paragraph 6), *bandolier* (paragraph 6), *bravado* (paragraph 9), *ad hoc* (paragraph 10), *labyrinthine* (paragraph 10), *cursory* (paragraph 11), *constitutionals* (paragraph 14).

FOR DISCUSSION IN CLASS OR ONLINE

What causes a person to be perceived as threatening?

WRITING ASSIGNMENTS

1. **Writing in your journal.** Although we admit that appearances can be deceiving, we often are influenced by the way others look. How do appearances affect the judgments we make about people? For example, how did the attacks on the World Trade Center and the Pentagon in September 2001 affect the way Arab Americans are sometimes perceived?
2. **Using cause-and-effect analysis for a purpose.** The purposes in the assignments are possibilities. You may establish whatever purpose you like, within your instructor's guidelines.
   - How safe do you feel walking alone on your campus or in your neighborhood? To relate experience, express feelings, and inform, explain why you feel the way you do and the effects of your feeling of security or insecurity.

- To relate experience, express feelings, and inform, explain how you think you are perceived by others and why you think you are perceived that way. Consider how one or more factors, such as your size, gender, skin color, age, manner of dress, and degree of attractiveness, affect how people judge your social class, economic level, degree of intelligence, occupation, and such. Then go on to explain how you are affected by the way you are perceived.

- If you have ever been perceived as a threat or if you have perceived someone else as a threat, explain what caused the perception and what its effects were in order to relate experience and express feelings.

3. **Combining patterns.** In paragraph 8, Staples comments on men and power: "It is, after all, only manly to embrace the power to frighten and intimidate." Do you agree that our concept of manliness is linked to the sense of power and the ability to intimidate? Agree or disagree by defining *manliness* (see Chapter 12) and explaining how men and women are affected by the concept.

4. **Analyzing and assessing.** Analyze Staples's use of description in the essay, and assess what it contributes to the piece, particularly how it helps the author achieve his writing purpose. To arrive at some conclusions, you might consider what the essay would be like without the descriptive language and description of people and places.

5. **Connecting and synthesizing the readings.** Explain how people react to those they perceive as "different." Also explain why you think people react the way they do. "Just Walk On By," "The Poncho Bearer" (page 212), and "Untouchables" (page 275) may give you some ideas.

6. **Drawing on sources.** Racial profiling occurs when the police make decisions based solely on race. For example, police officers who automatically stop and question young black males are practicing racial profiling. Summarize the arguments used to defend racial profiling and the arguments used to attack it. You can find information by typing in the phrase "racial profiling" at www.mywire.com or by looking up "racial profiling" in *The Reader's Guide to Periodical Literature* or the *New York Times Index.*

BACKGROUND: Child psychologist Dorothy Siegel is vice president emeritus for student services at Towson State University, Towson, Maryland, and founder of the Campus Violence Prevention Center at Towson, which has carried out significant research on issues related to campus violence. An authority on campus crime, Siegel has testified before Congress on the subject. The first director of Maryland's Institute Against Prejudice, Siegel also lectures and leads workshops about student services and campus violence and is a consultant to the U.S. Departments of Justice and Education. Siegel has written *Campuses Respond to Violent Tragedy* (1994), which discusses campus responses to assaults, deaths, and disasters and suggests how college officials can respond to crises. "What Is Behind the Growth of Violence on College Campuses?" first appeared in *USA Today Magazine* in 1994.

THE PATTERN AND ITS PURPOSE: In "What Is Behind the Growth of Violence on College Campuses?" Dorothy Siegel examines the *causes* of campus violence to **inform** readers. To make her points, Siegel often draws on statistics, some of which may surprise you.

WHAT IS BEHIND THE GROWTH OF VIOLENCE ON COLLEGE CAMPUSES?

BY DOROTHY SIEGEL

AMERICA'S COLLEGE CAMPUSES are not the war zones newspaper and magazine articles would lead the public to believe. Those crimes committed against students get major attention from the media probably because campuses are expected to be serene and safe. What is perhaps most troubling about campus crime is that the majority of the incidents, excluding theft, but including rape and other sexual assaults, are impulsive acts committed by students themselves, according to nationwide studies conducted by Towson State University's Campus Violence Prevention Center. Students are responsible for 80 percent of campus crime, although rarely with weapons.

> "Students are responsible for 80 percent of campus crime, although rarely with weapons."

As you read
Consider why Siegel wrote for the broad readership of *USA Today Magazine* rather than a publication aimed primarily at college students.

2   It is an uphill battle to ensure student safety. Schools provide escort services, tamper-proof windows, and continually upgraded state-of-the-art exterior lighting and electronic alarm systems. These institutional efforts frequently are undone by the immortal feelings of college-age men and women. That "it-can't-happen-to-me" attitude leads to lax security behaviors that literally leave the door open for an outside threat. Universities are challenged to help students develop and keep that awareness, except for the two weeks following an on-campus assault, when caution prevails.

3   The same students who sponsor night walks to check the lighting and grounds to increase safety will hold the door open for a stranger entering their residence hall. Despite frequent warnings, students—and even faculty, administrators, and other campus personnel—act less judiciously than they would elsewhere.

4   The mind-set of the students and probably of most of us is that crime is going to happen at night. Following a daylight abduction at one school, students demanded better lighting and evening patrols. They are loathe to follow the cautions about garages and out-of-the-way places during the day. They have trouble acknowledging, as we all probably do, that current criminal acts require new precautions, more appropriate to what is happening now.

5   Today, as part of the orientation programs at campuses across the nation, most administrators welcome students with information about crime on campus and ways they better can ensure their own safety. Because the Higher Education Security Act requires schools to report their previous year's crime statistics to the campus [community], colleges greet many new students and their parents with the previous year's count of violations and wise warnings. They are united in their efforts to command students' attention and enlist them as active partners in prevention. They use theater, video, discussions, posters, and circulars to inform students. Police statistics and reports are disseminated widely.

6   Despite this, if a stranger is seen entering a building, it is unlikely that any observers will notify the police, even if the potential assailant is dressed strangely and/or behaving oddly. If that stranger attacks someone the community will demand more protection. A series of seminars will produce good ideas and vigilant behavior for about two weeks, after which much of the more casual behavior about safety reappears.

7   When students discuss safety, it always is about dangers from outside the campus. Students are both the perpetrators and victims of most campus crime, yet it still is protection from trespassers that motivates most safety programs and is most in demand. It is an arduous and mostly unsuccessful process to convince students that they are more likely to be a victim of crime perpetrated by a member of their class or athletic team than by a stranger. It appears unthinkable that they themselves may become assailants. Although this message is included in many orientation programs for new students, it is nearly impossible to alert them to the potential danger from people they trust simply because they are members of the same community. Yet, eight percent of students report that they have been perpetrators and approximately 12 percent say they have been victims of assault.

> "It appears unthinkable that they themselves may become assailants."

8   Visitors to a campus during the day will see a reasonably civil society. Students will congregate in various common areas and study, talk, laugh, or even sleep. The homeless may gather on the campus benches while a non-student stands and shouts what he or she maintains is God's will. Literally thousands of people will pass without incident. If campus police are writing citations, it is likely to be for parking violations.

9   Yet, on any night from Thursday to Saturday on the same campus, the majority of students will be drinking, some excessively, and fights will erupt over seemingly trival issues—who can have the bedroom, the keys, the boyfriend or girlfriend, the Nintendo. Small differences may escalate into brawls when combined with drug and alcohol abuse. Student assistants in residence halls may write up hundreds of

classmates for violation of the campus alcohol policy. These reports are forwarded for administrative action. Few, if any, students will be arrested. Other drunk students will be returning from town where similar incidents may have occurred. Police rarely are called for fear of endangering the bar's liquor license. Still other students are on their way to parties, where recreational drinking is the featured attraction.

10   My first experience with campus violence came after I had spent two years in my current position as vice president for student services at Towson State University. One Friday evening, a drunk student trying to enter a residence hall to visit a friend beat the student worker who denied him access. The employee was hospitalized overnight. Although the student was criminally charged, the university immediately had to create procedures for an on-campus hearing to determine how the institution should respond. He was the first student suspended from the university because of assault charges stemming from a campus incident.

11   In the late 1970s, some students on campuses around the country reported being victims of assaults by fellow students. Residence directors observed increases in vandalism. Personnel at different schools thought they were experiencing situations unique to their own campuses. Rural and urban, large and small schools noted the existence of violent incidents, quantified in Towson State's surveys of over 1,000 colleges. Those studies became the nation's first national data on student-perpetrated violence. It documented that students were both victims and perpetrators of rape, other sexual violence, and physical assault.

UNITED STATES OF VIOLENCE

12   When sexual assaults and rapes are reported, an interviewer most frequently will learn that the two students have known each other, sometimes meeting at a party earlier that evening. Typically, they both will have been drinking. One may have accepted the other's invitation to share a room because a roommate was entertaining someone. He may make advances. She says she only will accept the offer of the room (or extend the offer) if it is a non-sexual relationship. He accepts the terms, but believes her accompanying him means she is willing. She thinks she has communicated effectively. He thinks he has understood. Such misunderstandings make one appreciate the clear consent to sex that Antioch College demands of its students as set forth in its most recent handbook.

13   One percent of students reported more physically brutal rapes. Four percent of female students stated that they had been raped, predominantly by other students. Researchers report that 74 percent of sexually related crimes were committed by fellow students. More than 30 percent of these sexual crimes were committed by fraternity members, while 14 percent were committed by athletes, some by friends of friends.

14   The majority of perpetrators indicated that they were drunk, high, or in need of drugs when the crimes were committed. Substance abuse is a direct correlate of violent campus behavior. Researchers from Towson State's Campus Violence Prevention Center reported in a study of responses from 1,800 college students nationwide that abuse of alcohol was heavier among victims and perpetrators than the rest of the campus population. A later study of more than 13,000 students

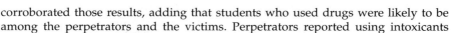

corroborated those results, adding that students who used drugs were likely to be among the perpetrators and the victims. Perpetrators reported using intoxicants more often than did victims. In turn, the victims reported heavier drinking habits than those who were neither victims nor assailants. Whether drunk or not, a substantial majority of victims and perpetrators said that, on the day of the crime, they had been drinking and/or using drugs. It is a logical conclusion that students usually will not become victims or perpetrators in student-to-student violence if they do not use drugs or abuse alcohol.

> "The majority of perpetrators indicated that they were drunk, high, or in need of drugs when the crimes were committed."

15   In spite of all the messages of abstinence that are drilled into the nation's youth from elementary school years on, many students come to higher education with histories of excessive drinking. Against the backdrop of violence that exists in American society, the loss of control heightened by substance abuse, including alcohol, often is accompanied by violent outbursts. The various preventive efforts such as mediation and conflict resolution offered by some schools are not effective techniques for preventing the acts fueled by the presence of alcohol.

16   Universities formerly had acted *in loco parentis.* When the national age of majority was lowered to 18, college administrators had to alter their relationship with students because institutions no longer could behave as substitute parents for youths who now could vote, drink, and go to war. While it is not documented how effective such supervision of students was, it is clear that those who wished to violate the rules had to work harder to do so. The current relationship is adult-to-adult, even though the institutions recognize that many students are not fully mature. That poses a continuing dilemma for campus personnel in helping students to develop control over their behavior, thus assuring their own safety and that of their peers.

17   Although the legal drinking age has been raised to 21 in each state, the national community of 18- to 20-year-olds simply does not accept this constraint. Some estimates are that as many as 80 percent of underage students carry fake proof-of-age identification. Drinking has become a standard pastime, and binge drinking—five or more drinks at a sitting—is condoned by 85 percent of college freshmen. The number of students who report excessive drinking is less in the sophomore year and decreases in each of the subsequent years. It has not been determined if the excessive drinkers have dropped out or changed their ways. It

> "It has not been determined if the excessive drinkers have dropped out or changed their ways."

probably is some of both. The people who have been most responsive to the substance abuse education programs are the casual users who reportedly are abstaining totally now. The laws are not effective despite substantial efforts. No way has been found to govern a population by laws they do not accept.

SEEKING UNDERSTANDING

18   College students are among the nation's brightest and most successful people. In general, they come from higher socioeconomic backgrounds than the non-college-attending members of their age group. Although there has been no formal study of their behavior after university attendance, it is unlikely that perpetrators of college incidents will commit other violent crimes later. Most do not repeat offenses on campus. A contributing factor may be that many schools require those responsible to attend substance abuse intervention programs as a condition of returning to or continuing to attend the university.

19   Administrators are at a loss to understand why such an increase in student violence has emerged in the past two decades. They have tried to study the problem from several approaches, but the only factor that remains the same in the majority of cases is alcohol abuse. It is not known if as many students in the past drank as much as current ones do. Research shows, though, that almost 50 percent of freshmen had been drunk within two weeks preceding the study.

20   Behaviors that lead to violence usually are tolerated by students. Resident students are reluctant to complain, even in cases where their rights and their living space are violated by the conduct of others. They may ask for alternate housing, but are not apt to make a formal complaint. Only victims report crimes. Most actions that lead to assaultive behaviors are tolerated by the student community. Students who dislike the rowdiness are more apt to move away than to assert their rights to a more appropriate living environment.

21   On more and more campuses, housing options available to students include alcohol-free residence halls. Those who choose them have quieter and less disruptive lives. Such an option is not successful when someone other than the students themselves makes those choices.

22   It is easy to prevent violence if each student is kept under lock and key. It is a more challenging problem in a society that values freedom. The message to students is that a safe community requires their participation. The role of police is to facilitate safety, not assure it. It is a challenge to have an environment appropriate for growth and learning and safety in today's society.

23   Student society evolves and changes. For instance, women increasingly are the assaulters. Though still in the single-digit numbers and not nearly as high as the amount of incidents with male perpetrators, the total is going up. More students are participating in communal efforts to help others, which may indicate that they are assuming more membership in the campus community. They increasingly are riding the escort vans that for so long were available, but appeared inconvenient. More are working actively for a civil environment. Although they continue to prop open doors for the pizza man, we are seeing some effort to make the school safer. More are complaining about the amount of drinking on campus, but they still are not willing to say that a roommate drinks too much. Many student governments, fraternities, and sororities have supported the efforts, but continue alcohol-dominated parties. Students at many colleges no longer sponsor dances because of the enforcement of alcohol laws by the institutions. More students are walking with others at night. Nevertheless, the struggle remains to help students pursue safer ways.

24   In our community of 10,000 full-time students, we held administrative hearings for 11 cases of physical assault in 1992. No sexual assaults were reported. Other years, the number of assaults was as high as 35, and the highest number of sexual assaults in any year was six. When colleges were required by the 1992 National Higher Education Security Act to inform their faculty, staff, and students about crime statistics on campuses, several reporters were sure that the colleges were hiding numbers. However, the amount of crimes on campuses never has been large. Still, even a single violent act requires that everyone become more discerning.

READING CLOSELY AND THINKING CRITICALLY

1. According to Siegel, what are the causes of campus violence?
2. One cause of campus violence, according to Siegel, is that students fail to report suspicious people and behavior. How do you explain this failure?
3. According to Siegel, why do students assume that the source of danger is outside campus, rather than within?
4. Explain the cause-and-effect relationship Siegel proposes between sexual assaults, including rapes, and ineffective communication.
5. Do you think that a return to *in loco parentis* would reduce the amount of crime on campus? Explain.
6. As a college student, how do you react to Siegel's message? Do you think most college students would react the way you do? Would they be surprised by any of the information or moved to alter their behavior in any way? Explain.

EXAMINING STRUCTURE AND STRATEGY

1. Why does Siegel mention her position as vice president for student services at Towson State University?
2. What are the sources of Siegel's details (personal experience, observation, research, television, and so on)?
3. Which paragraphs include statistics? How do those statistics help the author achieve her purpose? Should she have included the sources of her statistics? Explain.
4. Evaluate the effectiveness of the concluding paragraphs (paragraphs 23 and 24).
5. Why would the readers of *USA Today Magazine* be interested in Siegel's essay?

CONSIDERING LANGUAGE AND STYLE

1. In paragraph 16, Siegel says, "Universities formerly acted *in loco parentis.*" What does *in loco parentis* mean?
2. Paragraphs 1 and 2 open with metaphors. What are they? What effect do they create? (Metaphors are explained on page 128.)
3. Consult a dictionary if you are unsure of the meaning of any of these words: *perpetrators* (paragraph 7), *arduous* (paragraph 7), *corroborated* (paragraph 14).

If what Siegel says about the relationship between alcohol and violence is correct, do you think colleges should ban drinking on campus? Why or why not? If your campus already has a zero-tolerance policy toward alcohol, discuss its effectiveness.

WRITING ASSIGNMENTS

1. **Writing in your journal.** In a page or so, explain whether or not you feel safe on your campus and why you feel the way you do. Also note whether you plan to change your behavior as a result of reading the essay. If so, explain how; if not, explain why not.

2. **Using cause-and-effect analysis for a purpose.** The purposes in the assignments are possibilities. You may establish whatever purpose you like, within your instructor's guidelines.

   - Siegel says that "students usually will not become victims or perpetrators in student-to-student violence if they do not use drugs or abuse alcohol" (paragraph 14). With that in mind, explain what would happen if your school—in cooperation with local officials—initiated a policy making the college and surrounding area completely substance-free. Your purpose can be to inform and perhaps convince your reader that such a policy is or is not a good idea.

   - To inform, explain why "many students come to higher education with histories of excessive drinking" (paragraph 15). You can also offer solutions to the problem.

   - To inform, explain the causes or effects of another campus problem, such as cheating, declining enrollment, failure to graduate, or plagiarism.

3. **Combining patterns.** Using process analysis (explained in Chapter 8), write a procedure that you think will reduce campus violence. Then, using cause-and-effect analysis, explain how the process will affect students and their interactions. You might consider such campus activities as dating, attending sporting events, working in the library, walking across campus at night, and visiting members of the opposite sex in their residence halls or apartments.

4. **Analyzing and assessing.** The original audience for "What Is behind the Growth of Violence on College Campuses?" was readers of *USA Today Magazine,* a supplement to many metropolitan newspapers. If the essay were to be revised for inclusion in a supplement to your campus newspaper, what revisions would you recommend to make the piece more suitable for an audience of college students? Explain why you would recommend those changes. To illustrate one or more of the changes you recommend, include a revision of a paragraph or two of the essay.

5. **Connecting and synthesizing the readings.** Why do you think our country is as violent as it is? In addition to your own ideas, you can draw on the ideas in "What Is Behind the Growth of Violence on College Campuses?" and "Young Voices from the Cell" (page 613).

6. **Drawing on sources.** Visit the appropriate offices on your campus to learn how much and what kind of crime exists at your school. Also learn what measures are being taken to make your campus as safe as possible. Report your findings and whether you think more needs to be done. If so, state what; if not, explain why not.

BACKGROUND: Award-winning poet, screenwriter, fiction writer, and teacher Leslie Marmon Silko was born in Albuquerque, New Mexico, in 1948. Part Native American, part Mexican, and part Caucasian, she grew up on the Laguna Pueblo reservation. She graduated from the University of New Mexico in 1969 and was admitted to law school, but she decided instead to pursue graduate studies in English and a literary career. The dominant theme in Silko's work is the importance of preserving Native American traditions and ways of life. Her many works of poetry include *Rain* (1996). Her novels include *Ceremony* (1988) and *Storyteller* (1981). Her writing tells tales that convey the richness and unique qualities of the Native American heritage. Silko also uses prose and poetry to retell her own family's story. Her most recent works include *Yellow Woman and a Beauty of the Spirit: Essays on Native American Life Today* (1996) and *Gardens in the Dunes* (1999). "Lullaby" is taken from *Storyteller*. It was also adapted as a play by the author and Frank Chin.

COMBINED PATTERNS AND THEIR PURPOSES: "Lullaby" is a dark *narration* in which Leslie Marmon Silko **informs** readers of the *effects* on a Navajo family of the treatment they receive from individual whites and the American government. The story demonstrates how government policies and white racism *cause* the destruction of the family, alcoholism, loss of cultural identity, and despair. Much of this is revealed through the *contrast* of Ayah and Chato. Because much of Silko's writing draws on her own family history, "Lullaby" also **relates some of the experience** that is part of the author's background.

Lullaby

BY LESLIE MARMON SILKO

The sun had gone down but the snow in the wind gave off its own light. It came in thick tufts like new wool—washed before the weaver spins it. Ayah reached out for it like her own babies had, and she smiled when she remembered how she had laughed at them. She was an old woman now, and her life had become memories. She sat down with her back against the wide cottonwood tree, feeling the rough bark on her back bones; she faced east and listened to the wind and snow sing a high-pitched Yeibechei song. Out of the wind she felt warmer, and she could watch the wide fluffy snow fill in her tracks, steadily, until the direction she had come from was gone. By the light of the snow she could see the dark outline of the big arroyo[1] a few feet away. She was sitting on the edge of Cebolleta Creek, where in the springtime the thin cows would graze on grass already chewed flat to the ground. In the wide deep creek bed where only a trickle of water flowed in the summer, the skinny cows would wander, looking for new grass along winding paths splashed with manure.

As you read
Try to identify the differences between the two main characters, Ayah and Chato.

2   Ayah pulled the old Army blanket over her head like a shawl. Jimmie's blanket—the one he had sent to her. That was a long time ago and the green wool was faded, and it was unraveling on the edges. She did not want to think about Jimmie. So she thought about the weaving and the way her mother had done it. On the tall wooden loom set into the sand under a tamarack tree for shade. She

---

[1]A gully or ditch.

could see it clearly. She had been only a little girl when her grandma gave her the wooden combs to pull the twigs and burrs from the raw, freshly washed wool. And while she combed the wool, her grandma sat beside her, spinning a silvery strand of yarn around the smooth cedar spindle. Her mother worked at the loom with yarns dyed bright yellow and red and gold. She watched them dye the yarn in boiling black pots full of beeweed petals, juniper berries, and sage. The blankets her mother made were soft and woven so tight that rain rolled off them like birds' feathers. Ayah remembered sleeping warm on cold windy nights, wrapped in her mother's blankets on the hogan's[2] sandy floor.

3   The snow drifted now, with the northwest wind hurling it in gusts. It drifted up around her black overshoes—old ones with little metal buckles. She smiled at the snow which was trying to cover her little by little. She could remember when they had no black rubber overshoes; only the high buckskin leggings that they wrapped over their elkhide moccasins. If the snow was dry or frozen, a person could walk all day and not get wet; and in the evenings the beams of the ceiling would hang with lengths of pale buckskin leggings, drying out slowly.

4   She felt peaceful remembering. She didn't feel cold any more. Jimmie's blanket seemed warmer than it had ever been. And she could remember the morning he was born. She could remember whispering to her mother, who was sleeping on the other side of the hogan, to tell her it was time now. She did not want to wake the others. The second time she called to her, her mother stood up and pulled on her shoes; she knew. They walked to the old stone hogan together, Ayah walking a step behind her mother. She waited alone, learning the rhythms of the pains while her mother went to call the old woman to help them. The morning was already warm even before dawn and Ayah smelled the bee flowers blooming and the young willow growing at the springs. She could remember that so clearly, but his birth merged into the births of the other children and to her it became all the same birth. They named him for the summer morning and in English they called him Jimmie.

5   It wasn't like Jimmie died. He just never came back, and one day a dark blue sedan with white writing on its doors pulled up in front of the boxcar shack where the rancher let the Indians live. A man in a khaki uniform trimmed in gold gave them a yellow piece of paper and told them that Jimmie was dead. He said the Army would try to get the body back and then it would be shipped to them; but it wasn't likely because the helicopter had burned after it crashed. All of this was told to Chato because he could understand English. She stood inside the doorway holding the baby while Chato listened. Chato spoke English like a white man and he spoke Spanish too. He was taller than the white man and he stood straighter too. Chato didn't explain why; he just told the military man they could keep the body if they found it. The white man looked bewildered; he nodded his head and he left. Then Chato looked at her and shook his head, and then he told her, "Jimmie isn't coming home anymore," and when he spoke, he used the words to speak of the dead. She didn't cry then, but she hurt inside with anger. And she mourned him as the years passed, when a horse fell with Chato and broke his leg, and the white rancher told them he

---

[2]An earth-covered Navajo dwelling.

wouldn't pay Chato until he could work again. She mourned Jimmie because he would have worked for his father then; he would have saddled the big bag horse and ridden the fence lines each day, with wire cutters and heavy gloves, fixing the breaks in the barbed wire and putting the stray cattle back inside again.

6   She mourned him after the white doctors came to take Danny and Ella away. She was at the shack alone that day they came. It was back in the days before they hired Navajo women to go with them as interpreters. She recognized one of the doctors. She had seen him at the children's clinic at Cañoncito about a month ago. They were wearing khaki uniforms and they waved papers at her and a black ballpoint pen, trying to make her understand their English words. She was frightened by the way they looked at the children, like the lizard watches the fly. Danny was swinging on the tire swing on the elm tree behind the rancher's house, and Ella was around the front door, dragging the broomstick horse Chato made for her. Ayah could see they wanted her to sign the papers, and Chato had taught her to sign her name. It was something she was proud of. She only wanted them to go, and to take their eyes away from her children.

7   She took the pen from the man without looking at his face and she signed the papers in three different places he pointed to. She stared at the ground by their feet and waited for them to leave. But they stood there and began to point and gesture at the children. Danny stopped swinging. Ayah could see his fear. She moved suddenly and grabbed Ella into her arms; the child squirmed, trying to get back to her toys. Ayah ran with the baby toward Danny; she screamed for him to run and then she grabbed him around his chest and carried him too. She ran south into the foothills of juniper trees and black lava rock. Behind her she heard the doctors running, but they had been taken by surprise, and as the hills became steeper and the cholla cactus were thicker, they stopped. When she reached the top of the hill, she stopped to listen in case they were circling around her. But in a few minutes she heard a car engine start and they drove away. The children had been too surprised to cry while she ran with them. Danny was shaking and Ella's little fingers were gripping Ayah's blouse.

8   She stayed up in the hills for the rest of the day, sitting on a black lava boulder in the sunshine where she could see for miles all around her. The sky was light blue and cloudless, and it was warm for late April. The sun warmth relaxed her and took the fear and anger away. She lay back on the rock and watched the sky. It seemed to her that she could walk into the sky, stepping through clouds endlessly. Danny played with little pebbles and stones, pretending they were birds eggs and then little rabbits. Ella sat at her feet and dropped fistfuls of dirt into the breeze, watching the dust and particles of sand intently. Ayah watched a hawk soar high above them, dark wings gliding; hunting or only watching, she did not know. The hawk was patient and he circled all afternoon before he disappeared around the high volcanic peak the Mexicans called Guadalupe.

9   Late in the afternoon, Ayah looked down at the gray boxcar shack with the paint all peeled from the wood; the stove pipe on the roof was rusted and crooked. The fire she had built that morning in the oil drum stove had burned out. Ella was asleep in her lap now and Danny sat close to her, complaining that he was hungry; he asked when they would go to the house. "We will stay up here until your father

comes," she told him, "because those white men were chasing us." The boy remembered then and he nodded at her silently.

10   If Jimmie had been there he could have read those papers and explained to her what they said. Ayah would have known then, never to sign them. The doctors came back the next day and they brought a BIA policeman[3] with them. They told Chato they had her signature and that was all they needed. Except for the kids. She listened to Chato sullenly; she hated him when he told her it was the old woman who died in the winter, spitting blood; it was her old grandma who had given the children this disease. "They don't spit blood," she said coldly. "The whites lie." She held Ella and Danny close to her, ready to run to the hills again. "I want a medicine man first," she said to Chato, not looking at him. He shook his head. "It's too late now. The policeman is with them. You signed the paper." His voice was gentle.

11   It was worse than if they had died: to lose the children and to know that somewhere, in a place called Colorado, in a place full of sick and dying strangers, her children were without her. There had been babies that died soon after they were born, and one that died before he could walk. She had carried them herself, up to the boulders and great pieces of the cliff that long ago crashed down from Long Mesa; she laid them in the crevices of sandstone and buried them in fine brown sand with round quartz pebbles that washed down the hills in the rain. She had endured it because they had been with her. But she could not bear this pain. She did not sleep for a long time after they took her children. She stayed on the hill where they had fled the first time, and she slept rolled up in the blanket Jimmie had sent her. She carried the pain in her belly and it was fed by everything she saw: the blue sky of their last day together and the dust and pebbles they played with; the swing in the elm tree and broomstick horse choked life from her. The pain filled her stomach and there was no room for food or for her lungs to fill with air. The air and the food would have been theirs.

12   She hated Chato, not because he let the policeman and doctors put the screaming children in the government car, but because he had taught her to sign her name. Because it was like the old ones always told her about learning their language or any of their ways: it endangered you. She slept alone on the hill until the middle of November when the first snows came. Then she made a bed for herself where the children had slept. She did not lie down beside Chato again until many years later, when he was sick and shivering and only her body could keep him warm. The illness came after the white rancher told Chato he was too old to work for him anymore, and Chato and his old woman should be out of the shack by the next afternoon because the rancher had hired new people to work there. That had satisfied her. To see how the white man repaid Chato's years of loyalty and work. All of Chato's fine-sounding English talk didn't change things.

13   It snowed steadily and the luminous light from the snow gradually diminished into the darkness. Somewhere in Cebolleta a dog barked and other village dogs joined with it. Ayah looked in the direction she had come, from the bar where Chato was buying the wine. Sometimes he told her to go on ahead and wait; and then he

------

[3]Bureau of Indian Affairs officer.

never came. And when she finally went back looking for him, she would find him passed out at the bottom of the wooden steps to Azzie's Bar. All the wine would be gone and most of the money too, from the pale blue check that came to them once a month in a government envelope. It was then that she would look at his face and his hands, scarred by ropes and the barbed wire of all those years, and she would think, this man is a stranger; for forty years she had smiled at him and cooked his food, but he remained a stranger. She stood up again, with the snow almost to her knees, and she walked back to find Chato.

14 It was hard to walk in the deep snow and she felt the air burn in her lungs. She stopped a short distance from the bar to rest and readjust the blanket. But this time he wasn't waiting for her on the bottom step with his old Stetson hat[4] pulled down and his shoulders hunched up in his long wool overcoat.

15 She was careful not to slip on the wooden steps. When she pushed the door open, warm air and cigarette smoke hit her face. She looked around slowly and deliberately, in every corner, in every dark place that the old man might find to sleep. The bar owner didn't like Indians in there, especially Navajos, but he let Chato come in because he could talk Spanish like he was one of them. The men at the bar stared at her, and the bartender saw that she left the door open wide. Snowflakes were flying inside like moths and melting into a puddle on the oiled wood floor. He motioned to her to close the door, but she did not see him. She held herself straight and walked across the room slowly, searching the room with every step. The snow in her hair melted and she could feel it on her forehead. At the far corner of the room, she saw red flames at the mica window of the old stove door; she looked behind the stove just to make sure. The bar got quiet except for the Spanish polka-music playing on the jukebox. She stood by the stove and shook the snow from her blanket and held it near the stove to dry. The wet wool smell reminded her of new-born goats in early March, brought inside to warm near the fire. She felt calm.

16 In past years they would have told her to get out. But her hair was white now and her face was wrinkled. They looked at her like she was a spider crawling slowly across the room. They were afraid; she could feel the fear. She looked at their faces steadily. They reminded her of the first time the white people brought her children back to her that winter. Danny had been shy and hid behind the thin white woman who brought them. And the baby had not known her until Ayah took her into her arms, and then Ella had nuzzled close to her as she had when she was nursing. The blonde woman was nervous and kept looking at a dainty gold watch on her wrist. She sat on the bench near the small window and watched the dark snow clouds gather around the mountains; she was worrying about the unpaved road. She was frightened by what she saw inside too: the strips of venison drying on a rope across the ceiling and the children jabbering excitedly in a language she did not know. So they stayed for only a few hours. Ayah watched the government car disappear down the road and she knew they were already being weaned from these lava hills and from this sky. The last time they came was in early June, and Ella stared at her the way the men in the bar were now staring. Ayah did not try to pick her up; she smiled at her instead and spoke cheerfully to Danny. When he tried to answer her, he could not seem to

---

[4]A high-crowned, wide-brimmed "cowboy" hat.

remember and he spoke English words with the Navajo. But he gave her a scrap of paper that he had found somewhere and carried in his pocket; it was folded in half, and he shyly looked up at her and said it was a bird. She asked Chato if they were home for good this time. He spoke to the white woman and she shook her head. "How much longer?" he asked, and she said she didn't know; but Chato saw how she stared at the boxcar shack. Ayah turned away then. She did not say good-bye.

17   She felt satisfied that the men in the bar feared her. Maybe it was her face and the way she held her mouth with teeth clenched tight, like there was nothing anyone could do to her now. She walked north down the road, searching for the old man. She did this because she had the blanket, and there would be no place for him except with her and the blanket in the old adobe barn near the arroyo. They always slept there when they came to Cebolleta. If the money and the wine were gone, she would be relieved because then they could go home again; back to the old hogan with a dirt roof and rock walls where she herself had been born. And the next day the old man could go back to the few sheep they still had, to follow along behind them, guiding them, into dry sandy arroyos where sparse grass grew. She knew he did not like walking behind old ewes when for so many years he rode big quarter horses and worked with cattle. But she wasn't sorry for him; he should have known all along what would happen.

18   There had not been enough rain for their garden in five years; and that was when Chato finally hitched a ride into the town and brought back brown boxes of rice and sugar and big tin cans of welfare peaches. After that, at the first of the month they went to Cebolleta to ask the postmaster for the check; and then Chato would go to the bar and cash it. They did this as they planted the garden every May, not because anything would survive the summer dust, but because it was time to do this. The journey passed the days that smelled silent and dry like the caves above the canyon with yellow painted buffaloes on their walls.

19   He was walking along the pavement when she found him. He did not stop or turn around when he heard her behind him. She walked beside him and she noticed how slowly he moved now. He smelled strong of woodsmoke and urine. Lately he had been forgetting. Sometimes he called her by his sister's name and she had been gone for a long time. Once she had found him wandering on the road to the white man's ranch, and she asked him why he was going that way; he laughed at her and said, "You know they can't run that ranch without me," and he walked on determined, limping on the leg that had been crushed many years before. Now he looked at her curiously, as if for the first time, but he kept shuffling along, moving slowly along the side of the highway. His gray hair had grown long and spread out on the shoulders of the long overcoat. He wore the old felt hat pulled down over his ears. His boots were worn out at the toes and he had stuffed pieces of an old red shirt in the holes. The rags made his feet look like little animals up to their ears in snow. She laughed at his feet; the snow muffled the sound of her laugh. He stopped and looked at her again. The wind had quit blowing and the snow was falling straight down; the southeast sky was beginning to clear and Ayah could see a star.

20   "Let's rest awhile," she said to him. They walked away from the road and up the slope to the giant boulders that had tumbled down from the red sandrock mesa throughout the centuries of rainstorms and earth tremors. In a place where the

boulders shut out the wind, they sat down with their backs against the rock. She offered half of the blanket to him and they sat wrapped together.

21   The storm passed swiftly. The clouds moved east. They were massive and full, crowding together across the sky. She watched them with the feeling of horses—steely blue-gray horses startled across the sky. The powerful haunches pushed into the distances and the tail hairs streamed white mist behind them. The sky cleared. Ayah saw that there was nothing between her and the stars. The light was crystalline. There was no shimmer, no distortion through earth haze. She breathed the clarity of the night sky; she smelled the purity of the half moon and the stars. He was lying on his side with his knees pulled up near his belly for warmth. His eyes were closed now, and in the light from the stars and the moon, he looked young again.

22   She could see it descend out of the night sky: an icy stillness from the edge of the thin moon. She recognized the freezing. It came gradually, sinking snowflake by snowflake until the crust was heavy and deep. It had the strength of the stars in Orion, and its journey was endless. Ayah knew that with the wine he would sleep. He would not feel it. She tucked the blanket around him, remembering how it was when Ella had been with her; and she felt the rush so big inside her heart for the babies. And she sang the only song she knew to sing for babies. She could not remember if she had ever sung it to her children, but she knew that her grandmother had sung it and her mother had sung it:

> The earth is your mother,
>   she holds you.
> The sky is your father,
>   he protects you.
> Sleep,
> sleep.
> Rainbow is your sister,
>   she loves you.
> The winds are your brothers,
>   they sing to you.
> Sleep,
> sleep.
> We are together always
> We are together always
> There never was a time
> when this
> was not so.

CONSIDERING THE SHORT STORY

1.   How are whites depicted in "Lullaby"? What specific criticisms of whites does Silko imply? How can you tell?

2.   What caused Ayah to sign the paper turning her children over to the white doctors? What was the effect of her action?

3. How is Ayah and Chato's relationship affected by the way whites have treated them?
4. Explain the causes and effects of Chato's heavy drinking.
5. Twice in the story, Ayah is satisfied, once when she and Chato lose their home and once when she is feared in the bar. Why is she satisfied?
6. What are the chief differences between Ayah and Chato? Why are those differences important?

WRITING ASSIGNMENTS

1. **Writing in your journal.**
   - What kind of woman is Ayah? What are her chief characteristics? How can you tell?
   - Explain the meaning of the lullaby at the end of the story. Do you find it comforting? Why or why not?

2. **Using cause-and-effect analysis for a purpose.** "Lullaby," in part, is about culture clash—about what can happen when cultures fail to understand each other's traditions, history, and beliefs. To inform, explain the causes and/or effects of a culture clash that exists in society today. The purpose in the assignment is a possibility. You may establish whatever purpose you like, within your instructor's guidelines.

3. **Combining patterns.** "Lullaby," in part, is a story about what happens when change is forced on people. Narrate a story about a time you experienced a change that you did not initiate or welcome. (See Chapter 6 on narration.) What were the effects of the experience?

WRITING CAUSE-AND-EFFECT ANALYSIS

See pages 421 and 423 for strategies for writing cause-and-effect analysis and for a revising checklist.

1. Analyze the causes or effects of stress in college or high school students.

2. If you have difficulty with a particular subject (English, math, science, and so on), explain why the subject causes you problems and/or the effects of having difficulty with that subject.

3. Select a popular movie, television program, song, or book, and explain why it is popular. As an alternative, explain the popularity of an actor, comedian, or singer.

4. Explain why people lie.

5. Explain the effects on people or society of some aspect of the Internet, such as chat rooms, online shopping, access to information, online gambling, or online games.

6. Explain the techniques television commercials (or magazine ads) use to influence consumers. As an alternative, explain the effects of commercials (or magazine ads) on us.

7. Select a bad habit you have (for example, procrastinating, smoking, overeating, or nail biting), and explain its causes and effects.

8. Explain the effects of something that happened to you in school (for example, getting cut from the basketball team, being elected class president, becoming homecoming queen, or failing a course).

9. Select a problem on your campus (for example, inadequate student housing, high tuition, or limited course offerings), and analyze the effects on students to persuade those in authority to remedy the problem.

10. Analyze how the neighborhood in which you grew up affected you.

11. Explain why students cheat and the effects cheating has on students.

12. If you have a particular fear (of heights, of math, of failure, and so on), explain the causes and/or effects of that fear.

13. Pick a harmless human characteristic or behavior (for example, checking the alarm even though we know it is set, habitually choosing the wrong bank or supermarket line, or losing car keys). Then write a humorous essay that explains the causes and/or effects of this behavior or characteristic.

14. Select something inconsequential that Americans can no longer do, such as cook without a microwave, walk places, or change channels without a remote control. Then write a humorous account of the causes and effects of the "problem."

15. If you ever moved to a new town, explain how the move affected you.

16. If you have children, explain the effects of becoming a parent. If you want, you can make this essay humorous.

17. If you are an international student, explain how you have been affected by living and attending school in this country.

18. Explain why football (or baseball or basketball) is so popular in this country and how the sport affects American culture.

19. Select a person who has had a significant impact on you (for example, a coach, a clergyperson, a teacher, or a friend), and explain the effects this individual has had on you.

20. **Cause-and-effect analysis in context:** Assume you are a member of a consumer affairs panel that has secured a grant to study violence in the media. Write a report that explains why some people enjoy violent movies. Your audience is other members of the panel, and your purpose is to provide them with information.

You may be so accustomed to air-conditioned homes, stores, restaurants, offices, and schools that you fail to realize what a significant invention air-conditioning was. Think about life without air-conditioning, and write about the effects air-conditioning has on our health, on how and where we live, on recreation, on transportation, and on other aspects of life. For example, would shopping malls exist without air-conditioning? What about Las Vegas casinos?

Roz Chast/The New Yorker Collection/www.cartoonbank.com.

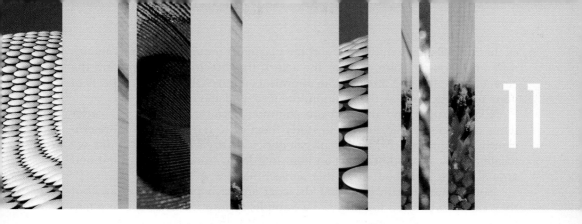

Classification and Division

CONSIDER THE PATTERN

The Roz Chast cartoon on the facing page classifies (groups) shoppers according to what they buy. Consider other ways grocery shoppers could be classified. For example, you might classify them according to how they behave in a checkout line.

THE PATTERN

Both classification and division are methods of grouping and ordering. **Classification** takes a number of items and groups them into categories; **division** takes one entity and breaks it down into its parts. Consider your college, for example. It orders courses in the catalog by placing them into groups according to the departments that offer those courses (English, biology, mathematics, and so on)—this is *classifying*. In addition, your college organizes itself by breaking into components (the School of Education, the School of Arts and Sciences, the School of Engineering, and so on)—this is *division*.

Examples of classification are everywhere. The Yellow Pages groups telephone numbers according to the kinds of businesses; your biology textbook classifies animals according to whether they are mammals, reptiles, and so on; your local grocery store arranges items in aisles by classifying them according to whether they are canned goods, cleaning products, pet products, meats, produce, or frozen foods.

Division is also common. A medical laboratory examines your blood by breaking it down into its components and studying each of them, such as the red cells, the white cells, and the plasma; a movie reviewer evaluates different parts of a film, such as the actors, the director, the script, and the cinematography; and a real estate appraisal analyzes the various aspects of your property, such as the location, the size, and the condition.

Classification and division are common because they help us order items or pieces of information to study them or to retrieve them more efficiently. Imagine a world without categories or divisions. How could we locate a book in the library or an item in a large store or study plant and animal life or just about any other subject matter?

Sometimes classification and division are each performed alone, but they can also be used together. For example, to inform, an article in a tennis magazine might classify the serves used by 10 top professional players and then break the serves down into their components (ball toss, arm motion, racquet speed, footwork, and so on).

---

www.mhhe.com/clousepatterns6	Classification

For more help with classification, click on
Writing > Paragraph Patterns
Writing > Writing Tutors: Classification

USING CLASSIFICATION AND DIVISION FOR A PURPOSE

You can classify or divide in order to *inform*. With classification, you can, for example, classify health clubs according to expense to help exercisers decide which club to join or classify kinds of nonverbal communication to help your readers understand the concept. With division, you can, for example, help people write effective grant proposals by dividing the proposal into its parts and describing the characteristics of each one. Sometimes you can classify or divide to give readers a fresh awareness of something familiar. For instance, in "White Lies," an essay in this chapter, Sissela Bok classifies white lies to help readers to a new understanding of their moral significance.

Classification and division can also allow you to *express feelings* and *relate experience*. This would be your purpose if you classified ways to celebrate Halloween to tell about your childhood Halloween experiences or if you divided your favorite Halloween celebration into its components.

Very often, classification and division have a *persuasive* purpose, as is the case with "The Ways of Meeting Oppression" in this chapter. In this essay, Dr. Martin Luther King, Jr., classifies the ways to deal with oppression to convince readers that one of those ways is more effective than the rest and should be employed.

Finally, you can write classification and division to *entertain*. For example, to amuse your audience, you could classify all your eccentric relatives according to their funny traits and behaviors, or you could examine your most eccentric relative by dividing that person's behavior and personality into the most amusing parts.

Combining Patterns for a Purpose

You can combine classification and division with other patterns to achieve your purpose for writing. For example, to *explain* Halloween to international students who don't celebrate the holiday in their countries, you might classify Halloween celebrations into the fun, the rowdy, and the scary. You could then give *examples* to illustrate the harmless pranks people play for a fun celebration; you could *describe* the frightening costumes people wear for a scary celebration; and you could *narrate* the story of your last Halloween celebration, which was of the rowdy sort. You could even use *process analysis* to inform about how to prepare for each kind of celebration.

To see how other patterns can be combined with division, study the following excerpt from "What's Really in Your Shampoo," an essay in this chapter that breaks shampoo down into its unappealing components. The author combines division with process analysis and cause-and-effect analysis.

EXCERPT FROM "WHAT'S REALLY IN YOUR SHAMPOO" COMBINING DIVISION WITH CAUSE-AND-EFFECT ANALYSIS AND PROCESS ANALYSIS

The highlighted division gives the components in shampoo.

The highlighted cause-and-effect in the first paragraph explains why ingredients are added, and in the second paragraph explains the cause of shiny hair.

The underscored process analysis explains how shampoo makes hair shiny.

Shampoo tends to use [seven] factors to help the
components discussed in essay
user feel good about it: shine, thickeners, lather, color, smell,

coatings, and exotic ingredients Those ingredients, though they

have nothing to do with cleansing, are part of the sell to

convince you that something beautiful happens to your hair.
first components discussed
Consumers value shininess in nearly everything,

including hair. For hair to shine, the cuticles of the

hair must lie flat. Imagine a strand of hair as a stack

of flimsy paper cups. When all the lips of the cup, called

imbrications, lie flat, hair shines. Dull hair has the cups'

lips sticking up. To get imbrications to lie flat hair needs to

be exposed to mildly acidic substances, so substances like
component
citric acid are added to make the imbrications lie down

and give hair that shiny look and to let yourself glow.

Classification and division can appear in essays developed primarily with other patterns. For example, in an essay explaining the causes and effects of age discrimination in the workplace, you could include a classification of the most common kinds of age discrimination (in hiring, promotion, responsibilities, and so on). Or in a process analysis explaining how to write effective e-mails in the workplace, you could divide an effective business e-mail into its parts.

Classification and Division beyond the Writing Classroom

Classification and division help writers achieve their purpose in many writing situations.

IN ACADEMIC WRITING AND READING   Outlining writing in any class involves classification and division because you divide your topic into ideas and group those ideas according to the point they develop. You will have many occasions to use classification and division in your college classes. In an education class, you might classify tasks in a lesson plan by types of learner they are particularly geared to in order to demonstrate that you can write a plan that meets the needs of diverse learners. In a business class, you might explain the components of a sound business plan to demonstrate that you could develop a plan, and in a marketing class, you might explain the components of an effective survey to show that you could construct one.

At times, you will write classification and division to show that you understand the different uses and merits of various categories of something. For example, in an advertising class, you could write a paper that classifies the kinds of direct mail campaigns, noting what kind of audience each approach appeals to and what kind of product each approach is best suited for.

Perhaps most frequently, you will write classification and division to demonstrate your comprehension of information. For example, in a biology class, you might classify the mating behaviors of birds, and in a communications class you might divide political rhetoric into its components.

Classification and division are found in many textbooks. In the following excerpt from *The World of Music,* for example, classification and division help inform students about kinds of American folk music and what each of those kinds is like.

The first sentence states what is being classified and the specific groupings.

The broad spectrum of American traditional folk music includes the following types of songs: narrative ballads, broadside ballads, lyric songs, work songs, children's songs, rally and protest songs, spirituals, and blues songs. Spirituals and the blues, however, are discussed in a later section of this chapter.

Narrative Ballads (Story Songs)

These songs originally came from New England, having been brought to America in the seventeenth, eighteenth, and nineteenth centuries by immigrants from the British Isles, particularly Scotland and Ireland. A ballad singer is a storyteller. The story has a beginning, a middle, and an end and may convey a romantic and sentimental mood or heroic action. Occasionally, dialogue between two characters in the story is inserted.

A narrative ballad may have many stanzas, each frequently comprised of four lines of poetry with a consistent rhyme scheme. The music often is strophic (the same music for each stanza regardless of the meaning and mood of the text).

This section gives the origin and the characteristics of songs in the first group.

Broadsides

These ballads are "folk songs" composed by professional songwriters. They flourished during the eighteenth and nineteenth centuries in western Europe and the United States. A broadside was a narrative accounting of current events and functioned somewhat as a newspaper in communities and regions. It was published on one large sheet of paper called a broadside. It may or may not have been published with musical notation. If only the words were published, sometimes instructions were included to sing them to a well-known tune. Broadsides were sold widely and cheaply and were considered popular songs of the day. Hundreds of British and American broadsides were published.

The origin of many folk songs has been traced to broadsides. Thus, we see a case where songs originally written down were eventually passed on by word of mouth; thus, they became part of the oral tradition we associate with traditional folk songs. . . . (Willoughby, *The World of Music*)

This section gives the origin and the characteristics of songs in the second group.

AT WORK AND IN THE COMMUNITY   On the job, classification and develop are essential. For example, to develop a solid business plan, you must group elements of the plan according to categories such as marketing, acquisition of capital, management structure, and growth potential. You may need to classify kinds of customer-incentive programs or group insurance plans to decide which one to use. Even before you get your job, you use classification and division to write a résumé, dividing and grouping your skills, education, and experience. In addition, when you write to-do lists to manage tasks for your personal, academic, professional, or civic responsibilities, you engage in classification and division if you divide the tasks into their parts and then group the parts according to their deadlines and importance so you can decide how to proceed.

THE PRINCIPLE OF CLASSIFICATION OR DIVISION

Most things can be classified more than one way. For example, you can classify colleges according to how much they cost, how rigorous their coursework is, what courses or degrees they offer, and so on. The basis of your classification is your *principle of classification*. Thus, in classifying colleges, your principle of classification might be the curriculum—the courses they offer.

If you have trouble deciding on your principle of classification, consider your audience and purpose. If you are classifying kinds of white lies, as one author does in this chapter, and you want to entertain your reader, your classifying principle probably will not be the degree of hurtfulness of the lies. Instead, a more plausible classifying principle might be the inventiveness of the lies. If your purpose is to inform, however, the degree of hurtfulness could be an appropriate classifying principle.

Principles of division are also important when you could divide your topic in various ways. For example, if your topic is elections, you might divide it by office (presidential elections, congressional elections, and so on) or by stage (campaigning for primaries, for nominations, and so on). Again, in deciding on a principle, consider your audience and purpose.

SUPPORTING DETAILS

For classification, your supporting details will likely indicate your groupings, the elements in each group, and the characteristics of the elements. For example, if you are classifying aerobics classes according to how much impact they have on the joints, your groupings might be high impact, moderate impact, and low impact. You would indicate which classes fit in each grouping (dance aerobics, step aerobics, kickboxing, walk aerobics, chair aerobics, and so on). Finally, you would explain the relevant aspects of the classes in each group, such as kinds of movements, speed of movements, number of repetitions, and amount of jumping. Similarly, for division, you will indicate the parts and their important characteristics.

When you select details, do not omit any categories or parts, or your classification or division will be incomplete. For example, if you are classifying the forms of financial aid to inform students of ways to get help paying for college, and you include loans, grants, and scholarships but omit work-study programs, your essay is less helpful than it could—and should—be. Similarly, if you are dividing an effective political campaign into its components, and you discuss grassroots support and publicity but omit financing, you won't have fully and accurately described campaigns.

On the other hand, avoid including groups incompatible with your principle of classification. For example, if you are classifying coaches according to how important winning is to them, you might have these categories: coaches who think winning is everything, coaches who emphasize winning but also value learning and having fun, and coaches who deemphasize winning. In this classification, you could not include as a category coaches who are inexperienced because that group is unrelated to the classifying principle.

ORGANIZING DETAILS

The thesis for classification or division can be handled a variety of ways. First, you can indicate what you are classifying or dividing and the principle you will use for classifying or dividing:

The current crop of television talk shows can be classified according to the kinds of guests that appear. (*Television talk shows will be classified; the classifying principle is the kinds of guests that appear.*)

Another way to handle the thesis is simply to indicate what you are classifying or dividing:

Although more talk shows are on television than ever before, all of these shows are one of three types. (*The thesis makes it clear that television talk shows will be classified, but the classifying principle is not given.*)

A third way to handle the thesis is to indicate what will be classified or divided, along with the groupings or parts to be discussed:

Television talk shows can be distinguished according to whether the guests are primarily entertainers, politicians, or oddballs. (*The thesis indicates that television talk shows will be classified and the categories will be those with guests who are entertainers, those with guests who are politicians, and those with guests who are oddballs.*)

Organizing a classification or division essay can be easier when you think of including topic sentences to introduce the discussion of each grouping or part. For example, if you were classifying talk shows, you might have topic sentences like these:

In the most common variety of talk show, the guests are entertainers. (*A discussion of talk shows with entertainers as guests would follow.*)

Somewhat more intellectual than the first type, another common variety of show has politicians for guests. (*A discussion of talk shows with politicians as guests would follow.*)

Increasingly popular is the talk show that showcases oddballs. (*A discussion of talk shows with oddballs as guests would follow.*)

To move smoothly from one grouping or part to another, you can include transitional phrases in your topic sentences:

Another category . . .

A more significant group . . .

A more common component . . .

A second part of . . .

When you order your details, consider your thesis. If it includes categories or divisions, present them in the same order they appear in the thesis. Otherwise, order is not much of an issue, unless your purpose is persuasive. Then you are likely to use progressive order, presenting the recommended category or the most important division last. In "The Ways of Meeting Oppression," for example, Dr. Martin Luther King, Jr., presents the method he wants people to adopt last.

When you are discussing the same characteristics for each category or division, present those characteristics in the same order each time. Thus, if you group Halloween celebrations and discuss decorations, costumes, and degree of scariness for each kind of celebration, discuss these features in the same order for each one.

TROUBLESHOOTING GUIDE

Maintaining Parallelism

If you have trouble expressing categories or divisions smoothly in your thesis, state them in the same grammatical form to maintain parallel structure. Here is a thesis that lacks parallelism:

> Television talk shows can be divided into three types: shows with entertainers for guests, those having guests who are politicians, and shows with oddballs for guests.

Notice that the following revision is much more pleasing because of the parallel structure:

> Television talk shows can be divided into three types: shows with entertainers for guests, shows with politicians for guests, and shows with oddballs for guests.

---

www.mhhe.com/clousepatterns6   Parallelism

For more help with maintaining parallelism, click on
Editing > Parallelism

CHAPTER 11   Classification and Division

VISUALIZING A CLASSIFICATION AND DIVISION ESSAY

The following chart can help you visualize the structure for a classification and division essay. Like all good models, however, this one can be altered as needed.

INTRODUCTION
- Creates interest in your essay
- States the thesis (underscored in the example), which can indicate what you are classifying or dividing, the principle of classification or division, and the groupings or divisions

EXAMPLE

Over the years, three kinds of horror movies have evolved. Originally, this movie genre was harmless enough, but today it has developed into stomach-turning trash.

↓

FIRST BODY PARAGRAPH
- Gives the first grouping or division (the first in the thesis, if mentioned), which can be stated in a topic sentence
- May include explanation and any patterns of development
- May arrange details in a progressive or other suitable order

EXAMPLE

At first, popular horror movies were the mass-destruction movies. These include The Blob, Invasion of the Body Snatchers, and the classic War of the Worlds. In these movies, the human race is threatened with destruction. . . .

↓

NEXT BODY PARAGRAPHS
- Continue until all the groupings or divisions (ordered as in the thesis, if mentioned there) are given
- May include explanation and any patterns of development
- May arrange details in a progressive or other suitable order

EXAMPLE

The supernatural thrillers came next. These movies tend to be very scary and rather nauseating, often dealing with the Satanic, the occult, vampires, and evil spirits. In The Exorcist, for example, . . .

↓

CONCLUSION
- Provides a satisfying finish
- Leaves the reader with a strong final impression

EXAMPLE

Horror movies should be disturbing and off-putting, but strangely audiences love them, returning for sequel after sequel. What does that say about us? Perhaps the answer is even scarier than the movies.

THINKING CRITICALLY ABOUT CLASSIFICATION AND DIVISION

Chapters 1 and 4 explain that thinking critically about your reading and writing requires analysis and assessment. To critically read and write classification and division, use what you learned in those chapters, and ask the following questions:

- **What is the purpose of the classification or division?** Sometimes classification or division can be used for harmful purposes. A blog that classifies Americans according to their ethnicity—Asian, Middle Eastern, Central American, and so on—and claims, for example, that those of some ethnicities are untrustworthy and those of others are lazy is suspect because the classification is advancing bigotry and hatred. However, a chart that classifies recent immigrants according to their ethnicity and country of origin in order to inform about immigration patterns has an appropriate purpose.

- **Are all the relevant categories or parts included, along with the important details?** Consider a car dealership advertisement that classifies the kinds of vehicles for sale. If the ad omits certain kinds of vehicles whose profit margin is low, customers get an incomplete classification—and incomplete information for making potential purchase decisions.

- **Does the classification avoid overgeneralizing and stereotypes?** A classification of ways people get their news should not say that those who watch *Fox News* are religious fundamentalists while those who watch MSNBC are liberals with socialist tendencies.

PROCESS GUIDELINES: STRATEGIES FOR WRITING CLASSIFICATION AND DIVISION

1. **Planning.** Write your principle of classification or division, and below that write each of your categories or divisions as the head for a column. (Three categories or divisions will give you three columns, four will give you four columns, and so on.) Under each column head, list the elements in the category or division.

2. **Generating supporting details.** To generate supporting details, look at the items within a column, and think about how you could develop them to give readers a clear sense of the group and its elements, or the part and its characteristics. Think about which patterns of development might be useful. Now look across columns—what you've listed in one might give you ideas about details to support points in other columns. Jot down whatever ideas occur to you.

3. **Organizing.** Number the columns on your sheet in the order you want to treat them. If you will be discussing similar characteristics in more than one column, order the items within each column so that

you discuss them in the same order across columns. You now have an outline to guide your draft.

4. **Revising.** As you evaluate your draft, consider everything in light of your audience and purpose. Be sure you have included all relevant categories or divisions and that they are compatible with your principle of classifying or dividing.

Using Sources for a Purpose

The paragraphs below are body paragraphs from an essay explaining the problems associated with computers. They illustrate how you can use sources from this book in your writing. The first paragraph includes a paraphrase and quotation from paragraph 5 of "Globalization: The Super-Story" on page 504.

THESIS We must be mindful of the serious problems associated with using computers.

WRITING PURPOSE AND AUDIENCE To inform computer users about the problems associated with computers.

Sentence 2 introduces the quotation and paraphrase in sentences 3–5. The paraphrase and quotation support the point made in sentence 1 by providing an example of someone who thinks the Internet connects people.

[1]People often say that the Internet connects people in profound ways. [2]Thomas L. Friedman's evaluation is typical of this perspective. [3]Friedman believes that the globalization that marks our times is characterized by an Internet-driven integration: "The globalization system is different [from the past Cold War system]. [4]It . . . has one overarching feature—and that is *integration*. . . . [5]In the globalization system we reach for the Internet, which is a symbol that we are all connected . . ." (505).

[6]I disagree. [7]We shop online rather than interact with others in stores. [8]We take classes online and sit alone rather than with classmates and teachers. [9]We research online and lose contact with reference librarians and students in the library. [10]We send Instant Messages, write e-mails, and meet on social-networking sites instead of talking in person. [11]For hours at a time, we surf the Web and play online video games, isolated from other humans. [12]In short, the overall effect of the Internet is to isolate us, not connect us to others.

AVOIDING PLAGIARISM

The excerpt illustrates the following points about avoiding plagiarism. (For more complete information on using source material, consult Chapters 4 and 15.)

- **Use brackets to add explanatory information or anything else not part of the original quotation.** As sentence 3 shows, use brackets to add material to a quotation for clarity or to work the quotation smoothly into your sentence.

(continued)

(continued)

- **Use ellipses for omitted words.** As sentence 4 illustrates, use three ellipsis points for words omitted from the middle of a quotation, and add a period to the ellipses when you omit the end of a quoted sentence. As sentence 5 shows, use three ellipsis points before the quotation mark, and place the final period after the parenthetical citation.

MYTHS ABOUT USING SOURCES

MYTH: Students should not disagree with ideas in source material.

FACT: Remember, critical readers evaluate material thoughtfully and form their own opinions. You can disagree with what you read, as long as you support your assertion.

Checklist for Revising Exemplification

You can use this checklist along with the one on page 76 to help you revise.

1. _____ All relevant categories or divisions are included.
2. _____ Your principle of classification or division is appropriate, and nothing is classified in an unfairly negative light.
3. _____ All categories or divisions are relevant to your principle of classifying or dividing.
4. _____ Your thesis indicates what you are classifying or dividing and, if appropriate, the principle you use and/or the categories or divisions.
5. _____ If appropriate, topic sentences introduce each category or division.
6. _____ Transitions help you move smoothly from one category or division to the next.
7. _____ If you have discussed the same characteristic for each category or division, they appear in the same order.

Student-author David Wolfe uses classification to inform his reader about the origins of some common expressions. Be sure to notice how the author uses examples to help make his point. After you read, you will have an opportunity to evaluate this essay.

Strictly Speaking
David Wolfe

Expressions derived from outdoor life are so ingrained in everyday English that we fail to notice them or consider their origins. However, it is interesting to pause and think about these terms, and one way to do that is to look at three basic categories of expressions: those derived from the use of firearms, those derived from hunting, and those derived from the characteristics of wildlife or game.

Some common sayings come directly from the use of firearms. For example, if we buy something "lock, stock, and barrel," we have purchased the whole object or believed the whole story. This expression originally meant to buy the whole gun by purchasing its three parts: the "lock" as in the flintlock, the wooden "stock," and the metal "barrel." We also talk about "going off half-cocked," which means taking action or setting out without being fully prepared. This expression goes back to having a gun on "half-cock." In the half-cocked position, the hammer is between the relaxed position and the fully cocked position, which means the gun is halfway between unready and fully ready for firing. Often we say we had our "sights set on" something or had a goal "in our sights." Both of these expressions refer to aiming a gun at something. Also, we can be "primed and ready," or fully prepared, as when a flintlock rifle is fully primed or prepared and ready to fire.

A second group of expressions is derived from hunting. For example, the word "hello" has its origins there. It comes from hunters calling out "hulloa" or "haloo" when they saw other hunters in the woods in order to attract attention and avoid being accidentally hurt. "Stop beating around the bush" is another example of a hunting expression. It comes from the European practice of using "beaters" or people to drive game out of the brush for the hunter to shoot at. To do the job properly, beaters had to get into the middle of the bush where the game was. Otherwise, they were not getting the job done because they were beating

Paragraph 1
This is the introduction. The thesis (the last sentence) indicates that Wolfe will use classification. It also indicates that expressions derived from outdoor life will be classified according to their sporting origins.

Paragraph 2
The first sentence is the topic sentence. It presents the first category given in the thesis. The supporting details are examples of expressions in the category.

Paragraph 3
The topic sentence is the first sentence. It presents the second category. The supporting details are examples. Note the transition provided by *a second group*, *for example*, *another example*, and *similarly*.

around the bush. If we "make tracks," we hurry. Originally, this expression referred to an animal going in a hurry and thus leaving behind a set of tracks that were easy to follow. Being on "the right trail" refers to doing something properly or going in the right direction, but its original meaning referred to a hunter being on the right trail while tracking game. Similarly, if we are "barking up the wrong tree," we are as mistaken as the hunting dogs that are howling up one tree when the raccoon is out on the limb of a different tree.

Paragraph 4
The first sentence is the topic sentence. It includes the transition *also* and presents the final category. The supporting details are examples.

Sayings related to wildlife or game are also interesting. We brag 4 about saving money when we are "feathering our nests" or "building up our nest eggs," the way a bird does in the spring. We may be called "owl-eyed" for wearing glasses or be "wise as an owl" for knowing the right answers. If we are "blind as a bat," we can't see very well, just as a bat has poor vision. If we have a bad disposition, we are "grouchy as a bear" or are told "don't be such a bear," since bears have angry temperaments. In addition, there are two ways we can get "skunked." We can actually get sprayed by a skunk, or we can lose a game of some kind very badly—in either case, we lose.

Paragraph 5
The conclusion repeats the idea in the introduction that these expressions are ingrained in English.

Expressions from the outdoors are so common that even those of 5 us who never hunt, shoot, or get close to animals will find ourselves drawing on vocabulary derived from these sources, a fact you may be more aware of from now on.

PEER REVIEW

Responding to "Strictly Speaking"

Analyze and assess "Strictly Speaking" by responding to these questions:

1. Does the essay hold your interest? Why or why not?
2. Is the thesis effective? Why or why not?
3. Are the categories clear and are the supporting details—the elements and their characteristics—adequate? Explain.
4. Is the organization effective? Why or why not?
5. What do you like best about the essay?
6. What single change do you think would make the essay better? How would it improve the essay?

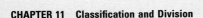

This advertisement has had wide distribution for a number of years. Perhaps you have seen it. Answering the questions that follow may help you analyze and assess the ad.

- What ordering principle is used for the division depicted in the advertisement?
- What kind of details explain the parts?
- Why is this kind of explanatory detail included?
- How do the words and image work together to achieve the advertisement's purpose?

BACKGROUND: Born in 1934 in Sweden to two Nobel Prize winners, writer and philosopher Sissela Bok was educated in Switzerland and France before coming to the United States. She earned her Ph.D. in philosophy from Harvard University. Bok is currently a senior visiting fellow at the Harvard Center for Population and Development Studies. She has written about ethics in medicine and government and has lectured on medical ethics at Harvard and the Massachusetts Institute of Technology. Bok won the Orwell Award for her book *Lying: Moral Choice in Private and Public Life* (1978, reissued in 1999), from which "White Lies" is taken. Her other books include *Secrets: On the Ethics of Concealment and Revelation* (1982); *A Strategy for Peace: Human Values and the Threat of War* (1989); *Alva Myrdal: A Daughter's Memoir* (1991), for which Bok received the Melcher Book Award; *Common Values* (1996); and *Mayhem: Violence as Public Entertainment* (1998). Bok has been a member of the Pulitzer Prize Board and a member of the Academic Advisory Council of the National Campaign Against Youth Violence.

COMBINED PATTERNS AND THEIR PURPOSES: In "White Lies," Sissela Bok *classifies* and *defines* white lies to **inform** readers of the various kinds. She also makes a **persuasive** point about the harm these lies cause, drawing on *examples* and *cause-and-effect analysis*.

White Lies

BY SISSELA BOK

As you read
Think about what life would be like if people did not tell white lies.

White lies are at the other end of the spectrum of deception from lies in a serious crisis. They are the most common and the most trivial forms that duplicity can take. The fact that they are so common provides their protective coloring. And their very triviality, when compared to more threatening lies, makes it seem unnecessary or even absurd to condemn them. Some consider *all* well-intentioned lies, however momentous, to be white; in this [essay], I shall adhere to the narrower usage: a white lie, in this sense, is a falsehood not meant to injure anyone, and of little moral import. I want to ask whether there *are* such lies; and if there are, whether their cumulative consequences are still without harm; and, finally whether many lies are defended as "white" which are in fact harmful in their own right.

2   Many small subterfuges may not even be intended to mislead. They are only "white lies" in the most marginal sense. Take, for example, the many social exchanges: "How nice to see you!" or "Cordially Yours." These and a thousand other polite expressions are so much taken for granted that if someone decided, in the name of total honesty, not to employ them, he might well give the impression of an indifference he did not possess. The justification for continuing to use such accepted formulations is that they deceive no one, except possibly those unfamiliar with the language.

3   A social practice more clearly deceptive is that of giving a false excuse so as not to hurt the feelings of someone making an invitation or request: to say one "can't" do what in reality one may not *want* to do. Once again, the false excuse may prevent unwarranted inferences of greater hostility to the undertaking than one may well feel. Merely to say that one can't do something, moreover, is not deceptive in the sense that an elaborately concocted story can be.

4   Still other white lies are told in an effort to flatter, to throw a cheerful interpretation on depressing circumstances, or to show gratitude for unwanted gifts. In the eyes of many, such white lies do not harm, provide needed support and cheer, and help dispel gloom and boredom. They preserve the equilibrium and often the humaneness of social relationships, and are usually accepted as excusable so long as they do not become excessive. Many argue, moreover, that such deception is so helpful and at times so necessary that it must be tolerated as an exception to a general policy against lying. Thus Bacon[1] observed:

> Doth any man doubt, that if there were taken out of men's minds vain opinions, flattering hopes, false valuations, imaginations as one would, and the like, but it would leave the minds of a number of men poor shrunken things, full of melancholy and indisposition, and unpleasing to themselves?

5   Another kind of lie may actually be advocated as bringing a more substantial benefit, or avoiding a real harm, while seeming quite innocuous to those who tell the lies. Such are the placebos given for innumerable common ailments, and the pervasive use of inflated grades and recommendations for employment and promotion.

6   A large number of lies without such redeeming features are nevertheless often regarded as so trivial that they should be grouped with white lies. They are the lies told on the spur of the moment, for want of reflection, or to get out of a scrape, or even simply to pass the time. Such are the lies told to boast or exaggerate, or on the contrary to deprecate and understate; the many lies told or repeated in gossip; Rousseau's[2] lies told simply "in order to say something"; the embroidering on facts that seem too tedious in their own right; and the substitution of a quick lie for the lengthy explanations one might otherwise have to provide for something not worth spending time on.

7   Utilitarians often cite white lies as the *kind* of deception where their theory shows the benefits of common sense and clear thinking. A white lie, they hold, is trivial; it is either completely harmless, or so marginally harmful that the cost of detecting and evaluating the harm is much greater than the minute harm itself. In addition, the white lie can often actually be beneficial, thus further tipping the scales of utility. In a world with so many difficult problems, utilitarians might ask: Why take the time to weigh the minute pros and cons in telling someone that his tie is attractive when it is an abomination, or of saying to a guest that a broken vase was worthless? Why bother even to define such insignificant distortions or make mountains out of molehills by seeking to justify them?

8   Triviality surely does set limits to when moral inquiry is reasonable. But when we look more closely at practices such as placebo-giving, it becomes clear that all lies defended as "white" cannot be so easily dismissed. In the first place, the harmlessness of lies is notoriously disputable. What the liar perceives as harmless or even beneficial may not be so in the eyes of the deceived. Second, the failure to look at

---

[1]Francis Bacon (1561–1626) was a British philosopher and statesman.
[2]Jean-Jacques Rousseau (1712–1778) was a French philosopher and author.

an entire practice rather than at their own isolated case often blinds liars to cumulative harm and expanding deceptive activities. Those who begin with white lies can come to resort to more frequent and more serious ones. Where some tell a few white lies, others may tell more. Because lines are so hard to draw, the indiscriminate use of such lies can lead to other deceptive practices. The aggregate harm from a large number of marginally harmful instances may, therefore, be highly undesirable in the end — for liars, those deceived, and honesty and trust more generally.

READING CLOSELY AND THINKING CRITICALLY

1. What does Bok mean when she says in paragraph 1, "The fact that [white lies] are so common provides their protective coloring"?
2. What kinds of white lies does Bok classify? What are the justifications for each of these kinds of white lies?
3. Who are the utilitarians that Bok refers to in paragraph 7? What is their view of white lies?
4. What is Bok's view of the white lie?
5. Is there any kind of white lie that Bok might find acceptable? Cite evidence from the selection to support your assertion.

EXAMINING STRUCTURE AND STRATEGY

1. What is Bok's ordering principle?
2. In what kind of order does Bok arrange her categories?
3. Bok introduces her categories with topic sentences. What are those topic sentences? What transitions appear in the topic sentences in paragraphs 4 and 5? What purpose do these transitions serve?

NOTING COMBINED PATTERNS

1. In paragraph 2, Bok gives examples of items in one of her categories. How do these examples help Bok achieve her purpose? Would any other paragraphs benefit from the addition of examples? Explain.
2. How does Bok use cause-and-effect analysis?
3. Is it possible to think of "White Lies" as a definition? Explain.

CONSIDERING LANGUAGE AND STYLE

1. What is a *placebo* (paragraphs 5 and 8), and how is it a form of lie?
2. Consult a dictionary if you are unsure of the meaning of any of these words: *spectrum* (paragraph 1), *duplicity* (paragraph 1), *innocuous* (paragraph 5), *utilitarians* (paragraph 7), *aggregate* (paragraph 8).

Discuss what day-to-day living would be like if people never told white lies. Would some kinds of lies be missed more than others?

WRITING ASSIGNMENTS

1. **Writing in your journal.** In a page or two, respond to these questions: How often do you tell white lies? What kinds of white lies do you usually tell? Have you ever told a white lie that has hurt someone? Have you ever been hurt by a white lie?

2. **Using classification and division for a purpose.** The purposes in the assignments are possibilities. You may establish whatever purpose you like, within your instructor's guidelines.

   • Rather than focus on white lies as Bok does, inform your reader with a classification of all lies. If you want, you can also persuade your reader that one kind of lie is more or less serious than the others. As an alternative, use division to break down one kind of lie into its components.

   • To inform and perhaps persuade your reader of the seriousness of the lies, classify the lies told in some specific context, such as in school, on a date, at a family gathering, or in the workplace.

   • To inform and perhaps persuade, classify the types of one kind of undesirable behavior, such as cheating, disloyalty, or procrastination. As an alternative, use division to break down one type of undesirable behavior into its components and evaluate its degree of harm.

3. **Combining patterns.** Classify the lies parents tell their children or the lies that teenagers tell their parents. Use exemplification to illustrate the lies and cause-and-effect analysis to explain the causes and effects of the lies.

4. **Analyzing and assessing.** Analyze Bok's argument and assess how convincing it is. You might look at her principle of classification, categories, examples, reasoning, details, or any other features of the essay you consider appropriate to examine.

5. **Connecting and synthesizing the readings.** White lies are a common—and even accepted—form of deception. Do you think that deception is so common that it is woven into the fabric of our society? Or do you think people are honest for the most part? Be sure to cite examples to support your assertion. You can draw on "White Lies," "Salvation" (page 203), and "Behind the Formaldehyde Curtain" (page 333) for ideas.

6. **Drawing on sources.** Select a kind of product frequently advertised, such as toothpaste, soft drinks, or laundry soap. Examine advertisements for the product type on television and/or in print, and write a classification of the ways the product is advertised. Draw a conclusion about how deceptive or truthful the advertising is.

BACKGROUND: The Reverend Dr. Martin Luther King, Jr., (1929–1968) was a Baptist minister and the most prominent civil rights leader of the 1950s and 1960s. He founded the Southern Christian Leadership Conference in 1957 and worked tirelessly to achieve racial integration through nonviolent means, especially peaceful demonstrations. Named *Time* magazine's Man of the Year in 1963, King became the youngest winner ever of the Nobel Peace Prize in 1964. King graduated from Morehouse College and went on to Crozer Theological Seminary to continue preparing for the ministry. In 1955, he received his doctorate from Boston University. While at Crozer, King attended a lecture on Indian pacifist Mahatma Gandhi. The lecture charted the course of King's philosophy of nonviolent resistance: "His message was so profound and electrifying," King later said, "that I left the meeting and bought a half dozen books on Gandhi's life and works." On April 4, 1968, King was assassinated in Memphis, Tennessee. King's writings include *Letter from Birmingham City Jail* (1963) and *Where Do We Go from Here: Chaos or Community* (1967). "The Ways of Meeting Oppression" is taken from *Stride toward Freedom* (1958).

www.mhhe.com/clousepatterns6   King

For more information on this author, go to

More resources > Chapter 11 > Martin Luther King, Jr.

COMBINED PATTERNS AND THEIR PURPOSES: Using *classification* combined with *cause-and-effect analysis* and *definition*, Martin Luther King, Jr., **informs** his readers of the options oppressed people have and works to **persuade** them that nonviolent resistance is the best way to oppose oppression.

The Ways of Meeting Oppression

BY MARTIN LUTHER KING, JR.

Oppressed people deal with their oppression in three characteristic ways. One way is acquiescence: the oppressed resign themselves to their doom. They tacitly adjust themselves to oppression, and thereby become conditioned to it. In every movement toward freedom some of the oppressed prefer to remain oppressed. Almost 2800 years ago Moses set out to lead the children of Israel from the slavery of Egypt to the freedom of the promised land. He soon discovered that slaves do not always welcome their deliverers. They become accustomed to being slaves. They would rather bear those ills they have, as Shakespeare pointed out, than flee to others that they know not of. They prefer the "fleshpots of Egypt" to the ordeals of emancipation.

As you read
Notice the biblical references and imagery.

2   There is such a thing as the freedom of exhaustion. Some people are so worn down by the yoke of oppression that they give up. A few years ago in the slum areas of Atlanta, a Negro guitarist used to sing almost daily: "Been down so long that down don't bother me." This is the type of negative freedom and resignation that often engulfs the life of the oppressed.

3   But this is not the way out. To accept passively an unjust system is to cooperate with that system; thereby the oppressed become as evil as the oppressor. Noncooperation with evil is as much a moral obligation as is cooperation with good. The oppressed must never allow the conscience of the oppressor to slumber. Religion reminds every man that he is his brother's keeper. To accept injustice or segregation passively is to say to the oppressor that his actions are morally right. It is a way of allowing his conscience to fall asleep. At this moment the oppressed fails to be his brother's keeper. So acquiescence—while often the easier way—is not the moral way. It is the way of the coward. The Negro cannot win the respect of his oppressor by acquiescing; he merely increases the oppressor's arrogance and contempt. Acquiescence is interpreted as proof of the Negro's inferiority. The Negro cannot win the respect of the white people of the South or the peoples of the world if he is willing to sell the future of his children for his personal and immediate comfort and safety.

4   A second way that oppressed people sometimes deal with oppression is to resort to physical violence and corroding hatred. Violence often brings about momentary results. Nations have frequently won their independence in battle. But in spite of temporary victories, violence never brings permanent peace. It solves no social problem; it merely creates new and more complicated ones.

5   Violence as a way of achieving racial justice is both impractical and immoral. It is impractical because it is a descending spiral ending in destruction for all. The old law of an eye for an eye leaves everybody blind. It is immoral because it seeks to humiliate the opponent rather than win his understanding; it seeks to annihilate rather than to convert. Violence is immoral because it thrives on hatred rather than love. It destroys community and makes brotherhood impossible. It leaves society in monologue rather than dialogue. Violence ends by defeating itself. It creates bitterness in the survivors and brutality in the destroyers. A voice echoes through time saying to every potential Peter, "Put up your sword."[1] History is cluttered with the wreckage of nations that failed to follow this command.

6   If the American Negro and other victims of oppression succumb to the temptation of using violence in the struggle for freedom, future generations will be the recipients of a desolate night of bitterness, and our chief legacy to them will be an endless reign of meaningless chaos. Violence is not the way.

7   The third way open to oppressed people in their quest for freedom is the way of nonviolent resistance. Like the synthesis in Hegelian philosophy,[2] the principle of nonviolent resistance seeks to reconcile the truths of two opposites—the acquiescence and violence—while avoiding the extremes and immoralities of both. The nonviolent resister agrees with the person who acquiesces that one should not be physically aggressive toward his opponent; but he balances the equation by agreeing with the person of violence that evil must be resisted. He avoids the nonresistance of the former and the violent resistance of the latter. With nonviolent resistance,

---

[1]The apostle Peter had drawn his sword to defend Christ from arrest. The voice was Christ's, who surrendered himself for trial and crucifixion (John 18:11).

[2]Georg Wilhelm Hegel (1770–1831) was a German philosopher who said that contradictions could be synthesized to achieve truth.

no individual or group need submit to any wrong, nor need anyone resort to violence in order to right a wrong.

8   It seems to me that this is the method that must guide the actions of the Negro in the present crisis in race relations. Through nonviolent resistance the Negro will be able to rise to the noble height of opposing the unjust system while loving the perpetrators of the system. The Negro must work passionately and unrelentingly for full stature as a citizen, but he must not use inferior methods to gain it. He must never come to terms with falsehood, malice, hate, or destruction.

9   Nonviolent resistance makes it possible for the Negro to remain in the South and struggle for his rights. The Negro's problem will not be solved by running away. He cannot listen to the glib suggestion of those who would urge him to migrate en masse to other sections of the country. By grasping his great opportunity in the South he can make a lasting contribution to the moral strength of the nation and set a sublime example of courage for generations yet unborn.

10   By nonviolent resistance, the Negro can also enlist all men of good will in his struggle for equality. The problem is not a purely racial one, with Negroes set against whites. In the end, it is not a struggle between people at all, but a tension between justice and injustice. Nonviolent resistance is not aimed against oppressors but against oppression. Under its banner consciences, not racial groups, are enlisted.

READING CLOSELY AND THINKING CRITICALLY

1.   According to King, what are the problems with acquiescence? With physical violence?

2.   In paragraph 2, King refers to the "freedom of exhaustion." What does this phrase mean?

3.   In paragraph 1, King says that some "would rather bear those ills they have . . . than flee to others they know not of." What does King mean? Why do you think that he makes this point?

4.   According to King, how does nonviolent resistance balance the approaches of those who acquiesce and those who engage in physical violence?

5.   Why does King advocate nonviolent resistance?

EXAMINING STRUCTURE AND STRATEGY

1.   What ordering principle does King use? What are his categories?

2.   Which sentence is the thesis of "The Ways of Meeting Oppression"?

3.   King presents his categories in topic sentences. What are those topic sentences?

4.   Where in the essay does King make his persuasive purpose clear? Why do you think he establishes his persuasive point at this stage of his essay?

NOTING COMBINED PATTERNS

1. Cause-and-effect analysis appears in paragraphs 5, 6, and 8–10. (Cause-and-effect analysis is discussed in Chapter 10.) How does the analysis help advance the classification?
2. Which paragraph includes definition? (Definition is discussed in Chapter 12.) What purpose does that definition serve? What paragraphs include examples? What purpose do those examples serve?

CONSIDERING LANGUAGE AND STYLE

1. Paragraph 5 includes two biblical references: the mention of "an eye for an eye" and the mention of Peter. Explain these references and evaluate their appropriateness. Why is it natural for King to use biblical references?
2. "The Ways of Meeting Oppression" comes from King's 1958 book *Stride toward Freedom*. What elements of King's language are clues to the era in which King was writing? Do these dated elements in any way detract from the essay? Explain.
3. Consult a dictionary if you are unsure of the meaning of any of these words: *tacitly* (paragraph 1), *fleshpots* (paragraph 1), *desolate* (paragraph 6), *legacy* (paragraph 6), *perpetrators* (paragraph 8), *glib* (paragraph 9), *en masse* (paragraph 9).

FOR DISCUSSION IN CLASS OR ONLINE

Martin Luther King's birthday is a national holiday celebrated in January. Do Americans celebrate King's birthday as it should be celebrated? Explain.

WRITING ASSIGNMENTS

1. **Writing in your journal.** Write about a time when you witnessed, experienced, or heard about some form of oppression or discrimination. Describe the incident and how it made you feel.
2. **Using classification and division for a purpose.** The purposes in the assignments are possibilities. You may establish whatever purpose you like, within your instructor's guidelines.
   - To inform readers and persuade them that one way is better than the others, classify the ways of dealing with a bully. Give the chief advantages and/or disadvantages of each way.
   - To inform readers and persuade them that one way is better than the others, classify the ways of dealing with either stress or depression. Give the chief advantages and disadvantages of each way.
   - To inform readers and persuade them that one way is better than the others, classify the ways of dealing with gender discrimination, age discrimination, or sexual harassment. Give the chief advantages and disadvantages of each way.
3. **Combining patterns.** Using definition (explained in Chapter 12), explain what a *bully* is, and classify ways of dealing with one, being sure to indicate the methods that are

most effective. As an alternative, classify kinds of bullying behavior, indicating which are the most harmful.

4. **Analyzing and assessing.** Analyze King's use of language and assess whether it is effective, and why. You might consider the biblical and other references, the word choice, the level of language, and anything else you judge relevant.

5. **Connecting and synthesizing the readings.** Read "Untouchables" (page 275) and "What Is Poverty?" (page 546). Then write an essay that explains to what extent the homeless and poor are victims of oppression. Indicate whether you think King's policy of nonviolent resistance would help the homeless and poor, and explain why you believe as you do.

6. **Drawing on sources.** On April 8, 1968, four days after Martin Luther King, Jr., was assassinated, U.S. Representative John Conyers, a Michigan Democrat, introduced legislation to make King's birthday a national holiday. However, it was not until August 2, 1983, that the House of Representatives approved legislation to commemorate King in this way. Research the events leading up to the creation of Martin Luther King Day, and classify the ways we celebrate it. How appropriate are these celebrations? For information, use the phrase "Martin Luther King Day" in your favorite search engine, or look under the entry "Martin Luther King, Jr." in *Africana* in your library.

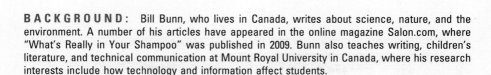

BACKGROUND: Bill Bunn, who lives in Canada, writes about science, nature, and the environment. A number of his articles have appeared in the online magazine Salon.com, where "What's Really in Your Shampoo" was published in 2009. Bunn also teaches writing, children's literature, and technical communication at Mount Royal University in Canada, where his research interests include how technology and information affect students.

COMBINED PATTERNS AND THEIR PURPOSES: In "What's Really in Your Shampoo," Bill Bunn uses *division, process analysis,* and *cause-and-effect analysis* to **inform** readers about the ingredients in shampoo and what those ingredients do — and don't do. You will notice that Bunn also has a **persuasive** purpose: to convince readers that most shampoos are not necessary or desirable products. See if you're convinced.

WHAT'S REALLY IN YOUR SHAMPOO

BY BILL BUNN

There are two types of ingredients in shampoo. One type cleans your hair. The other type strokes your emotions. I'm holding a bottle of Pantene Pro V, one of the world's most popular shampoos. Of the 22 ingredients in this bottle of shampoo, three clean hair. The rest are in the bottle not for the hair, but for the psychology of the person using the shampoo. At least two-thirds of this bottle, by volume, was put there just to make me feel good.

As you read Consider Bunn's tone and whether it advances or undermines his persuasive purpose.

2   The world spends around $230 billion on beauty products every year. Of this figure, $40 billion go to shampoo purchases. North Americans blow almost $11 billion on shampoo and conditioner each year. So most soap manufacturers aren't willing to rely on a product that merely works. The bigger job is convincing the consumer that their soap is adding value to the consumer's life. So shampoo bottles include an extra concoction aimed at convincing the man or woman in the shower that the soap is more "luxurious" or "effective." Because beautiful hair doesn't just happen.

3   Have you got the greasies? One shampoo ingredient is all you need: detergent. Detergents are chemicals designed to bond to both water and grease. When the shampooer massages shampoo into the scalp, the detergent adheres to the grease. The detergent attaches to the rinse water and leaves, taking the grease (sebum) with it.

4   The most common shampoo detergents are ammonium lauryl sulphate and one of its molecular sidekicks, ammonium laureth sulphate. These viscous, yellow liquids, with the water of a shower, are enough to make your hair clean. They help stop the greasies.

5   Shampoo tends to use [seven] factors to help the user feel good about it: shine, thickeners, lather, color, smell, coatings and exotic ingredients. Those ingredients, though they have nothing to do with cleansing, are part of the sell to convince you that something beautiful happens to your hair.

6   Consumers value shininess in nearly everything, including hair. For hair to shine, the cuticles of the hair must lie flat. Imagine a strand of hair as a stack of flimsy paper cups. When all the lips of the cup, called imbrications, lie flat, hair shines. Dull hair has the cups' lips sticking up. To get imbrications to lie flat, hair

needs to be exposed to mildly acidic substances, so substances like citric acid are added to make the imbrications lie down and give hair that shiny look and to let yourself glow.

7   Consumers believe that thick is better. Which may explain why George Bush was a two-termer. Shampooers trust the velvet heft of the shampoo in the palms of their hands. So five of the 20 ingredients on the list are there because they help thicken the soap. Thickness also guarantees that people use more shampoo than necessary. There's salt, glycol distearate, cetyl alcohol, ammonium xylene sulfonate and others: body on tap.

8   And where would we be without suds? Cleaning agents do tend to foam a little when they're used, but the bubbles don't affect the cleansing much. However, the extra lather helps convince the shampooer that the soap is working. Lathering agents are added to boost the suds, chemicals like cocamide MEA. This little devil, besides being toxic in a few ways, also helps the lather to stay once it's been raised, a sudsy Viagra, with the help of known associates like the plastic PEG-7M. Great lather for great-looking hair.

9   Consumers tend to believe that good things must also be pretty. So shampoo manufacturers add colors, like purple and green, with reflective particulates to form blossoming clouds. Colors are often a problem either for humans or for the environment, like good old red dye no. 3, banned in 1990, eight years after a number of reliable studies revealed its cancer-causing tendency. Don't hate it for being beautiful.

10   Smell is important, because after the bathers have washed their hair, smell reminds them that the soap has done its job. Gee, some hair smells terrific. Smell is often associated with a brand, and smell helps to form the most intimate psychological connection a soap can make with its user. But the more "natural" the smell, the less natural the machinations behind it. That lovely apple smell has about as much to do with apples as Dick Cheney with world peace. And fragrance can be particularly dangerous because it's not specifically labeled. It's a combination of ingredients that could be harmless, on one hand or, on the other, noxious.

11   Once the natural oils have been removed from scalp and hair, shampoo often replaces them with conditioners derived from animals or plants. These conditioners coat the air and smooth its surface. The bottle of shampoo I'm holding uses dimethicone to coat the hair (it also helps to thicken the shampoo). It's a silicone-based chemical that coats hair and skin. You'll also find it in caulking, Silly Putty, and herbicides. No more tears. No more tangles.

12   Some shampoo sounds more like chicken marinade than shampoo, boasting of vitamins, minerals, protein and herbs. But the vitamins and minerals and exotic extras play a useless role. So whether the shampoo brags that it is "infused" with real beer, exotic proteins, vitamins, antioxidants, or extracts from some fabulously endangered species, the additive saturates the users' minds, not their hair.

13   All these ingredients would go bad were it not for preservatives, a chemical equivalent of the right to bear arms. Sodium benzoate, for example, is handy because it kills nearly every living thing that might start to grow in a shampoo bottle. Ironically, in most cases the detergents won't go bad. It's the psychological ingredients that need preservation.

14   And these chemicals are tough to track down because tracking chemical names, it turns out, is a little like tracking criminals. Most have several aliases and fake IDs, play a role in many different products, and are shifty when caught and questioned. Some have long toxicity records; others are suspects in a range of problems. Of the 22 shampoo ingredients in my hand, all except three have proved to contribute, or are suspected of contributing, to health or environmental problems. Most of these ingredients, though known toxins, are permitted for use, because the small quantities limit human and environmental exposure.

15   Most of the ingredients in shampoo "may" cause health concerns. The word "may" is used because most chemicals have never been tested. Of the more than 80,000 chemicals registered and used in the U.S. since World War II, fewer than 500 have ever been properly studied for their effects on humans and the environment. So it's hard to say exactly how dangerous it is to use shampoo every day.

16   In May 2008, Jane Houlihan, director of research for the Environmental Working Group, reported on the dangers of cosmetics and personal care products to a House subcommittee. She believes that these products, including shampoo, are the biggest source of human exposure to dangerous chemicals. According to Houlihan, "companies are free to use almost any ingredient they choose in personal care products, with no proof of safety required." Consumers are not properly warned of possible dangers because of a "lack of standards and labeling loopholes." Let's just say that the less you hang out with any of these chemicals, the better off you are, we all are.

17   Mount Sinai Hospital reports that 2.5 billion pounds of toxic chemicals are released in the U.S. each year, the equivalent of 37,100 tanker trucks of noxious chemicals. A lot of these chemicals are released from homes every day. Daily, 45 billion gallons of wastewater go down the drain to be treated at one of the 16,000 water treatment plants in the U.S. But wastewater plants are designed to handle only the major pollutants. They can't remove the diversity of chemicals that humans flush every day.

18   This is the big problem with the shampoo ingredients: When a man rinses his hair, all the ingredients wash down the drain, carrying the grease to boot. And as one man's shampoo travels down the pipe, it meets up with a woman's, and so on, and so on, and so on. At least 350 million gallons of shampoo and its unregulated ingredients flow down U.S. drains every year. And many of these chemicals flow straight into our freshwater systems.

19   Shampoo, for example, contributes to high levels of estrogen and estrogen-like substances (endocrine disrupters) in freshwater downstream of sewage treatment plants that damage fish populations and cause male fish to grow ovaries, a sort of liquid feminism. My hometown of Calgary, Canada, studied the fish downstream of where we add our treated sewage to the river and discovered that female fish outnumber male fish 9 to 1. Estrogen runs through it. One study identifies more than 200 chemicals that are still present in wastewater after treatment. But the problem is likely much larger: environmental damage is difficult to estimate because we're dumping chemicals into the environment that have never been studied.

20   As we get to know some of these chemicals better, we discover that they should not be trusted. Health Canada banned two common shampoo ingredients a while

ago, siloxanes D4 and D5, aka octamethylcyclotetrasiloxane and decamethylcyclopentasiloxane, respectively. D4 and D5 did make hair silky soft, easier to dry and easier to work with. They're also handy in making plastics and paint. Sometimes you need a little D4 or D5. Sometimes you need a lot. But Health Canada strongly suspects that D4 and D5 are significantly affecting fish and aquatic organisms. But, oh, how hair shines.

21   So I can live without the bottled psychology. My new shampoo, Sunlight Dish Detergent, has just four ingredients. It's runny and slightly acidic, smells vaguely lemony, doesn't foam excessively and looks anemic. It's not perfect, just better. I need to apply it only once when I shampoo. With each shampoo, I use a 10th of the volume that regular shampoo requires. The bottle will last at least a year, as my last one did. And though its ingredients aren't worth celebrity endorsement, my hair gets clean and I expose my body and the environment to less risk.

READING CLOSELY AND THINKING CRITICALLY

1.   Bunn explains that the only shampoo ingredient that cleans hair is detergent. Why, then, are all the other ingredients added to the product?

2.   According to Bunn, what do consumers value in shampoo? Do you agree? If so, explain why consumers value these elements. If you disagree, explain what you think consumers *do* value.

3.   Bunn uses division to explain the components of shampoo. How are his details similar to ones a reader might find in a science or reference book? How are they different?

4.   In paragraph 16, Bunn cites Jane Houlihan; in paragraph 17, he references Mount Sinai Hospital. How do these references help the author achieve his purposes?

5.   Is Bunn politically more of a liberal or a conservative? How can you tell? Are his politics relevant in this essay? Should he have avoided any mention of politics? Explain.

EXAMINING STRUCTURE AND STRATEGY

1.   Which sentences form the thesis of "What's Really in Your Shampoo"? What words indicate the author's assertion about his subject?

2.   What is the purpose of paragraphs 1–4?

3.   Which paragraphs include topic sentences that present a division to be considered?

4.   One ingredient that is part of the division—preservatives—is not mentioned in the thesis, although it is discussed in paragraph 13. Why is this ingredient not mentioned in the thesis? Should it have been included there?

5.   What do you think of the conclusion? How does it help Bunn achieve his purpose for writing?

1. Cause-and-effect analysis is an important part of "What's Really in Your Shampoo." How does Bunn use cause-and-effect analysis to achieve his writing purposes?
2. Which paragraphs include process analysis? How does the process analysis help Bunn achieve his writing purposes?

CONSIDERING LANGUAGE AND STYLE

1. What is the tone of the essay? (See page 69 on tone.) What are some sentences that especially exemplify this tone?
2. Consult a dictionary if you are unsure of the meaning of these words: *viscous* (paragraph 4), *machinations* (paragraph 10).

FOR DISCUSSION IN CLASS OR ONLINE

Are readers likely to follow Bunn's lead and use Sunlight dishwashing liquid (or a similar product) as shampoo? Why or why not?

WRITING ASSIGNMENTS

1. **Writing in your journal.** What is your reaction to what you learned about the makeup of shampoo? Why do you react this way? Have your opinions of shampoo and shampoo advertising changed? Answer these questions in a page or so.

2. **Using classification and division for a purpose.** The purposes given in the assignments are possibilities. You may establish whatever purpose you like, within your instructor's guidelines.

   - Shampoo is widely advertised on television and in print media. Shampoo advertisements, even for different brands, have much in common. To inform readers, use division to analyze the common components of shampoo advertisements. Alternatively, write a classification of kinds of print or television advertisements for shampoo.

   - To inform and perhaps entertain, use division to analyze the characteristics of consumers of a particular type of grooming product, such as hair color, hair gel, shaving cream, or cologne. Alternatively, write a classification of kinds of print or television advertisements for a particular type of grooming product.

3. **Combining patterns.** Bunn aims to convince readers that a commonly used product is unnecessary and undesirable. Try to convince readers that a product or activity they consider unappealing is really desirable. Use division to show the product or activity's parts. In addition, use process analysis to show how the product or activity works and/or cause-and-effect analysis to explain the effects of the product or activity. Consider products and activities that some people are resistant to, such as tofu, soy milk, weight lifting, donating blood, or carpooling.

4. **Analyzing and assessing.** Use specific evidence from the essay to describe Bunn's opinion of consumers, manufacturers, advertisers, and marketers of shampoo, as well as his readers.

5. **Connecting and synthesizing the readings.** Drawing on "What's Really in Your Shampoo" and "The Beguiling Truth about Beauty" (page 442), explain how our use of beauty and grooming products—along with advertisements for those products— affects how attractive or unattractive we consider ourselves.

6. **Drawing on sources.** Personal care products such as shampoo are not alone in containing chemical additives. Most of our food products do as well. Read the labels on several kinds of packaged food, such as canned and frozen vegetables, breakfast cereals, lunch meats, bottled salad dressings, and cookies. List the most frequently occurring additives, and then look those additives up to learn what purpose they serve. You can check the *Social Sciences Index* under "food additives" or visit the Web site of the U.S. Food and Drug Administration (http://www.fda.gov) and type "food additives" into the search box. Write a classification of the most frequently occurring additives you found, using their purpose as your principle of classification.

BACKGROUND: Three-time Pulitzer Prize–winning author Thomas Friedman (b. 1953) writes a foreign affairs column for the *New York Times* that is syndicated to 700 papers worldwide. He has reported on many subjects, including the end of the Cold War, international economics, oil-related news, and terrorist threats. An authority on the Middle East who has been a visiting professor at Harvard University, Friedman was the *Times* correspondent in Beirut and bureau chief in Jerusalem. His books include *From Beirut to Jerusalem* (1989), which won the National Book Award for nonfiction; *The Lexus and the Olive Tree: Understanding Globalization* (1999); *Longitudes and Attitudes: Explaining the World after September 11* (2002), which included many of the *New York Times* columns; *The World Is Flat: A Brief History of the Twenty-First Century* (2005); and *Hot, Flat, and Crowded: Why We Need a Green Revolution—And How It Can Renew America* (2008). "Globalization: The Super-Story" first appeared in *Longitudes and Attitudes* as "Prologue: The Super-Story."

COMBINED PATTERNS AND THEIR PURPOSE: With clarity and insight, Thomas L. Friedman combines *classification and division, comparison-contrast,* and *exemplification* to **inform** readers about the nature of globalization. His explanation includes the categories of balance that compose globalization and how these different kinds of balance influence events.

Globalization: The Super-Story

BY THOMAS L. FRIEDMAN

I am a big believer in the idea of the super-story, the notion that we all carry around with us a big lens, a big framework, through which we look at the world, order events, and decide what is important and what is not. The events of 9/11 did not happen in a vacuum. They happened in the context of a new international system—a system that cannot explain everything but *can* explain and connect more things in more places on more days than anything else. That new international system is called globalization. It came together in the late 1980s and replaced the previous international system, the cold war system, which had reigned since the end of World War II. This new system is the lens, the super-story, through which I viewed the events of 9/11.

As you read Consider whether Friedman's classification will stay with you to influence the way you interpret national and international news.

2   I define globalization as the inexorable integration of markets, transportation systems, and communication systems to a degree never witnessed before—in a way that is enabling corporations, countries, and individuals to reach around the world farther, faster, deeper, and cheaper than ever before, and in a way that is enabling the world to reach into corporations, countries, and individuals farther, faster, deeper, and cheaper than ever before.

3   Several important features of this globalization system differ from those of the cold war system in ways that are quite relevant for understanding the events of 9/11. I examined them in detail in my previous book, *The Lexus and the Olive Tree,* and want to simply highlight them here.

4   The cold war system was characterized by one overarching feature—and that was *division.* That world was a divided-up, chopped-up place, and whether you were a country or a company, your threats and opportunities in the cold war system

tended to grow out of who you were divided from. Appropriately, this cold war system was symbolized by a single word—*wall,* the Berlin Wall.

5   The globalization system is different. It also has one overarching feature—and that is *integration.* The world has become an increasingly interwoven place, and today, whether you are a company or a country, your threats and opportunities increasingly derive from who you are connected to. This globalization system is also characterized by a single word—*web,* the World Wide Web. So in the broadest sense we have gone from an international system built around division and walls to a system increasingly built around integration and webs. In the cold war we reached for the hotline, which was a symbol that we were divided but at least two people were in charge—the leaders of the United States and the Soviet Union. In the globalization system we reach for the Internet, which is a symbol that we are all connected and nobody is quite in charge.

6   Everyone in the world is directly or indirectly affected by this new system, but not everyone benefits from it, not by a long shot, which is why the more it becomes diffused, the more it also produces a backlash by people who feel overwhelmed by it, homogenized by it, or unable to keep pace with its demands.

7   The other key difference between the cold war system and the globalization system is how power is structured within them. The cold war system was built primarily around nation-states. You acted on the world in that system through your state. The cold war was a drama of states confronting states, balancing states, and aligning with states. And, as a system, the cold war was balanced at the center by two superstates, two superpowers: The United States and the Soviet Union.

8   The globalization system, by contrast, is built around three balances, which overlap and affect one another. The first is the traditional balance of power between nation-states. In the globalization system, the United States is now the sole and dominant superpower and all other nations are subordinate to it to one degree or another. The shifting balance of power between the United States and other states, or simply between other states, still very much matters for the stability of this system. And it can still explain a lot of the news you read on the front page of the paper, whether it is the news of China balancing Russia, Iran balancing Iraq, or India confronting Pakistan.

9   The second important power balance in the globalization system is between nation-states and global markets. These global markets are made up of millions of investors moving money around the world with the click of a mouse. I call them the Electronic Herd, and this herd gathers in key global financial centers—such as Wall Street, Hong Kong, London, and Frankfurt—which I call the Supermarkets. The attitudes and actions of the Electronic Herd and the Supermarkets can have a huge impact on nation-states today, even to the point of triggering the downfall of governments. Who ousted Suharto in Indonesia in 1998? It wasn't another state, it was the Supermarkets, by withdrawing their support for, and confidence in, the Indonesian economy. You also will not understand the front page of the newspaper today unless you bring the Supermarkets into your analysis. Because the United States can destroy you by dropping bombs, but the Supermarkets can destroy you by downgrading your bonds. In other words, the United States is the dominant player in maintaining the globalization game board, but it is hardly alone in influencing the moves on that game board.

10   The third balance that you have to pay attention to—the one that is really the newest of all and the most relevant to the events of 9/11—is the balance between individuals and nation-states. Because globalization has brought down many of the walls that limited the movement and reach of people, and because it has simultaneously wired the world into networks, it gives more power to *individuals* to influence both markets and nation-states than at any other time in history. Whether by enabling people to use the Internet to communicate instantly at almost no cost over vast distances, or by enabling them to use the Web to transfer money or obtain weapons designs that normally would have been controlled by states, or by enabling them to go into a hardware store now and buy a five-hundred-dollar global positioning device, connected to a satellite, that can direct a hijacked airplane—globalization can be an incredible force-multiplier for individuals. Individuals can increasingly act on the world stage directly, unmediated by a state.

11   So you have today not only a superpower, not only Supermarkets, but also what I call "super-empowered individuals." Some of these super-empowered individuals are quite angry, some of them quite wonderful—but all of them are now able to act much more directly and much more powerfully on the world stage.

12   Osama bin Laden declared war on the United States in the late 1990s. After he organized the bombing of two American embassies in Africa, the U.S. Air Force retaliated with a cruise missile attack on his bases in Afghanistan as though he were another nation-state. Think about that: on one day in 1998, the United States fired 75 cruise missiles at bin Laden. The United States fired 75 cruise missiles, at $1 million apiece, at a person! That was the first battle in history between a superpower and a super-empowered angry man. September 11 was just the second such battle.

13   Jody Williams won the Nobel Peace Prize in 1997 for helping to build an international coalition to bring about a treaty outlawing land mines. Although nearly 120 governments endorsed the treaty, it was opposed by Russia, China, and the United States. When Jody Williams was asked, "How did you do that? How did you organize one thousand different citizens' groups and nongovernmental organizations on five continents to forge a treaty that was opposed by the major powers?" she had a very brief answer: "E-mail." Jody Williams used e-mail and the networked world to super-empower herself.

14   Nation-states, and the American superpower in particular, are still hugely important today, but so too now are Supermarkets and super-empowered individuals. You will never understand the globalization system, or the front page of the morning paper—or 9/11—unless you see each as a complex interaction between all three of these actors: states bumping up against states, states bumping up against Supermarkets, and Supermarkets and states bumping up against super-empowered individuals—many of whom, unfortunately, are super-empowered angry men.

READING CLOSELY AND THINKING CRITICALLY

1.   In your own words, explain what a super-story is. Why is it important?

2.   How does the globalization system differ from the Cold War system? Why is it important to understand the difference between the systems?

Why is the balance between individuals and nation-states so important?
4. According to Friedman, how does globalization explain the attacks of September 11, 2001? What do you think of his explanation?

EXAMINING STRUCTURE AND STRATEGY

1. Friedman uses both division and classification. What does he divide into parts, and what does he group into categories?
2. The classification and division does not begin until paragraph 8. What is the purpose of the first seven paragraphs?
3. Friedman uses topic sentences to introduce each category of balance. Identify those topic sentences and explain how they help the author achieve his purpose for writing.
4. Why does Friedman discuss the balance between nations and individuals last?

NOTING COMBINED PATTERNS

1. Which paragraphs include definition? Given Friedman's audience and purpose, why are the definitions important? (See the headnotes for helpful information.)
2. Which paragraphs include comparison-contrast? How does that comparison-contrast help Friedman achieve his writing purpose?
3. How do the examples in paragraphs 9, 12, and 13 help Friedman achieve his writing purpose?

CONSIDERING LANGUAGE AND STYLE

1. How would you characterize the tone of the essay? (Tone is discussed on page 69.) Is the tone appropriate? Explain.
2. Consult a dictionary if you are unsure of the meaning of *inexorable* (paragraph 2).

FOR DISCUSSION IN CLASS OR ONLINE

Consider ways we can encourage the efforts of super-empowered individuals like Jody Williams (people who are forces of good) and discourage super-empowered individuals like Osama bin Laden (those who are forces of destruction).

WRITING ASSIGNMENTS

1. **Writing in your journal.** How we react to events in our personal lives is often influenced by just one or two factors that form a personal super-story, factors such as being a working student, becoming a new parent, or coping with a disability. What is your personal super-story, the "big lens . . . through which [you] look at the world" (paragraph 1)? In a page or two, explain what influences the way you react to events.

2. **Using classification and division for a purpose.** The purposes given in the assignments are possibilities. You may establish whatever purpose you like, within your instructor's guidelines.

   - To inform your classmates, family members, or co-workers, use classification and division to discuss the ways power or status is ascribed and maintained on your campus, in your family, or at work.
   - In paragraph 6, Friedman says that "not everyone benefits from [globalization]." Classify the people who do or do not benefit from globalization. Your purpose is to inform and perhaps convince readers to take action to help those who do not benefit.
   - Classify the ways you get news of the world to convince readers that the news sources are adequate and diverse.
   - Divide a news source, such as a print or online newspaper, a news magazine, or a cable or network news broadcast, into its components. Your purpose is to evaluate the quality of the source.

3. **Combining patterns.** Friedman says that division was a primary feature of the Cold War and that integration is a primary feature of globalization. Classify the kinds of integration or the kinds of division that exist on your campus or that existed at your high school. Use examples to illustrate your categories, and, if you like, explain the causes or effects of the integration or division.

4. **Analyzing and assessing.** Friedman discusses complex ideas and events. How does he make this complex material understandable to general readers? Consider such elements as vocabulary, sentence structure, supporting details, and organization.

5. **Connecting and synthesizing the readings.** Classify the ways computers connect people, drawing on your own experience along with the information in "Globalization: The Super-Story" and "The Snoop Next Door" (page 255).

6. **Drawing on sources.** Like most everything, globalization has both positive and negative effects. Research globalization to discover those positive and negative effects, and then write an essay that explains what the most significant ones are. For information, go to http://scholar.google.com/, and type "globalization effects" in the search box. Alternatively, you can check the *New York Times Index* in your campus library reference room.

B A C K G R O U N D : William Zinsser was born in New York City in 1922. A 1944 graduate of Princeton University, he has been a writer and film critic. He has written for the New York *Herald Tribune,* the *New York Times,* the *Atlantic Monthly,* and *Life* magazine. He has also been an English teacher at Yale University, where, as mentioned in the essay, he was master of Branford College. He has taught at the New School in New York. From 1979 to 1987, he was the general editor of the Book-of-the-Month Club. An astute observer of American culture, Zinsser has written 15 books on topics ranging from jazz to baseball, including the influential books on writing *On Writing Well* (1980), *Writing to Learn* (1988), *American Places: A Writer's Pilgrimage to 15 of This Country's Most Visited and Cherished Sites* (1992), and *Writing Places: The Life Journey of a Writer and Teacher* (2009). "College Pressures," first published in *Blair & Ketchum's Country Journal* in 1979, still resonates with today's college students.

www.mhhe.com/clousepatterns6	William Zinsser

For more information on this author, go to

More resources > Chapter 11 > William Zinsser

COMBINED PATTERNS AND THEIR PURPOSES: In "College Pressures," William Zinsser combines *classification, exemplification,* and *cause-and-effect analysis* to **inform** of the nature and extent of the pressures Yale students face. The author also has a **persuasive** purpose: He argues that students themselves must eliminate the pressures they face.

COLLEGE PRESSURES

BY WILLIAM ZINSSER

DEAR CARLOS: I desperately need a dean's excuse for my chem midterm which will begin in about 1 hour. All I can say is that I totally blew it this week. I've fallen incredibly, inconceivably behind.

2   Carlos: Help! I'm anxious to hear from you. I'll be in my room and won't leave it until I hear from you. Tomorrow is the last day for . . .

As you read
Decide whether or not you agree with Zinsser.

3   Carlos: I left town because I started bugging out again. I stayed up all night to finish a take home make-up exam & am typing it to hand in on the 10th. It was due on the 5th. P.S. I'm going to the dentist. Pain is pretty bad.

4   Carlos: Probably by Friday I'll be able to get back to my studies. Right now I'm going to take a long walk. This whole thing has taken a lot out of me.

> "Carlos: Probably by Friday I'll be able to get back to my studies. Right now I'm going to take a long walk. This whole thing has taken a lot out of me."

5   Carlos: I'm really up the proverbial creek. The problem is I really *bombed* the history final. Since I need that course for my major . . .

6   Carlos: Here follows a tale of woe. I went home this weekend, had to help my Mom, & caught a fever so didn't have much time to study. My professor . . .

7   Carlos: Aargh! Nothing original but everything's piling up at once. To be brief, my job interview . . .

8   Hey Carlos, good news! I've got mononucleosis.

9   Who are these wretched supplicants, scribbling notes so laden with anxiety, seeking such miracles of postponement and balm? They are men and women who belong to Branford College, one of the twelve residential colleges at Yale University, and the messages are just a few of the hundreds that they left for their dean, Carlos Hortas—often slipped under his door at 4 A.M.—last year.

10   But students like the ones who wrote those notes can also be found on campuses from coast to coast—especially in New England and at many other private colleges across the country that have high academic standards and highly motivated students. Nobody could doubt that the notes are real. In their urgency and their gallows humor they are authentic voices of a generation that is panicky to succeed.

11   My own connection with the message writers is that I am master of Branford College. I live in its Gothic quadrangle and know the students well. (We have 485 of them.) I am privy to their hopes and fears—and also to their stereo music and their piercing cries in the dead of night ("Does anybody ca-a-are?"). If they went to Carlos to ask how to get through tomorrow, they come to me to ask how to get through the rest of their lives.

12   Mainly I try to remind them that the road ahead is a long one and that it will have more unexpected turns than they think. There will be plenty of time to change jobs, change careers, change whole attitudes and approaches. They don't want to hear such liberating news. They want a map—right now—that they can follow unswervingly to career security, financial security, Social Security and, presumably, a prepaid grave.

> "What I wish for all students is some release from the clammy grip of the future."

13   What I wish for all students is some release from the clammy grip of the future. I wish them a chance to savor each segment of their education as an experience in itself and not as a grim preparation for the next step. I wish them the right to experiment, to trip and fall, to learn that defeat is as instructive as victory and is not the end of the world.

14   My wish, of course, is naive. One of the few rights that America does not proclaim is the right to fail. Achievement is the national god, venerated in our media—the million-dollar athlete, the wealthy executive—and glorified in our praise of possessions. In the presence of such a potent state religion, the young are growing up old.

15   I see four kinds of pressure working on college students today: economic pressure, parental pressure, peer pressure, and self-induced pressure. It is easy to look around for villains—to blame the colleges for charging too much money, the professors for assigning too much work, the parents for pushing their children too far, the students for driving themselves too hard. But there are no villains, only victims.

16   "In the late 1960s," one dean told me, "the typical question that I got from students was 'Why is there so much suffering in the world?' or 'How can I make a contribution?' Today it's 'Do you think it would look better for getting into law

school if I did a double major in history and political science, or just majored in one of them?'" Many other deans confirmed this pattern. One said: "They're trying to find an edge—the intangible something that will look better on paper if two students are about equal."

17   Note the emphasis on looking better. The transcript has become a sacred document, the passport to security. How one appears on paper is more important than how one appears in person. *A* is for Admirable and *B* is for Borderline, even though, in Yale's official system of grading, *A* means "excellent" and *B* means "very good." Today, looking very good is no longer good enough, especially for students who hope to go on to law school or medical school. They know that entrance into the better schools will be an entrance into the better law firms and better medical practices where they will make a lot of money. They also know that the odds are harsh. Yale Law School, for instance, matriculates 170 students from an applicant pool of 3,700; Harvard enrolls 550 from a pool of 7,000.

18   It's all very well for those of us who write letters of recommendation for our students to stress the qualities of humanity that will make them good lawyers or doctors. And it's nice to think that admission officers are really reading our letters and looking for the extra dimension of commitment or concern. Still, it would be hard for a student not to visualize these officers shuffling so many transcripts studded with *A*s that they regard a *B* as positively shameful.

19   The pressure is almost as heavy on students who just want to graduate and get a job. Long gone are the days of the "gentleman's C," when students journeyed through college with a certain relaxation, sampling a wide variety of courses—music, art, philosophy, classics, anthropology, poetry, religion—that would send them out as liberally educated men and women. If I were an employer I would rather employ graduates who have this range and curiosity than those who narrowly pursued safe subjects and high grades. I know countless students whose inquiring minds exhilarate me. I like to hear the play of their ideas. I don't know if they are getting *A*s or *C*s, and I don't care. I also like them as people. The country needs them, and they will find satisfying jobs. I tell them to relax. They can't.

20   Nor can I blame them. They live in a brutal economy. Tuition, room, and board at most private colleges now comes to at least $7,000,[1] not counting books and fees. This might seem to suggest that the colleges are getting rich. But they are equally battered by inflation. Tuition covers only 60 percent of what it costs to educate a student, and ordinarily the remainder comes from what colleges receive in endowments, grants, and gifts. Now the remainder keeps being swallowed by the cruel costs—higher every year—of just opening the doors. Heating oil is up. Insurance is up. Postage is up. Health-premium costs are up. Everything is up. Deficits are up. We are witnessing in America the creation of a brotherhood of paupers—colleges, parents, and students, joined by the common bond of debt.

21   Today it is not unusual for a student, even if he works part time at college and full time during the summer, to accrue $5,000[2] in loans after four years—loans that

---

[1] In 2009, tuition, room, and board averaged $15,000 a year for public schools and $36,000 for private schools.

[2] In 2009, students graduated with an average of $20,000 of debt.

he must start to repay within one year after graduation. Exhorted at commencement to go forth into the world, he is already behind as he goes forth. How could he not feel under pressure throughout college to prepare for this day of reckoning? I have used "he," incidentally, only for brevity. Women at Yale are under no less pressure to justify their expensive education to themselves, their parents, and society. In fact, they are probably under more pressure. For although they leave college superbly equipped to bring fresh leadership to traditionally male jobs, society hasn't yet caught up with this fact.

22   Along with economic pressure goes parental pressure. Inevitably, the two are deeply intertwined.

23   I see many students taking pre-medical courses with joyless tenacity. They go off to their labs as if they were going to the dentist. It saddens me because I know them in other corners of their life as cheerful people.

24   "Do you want to go to medical school?" I ask them.

25   "I guess so," they say, without conviction, or "Not really."

26   "Then why are you going?"

27   "Well, my parents want me to be a doctor. They're paying all this money and . . ."

28   Poor students, poor parents. They are caught in one of the oldest webs of love and duty and guilt. The parents mean well; they are trying to steer their sons and daughters toward a secure future. But the sons and daughters want to major in history or classics or philosophy—subjects with no "practical" value. Where's the payoff on the humanities? It's not easy to persuade such loving parents that the humanities do indeed pay off. The intellectual faculties developed by studying subjects like history and classics—an ability to synthesize and relate, to weigh cause and effect, to see events in perspective—are just the faculties that make creative leaders in business or almost any general field. Still, many fathers would rather put their money on courses that point toward a specific profession—courses that are pre-law, pre-medical, pre-business, or, as I sometimes heard it put, "pre-rich."

> "It's not easy to persuade such loving parents that the humanities do indeed pay off."

29   But the pressure on students is severe. They are truly torn. One part of them feels obligated to fulfill their parents' expectations; after all, their parents are older and presumably wiser. Another part tells them that the expectations that are right for their parents are not right for them.

30   I know a student who wants to be an artist. She is very obviously an artist and will be a good one—she has already had several modest exhibits. Meanwhile she is growing as a well-rounded person and taking humanistic subjects that will enrich the inner resources out of which her art will grow. But her father is strongly opposed. He thinks that an artist is a "dumb" thing to be. The student vacillates and tries to please everybody. She keeps up with her art somewhat furtively and takes some of the "dumb" courses her father wants her to take—at least they are dumb courses for her. She is a free spirit on a campus of tense students—no small achievement in itself—and she deserves to follow her muse.

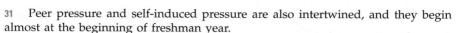

31   Peer pressure and self-induced pressure are also intertwined, and they begin almost at the beginning of freshman year.

32   "I had a freshman student I'll call Linda," one dean told me, "who came in and said she was under terrible pressure because her roommate, Barbara, was much brighter and studied all the time. I couldn't tell her that Barbara had come in two hours earlier to say the same thing about Linda."

33   The story is almost funny—except that it's not. It's symptomatic of all the pressure put together. When every student thinks every other student is working harder and doing better, the only solution is to study harder still. I see students going off to the library every night after dinner and coming back when it closes at midnight. I wish they could sometimes forget about their peers and go to a movie. I hear the clacking of typewriters in the hours before dawn. I see the tension in their eyes when exams are approaching and papers are due: *Will I get everything done?*

34   Probably they won't. They will get sick. They will get "blocked." They will sleep. They will oversleep. They will bug out. *Hey Carlos, help!*

35   Part of the problem is that they do more than they are expected to do. A professor will assign five-page papers. Several students will start writing ten-page papers to impress him. Then more students will write ten-page papers, and a few will raise the ante to fifteen. Pity the poor student who is still just doing the assignment.

"Part of the problem is that they do more than they are expected to do."

36   "Once you have twenty or thirty percent of the student population deliberately overexerting," one dean points out, "it's bad for everybody. When a teacher gets more and more effort from his class, the student who is doing normal work can be perceived as not doing well. The tactic works, psychologically."

37   Why can't the professor just cut back and not accept longer papers? He can, and he probably will. But by then the term will be half over and the damage done. Grade fever is highly contagious and not easily reversed. Besides, the professor's main concern is with his course. He knows his students only in relation to the course and doesn't know that they are also overexerting in their other courses. Nor is it really his business. He didn't sign up for dealing with the student as a whole person and with all the emotional baggage the student brought along from home. That's what deans, masters, chaplains, and psychiatrists are for.

38   To some extent this is nothing new: a certain number of professors have always been self-contained islands of scholarship and shyness, more comfortable with books than with people. But the new pauperism has widened the gap still further, for professors who actually like to spend time with students don't have as much time to spend. They also are overexerting. If they are young, they are busy trying to publish in order not to perish, hanging by their fingernails onto a shrinking profession. If they are old and tenured, they are buried under the duties of administering departments—as departmental chairmen or members of committees—that have been thinned out by the budgetary axe.

39   Ultimately it will be the students' own business to break the circles in which they are trapped. They are too young to be prisoners of their parents' dreams and their classmates' fears. They must be jolted into believing in themselves as unique men and women who have the power to shape their own future.

40   "Violence is being done to the undergraduate experience," says Carlos Hortas. "College should be open-ended: at the end it should open many, many roads. Instead, students are choosing their goal in advance, and their choices narrow as they go along. It's almost as if they think that the country has been codified in the type of jobs that exist — that they've got to fit into certain slots. Therefore, fit into the best-paying slot.

> "Violence is being done to the undergraduate experience," says Carlos Hortas.

41   "They ought to take chances. Not taking chances will lead to a life of colorless mediocrity. They'll be comfortable. But something in the spirit will be missing."

42   I have painted too drab a portrait of today's students, making them seem a solemn lot. That is only half of their story; if they were so dreary I wouldn't so thoroughly enjoy their company. The other half is that they are easy to like. They are quick to laugh and to offer friendship. They are not introverts. They are usually kind and are more considerate of one another than any student generation I have known.

43   Nor are they so obsessed with their studies that they avoid sports and extracurricular activities. On the contrary, they juggle their crowded hours to play on a variety of teams, perform with musical and dramatic groups, and write for campus publications. But this in turn is one more cause of anxiety. There are too many choices. Academically, they have 1,300 courses to select from; outside class they have to decide how much spare time they can spare and how to spend it.

44   This means that they engage in fewer extracurricular pursuits than their predecessors did. If they want to row on the crew and play in the symphony they will eliminate one; in the '60s they would have done both. They also tend to choose activities that are self-limiting. Drama, for instance, is flourishing in all twelve of Yale's residential colleges as it never has before. Students hurl themselves into these productions — as actors, directors, carpenters, and technicians — with a dedication to create the best possible play, knowing that the day will come when the run will end and they can get back to their studies.

45   They also can't afford to be the willing slave of organizations like the *Yale Daily News*. Last spring at the one-hundredth anniversary banquet of that paper — whose past chairmen include such once and future kings as Potter Stewart, Kingman Brewster, and William F. Buckley, Jr.[3] — much was made of the fact that the editorial staff used to be small and totally committed and that "newsies" routinely worked fifty hours a week. In effect they belonged to a club; Newsies is how they defined themselves at Yale. Today's student will write one or two articles a week, when he

---

[3]Stewart was a U.S. Supreme Court justice; Brewster was a president of Yale; and Buckley was a conservative editor and writer.

can, and he defines himself as a student. I've never heard the word Newsie except at the banquet.

46   If I have described the modern undergraduate primarily as a driven creature who is largely ignoring the blithe spirit inside who keeps trying to come out and play, it's because that's where the crunch is, not only at Yale but throughout American education. It's why I think we should all be worried about the values that are nurturing a generation so fearful of risk and so goal-obsessed at such an early age.

47   I tell students that there is no one "right" way to get ahead—that each of them is a different person, starting from a different point and bound for a different destination. I tell them that change is a tonic and that all the slots are not codified nor the frontiers closed. One of my ways of telling them is to invite men and women who have achieved success outside the academic world to come and talk informally with my students during the year. They are heads of companies or ad agencies, editors of magazines, politicians, public officials, television magnates, labor leaders, business executives, Broadway producers, artists, writers, economists, photographers, scientists, historians—a mixed bag of achievers.

48   I ask them to say a few words about how they got started. The students assume that they started in their present profession and knew all along that it was what they wanted to do. Luckily for me, most of them got into their field by a circuitous route, to their surprise, after many detours. The students are startled. They can hardly conceive of a career that was not pre-planned. They can hardly imagine allowing the hand of God or chance to nudge them down some unforeseen trail.

READING CLOSELY AND THINKING CRITICALLY

1.   According to Zinsser, what factors cause the pressure that college students experience?

2.   Make a list of at least five words or phrases Zinsser uses to describe the contemporary college student.

3.   In a sentence or two, summarize Zinsser's advice to college students. What do you think of this advice?

4.   According to Zinsser, how can college pressures be reduced?

5.   Are the author's description of Yale students and his classification of the pressures they face representative of students and their pressures in general? Explain.

EXAMINING STRUCTURE AND STRATEGY

1.   In your own words, write out Zinsser's thesis.

2.   In which paragraph does Zinsser's classification begin, and in which paragraph does it end?

3.   What is Zinsser classifying? What does the classification contribute to the essay? That is, what purpose does it serve?

NOTING COMBINED PATTERNS

1. What element of cause-and-effect analysis appears in the essay? What does the analysis contribute to the essay?
2. What is the purpose of the opening examples of notes written to Carlos Hortas?

CONSIDERING LANGUAGE AND STYLE

1. Zinsser uses *he* to refer to college students and professors. He says, however, in paragraph 21 that he uses this pronoun for "brevity"; he recognizes that women, too, are under pressure. Do you think Zinsser should have used language that includes women? Explain.
2. What metaphor appears in paragraph 9? Do you find the metaphor appropriate? Explain. (Metaphors are explained on page 128.)
3. Consult a dictionary if you are unsure of the meaning of any of these words: *supplicants* (paragraph 9), *gallows humor* (paragraph 10), *privy* (paragraph 11), *venerated* (paragraph 14), *matriculates* (paragraph 17), *accrue* (paragraph 21), *exhorted* (paragraph 21), *muse* (paragraph 30), *blithe* (paragraph 46), *circuitous* (paragraph 48).

FOR DISCUSSION IN CLASS OR ONLINE

In paragraph 47, Zinsser tells of inviting people to speak to his students. Do you think these classroom visits changed the attitudes of many students? Why or why not?

WRITING ASSIGNMENTS

1. **Writing in your journal.** In two or three pages, describe the kinds and amount of pressure you experience as a college student. Then explain the effects this pressure has on you.
2. **Using classification and division for a purpose.** The purposes in the assignments are possibilities. You may establish whatever purpose you like, within your instructor's guidelines.
   - To inform readers, write a classification of the kinds of college students. Use examples from your own experience and observation to illustrate your categories. As an alternative, use division to explain the aspects of a typical college student.
   - To inform, classify the pressures in some nonacademic setting, such as the pressures of parenthood, of being an only child, of working as a table server, of being a lifeguard, or of being a student athlete. Like Zinsser, offer some advice for overcoming the pressures.
   - In paragraph 41, Zinsser notes that Carlos Hortas says students "'ought to take chances. Not taking chances will lead to a life of colorless mediocrity.'" To inform, classify the kinds of risks people should take.

3. **Combining patterns.** In paragraph 12, Zinsser says that students "want a map—right now—that they can follow unswervingly to career security, financial security, Social Security and, presumably, a prepaid grave." If you disagree, or if you think students want more than a map, inform and persuade your reader with your classification of things students want. Use cause-and-effect analysis (discussed in Chapter 10) to explain why students want what they do.

4. **Analyzing and assessing.** The "Background" headnote to this essay on page 509 says that although "College Pressures" was first published in 1979, the essay "still resonates with today's college students." Drawing on as many of the essay's features as you find pertinent, agree or disagree with that statement.

5. **Connecting and synthesizing the readings.** How do the pressures that college students face create situations conducive to the panic and choking explained in "The Art of Failure" (p. 551)? What, if anything, can be done to prevent panic and choking among college students?

6. **Drawing on sources.** Interview 10 students, either in person or by e-mail, to learn about the pressures characteristic of students on your campus. Then classify those pressures. Explain how your classification compares to Zinsser's. Have college pressures changed since Zinsser wrote his essay?

BACKGROUND: Welsh poet Dylan Thomas (1914–1953) made a living in various ways—as an actor, a reporter, a reviewer, a scriptwriter, and a handyman. During World War II, he was an anti-aircraft gunner, and after the war, he was a poetry commentator for the British Broadcasting Company (BBC). He published his first book of poetry, *Eighteen Poems* (1934), when he was only 19 years old. Thomas's second and third volumes were *Twenty-five Poems* (1936) and *The Map of Love* (1939). The poems of his first three volumes were collected in *The World I Breathe* (1939). He also wrote *A Portrait of the Artist as a Young Dog* (1940), a collection of humorous autobiographical sketches; *Deaths and Entrances* (1946); and *In Country Sleep* (1951). *Collected Poems, 1934–1953* (1953) contains all of his poetry that he wished to preserve. The dominant themes of Thomas's poetry are divine purpose and the cycle of birth and death. "Do Not Go Gentle into That Good Night" comes from *Poems of Dylan Thomas* (1952).

THE PATTERN AND ITS PURPOSES: In "Do Not Go Gentle into That Good Night," Dylan Thomas *classifies* the ways different men face death to **persuade** his dying father to resist his own death. The poem also allows Thomas to **express his feelings.**

Do Not Go Gentle into That Good Night
BY DYLAN THOMAS

As you read
Look for the different metaphors Thomas uses to refer to death.

Do not go gentle into that good night,
Old age should burn and rave at close of day;
Rage, rage against the dying of the light.

Though wise men at their end know dark is right,
Because their words had forked no lightning they   5
Do not go gentle into that good night.

Good men, the last wave by, crying how bright
Their frail deeds might have danced in a green bay,
Rage, rage against the dying of the light.

Wild men who caught and sang the sun in flight,   10
And learn, too late, they grieved it on its way
Do not go gentle into that good night.

Grave men, near death, who see with blinding sight
Blind eyes could blaze like meteors and be gay,
Rage, rage against the dying of the light.   15

And you, my father, there on the sad height,
Curse, bless, me now with your fierce tears, I pray.
Do not go gentle into that good night.
Rage, rage against the dying of the light.

CONSIDERING THE POEM

1. What are Thomas's categories? What is his ordering principle?
2. How does the classification help Thomas achieve his purpose?
3. What metaphors does Thomas use to refer to death? (Metaphors are explained on page 128.)
4. What is Thomas asking of his father in the last stanza? Why does he ask to be cursed *and* blessed?
5. Why do the men of the poem "rage against the dying of the light"?
6. Explain the double meaning of "grave" in the fifth stanza.

WRITING ASSIGNMENTS

1. **Writing in your journal.**
   - In a page or two, give your specific reactions to the poem. Do you enjoy it? Why or why not?
   - In a page or two, relate your own views about death.
   - Write your own poem about death or loss. This is not for sharing, so feel free to experiment.
2. **Using classification and division for a purpose.** The purposes in the assignments are possibilities. You may establish whatever purpose you like, within your instructor's guidelines.
   - To inform, classify approaches to death or serious illness.
   - To inform, classify approaches to a particular life cycle event, such as graduation, marriage, birth, confirmation, or bar or bat mitzvah.

WRITING CLASSIFICATION AND DIVISION

See pages 482–484 for strategies for writing classification and division and for a revising checklist.

1. Classify popular music to inform people who do not know much about this music.

2. Classify television talk shows, reality shows, or sit-coms to explain the nature of these forms of entertainment. As an alternative, use division to break down one of these shows into its various parts.

3. Classify teachers you have had.

4. Classify baseball pitchers, football quarterbacks, basketball forwards, or others who play a particular position on a sports team.

5. Classify movie superstars to explain their appeal. As an alternative, use division to break down the typical superstar into his or her components.

6. Classify kinds of shoppers.

7. Classify radio disc jockeys or television newscasters or talk show hosts.

8. Classify sources of frustration.

9. Classify kinds of dishonesty.

10. Classify types of inner strength or types of courage.

11. To help explain their appeal, classify horror movies or break them down into their various parts.

12. Classify parenting styles. If you wish, your purpose can be to persuade your reader that a particular style is the best.

13. Classify types of drivers. If you like, your purpose can be to entertain.

14. Classify soft drink advertisements on television or makeup advertisements in magazines to inform your reader of the persuasive strategies that are employed. As an alternative, analyze the components of a typical advertisement for one of these products.

15. Classify the kinds of parties college students attend. As an alternative, use division to present the various aspects of a college party.

16. Classify football, baseball, or basketball fans.

17. Classify the kinds of neighbors people can have.

18. Write a classification of the kinds of good luck or bad luck.

19. Classify the different kinds of blogs.

20. **Classification and division in context:** Assume you are the entertainment editor for your campus newspaper. For the first issue of the fall term, write an article that classifies the kinds of entertainment available to students at your school. Your purpose is to inform first-year students of the options available to them and the chief features of each kind of entertainment in order to help them adjust to your campus.

The following graphic is a Venn diagram. A *Venn diagram,* composed of overlapping circles, is often used for examining how items relate to one another. This particular Venn diagram divides a criminal event into its components. Analyze the diagram for the following information:

- What do the overlaps mean?
- What elements are generally present when a crime is committed?
- What are "suitable target," "likely offender," and "capable guardian"?
- What does this diagram suggest about how crime can be prevented?

After analyzing the diagram, read a newspaper account of a crime, and explain what took place and whether the crime conforms to the division given in the diagram.

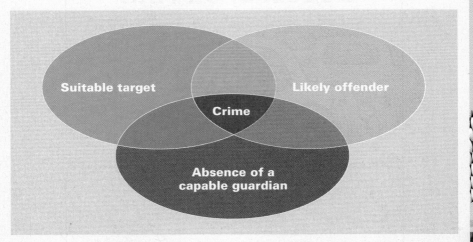

From Freda Adler, Gerhard O. Mueller, and William S. Laufer in *Criminology,* 4th Ed. New York: McGraw-Hill, 2001, p. 241. Copyright © 2001 The McGraw-Hill Companies. Reprinted with permission of The McGraw-Hill Companies.

Reprinted with permission from Andy Singer.

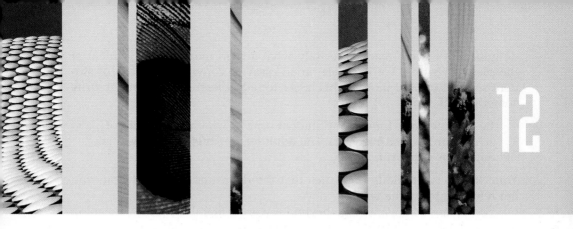

Definition

The cartoon on the facing page defines the successful man and the unsuccessful man. However, as the image suggests, many concepts and terms, including *successful man* and *unsuccessful man*, can be defined in multiple ways. How would you define a successful person or an unsuccessful person?

THE PATTERN

The dictionary may be the most frequently consulted reference source. Since grade school, we have gone to the dictionary to check the meaning of a word we don't know. When we work on the computer, striking a key or two, we can consult an online dictionary quickly. A dictionary gives a **formal definition,** which often explains a term by giving the class it belongs to and indicating how it differs from other members of that class.

term	**class**	**differentiation**
↓	↓	↓
A formula is	a set of words	that indicates a procedure to be followed.

Formal definitions often include synonyms, so a *formula* may be defined as a "method" or a "procedure." Textbooks often include formal definitions to help students understand new terminology.

Another kind of definition is the **stipulative definition,** which states the specific way the writer is using a term. Writers can include a stipulative definition to tell the reader precisely what a term means in the context of the piece a writing. For example, in an essay to convince the dean of student services to offer more night classes for adult learners, you might write something like this:

> By adult learner, I mean any student over 25 who has been out of school for at least five years. The adult learner typically holds a job and helps support a family.

Your stipulative definition ensures that the dean understands whom you are referring to by the term.

Sometimes you want to go beyond a word's literal dictionary meaning to explain the broader significance, associations, and private meanings the word may have. This information can come from an **extended definition,** the kind of essay this chapter treats. For example, consider the word *sled.* A dictionary will tell a reader that it is a vehicle on runners used for coasting on snow. However, an extended definition can tell the reader that a sled contributed to the happiest times you shared with your brother and father. Now consider the word *prejudice,* which can mean different things to different people. An extended definition allows you to explain the meaning and significance *you* ascribe to the word. Thus, an extended definition affords a writer the opportunity to express feelings and relate experiences, as well as convey opinions, knowledge, and personal understandings associated with a word.

www.mhhe.com/clousepatterns6	Definition

For more help with definition, click on

Writing > Paragraph Patterns
Writing > Writing Tutor: Definition

USING DEFINITION FOR A PURPOSE

An extended definition usually *informs.* Sometimes you inform by clarifying something that is complex. For example, an essay that defines *freedom* can help your reader understand this difficult concept. A definition can also inform by bringing your reader to a fresh appreciation of something familiar or taken for granted. For example, you might define *free speech* to help readers more fully appreciate this important liberty. A definition can also bring your reader to an understanding of something unfamiliar. In "What Is Poverty?" (page 546), for example, the author defines poverty for an audience who has not experienced it and hence does not fully understand what it means.

An extended definition can also *express feelings* and *relate experiences.* For example, you could define *teenager* by explaining what your own teenage years were like, connecting your experience to the term. An extended definition can also *entertain,* as when you write a humorous definition of *first-year student.* Finally, an extended definition can serve a *persuasive* purpose, particularly when it points to a conclusion about a controversial issue. For example, Jo Goodwin Parker presents a powerful, graphic definition of *poverty* in "What Is Poverty?" to move readers to take steps to end poverty.

Combining Patterns for a Purpose

You can combine definition with other patterns to achieve your writing purpose. For example, if you define *sinus headache* to *relate your own experiences* of this misery, you could *describe* the pain. To define *math anxiety* to *inform* the reader of what this condition is like, you could also *narrate* an account of a time you experienced this anxiety. To define a *good teacher* to *persuade* your reader of what teachers should be like, you could include *examples* of good teachers from your past. To define *maturity* to *inform* readers about this concept, you could include a *contrast* of maturity with immaturity.

To see how other patterns can be combined with definition, study the following excerpt from "Conspiracy Theories 101," an essay in this chapter that defines *academic freedom.* The excerpt combines exemplification and cause-and-effect analysis with the definition to clarify one characteristic of the term (the liberty to teach seemingly trivial subjects).

EXCERPT FROM "CONSPIRACY THEORIES 101"
COMBINING DEFINITION AND EXEMPLIFICATION

Definition gives a characteristic of the term *academic freedom:* Instructors can teach seemingly trivial subjects if the subjects have an intellectual component.

definition
Academic freedom means that if I think there may
be an intellectual payoff to be had by turning an academic lens on material others consider trivial — golf tees,

examples
gourmet coffee, lingerie ads, convenience stores, street

Examples explain the characteristic by illustrating subjects that are seemingly trivial.

examples
names, whatever — I should get a chance to try. If I man-

cause-and-effect analysis
age to demonstrate to my peers and students that studying this material yields insights into matters of general

Cause-and-effect analysis explains the characteristic by giving its effect: Teaching seemingly trivial material that has an intellectual component can lead to a new area of study.

intellectual interest, there is a new topic under the academic sun and a new subject for classroom discussion.

In addition to using definition as your sole or primary pattern of development, you can use it as a secondary pattern to achieve your writing purpose. For example, in an essay classifying folk art, you might include a definition of *folk art*—perhaps in your first body paragraph. In an essay on courage, exemplification might be your primary pattern, but you might include your personal definition of *courage*.

Definition beyond the Writing Classroom

Definition helps writers achieve their purpose in many writing situations.

IN ACADEMIC WRITING AND READING   College work requires you to learn the meaning of terms and concepts and to demonstrate your understanding of these terms and concepts by writing definitions. Sometimes these definitions will be extended, as when you define *existentialism* in a paper for a philosophy class, or *naturalism* in an essay for an American literature class, or *natural selection* for a biology exam.

Many times you will incorporate formal definition with other patterns of development. For example, a history paper might require you to define the *chivalric code* and explain its effects. Similarly, a paper for an introductory psychology course might require you to define and classify *defense mechanisms* and then give examples of each kind.

Definition is an important part of college textbooks. Here is one example, taken from the introductory textbook *Sociology*.

To clarify unfamiliar terms and concepts, textbooks often follow definitions with examples. *Ethnocentrism* is defined in the first paragraph and exemplified in the second paragraph.

It is tempting to evaluate the practices of other cultures on the basis of our own perspectives. Sociologist William Graham Sumner (1906) coined the term *ethnocentrism* to refer to the tendency to assume that one's culture and way of life constitute the norm or are superior to all others. The ethnocentric person sees his or her own group as the center or defining point of culture and views all other cultures as deviations from what is "normal."

Those westerners who are contemptuous of India's Hindu religion and culture because of its view of cattle as sacred are engaged in ethnocentrism. As another manifestation of ethnocentrism, people in one culture may dismiss as unthinkable the mate selection or child rearing practices of another culture . . . (Schaefer, *Sociology*).

AT WORK AND IN THE COMMUNITY   On the job, definition is also important. A teacher might write a stipulative definition of *competency testing* in an e-mail to parents in order to help them understand how the tests are used in their children's classrooms. A dietician might write formal definitions of *good cholesterol* and *bad cholesterol* to help clients make better food choices. A human resources manager might combine formal, stipulative, and extended definitions of *mutual gains bargaining* to persuade a labor union to adopt this negotiating practice.

Writers have many other occasions to use definition. As editor of your religious congregation's newsletter, you might write an editorial that is an extended definition of *charity* to encourage congregants to give more generously. In a letter to the editor of your local newspaper, you might define *good citizen* to encourage readers to vote.

SUPPORTING DETAILS

In general, an extended definition presents the characteristics of what is being defined. Thus, to define *courage,* you might note that its characteristics include doing what needs to be done without regard to personal cost or fear.

Sometimes you should explain what your subject is *not,* especially if you need to correct a misconception. For example, if you were defining *poverty,* you could note that it is not necessarily something that people can escape if they just try hard enough.

When you write your definition, avoid stating the obvious. For example, if you are defining *mother*, you need not state that a mother is a female parent. Also avoid using a dictionary style, unless you are writing a formal definition. A *dictionary style* in an extended definition is likely to bore your reader because it is stiff and unnatural. Thus, avoid defining *teenager* as "a person in that developmental period of hormonal and social change marking the transition from childhood to adulthood."

ORGANIZING DETAILS

Your thesis for an extended definition can state what you are defining and your assertion about what you are defining, like this:

Adolescence is not the happy time many people remember it to be.

This thesis indicates that you will define *adolescence* and show that it can be a difficult period.

Avoiding Circular Definitions

If you have trouble avoiding circular definitions, remember to avoid repeating the words you are defining or merely using synonyms for those words.

CIRCULAR	**Male liberation is the liberation of men.**
CIRCULAR	**Male liberation involves freeing men.**
BETTER	**Male liberation allows men to relinquish their traditional roles to assume roles formerly held only by women.**

As you can see, circular definitions communicate too little to be helpful.

TROUBLESHOOTING GUIDE

You can also shape a thesis by stating what you will define and noting why it is important to understand the term, like this:

If we do not understand the meaning of free speech, we risk losing it.

To create interest in your essay, your introduction can explain the significance of the definition. Thus, if you are defining *homelessness,* you can note the extent of homelessness in this country to show why readers need to understand it. Your introduction can also create interest by telling a story related to what you are defining. If you are defining *attention deficit disorder,* you can create interest by narrating the story of the time your mind wandered in an important business meeting. If the meaning of your term has changed over the years, in your introduction, you can also explain what your term used to mean. For example, if you are defining *dating,* you could open by noting that dating used to mean sitting in the parlor with a girl's parents or attending a church social together.

Since an essay whose primary purpose is definition often includes other patterns, the order of details will be influenced by these other patterns. Thus, narrations will use chronological order, cause-and-effect analysis will reproduce causal chains, and so on. Purpose, too, can influence order. Thus, if your purpose is persuasive, you may want to place the characteristics of what you are defining in a progressive order to save the most important points for last.

VISUALIZING A DEFINITION ESSAY

The chart on page 529 can help you visualize the structure for a definition essay. Like all good models, however, this one can be altered as needed.

THINKING CRITICALLY ABOUT DEFINITION

As you know from Chapters 1 and 4, to think critically about your reading and writing, you must engage in analysis and assessment. To read and write critically about definition, use what you learned in those chapters, and ask these questions:

- **Is the definition accurate?** A definition that characterizes a *working mother* as someone who voluntarily remains in the workforce to advance her career fails to acknowledge mothers who work mainly in order to pay the bills. This definition is at best incomplete and, therefore, inaccurate. A definition of *social drinkers* as people who get drunk at parties overlooks all those who drink responsibly at such gatherings. In fact, since social drinkers are those who drink in moderation and especially on social occasions, this definition is completely inaccurate.
- **Is the definition responsible?** An irresponsible definition not only fails to be accurate but also can cause harm. For example, an employer who defines *manager* as someone under 50 years old unfairly excludes older people from applying for a job as manager.

INTRODUCTION
- Creates interest in your essay, perhaps by explaining the significance of the definition, telling a story related to the term, or explaining how the term's meaning has changed over the years
- States the thesis (underlined in the example), which mentions the term you will define and can give your assertion about the term or explain why it is important to understand the term

EXAMPLE

Depending on what statistic you read, one in four, or one in five, or one in six people has attention deficit disorder, commonly called ADD. I am one of those people. It's not easy having ADD, but <u>it would be easier if more people understood the nature of the condition.</u>

FIRST BODY PARAGRAPH
- Gives and explains the first characteristic of the term
- May include any patterns of development
- May explain what the term is not
- Avoids statements of the obvious, circular definitions, and dictionary style
- Arranges details according to the patterns used

EXAMPLE

ADD is a condition characterized by distractibility and inattention. For example, when my stomach growls while I am listening to a class lecture, it makes me think of food, which makes me realize I have to go to the grocery store, which makes me think about what to buy, and the next thing I know, I've missed five minutes of the lecture. . . .

NEXT BODY PARAGRAPHS
- Continue until all the characteristics are given and explained
- May include any patterns of development
- May explain what the term is not
- Avoid statements of the obvious, circular definitions, and dictionary style
- Arrange details according to the patterns used

EXAMPLE

ADD is also marked by impulsiveness and difficulty with self-control. People with ADD often make poor choices because they do not think before they act. For example, . . .

CONCLUSION
- Provides a satisfying finish
- Leaves the reader with a strong final impression

EXAMPLE

Like many people with ADD, I control my symptoms with medication and behavioral tools. That said, the more people understand the condition, the easier it will be for those of us who must contend with it.

Similarly, a hate group that defines *Arabs* as terrorists encourages animosity toward an ethnic group.

- **Are formal definitions from sources properly acknowledged?** Extended-definition essays often include formal definitions from sources. If a definition is quoted from a source, be sure it appears in quotation marks and is documented according to the conventions given in Chapter 15.

PROCESS GUIDELINES: STRATEGIES FOR WRITING DEFINITION

1. **Selecting a topic.** Consider the roles you play in your life and the aspects of those roles. If you are an athlete, for example, you can define *student athlete* or *competition*. Or consider emotions and moods you have experienced lately. Perhaps you can define *love, anger, anxiety,* or *jealousy.*

2. **Generating ideas.** List all the characteristics of your term. Then circle the ones you want to treat.
   - For each circled characteristic, ask whether you can usefully develop it by giving examples, describing, comparing or contrasting the characteristic, explaining a related process, or identifying causes and effects.
   - Decide whether you need to clear up any reader misconceptions by explaining what your subject is *not*.
   - Write a statement of the significance of your term and why it is important to define it. You can use a version of this statement in your introduction, as your thesis, or in your conclusion.

3. **Organizing.** Number your characteristics in the order you will discuss them, possibly in a progressive order.

Checklist for Revising Definition

You can use this checklist along with the one on page 76 to help you revise.

1. _____ Your thesis notes what you are defining.
2. _____ You have stated or strongly implied the significance of your definition.
3. _____ You have avoided stating the obvious.
4. _____ You have avoided an inappropriate dictionary style.
5. _____ You have avoided circular definitions.
6. _____ You have developed all the relevant characteristics of your term.
7. _____ You have used appropriate patterns of development and organized accordingly.
8. _____ You have explained what your term is *not,* as needed.

Using Sources for a Purpose

Below is a body paragraph for an essay about why students cheat. It illustrates how to use sources from this book in your writing. The quotation from paragraph 4 of "The Art of Failure" on page 551 helps the author achieve an informational purpose.

THESIS Students cheat for a variety of reasons, many of them linked to societal pressures.

WRITING PURPOSE AND AUDIENCE To inform university instructors about why students cheat.

[1]We may learn more from failure than from success, but our society has little tolerance for failure. [2]An athlete who fails to make the game-winning point is rarely praised for a good effort. [3]When a company's profits falter, the CEO is fired before being given a chance to lead a recovery. [4]A movie that doesn't reach blockbuster status its first week is considered a disappointment, even if it makes a profit. [5]We do, in fact, "live in an age obsessed with success," as Malcolm Gladwell puts it (552). [6]This obsession often leads students to cheat. [7]Students are so afraid of failure that they will do anything to avoid it. [8]Students who fear failure can be so desperate that they will turn in a plagiarized paper if they think the one they wrote is unlikely to get an A or steal a look at a classmate's exam if they think they do not know an answer themselves. [9]Of course, students who cheat miss the irony that cheating actually makes them failures because they are not really looking to avoid failure; they are looking to avoid the *appearance* of failure.

> The quotation in sentence 5 helps the writer inform about a reason for cheating: It confirms the writer's statement that our society does not tolerate failure, and it helps the writer transition to the idea that students cheat because that lack of tolerance causes them to fear failure.

AVOIDING PLAGIARISM

The paragraph illustrates the following points about avoiding plagiarism. (For more complete information on using source material, consult Chapters 4 and 15.)

- **Attribute quotations correctly.** The attribution most often appears before the source material, but as sentence 5 shows, the attribution can instead follow the source material.

- **Understand how to quote part of a sentence.** In quoting part of a sentence, as in sentence 5, you must not alter the author's original meaning. Sentence 5 does not alter meaning (see paragraph 4 on page 552 to check the full sentence in the source).

MYTHS ABOUT USING SOURCES

MYTH: Source material is authoritative, so it stands on its own and does not have to be linked to details around it.

FACT: You need coherence devices to show how source material connects to your other ideas. To illustrate, sentences 4–6 are reprinted below, with the transitions that connect source material and the writer's ideas underlined. (See pages 67–69 on coherence.)

A movie that doesn't reach blockbuster status its first week is considered a disappointment, even if it makes a profit. We do, in fact, "live in an age obsessed with success," as Malcolm Gladwell puts it (552)." This obsession often leads students to cheat.

Annotated Student Essay

Student-writer Nick Hickman defines a technical term for a nontechnical reader in order to inform and—surprisingly—entertain. To address the needs of his audience, Nick uses process analysis, exemplification, and an image. After you read, you will have an opportunity to evaluate the essay.

Why Did the Chicken Cross the Möbius Strip?
(Or Babysitting for Dummies)
Nick Hickman

Paragraph 1
The introduction creates interest with a twist on a children's riddle. The thesis is the last two sentences. It combines a formal technical definition with the intriguing notion (that also creates interest) that the Möbius strip is "seemingly impossible."

Ask anyone over the age of three why the chicken crossed the road, 1 and you will immediately get the response: "to get to the other side." Ask the question in the title (Why did the chicken cross the Möbius strip?), and you will get a far different response: "What is a Möbius strip?" The answer is that the *Möbius strip* is an example of a nonorientable surface. It is a seemingly impossible object of great interest to mathematicians, yet a person can hold it in the palm of one hand.

Paragraph 2
The paragraph opens with a topic sentence that notes a necessary background definition will be given (of *surface*). The supporting details give a characteristic of the term being defined and explain the characteristic with examples.

To understand the Möbius strip, a person must know what a non- 2 orientable surface is, which means first knowing the definition of a surface. Think of a *surface* as anything that can be created by taping together sheets of paper. The only restriction is that the sheets must be taped flat-side-to-flat-side or edge-to-edge. In other words, long strips of paper are surfaces, and an L-shape made by two sheets taped at their edges is a surface. A cylinder can be thought of as a surface in two different ways—by putting two pieces of paper together or by connecting the opposite edges of one sheet. A person who gets really creative can even build a pair of pants or a shirt this way but not a set of bookshelves. Bookshelves cannot be a surface because the edges and back of each shelf make a T-shape with the outer casing.

Paragraph 3
The topic sentence is the last sentence. It notes that another background definition *(orientable surface)* is given. The supporting details give a characteristic of the term, which is explained with examples.

In addition to all of them being surfaces, a cylinder, a pair of pants, 3 and a shirt have something else in common. They all have a clearly distinguishable inside and outside. That is, a person who touches a pair of pants with a finger can readily tell whether the outside or the inside of the object is being touched. The same is true for a tabletop, a drinking glass, or a funhouse mirror because all of these are surfaces with a well-defined front and back, inside and outside, or top and bottom. This is what it means to be an *orientable surface.*

Obviously, that means that a *nonorientable surface* must be a surface with only one side! Orientable surfaces are boring everyday objects—certainly no fun at parties—but a one-sided object could really be something to show off to a crowd!

The best way to demonstrate that a Möbius strip is a nonorientable surface is to construct one. Take a standard pants belt, unbuckled. Bring the tip around toward the buckle, just as if you were putting the belt around your waist, but do not buckle it. Notice that if you buckled the belt normally it would clearly have two sides, an inside and an outside. Now take the tip and give it half a twist so the "inside" is facing out, and buckle it in this position. This is a Möbius strip, a one-sided surface right in your own home that looks like this:

To test for nonorientability, take your finger and place it by the buckle. Now trace the belt around until it gets back to the buckle again. Your finger should be on the "other side" of the belt. Without lifting your finger, keep tracing. When you get back to the buckle a second time, your finger will have returned to the "correct side" of the belt. You have now touched every part of the surface, but you changed sides without lifting your finger!

To mathematicians, a nonorientable surface is a two-dimensional manifold with no consistent choice of fundamental class in its second homology group. The Möbius strip, which was discovered by German mathematician August Ferdinand Möbius in 1868, can be thought of as one of two canonical vector bundles over the circle or as a topological quotient space of the closed unit square. At heart, though, a Möbius strip is just a twisted belt. Advanced abstract mathematics is actually that close to our boring everyday lives, and if you don't think a twisted belt

Paragraph 4
This is a transitional paragraph, linking the definitions of orientable and nonorientable surfaces. Notice the touch of humor. How is it likely to appeal to the author's intended audience?

Paragraph 5
The paragraph opens with a topic sentence that notes the paragraph will be about how to make a Möbius strip. Knowing how to make the strip helps the reader understand its nature. The detail is process analysis.

The drawing helps the reader visualize the strip. How important is the drawing?

Paragraph 6
The process analysis further clarifies the nature of the term.

Paragraph 7
This paragraph contrasts a technical definition with a nontechnical one and brings the technical down to the everyday level for the average reader. Notice the energetic, non-scientific tone.

Paragraph 8
The conclusion provides closure by connecting to the introduction and cleverly playing on the opening riddle.

is really all that exciting, give one to a child and explain how the finger-tracing works. Imagine a house cat trying to come to terms with a hologram of a mouse, and you will understand how the Möbius strip can be an amazing babysitting tool.

So, why did the chicken cross the Möbius strip? You should have 8 figured that out by now: to get to the same side.

PEER REVIEW

Responding to "Why Did the Chicken Cross the Möbius Strip? (Or Babysitting for Dummies)"

Analyze and assess "Why Did the Chicken Cross the Möbius Strip? (Or Babysitting for Dummies)" by responding to these questions:

1. Does the essay hold your interest? Why or why not?
2. Is the thesis effective? Why or why not?
3. Is there enough of the right kind of detail to define the term adequately? Explain.
4. Is the organization effective? Why or why not?
5. Is the image effective and helpful? Explain.
6. What do you like best about the essay?
7. What single change do you think would make the essay better? How would it improve the essay?

EXAMINING VISUALS   Definition in a Photograph

A gift from France in the nineteenth century, the Statue of Liberty has become one of the United States' most powerful symbols. Its meaning, however, can vary from person to person.

- Why does the Statue of Liberty mean different things to different people?
- Why are recent immigrants, longtime citizens, those longing to move to the United States, and anti-American extremists likely to define the statue differently?
- Select two of the above groups. How might their definitions of the Statue of Liberty differ?

BACKGROUND: A literary, social, and political theorist, Stanley Fish (b. 1938) is the dean emeritus of the College of Liberal Arts and Sciences at the University of Illinois, and he also teaches law at Florida International University. He has been professor of law and chair of the English Department at Duke University. Fish is particularly well known for his theory about the role of the reader in literature (known as reader-response theory). Fish has written *Is There a Text in This Class? The Authority of Interpretive Communities* (1980); *There's No Such Thing as Free Speech, and It's a Good Thing, Too* (1994); *The Trouble with Principle* (1999); *How Milton Works* (2001); and *Save the World on Your Own Time* (2008). "Conspiracy Theories 101" first appeared on the op-ed page of the *New York Times* (2006).

THE PATTERN AND ITS PURPOSE: In "Conspiracy Theories 101" Fish *defines* academic freedom and reframes the issue to **persuade** readers that the concept should not focus on content.

Conspiracy Theories 101

BY STANLEY FISH

Kevin Barrett, a lecturer at the University of Wisconsin at Madison, has now taken his place alongside Ward Churchill[1] of the University of Colorado as a college teacher whose views on 9/11 have led politicians and ordinary citizens to demand that he be fired.

2   Mr. Barrett, who has a one-semester contract to teach a course titled "Islam: Religion and Culture," acknowledged on a radio talk show that he has shared with students his strong conviction that the destruction of the World Trade Center was an inside job perpetrated by the American government. The predictable uproar ensued, and the equally predictable battle lines were drawn between those who disagree about what the doctrine of academic freedom does and does not allow.

As you read
Consider how your own classrooms would or would not differ if everyone adhered to Fish's assertion.

3   Mr. Barrett's critics argue that academic freedom has limits and should not be invoked to justify the dissemination of lies and fantasies. Mr. Barrett's supporters (most of whom are not partisans of his conspiracy theory) insist that it is the very point of an academic institution to entertain all points of view, however unpopular. (This was the position taken by the university's provost, Patrick Farrell, when he ruled on July 10 that Mr. Barrett would be retained: "We cannot allow political pressure from critics of unpopular ideas to inhibit the free exchange of ideas.")

4   Both sides get it wrong. The problem is that each assumes that academic freedom is about protecting the content of a professor's speech; one side thinks that no content should be ruled out in advance; while the other would draw the line at propositions (like the denial of the Holocaust or the flatness of the world) considered by almost everyone to be crazy or dangerous.

---

[1]As a professor of ethnic studies at the University of Colorado, Ward Churchill was widely criticized for stating that many of the people killed in the World Trade Center attacks were "technocrats" and "little *Eichmanns*."

5   But in fact, academic freedom has nothing to do with content. It is not a subset of the general freedom of Americans to say anything they like (so long as it is not an incitement to violence or is treasonous or libelous). Rather, academic freedom is the freedom of academics to study anything they like; the freedom, that is, to subject any body of material, however unpromising it might seem, to academic interrogation and analysis.

6   Academic freedom means that if I think that there may be an intellectual payoff to be had by turning an academic lens on material others consider trivial—golf tees, gourmet coffee, lingerie ads, convenience stores, street names, whatever—I should get a chance to try. If I manage to demonstrate to my peers and students that studying this material yields insights into matters of general intellectual interest, there is a new topic under the academic sun and a new subject for classroom discussion.

7   In short, whether something is an appropriate object of academic study is a matter not of its content—a crackpot theory may have had a history of influence that well rewards scholarly scrutiny—but of its availability to serious analysis. This point was missed by the author of a comment posted to the blog of a University of Wisconsin law professor, Ann Althouse: "When is the University of Wisconsin hiring a professor of astrology?" The question is obviously sarcastic; its intention is to equate the 9/11-inside-job theory with believing in the predictive power of astrology, and to imply that since the university wouldn't think of hiring someone to teach the one, it should have known better than to hire someone to teach the other.

8   But the truth is that it would not be at all outlandish for a university to hire someone to teach astrology—not to profess astrology and recommend it as the basis of decision-making (shades of Nancy Reagan[2]), but to teach the history of its very

---

[2]In a tell-all book, former presidential aide Donald Regan claimed that during Ronald Reagan's presidency, First Lady Nancy Reagan consulted an astrologer about all major White House decisions.

long career. There is, after all, a good argument for saying that Shakespeare, Chaucer and Dante, among others, cannot be fully understood unless one understands astrology.

9   The distinction I am making—between studying astrology and proselytizing for it—is crucial and can be generalized; it shows us where the line between the responsible and irresponsible practice of academic freedom should always be drawn. Any idea can be brought into the classroom if the point is to inquire into its structure, history, influence and so forth. But no idea belongs in the classroom if the point of introducing it is to recruit your students for the political agenda it may be thought to imply.

10   And this is where we come back to Mr. Barrett, who, in addition to being a college lecturer, is a member of a group calling itself Scholars for 9/11 Truth, an organization with the decidedly political agenda of persuading Americans that the Bush administration "not only permitted 9/11 to happen but may even have orchestrated these events."

11   Is the fact of this group's growing presence on the Internet a reason for studying it in a course on 9/11? Sure. Is the instructor who discusses the group's arguments thereby endorsing them? Not at all. It is perfectly possible to teach a viewpoint without embracing it and urging it. But the moment a professor does embrace and urge it, academic study has ceased and been replaced by partisan advocacy. And that is a moment no college administration should allow to occur.

12   Provost Farrell doesn't quite see it that way, because he is too hung up on questions of content and balance. He thinks that the important thing is to assure a diversity of views in the classroom, and so he is reassured when Mr. Barrett promises to surround his "unconventional" ideas and "personal opinions" with readings "representing a variety of viewpoints."

13   But the number of viewpoints Mr. Barrett presents to his students is not the measure of his responsibility. There is, in fact, no academic requirement to include more than one view of an academic issue, although it is usually pedagogically useful to do so. The true requirement is that no matter how many (or few) views are presented to the students, they should be offered as objects of analysis rather than as candidates for allegiance.

14   There is a world of difference, for example, between surveying the pro and con arguments about the Iraq war, a perfectly appropriate academic assignment, and pressing students to come down on your side. Of course the instructor who presides over such a survey is likely to be a partisan of one position or the other—after all, who doesn't have an opinion on the Iraq war?—but it is part of a teacher's job to set personal conviction aside for the hour or two when a class is in session and allow the techniques and protocols of academic research full sway.

15   This restraint should not be too difficult to exercise. After all, we require and expect it of judges, referees and reporters. And while its exercise may not always be total, it is both important and possible to make the effort.

16   Thus the question Provost Farrell should put to Mr. Barrett is not "Do you hold these views?" (he can hold any views he likes) or "Do you proclaim them in public?" (he has that right no less than the rest of us) or even "Do you surround them with the views of others?"

17 Rather, the question should be: "Do you separate yourself from your partisan identity when you are in the employ of the citizens of Wisconsin and teach subject matter—whatever it is—rather than urge political action?" If the answer is yes, allowing Mr. Barrett to remain in the classroom is warranted. If the answer is no, (or if a yes answer is followed by classroom behavior that contradicts it) he should be shown the door. Not because he would be teaching the "wrong" things, but because he would have abandoned teaching for indoctrination.

18 The advantage of this way of thinking about the issue is that it outflanks the sloganeering and posturing both sides indulge in: on the one hand, faculty members who shout "academic freedom" and mean by it an instructor's right to say or advocate anything at all with impunity; on the other hand, state legislators who shout "not on our dime" and mean by it that they can tell academics what ideas they can and cannot bring into the classroom.

19 All you have to do is remember that academic freedom is just that: the freedom to do an academic job without external interference. It is not the freedom to do other jobs, jobs you are neither trained for nor paid to perform. While there should be no restrictions on what can be taught—no list of interdicted ideas or topics—there should be an absolute restriction on appropriating the scene of teaching for partisan political ideals. Teachers who use the classroom to indoctrinate make the enterprise of higher education vulnerable to its critics and shortchange students in the guise of showing them the true way.

READING CLOSELY AND THINKING CRITICALLY

1. Explain how academic freedom is defined by those who support Kevin Barrett and the different way it is defined by those who do not support him.
2. How does Stanley Fish define *academic freedom*?
3. Why is Provost Farrell reassured because Barrett promises to include readings that reflect a "variety of viewpoints"?
4. If a woman felt uncomfortable with a discussion of sexual harassment in a college classroom, what do you think Fish would say to her?
5. Why does Fish believe proselytizing is not protected as a form of academic freedom?

EXAMINING STRUCTURE AND STRATEGY

1. Why does Fish mention in paragraph 3 that most of Barrett's supporters do not agree with Barrett's theory?
2. In which paragraphs does Fish use examples? What purpose do the examples serve?
3. In which paragraphs does Fish use comparison-contrast? What purpose does the comparison-contrast serve?
4. In which paragraphs does Fish explain what academic freedom is *not*? How does that information help him achieve his writing purpose?
5. What approach does Fish take to his conclusion? Do you think the conclusion is a good one? Why or why not?

CONSIDERING LANGUAGE AND STYLE

1. In paragraph 2, why does Fish refer to both the uproar and the drawn battle lines as "predictable"? What does the word imply? Do you agree that the uproar and drawn battle lines were predictable?

2. Consult a dictionary if you are unsure of the meaning of these words: *proselytizing* (paragraph 9), *impunity* (paragraph 18).

FOR DISCUSSION IN CLASS OR ONLINE

Agree or disagree with Stanley Fish's definition of academic freedom, being sure to give reasons for your assertion.

WRITING ASSIGNMENTS

1. **Writing in your journal.** Do your classrooms adhere to Fish's definition of academic freedom? If your classrooms do not adhere to the definition, what would they be like if they did? If your classrooms *do* adhere to the definition, what would they be like if they did not?

2. **Using definition for a purpose.** The purposes given in the assignments are possibilities. You may establish whatever purpose you like, within your instructor's guidelines.

   - If you disagree with Fish, write your own definition of *academic freedom* to convince members of the academic community to adopt your definition.

   - To inform new students, write a definition of *plagiarism* suitable for publication in your college's student handbook.

   - To inform readers, define *education*. Like Fish, explain what your term is *not*.

   - To entertain your readers, write a humorous definition of *college student* suitable for publication in your campus newspaper. As an alternative, write a humorous definition of *working student* or *student athlete*.

3. **Combining patterns.** In paragraph 6, Fish mentions a number of seemingly trivial subjects that could come under legitimate academic scrutiny. Select a subject that some people might consider unworthy of college-level consideration—such as reality TV, popular films, hairstyles, or hip-hop music lyrics. First define the subject, and then use examples to demonstrate that the subject can be a legitimate focus for academic study.

4. **Analyzing and assessing.** In paragraph 6, Fish says academic freedom means that instructors can teach anything that might have an "intellectual payoff" or that "yields insights into matters of general intellectual interest." In paragraph 7, he says anything with "availability to serious analysis" can be taught. He does not, however, define or explain these phrases. Can we understand Fish's definition and accept his assertion without a clarification of these terms? How do you think Fish means them? Will the average reader share that meaning?

5. **Connecting and synthesizing the readings.** Write an essay that explains the importance of academic freedom. The ideas in "Conspiracy Theories 101," "Speech Codes: Alive and Well at Colleges" (page 632), and "Fan Profanity" (page 639) may help you.

6. **Drawing on sources.** Find out what your school's academic freedom policy is and then argue that the policy is (or is not) a good one. Alternatively, argue for a particular change in your school's policy.

BACKGROUND: A senior writer for the *National Journal,* a nonpartisan journal on government and public policy, political writer and journalist Jonathan Rauch (b. 1960) is also a contributing editor for the *Atlantic Monthly* and a guest scholar at the Brookings Institution think tank. A 1982 graduate of Yale, Rauch writes on a range of topics, including American politics, economic issues, and animal rights. He has written for many periodicals, including London's *Economist,* the *Winston-Salem* (North Carolina) *Journal,* and *the New Republic.* Rauch's books include *Kindly Inquisitors: The New Attacks on Free Thought* (1993), *Government's End: Why Washington Stopped Working* (1999), and *Gay Marriage: Why It Is Good for Gays, Good for Straights, and Good for America* (2004). "Caring for Your Introvert" first appeared in the *Atlantic Monthly* (2003).

COMBINED PATTERNS AND THEIR PURPOSES: In "Caring for Your Introvert," Jonathan Rauch combines a *definition* of *introvert* with *contrast* to **inform** readers of the characteristics of a little-understood personality type. In addition, Rauch works to **persuade** readers that although introverts are an oppressed group, they are superior to extroverts. You will, no doubt, notice elements of humor in the essay that **entertain** readers.

CARING FOR YOUR INTROVERT BY JONATHAN RAUCH

DO YOU KNOW SOMEONE who needs hours alone every day? Who loves quiet conversations about feelings or ideas, and can give a dynamite presentation to a big audience, but seems awkward in groups and maladroit at small talk? Who has to be dragged to parties and then needs the rest of the day to recuperate? Who growls or scowls or grunts or winces when accosted with pleasantries by people who are just trying to be nice?

As you read
Consider why Rauch organizes part of his essay with a question-and-answer format.

2 If so, do you tell this person he is "too serious," or ask if he is okay? Regard him as aloof, arrogant, rude? Redouble your efforts to draw him out?

3 If you answered yes to these questions, chances are that you have an introvert on your hands—and that you aren't caring for him properly. Science has learned a good deal in recent years about the habits and requirements of introverts. It has even learned, by means of brain scans, that introverts process information differently from other people (I am not making this up). If you are behind the curve on this important matter, be reassured that you are not alone. Introverts may be common, but they are also among the most misunderstood and aggrieved groups in America, possibly the world.

4 I know. My name is Jonathan, and I am an introvert.

5 Oh, for years I denied it. After all, I have good social skills. I am not morose or misanthropic. Usually. I am far from shy. I love long conversations that explore intimate thoughts or passionate interests. But at last I have self-identified and come out to my friends and colleagues. In doing so, I have found myself liberated from any number of damaging misconceptions and stereotypes. Now I am here to tell you what you need to know in order to respond sensitively and supportively to

> "My name is Jonathan, and I am an introvert."

your own introverted family members, friends, and colleagues. Remember, someone you know, respect, and interact with every day is an introvert, and you are probably driving this person nuts. It pays to learn the warning signs.

What Is Introversion?

6   In its modern sense, the concept goes back to the 1920s and the psychologist Carl Jung. Today it is a mainstay of personality tests, including the widely used Myers-Briggs Type Indicator. Introverts are not necessarily shy. Shy people are anxious or frightened or self-excoriating in social settings; introverts generally are not. Introverts are also not misanthropic, though some of us do go along with Sartre[1] as far as to say "Hell is other people at breakfast." Rather, introverts are people who find other people tiring.

7   Extroverts are energized by people, and wilt or fade when alone. They often seem bored by themselves, in both senses of the expression. Leave an extrovert alone for two minutes and he will reach for his cell phone. In contrast, after an hour or two of being socially "on," we introverts need to turn off and recharge. My own formula is roughly two hours alone for every hour of socializing. This isn't anti-social. It isn't a sign of depression. It does not call for medication. For introverts, to be alone with our thoughts is as restorative as sleeping, as nourishing as eating. Our motto: "I'm okay, you're okay—in small doses."[2]

How Many People Are Introverts?

8   I performed exhaustive research on this question, in the form of a quick Google search. The answer: About 25 percent. Or: Just under half. Or—my favorite—"a minority in the regular population but a majority in the gifted population."

Are Introverts Misunderstood?

9   Wildly. That, it appears, is our lot in life. "It is very difficult for an extrovert to understand an introvert," write the education experts Jill D. Burruss and Lisa Kaenzig. (They are also the source of the quotation in the previous paragraph.) Extroverts are easy for introverts to understand, because extroverts spend so much of their time working out who they are in voluble, and frequently inescapable, interaction with other people. They are as inscrutable as puppy dogs. But the street does not run both ways. Extroverts have little or no grasp of introversion. They assume that company, especially their own, is always welcome. They cannot imagine why someone would need to be alone; indeed, they often take umbrage at the suggestion. As often as I have tried to explain the matter to extroverts, I have never sensed that any of them really understood. They listen for a moment and then go back to barking and yipping.

Are Introverts Oppressed?

10   I would have to say so. For one thing, extroverts are overrepresented in politics, a profession in which only the garrulous are really comfortable. Look at

---

[1]Jean-Paul Sartre (1905–1980) was a French philosopher; "Hell is other people" is a quotation from his 1944 play *No Exit*.

[2]*I'm OK—You're OK* (1967) is a self-help book by Thomas Harris, M.D.

George W. Bush. Look at Bill Clinton. They seem to come fully to life only around other people. To think of the few introverts who did rise to the top in politics— Calvin Coolidge, Richard Nixon—is merely to drive home the point. With the possible exception of Ronald Reagan, whose fabled aloofness and privateness were probably signs of a deep introverted streak (many actors, I've read, are introverts, and many introverts, when socializing, feel like actors), introverts are not considered "naturals" in politics.

11   Extroverts therefore dominate public life. This is a pity. If we introverts ran the world, it would no doubt be a calmer, saner, more peaceful sort of place. As Coolidge is supposed to have said, "Don't you know that four fifths of all our troubles in this life would disappear if we would just sit down and keep still?" (He is also supposed to have said, "If you don't say anything, you won't be called on to repeat it." The only thing a true introvert dislikes more than talking about himself is repeating himself.)

12   With their endless appetite for talk and attention, extroverts also dominate social life, so they tend to set expectations. In our extrovertist society, being outgoing is considered normal and therefore desirable, a mark of happiness, confidence, leadership. Extroverts are seen as big-hearted, vibrant, warm, empathic. "People person" is a compliment. Introverts are described with words like "guarded," "loner," "reserved," "taciturn," "self-contained," "private"—narrow, ungenerous words, words that suggest emotional parsimony and smallness of personality. Female introverts, I suspect, must suffer especially. In certain circles, particularly in the Midwest, a man can still sometimes get away with being what they used to call a strong and silent type; introverted women, lacking that alternative, are even more likely than men to be perceived as timid, withdrawn, haughty.

Are Introverts Arrogant?

13   Hardly. I suppose this common misconception has to do with our being more intelligent, more reflective, more independent, more level-headed, more refined, and more sensitive than extroverts. Also, it is probably due to our lack of small talk, a lack that extroverts often mistake for disdain. We tend to think before talking, whereas extroverts tend to think *by* talking, which is why their meetings never last less than six hours. "Introverts," writes a perceptive fellow named Thomas P. Crouser, in an online review of a recent book called *Why Should Extroverts Make All the Money?* (I'm not making *that* up, either), "are driven to distraction by the semi-internal dialogue extroverts tend to conduct. Introverts don't outwardly complain, instead roll their eyes and silently curse the darkness." Just so.

14   The worst of it is that extroverts have no idea of the torment they put us through. Sometimes, as we gasp for air amid the fog of their 98-percent-content-free talk, we wonder if extroverts even bother to listen to themselves. Still, we endure stoically, because the etiquette books—written, no doubt, by extroverts—regard declining to banter as rude and gaps in conversation as awkward. We can only dream that someday, when our condition is more widely understood, when perhaps an Introverts' Rights movement has blossomed and borne fruit, it will not be impolite to say "I'm an introvert. You are a wonderful person and I like you. But now please shush."

How Can I Let the Introvert in My Life Know That I Support Him and Respect His Choice?

15 First, recognize that it's not a choice. It's not a lifestyle. It's an *orientation*.

16 Second, when you see an introvert lost in thought, don't say "What's the matter?" or "Are you all right?"

17 Third, don't say anything else, either.

READING CLOSELY AND THINKING CRITICALLY

1. Which sentence is the thesis of the essay?

2. Why does Rauch want readers to understand what introverts are like? That is, what is the significance of the definition?

3. Some of the essay is humorous, and some of the points are exaggerated. Cite one humorous detail and one exaggerated detail. Given the humor and exaggeration, how serious is Rauch?

4. According to Rauch, what misconceptions do people have about introverts?

5. Rauch says the fact that Calvin Coolidge and Richard Nixon were introverts helps make the point that introverts are not natural politicians. Explain what Rauch means.

EXAMINING STRUCTURE AND STRATEGY

1. Why does Rauch open his essay with questions that include the characteristics of an introvert rather than state the introvert's characteristics in declarative sentences?

2. Rauch cites scientific and other sources throughout the essay. (See, for example, paragraphs 3 and 6.) How does this material help the author achieve his purpose?

3. Why does Rauch use the question-and-answer format in paragraphs 6–17? Do you think this format provides an effective organizational structure? Explain.

4. What techniques does Rauch use to create humor and entertain his reader?

NOTING COMBINED PATTERNS

1. What is the purpose of the contrast in paragraphs 6 and 7?

2. What is the purpose of the contrast in paragraphs 10–12?

3. What is the purpose of the contrast in paragraphs 13 and 14?

CONSIDERING LANGUAGE AND STYLE

1. At times, Rauch uses exaggeration and mock seriousness. For example, in paragraph 3, he exaggerates by saying that introverts are one of the "most misunderstood and aggrieved groups in America, possibly the world." Cite three other examples of exaggeration or mock seriousness.

2. At times, Rauch adopts the language of sexual orientation. He even uses introversion as a metaphor for being gay. Cite two examples of this use of language.

3. Consult a dictionary if you are unsure of the meaning of these words: *maladroit* (paragraph 1), *misanthropic* (paragraph 5, 6), *self-excoriating* (paragraph 6), *garrulous* (paragraph 10), *parsimony* (paragraph 12).

FOR DISCUSSION IN CLASS OR ONLINE

Rauch says that extroverts "dominate public life" (paragraph 11). Is it possible for introverts to dominate public life? Why or why not?

WRITING ASSIGNMENTS

1. **Writing in your journal.** In a page or so, explain whether you are an introvert or an extrovert. Cite examples to illustrate your characterization.

2. **Using definition for a purpose.** The purposes in the assignments are possibilities. You may establish whatever purpose you like, within your instructor's guidelines.
   - To inform and perhaps entertain, write your own definition of *introvert.*
   - To inform and perhaps entertain, define *extrovert.* You can also try to convince readers that extroverts are superior to introverts.
   - Rauch says that introverts are oppressed. To entertain your reader, define another such oppressed group, perhaps impulsive people, procrastinators, the fashion-challenged, or clumsy people.
   - In paragraph 12, Rauch says that "being outgoing is considered normal." To inform, and perhaps persuade or entertain, define *normal.*

3. **Combining patterns.** Define some characteristic or condition that you have, such as shyness, self-consciousness, attention deficit disorder, dyslexia, or hearing impairment. Using narration (explained in Chapter 6), tell one or more brief stories to illustrate how you are affected by the characteristic or condition.

4. **Analyzing and assessing.** Analyze how Rauch plays with the conventions of articles in popular magazines that claim to help people improve their lives or the lives of others, and assess what he is saying about those articles and conventions.

5. **Connecting and synthesizing the readings.** Using the information in "The Poncho Bearer" (page 212), "Caring for Your Introvert," and your own experience and observation, discuss what it means to be either an introvert or an extrovert in high school.

6. **Drawing on sources.** Observe people in gatherings you are regularly a part of, such as those that occur in the classroom, at social functions, with your friends, at the gym, in houses of worship, and in grocery stores. What differences do you notice between introverts and extroverts? Do you agree with Rauch's characterizations of introverts and extroverts? Do you agree with his conclusion that extroverts "dominate public life" (paragraph 11)? Support your responses with examples of the people you observe.

BACKGROUND: When University of Oklahoma professor George Henderson was gathering material for his book *America's Other Children: Public Schools outside Suburbia* (1971), "What Is Poverty?" was mailed to him from West Virginia. Henderson, who included the essay in his book, says it was a speech delivered in De Land, Florida, in 1965. We do not know for sure whether Parker is writing of herself or acting as a spokesperson for others. Either way, her definition of poverty is so startlingly vivid that it has become a frequently reprinted example of definition.

COMBINED PATTERNS AND THEIR PURPOSES: In addition to **informing** her audience about the nature of poverty, Parker's *definition* works to **persuade** the reader to help solve the problem. As you read, you will notice a great deal of *description*, some *cause-and-effect analysis*, and *exemplification*.

What Is Poverty?

BY JO GOODWIN PARKER

You ask me what is poverty? Listen to me. Here I am, dirty, smelly, and with no "proper" underwear on and the stench of my rotting teeth near you. I will tell you. Listen to me. Listen without pity. I cannot use your pity. Listen with understanding. Put yourself in my dirty, worn out, ill-fitting shoes, and hear me.

2 Poverty is getting up every morning from a dirt- and illness-stained mattress. The sheets have long since been used for diapers. Poverty is living in a smell that never leaves. This is a smell of urine, sour milk, and spoiling food sometimes joined with the strong smell of long-cooked onions. Onions are cheap. If you have smelled this smell, you did not know how it came. It is the smell of the outdoor privy. It is the smell of young children who cannot walk the long dark way in the night. It is the smell of the mattresses where years of "accidents" have happened. It is the smell of the milk which has gone sour because the refrigerator long has not worked, and it costs money to get it fixed. It is the smell of rotting garbage. I could bury it, but where is the shovel? Shovels cost money.

> **As you read**
> Notice that many paragraphs begin "Poverty is . . ." What effect does the repetition of those words have on you?

3 Poverty is being tired. I have always been tired. They told me at the hospital when the baby came that I had chronic anemia caused from poor diet, a bad case of worms, and that I needed a corrective operation. I listened politely—the poor are always polite. The poor always listen. They don't say that there is no money for iron pills, or better food, or worm medicine. The idea of an operation is frightening and costs so much that, if I had dared, I would have laughed. Who takes care of my children? Recovery from an operation takes a long time. I have three children. When I left them with "Granny" the last time I had a job, I came home to find the baby covered with fly specks, and a diaper that had not been changed since I left. When the dried diaper came off, bits of my baby's flesh came with it. My other child was playing with a sharp bit of broken glass, and my oldest was playing alone at the edge of a lake. I made twenty-two dollars a week, and a good nursery school costs twenty dollars a week for my three children. I quit my job.

4 Poverty is dirt. You say in your clean clothes coming from your clean house, "Anybody can be clean." Let me explain about housekeeping with no money. For

breakfast I give my children grits with no oleo[1] or cornbread without eggs and oleo. This does not use up many dishes. What dishes there are, I wash in cold water and with no soap. Even the cheapest soap has to be saved for the baby's diapers. Look at my hands, so cracked and red. Once I saved for two months to buy a jar of Vaseline for my hands and the baby's diaper rash. When I had saved enough, I went to buy it and the price had gone up two cents. The baby and I suffered on. I have to decide every day if I can bear to put my cracked, sore hands into the cold water and strong soap. But you ask, why not hot water? Fuel costs money. If you have a wood fire it costs money. If you burn electricity, it costs money. Hot water is a luxury. I do not have luxuries. I know you will be surprised when I tell you how young I am. I look so much older. My back has been bent over the wash tubs for so long, I cannot remember when I ever did anything else. Every night I wash every stitch my school-age child has on and just hope her clothes will be dry by morning.

5   Poverty is staying up all night on cold nights to watch the fire, knowing one spark on the newspaper covering the walls means your sleeping children die in flames. In summer poverty is watching gnats and flies devour your baby's tears when he cries. The screens are torn and you pay so little rent you know they will never be fixed. Poverty means insects in your food, in your nose, in your eyes, and crawling over you when you sleep. Poverty is hoping it never rains because diapers won't dry when it rains and soon you are using newspapers. Poverty is seeing your children forever with runny noses. Paper handkerchiefs cost money and all your rags you need for other things. Even more costly are antihistamines. Poverty is cooking without food and cleaning without soap.

6   Poverty is asking for help. Have you ever had to ask for help, knowing your children will suffer unless you get it? Think about asking for a loan from a relative, if this is the only way you can imagine asking for help. I will tell you how it feels. You find out where the office is that you are supposed to visit. You circle that block four or five times. Thinking of your children, you go in. Everybody is very busy. Finally, someone comes out and you tell her that you need help. That never is the person you need to see. You go see another person, and after spilling the whole shame of your poverty all over the desk between you, you find that this isn't the right office after all—you must repeat the whole process, and it never is any easier at the next place.

7   You have asked for help, and after all it has a cost. You are again told to wait. You are told why, but you don't really hear because of the red cloud of shame and the rising black cloud of despair.

8   Poverty is remembering. It is remembering quitting school in junior high because "nice" children had been so cruel about my clothes and my smell. The attendance officer came. My mother told him I was pregnant. I wasn't but she thought that I could get a job and help out. I had jobs off and on, but never long enough to learn anything. Mostly I remember being married. I was so young then. I am still young. For a time, we had all the things you have. There was a little house in another town, with hot water and everything. Then my husband lost his

---

[1]Oleo is short for oleomargarine, more frequently abbreviated to margarine.

job. There was unemployment insurance for a while and what few jobs I could get. Soon, all our nice things were repossessed and we moved back here. I was pregnant then. This house didn't look so bad when we first moved in. Every week it gets worse. Nothing is ever fixed. We now had no money. There were a few odd jobs for my husband, but everything went for food then, as it does now. I don't know how we lived through three years and three babies, but we did. I'll tell you something, after the last baby I destroyed my marriage. It had been a good one, but could you keep on bringing children in this dirt? Did you ever think how much it costs for any kind of birth control? I knew my husband was leaving the day he left, but there were no good-byes between us. I hope he has been able to climb out of this mess somewhere. He never could hope with us to drag him down.

9   That's when I asked for help. When I got it, you know how much it was? It was, and is, seventy-eight dollars a month for the four of us; that is all I ever can get. Now you know why there is no soap, no needles and thread, no hot water, no aspirin, no worm medicine, no hand cream, no shampoo. None of these things forever and ever and ever. So that you can see clearly, I pay twenty dollars a month rent, and most of the rest goes for food. For grits and cornmeal, and rice and milk and beans. I try my best to use only the minimum electricity. If I use more, there is that much less for food.

10   Poverty is looking into a black future. Your children won't play with my boys. They will turn to other boys who steal to get what they want. I can already see them behind the bars of their prison instead of behind the bars of my poverty. Or they will turn to the freedom of alcohol or drugs, and find themselves enslaved. And my daughter? At best, there is for her life like mine.

11   But you say to me, there are schools. Yes, there are schools. My children have no extra books, no magazines, no extra pencils, or crayons, or paper and the most important of all, they do not have health. They have worms, they have infections, they have pink-eye all summer. They do not sleep well on the floor, or with me in my one bed. They do not suffer from hunger, my seventy-eight dollars keeps us alive, but they do suffer malnutrition. Oh yes, I do remember what I was taught about health in school. It doesn't do much good. In some places there is a surplus commodities program. Not here. The county said it cost too much. There is a school lunch program. But I have two children who will already be damaged by the time they get to school.

12   But, you say to me, there are health clinics. Yes, there are health clinics and they are in the towns. I live out here eight miles from town. I can walk that far (even if it is sixteen miles both ways), but can my little children? My neighbor will take me when he goes; but he expects to get paid, *one way or another.* I bet you know my neighbor. He is that large man who spends his time at the gas station, the barbershop, and the corner store complaining about the government spending money on the immoral mothers of illegitimate children.

13   Poverty is an acid that drips on pride until all pride is worn away. Poverty is a chisel that chips on honor until honor is worn away. Some of you say that you would do *something* in my situation, and maybe you would, for the first week or the first month, but for year after year?

14   Even the poor can dream. A dream of a time when there is money. Money for the right kinds of food, for worm medicine, for iron pills, for toothbrushes, for hand cream, for a hammer and nails and a bit of screening, for a shovel, for a bit of paint, for some sheeting, for needles and thread. Money to pay *in money* for a trip to town. And, oh, money for hot water and money for soap. A dream of when asking for help does not eat away the last bit of pride. When the office you visit is as nice as the offices of other governmental agencies, when there are enough workers to help you quickly, when workers do not quit in defeat and despair. When you have to tell your story to only one person, and that person can send you for other help and you don't have to prove your poverty over and over and over again.

15   I have come out of my despair to tell you this. Remember I did not come from another place or another time. Others like me are all around you. Look at us with an angry heart, anger that will help you help me. Anger that will let you tell of me. The poor are always silent. Can you be silent too?

READING CLOSELY AND THINKING CRITICALLY

1.   According to Parker, what are the chief characteristics of poverty?
2.   What are the effects of poverty on children?
3.   According to the author, why doesn't education provide a way out of poverty for children?
4.   In paragraphs 11–13, Parker addresses people who say that schools, health clinics, and the poor themselves can help alleviate poverty. How does she counter the argument these people make? Why does she bother to address this argument?
5.   Paragraph 8 describes a vicious cycle that is part of poverty. What other vicious cycles can you detect as a result of reading the essay?
6.   Who do you think would make the best audience for "What Is Poverty?" Why?

EXAMINING STRUCTURE AND STRATEGY

1.   "What Is Poverty?" was originally delivered as a speech. Is the opening question equally appropriate for speech and writing? Explain. What approach does Parker take to the rest of the introduction?
2.   Parker addresses her audience directly with frequent use of "you." Why does she do so?
3.   What approach does the author take to the conclusion?

NOTING COMBINED PATTERNS

1.   Parker uses a great deal of description. Is this description objective or expressive? (See page 124 on objective and expressive details.) How does the descriptive detail help Parker achieve her purpose?

2. In which paragraph does Parker use examples? How do these examples help Parker achieve her purpose?

3. In which paragraph does Parker use cause-and-effect analysis? How does the analysis help Parker achieve her purpose?

CONSIDERING LANGUAGE AND STYLE

1. Many of Parker's paragraphs begin with the words "Poverty is . . ." Is this technique effective? Explain.

2. Consult a dictionary if you are unsure of the meaning of any of these words: *privy* (paragraph 2), *antihistamines* (paragraph 5), *repossessed* (paragraph 8).

FOR DISCUSSION IN CLASS OR ONLINE

Do you think Jo Goodwin Parker wrote "What Is Poverty?" about herself, or do you think it was meant to be representative of living in poverty? (See the headnote.) Explain your opinion.

WRITING ASSIGNMENTS

1. **Writing in your journal.** Compare and contrast your understanding of poverty before and after you read "What Is Poverty?" How has your understanding changed?

2. **Using definition for a purpose.** The purposes in the assignments are possibilities. You may establish whatever purpose you like, within your instructor's guidelines.
   - To relate your experience, inform, and persuade, define a social problem you have firsthand knowledge of, such as drug use, alcohol abuse, peer pressure, sexual harassment, or greed. Like Parker, try to arouse your audience to take action to help solve the problem.
   - To relate experience, express feelings, and inform, define a school problem, such as pressure for grades, cheating, competition, or math anxiety. If you like, you can use description and exemplification, as Parker does.
   - To relate experience and express feelings, draw on personal experience to define one of the following: fear, ambition, pride, jealousy, satisfaction, depression, or serenity.

3. **Combining patterns.** Write a definition of wealth, drawing on description and exemplification to help make your points. If you like, you can also include cause-and-effect analysis.

4. **Analyzing and assessing.** Explain your reaction to "What Is Poverty?" and analyze how the various features of the piece contribute to that reaction, features such as word choice, tone, and supporting details.

5. **Connecting and synthesizing the readings.** Using information from "What Is Poverty?" and "Untouchables" (page 275), write an essay to persuade legislators to increase their effort to aid the poor and homeless.

6. **Drawing on sources.** Poverty is a problem both in the United States and worldwide. In an essay, define one aspect of poverty, such as hunger, despair, uncertainty, or chronic illness. Then go on to suggest something college students can do to help alleviate the problem. You can find information in your library by looking up "poor" in the *Reader's Guide to Periodical Literature* or "poverty" in the *Social Sciences Index*. On the Internet, go to www.worldbank.org/poverty.

BACKGROUND: Named one of *Time* magazine's 100 most influential people, Malcolm Gladwell was born in 1963 in England to a Jamaican mother and an English father. He grew up in Canada and graduated with a degree in history from the University of Toronto in 1984. He is a former business and science writer and one-time New York City bureau chief for the *Washington Post*. Since 1996, he has been a staff writer for the *New Yorker* magazine. His *New Yorker* essays have been on a wide range of topics, including risk theory, the drop in New York City's crime rate in the 1990s, advertising for hair dye, a Chicago grandmother who seems to know everybody, and physical genius. His book *The Tipping Point: How Little Things Can Make a Difference* (2000) has been on both the *New York Times* best-seller list and the business best-seller list of the *Wall Street Journal*. His most recent books *Blink* (2005) and *Outliers: The Story of Success* (2008) were also best-sellers. "The Art of Failure" was originally published in the *New Yorker* in 2000.

COMBINED PATTERNS AND THEIR PURPOSE: In "The Art of Failure," Malcolm Gladwell *defines* several things, including panicking, choking, and stereotype threat. He ties the definitions together to **inform** the reader about why people—even ones who usually succeed—fail. To clarify his definitions, the author uses many patterns of development, including *narration, process analysis, comparison-contrast,* and *cause-and-effect analysis.*

THE ART OF FAILURE BY MALCOLM GLADWELL

THERE WAS A MOMENT, in the third and deciding set of the 1993 Wimbledon final, when Jana Novotna seemed invincible. She was leading 4–1 and serving at 40–30, meaning that she was one point from winning the game, and just five points from the most coveted championship in tennis. She had just hit a backhand to her opponent, Steffi Graf, that skimmed the net and landed so abruptly on the far side of the court that Graf could only watch, in flat-footed frustration. The stands at Center Court were packed. The Duke and Duchess of Kent were in their customary place in the royal box. Novotna was in white, poised and confident, her blond hair held back with a headband—and then something happened. She served the ball straight into the net. She stopped and steadied herself for the second serve—the toss, the arch of the back—but this time it was worse. Her swing seemed half-hearted, all arm and no legs and torso. Double fault. On the next point, she was slow to react to a high shot by Graf, and badly missed on a forehand volley. At game point, she hit an overhead straight into the net. Instead of 5–1, it was now 4–2. Graf to serve: an easy victory, 4–3. Novotna to serve. She wasn't tossing the ball high enough. Her head was down. Her movements had slowed markedly. She double-faulted once, twice, three times. Pulled wide by a Graf forehand, Novotna inexplicably hit a low, flat shot directly at Graf, instead of a high crosscourt forehand that would have given her time to get back into position: 4–4. Did she suddenly realize how terrifyingly close she was to victory? Did she remember that she had never won a major tournament before? Did she look across the net and see Steffi Graf—Steffi Graf!—the greatest player of her generation?

2   On the baseline, awaiting Graf's serve, Novotna was now visibly agitated, rocking back and forth, jumping up and down. She talked to herself under her breath.

As you read
Decide whether the distinction between pan-icking and choking is an important one.

"Jana Novotna seemed invincible."

Her eyes darted around the court. Graf took the game at love; Novotna, moving as if in slow motion, did not win a single point: 5–4, Graf. On the sidelines, Novotna wiped her racquet and her face with a towel, and then each finger individually. It was her turn to serve. She missed a routine volley wide, shook her head, talked to herself. She missed her first serve, made the second, then, in the resulting rally, mis-hit a backhand so badly that it sailed off her racquet as if launched into flight. Novotna was unrecognizable, not an elite tennis player but a beginner again. She was crumbling under pressure, but exactly why was as baffling to her as it was to all those looking on. Isn't pressure supposed to bring out the best in us? We try harder. We concentrate harder. We get a boost of adrenaline. We care more about how well we perform. So what was happening to her?

3   At championship point, Novotna hit a low, cautious, and shallow lob to Graf. Graf answered with an unreturnable overhead smash, and, mercifully, it was over. Stunned, Novotna moved to the net. Graf kissed her twice. At the awards ceremony, the Duchess of Kent handed Novotna the runner-up's trophy, a small silver plate, and whispered something in her ear, and what Novotna had done finally caught up with her. There she was, sweaty and exhausted, looming over the delicate white-haired Duchess in her pearl necklace. The Duchess reached up and pulled her head down onto her shoulder, and Novotna started to sob.

4   Human beings sometimes falter under pressure. Pilots crash and divers drown. Under the glare of competition, basketball players cannot find the basket and golfers cannot find the pin. When that happens, we say variously that people have "panicked" or, to use the sports colloquialism, "choked." But what do those words mean? Both are pejoratives. To choke or panic is considered to be as bad as to quit. But are all forms of failure equal? And what do the forms in which we fail say about who we are and how we think? We live in an age obsessed with success, with documenting the myriad ways by which talented people overcome challenges and obstacles. There is as much to be learned, though, from documenting the myriad ways in which talented people sometimes fail.

> "To choke or to panic is considered to be as bad as to quit."

5   "Choking" sounds like a vague and all-encompassing term, yet it describes a very specific kind of failure. For example, psychologists often use a primitive video game to test motor skills. They'll sit you in front of a computer with a screen that shows four boxes in a row, and a keyboard that has four corresponding buttons in a row. One at a time, x's start to appear in the boxes on the screen, and you are told that every time this happens you are to push the key corresponding to the box. According to Daniel Willingham, a psychologist at the University of Virginia, if you're told ahead of time about the pattern in which those x's will appear, your reaction time in hitting the right key will improve dramatically. You'll play the game very carefully for a few rounds, until you've learned the sequence, and then you'll get faster and faster. Willingham calls this "explicit learning." But suppose you're not told that the x's appear in a regular sequence, and even after playing the game for a while you're not aware that there is a pattern. You'll *still* get faster: you'll learn the sequence unconsciously. Willingham calls that "implicit learning"—learning that takes place outside of awareness. These two learning

systems are quite separate, based in different parts of the brain. Willingham says that when you are first taught something—say, how to hit a backhand or an overhead forehand—you think it through in a very deliberate, mechanical manner. But as you get better the implicit system takes over: you start to hit a backhand fluidly, without thinking. The basal ganglia, where implicit learning partially resides, are concerned with force and timing, and when that system kicks in you begin to develop touch and accuracy, the ability to hit a drop shot or place a serve at a hundred miles per hour. "This is something that is going to happen gradually," Willingham says. "You hit several thousand forehands, after a while you may still be attending to it. But not very much. In the end, you don't really notice what your hand is doing at all."

6   Under conditions of stress, however, the explicit system sometimes takes over. That's what it means to choke. When Jana Novotna faltered at Wimbledon, it was because she began thinking about her shots again. She lost her fluidity, her touch. She double-faulted on her serves and mis-hit her overheads, the shots that demand the greatest sensitivity in force and timing. She seemed like a different person— playing with the slow, cautious deliberation of a beginner—because, in a sense, she *was* a beginner again: she was relying on a learning system that she hadn't used to hit serves and overhead forehands and volleys since she was first taught tennis, as a child. The same thing has happened to Chuck Knoblauch, the New York Yankees' second baseman, who inexplicably has had trouble throwing the ball to first base. Under the stress of playing in front of forty thousand fans at Yankee Stadium, Knoblauch finds himself reverting to explicit mode, throwing like a Little Leaguer again.

> "She lost her fluidity, her touch."

7   Panic is something else altogether. Consider the following account of a scuba-diving accident, recounted to me by Ephimia Morphew, a human-factors specialist at NASA: "It was an open-water certification dive, Monterey Bay, California, about ten years ago. I was nineteen. I'd been diving for two weeks. This was my first time in the open ocean without the instructor. Just my buddy and I. We had to go about forty feet down, to the bottom of the ocean, and do an exercise where we took our regulators out of our mouth, picked up a spare one that we had on our vest, and practiced breathing out of the spare. My buddy did hers. Then it was my turn. I removed my regulator. I lifted up my secondary regulator. I put it in my mouth, exhaled, to clear the lines, and then I inhaled, and, to my surprise, it was water. I inhaled water. Then the hose that connected that mouthpiece to my tank, my air source, came unlatched and air from the hose came exploding into my face.

8   "Right away, my hand reached out for my partner's air supply, as if I was going to rip it out. It was without thought. It was a physiological response. My eyes are seeing my hand do something irresponsible. I'm fighting with myself. *Don't do it.* Then I searched my mind for what I could do. And nothing came to mind. All I could remember was one thing: If you can't take care of yourself, let your buddy take care of you. I let my hand fall back to my side, and I just stood there."

9   This is a textbook example of panic. In that moment, Morphew stopped thinking. She forgot that she had another source of air, one that worked perfectly well

and that, moments before, she had taken out of her mouth. She forgot that her partner had a working air supply as well, which could easily be shared, and she forgot that grabbing her partner's regulator would imperil both of them. All she had was her most basic instinct: *get air.* Stress wipes out short-term memory. People with lots of experience tend not to panic, because when the stress suppresses their short-term memory they still have some residue of experience to draw on.

> "Stress wipes out short-term memory."

But what did a novice like Morphew have? *I searched my mind for what I could do. And nothing came to mind.*

10   Panic also causes what psychologists call perceptual narrowing. In one study, from the early seventies, a group of subjects were asked to perform a visual-acuity task while undergoing what they thought was a sixty-foot dive in a pressure chamber. At the same time, they were asked to push a button whenever they saw a small light flash on and off in their peripheral vision. The subjects in the pressure chamber had much higher heart rates than the control group, indicating that they were under stress. That stress didn't affect their accuracy at the visual-acuity task, but they were only half as good as the control group at picking up the peripheral light. "You tend to focus or obsess on one thing," Morphew says. "There's a famous airplane example, where the landing light went off, and the pilots had no way of knowing if the landing gear was down. The pilots were so focussed on that light that no one noticed the autopilot had been disengaged, and they crashed the plane." Morphew reached for her buddy's air supply because it was the only air supply she could see.

11   Panic, in this sense, is the opposite of choking. Choking is about thinking too much. Panic is about thinking too little. Choking is about loss of instinct. Panic is reversion to instinct. They may look the same, but they are worlds apart.

12   Why does this distinction matter? In some instances, it doesn't much. If you lose a close tennis match, it's of little matter whether you choked or panicked; either way, you lost. But there are clearly cases when *how* failure happens is central to understanding *why* failure happens.

13   Take the plane crash in which John F. Kennedy, Jr., was killed last summer. The details of the flight are well known. On a Friday evening last July, Kennedy took off with his wife and sister-in-law for Martha's Vineyard. The night was hazy, and Kennedy flew along the Connecticut coastline, using the trail of lights below him as a guide. At Westerly, Rhode Island, he left the shoreline, heading straight out over Rhode Island Sound, and at that point, apparently disoriented by the darkness and haze, he began a series of curious maneuvers: He banked his plane to the right, farther out into the ocean, and then to the left. He climbed and descended. He sped up and slowed down. Just a few miles from his destination, Kennedy lost control of the plane, and it crashed into the ocean.

> "Just a few miles from his destination, Kennedy lost control of the plane, and it crashed into the ocean."

14   Kennedy's mistake, in technical terms, was that he failed to keep his wings level. That was critical, because when a plane banks to one side it begins to turn and its wings lose some of their vertical lift. Left unchecked, this process accelerates. The angle of the bank increases, the turn gets sharper and sharper, and the plane starts to dive toward the ground in an ever-narrowing corksrew. Pilots call this the graveyard spiral. And why didn't Kennedy stop the dive? Because, in times of low visibility and high stress, keeping your wings level—indeed, even knowing whether you are in a graveyard spiral—turns out to be surprisingly difficult. Kennedy failed under pressure.

15   Had Kennedy been flying during the day or with a clear moon, he would have been fine. If you are the pilot, looking straight ahead from the cockpit, the angle of your wings will be obvious from the straight line of the horizon in front of you. But when it's dark outside the horizon disappears. There is no external measure of the plane's bank. On the ground, we know whether we are level even when it's dark, because of the motion-sensing mechanisms in the inner ear. In a spiral dive, though, the effect of the plane's G-force on the inner ear means that the pilot *feels* perfectly level even if his plane is not. Similarly, when you are in a jetliner that is banking at thirty degrees after takeoff, the book on your neighbor's lap does not slide into your lap, nor will a pen on the floor roll toward the "down" side of the plane. The physics of flying is such that an airplane in the midst of a turn always feels perfectly level to someone inside the cabin.

16   This is a difficult notion, and to understand it I went flying with William Langewiesche, the author of a superb book on flying, "Inside the Sky." We met at San Jose Airport, in the jet center where the Silicon Valley billionaires keep their private planes. Langewiesche is a rugged man in his forties, deeply tanned, and handsome in the way that pilots (at least since the movie "The Right Stuff") are supposed to be. We took off at dusk, heading out toward Monterey Bay, until we had left the lights of the coast behind and night had erased the horizon. Langewiesche let the plane bank gently to the left. He took his hands off the stick. The sky told me nothing now, so I concentrated on the instruments. The nose of the plane was dropping. The gyroscope told me that we were banking, first fifteen, then thirty, then forty-five degrees. "We're in a spiral dive," Langewiesche said calmly. Our airspeed was steadily accelerating, from a hundred and eighty to a hundred and ninety to two hundred knots. The needle on the altimeter was moving down. The plane was dropping like a stone, at three thousand feet per minute. I could hear, faintly, a slight increase in the hum of the engine, and the wind noise as we picked up speed. But if Langewiesche and I had been talking I would have caught none of that. Had the cabin been unpressurized, my ears might have popped, particularly as we went into the steep part of the dive. But beyond that? Nothing at all. In a spiral dive, the G-load—the force of inertia—is normal. As Langewiesche puts it, the plane *likes* to spiral-dive. The total time elapsed since we started diving was no more than six or seven seconds. Suddenly, Langewiesche

"We met at San Jose Airport, in the jet center where the Silicon Valley billionaires keep their private planes."

straightened the wings and pulled back on the stick to get the nose of the plane up, breaking out of the dive. Only now did I feel the full force of the G-load, pushing me back in my seat. "You feel no G-load in a bank," Langewiesche said. "There's nothing more confusing for the uninitiated."

17   I asked Langewiesche how much longer we could have fallen. "Within five seconds, we would have exceeded the limits of the airplane," he replied, by which he meant that the force of trying to pull out of the dive would have broken the plane into pieces. I looked away from the instruments and asked Langewiesche to spiral-dive again, this time without telling me. I sat and waited. I was about to tell Langewiesche that he could start diving anytime, when, suddenly, I was thrown back in my chair. "We just lost a thousand feet," he said.

18   This inability to sense, experientially, what your plane is doing is what makes night flying so stressful. And this was the stress that Kennedy must have felt when he turned out across the water at Westerly, leaving the guiding lights of the Connecticut coastline behind him. A pilot who flew into Nantucket that night told the National Transportation Safety Board that when he descended over Martha's Vineyard he looked down and there was "nothing to see. There was no horizon and no light . . . I thought the island might [have] suffered a power failure." Kennedy was now blind, in every sense, and he must have known the danger he was in. He had very little experience in flying strictly by instruments. Most of the time when he had flown up to the Vineyard the horizon or lights had still been visible. That strange, final sequence of maneuvers was Kennedy's frantic search for a clearing in the haze. He was trying to pick up the lights of Martha's Vineyard, to restore the lost horizon. Between the lines of the National Transportation Safety Board's report on the crash, you can almost feel his desperation:

> "This inability to sense, experientially, what your plane is doing is what makes night flying so stressful."

19   About 2138 the target began a right turn in a southerly direction. About 30 seconds later, the target stopped its descent at 2200 feet and began a climb that lasted another 30 seconds. During this period of time, the target stopped the turn, and the airspeed decreased to about 153 KIAS. About 2139, the target leveled off at 2500 feet and flew in a south-easterly direction. About 50 seconds later, the target entered a left turn and climbed to 2600 feet. As the target continued in the left turn, it began a descent that reached a rate of about 900 fpm.

20   But was he choking or panicking? Here the distinction between those two states is critical. Had he choked, he would have reverted to the mode of explicit learning. His movements in the cockpit would have become markedly slower and less fluid. He would have gone back to the mechanical, self-conscious application of the lessons he had first received as a pilot—and that might have been a good thing. Kennedy *needed* to think, to concentrate on his instruments, to break away from the instinctive flying that served him when he had a visible horizon.

21   But instead, from all appearances, he panicked. At the moment when he needed to remember the lessons he had been taught about instrument flying, his

mind—like Morphew's when she was underwater—must have gone blank. Instead of reviewing the instruments, he seems to have been focussed on one question: Where are the lights of Martha's Vineyard? His gyroscope and his other instruments may well have become as invisible as the peripheral lights in the underwater-panic experiments. He had fallen back on his instincts—on the way the plane *felt*—and in the dark, of course, instinct can tell you nothing. The N.T.S.B. report says that the last time the Piper's wings were level was seven seconds past 9:40, and the plane hit the water at about 9:41, so the critical period here was less than sixty seconds. At twenty-five seconds past the minute, the plane was tilted at an angle greater than forty-five degrees. Inside the cockpit it would have felt normal. At some point, Kennedy must have heard the rising wind outside, or the roar of the engine as it picked up speed. Again, relying on instinct, he might have pulled back on the stick, trying to raise the nose of the plane. But pulling back on the stick without first levelling the wings only makes the spiral tighter and the problem worse. It's also possible that Kennedy did nothing at all, and that he was frozen at the controls, still frantically searching for the lights of the Vineyard, when his plane hit the water. Sometimes pilots don't even try to make it out of a spiral dive. Langewiesche calls that "one G all the way down."

22   What happened to Kennedy that night illustrates a second major difference between panicking and choking. Panicking is conventional failure, of the sort we tacitly understand. Kennedy panicked because he didn't know enough about instrument flying. If he'd had another year in the air, he might not have panicked, and that fits with what we believe—that performance ought to improve with experience, and that pressure is an obstacle that the diligent can overcome. But choking makes little intuitive sense. Novotna's problem wasn't lack of diligence; she was as superbly conditioned and schooled as anyone on the tennis tour. And what did experience do for her? In 1995, in the third round of the French Open, Novotna choked even more spectacularly than she had against Graf, losing to Chanda Rubin after surrendering a 5–0 lead in the third set. There seems little doubt that part of the reason for her collapse against Rubin was her collapse against Graf—that the second failure built on the first, making it possible for her to be up 5–0 in the third set and yet entertain the thought *I can still lose.* If panicking is conventional failure, choking is paradoxical failure.

23   Claude Steele, a psychologist at Stanford University, and his colleagues have done a number of experiments in recent years looking at how certain groups perform under pressure, and their findings go to the heart of what is so strange about choking. Steele and Joshua Aronson found that when they gave a group of Stanford undergraduates a standardized test and told them that it was a measure of their intellectual ability, the white students did much better than their black counterparts. But when the same test was presented simply as an abstract laboratory tool, with no relevance to ability, the scores of blacks and whites were virtually identical. Steele and Aronson attribute this disparity to what they call "stereotype threat": when black students are put into a situation where they are directly confronted with a stereotype about their group—in this case, one having to do with intelligence—the resulting pressure causes their performance to suffer.

24   Steele and others have found stereotype threat at work in any situation where groups are depicted in negative ways. Give a group of qualified women a math test and tell them it will measure their quantitative ability and they'll do much worse than equally skilled men will; present the same test simply as a research tool and they'll do just as well as the men. Or consider a handful of experiments conducted by one of Steele's former graduate students, Julio Garcia, a professor at Tufts University. Garcia gathered together a group of white, athletic students and had a white instructor lead them through a series of physical tests: to jump as high as they could, to do a standing broad jump, and to see how many pushups they could do in twenty seconds. The instructor then asked them to do the tests a second time, and, as you'd expect, Garcia found that the students did a little better on each of the tasks the second time around. Then Garcia ran a second group of students through the tests, this time replacing the instructor between the first and second trials with an African-American. Now the white students ceased to improve on their vertical leaps. He did the experiment again, only this time he replaced the white instructor with a black instructor who was much taller and heavier than the previous black instructor. In this trial, the white students actually jumped less high than they had the first time around. Their performance on the pushups, though, was unchanged in each of the conditions. There is no stereotype, after all, that suggests that whites can't do as many push-ups as blacks. The task that was affected was the vertical leap, because of what our culture says: *white men can't jump.*

25   It doesn't come as news, of course, that black students aren't as good at test taking as white students, or that white students aren't as good at jumping as black students. The problem is that we've always assumed that this kind of failure under pressure is panic. What is it we tell underperforming athletes and students? The same thing we tell novice pilots or scuba divers: to work harder, to buckle down, to take the tests of their ability more seriously. But Steele says that when you look at the way black or female students perform under stereotype threat you don't see the wild guessing of a panicked test taker. "What you tend to see is carefulness and second-guessing," he explains. "When you go and interview them, you have the sense that when they are in the stereotype-threat condition they say to themselves, 'Look, I'm going to be careful here. I'm not going to mess things up.' Then, after having decided to take that strategy, they calm down and go through the test. But that's not the way to succeed on a standardized test. The more you do that, the more you will get away from the intuitions that help you, the quick processing. They think they did well, and they are trying to do well. But they are not." This is choking, not panicking. Garcia's athletes and Steele's students are like Novotna, not Kennedy. They failed because they were good at what they did: only those who care about how well they perform ever feel the pressure of stereotype threat. The usual prescription for failure — to work harder and take the test more seriously — would only make their problems worse.

26   That is a hard lesson to grasp, but harder still is the fact that choking requires us to concern ourselves less with the performer and more with the situation in which the performance occurs. Novotna herself could do nothing to prevent her

collapse against Graf. The only thing that could have saved her is if—at that critical moment in the third set—the television cameras had been turned off, the Duke and Duchess had gone home, and the spectators had been told to wait outside. In sports, of course, you can't do that. Choking is a central part of the drama of athletic competition because the spectators *have* to be there—and the ability to overcome the pressure of the spectators is part of what it means to be a champion. But the same ruthless inflexibility need not govern the rest of our lives. We have to learn that sometimes a poor performance reflects not the innate ability of the performer but the complexion of the audience; and that sometimes a poor test score is the sign not of a poor student but of a good one.

27   Through the first three rounds of the 1996 Masters golf tournament, Greg Norman held a seemingly insurmountable lead over his nearest rival, the Englishman Nick Faldo. He was the best player in the world. His nickname was the Shark. He didn't saunter down the fairways; he stalked the course, blond and broad-shouldered, his caddy behind him, struggling to keep up. But then came the ninth hole on the tournament's final day. Norman was paired with Faldo, and the two hit their first shots well. They were now facing the green. In front of the pin, there was a steep slope, so that any ball hit short would come rolling back down the hill into oblivion. Faldo shot first, and the ball landed safely long, well past the cup.

28   Norman was next. He stood over the ball. "The one thing you guard against here is short," the announcer said, stating the obvious. Norman swung and then froze, his club in midair, following the ball in flight. It was short. Norman watched, stone-faced, as the ball rolled thirty yards back down the hill, and with that error something inside of him broke.

29   At the tenth hole, he hooked the ball to the left, hit his third shot well past the cup, and missed a makable putt. At eleven, Norman had a three-and-a-half-foot putt for par—the kind he had been making all week. He shook out his hands and legs before grasping the club, trying to relax. He missed: his third straight bogey. At twelve, Norman hit the ball straight into the water. At thirteen, he hit it into a patch of pine needles. At sixteen, his movements were so mechanical and out of synch that, when he swung, his hips spun out ahead of his body and the ball sailed into another pond. At that, he took his club and made a frustrated scythelike motion through the grass, because what had been obvious for twenty minutes was now official: he had fumbled away the chance of a lifetime.

30   Faldo had begun the day six strokes behind Norman. By the time the two started their slow walk to the eighteenth hole, through the throng of spectators, Faldo had a four-stroke lead. But he took those final steps quietly, giving only the smallest of nods, keeping his head low. He understood what had happened on the greens and fairways that day. And he was bound by the particular etiquette of choking, the understanding that what he had earned was something less than a victory and what Norman had suffered was something less than a defeat.

31   When it was all over, Faldo wrapped his arms around Norman. "I don't know what to say—I just want to give you a hug," he whispered, and then he said the only thing you can say to a choker. "I feel horrible about what happened. I'm so sorry." With that, the two men began to cry.

1. What is implicit learning, and what is explicit learning?
2. According to Gladwell, what is choking? What is panicking? How are choking and panicking alike, and how are they different?
3. What caused Jana Novotna to choke at Wimbledon? What caused Ephimia Morphew to panic during her dive? How is Novotna's experience an example of choking? How is Morphew's experience an example of panicking?
4. Gladwell says that it doesn't matter whether Novotna panicked or choked, but it *does* matter that John F. Kennedy, Jr., panicked rather than choked. Why does the distinction matter in one situation but not the other?
5. What is stereotype threat, and how is it related to choking?

EXAMINING STRUCTURE AND STRATEGY

1. How does Gladwell achieve transition between paragraphs 3 and 4? Between paragraphs 5 and 6? Between paragraphs 7 and 8? Between paragraphs 9 and 10? Between paragraphs 11 and 12? Between paragraphs 15 and 16?
2. Where does Gladwell give the significance of his definitions of *choking* and *panic*?
3. Why does Gladwell close his essay with the narration of what happened between Greg Norman and Nick Faldo?

NOTING COMBINED PATTERNS

1. How does the comparison-contrast in paragraphs 5 and 11 help Gladwell achieve his purpose?
2. How does the cause-and-effect analysis in paragraphs 6, 10, and 15 help Gladwell achieve his purpose?
3. Gladwell includes a number of narrations for specific reasons. Explain the purpose of each of the following narrations, the concept each narration describes, and the contribution each makes to the definition:
   a. Jana Novotna's deciding set against Steffi Graf (paragraphs 1–3).
   b. Ephimia Morphew's diving experience (paragraphs 7–9).
   c. Gladwell's experience flying with Langewiesche (paragraphs 16–17).
   d. Greg Norman's experience at the 1996 Masters (paragraphs 27–31).
4. Gladwell includes process analysis in paragraph 5 and in paragraphs 14–15. How does that process analysis help him achieve his purpose?

CONSIDERING LANGUAGE AND STYLE

1. Gladwell often uses descriptive language. For example, in paragraph 1, he writes that Novotna "had just hit a backhand . . . that skimmed the net and landed so abruptly on the far side of the court that Graf could only watch, in flat-footed frustration." Cite three other examples of descriptive language. How does the description help Gladwell achieve his purpose?

2. A *rhetorical question* requires no answer from the reader or listener. Explain the purpose of the rhetorical questions in paragraphs 1, 2, and 4.

3. Consult a dictionary if you do not know the meaning of these words: *invincible* (paragraph 1), *coveted* (paragraph 1), *inexplicably* (paragraph 1), *colloquialism* (paragraph 4), *pejoratives* (paragraph 4), *myriad* (paragraph 4), *acuity* (paragraph 10), *inertia* (paragraph 16).

FOR DISCUSSION IN CLASS OR ONLINE

What implications does stereotype threat have for teachers? Should educators take specific steps to deal with stereotype threat? Explain.

WRITING ASSIGNMENTS

1. **Writing in your journal.** Write about a time when you choked or panicked. Does anything in the essay help you better understand your experience? Explain.

2. **Using definition for a purpose.** The purposes in the assignments are possibilities. You may establish whatever purpose you like, within your instructor's guidelines.
   - To inform, define *failure.* Try to illustrate aspects of your definition with narrations.
   - To inform, define *pressure* or *stress.* Try to illustrate aspects of your definition with narration.
   - To inform and perhaps relate experience and express feelings, define *good sport.* Try to illustrate aspects of your definition with narration.

3. **Combining patterns.** In paragraph 4, Gladwell says, "We live in an age obsessed with success. . . ." Define *success* and agree or disagree with Gladwell, using exemplification (explained in Chapter 7) to support your assertion.

4. **Analyzing and assessing.** Discuss the significance of choking, panicking, and stereotype threat. Then note what applications these phenomena have in the classroom for teachers and/or students.

5. **Connecting and synthesizing the readings.** The account of her struggle to stay alive in "Struck by Lightning" (page 156) shows that Gretel Ehrlich neither choked nor panicked. Contrast Ehrlich's actions with those of Novotna, Kennedy, Norman, or Morphew.

6. **Drawing on sources.** Read accounts of the death of John F. Kennedy, Jr., in four different newspapers, magazines, or online sources. Drawing on the accounts that you read for examples, define *responsible reporting.*

BACKGROUND: Award-winning writer and artist José Antonio Burciaga (1940–1996) was an illustrator, muralist, newspaper columnist, and poet. He was also a founding performer of Culture Clash, a comedy troupe with a Latino perspective and a blending of the points of view of Mexican and American culture. His prose and poetry are known for this same Latino perspective. His prose collections include *Drink Cultura: Chicanismo* (1993) and *Spilling the Beans* (1995); his poetry collections include *Undocumented Love/Amor Indocumentado: A Personal Anthology of Poetry* (1992). His book of essays, *Weedee Peepo* (1988, 1992), includes "I Remember Masa."

COMBINED PATTERNS AND THEIR PURPOSES: In "I Remember Masa," José Antonio Burciaga combines *definition* with *description, narration,* and *exemplification* to **inform** readers about the nature of tortillas and to **express his feelings** about and **relate his experience** with this staple of Mexican cuisine.

I Remember Masa[1]

BY JOSÉ ANTONIO BURCIAGA

My earliest memory of *tortillas* is my *Mamá* telling me not to play with them. I had bitten eyeholes in one and was wearing it as a mask at the dinner table.

2   As a child, I also used *tortillas* as hand warmers on cold days, and my family claims that I owe my career as an artist to my early experiments with *tortillas*. According to them, my clowning around helped me develop a strong artistic foundation. I'm not so sure, though. Sometimes I wore a *tortilla* on my head, like a *yarmulke*,[2] and yet I never had any great urge to convert from Catholicism to Judaism. But who knows? They may be right.

As you read
Think about why tortillas are so important to the author.

3   For Mexicans over the centuries, the *tortilla* has served as the spoon and the fork, the plate and the napkin. *Tortillas* originated before the Mayan civilizations, perhaps predating Europe's wheat bread. According to Mayan mythology, the great god Quetzalcoatl, realizing that the red ants knew the secret of using maize as food, transformed himself into a black ant, infiltrated the colony of red ants, and absconded with a grain of corn. (Is it any wonder that to this day, black ants and red ants do not get along?) Quetzalcoatl then put maize on the lips of the first man and woman, Oxomoco and Cipactonal, so that they would become strong. Maize festivals are still celebrated by many Indian cultures of the Americas.

4   When I was growing up in El Paso, *tortillas* were part of my daily life. I used to visit a *tortilla* factory in an ancient adobe building near the open *mercado*[3] in Ciudad Juárez. As I approached, I could hear the rhythmic slapping of the *masa* as the skilled vendors outside the factory formed it into balls and patted them into perfectly round corn cakes between the palms of their hands. The wonderful aroma and the speed with which the women counted so many dozens of *tortillas* out of warm wicker baskets still linger in my mind. Watching them at work convinced me

---

[1]Masa is a dough; often made with dried corn.

[2]A yarmulke is a skullcáp worn by religious Jewish men and boys.

[3]A *mercado* is a market.

that the most handsome and *deliciosas tortillas* are handmade. Although machines are faster, they can never adequately replace generation-to-generation experience. There's no place in the factory assembly line for the tender slaps that give each *tortilla* character. The best thing that can be said about mass-producing *tortillas* is that it makes it possible for many people to enjoy them.

5   In the *mercado* where my mother shopped, we frequently bought *taquitos de nopalitos,* small tacos filled with diced cactus, onions, tomatoes, and *jalapeños.* Our friend Don Toribio showed us how to make delicious, crunchy *taquitos* with dried, salted pumpkin seeds. When you had no money for the filling, a poor man's *taco* could be made by placing a warm *tortilla* on the left palm, applying a sprinkle of salt, then rolling the *tortilla* up quickly with the fingertips of the right hand. My own kids put peanut butter and jelly on *tortillas,* which I think is truly bicultural. And speaking of fast foods for kids, nothing beats a *quesadilla,* a *tortilla* grilled-cheese sandwich.

6   Depending on what you intend to use them for, *tortillas* may be made in various ways. Even a run-of-the-mill *tortilla* is more than a flat corn cake. A skillfully cooked homemade *tortilla* has a bottom and a top; the top skin forms a pocket in which you put the filling that folds your *tortilla* into a taco. Paper-thin *tortillas* are used specifically for *flautas,* a type of taco that is filled, rolled, and then fried until crisp. The name *flauta* means *flute,* which probably refers to the Mayan bamboo flute; however, the only sound that comes from an edible *flauta* is a delicious crunch that is music to the palate. In México *flautas* are sometimes made as long as two feet and then cut into manageable segments. The opposite of *flautas* is *gorditas,* meaning *little fat ones.* These are very thick small *tortillas.*

7   The versatility of *tortillas* and corn does not end here. Besides being tasty and nourishing, they have spiritual and artistic qualities as well. The Tarahumara Indians of Chihuabua, for example, concocted a corn-based beer called *tesgüino,* which their descendants still make today. And everyone has read about the woman in New Mexico who was cooking her husband a *tortilla* one morning when the image of Jesus Christ miraculously appeared on it. Before they knew what was happening, the man's breakfast had become a local shrine.

8   Then there is *tortilla* art. Various Chicano artists throughout the Southwest have, when short of materials or just in a whimsical mood, used a dry *tortilla* as a small, round canvas. And a few years back, at the height of the Chicano movement, a priest in Arizona got into trouble with the Church after he was discovered celebrating mass using a *tortilla* as the host. All of which only goes to show that while the *tortilla* may be a lowly corn cake, when the necessity arises, it can reach unexpected distinction.

READING CLOSELY AND THINKING CRITICALLY

1.   Burciaga defines *tortilla.* What characteristics of his subject does he mention?

2.   Why are tortillas so important to the author?

3.   Why does Burciaga consider peanut butter and jelly on a tortilla to be a bicultural phenomenon?

4.   In paragraph 7, the author says that tortillas have "spiritual and artistic qualities." Is he serious? That is, can food really be spiritual and artistic?

EXAMINING STRUCTURE AND STRATEGY

1. The thesis of the essay is not in the introduction. What is the thesis, and where is it found? What point does it say can be drawn from the definition?
2. For what audience do you think Burciaga wrote? How familiar is that audience with tortillas?
3. Why does the author include the Mayan myth? How does it help him achieve his writing purpose?
4. What approach does Burciaga take to his conclusion? Is the conclusion a good one? Explain.

NOTING COMBINED PATTERNS

1. Burciaga uses description in paragraphs 4–6. How does that description help him achieve his writing purpose?
2. Burciaga uses narration in paragraph 3. How does that pattern help him achieve his writing purpose?
3. How does the exemplification in paragraphs 7 and 8 help the author achieve his writing purpose?

CONSIDERING LANGUAGE AND STYLE

1. In paragraph 4, Burciaga mentions "the tender slaps that give each *tortilla* character." What does he mean?
2. Consult a dictionary if you are unfamiliar with this word: *absconded* (paragraph 3).

FOR DISCUSSION IN CLASS OR ONLINE

Part of "I Remember Masa" notes the importance of tortillas in the author's family life when he was a child. In general, how important is food in family life? Cite examples to support your opinion.

WRITING ASSIGNMENTS

1. **Writing in your journal.** In a page or two, write about your earliest memory of food or something associated with food, such as shopping or cooking.
2. **Using definition for a purpose.** The purposes given in the assignments are possibilities. You may establish whatever purpose you like, within your instructor's guidelines.
   - To entertain and perhaps share feelings, write a definition of a food many people do not like, such as liver or headcheese. Try to convey what makes the food so unappealing.
   - To inform, write a definition of an ethnic term, such as *chutzpah, gringo,* or *machismo.*

- To inform about why people like certain television programs, define the nature of a successful (popular, not necessarily good) television show. Be sure to include the important characteristics of the show.
- To inform readers and, perhaps, express feelings and relate experience, define a holiday celebration or ceremony associated with your religion or ethnicity, such as Cinco de Mayo, the Sabbath, Ramadan, Holy Communion, Easter, or Chanukah. Note the chief characteristics of the event, including how it is celebrated and its significance to you.

3. **Combining patterns.** Write a definition of a food that is mass produced, and contrast its factory and handmade versions. Some possibilities include pizza, bread, salad dressing, bagels, and egg rolls.

4. **Analyzing and assessing.** Some of the material in the essay is humorous, exaggerated, or whimsical, so it is not meant to be taken literally. Which details are to be taken at face value, and which should not be taken literally? What does the humor, exaggeration, and whimsy add to the essay?

5. **Connecting and synthesizing the readings.** Using the information in "I Remember Masa," "Am I Blue?" (page 379), and your own experience and observation, explain the significance of food beyond its role of providing sustenance. You might consider its political, social and/or cultural ramifications.

6. **Drawing on sources.** Research the history of a food that has been around for a long time, such as corn, chocolate, wheat, butter, tea, coffee, candy bars, or corn flakes. Then summarize the history and explain whether the importance of the food is different today than it was in the past. In your campus library, you can check the *Cambridge World History of Food* for information. On the Internet, type "history of _____" in your favorite search engine.

BACKGROUND: El Paso, Texas, native Pat Mora was born in 1942. Both sets of her grandparents left Mexico for El Paso to escape the turmoil of the Mexican revolution of the early twentieth century. Mora earned her M.A. from the University of Texas at El Paso and then became a teacher, a college administrator, and a public radio host for a show called *Voices: The Mexican-American in Perspective*. Her many awards include a Kellogg National Fellowship to study ways of preserving cultures and a National Endowment for the Arts Fellowship. A prolific author of children's stories, poetry, and essays, Mora often bases her material on family members and personal experience. Much of her poetry treats her Chicana heritage and Southwest experience. Mora's children's books include *A Birthday Basket for Tía* (1992), *Pablo's Tree* (1994), and *Doña Flor* (2005). Her poetry collections include *Borders* (1986), in which "Immigrants" appears; *My Own True Name* (2000); *Adobe Odes* (2006); and *Dizzy in Your Eyes* (2010).

COMBINED PATTERNS AND THEIR PURPOSES: In "Immigrants," Pat Mora *defines* Americans from the perspective of people new to the United States. She also explains a *process* some immigrants employ to help their children assimilate into American culture. While the poem **informs,** Mora also uses it to **express her feelings** about assimilation and conformity.

Immigrants

BY PAT MORA

As you read
Try to determine how Mora feels about assimilation and conformity.

wrap their babies in the American flag,
feed them mashed hot dogs and apple pie,
name them Bill and Daisy,
buy them blonde dolls that blink blue
eyes or a football and tiny cleats   5
before the baby can even walk,
speak to them in thick English,
    hallo, babee, hallo,
whisper in Spanish or Polish
when the babies sleep, whisper   10
in a dark parent bed, that dark
parent fear, "Will they like
our boy, our girl, our fine american
boy, our fine american girl?"

CONSIDERING THE POEM

1. How are Americans defined in the poem? Whose definition is given? Is that definition accurate? Explain.
2. What is ironic about the definition of Americans in the poem?
3. Is Mora suggesting that some immigrants literally "wrap their babies in the American flag" (line 1)? Explain.

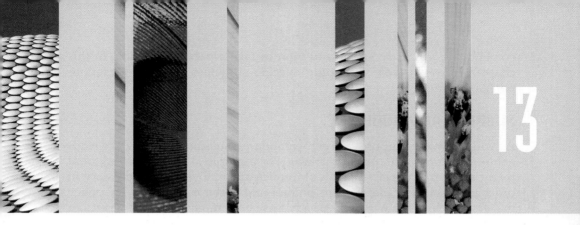

The Law and Society:
A Casebook for Argumentation-Persuasion

The cartoon on the facing page makes the point that freedom of speech has led to what some consider to be obscene speech on radio and television. Nevertheless, some restrictions do apply. What restrictions do you think there should be? Why?

THE DIFFERENCE BETWEEN ARGUMENTATION AND PERSUASION

Argumentation relies on sound reasoning, compelling evidence, and logic to convince readers to agree with an assertion; **persuasion** appeals to emotions, values, and beliefs. Both argumentation and persuasion have persuasive purposes. Suppose you want to convince a friend that a particular candidate would make a good governor. You would employ argumentation if you built a case based on the candidate's prior experience in the state legislature and her position on issues. You would employ persuasion if you discussed how great it would be to see more women in high political office. In order to convince readers to think or act in a particular way—that is, in order to achieve a persuasive purpose—writers very often combine argumentation and persuasion. Furthermore, writers often incorporate one or more of the patterns already discussed in this book as part of their argumentation-persuasion strategy.

In this book, you have read many essays with a persuasive purpose because each chapter of readings included one or more selections meant to convince readers to accept an assertion or take a particular action. In this chapter, however, you will study specific strategies for argumentation-persuasion in greater detail.

PURPOSE AND AUDIENCE

As you know, the purpose of argumentation-persuasion is to convince readers to think or act in a particular way. For example, a newspaper editorial might argue that the city's layoff of municipal employees is unnecessary in order to convince readers of this point—and perhaps convince city policy makers to rehire the workers. An advertisement might extol the virtues of a car to persuade people to buy it.

Sometimes you have no hope of convincing your reader, so you must establish a less ambitious goal, such as softening your reader's objection or convincing your reader that your assertion has some merit. Suppose you are arguing that the governor should increase the sales tax to support public education. If your reader has children in school, you can reasonably aim to convince your reader to agree with you. However, if your reader is a retired person on a fixed income, expecting agreement may be unreasonable. In this case, a more suitable goal may be to convince your reader that there are some good reasons to raise the sales tax—even if he or she does not fully support the idea. Perhaps you are wondering what good it is to soften a reader's objection or convince that person that your assertion has some merit. The answer is that if you can do this, your reader may come around to your thinking eventually, or at least work less hard to oppose you. Thus, if you convince a retired person that there are some valid reasons for the sales tax, he or she still might not vote for it but also might not campaign actively against it.

Audience assessment is particularly important in argumentation-persuasion. You must assess your reader in order to establish a reasonable goal for your writing and to understand which points need to be stated and proven, what kind of evidence will be the most effective, how hard you must work to convince your reader, and how your reader will respond to emotional appeal. In short, you must know your reader in order to establish and achieve a reasonable persuasive purpose.

Combining Patterns for a Purpose

To explain and back up reasons for your assertion in order to convince your reader, you can use any of the patterns of development in any combination. For instance, to convince your reader that couples should marry rather than just live together, you can *narrate* an account of the trouble that occurred when your brother and his girlfriend lived together. You can also provide *examples* of the complications couples must endure when they do not marry. You can *contrast* the benefits of marriage with the drawbacks of living together, and you can *describe* the embarrassment of older relatives of some unmarried couples.

To see how other patterns can be combined in argumentation-persuasion in order to achieve a persuasive purpose, study the following excerpt from

RESPONDING TO AN IMAGE

The largest retailer and largest corporation in the world, Walmart is controversial. Some praise it, citing the low prices, employment opportunities, and economic impetus it provides; others condemn it, criticizing its employment practices, trade policies, and effect on competition. What is your opinion? Write a definition of *Walmart* that makes clear your opinion of the retail giant. As an alternative, define something else whose value people disagree about, such as a fast-food meal, oil companies, or labor unions.

caglecartoons.com

Copyright © 2004 Larry Wright, *The Detroit News* and PoliticalCartoons.com. Reprinted with permission.

"Speech Codes: Alive and Well at Colleges," an essay in this chapter. In this passage, the author combines definition with cause-and-effect analysis to help convince readers of his assertion that "speech zones" are a form of harmful censorship that exists on many college campuses.

EXCERPT FROM "SPEECH CODES: ALIVE AND WELL AT COLLEGES" COMBINING DEFINITION AND CAUSE-AND-EFFECT ANALYSIS

The definition of *speech code* is important for demonstrating that speech zone policies, explained in the next paragraph, are really forms of speech codes.

But speech codes are alive and well, if one is realistic about what makes a campus regulation a speech code. The definition Foundation for Individual Rights in Education defines a speech code as *any campus regulation that punishes, forbids, heavily regulates, or restricts a substantial amount of protected* significance of the definition *speech.* Thus defined, speech codes are the rule rather than the exception in higher education.

The cause-and-effect analysis in the first two sentences explains why colleges no longer use the term *speech code*. The cause-and-effect analysis in the rest of the paragraph explains why colleges have speech zones and what the effect of those zones is. Most readers will infer from the cause-and-effect analysis that the author is arguing against speech zones.

cause-and-effect analysis

Why does virtually no college call its speech code by that name? For one thing, in the 1980s and 90s, every legal challenge of a clearly identified speech code at a public cause-and-effect analysis institution was successful. To maintain a weapon against speech that is "offensive" or "uncivil" (or merely too robust), the authors of the current stealthier generation of speech codes have adopted highly restrictive "speech zone" policies, e-mail policies that ban "offensive" speech, "diversity statements" with provisions that punish those uttering any "intolerant expression," and, of course, the ubiquitous "harassment policies" aimed at "hostile" viewpoints and words that operate by redefining speech as a form of conduct.

Argumentation-Persuasion beyond the Writing Classroom

Argumentation-persuasion helps writers achieve their purpose in many writing situations.

IN ACADEMIC WRITING AND READING   Argumentation is a big part of college writing. To show that you have thoughtfully considered information from a text or a lecture, you will be asked not merely to restate it but to analyze it, consider different points of view, draw your own conclusions, and present and defend these conclusions.

For example, in an ethics class, you may need not only to explain genetic screening but also to develop guidelines governing genetic screening and to argue for their acceptance. In a history class, you may need to explain why the atomic bomb was dropped during World War II and then argue that it should or should not have been used to end the war with Japan; in a business course, you may need to define inflation, explain strategies for combating it, and then go on to argue which strategy is the best.

Although textbooks emphasize objective presentation of information and generally try to cover all sides of an issue evenhandedly, at times a text, especially an upper-level text, may use argumentation-persuasion. Here is an example taken from the textbook *Teachers, Schools, and Society* by Myra and David Sadker:

The authors argue their assertion that textbooks do not do a good job of discussing some religious issues, an assertion they support by paraphrasing Goodman.	There is an important difference between *teaching about* religion and *promoting* religion. Today's texts fail to discuss adequately many religious issues that are intellectually complex and socially controversial. Columnist Ellen Goodman suggests that as publishers retreat from controversy, they also retreat from many important lessons. Goodman points out that the strength of our nation, what children really need to learn, is that our history has not always had happy endings, and that we have not yet resolved all our differences. In fact, Americans may never resolve all of their differences. The lesson to be taught to children is that we can live together as a people and not agree on everything.

AT WORK AND IN THE COMMUNITY   Argumentation-persuasion is also frequently required in the workplace. For example, copywriters compose advertisements to persuade consumers to buy products. Attorneys write briefs to convince judges of the merits of their case. Public health officials draw on research to persuade people to improve their eating habits. Artists write proposals to convince arts councils to fund their projects. Managers write reports to convince supervisors to purchase a particular phone service or to reorganize an office.

You will also use argumentation-persuasion in your personal writing. For example, you might write a letter to the editor to persuade others to accept your assertion about an issue important to you, an e-mail to a friend to convince him or her to join you on a cross-country trip, a letter to a customer service rep to persuade a business to give you a refund for a faulty product, or a speech to convince school board members to change a school bus route.

SUPPORTING DETAILS

The ancient Greeks identified three elements of a successful argument: logos, pathos, and ethos. **Logos** (from which our word *logical* derives) refers to the sound reasoning of the argument. It includes the evidence, facts, statistics, examples, and authoritative statements that back up your assertion. **Pathos** (from which our word *pathetic* derives) refers to the emotional component of persuasion; it appeals to the reader's feelings, values, attitudes, and beliefs. Assume you want to persuade your reader to buy a particular stock. If you say that failure to buy the stock could mean missing the opportunity of a lifetime, you are using pathos by appealing to the reader's fear of passing up an opportunity. If you explain that the stock is undervalued and part of a growing market sector, you are relying on logos, appealing to the reader's intellect. **Ethos** (from which our word *ethical* derives) refers to establishing your honesty, integrity, and reliability so your reader will trust you and, therefore, believe what you say. You must present yourself as knowledgeable and thoughtful, as someone who carefully weighs all evidence before drawing conclusions. If your reader thinks you are impetuous, careless, or biased, he or she may not accept your assertion, no matter how well argued it is.

Logos

To present your argument soundly, you must reason logically and avoid the errors in logic discussed on pages 7–9. Logos is the core of argumentation. For the most part, your argumentative detail will be the reasons underlying your assertion and your support for these reasons. If you want to convince your reader that the federal government should pay day care expenses for working parents, you would give all the reasons this idea is a good one, *and* you would back up each reason with support. Say you argue that the family is in trouble, and you give the divorce rate as one reason. You must then back up this reason, perhaps by giving a statistic about how high the divorce rate is and by explaining the specific negative effects of divorce on the family.

To back up your reasons, you can use personal experience and observation, facts and statistics, quotations and paraphrases, interviews, and speculation about the effects of adopting or not adopting your assertion—all of which are explained next—as well as the patterns of development.

Draw on Personal Experience and Observation

Suppose that one of the reasons you give for supporting federally funded day care is that children of working parents do not always get satisfactory care without it. To back up this reason, you could draw on observation by telling about your neighbor, who cannot afford decent care for her child while she is at work. If your own experience as a working parent supports the point, you could also write about that experience to back up your claim.

Use Facts and Statistics

To convince your reader that we need a fresh approach to the problem of juvenile crime, you could show that our current approach is not working by citing Linda J. Collier's claim in "Adult Crime, Adult Time" (page 608) that since 1965 the number of arrests for crimes of violence has increased twofold for 12-year-olds and threefold for 13- and 14-year-olds. If you use facts and statistics from sources, be sure to document this information according to the conventions explained in Chapters 4 and 15.

Use Quotations and Paraphrases

To argue that racist speech should not be protected by the First Amendment, you could quote or paraphrase Charles R. Lawrence III, who says in "The Debate over Placing Limits on Racist Speech Must Not Ignore the Damage It Does to Its Victims" (page 627), "Whenever we decide that racist speech must be tolerated because of the importance of maintaining societal tolerance for all unpopular speech, we are asking blacks and other subordinated groups to bear the burden for the good of all." If you use quotations or paraphrases, be sure to follow the guidelines given in Chapters 4 and 15.

www.mhhe.com/clousepatterns6 | Using Sources

For more help with incorporating quotes and paraphrases, click on
Research > Incorporating Source Information

Conduct Interviews

Suppose that to argue for federally funded day care you note that the day care fees are too high for some individuals. To support this reason, you could interview the owners of local day care centers to learn the cost of enrollment. You could then interview parents of young children for thoughts on the enrollment fees you discovered.

Speculate about What Would Happen If the Proposal in Your Thesis Were or Were Not Adopted

Sometimes you can argue your case by explaining the good that would result if the proposal in your thesis were adopted or the harm that would result if it were not. Say you want to argue for the elimination of the foreign language requirement for mathematics and science majors. You could argue that if the requirement is eliminated, science and math majors will have more time to participate in valuable internship programs. Or you could argue that if the requirement is not abolished, many prospective math and science majors will attend school at the nearby colleges that do not require a foreign language.

---

www.mhhe.com/clousepatterns6   Paragraph Patterns

For more help with patterns of paragraph development, click on

Writing > Paragraph Patterns

Pathos

In addition to appealing to your reader's intellect with sound reasons, you can appeal to your reader's emotions, needs, values, beliefs, and concerns. For example, to persuade your reader to support proposed legislation permitting assisted suicide, you can move the reader to compassion by describing the agony of a patient who must linger in pain with no hope of recovery. Similarly, to convince your reader that the federal government should fund day care, you can stir up the reader's emotions with a graphic explanation of the substandard care the child next door is getting.

Appealing to your reader's emotions is a valid strategy, but do not overdo it. Emotional appeal should be restrained. It is fine to arouse compassion for a gay couple who want to marry, but it would be unfair to say that all gay couples who cannot marry are therefore totally unfulfilled. Further, the number of emotional appeals should be reasonable. Most often, they should appear *in addition to* logical reasons—not *instead of* them. Rely mostly on logical reasons, and supplement those reasons with emotional appeal when appropriate.

Ethos

If you have particular knowledge or experience that makes you authoritative, you can mention it to establish your credentials. For example, if you are arguing that your community should update its zoning laws, you can note that you were on the zoning board for five years.

Part of ethos is also presenting yourself as a thoughtful person who weighs all sides of an issue before forming an opinion. No matter what stand you take on an issue, some reasonable people will disagree with you, and those people will have valid points to support their own stand. Ignoring this opposition will diminish your ethos because you will not come across as someone who has carefully examined all sides. Furthermore, even if you ignore the opposition, your reader might not. If your reader thinks of points that work against your assertion and you do not deal with those points, you may fail to convince him or her. Thus, you must acknowledge the opposing arguments and find a way to make them less compelling, a process called *raising and countering objections*.

In general, you can counter objections in any of three ways:

1. **State that the opposition has a point but so do you.**

   Many people are concerned because federally funded day care will raise taxes [*objection raised*]. However, children who are currently given substandard care because we lack a comprehensive, federally funded program will not thrive. Children who do not thrive fail to realize their potential or they develop problems, both of which end up costing society more money than day care [*objection countered*].

2. **State that the opposition has a point but your point is better.**

   Although some are concerned about the cost of federally funded day care [*objection raised*], we cannot put a price tag on the well-being of our children because they are our hope for a better future [*objection countered*].

3. **State that the opposition's point is untrue.**

   There are those who maintain that parents do not need help with federally funded day care [*objection raised*]. However, the number of mothers who must work outside the home is very high, and many of these working mothers are the sole support of their children and could not stay home even if they wanted to. As a result, many parents are forced into substandard, or even downright dangerous, child care arrangements [*objection countered*].

Raising and countering objections helps strengthen your case, but you need not deal with every opposition point. Instead, identify the most compelling objections and deal with those.

How Logos, Pathos, and Ethos Relate to Purpose and Audience

When you write argumentation-persuasion, you will usually employ some combination of logos, pathos, and ethos. To determine the proportions of these elements, consider your purpose and audience. Is your purpose to convince your audience that additional campaign finance reform is a good idea? Then you can emphasize sound reasons (logos) and your own trustworthiness (ethos). Or do you want your reader to take action and write members of Congress to encourage them to vote for campaign finance reform? That purpose may require the addition of emotional appeal (pathos), perhaps by moving your reader to anger over the current method for financing campaigns.

With your purpose in mind, assess whether your reader is supportive, wavering, or hostile:

- A *supportive reader* is already on your side. This reader trusts you and shares some or all of your positions. If you were arguing for strengthening the sex education curriculum in local schools, a supportive audience would include members of Planned Parenthood. With this audience, you can draw on your trustworthiness to establish your bond with them and rely more heavily on emotional appeals to tap into shared beliefs, attitudes, and emotions and solidify support for your assertion. You will also include some elements of logos, as by reminding the reader of facts and presenting new facts, and thereby reaffirming agreement.

- A *wavering reader* can be brought to your side but is currently not committed to your assertion. Such a reader may be insufficiently informed about the issue, may not have made up his or her mind, or may not have a reason to care. If you were arguing for strengthening the sex education curriculum in local schools, a wavering audience might be parents with very young children, parents who have not yet turned their attention to this issue, or parents who are uncertain about what will be best for their children. For a wavering audience, you must draw on reliable evidence and sound reasoning to convince them of the validity of your position and of your own trustworthiness and, if possible, mention credentials that would add to your trustworthiness (perhaps the fact that you are a parent yourself). In other words, logos and ethos will be very important. Emotional appeals (pathos) can be used, but they must be very restrained, or you could alienate your readers by seeming manipulative.

- A *hostile reader* is the most difficult to persuade. This reader is strongly opposed to your assertion or difficult to reach for some other reason, such as reluctance to consider opposing viewpoints. With a hostile audience, you must shape your purpose realistically. You may not have a chance of changing a reader's mind, but you may be able to soften that person's objection or earn some respect for your assertion. For example, if your reader has strong moral beliefs that sex education belongs in the home and not in schools, you will not be able to convince that person to support a stronger sex education curriculum. However, you may be able to help that person see that sex education has some positive aspects. With a hostile reader, emphasize logos. Give your audience your best facts and reasoning, and hope they have some impact.

THE TOULMIN MODEL

In his book *The Uses of Argument* (1958), Stephen Toulmin identifies three parts of an argument. An adaptation of his division is given here. You may find it helpful as you critically read the arguments of others and write your own arguments.

In the Toulmin model, you can think of argumentation-persuasion as having three parts: the claim, the support, and the assumption.

The *claim* is the assertion you are trying to convince your reader of. Here are some examples of claims.

CLAIM	This university should switch from its current quarter system to the semester system.
CLAIM	Teachers should not be permitted to engage in labor strikes.
CLAIM	The United States' immigration policy creates many problems.

In argumentation-persuasion, the claim appears in the thesis.

The *support* is the ideas and information you include to convince the reader of your claim. It can be evidence used for logical appeals—statistics and facts, for example—or for appeals to emotions, values, and beliefs. Here are examples of both kinds of support.

CLAIM	This university should switch from its current quarter system to the semester system.
SUPPORT (BASED ON A FACT)	The administration says that the switch would save the university money because fewer terms would reduce the cost of registering and advising students.
SUPPORT (APPEAL TO BELIEF)	Semesters allow students to study subjects at a more comfortable pace. (*An appeal to the belief that it is better to study something for 15 weeks than for 10.*)

In argumentation-persuasion, the support will be the supporting details.

The third part of argumentation-persuasion is the *assumption,* which is the inference that connects the claim and the support. To see how the assumption connects the claim and support, study this example.

CLAIM	This university should switch from its current quarter system to the semester system.
SUPPORT (REASON)	The administration says that the switch would save the university money because fewer terms would reduce the cost of registering and advising students.
UNSTATED ASSUMPTIONS	The administration is trustworthy, so it can be believed when it says that money will be saved. Saving the administration money is good.

If the reader trusts the administration, the assumption is accepted and the support is convincing. However, if the reader does not trust the administration, then the assumption is not accepted and the support fails to convince. When a reader might not accept an assumption automatically, you must support the assumption to make it convincing.

| STATED ASSUMPTION WITH SUPPORT | The administration says that the switch would save the university money because fewer terms would reduce the cost of registration and advisement. They arrived at this conclusion after surveying 200 schools that have switched from the quarter to the semester system. |

Sometimes an assumption is a value or belief.

CLAIM	Teachers should not be allowed to engage in labor strikes.
SUPPORT	When teachers strike, they cause a great deal of harm.
ASSUMPTION	Teachers are different from other workers who engage in strikes that create problems and yet have the right to strike.

As this example suggests, the assumption is often what will or will not incline the reader to move from the support to accepting the claim. To prove that teachers should not strike, you would have to prove the assumption and show how teachers are different from others who strike—steelworkers, truck drivers, television writers, and so forth.

Sometimes the assumption is self-evident, so it need not be written. Say you want to argue that we should censor the Internet to protect children from predatory adults. The assumption that we do not want children harmed is so obvious that it need not be stated. Now say that you want to argue that teenagers who commit murder should be tried as adults. In this case, the assumption that some teenagers are emotionally and intellectually mature needs to be stated and proven. Otherwise, your reader may have difficulty moving from your support to accepting your claim.

INDUCTIVE AND DEDUCTIVE REASONING

Induction and deduction are two methods of reasoning especially helpful for supporting a claim.

Induction

Induction is a form of reasoning that moves from specific evidence to a general conclusion. To reason inductively, examine specific facts, cases, examples, and other available evidence, and then draw a reasonable conclusion based on that information. Induction is used all the time: A doctor ponders a patient's symptoms and test results, and reasons inductively to reach a diagnosis; a jury considers the evidence presented at the trial and reasons inductively to reach a verdict; a police officer studies the crime scene, examines clues, and reasons inductively to establish a list of suspects.

In argumentation-persuasion, you will often employ inductive reasoning. Assume, for example, that you wish to argue the need for a traffic light at the corner of First Street and Third Avenue. You could first present your specific evidence: In the last year, traffic accidents at that intersection have increased 80 percent; five people have died there, including two children;

traffic at that intersection has increased since the shopping mall opened a mile away; the Highway Patrol has said that a traffic light there could reduce the number of accidents. After offering this evidence, you could present your assertion—your claim—in the form of a generalization that follows from the evidence: We need a traffic light at the corner of First Street and Third Avenue. This generalization would be your thesis.

No matter how compelling your evidence seems to be, you cannot always be certain of the reliability of the generalization it leads you to. Thus, it may well be true that a traffic light would solve the problem at First Street and Third Avenue, but it could also be true that the real problem is the speed limit, and a better solution would be to reduce it from 55 mph to 35 mph. Because the conclusion drawn in inductive reasoning is rarely certain beyond a doubt, that conclusion is called an **inference.** To increase the likelihood that your inferences are accurate, be sure that your evidence is sound. Supply enough evidence and verify that the evidence is accurate, recent, specific, and representative.

Deduction

In a broad sense, deduction involves reasoning from the general to the specific, but you should not think of deduction as the opposite of induction. Instead, **deduction** moves from a generalization (called a *major premise*) and a specific instance (called a *minor premise*) to a conclusion, like this.

MAJOR PREMISE (GENERALIZATION)	This state allows all juveniles accused of murder to be tried as adults.
MINOR PREMISE (SPECIFIC INSTANCE)	Sixteen-year-old John Smith is accused of murdering his father in this state.
CONCLUSION	Therefore, 16-year-old John Smith can be tried as an adult.

Recall that with inductive reasoning, the conclusion is an inference rather than a certainty. In contrast, with deductive reasoning, if the two premises are accurate, then the conclusion will follow inescapably. If one or both of the premises are wrong, however, the conclusion will not follow, as is the case in this example.

MAJOR PREMISE	All college students drink beer.
MINOR PREMISE	Chris is a college student.
CONCLUSION	Therefore, Chris drinks beer.

Notice that the conclusion cannot be accepted because the major premise is untrue: Not all college students drink beer; therefore, we cannot conclude inescapably that college student Chris drinks beer.

Deductive reasoning can provide a useful framework for argumentation-persuasion. You can organize your essay so that your supporting details present the evidence demonstrating the truth of each premise. With the premises proven, your reader will accept your thesis, which is the point you are arguing.

ORGANIZING ARGUMENTATION-PERSUASION

You can handle the introduction of your argumentation-persuasion essay many ways. Explaining why the issue is important can be effective because it helps your reader understand the seriousness of your purpose. Thus, if you are arguing that high schools should have day care centers for the children of students who are mothers, your introduction can note the large number of teen mothers who drop out of school because they have no child care. This figure should help your reader appreciate the urgency of the issue. If your reader needs certain background information in order to appreciate your argument, your introduction can be a good place to provide that information. Thus, if you are arguing the need to return to homogeneous groupings in classrooms, you should explain what a homogeneous grouping is if your reader is not likely to know. Your introduction can also be a good place to establish your ethos. Thus, if you are arguing in favor of increasing the city sales tax, you can note that you have worked in the city's finance department for three years and can confirm the recent claims of shortfalls.

Your thesis, whether it appears in the opening paragraphs or elsewhere, should state the issue and your assertion about that issue, as in these examples:

> The United States desperately needs federally funded day care.
> (*issue:* federally funded day care; *assertion:* in favor of it)
>
> Federally funded day care would create more problems than it solves.
> (*issue:* federally funded day care; *assertion:* against it)

In general, arranging your points in a progressive order (from least to most compelling) is effective. This way, your reader leaves your essay with your most compelling arguments fresh in mind. Or you can place your strongest arguments first *and* last for a big opening and finish.

If you are reasoning inductively, you can place your thesis at the end of your essay, after you have presented all the specific evidence pointing to the inference that stands as your thesis. Placing the thesis at the end can work well for a hostile reader. You can build your case and then present your assertion about the issue. If you are reasoning deductively, you can first present the evidence to support your major premise and then present the evidence to support your minor premise.

Topic sentences can help you to structure your essay and can help your reader to follow it. You can place each reason for your thesis in its own topic sentence and follow each topic sentence with the appropriate support. An essay arguing that we should pay college athletes rather than give them scholarships could have these topic sentences:

> If we pay college athletes, the players can use the money for tuition and books.
>
> If we pay college athletes, we can dispel the myth that players are always students first.

Finally, once we pay college athletes, colleges can acknowledge openly that they are farm clubs for professional teams.

You can raise and counter objections wherever a point to be countered logically emerges. Alternatively, you can raise and counter objections together in one or two paragraphs at the beginning or end of the essay.

To conclude, you can reaffirm your assertion for emphasis, summarize your chief arguments if your reader is likely to appreciate the reminder, or present your most persuasive point. In addition, you can call your audience to action by explaining what you want the reader to do. Or you can recommend a particular solution to a problem. Explaining what would happen if the proposal in your thesis were or were not adopted can also be an effective closing.

www.mhhe.com/clousepatterns6	Arguments

For more help with writing an argument essay, click on
Writing > Writing Tutor: Arguments

VISUALIZING AN ARGUMENTATION-PERSUASION ESSAY

The chart on page 585 can help you visualize the structure for an argumentation-persuasion essay. Like all good models, however, this one can be altered as needed.

THINKING CRITICALLY ABOUT ARGUMENTATION-PERSUASION

Chapters 1 and 4 explained that thinking critically about your reading and writing requires analysis and assessment. To read and write critically about argumentation-persuasion, use what you learned in those chapters, and ask the following questions:

- **Are reasons supporting the assertion backed up with evidence, and is that evidence both appropriate and accurate?** For example, saying that most Americans support raising the minimum driving age is not credible without evidence to back up that claim. In this case, poll data would be an appropriate kind of evidence; personal experience and observation would not be. And if evidence from polls is mixed, it would be inaccurate to cite only polls in which most respondents favored raising the driving age.
- **Are emotional appeals fair and restrained?** Appealing to readers' emotions should not involve manipulating their fears and vulnerabilities. For example, a writer can fairly appeal to Americans'

INTRODUCTION

- Creates interest in your essay, perhaps by explaining why the issue is important; may provide background information and may establish your reliability
- May state the thesis (underlined in the example), which gives the issues and your assertion; if deduction is used, the thesis may appear in the conclusion

EXAMPLE

We are commonly called an "urban university." What this euphemism really means is that we are located in the inner city—in other words, in a high-crime area. In the blocks just beyond the perimeter of campus, car thefts, muggings, sexual assaults, and even murders occur. Unfortunately, criminal activities are not limited to areas beyond campus; they occur here as well. For this reason, we must permit our campus police officers to carry guns.

FIRST BODY PARAGRAPH

- Gives and explains the first point to support your assertion
- May rely on logos, pathos, and/or ethos
- May raise and counter objections
- May rely on inductive or deductive reasoning
- Generally, arranges details in progressive order

EXAMPLE

That crime—serious crime—occurs on our campus cannot be denied. Almost weekly, the campus newspaper reports that a car has been stripped in one of our parking lots. Sadly, there have been several rapes and other assaults. . . . Our current crime rate is this high because without guns our police officers do not act as a deterrent.

NEXT BODY PARAGRAPHS

- Continue until all the points to support the assertion are made
- May rely on logos, pathos, and/or ethos
- May raise and counter objections
- May rely on inductive or deductive reasoning
- Generally, arrange details in progressive order

EXAMPLE

Some people oppose arming campus police because they believe doing so will promote violence. However, the opposite is true. . . .

CONCLUSION

- Can reaffirm your assertion or present your most persuasive point
- Can call your reader to action or recommend a solution to a problem
- Can explain what would happen if the proposal in your thesis were or were not adopted
- Can state the thesis if deduction has been used

EXAMPLE

Thus, we should arm campus police to increase the safety of everyone on campus and to save the university money by reducing the amount of stolen and damaged property. If we do not arm the campus police, we may soon have to arm ourselves because the amount of crime is increasing.

concerns about airline security by arguing that a ticket surcharge to pay for more sophisticated luggage scanners will make flying safer. However, stating that failure to implement such a surcharge will ensure that terrorists kill more Americans in the air is unfair and inflammatory.

- **Are objections valid and accurately stated?** Raising and countering objections is an effective strategy, but objections must not be misrepresented. Suppose that, in arguing in favor of establishing charter schools, a writer counters the objection that they're not needed for purposes of innovation since existing public schools can innovate. A writer who represented the objection as a claim that school systems do not need to innovate would be misrepresenting the objection.

- **Is the writer's self-characterization accurate?** Building ethos is important, but, for example, a writer cannot claim to be an expert without the appropriate training and experience.

PROCESS GUIDELINES: STRATEGIES FOR WRITING ARGUMENTATION-PERSUASION

1. **Selecting a topic.** If you need help discovering a topic, try one of these strategies.
   - Review the essays in this book for ideas. Or review local and campus newspapers to learn about important controversial issues.
   - Fill in the blank in one of these sentences:

     It is unfair that _____.

     It makes me angry that _____.

     I disagree with people who believe that _____.

     The quality of life in my community would be better if _____.

     People of my generation would be more confident about our future if _____.

     Opportunities for children would be enhanced if _____.
   - Try a Google search on a subject of interest.

2. **Determining purpose and assessing audience.** Answer these questions:
   - Do you want to convince your reader to think a particular way about an issue? If so, what do you want your reader to think?
   - Do you want your reader to take a particular action? If so, what do you want your reader to do?
   - Is your reader supportive, wavering, or hostile? Is your purpose reasonable for such an audience?

3. **Generating ideas.** Answering the following questions can help you generate ideas:
   - Based on your purpose and audience, how will you balance logos, pathos, and ethos?
   - Why is your issue important? To whom is it important?
   - What would happen if your thesis were adopted? If it were not adopted?
   - What are the chief objections to your thesis? How can you logically and constructively counter those objections?
   - How can you appeal to your reader's emotions?
   - How can you present yourself as trustworthy?
4. **Revising.** Ask two reliable readers to review your draft to be sure that you have avoided errors in logic and have countered important objections.

Using Sources for a Purpose

The body paragraph below is for an essay about how to keep children safe, and it illustrates how to use sources from this book in your writing. It also includes a long quotation of paragraph 10 of "Young Voices from the Cell" on page 613.

THESIS Parents today must protect their children from dangers that parents in previous generations never had to think about.

WRITING PURPOSE AND AUDIENCE To inform parents about how to protect their children from the unique dangers threatening today's children.

[1]Children are reluctant to tell on friends who plan or do something wrong (widely known as "snitching") because doing so is considered disloyal. [2]In the past, snitching was about such issues as whether to tell on a grounded friend who sneaked out of the house to attend a concert. [3]Today, the stakes are higher, so parents must teach children that snitching can be the right thing to do, even if they lose friends in the process. [4]And if children fail to believe parents who explain that snitching is sometimes acceptable, they might believe Evan Ramsey, who opened fire in his high school, killing the principal and a fellow student and wounding two others. [5]Roche and Bower report that Ramsey wishes someone had snitched on him:

> [6]Among Ramsey's wishes is that one of the two friends to whom he confided his lethal plan would have turned him in. [7]Last week a blue-ribbon panel that studied the Columbine massacre criticized police, school officials and the killers' parents for not intervening to stop Klebold and Harris, after being given signs of their murderous intent. [8]"That would

The long quotation helps the writer achieve an informational purpose by supporting the idea that parents should teach children that under some circumstances, snitching is the right thing to do.

(continued)

(continued)

> have been one of the best things a person could have done," says Ramsey
> of his own case. ⁹Instead, Ramsey's buddies egged him on. (615)

AVOIDING PLAGIARISM

The paragraph, which includes a long quotation, illustrates these points about avoiding plagiarism. (For more complete information on using source material, consult Chapters 4 and 15.)

- **Know how to handle a long quotation.** A long quotation is one that runs more than 4 typed lines in your paper. As sentences 5–9 illustrate, double-space a long quotation and indent it instead of using quotation marks. Do not indent the first word more than the rest, even if it begins a paragraph in the source. Place the parenthetical citation after the final period, and most often follow the introduction with a colon (see sentence 5).

- **Use quotation marks for a quote within a quote.** Long quotations are not set off with quotation marks. However, as sentence 8 illustrates, when quotation marks appear in the source, use double quotation marks for that material.

MYTHS ABOUT USING SOURCES

MYTH: If I copy material from the Internet and paste it into my paper, I do not have to document the material, use quotation marks, or indent.

FACT: Material copied and pasted from the Internet is treated the same way as source material taken from print sources. Document it appropriately (see Chapters 4 and 15).

Checklist for Revising Argumentation-Persuasion

You can use this checklist along with the one on page 76 to help you revise.

1. _____ Your thesis gives the issue and your assertion.
2. _____ Your introduction explains why your topic is important or otherwise engages your readers' interest and, if necessary, provides background information.
3. _____ All your points are true, clarified, and supported.
4. _____ Logos, pathos, and ethos are balanced in a way that is appropriate for your purpose and audience.
5. _____ If necessary, you have stated and supported the assumptions that connect your claims and support.
6. _____ You have appealed to emotion, values, and beliefs with appropriate restraint.
7. _____ You have avoided problems with logic.
8. _____ You have raised and countered compelling objections.
9. _____ Paraphrases and quotations are documented according to the conventions given in Chapters 4 and 15.
10. _____ Your conclusion brings the essay to a strong close (and, perhaps, states the thesis if you used deduction).

Student-author Hannah Scheels uses argumentation to convince readers that the Kansas attorney general's acceptance of only 1,600 free CDs out of a total 51,000 is a serious form of censorship. She also works to move readers to take action against this censorship. Notice that she draws on sources and synthesizes them. After you read the essay, you will have an opportunity to evaluate it.

Cast Out of Kansas: Music Censorship in Public Libraries

Hannah Scheels

In the summer of 2004, Kansas was one of forty states nationwide 1 to receive several thousand free compact disks as part of a settlement to resolve charges that the music industry had fixed prices for recordings. The disks were intended to be given, free of charge, to public libraries in these forty states, where they would be made available to anyone who wished to listen to them. However, library patrons in Kansas will not be able to listen to more than 1,600 of these recordings (out of a total 51,000) because, as CNN reports, the Kansas attorney general found that they "did not mesh with the values of a majority of Kansans" ("'OutKast'"). This chilling example of state-sponsored censorship interferes with the ability of Kansas citizens—and their librarians—to determine their own "values" for themselves. Left unchallenged, the actions of the Kansas attorney general set a dangerous precedent that undermines First Amendment rights to free speech guaranteed to all by the U.S. Constitution.

According to *CNN.com,* the rejected disks include works by the rap 2 artists OutKast and Notorious B.I.G., the popular alternative rock bands Stone Temple Pilots and Rage Against the Machine, and classic alternative voices ranging from Lou Reed to Devo ("'OutKast'"). All of these artists have well-earned reputations for the quality and expressiveness of their lyrics as well as their innovative music. Another quality these artists share is their status as "alternative." Even though many of these artists are Grammy winners (a testament to their popularity and the enormous sales of their music), they are more importantly critically acclaimed. Rap artists OutKast have merged funk, rhythm and blues, and hip-hop in a significantly creative fashion. At the same time, their music videos brilliantly send up stereotypical images of black musicians. Notorious B.I.G.'s lyrics capture the very real violence that defines the lives of so many urban Americans. Lou Reed's deadpan lyrics describe the alternative lifestyles of the 1960s

Title
Notice the word play: "Cast Out" is a clever reference to OutKast.

Paragraph 1
This introductory paragraph gives background information—the details of the settlement. The thesis is the last sentence. The issue is the action of the Kansas attorney general; the assertion is that the action undermines the First Amendment. Notice the use of quotation.

Paragraph 2
The topic sentence idea (library patrons are denied access to important music) is implied. The details establish that the rejected music is important, which helps support the idea that the attorney general did the wrong thing. Notice that the source of information is acknowledged.

and 1970s in unforgettable images. And both the Stone Temple Pilots and Rage Against the Machine evoke, in both their lyrics and their musical arrangements, the frustration and lack of opportunity felt by so many young people in an age of increasing cultural and economic conformity.

Paragraph 3
The topic sentence (the first sentence) presents an objection, and the rest of the paragraph counters that objection.

3   It is true that these artists, in their desire to tell the truth as they see it and express the realities they believe we should all at least acknowledge, often use explicit language and create images that can be disturbing. Sometimes, as in the work of OutKast, the sexual language and imagery can be pornographic. This is why the recording industry puts parental advisory stickers on disks that contain violent or explicit language, and why many artists (including OutKast) also release "clean" versions of their albums that digitally remove the potentially offensive language without interfering with the overall integrity of the music.

Paragraph 4
The topic sentence (the second sentence) gives the next reason supporting the assertion. The rest of the paragraph relies on sound reasoning (logos) for support. Notice that transition is achieved with the synonym "decision." Also notice the quotation, which is credited in parentheses.

4   What is most disturbing about the decision of the Kansas attorney general is that he has made his decision based on "Internet databases of lyrics" (" 'OutKast' "). In other words, these artists are being censored as writers, not just as musicians. If these musicians published their lyrics as poetry or short stories instead of albums, this decision would seem to set a precedent that would allow a state attorney general to remove books from a library—or, as in this case, prevent some books from ever even reaching a library's shelves.

Paragraph 5
The topic sentence (the first sentence) gives the next reason supporting the assertion. The rest of the paragraph relies on sound reasoning (logos) for support. Notice the quotation and that the source is given.

5   The actions of the Kansas attorney general also override the expertise, experience, and responsibilities of local librarians. Even though the executive director of the Kansas Library Association is quoted in the *CNN.com* article as saying that the attorney general "did libraries a big favor by selecting these CDs because there's no way libraries could have said what they wanted" (" 'OutKast' "), the fact is that librarians had no say at all in this decision. Local librarians are trained to be sensitive to the needs and "values" of their particular neighborhoods and communities. By abdicating their responsibility to a state attorney general—an elected official with a political agenda—the librarians of Kansas have damaged the First Amendment rights of Kansas citizens. Further, they have violated the Code of Ethics of the American Library Association, which states that librarians must "uphold the

principles of intellectual freedom and resist all efforts to censor library resources" (American Library Association).

Furthermore, this decision is grossly unfair to those citizens who 6 either cannot afford to purchase CDs, or who wish to sample a recording before purchasing it (or allowing their children to purchase it). Paradoxically, in an age where major retailers such as Wal-Mart are themselves curtailing (based on "values") the kinds of music, DVDs, books, and magazines they make available to consumers, public libraries may in some communities be the *only* place people can turn to for a genuinely diverse and fair selection of media.

Patrons of libraries nationwide should actively protest what is hap- 7 pening in Kansas, unless they want their acquisitions and holdings to be managed by lawyers rather than librarians. The issue here is not about the "decency" of certain musicians, but about the freedom of Americans to determine their values for themselves.

Works Cited

American Library Association. *Code of Ethics. ALA.org.* American Library
> Association, 28 June 1997. Web. 12 Sept. 2004.

"'OutKast' Not Allowed in Kansas Libraries." *CNN.com.* Cable News
> Network, 6 Aug. 2004. Web. 12 Sept. 2004.

Paragraph 6
The topic sentence (the first sentence) gives the next reason supporting the assertion. The rest of the paragraph relies on sound reasoning (logos) for support. Notice the transition "furthermore."

Paragraph 7
This is the conclusion. The essay ends with a call to action.

Works Cited
For information on how to document paraphrases and quotations, including how to write a works cited citation, see Chapters 4 and 15.

PEER REVIEW

Responding to "Cast Out of Kansas: Music Censorship in Public Libraries"

Analyze and assess "Cast Out of Kansas: Music Censorship in Public Libraries" by responding to these questions:

1. Is the essay persuasive? Why or why not?
2. Should the essay employ more logos, ethos, or pathos? Explain.
3. Are significant objections raised and countered effectively? Explain.
4. Are there any problems with logic?
5. Do paraphrases and quotations help the writer achieve her persuasive purpose?
6. What do you like best about the essay?
7. What single change do you think would improve the essay?

SHOULD THE LAW ALLOW PAYMENT TO ORGAN DONORS?

BACKGROUND: "Financial Incentives for Organ Donation" is a position paper adopted by the National Kidney Foundation in 2003. On its Web site, where the position paper is posted, the foundation describes itself as a nonprofit organization "dedicated to preventing kidney and urinary tract diseases, improving the health and well-being of individuals and families affected by kidney disease and increasing the availability of all organs for transplantation."

THE PATTERN AND ITS PURPOSE: To **persuade** readers that legalizing compensation for organ donation would be harmful, the position paper relies on *cause-and-effect analysis.*

FINANCIAL INCENTIVES FOR ORGAN DONATION
BY THE NATIONAL KIDNEY FOUNDATION

The National Kidney Foundation opposes all efforts to legalize payments for human organs for use in transplantation and urges the federal government to retain the prohibition against the purchase of organs that is codified in Title III of the National Organ Transplant Act of 1984.

As you read
Notice why the NKF believes that payment will not increase the number of organ donations.

2   Offering direct or indirect economic benefits in exchange for organ donation is inconsistent with our values as a society. Any attempt to assign a monetary value to the human body, or body parts, either arbitrarily, or through market forces, diminishes human dignity. By treating the body as property, in the hope of increasing organ supply, we risk devaluating the very human life we seek to save. Providing any form of compensation for organs may be an affront to the thousands of donor families and living donors who have already made an altruistic gift of life and it could alienate Americans who are prepared to donate life-saving organs out of humanitarian concern. In addition, it disregards families who are unable to donate organs but do consent to tissue donation.

3   Offering money for organs can be viewed as an attempt to coerce economically disadvantaged Americans to participate in organ donation. Furthermore, since the economically disadvantaged have been shown to be less likely to be organ transplant candidates, financial incentives for organ donation could be characterized as exploitation.

4   While payment for organs has real potential to undermine the transplant system in this country, its ability to increase the supply of organs for transplantation is questionable. In a recent survey of families who refused to donate organs of their loved ones who have died, 92% said that payment would not have persuaded them to donate. Public opinion polls and focus groups have disclosed that many Americans are not inclined to be organ donors because they distrust the U.S. health care system, in general, and, in particular, because they are concerned that the health care of potential organ donors might be compromised if their donor status were known. A program of financial incentives for organ donation is not likely to change these perceptions and, indeed, may aggravate mistrust. This is true even with the

suggested subterfuge of paying the money to funeral homes. That strategy would most likely simply raise the price of a funeral without benefiting the family at all. Making financial incentives available at the time of death opens the possibility of creating new sources of tension and dissension between family members who are faced with the option of organ donation. Finally, a program of financial incentives for organ donation could expose transplant recipients to unnecessary risks because living donors and donor families would have an incentive to withhold information concerning the donor's health status so that they can be assured a financial benefit.

5   Proponents of financial incentives for organ donation assert that a demonstration project is necessary to confirm or refute the types of concerns mentioned above. The American Medical Association, the United Network for Organ Sharing and the Ethics Committee of the American Society of Transplant Surgeons have called for pilot studies of financial incentives. Conversely, the National Kidney Foundation maintains that it would not be feasible to design a pilot project that would definitively demonstrate the efficacy of financial incentives for organ donation. Moreover, the implementation of a pilot project would have the same corrosive effect on the ethical, moral and social fabric of this country that a formal change in policy would have. Finally, a demonstration project is objectionable because it will be difficult to revert to an altruistic system once payment is initiated, even if it becomes evident that financial incentives don't have a positive impact on organ donation.

6   The National Kidney Foundation believes that payment for organs is wrong. Such a practice should not be started or tested since its negative message could not be undone if, as research indicates, it will not work. The headline "Local Family Offered Money for Loved One's Organs" should never appear.

7   The National Kidney Foundation remains committed to doing everything that can rightly be done to alleviate the critical organ shortage. However, better understanding by the public, better practices from medical and procurement professionals, better organ-preserving care for post-transplant patients and increased living donation will help, not money. Any attempt to pay families to say yes is wrong.

READING CLOSELY AND THINKING CRITICALLY

1. Why does the National Kidney Foundation (NKF) oppose financial incentives for organ donation?

2. How does the NKF say that financial incentives for donation can exploit the poor? How might you counter that objection to incentives?

3. Why does the NKF believe that financial incentives for donation are unlikely to increase the number of organs available for transplantation?

4. The NKF is opposed to instituting a pilot program to try out incentives. Why?

5. What assumption connects the claim with the support in paragraph 2? (See page 580 on assumptions and claims in the Toulmin model.)

EXAMINING STRUCTURE AND STRATEGY

1. What element of ethos appears in paragraph 1? Does that element help make the introduction effective? Explain.

2. Cause-and-effect analysis appears throughout the essay. How does it help the essay achieve its persuasive purpose?

3. For paragraphs 2, 4, and 5, indicate whether the details rely on logos, pathos, or ethos, or a combination.

4. How does mentioning the NKF at the beginning and the end help the essay achieve its persuasive purpose?

5. Only one objection is raised and countered in the piece. What is that objection and how is it countered? How effective is the counter?

CONSIDERING LANGUAGE AND STYLE

1. In paragraph 4, the plan to pay funeral homes a financial incentive is referred to as a "subterfuge." How does the connotation of that word help the essay achieve its persuasive purpose?

2. Is the headline in paragraph 6 an effective persuasive strategy? Why or why not?

3. Consult a dictionary if you are unfamiliar with these words: *altruistic* (paragraph 2), *corrosive* (paragraph 5).

For discussion and writing assignments based on "Financial Incentives for Organ Donation," see page 597.

BACKGROUND: A former professor of psychiatry at Yale, Sally Satel is a resident scholar at the American Enterprise Institute, a nonprofit conservative think tank. She is also the staff psychiatrist at the Oasis Clinic in Washington, D.C. She has published a number of articles in medical journals and magazines on the cultural aspects of science and medicine, including "The Case for Paying Organ Donors," which first appeared in the *Wall Street Journal* in 2009. Her books include *Drug Treatment: The Case for Coercion* (1999), *PC, M.D.: How Political Correctness Is Corrupting Medicine* (2001), *One Nation under Therapy* (2005), and *When Altruism Isn't Enough: The Case for Compensating Kidney Donors* (2009).

THE PATTERN AND ITS PURPOSE: To **persuade** readers that legalizing compensation for organ donation would be beneficial, Sally Satel, relies on *cause-and-effect analysis*.

The Case for Paying Organ Donors

BY SALLY SATEL

Last week the Council of Europe and the United Nations issued a joint study on trafficking in human organs. According to the study, up to 10% of all kidneys transplanted worldwide are obtained in the organ bazaars of Africa, Asia, Eastern Europe and South America.

2   These underground markets exist, the paper rightly says, because of "the desperation of patients waiting for transplant." But its two-pronged solution won't solve the problem. It will likely make it even worse.

3   Let me explain. First, the study calls for a ban on organ trafficking. At first blush, this seems reasonable. After all, the depredations of illicit organ markets are stark: Corrupt brokers deceive indigent and illiterate donors about the nature of surgery, cheat them out of payment, and ignore their post-surgical needs.

As you read Think about whether the author's personal experience adds weight to her argument.

4   But this brings us to the second prong of the study's approach: Prohibiting the legal compensation of donors, which could be used to increase the number of organs available for transplant. A number of countries such as Singapore, the Netherlands, Israel, the U.S. and Saudi Arabia have contemplated offering benefits such as lifetime health insurance to kidney donors, or plan to do so. International prohibitions on the practice, as championed in the joint study, would undermine their efforts and stifle humane pilot programs elsewhere.

5   Together, these two approaches spell disaster. Clamping down on unlawful organ sales without first expanding the organ pool will mean not less criminal activity, but more patient deaths. I say this as an American who contemplated going overseas to find a kidney when I needed a transplant a few years ago.

6   Most likely, the efforts to stamp out trafficking will also drive corruption rings further underground, thereby increasing the risks to recipients and donors or cause markets to blossom elsewhere around the globe.

7   Without question, more countries need to improve their rates of obtaining organs at death from volunteers. But even in Spain, which is famously successful

at retrieving organs from the newly-deceased because of its robust procurement infrastructure, there are still patients dying on its waiting list.

8   The bold fact is that organ trafficking will stop only when the dire shortage recedes. How to make this happen? Enable more patients in wealthy countries to obtain transplants at home by empowering their governments, under strict regulation, to offer incentives to prospective donors.

9   Regrettably, the U.N. and Council of Europe renounce this approach. One reason is practical, the other abstract. First, the task force is worried that buying organs, even if done legally, will encourage very poor people to sell their organs out of desperation. A fair point. The answer is a plan that circumvents donor exploitation. If in-kind rewards were offered to donors, such as a contribution to a retirement fund, an income tax credit, or tuition vouchers for their children—rather than lump-sum cash payments—the program would not attract desperate people who might otherwise rush to donate for a large sum of instant cash.

10   Such an incentive program would carefully screen would-be donors for physical and emotional health, as is currently done for all volunteer living kidney donors everywhere. A months-long waiting period would ensure that donors are not acting impulsively or with less than fully informed consent. Finally, all donors would be guaranteed follow-up medical care for any complications.

11   Notably, the incentives would be provided by a third party such as a governmental entity, charity or insurer; not by individual patients. Thus, organs procured in this manner would be distributed to the next needy patient in line—with no special advantage to the well-off.

12   Not only would more lives be saved through legal means of donor rewards, but it would also result in fewer people from rich countries paying kidney brokers to haunt the back alleys of China, Pakistan, Egypt, Colombia, and Eastern Europe in search of hapless donors.

13   This plan, alas, runs afoul of the principle of altruistic giving. "Altruism is the bioethical foundation . . . for obtaining organs in a manner consistent with human dignity," the joint study says. "Organs should not give rise to financial gain."

14   I reject this logic. Dignity is affirmed when we respect the capacity of individuals to make decisions in their own best interest, protect their health and express gratitude for their sacrifice. Financial gain, *per se,* is not inconsistent with this. The true indignity is to stand by smugly while thousands of people die each year for want of an organ.

15   As for the donor, why shouldn't he be able to accept a reward for saving the life of another human being? After all, he is the one who takes a risk and relinquishes the precious good. The doctors, nurses, and hospital all receive compensation when a transplant occurs—yet no one insists they volunteer their services. And rightly so, because the more transplants performed, the more suffering averted and the more lives saved.

16   Although I am a blessed beneficiary of someone's altruism—a glorious friend donated one of her kidneys to me in 2006—I know that altruism is not enough. Twelve citizens in the European Union die daily because they could not survive the wait for a transplant. In the U.S., 18 people die each day.

17   But instead of forging solutions, the Joint Council wants to reinforce the status quo. "Changes in the relevant values might well alienate the public who have grown used to the existing bioethical framework," the report says.

18   Grown *used to?* What a poor excuse for global leadership. New ideas are imperative when a tired policy regime has proven itself inadequate. Sadly, the study's prescription ensures more needless death and suffering—a dire outcome that we must refuse to grow used to.

READING CLOSELY AND THINKING CRITICALLY

1.   What is the Council of Europe and the United Nations' "two-pronged solution" (paragraph 2) to the problem of trafficking in human organs?

2.   Why does Satel oppose the two-pronged solution?

3.   What safeguards does Satel recommend to ensure that an incentive program does not attract donors who give organs for the wrong reasons?

4.   Evaluate the logic of paragraph 15. What flaw do you notice?

EXAMINING STRUCTURE AND STRATEGY

1.   Why does Satel open with a statistic? Why does she open with a study whose recommendation she wants to counter?

2.   What objections to financial incentives for organ donors does Satel raise? How does she counter those objections?

3.   How does Satel use cause-and-effect analysis to achieve her persuasive purpose?

4.   For paragraphs 5, 8, 14, and 16, indicate whether the details rely on logos, pathos, or ethos, or a combination.

CONSIDERING LANGUAGE AND STYLE

1.   Why are the places where organs are procured illegally called "organ bazaars"?

2.   Consult a dictionary if you are unfamiliar with these words: *trafficking* (paragraph 1), *indigent* (paragraph 3), *per se* (paragraph 14).

For discussion and writing assignments based on "The Case for Paying Organ Donors," see below.

ASSIGNMENTS FOR DISCUSSION AND WRITING

"Financial Incentives for Organ Donation" and "The Case for Paying Organ Donors"

1.   **For discussion in class or online.** Both the National Kidney Foundation and Sally Satel make reasonable arguments. What are the best arguments for the side of the debate with which you disagree? Why are these arguments compelling?

2. **Writing in your journal.** Live kidney donors undergo surgery that can last five hours. The process can involve a two-to-three day hospital stay, four to six weeks of recovery, and significant pain. In a page or so, explain whether you would be a living kidney donor. What about upon your death? Why do you feel the way you do?

3. **Using argumentation for a purpose.** The purposes in the assignments are possibilities. You may establish whatever purpose you like, within your instructor's guidelines.

   - The National Kidney Foundation says, "Offering direct or indirect economic benefits in exchange for organ donation is inconsistent with our values as a society" (paragraph 2). To convince readers who are undecided about whether to pay organ donors, agree or disagree with this statement.

   - On its Web site, the National Kidney Foundation says its vision is "to enhance the lives of everyone with, at risk of or affected by kidney disease." To convince readers who believe financial incentives should be offered to organ donors, argue that the foundation's position on incentives is not compatible with its statement of vision.

   - Design a pilot program to test offering financial incentives for organ donors, and then argue for its adoption. Your purpose is to convince average readers that the program should be given a trial run.

   - Satel suggests a number of safeguards to prevent abuses of organ donor incentives. Are her safeguards adequate? Argue your assertion for an undecided audience.

4. **Analyzing and assessing.** Analyze "Financial Incentives for Organ Donation" and "The Case for Paying Organ Donors," and assess which essay is more persuasive. Consider all the aspects of argumentation-persuasion you have been studying: audience and purpose; logos, pathos, and ethos; the kind and quality of supporting details; raising and countering objections; and so on.

5. **Connecting and synthesizing the readings.** Using the information in "Financial Incentives for Organ Donation," "The Case for Paying Organ Donors," and "One Room, 3000 Brains" (page 677), discuss whether the issues surrounding donating all or part of our bodies to science for research are the same as those surrounding organ donation. Should financial incentives exist to encourage people to donate all or part of their bodies to science?

6. **Drawing on sources.** In your campus library or on the Internet, read a variety of opinions on organ donation. In the library, you can use *Infotrac, The Reader's Guide to Periodical Literature,* or the *New York Times Index* to find information. On the Internet, you can use your favorite search engine. Read the opinions you discover, and write a summary and synthesis of the most compelling ones.

BACKGROUND: In 2000, Nathaniel Brazill was sentenced to the minimum of 25 years for shooting his seventh-grade teacher, Barry Grunow, with a semiautomatic pistol. Brazill was 13 at the time of the shooting and could have received a life sentence without parole. At 14, Lionel Tate became the youngest person sentenced to life in prison. He was convicted of stomping a 6-year-old playmate to death. Three years later, in 2004, an appeals court ruled that his mental competency should have been evaluated before the trial, and he was granted bond and released. Both children were tried as adults. After these Florida murder trials made particularly visible the trend toward trying minors as adults, public debate about how to deal with violent juvenile offenders heated up. Some of that debate took place on the editorial pages of our nation's newspapers. "Little Adult Criminals" first appeared on the editorial page of the *New York Times* in May 2001.

COMBINED PATTERNS AND THEIR PURPOSE: "Little Adult Criminals" advances the argument that children age 12 or 14 have insufficient emotional maturity to control their impulses or to comprehend the consequences of their actions. To achieve its **persuasive** purpose, the editorial includes *cause-and-effect analysis* and *exemplification*.

Little Adult Criminals

NEW YORK TIMES EDITORIAL

Spurred by news of teenagers with easy access to guns and other weapons committing increasingly violent crimes, all but three states have made it easier in recent years to try minors as adults. The idea was that certain types of violent crime are so serious that they do not belong in a juvenile court system designed not only to punish delinquents but to rehabilitate them before they reach adulthood. Two high-profile murder trials in Florida this year have sounded a warning that the trend may have gone too far.

2   In the first case, Lionel Tate, a 14-year-old, was convicted in January of first-degree murder for beating to death a 6-year-old playmate when he was 12. He was sentenced in March to life without parole. His mother had foolishly refused to accept a plea bargain that would have carried only a three-year sentence in a youth facility followed by 10 years of probation.

3   Then this month, a jury convicted Nathaniel Brazill, also 14, of second-degree murder. When he was 13 he shot and killed a teacher who would not allow him back into class after he had been suspended for throwing water balloons. "Not too bad," was the youth's reaction to the verdict, which carries a sentence of 25 years to life in prison. In his case we are again left wondering whether the disciplinary troubles of a teenager would have escalated into a crime if he had lived in a place where guns were not so readily available.

As you read
Notice that the author offers a compromise. Determine whether that compromise adds to the persuasive quality of the editorial.

4   A civilized society must not easily give up hope of rehabilitating a child who commits a crime. While a 17-year-old repeat offender may warrant trial as an adult criminal, children who are 12 or 14 do not possess the emotional maturity to control

their impulses, or to fully understand the consequences of their actions. It is more than social development; recent medical research has found that the brain continues to develop into one's teenage years. In no instance does a juvenile belong in adult prisons.

5   In Florida, it was evident that the two defendants did not fully grasp the significance of the proceedings. Some of the jurors in each case later questioned the wisdom of trying the boys in an adult court, and even Gov. Jeb Bush said that Nathaniel should not have been tried as an adult. "There should be a sensitivity to the fact that a 14-year-old is not a little adult," he said.

6   The governor can act upon this belief in reviewing the clemency petitions of both boys. He should also press for review of whether juvenile court judges, instead of prosecutors or state legislatures, should determine whether a particular minor ought to be tried in an adult criminal system whose procedures, sentencing guidelines and prisons make no allowances for minors. Florida, like many other states, has wrongly granted prosecutors too much discretion in making that call.

7   Reasserting the role of the juvenile criminal system, traditionally charged with acting in the best interests of a minor, does not mean society's interest in public safety is shortchanged. Juvenile courts have rarely hesitated to transfer minors to adult court where necessary, such as when a 17-year-old with a history of violent behavior commits a heinous, premeditated crime.

8   Moreover, studies have shown that minors who have gone through the juvenile system, with its emphasis on rehabilitation through counseling, mentoring, education and vocational training, are less likely to be arrested again after being released

than those who have served time in ordinary prisons. A sensible approach is to have minors convicted in criminal court serve time in juvenile detention facilities, and have their sentences reviewed when they come of age. The criminal justice system is charged with determining an individual's level of culpability, and it must factor a minor's age into that equation.

9   To send 14-year-olds directly to adult prisons for a quarter-century is to give up on them. It may even ensure that they become lifetime criminals.

READING CLOSELY AND THINKING CRITICALLY

1. According to the editorial, why have so many states made it easier to try juveniles in adult courts?
2. For what reasons is the author opposed to trying juveniles as adults?
3. What is the author's position on gun ownership? How can you tell?
4. What compromise solution does the author offer to resolve the question of whether to try juveniles as adults? Does the compromise help achieve the author's persuasive purpose? Explain.

EXAMINING STRUCTURE AND STRATEGY

1. Why does the author mention that Lionel Tate's mother refused a plea bargain? How does that information contribute to the author's persuasive purpose?
2. What objections does the author raise and counter? Are the counterarguments effective? Explain.
3. Does the author support points to your satisfaction? Explain.
4. What does the editorial's conclusion contribute to its persuasive purpose?

NOTING COMBINED PATTERNS

1. How does the editorial writer use cause-and-effect analysis as part of the editorial's introduction?
2. How does the writer use cause-and-effect analysis in paragraphs 8 and 9 as part of the argument?
3. How do examples in paragraphs 2, 3, and 5 help support the argument?

CONSIDERING LANGUAGE AND STYLE

1. In the second sentence in paragraph 1, sentence 2, why did the author include the phrase "designed not only to punish delinquents but to rehabilitate them before they reach adulthood"?
2. Consult your dictionary if you do not know the meaning of these words: *clemency* (paragraph 6), *heinous* (paragraph 7), *premeditated* (paragraph 7), *mentoring* (paragraph 8), *culpability* (paragraph 8).

For discussion and writing assignments based on "Little Adult Criminals," see page 620.

BACKGROUND: Laurence Steinberg is the Distinguished University Professor of Psychology at Temple University and the director of the John D. and Catherine T. MacArthur Foundation Research Network on Adolescent Development and Juvenile Justice. He is an expert on the psychological development of adolescents, parent–child relationships, high school reform, and juvenile justice. He is a member of the National Academy of Science's Panel on the Health Implications of Child Labor and a consultant to federal agencies on child labor and juvenile justice policy. The author of more than 150 scholarly articles, he is also the author or editor of many books, including *You and Your Adolescent: A Parent's Guide for Ages 10–20* (1997), *Handbook of Adolescent Psychology* (2004), *The Ten Basic Principles of Good Parenting* (2004), and the best-selling textbook *Adolescence,* now in its eighth edition (2007). "Should Juvenile Offenders Be Tried as Adults?" first appeared in *USA Today Magazine* in January 2001.

COMBINED PATTERNS AND THEIR PURPOSES: In "Should Juvenile Offenders Be Tried as Adults?" Laurence Steinberg draws on several patterns of development, including *definition, contrast,* and *cause-and-effect analysis* to **inform** readers about the nature of the juvenile justice system and how it differs from the adult system. He also **argues** that children of a certain age should not be tried as adults unless they are assessed and judged to be sufficiently competent to enter the adult system.

SHOULD JUVENILE OFFENDERS BE TRIED AS ADULTS?

BY LAURENCE STEINBERG

FEW ISSUES CHALLENGE a society's ideas about the natures of human development and justice as much as serious juvenile crime. Because people neither expect children to be criminals nor expect crimes to be committed by them, the unforeseen intersection between childhood and criminality creates a dilemma that most of us find difficult to resolve. The only way out of this dilemma is either to redefine the offense as something less serious than a crime or to redefine the offender as someone who is not really a child.

As you read
Pay attention to where Steinberg raises and counters an objection, and determine why he does so at that point.

2   For the past 100 years, American society has most often chosen the first approach. It has redefined juvenile offenses by treating most of them as delinquent acts to be adjudicated within a separate juvenile justice system that is theoretically designed to recognize the special needs and immature status of young people and emphasize rehabilitation over punishment. Two guiding beliefs about young people have prevailed: first, that juveniles have different competencies than adults (and therefore need to be adjudicated in a different type of venue); and second, that they have different potential for change than adults (and therefore merit a second chance and an attempt at rehabilitation). States have recognized that conduct alone—that is, the alleged criminal act—should not by itself determine whether to invoke the heavy hand of the adult criminal justice system.

"States have determined that conduct alone should not by itself determine whether to invoke the heavy hand of the adult criminal justice system."

3   In recent years, though, there has been a dramatic shift in the way juvenile crime is viewed by policymakers and the general public, one that has led to widespread changes in policies and practices concerning the treatment of juvenile offenders. Rather than choosing to define offenses committed by youth as delinquent, society increasingly is opting to redefine them as adults and transfer them to the adult court and criminal justice system.

4   Most reasonable people agree that a small number of young offenders should be transferred to the adult system because they pose a genuine threat to the safety of other juveniles, the severity of their offense merits a relatively more severe punishment, or their history of repeated offending bodes poorly for their ultimate rehabilitation. However, this does not describe the tens of thousands of young people who currently are being prosecuted in the adult system, a large proportion of whom have been charged with nonviolent crimes. When the wholesale transfer to criminal court of various categories of juvenile offenders starts to become the rule rather than the exception, this represents a fundamental challenge to the very premise that the juvenile court was founded on—that adolescents and adults are different.

5   There are many lenses through which one can view debates about transfer policies. As a developmental psychologist, I ask whether the distinctions we draw between people of different ages under the law are sensible in light of what we know about age differences in various aspects of intellectual, emotional, or social functioning. More specifically, on the basis of what we know about development, should a boundary be drawn between juveniles and adults in criminal matters and, if so, at what age should we draw it?

6   Developmental psychology, broadly defined, concerns the scientific study of changes in physical, intellectual, emotional, and social development over the life cycle. Developmental psychologists are mainly interested in the study of "normative" development. My concern is whether the study of normative development indicates that there are scientific reasons to warrant the differential treatment of young people and adults within the legal system, especially with regard to the age period most under current political scrutiny—the years between 12 and 17.

7   First, this age range is an inherently transitional time. There are rapid and dramatic changes in individuals' physical, intellectual, emotional, and social capabilities. If there is a period in the life span during which one might choose to draw a line between incompetent and competent individuals, this is it.

8   Second, adolescence is a period of potential malleability. Experiences in the family, peer group, school, and other settings still have a chance to influence the course of development. To the extent that malleability is likely, transferring juveniles into a criminal justice system that precludes a rehabilitative response may not be very sensible public policy. However, to the extent that amenability is limited, their transfer to the adult system is less worrisome.

"Adolescence is a period of potential malleability."

9   Finally, adolescence is a formative period during which a number of developmental trajectories become firmly established and increasingly difficult to alter. Many adolescent experiences have a tremendous cumulative impact. Bad decisions or poorly

THE SUPREME COURT ALLOWS JUVENILE EXECUTIONS...

Copyright © 2002 by Mike Keefe. *The Denver Post,* October 25, 2002. Reprinted with permission.

formulated policies pertaining to juvenile offenders may have unforeseen and harmful consequences that are very hard to undo.

10   It is only fair to ask whether or why a developmental perspective is even relevant to contemporary discussions of trying juvenile offenders in the adult criminal system. After all, current discussions about trying juveniles in adult court are typically not about the characteristics of the offender, but about the seriousness and harmfulness of the offense—factors independent of the offender's age or maturity. "Adult time for adult crime"—the mantra of the get-tough-on-juvenile-crime lobby—says nothing about the age of the offender, except for the fact that it ought to be considered irrelevant.

11   I believe that it is logically impossible to make the age of the offender irrelevant in discussions of criminal justice policy. A fair punishment to an adult is unfair when applied to a child who did not understand the consequences of his or her actions. The ways we interpret and apply laws should rightfully vary when the case at hand involves a defendant whose understanding of the law is limited by intellectual immaturity or whose judgment is impaired by emotional immaturity. Moreover, the implications and consequences of administering a long and harsh punishment are very different when the offender is young than when he or she is an adult.

12   Transferring juveniles to criminal court has three sets of implications that need to be considered in discussions about whether they should be tried as adults. First, transfer to adult court alters the legal process by which a minor is tried. Criminal court is based on an adversarial model, while juvenile court is based, at least in theory, on a more cooperative model. This difference in the climates of juvenile vs.

adult courts is significant because it is unclear at what age individuals have sufficient understanding of the ramifications of the adversarial process and the different vested interests of prosecutors, defense attorneys, and judges. Young defendants may simply not have what it takes—by the standards established in the Constitution—to be able to defend themselves in criminal court.

> "Transfer to adult court alters the legal process by which a minor is tried."

13   Second, the legal standards applied in adult and juvenile courts are different. For example, competence to stand trial is presumed among adult defendants unless they suffer from a serious mental illness or substantial mental retardation. We do not know if the presumption of competence holds for juveniles, who, even in the absence of mental retardation or mental illness, may lack sufficient competence to participate in the adjudicative process. Standards for judging culpability may be different in juvenile and adult courts as well. In the absence of mental illness or substantial deficiency, adults are presumed to be responsible for their own behavior. We do not know the extent to which this presumption applies to juveniles, or whether the validity of this presumption differs as a function of the juvenile's age.

14   Finally, the choice of trying a young offender in adult vs. juvenile court determines the possible outcomes of the adjudication. In adult court, the outcome of being found guilty of a serious crime is nearly always some sort of punishment. In juvenile court, the outcome of being found delinquent may be some sort of punishment, but juvenile courts typically retain the option of a rehabilitative disposition, in and of itself or in combination with some sort of punishment. This has two significant ramifications: the stakes of the adjudication are substantially greater and, in juvenile court, offenders generally are presumed amenable unless the prosecutor demonstrates otherwise. In adult court, amenability is not presumed, and must instead be shown by the defendant's counsel.

15   In other words, decisionmakers within the juvenile and criminal justice systems bring different presumptions to the table. The juvenile court operates under the presumption that offenders are immature, in three different senses of the word: Their development is incomplete; their judgment is less than mature; and their character is still developing. The adult court, in contrast, presumes that defendants are mature, competent, responsible, and unlikely to change.

16   Which of these presumptions best characterizes individuals between the ages of 12 and 17? Is there an approximate age where the presumptions of the criminal court become more applicable to an offender than the presumptions of the juvenile court? Although developmental psychology does not point to any one age that politicians and practitioners should use in formulating transfer policies or practices, it does point to age-related trends in certain legally relevant attributes, such as the intellectual or emotional capabilities that affect decisionmaking in court and on the street.

> "This does not mean that we should let them off the hook or fail to punish them."

17   It is appropriate, based on developmental research, to raise serious concerns about the transfer of individuals 12 and under to adult court, because of their limited adjudicative competence as well as the very real possibility that most children this young will not prove to be

sufficiently blameworthy to warrant exposure to the harsh consequences of a criminal court adjudication. For this reason, individuals 12 and under should continue to be viewed as juveniles, regardless of the nature of their offense. This does not mean that we should let them off the hook or fail to punish them. It merely means that they should be punished and held responsible within a system designed to treat children, not fully mature adults.

18 At the other end of the continuum, it appears appropriate to conclude that the vast majority of individuals older than 16 are not appreciably different from adults in ways that would prohibit their fair adjudication within the criminal justice system. My view is that variability among individuals older than 12, but younger than 16, requires that some sort of individualized assessment of an offender's competence to stand trial, blameworthiness, and likely amenability to treatment be made before reaching a transfer decision. The relevant decisionmakers (e.g., judges, prosecutors, and defense attorneys) should be permitted to exercise judgment about individual offenders' maturity and eligibility for transfer.

19 It is true that a bullet wound hurts just as much when the weapon is fired by a child as when it is fired by an adult, but this argument is a red herring, since we comfortably acknowledge that there are numerous situations where mitigating factors should be taken into account when trying a defendant, such as insanity, emotional duress, or self-defense. Immaturity is another mitigating factor. People may differ in their opinions about the extent to which, the ways in which, and the age at which an offender's maturity should be considered in court decisions. One person might believe that a boundary should be drawn at 18, another at 15, and yet another at 13. Nevertheless, ignoring the offender's age entirely is like trying to ignore an elephant that has wandered into the courtroom. You can do it, but most people will notice that something smells foul.

"Ignoring the offender's age entirely is like trying to ignore an elephant that has wandered into the courtroom."

READING CLOSELY AND THINKING CRITICALLY

1. What is Steinberg arguing? What are the issues and his assertion?

2. Steinberg says that we have two ways to deal with children who commit crimes. What are they? Which option has American society chosen most often over the past 100 years?

3. How is the American juvenile justice system designed to treat the youthful offender?

4. Steinberg notes a recent change in the nation's handling of juvenile crime. What is the change? How extensive is it?

5. Why does Steinberg consider the age span 12–17 so significant? Why is it important to handle properly the juvenile offenders in this group?

6. Some people believe the age of the offender is irrelevant. Instead, the nature of the crime should determine the punishment. Does Steinberg agree? Explain.

EXAMINING STRUCTURE AND STRATEGY

1. In paragraph 5, the author identifies himself as a developmental psychologist. In what way is that information a form of ethos? How does it help the author achieve his persuasive purpose?
2. How does the author develop his ethos in paragraphs 10 and 11?
3. In paragraph 19, what objection does Steinberg raise? How does he counter that objection? Why does he raise and counter the objection at the end of the essay?

NOTING COMBINED PATTERNS

1. Paragraph 6 includes definition. How does that definition help Steinberg achieve his persuasive purpose?
2. What is contrasted in paragraphs 12–14? Where does cause-and-effect analysis appear in the essay?
3. How do the contrast and cause-and-effect analysis help Steinberg achieve his persuasive purpose?

CONSIDERING LANGUAGE AND STYLE

1. In paragraph 19, Steinberg refers to an argument as a "red herring." What does he mean?
2. Paragraph 4 opens with the words, "Most reasonable people agree." What is the effect of that clause?
3. Consult a dictionary if you are unsure of these words: *adjudicate* (paragraph 2), *venue* (paragraph 2), *malleability* (paragraph 8), *amenability* (paragraph 8), *trajectories* (paragraph 9), *mantra* (paragraph 10), *culpability* (paragraph 13).

For discussion and writing assignments based on this essay, see page 620.

BACKGROUND: Linda J. Collier is an attorney who has worked in juvenile courts. Currently the dean of public services and social sciences at Delaware County Community College, she earned her Bachelor of Arts and Juris Doctorate degrees from Howard University and her Master of Science in criminal justice from St. Joseph's University. Collier has been a special assistant for legal affairs to the presidents at both Cheyney and Lincoln universities and has taught courses in English, political justice, sociology, and criminal justice. She has also been the director of student legal services at Penn State University. "Adult Crime, Adult Time" originally appeared in the *Washington Post* in 1998 as "Adult Crime, Adult Time: Outdated Juvenile Laws Thwart Justice."

COMBINED PATTERNS AND THEIR PURPOSES: In "Adult Crime, Adult Time," Linda Collier uses *process analysis* to **inform** readers about how the juvenile justice system works, and she discusses the *effects* of those procedures in part with *exemplification*. Her goal is to **persuade** readers that the current system is inadequate and that we should be trying juveniles as adults if they commit violent crimes.

Adult Crime, Adult Time

BY LINDA J. COLLIER

When prosecutor Brent Davis said he wasn't sure if he could charge 11-year-old Andrew Golden and 13-year-old Mitchell Johnson as adults after Tuesday afternoon's slaughter in Jonesboro, Ark.,[1] I cringed. But not for the reasons you might think.

2   I knew he was formulating a judgment based on laws that have not had a major overhaul for more than 100 years. I knew his hands were tied by the long-standing creed that juvenile offenders, generally defined as those under the age of 18, are to be treated rather than punished. I knew he would have to do legal cartwheels to get the case out of the juvenile system. But most of all, I cringed because today's juvenile suspects—even those who are accused of committing the most violent crimes—are still regarded by the law as children first and criminals second.

As you read Consider how compelling Collier's supporting detail is.

3   As astonishing as the Jonesboro events were, this is hardly the first time that children with access to guns and other weapons have brought tragedy to a school. Only weeks before the Jonesboro shootings, three girls in Paducah, Ky., were killed in their school lobby when a 14-year-old classmate allegedly opened fire on them. Authorities said he had several guns with him, and the alleged murder weapon was one of seven stolen from a neighbor's garage. And the day after the Jonesboro shootings, a 14-year-old in Daly City, Calif., was charged as a juvenile after he allegedly fired at his middle-school principal with a semiautomatic handgun.

---

[1]Fourteen-year-old Mitchell Johnson and 12-year-old Andrew Golden were convicted of shooting four classmates and a teacher in Jonesboro, Arkansas, in 1998. After the article was written, the two boys were sentenced to the maximum penalty allowed by Arkansas law—confinement in a juvenile center until they turn 21.

4   It's not a new or unusual phenomenon for children to commit violent crimes at younger and younger ages, but it often takes a shocking incident to draw our attention to a trend already in progress. According to the U.S. Department of Justice, crimes committed by juveniles have increased by 60 percent since 1984. Where juvenile delinquency was once limited to truancy or vandalism, juveniles now are more likely to be the perpetrators of serious and deadly crimes such as arson, aggravated assault, rape and murder. And these violent offenders increasingly include those as young as the Jonesboro suspects. Since 1965, the number of 12-year-olds arrested for violent crimes has doubled and the number of 13- and 14-year-olds has tripled, according to government statistics.

5   Those statistics are a major reason why we need to revamp our antiquated juvenile justice system. Nearly every state, including Arkansas, has laws that send most youthful violent offenders to the juvenile courts, where they can only be found "delinquent" and confined in a juvenile facility (typically not past age 21). In recent years, many states have enacted changes in their juvenile crime laws, and some have lowered the age at which a juvenile can be tried as an adult for certain violent crimes. Virginia, for example, has reduced its minimum age to 14, and suspects accused of murder and aggravated malicious wounding are automatically waived to adult court. Illinois is now sending some 13-year-olds to adult court after a hearing in juvenile court. In Kansas, a 1996 law allows juveniles as young as 10 to be prosecuted as adults in some cases. These are steps in the right direction, but too many states still treat violent offenders under 16 as juveniles who belong in the juvenile system.

6   My views are not those of a frustrated prosecutor. I have represented children as a court-appointed guardian ad litem, or temporary guardian, in the Philadelphia juvenile justice system. Loosely defined, a guardian ad litem is responsible for looking after the best interest of a neglected or rebellious child who has come into the juvenile courts. It is often a humbling experience as I try to help children whose lives have gone awry, sometimes because of circumstances beyond their control.

7   My experience has made me believe that the system is doing a poor job at treatment as well as punishment. One of my "girls," a chronic truant, was a foster child who longed to be adopted. She often talked of how she wanted a pink room, a frilly bunk bed and sisters with whom she could share her dreams. She languished in foster care from ages 2 to 13 because her drug-ravaged mother would not relinquish her parental rights. Initially, the girl refused to tolerate the half-life that the state had maintained was in her best interest. But as it became clear that we would never convince her mother to give up her rights, the girl became a frequent runaway. Eventually she ended up pregnant, wandering from place to place and committing adult crimes to survive. No longer a child, not quite a woman, she is the kind of teenage offender for whom the juvenile system has little or nothing to offer.

8   A brief history: Proceedings in juvenile justice began in 1890 in Chicago, where the original mandate was to save wayward children and protect them from the ravages of society. The system called for children to be processed through an appendage of the family court. By design, juveniles were to be kept

away from the court's criminal side, the district attorney and adult correctional institutions.

9   Typically, initial procedures are informal, nonthreatening and not open to public scrutiny. A juvenile suspect is interviewed by an "intake" officer who determines the child's fate. The intake officer may issue a warning, lecture and release; he may detain the suspect; or, he may decide to file a petition, subjecting the child to juvenile "adjudication" proceedings. If the law allows, the intake officer may make a recommendation that the juvenile be transferred to adult criminal court.

10   An adjudication is similar to a hearing, rather than a trial, although the juvenile may be represented by counsel and a juvenile prosecutor will represent the interests of the community. It is important to note that throughout the proceedings, no matter which side of the fence the parties are on, the operating principle is that everyone is working in the best interests of the child. Juvenile court judges do not issue findings of guilt, but decide whether a child is delinquent. If delinquency is found, the judge must decide the child's fate. Should the child be sent back to the family—assuming there is one? Declare him or her "in need of supervision," which brings in the intense help of social services? Remove the child from the family and place him or her in foster care? Confine the child to a state institution for juvenile offenders?

11   This system was developed with truants, vandals and petty thieves in mind. But this model is not appropriate for the violent juvenile offender of today. Detaining a rapist or murderer in a juvenile facility until the age of 18 or 21 isn't even a slap on the hand. If a juvenile is accused of murdering, raping or assaulting someone with a deadly weapon, the suspect should automatically be sent to adult criminal court. What's to ponder?

12   With violent crime becoming more prevalent among the junior set, it's a mystery why there hasn't been a major overhaul of juvenile justice laws long before now. Will the Jonesboro shootings be the incident that makes us take a hard look at the current system? When it became evident that the early release of Jesse Timmendequas—whose murder of 7-year-old Megan Kanka in New Jersey sparked national outrage—had caused unwarranted tragedy, legislative action was swift. Now New Jersey has Megan's Law, which requires the advance notification of a sexual predator's release into a neighborhood. Other states have followed suit.

13   It is unequivocally clear that the same type of mandate is needed to establish a uniform minimum age for trying juveniles as adults. As it stands now, there is no consistency in state laws governing waivers to adult court. One reason for this lack of uniformity is the absence of direction from the federal government or Congress. The Bureau of Justice Statistics reports that adjacent states such as New York and Pennsylvania respond differently to 16-year-old criminals, with New York tending to treat offenders of that age as adults and Pennsylvania handling them in the juvenile justice system.

14   Federal prosecution of juveniles is not totally unheard of, but it is uncommon. The Bureau of Justice Statistics estimates that during 1994, at least 65 juveniles were referred to the attorney general for transfer to adult status. In such cases, the U.S. attorney's office must certify a substantial federal interest in the case and show that one of the following is true: The state does not have jurisdiction; the state refuses to assume jurisdiction or the state does not have adequate services for juvenile offenders; the offense is a violent felony, drug trafficking or firearm offense as defined by the U.S. Code.

15   Exacting hurdles, but not insurmountable. In the Jonesboro case, prosecutor Davis has been exploring ways to enlist the federal court's jurisdiction. Whatever happens, federal prosecutions of young offenders are clearly not the long-term answer. The states must act. So as far as I can see, the next step is clear: Children who knowingly engage in adult conduct and adult crimes should automatically be subject to adult rules and adult prison time.

READING CLOSELY AND THINKING CRITICALLY

1. Which sentence is the thesis of "Adult Crime, Adult Time"?

2. Collier says that she cringed—but not for the reasons the reader might think—when she heard that the prosecutor "wasn't sure if he could charge" Andrew Golden and Mitchell Johnson as adults. Why did she cringe? For what reasons does she think her readers will cringe?

3. In paragraph 7, Collier cites the example of a girl who began committing adult crimes. Does this example effectively support the author's assertion? Explain.

4. Can the example of the girl in paragraph 7 be used to argue *against* trying juveniles as adults? Why or why not?

5. What reasons does Collier give for her assertion? Does she provide sufficient support for it? Explain.

EXAMINING STRUCTURE AND STRATEGY

1. In paragraph 4, Collier includes government statistics. How do these statistics help her achieve her purpose?
2. In paragraph 6, Collier identifies herself as a person who has been a court-appointed guardian for juveniles. She also says that she is not a frustrated prosecutor. Why does she make these points?
3. In paragraph 8, Collier gives a brief history of the juvenile justice system. Does this information help her achieve her purpose? Explain.
4. A *rhetorical question* is not meant to elicit a reply. Does the rhetorical question in paragraph 11 help Collier achieve her persuasive purpose? Why or why not?
5. Is Collier's reasoning inductive or deductive? How do you know?

NOTING COMBINED PATTERNS

1. What purpose do the examples in paragraphs 3 and 5 serve?
2. How does the process analysis in paragraphs 9 and 10 help Collier support her thesis?
3. In what way is cause-and-effect analysis important to Collier's persuasive strategy?

CONSIDERING LANGUAGE AND STYLE

1. Explain the metaphor *legal cartwheels* in paragraph 2. What does it mean? Is it effective? (Metaphors are explained on page 128.)
2. Paragraph 15 opens with a sentence fragment rather than with a sentence. How is the fragment used? Would a sentence have been more effective? Explain.
3. Consult a dictionary if you are unsure of the meaning of these words: *creed* (paragraph 2), *truancy* (paragraph 4), *awry* (paragraph 6), *languished* (paragraph 7), *ravages* (paragraph 8), *appendage* (paragraph 8).

For discussion and writing assignments based on this essay, see page 620.

BACKGROUND: Timothy Roche (1968–2006) was an award-winning investigative reporter who began writing for newspapers while he was still in high school. He became a bureau chief for *Time* magazine in 2002. Roche wrote on a wide range of national issues, including the controversy surrounding the painkiller OxyContin, the murder in Georgia of sheriff-elect Derwin Brown, the crisis of foster care, the controversy surrounding the election of George W. Bush, segregation, and school prayer. Amanda Bower frequently writes the "Milestones" section of *Time*, which notes important events in the lives of famous people, and articles on health issues. In addition, she has written articles on green architecture, Mother Teresa, and the 2001 disappearance of Washington intern Chandra Levy. "Young Voices from the Cell" first appeared in *Time* in May 2001.

COMBINED PATTERNS AND THEIR PURPOSE: In "Young Voices from the Cell," Timothy Roche and Amanda Bower use *cause-and-effect analysis* to **inform** the reader of why young boys go on killing rampages at their schools and what happens when they are incarcerated in adult prisons. To make their points, the authors use *exemplification* by describing the lives of 12 teenagers who opened fire on students and teachers at their schools.

YOUNG VOICES FROM THE CELL

BY TIMOTHY ROCHE AND AMANDA BOWER

"NOT TOO BAD," that's what the boy killer murmured to his lawyer when the verdict came in. He was right that it could have been worse. The Florida jury might have gone for murder one but instead convicted Nathaniel Brazill, 14, of murder in the second degree for pointing a gun between the eyes of his favorite teacher and pulling the trigger a year ago. "I'm O.K.," he mouthed to his mother Polly, seated in the courtroom's second row. Then he gave a little wave to a young cousin, sitting nearby.

As you read
Consider how the authors use direct quotation to help them achieve their persuasive purpose.

2   If Brazill didn't at that instant grasp the grim future that awaits him, it probably won't take him long. Next month the judge will mete out a sentence that could mean a lifetime in prison.[1] And if Brazill needs a clearer picture of what's in store for him, the prison life of other school shooters will give him an idea. These young gunmen, at the moment of their wrathful outbursts, were often filled with a sense of potency and triumph or at least relief that whatever or whoever was troubling them had been exorcised. But those sensations generally prove fleeting. As they settle into the monotony and isolation of prison life, these boys tend to experience feelings of profound regret, remorse and loss as they come to terms with what they have done to their victims and what they have done to themselves.

3   For eight weeks, *Time* delved into the lives of 12 convicted school shooters—who had terrified their classmates and periodically traumatized the nation since 1997. Among them, they fired 135 shots, killing 21 people and wounding 62. If they were not suffering overtly from mental illness before their crimes, many clearly are now, with varying degrees of treatment available. Psychologists say they are likely to be suicidal for much of their lives and suffer repeated flashbacks to the single day

---

[1]Brazill was sentenced to 25 years in prison, the minimum term.

when everything changed, when they killed beloved teachers or gunned down schoolmates they did not know, when they went from good sons to the young terrorists among us.

4   Within the system and in their own personal circles, these boys engender a wide range of reactions. Prosecutors label many of them unredeemable sociopaths; defenders say that with education and counseling, they can be restored. Even loved ones take varying positions. Some offer support, while others abandon their own.

5   To this day, a few of the boys refuse to explain themselves. And it is fair to ask why we would want to hear from any of them anyway or have sympathy for what they have to say. But many have developed, sometimes with the help of psychologists, a better understanding of what led them to murderous fury—an understanding that could help others avoid such atrocities in the future. Almost all the shooters were expressing rage, either against a particular person for a particular affront or, more often, against a whole cohort of bullying classmates. Some of their stories confirm the notion that school shootings are a contagion, that the perpetrators are imitating the gross acts of carnage they've seen reported in other places. On the day that he brought to school a .25-cal. semiautomatic handgun that he had stolen from his grandfather's desk drawer, Brazill boasted to a classmate that he would be "all over the news."

> "To this day, a few of the boys refuse to explain themselves."

6   If these kids felt empowered by the notorious shooters who came before them, however, at least some—the most self-aware of the group—now want to set a new example for students tempted to perpetuate the cycle. Don't look to Columbine's Dylan Klebold and Eric Harris, the most notorious of the school avengers, this group is saying. Those boys killed themselves and never had to face the aftermath of their rampage. Instead, this group says, look to us, who are living the postscript, and don't let it happen to you. Even Brazill, in an interview with *Time* six weeks before his conviction, had come that far. Asked what he would like to tell the student groups who sometimes tour his jail, he replied, "Don't pick up a gun. You don't know what's going to happen."

THE PRICE

7   Evan Ramsey knows. Four years ago, he brought a pump-action shotgun to his Alaska high school and opened up, killing the principal and one student. Now he is serving a 210-year term in a maximum-security prison in the Alaskan mountains. Every night, before crashing in the tiny cell he shares with a fellow murderer, he mops the prison floors, a job that earns him $21 a month, just enough to buy soap, shampoo and stationery, which the Spring Creek Correctional Center does not supply for free. His face pasty white from lack of sun, Ramsey told *Time* his biggest complaint is the total absence of privacy. The light is always on in his cell, and the toilet sits in the open at the end of his bunk.

8   A school shooter with one of the longest sentences, Ramsey has encountered some of the harder edges of prison life. He spent six months in solitary confinement after beating a fellow inmate with a sock packed with batteries when the prisoner reneged on a gambling debt of four candy bars. Ramsey has heard that an uncle of the student he killed is in the same prison and that the man "wants to do a bunch of different things to me."

9   Ramsey says he committed his rampage because he was sick of being picked on in school, where he was nicknamed "Screech'" after the geeky character in the TV show "Saved by the Bell." "Nobody liked me, and I could never understand why," he says. "It was pretty bad then, but it's a lot worse now." Sometimes Ramsey will be starkly reminded of the shooting, for instance, when he recently received papers on a civil suit his victims' families have filed against the school district. "I sit there, and I wish, I wish, I wish, I wish I didn't do what I did," he says. "I wish I would have known the things that I know now."

10   Among Ramsey's wishes is that one of the two friends to whom he confided his lethal plan would have turned him in. Last week a blue-ribbon panel that studied the Columbine massacre criticized police, school officials and the killers' parents for not intervening to stop Klebold and Harris, after being given signs of their murderous intent. "That would have been one of the best things a person could have done," says Ramsey of his own case. Instead, Ramsey's buddies egged him on.

11   Maintaining relationships from within prison walls is a trial. Some of these kids have devoted parents and friends. A number have attracted admirers. Ramsey has a pen-pal fiancée. Kip Kinkel, who is serving a 112-year term for killing his parents and then two students in his Oregon high school in 1998, has received money in the mail from strangers. Charles (Andy) Williams, who is in prison on charges of killing two students in his Santee, Calif., school in March, gets more letters than he can answer—as many as 40 a week, according to his lawyer. There are five different clubs on Yahoo! dedicated to him, as well as a dozen homemade websites. But the real, deepest ties these kids have to their communities are often shredded. Ramsey's family visits only once a year. At one point, they went nine months without even calling.

> "There are five different clubs on Yahoo! dedicated to him, as well as a dozen homemade websites."

12   The father of Mitchell Johnson, who with buddy Andrew Golden killed four kids and a teacher when they attacked their Jonesboro, Ark., school with an arsenal of weapons in 1998, has severed contact with him. Mitchell told his mother that his father said to him on the phone, "You're the reason I quit praying" and hung up. After T. J. Solomon of Conyers, Ga., shot and wounded six classmates with a sawed-off shotgun in 1999, his mother demanded to know why he hadn't blasted himself. "You were going to kill yourself, I understand. How did that not happen?" she asked him just after his arrest. "I don't understand how you took innocent children, but you were too afraid to do anything to you. That really has me puzzled. You didn't think twice about doing it to them."

13   Luke Woodham, who killed two classmates in Pearl, Miss., in 1997 after beating and stabbing his mother to death, gets very few visitors. The school friends of Michael Carneal, who killed three classmates in West Paducah, Ky., in 1997, largely shun him. From jail, Brazill continued to write love letters to Dinora Rosales, one of the girls he wanted to see when the teacher he killed, Barry Grunow, refused to allow Brazill inside the classroom because he had been suspended for throwing water balloons. But the 14-year-old Rosales, feeling threatened, turned the mash notes over to the police.

Nick Creson (the Person Jacob Davis Shot) Being Attended to in the School Parking Lot

THE REMORSE

14   After Jacob Davis used a magnum bolt-action rifle to mow down his girlfriend's ex-lover at his Tennessee high school in 1998, he dropped down beside the bleeding body. A friend came over and said to Davis, "Man, you just flushed your life down the toilet." Davis replied, "Yes, but it's been fun." The fun didn't last. Today Davis is serving a 52-year term at a medium-security correctional facility in Clifton, Tenn. Before the shooting, he had received an academic scholarship to study computer science at Mississippi State University. Instead, he takes a prison course to learn the low-tech skill of computer refurbishment. Dressed in prison blues, Davis spoke to *Time* while seated at a small wooden table in a visitor's room, with a security guard standing watch in the corner.

15   "When you got someone else's blood on your hands, it's not an easy thing to deal with," Davis says, looking downward. "I will suffer my own personal hell the rest of my life. There's nothing you can do to make it go away. I'm truly remorseful for what happened. He's gone," Davis says of Nick Creson, the 18-year-old boy he killed, "and I can't do anything to change it and bring him back."

16   Davis is plagued by nightmares and insomnia, as are many of the other gunmen. And when he awakens each day, he often confronts anew the calamitous effects of his act on Creson's family and his own. "It's kind of hard not to when you wake up every morning in a prison cell," he says. If Johnson didn't understand at the time the consequences of his murders, he does now, says his mother, Gretchen Woodard. "He's older. He knows now the permanence of it," she says. "If words from him would not hurt those families, he'd write them."

> "Davis is plagued by nightmares and insomnia, as are many of the other gunmen."

17   For many of the young shooters, news of another school rampage sets off bouts of emotional turmoil. Carneal became "seriously depressed" after the Columbine attack, according to Kentucky juvenile-justice commissioner Ralph Kelly. "He really

took a setback from that. He felt a lot of responsibility for that happening." Kinkel also blamed himself for Columbine. On hearing the news, Kinkel told a psychologist, "I flipped out, started blaming myself." According to a friend, the March school shooting in Santee also disturbed Kinkel. Victor Cordova, incarcerated in a juvenile-treatment facility in New Mexico for shooting a schoolmate in the head, was so upset by a TV report on the Santee case that he asked to be released from the requirement that residents watch the evening news each day. Brazill, the night of his conviction, couldn't stomach even an episode of "Law & Order" that featured a school shooting; he retreated from the common room to his cell.

18   Woodham, whom many investigators believe started the chain of recent school shootings with his killing spree in 1997, is haunted by that burden. "If there's any way that I can, I would like to help stop these shootings," he wrote in a letter to *Time*. Davis has the same idea and a plan. He's writing a book about his experiences. "I want somebody to learn from the mistakes I've gone through," he says. "I want to be a part of changing all this crap that's going on."

19   One way to do that is to try to understand the triggers for these crimes. Davis says for him the proximate cause was jealous rage. After his girlfriend, Tonya Bishop, confided that she had had sex with Creson, Davis became increasingly obsessed over a period of three months with hatred for Creson. Davis' stepmother Phyllis thought this was "just like any other" teen-romance drama and assumed that "just like everybody else, he'd get over it." He didn't. He was besotted with Bishop but didn't trust her. He started sleeping just a few hours a night. His grades fell from A's to D's and F's. One day, after a glaring match with Creson in a hallway, Davis recalls, "it was just like something clicked in my head. I had been going downhill for so long. I got stuck thinking about all the pain I'd suffered. And I couldn't put all that out of my head." He went home, got his hunting rifle and ambushed Creson in the school parking lot.

20   With the benefit of antidepressant medication, Davis now believes that mental illness was at the root of his behavior. The psychiatrists who examined him agree, having determined that at the time of the shooting, Davis was suffering from serious depression with psychotic features. Eight of the other 11 convicted kids that *Time* reviewed have had some sort of mental disorder diagnosed since their crimes, mostly depression but also personality disorders and schizophrenia or its precursors. Six of the kids have had behavior-altering psychotropic drugs prescribed.

"Carneal . . . told a psychiatrist that he felt going to prison would be better than continuing to endure the bullying in school."

21   The presence of mental illness may help explain why some kids snap when faced with the usual torments of adolescence and others don't. Of course, some kids consider their vexations extraordinary. Carneal, who at the time of his crime was a freshman who got picked on for his small stature and quiet manner, told a psychiatrist that he felt going to prison would be better than continuing to endure the bullying in school.

22   Psychiatrist Stuart Twemlow, director of the Erik H. Erikson Institute for Education and Research in Stockbridge, Mass., notes that a significant subgroup of the

school shooters consists of kids who come from relatively affluent families, who are academically above average, if not gifted, and who rarely have the qualities expected of violent offenders—such as a history of substance abuse or mental disorder. In Twemlow's view, this is no coincidence. "Bullying is more common in affluent schools probably than in the low-income schools," he says. It is spurred, he believes, by "the dynamics that come out of our typical hard-nosed, competitive" middle class.

23   Park Dietz, a forensic psychiatrist who has interviewed numerous school shooters, says they tend to have in common "some degree of depression, considerable anger, access to weapons that they aren't ready to have, and a role model salient in their memory. So far," he told a *Time* reporter, "it's always been a mass murderer who has been given ample coverage in your magazine." Describing his pre-rampage mind-set, Solomon once wrote, "I felt the next thing left to release my anger would be through violence. I had just gotten the idea from the shooting at Columbine High School on April 20." Solomon opened fire precisely one month after that date. Seth Trickey, who in 1999 shot and wounded five classmates in Fort Gibson, Okla., told a psychiatrist he had become preoccupied with previous school shooters and wondered how he would hold up in their shoes. Woodham told the cops who took his confession, "I guess everyone is going to remember me now."

THE REHABILITATION

24   Though Woodham has since expressed remorse, prison authorities aren't especially interested in his redemption. Woodham receives no schooling or counseling. "We don't make any pretense about trying to rehabilitate someone who is going to spend their natural life in prison," says Robert Johnson, commissioner of Mississippi's Department of Corrections. "What's the use?"

25   Most of the rest of the boys are working toward high school diplomas. A couple hope to move on to college correspondence courses. Seven of the shooters are offered regular psychological counseling, ranging from daily to weekly sessions. However, some lawyers and relatives have begun to question the treatment and challenge the qualifications of prison psychologists, who increasingly are overburdened and underfunded as overall inmate populations grow.

26   In Pennsylvania, the mother of Andrew Wurst, who opened fire on his middle-school dance in 1998, killing a teacher, has battled prison officials to upgrade her son's therapy. She has been rebuffed. So Wurst remains totally delusional, according to psychiatrist Robert Sadoff, who examined him. Sadoff wrote that Wurst believes "he is real but everyone else is unreal." That includes the teacher he killed, John Gilette, who in Wurst's mind "was already dead or unreal." Wurst told Sadoff that, excepting himself, everyone has been programmed by the government by means of "time tablets" that control people's thoughts.

"Wurst believes 'he is real but everyone else is unreal.'"

27   There are other kids lost in their own worlds. Trickey, according to a report of the Oklahoma Office of Juvenile Affairs, "does not show any remorse for his crime and has little insight into his problems." Father John Kiernan, who used to visit Solomon regularly, says he seemed unaware of the consequences of his rampage. But in 1999, Solomon carved an X across his chest, apparently with a fingernail, and

last January he attempted suicide by swallowing 22 pills of the antidepressant Elavil that he had bought from another inmate.

28   Many years will pass before most of the shooters come up for possible release. Three of them expect never to be paroled. Others will be men of 50 or even 70 before they have that option. But a handful of these boys, sentenced in more lenient states, will be released during the next five to seven years. Trickey's continued detention is reviewed every six months, and he will certainly go free by the time he turns 19. Cordova gets out at age 21. So do Johnson and Golden.

"For his part, Solomon is in for 40 years. He's likely to be haunted by nightmares for much of that duration."

29   For his part, Solomon is in for 40 years. He's likely to be haunted by nightmares for much of that duration. "I've been having dreams and many flashbacks, and most recently, I have been hearing screams," he wrote after his arrest. "I know that it's just in my mind, [but] it's like I'm really hearing them, as if someone were screaming in my face. Usually when it's time to go to sleep and everything is quiet is when my thoughts get worst, because it's all I can hear." Of a dream, he said, "I see myself standing there, shooting me." In his sleep, he is his own victim. And when he wakes up, he is too.

READING CLOSELY AND THINKING CRITICALLY

1. How do family, friends, and others react to the 12 boys in the essay who gunned down teachers and schoolmates?
2. What prompted the boys in the essay to kill? How are they responding to their incarceration in adult prisons?
3. The authors indicate that some young killers may have been mentally ill at the time they committed their crimes. Should mental illness influence whether juveniles are tried in the adult system? Why or why not?
4. Why do some affluent young people become school shooters?
5. In paragraph 23, the authors present evidence that the publicity surrounding school shootings contributes to other school shootings. Should media coverage of these events be limited? Why or why not?
6. Do the authors advance a particular point of view, or is the essay unbiased? Explain.

EXAMINING STRUCTURE AND STRATEGY

1. Do the opening paragraphs of the essay engage your interest? Why or why not?
2. The authors include direct quotations of the words of the jailed boys. What is the effect of those quotations? Do they help the authors achieve their purpose? Explain.
3. In paragraph 8, the authors suggest a little about the exploitation and abuse experienced by juveniles in the adult system. Should they have included more information about the horrors of prison life? Why or why not?

4. In paragraph 3, the authors tell how many prisoners they studied, how long they studied them, how many people the prisoners killed, and how many they wounded. Why do they provide this information?

5. The authors conclude by mentioning Solomon's nightmares. What effect does that conclusion create?

NOTING COMBINED PATTERNS

1. The authors use cause-and-effect analysis for more than one informational purpose. What informational purposes does the cause-and-effect analysis serve?

2. The authors use exemplification for more than one informational purpose. What informational purposes does the exemplification serve?

CONSIDERING LANGUAGE AND STYLE

1. In the first sentence, the authors refer to Nathaniel Brazill as "the boy killer." Why do they use that phrase?

2. Consult your dictionary if you do not know the meaning of these words and phrases: *mete out* (paragraph 2), *engender* (paragraph 4), *sociopaths* (paragraph 4), *cohort* (paragraph 5), *contagion* (paragraph 5), *reneged* (paragraph 8), *affluent* (paragraph 22), *salient* (paragraph 23).

For discussion and writing assignments based on "Young Voices from the Cell," see below.

ASSIGNMENTS FOR DISCUSSION AND WRITING

"Little Adult Criminals," "Should Juvenile Offenders Be Tried as Adults?" "Adult Crime, Adult Time," and "Young Voices from the Cell"

1. **For discussion in class or online.** Answer any or all of the following questions: How much bullying goes on in schools? Have you witnessed or experienced bullying? If so, how did you deal with it? How can schools deal with bullying? If your instructor directs you to do so, post your responses to your class Web site.

2. **Writing in your journal.** In "Young Voices from the Cell," the authors describe life in prison. How do you react to that description?

3. **Using argumentation for a purpose.** The purposes in the assignments are possibilities. You may establish whatever purpose you like, within your instructor's guidelines.

    •   Write a guest editorial for your local newspaper arguing for instituting conflict resolution classes and initiatives to deal with bullying in elementary and middle schools. Your purpose can be to convince readers to write members of the state board of education to petition for these changes.

    •   In paragraph 10 of "Young Voices from the Cell," the authors note that Evan Ramsey's friends encouraged him to commit murder and that parents and school officials were criticized for not trying to stop the Columbine shooters. Should we prosecute those who have reason to believe a shooting might occur but fail to report their knowledge to police? Argue your assertion to soften the objections of a hostile reader.

- Paragraph 24 of "Young Voices from the Cell" quotes Robert Johnson, commissioner of Mississippi's Department of Corrections, as saying, "We don't make any pretense about trying to rehabilitate someone who is going to spend their natural life in prison." Agree or disagree with this position to convince a wavering reader.
- Write a speech suitable for a middle school assembly to be held at the beginning of the school year. Your purpose is to convince students not to engage in bullying and to show students how to behave if they are the targets of or witnesses to bullying.
- Currently, juveniles cannot be executed for committing murder. They can, however, be incarcerated for life. Argue for or against life sentences for juveniles convicted of murder: alternatively, argue for the death penalty for juveniles found guilty of murder. Your audience is average readers of your local newspaper.

4. **Analyzing and assessing.** Write a review of "Little Adult Criminals," "Should Juvenile Offenders Be Tried as Adults?" "Adult Crime, Adult Time," and "Young Voices from the Cell" by noting what their main points are, which of the points are the most compelling or best argued, and which are the least compelling and least argued. Be sure to explain the reasons for your assessments.

5. **Connecting and synthesizing the readings.** Explain why adolescents become violent and whether there is more we can do to prevent teen violence. In addition to the readings in this section and your own experience and observation, you can draw on these readings that say something about adolescence: "Salvation" (page 203), "The Poncho Bearer" (page 212), "Ring Leader" (page 217), and "College Pressures" (page 509).

6. **Drawing on sources.** Agree or disagree with the concept "adult time for adult crime." Be sure to raise and counter significant objections to your assertion. If you would like to read more on the subject, visit the Public Broadcasting System's *Frontline* Web site at www.pbs.org/wgbh/pages/frontline/shows/juvenile or look up "juvenile justice" in the *Social Sciences Index* in your library reference room.

BACKGROUND: Conservative political commentator Cinnamon Stillwell is a one-time columnist and contributing editor for *SFGate.com,* the online sister of the *San Francisco Chronicle.* She was also a staff writer for the New Media Alliance and is currently the West Coast representative for Campus Watch, a Middle East Forum think-tank affiliated with Daniel Pipes, who is mentioned in paragraph 8. For Campus Watch, Stillwell monitors Middle East studies programs in northern California colleges. A frequent blogger at a number of sites, including *Kesher Talk,* Stillwell has written for *the World Jewish News Agency, Front Page Magazine, Accuracy in Media, Intellectual Conservative,* and *the Conservative Voice.* She has written on immigration issues, Somalia, the post-9/11 world, anti-Semitism, media bias, and the Iraq war. "Mob Rule on College Campuses" first appeared on *SFGate.com* in 2006.

COMBINED PATTERNS AND THEIR PURPOSES: With *exemplification,* Cinnamon Stillwell **informs** readers that conservative speakers on college campuses have often been unable to speak freely because of what she characterizes as the bullying behavior of student liberals. Stillwell also uses *cause-and-effect analysis* to **persuade** her readers of the negative effects of this suppression of speech and (by extension) of the fact that it should stop.

Mob Rule on College Campuses

BY CINNAMON STILLWELL

America's college campuses, once thought to be bastions of free speech, have become increasingly intolerant toward the practice. Visiting speakers whose views do not conform to the prevailing left-leaning political mind-set on most campuses are at particular risk of having their free speech rights infringed upon.

2   While academia has its own crimes to atone for, it's the students who have become the bullies as of late. A disturbing number seem to feel that theirs is an inviolate world to which no one of differing opinion need apply. As a result, everything from pie throwing to disrupting speeches to attacks on speakers has become commonplace.

As you read
Notice how Stillwell chooses words to move her readers' emotions.

3   Conservative speakers have long been the targets of such illiberal treatment. The violent reception given to Jim Gilchrist, founder of the Minuteman Project, an anti-illegal immigration group, at Columbia University in October is a recent example. Gilchrist had been invited to speak by the Columbia University College Republicans, but was prevented from doing so by an unruly mob of students. What could have been mere heckling descended into yelling, screaming, kicking and punching, culminating in the rushing of the stage and Gilchrist being shuttled off by security.

4   The fact that the rioting students could be heard yelling, "He has no right to speak!" was telling. Apparently, in their minds, neither Gilchrist nor anyone else with whom they disagree has a right to express their viewpoints. In any other setting this would be called exactly what it is—totalitarianism. But in the untouchable Ivy League world of Columbia, it was chalked up to student activism gone awry. While condemning the incident, Columbia University President Lee Bollinger has yet to apologize to Gilchrist or to conclude the supposed investigation into the affair. In other words, mob rule won the day.

BAY AREA PC INTOLERANCE

5   Such behavior is certainly not limited to East Coast universities. Last February at San Francisco State University, former liberal activist-author turned conservative activist-author David Horowitz had his entire speech shouted down by a group of protesters. Composed primarily of students and other members of the Spartacus Youth Club, a Trotskyist organization, the group stood in the back of the room shouting slogans and comments at every turn.

6   Even this was not enough to warrant their removal, so Horowitz and his audience, which included me, simply had to suffer through the experience. Horowitz, whose speech centered on his Academic Bill of Rights,[1] took on his critics and attempted to engage them in dialogue, with varying degrees of success. But those who actually came to hear him speak, whether out of sympathy for his views or out of a desire to tackle them intellectually, were unable to do so fully because of the actions of a few bullies.

7   It is not only conservative speakers who are at risk of having their free speech rights trampled upon on American college campuses. Those who dare criticize radical Islam in any way, shape or form tend to suffer the same fate.

8   In 2004, UC Berkeley became the locus for bullying behavior during a speech by Islam scholar Daniel Pipes. I was witness to the spectacle, one I'll never forget. Members of the Muslim Student Association and other protesters formed a disruptive group in the audience, shouting, jeering and chanting continually. They booed loudly throughout and called Pipes everything from "racist" and "Zionist" (which in their minds is an insult) to "racist Jew"—all because Pipes had the audacity to propose that moderate Muslims distance themselves from extremist elements in their midst; that in tackling terrorism authorities take into account the preponderance of Muslim perpetrators and that Israel has a right to exist peacefully among its neighbors.

9   This was hardly the first time that UC Berkeley students had espoused hostility toward speakers with "unpopular" views or those hailing from "unpopular" countries such as Israel. Nonetheless, it was a wake-up call for many in the audience who had not yet experienced first-hand the intimidation of the mob.

---

[1]The Academic Bill of Rights emphasizes "intellectual diversity" and lists the rights of students not to be indoctrinated by political propagandists in the classroom. Some say that the underlying purpose is to force colleges to hire conservative professors.

ARAB REFORMERS SILENCED

10   Recently, reformers from within the Arab world itself have been on the receiving end of such treatment. Whether it be the work of student groups or of faculty, insurmountable security restrictions and last-minute cancellations have a strange way of arising whenever such figures are invited to speak on college campuses.

11   Arab American activist and author Nonie Darwish was to speak at Brown University earlier this month, when the event was canceled because her views were deemed "too controversial" by members of the Muslim Students' Association. Given that Darwish is the author of the recently released book *Now They Call Me Infidel: Why I Renounced Jihad for America, Israel and the War on Terror,* such claims are hardly unpredictable. Like most Arab reformers, Darwish must overcome the resistance within her own community, aided and abetted by misguided liberal sympathizers, in order to get her message across.

12   Darwish was born and raised a Muslim in Egypt and later lived in Gaza. It was during this time that she had several experiences that led her to reject the anti-Semitism and anti-Americanism with which she was indoctrinated as a child. She eventually converted to Christianity and emigrated to the United States. She has since dedicated her life to exposing the ways that hatred and intolerance are crippling the Muslim world and leading to violence against non-Muslims.

13   Her pro-Israel views led to an invitation from the campus Jewish group Hillel to speak at Brown University. Unfortunately, the very same organization later backed out, fearing that their relationship with the Muslim Students' Association would be harmed by the experience. But if such a relationship is based on mutually assured censorship, then it's hardly worth preserving. In the end, all of Brown's students missed out on what would undoubtedly have been a thought-provoking experience.

14   Word has it that Brown University has re-invited Darwish to speak, no doubt in response to the furor, so perhaps students will have that opportunity after all.

TERRORISTS RECANT

15   Walid Shoebat, a former PLO terrorist turned Christian convert and outspoken anti-jihadist, fared slightly better at Columbia University in October. Shoebat is the author of *Why I Left Jihad: The Root of Terrorism and the Return of Radical Islam.* He was invited to speak by the Columbia College Republicans, along with former Lebanese terrorist Zachariah Anani and former Nazi Hitler Youth member and German soldier Hilmar von Campe. All three have renounced their former anti-Semitic views and dedicated themselves to exposing radical Islam in a no-holds-barred fashion.

16   They managed to give their presentation, but the turnout was greatly impacted by last-minute changes to security policies implemented in the wake of the Jim Gilchrist debacle. As a result, 75 to 120 people who had RSVP'd for the event were turned away at the door because only Columbia students and 20 guests were allowed to attend. An e-mail sent out 3 hours before the event was the only forewarning, and as one would expect, most of those planning to attend didn't receive it in time. The event had been widely advertised in the blogosphere, and those denied entry were not only greatly inconvenienced but also greatly disappointed.

17   Members of student groups who had boycotted the event were much cheerier at the prospect of a low turnout. A post at the blog for the Blue and White, Columbia's

undergraduate magazine, expressed eagerness for "pretty pictures of empty chairs." Unfortunately, they got their wish, to the detriment of open discourse at Columbia.

ILLIBERAL MOB RULE

18   It's a sad state of affairs indeed when the figures of moderation and reform that many who call themselves liberal or progressive should in theory support are instead shunned in the name of political correctness. For how can one expect to promote progress while helping to stifle the voices at its heart?

19   People such as Shoebat and Darwish, who literally risk their lives to call attention to a grave threat to all our rights, are the true freedom fighters of our day. But far too many accord that label to those who choose to effect political change by blowing themselves up in a crowd of civilians or by randomly lobbing rockets into homes and schools or by promoting hatred of other religions. By excusing such behavior and simultaneously helping to suppress reformers, liberal student groups are in fact aiding the very totalitarian forces they claim to oppose. They have in effect become part of the problem, not part of the solution.

20   It would be nice if we could look to our colleges and universities as the bearers of progress, but at this rate it seems an unlikely prospect. If we are to truly promote an atmosphere of intellectual openness, respectful political debate and the free flow of ideas on campus, then we must stem the tide of thuggery, bullying and intolerance that threatens to subsume future generations.

21   Otherwise, we cede the day to mob rule.

Copyright © 2001 Larry Wright, *The Detroit News* and PoliticalCartoons.com. Reprinted with permission.

READING CLOSELY AND THINKING CRITICALLY

1. What issue is Stillwell arguing, and what is her assertion about that issue?
2. According to the author, in what way are some student liberals guilty of "mob rule"? Why does she think these liberal students are suppressing speech rather than exercising their own right to free speech?
3. Why do you think that some university administrators fail to punish those who disrupt or prevent the speech of conservative speakers?
4. What assumptions connect Stillwell's claim and her support?
5. In paragraph 18, Stillwell says that conservative speakers whose speech is disrupted are victims of political correctness. How so?

EXAMINING STRUCTURE AND STRATEGY

1. Where does Stillwell state the issue and assertion?
2. What element of logos appears in the essay?
3. How does Stillwell establish her credibility and, therefore, add an element of ethos to her argument?
4. How would you describe Stillwell's tone? (See page 69 on tone.)
5. Why do the words *unpopular* and *too controversial* appear in quotation marks in paragraphs 9 and 11?

NOTING COMBINED PATTERNS

1. How does Stillwell use examples to help her fulfill her writing purpose?
2. How does Stillwell use cause-and-effect analysis to help her achieve her writing purpose?

CONSIDERING LANGUAGE AND STYLE

1. How does Stillwell's word choice contribute to the emotional appeal—the pathos—of the essay?
2. Stillwell refers to totalitarianism in paragraph 4 and to a Trotskyist in paragraph 5. How do these words play on readers' emotions and help achieve the author's persuasive purpose?
3. Consult a dictionary if you are unsure of the meaning of these words: *bastions* (paragraph 1), *academia* (paragraph 2), *inviolate* (paragraph 2), *locus* (paragraph 8), *subsume* (paragraph 20).

For discussion and writing assignments based on "Mob Rule on College Campuses," see page 650.

BACKGROUND: An award-winning professor, Charles R. Lawrence began his teaching career at the University of San Francisco and went on to teach at Stanford University. Currently, he is law professor at Georgetown University. He is an expert on antidiscrimination law, equal protection, and theories of race. He has written two books with Mari Matsuda: *Words That Wound: Critical Race Theory, Assaultive Speech, and the First Amendment* (1993) and *We Won't Go Back: Making the Case for Affirmative Action* (1997). Lawrence adapted the following essay from a speech he delivered to the American Civil Liberties Union. This written version was first published in the *Chronicle of Higher Education* (1989), which is read primarily by college faculty and administrators.

THE PATTERN AND ITS PURPOSE: In his essay, Charles R. Lawrence uses *cause-and-effect analysis* to **persuade** readers that hate speech on college campuses should not be protected.

The Debate over Placing Limits on Racist Speech Must Not Ignore the Damage It Does to Its Victims

BY CHARLES R. LAWRENCE III

I have spent the better part of my life as a dissenter. As a high school student, I was threatened with suspension for my refusal to participate in a civil-defense drill, and I have been a conspicuous consumer of my First Amendment liberties ever since. There are very strong reasons for protecting even racist speech. Perhaps the most important of these is that such protection reinforces our society's commitment to tolerance as a value, and that by protecting bad speech from government regulation, we will be forced to combat it as a community.

2   But I also have a deeply felt apprehension about the resurgence of racial violence and the corresponding rise in the incidence of verbal and symbolic assault and harassment to which blacks and other traditionally subjugated and excluded groups are subjected. I am troubled by the way the debate has been framed in response to the recent surge of racist incidents on college and university campuses and in response to some universities' attempts to regulate harassing speech. The problem has been framed as one in which the liberty of free speech is in conflict with the elimination of racism. I believe this has placed the bigot on the moral high ground and fanned the rising flames of racism.

3   Above all, I am troubled that we have not listened to the real victims, that we have shown so little understanding of their injury, and that we have abandoned those whose race, gender, or sexual preference continues to make them second-class citizens. It seems to me a very

sad irony that the first instinct of civil libertarians has been to challenge even the smallest, most narrowly framed efforts by universities to provide black and other minority students with the protection the Constitution guarantees them.

4   The landmark case of *Brown* v. *Board of Education* is not a case that we normally think of as a case about speech. But *Brown* can be broadly read as articulating the principle of equal citizenship. *Brown* held that segregated schools were inherently unequal because of the *message* that segregation conveyed—that black children were an untouchable caste, unfit to go to school with white children. If we understand the necessity of eliminating the system of signs and symbols that signal the inferiority of blacks, then we should hesitate before proclaiming that all racist speech that stops short of physical violence must be defended.

5   University officials who have formulated policies to respond to incidents of racial harassment have been characterized in the press as "thought police," but such policies generally do nothing more than impose sanctions against intentional face-to-face insults. When racist speech takes the form of face-to-face insults, catcalls, or other assaultive speech aimed at an individual or small group of persons, it falls directly within the "fighting words" exception to First Amendment protection. The Supreme Court has held that words which "by their very utterance inflict injury or tend to incite an immediate breach of the peace" are not protected by the First Amendment.

6   If the purpose of the First Amendment is to foster the greatest amount of speech, racial insults disserve that purpose. Assaultive racist speech functions as a preemptive strike. The invective is experienced as a blow, not as a proffered idea, and once the blow is struck, it is unlikely that a dialogue will follow. Racial insults are particularly undeserving of First Amendment protection because the perpetuator's intention is not to discover truth or initiate dialogue but to injure the victim. In most situations, members of minority groups realize that they are likely to lose if they respond to epithets by fighting and are forced to remain silent and submissive.

7   Courts have held that offensive speech may not be regulated in public forums such as streets where the listener may avoid the speech by moving on, but the regulation of otherwise protected speech has been permitted when the speech invades the privacy of the unwilling listener's home or when the unwilling listener cannot avoid the speech. Racist posters, fliers, and graffiti in dormitories, bathrooms, and other common living spaces would seem to clearly fall within the reasoning of these cases. Minority students should not be required to remain in their rooms in order to avoid racial assault. Minimally, they should find a safe haven in their dorms and in all other common rooms that are a part of their daily routine.

8   I would also argue that the university's responsibility for ensuring that these students receive an equal educational opportunity provides a compelling justification for regulations that ensure them safe passage in all common areas. A minority student should not have to risk becoming the target of racially assaulting speech every time he or she chooses to walk across campus. Regulating vilifying speech that cannot be anticipated or avoided would not preclude announced speeches and rallies—situations that would give minority-group members and their allies the chance to organize counterdemonstrations or avoid the speech altogether.

9   The most commonly advanced argument against the regulation of racist speech proceeds something like this: We recognize that minority groups suffer pain and

injury as the result of racist speech, but we must allow this hate mongering for the benefit of society as a whole. Freedom of speech is the lifeblood of our democratic system. It is especially important for minorities because often it is their only vehicle for rallying support for the redress of their grievances. It will be impossible to formulate a prohibition so precise that it will prevent the racist speech you want to suppress without catching in the same net all kinds of speech that it would be unconscionable for a democratic society to suppress.

10   Whenever we make such arguments, we are striking a balance on the one hand between our concern for the continued free flow of ideas and the democratic process dependent on that flow, and, on the other, our desire to further the cause of equality. There can be no meaningful discussion of how we should reconcile our commitment to equality and our commitment to free speech until it is acknowledged that there is real harm inflicted by racist speech and that this harm is far from trivial.

11   To engage in a debate about the First Amendment and racist speech without a full understanding of the nature and extent of that harm is to risk making the First Amendment an instrument of domination rather than a vehicle of liberation. We have not all known the experience of victimization by racist, misogynist, and homophobic speech, nor do we equally share the burden of the societal harm it inflicts. We are often quick to say that we have heard the cry of the victims when we have not.

12   The *Brown* case is again instructive because it speaks directly to the psychic injury inflicted by racist speech by noting that the symbolic message of segregation affected "the hearts and minds" of negro children "in a way unlikely ever to be undone." Racial epithets and harassment often cause deep emotional scarring and feelings of anxiety and fear that pervade every aspect of a victim's life.

13   *Brown* also recognized that black children did not have an equal opportunity to learn and participate in the school community if they bore the additional burden of being subjected to the humiliation and psychic assault contained in the message of segregation. University students bear an analogous burden when they are forced to live and work in an environment where at any moment they may be subjected to denigrating verbal harassment and assault. The same injury was addressed by the Supreme Court when it held that sexual harassment that creates a hostile or abusive work environment violates the ban on sex discrimination in employment of Title VII of the Civil Rights Act of 1964.

14   Carefully drafted university regulations would bar the use of words as assault weapons and leave unregulated even the most heinous of ideas when those ideas are presented at times and places and in manners that provide an opportunity for reasoned rebuttal or escape from immediate injury. The history of the development of the right to free speech has been one of carefully evaluating the importance of free expression and its effects on other important societal interests. We have drawn the line between protected and unprotected speech before without dire results. (Courts have, for example, exempted from the protection of the First Amendment obscene speech and speech that disseminates official secrets, that defames or libels another person, or that is used to form a conspiracy or monopoly.)

15   Blacks and other people of color are skeptical about the argument that even the most injurious speech must remain unregulated because, in an unregulated market-place of ideas, the best ones will rise to the top and gain acceptance. Our experience

tells us quite the opposite. We have seen too many demagogues elected by appealing to America's racism. We have seen too many good liberal politicians shy away from the issues that might brand them as being too closely allied with us.

16 Whenever we decide that racist speech must be tolerated because of the importance of maintaining societal tolerance for all unpopular speech, we are asking blacks and other subordinated groups to bear the burden for the good of all. We must be careful that the ease with which we strike the balance against the regulation of racist speech is in no way influenced by the fact that the cost will be borne by others. We must be certain that those who will pay that price are fairly represented in our deliberations and that they are heard.

17 At the core of the argument that we should resist all government regulation of speech is the ideal that the best cure for bad speech is good, that ideas that affirm equality and the worth of all individuals will ultimately prevail. This is an empty ideal unless those of us who would fight racism are vigilant and unequivocal in that fight. We must look for ways to offer assistance and support to students whose speech and political participation are chilled in a climate of racial harassment.

18 Civil-rights lawyers might consider suing on behalf of blacks whose right to an equal education is denied by a university's failure to ensure a nondiscriminatory educational climate or conditions of employment. We must embark upon the development of a First Amendment jurisprudence grounded in the reality of our history and our contemporary experience. We must think hard about how best to launch legal attacks against the most indefensible forms of hate speech. Good lawyers can create exceptions and narrow interpretations that limit the harm of hate speech without opening the floodgates of censorship.

19 Everyone concerned with these issues must find ways to engage actively in actions that resist and counter the racist ideas that we would have the First Amendment protect. If we fail in this, the victims of hate speech must rightly assume that we are on the oppressors' side.

READING CLOSELY AND THINKING CRITICALLY

1. Lawrence expresses discomfort with the way the debate over hate speech has been framed. What problems does he see?

2. What irony does Lawrence identify in the debate over hate speech? (See page 205 on irony.)

3. Lawrence offers the landmark Supreme Court decision in *Brown* v. *The Board of Education* as one reason to punish hate speech. Explain his reasoning. Do you agree with his reasoning? Why or why not?

4. Why does Lawrence believe that racial insults do not deserve First Amendment protection?

5. What support and assumption does Lawrence use for his argument in paragraph 12?

6. Lawrence delivered an earlier version of the essay as a speech before members of the American Civil Liberties Union. Characterize the audience for the speech, and consider how that audience was likely to react to Lawrence's thesis. What kind of persuasive goal do you think Lawrence could reasonably have established for the speech?

1. Lawrence opens by noting that he has been a longtime dissenter. Why does he make this opening remark? What does this statement suggest about Lawrence's view of his audience?

2. What objections does Lawrence raise, and how does he counter them?

3. Does Lawrence rely more on logical reasoning or emotional appeal to persuade his reader?

4. In paragraph 14, Lawrence notes historical exemptions to free speech. Does that information contribute to the persuasive quality of the essay? Explain.

5. Lawrence uses deductive reasoning to present his argument. What are his major and minor premises?

6. Which paragraphs form the conclusion of the essay? What approach does Lawrence take to that conclusion?

CONSIDERING LANGUAGE AND STYLE

1. In paragraph 2, Lawrence mentions symbolic assaults. Cite examples of symbolic (nonverbal) language that is threatening to some people.

2. Consult a dictionary if you are unfamiliar with any of these words: *catcalls* (paragraph 5), *preemptive strike* (paragraph 6), *invective* (paragraph 6), *epithets* (paragraph 6), *vilifying* (paragraph 8), *hate mongering* (paragraph 9), *unconscionable* (paragraph 9), *misogynist* (paragraph 11), *heinous* (paragraph 14), *demagogues* (paragraph 15).

For discussion and writing assignments based on this essay, see page 650.

BACKGROUND: Harvey A. Silverglate (b. 1942) is a Boston attorney who specializes in civil liberties, academic freedom, and student rights law. He is also a founder and director of the Foundation for Individual Rights for Education (FIRE), an organization mentioned in the essay that monitors and advocates for free-speech issues on college campuses. A three-decade member of the Massachusetts American Civil Liberties Union (ACLU), Silverglate has taught at Harvard Law School. With Alan Charles Kors, he wrote *The Shadow University* (1999). He has also written for the *National Law Journal,* the *Wall Street Journal,* the *Boston Globe,* and *Media Studies Journal.* Attorney Greg Lukianoff is president of FIRE. A frequent guest on local and national radio and television programs, he has also testified before Congress about free speech issues on college campuses. Lukianoff has written for several publications, including the *The Huffington Post, Chronicle of Higher Education,* the *Stanford Technology Law Review,* the *Daily Journal of Los Angeles,* and the *Daily Journal of San Francisco.* "Speech Codes: Alive and Well at Colleges" was published in 2003 in the *Chronicle of Higher Education,* a periodical for university faculty and administrators.

COMBINED PATTERNS AND THEIR PURPOSE: To **persuade** readers that campus speech codes are a harmful form of censorship, Silverglate and Lukianoff rely heavily on *exemplification* and *cause-and-effect analysis.* An element of *definition* also appears because the meaning of important terms must be clarified.

Speech Codes: Alive and Well at Colleges

BY HARVEY A. SILVERGLATE AND GREG LUKIANOFF

Five years ago, a higher-education editor for *The New York Times* informed one of us, Harvey Silverglate, that Neil L. Rudenstine—then president of Harvard University—had insisted that Harvard did not have, much less enforce, any "speech codes." Silverglate suggested the editor dig deeper, because virtually any undergraduate could contest the president's claim.

2   A mere three years earlier, the faculty of the Harvard Law School had adopted "Sexual Harassment Guidelines" targeted at "seriously offensive" speech. The guidelines were passed in response to a heated campus controversy involving a law-student parody of an expletive-filled *Harvard Law Review* article that promoted a postmodernist, gender-related view of the nature of law. In response to an outcry by outraged campus feminists and their allies, a law professor lodged a formal complaint against the parodists with the college's administrative board.

As you read
Ask yourself why colleges adopt speech codes.

3   When the board dismissed the charge on the technicality that the law school had no speech code that would specifically outlaw such a parody, the dean at the time appointed a faculty committee to draft the guidelines, which remain in force today. The intention was to prevent, or punish if necessary, future offensive gender-related speech that might create a "hostile environment" for female law students at Harvard. As far as Silverglate (who lives and works near the Harvard campus and follows events there closely) has observed, there has not been a truly biting parody on hot-button issues related to gender politics at the law school since.

4   Last fall, officials at Harvard Business School admonished and threatened with punishment an editor of the school's student-run newspaper for publishing a cartoon critical of the administration. He resigned in protest over the administration's assault on the paper's editorial independence.

5   At virtually the same time, after a controversy in which a law student was accused of racially insensitive speech, a cry went up for adopting "Discriminatory Harassment Guidelines" to parallel the code that outlawed gender-based insults. As the controversy progressed, some students accused two professors of insensitivity for trying to discuss the issues in class. Soon after the Black Law Students Association demanded that one of those professors be disciplined and banned from teaching required first-year classes, he announced that he would not teach his course for the rest of the semester. The other professor insisted on continuing to teach, but the dean's office announced that all of his classes had to be tape-recorded so that any students who felt offended being in his presence could instead listen to the recorded lecture.

6   All of that at a university that, as President Rudenstine supposedly assured *The New York Times*, did not have, much less enforce, a speech code.

7   Today, many in higher education still share Rudenstine's apparent belief that a speech code exists only if it is prominently stamped SPEECH CODE in the student handbook. To them, any speech code is an anachronism, a failed relic of the 1980s that has disappeared from all but the most repressive backwaters of academe.

8   But speech codes are alive and well, if one is realistic about what makes a campus regulation a speech code. The Foundation for Individual Rights in Education defines a speech code as *any campus regulation that punishes, forbids, heavily regulates, or restricts a substantial amount of protected speech.*[1] Thus defined, speech codes are the rule rather than the exception in higher education.

9   Why does virtually no college call its speech code by that name? For one thing, in the 1980s and 90s, every legal challenge of a clearly identified speech code at a public institution was successful. To maintain a weapon against speech that is "offensive" or "uncivil" (or merely too robust), the authors of the current stealthier generation of speech codes have adopted highly restrictive "speech zone" policies, e-mail policies that ban "offensive" speech, "diversity statements" with provisions that punish those uttering any "intolerant expression," and, of course, the ubiquitous "harassment policies" aimed at "hostile" viewpoints and words that operate by redefining speech as a form of conduct.

10   FIRE initiated, in April, a litigation project aimed at abolishing such codes at public colleges and universities, beginning with a lawsuit charging that various policies at Shippensburg University are unconstitutional. Shippensburg promises only to protect speech that does not "provoke, harass, demean, intimidate, or harm another." Shippensburg's "Racism and Cultural Diversity" statement (modified by the university after FIRE filed suit) defined harassment as "unsolicited, unwanted conduct which annoys, threatens, or alarms a person or group." Shippensburg also has "speech zones" that restrict protests to only two areas on the campus.

---

[1]Protected speech is the communication guaranteed by the First Amendment to the Constitution to be unrestricted by the government.

11   In a recent *Chronicle* article, Shippensburg's president, Anthony F. Ceddia, complained that FIRE had "cobbled together words and expressions of different policies and procedures." That is true; it found unconstitutional provisions in many different places—the student handbook and the university's Web site, to cite just two—and is challenging all of them.

12   FIRE has been developing an online database of policies that restrict speech on both private and public campuses. Given the longstanding assumption that academic freedom at liberal arts colleges protects offensive and unpopular speech, the number and variety of such policies are startling. FIRE's still-in-progress survey and analysis demonstrates that a clear majority of higher-education institutions have substantial speech restrictions and many others have lesser restrictions that still, arguably, infringe on academic freedom.

13   Some codes, of course, are worse than others. Some are patently unconstitutional; others, artfully written by offices of general counsels, seek to obfuscate their intention to prohibit or discourage certain speech. However, there is no excuse for a liberal-arts institution, public or private, to punish speech, no matter how impolite, impolitic, unpopular, or ornery.

14   No one denies that a college can and should ban true harassment—but a code that *calls* itself a "racial-harassment code" does not thereby magically inoculate itself against free-speech and academic-freedom obligations. The recent controversy over "racial harassment" at Harvard Law School has been replicated on campuses across the country, often with outcomes as perilous to academic freedom. For example, in 1999, a professor at the Columbia University School of Law administered a criminal law exam posing a complex question concerning the issues of feticide, abortion, violence against women, and consent to violence. Some women in the class complained to two faculty members, who then told the law-school dean that the professor's exam was so insensitive to the women in the class that it may have constituted harassment. The dean brought the case to Columbia's general counsel before concluding—correctly of course—after a dialogue with FIRE that academic freedom absolutely protected the professor.

15   Such examples demonstrate the persistence of the notion that administrators may muzzle speech that some students find "offensive," in the name of protecting civil rights. Further, the continuing existence of these codes relies on people's unwillingness to criticize any restriction that sports the "progressive" veneer of preventing racial or sexual "harassment"—even when the codes themselves go far beyond the traditional boundaries of academic and constitutional freedom. Fortunately, some see these codes for what they are and recognize that there is nothing progressive about censorship.

16   It should be obvious that allowing colleges to promulgate broad and amorphous rules that can punish speech, regardless of the intention, will result in self-censoring and administrative abuses. Consider the case of Mercedes Lynn de Uriarte, a professor at the University of Texas at Austin. In 1999, after filing an employment grievance, she received notice that the campus's office of equal employment opportunity had chosen to investigate her for "ethnic harassment" of another professor in her department. Both de Uriarte and the accusing professor were Mexican-American. The facts suggest that the ethnic-harassment accusation was little more than an excuse for the university to retaliate against de Uriarte for filing

Copyright © John Pritchett. Reprinted with permission.

the grievance. After nine months of pressing de Uriarte to answer personal questions about her beliefs and why she disliked the other professor, the EEO office concluded that there was no evidence of "ethnic harassment" but scolded de Uriarte for "harboring personal animosity" toward the other professor and for not being sufficiently cooperative with the investigating dean.

17   In 2001 at Tufts University, a female undergraduate filed sexual-harassment charges against a student publication, citing a sexual-harassment code and claiming a satirical cartoon and text made her a "sex object." A vocal member of the Student Labor Action Movement, she was offended when the paper mocked "oh-so-tight" slam tank tops (amid other jokes about Madonna and President Bush). Hearings were initiated. FIRE successfully persuaded the hearing panel to reject the attempted censorship.

18   Those are just two examples among dozens that FIRE has seen recently where speech codes are used against students or faculty members. They illustrate not only that these codes are enforced, but that they are enforced against speech that would be clearly protected in the larger society.

19   Moreover, virtually none of the cases that FIRE has dealt with have followed the paradigm that "hate-speech codes" were supposedly crafted to combat: the intentional hurling of an epithet at a member of a racial or sexual minority. Overwhelmingly, speech codes are used against much milder expression, or even against expression of a particular unpopular or officially disfavored viewpoint.

20   The situation of Steve Hinkle, a student at California Polytechnic State University, is another case in point. In the fall of 2002, he posted fliers for a speech by C. Mason Weaver, the author of *It's OK to Leave the Plantation.* In his book, Weaver, an African-American writer, argues that government-assistance programs place many black people in a cycle of poverty and dependence similar to slavery. The flier included the place and time of the speech, the name of the book, and the author's picture. When Hinkle tried to post a flier in one public area, several students approached him and demanded that he not post the "offensive" flier. One student actually called the campus police, whose reports note that the students complained of "a suspicious white male passing out literature of an offensive racial nature." Hinkle was subjected to administrative hearings over the next half year and was found guilty of "disruption" for trying to post the flier.

21   Unless one considers posting a flier with factually accurate information a "hate crime," it is clear such speech codes are used to punish speech that administrators or students simply dislike. That should not come as a surprise to any student of history. When broad powers and unchecked authority are granted to officials—even for what are claimed to be the noblest of goals—those powers will be abused. Indeed, the Supreme Court has ruled unequivocally that "hate-speech laws," in contrast to "hate-crimes laws," are unconstitutional. Yet most of the speech prosecuted on college campuses does not even rise to the level of hate speech.

22   Some argue that speech codes communicate to students the kind of society to which we all *should* aspire. That is perhaps the most pernicious of all justifications, for it makes unexamined assumptions about the power of administrators to reach intrusively into the hearts and consciences of students. There is nothing ideal about a campus where protests and leaflets are quarantined to tiny, remote "speech zones," or where being inoffensive is a higher value than intellectual engagement.

23   Yet even if one agrees with such "aspirations," it is antithetical to a liberal arts college to coerce others into sharing them. The threat of sanctions crosses the clear line between *encouraging* such aspirations and *coercing* fealty to them, whether genuine or affected. An administrator's employing the suasion of the bully pulpit differs crucially from using authority to bully disfavored opinions into submission.

24   Some people contend that the codes are infrequently enforced. The facts demonstrate otherwise, but even if a campus never enforced its speech code, the code would remain a palpable form of coercion. As long as the policy exists, the *threat* of enforcement remains real and will inevitably influence some people's speech. In First Amendment law, that is known as a "chilling"effect:[2] Merely by disseminating the codes in student handbooks, administrators can prevent much of the speech they disfavor. Students, seeing what is banned—or even guessing at what might be banned as they struggle with the breadth or vagueness of the definitions—will play it safe and avoid engaging in speech that, even though constitutionally protected, may offend a student or a disciplinary board.

---

[2]A "chilling effect" occurs when regulations or a particular atmosphere discourage free speech.

25   In the long run, speech codes—actively enforced or not—send the message that it is OK to ban controversial or arguably ugly expressions that some do not wish to hear. Students will not forget that lesson once they get their diplomas. A whole generation of American students is learning that its members should hide their deeply held unpopular beliefs, while other students realize that they have the power, even the right, to censor opinions they dislike.

26   Take the case at Ithaca College last spring, when the College Republicans brought to campus Bay Buchanan, the sister of Patrick Buchanan, for a speech entitled "The Failures of Feminism." Instead of protesting the speech or debating Buchanan's points, several students demanded that the campus police stop the event and declare it a "bias-related incident"—a punishable offense. The "Bias-Related Incidents Committee" ultimately declared the speech protected but then announced that it would explore developing policies that could prohibit similar future speeches. Outrageous though it seems, the students' reaction is understandable. Ithaca College teaches that it is okay to ban "biased" speech. The "Bias-Related Incidents Committee" shunned free speech as a sacred value and instead sought ways to punish disagreeable viewpoints in the future.

27   FIRE generally eschews litigation in favor of reasoning with campus administrators in detailed philosophical, academic, and moral arguments made in memorandums and letters. However, speech codes have proved remarkably impervious to reasoned arguments, for while FIRE often can snatch individual students from the jaws of speech prosecutions, administrators rarely abandon the codes themselves. (A happy exception was when in 1999 the Faculty Senate of the University of Wisconsin at Madison voted to repeal the longstanding code that restricted faculty speech.) FIRE thus initiated its litigation campaign.

28   Shippensburg is the beginning. In cooperation with FIRE's Legal Network, attorney Carol Sobel in May challenged a speech code at Citrus College, in California, where students were allocated three remote areas—less than 1 percent of the campus—for protest activities. Even if they were to protest within the ironically named "free speech area," students had to get permission in advance, alert campus security of the intended message, and provide any printed materials that they wished to distribute, in addition to a host of other restrictions. Further, this free-speech area was open only from "8 A.M. through 6 P.M. Monday through Friday." Citrus's student-conduct code banned "lewd, indecent, obscene or offensive conduct [and] expression," and included a number of other highly restrictive provisions. Just two weeks after the lawsuit was filed, the administration yielded and rescinded all of the provisions listed above. It is unfortunate that it took a lawsuit to demonstrate that restrictions on words have no place on the modern liberal-arts campus.

29   Colleges must recognize that growth, progress, and innovation require the free and occasionally outrageous exchange of views. Without speech codes, students are more likely to interact honestly. Having one's beliefs challenged is not a regrettable side effect of openness and intellectual diversity, but an essential part of the educational process. And, in fact, liberty is more than simply a prerequisite for progress; it is, at the deepest level, a fundamental and indispensable way of being human.

READING CLOSELY AND THINKING CRITICALLY

1. Was Neil L. Rudenstine lying when he said that Harvard did not have any speech codes? Explain.
2. Why is it surprising that colleges have speech codes?
3. Why do so many colleges adopt and defend speech codes? Why is it difficult for people to object to speech codes?
4. What are speech zones? How do speech zones affect free speech on college campuses?
5. List the negative effects of speech codes. Can you think of any positive effects?

EXAMINING STRUCTURE AND STRATEGY

1. The thesis of the essay is delayed until paragraph 8. What do the paragraphs before the thesis accomplish?
2. In which paragraphs do the authors raise and counter objections?
3. Do the authors rely mostly on logos, ethos, or pathos? Why?
4. The authors write a strong conclusion. What makes it so effective?

NOTING COMBINED PATTERNS

1. Silverglate and Lukianoff use many examples throughout the essay. Cite four paragraphs that include examples. What purpose do the examples serve? Would the essay be as persuasive without them? Explain.
2. The authors use definition in paragraphs 8–10 and 24. Why?
3. How does the cause-and-effect analysis in the essay help the authors achieve their persuasive purpose?

CONSIDERING LANGUAGE AND STYLE

1. List three words or phrases that describe the authors' writing style in "Speech Codes: Alive and Well at Colleges."
2. The audience for the *Chronicle of Higher Education,* where "Speech Codes: Alive and Well at Colleges" first appeared, is college professors and administrators. How would the language, style, and emphasis of the essay be different if the audience were college students?
3. Consult a dictionary if you are unsure of the meaning of any of these words: *postmodernist* (paragraph 2), *anachronism* (paragraph 7), *ubiquitous* (paragraph 9), *obfuscate* (paragraph 13), *amorphous* (paragraph 16), *paradigm* (paragraph 19), *fealty* (paragraph 23), *suasion* (paragraph 23), *bully pulpit* (paragraph 23).

For discussion and writing assignments based on "Speech Codes: Alive and Well at Colleges," see page 650.

BACKGROUND: An assistant professor of law at Florida International University College of Law, Howard M. Wasserman is an expert on issues related to civil procedure, civil rights, and free speech. Before joining the faculty of FIU, Wasserman was an attorney in Chicago and later a clerk for a U.S. district court judge and for a U.S. court of appeals judge. His many publications include pieces in the Emory, Tulane, and Kentucky law reviews and in the *William and Mary Bill of Rights Journal*. "Fan Profanity" was written for the First Amendment Center's Web site. Operated by Vanderbilt University, this site offers comprehensive coverage of First Amendment issues, including research, commentary, and analysis by legal specialists. You can visit the site at www.firstamendmentcenter.org.

COMBINED PATTERNS AND THEIR PURPOSES: Howard M. Wasserman uses *exemplification* to **inform** readers about the kinds of profane speech used by college sports fans. To **persuade** readers that such speech is protected by the First Amendment, Wasserman draws on *comparison* and *cause-and-effect analysis*. Finally, to clarify terms, Wasserman uses *definition*.

FAN PROFANITY

BY HOWARD M. WASSERMAN

MANY FREE-SPEECH CONTROVERSIES, especially on college campuses, are grounded in concerns for civility, politeness, and good taste. They also tend to follow the same path and end the same way. A government entity regulates speech in an effort to elevate discourse, limit the profane and protect public and personal sensitivities; courts strike down the regulations as violating the First Amendment freedom of speech; and we end up right where we started.

As you read
Consider why university officials are concerned about fan profanity.

2   Colleges may be pursuing a similar course in trying to deal with objectionable cheering by students at sporting events. University of Maryland officials expressed anger and embarrassment following a men's basketball game against conference rival Duke University in January 2004, when fans chanted and sported T-shirts with the slogan "F - - - Duke" and directed epithets at Duke players. This was one of many incidents of offensive or obnoxious cheering by students throughout the country during the 2004 college basketball season.

"...fans chanted and sported T-shirts with the slogan 'F - - - Duke' ..."

3   John K. Anderson, chief of the Educational Affairs Division of the Maryland Attorney General's Office, advised the university that a written code of fan conduct applicable at a university-owned and -operated athletic facility, if "carefully drafted," would be constitutionally permissible. University of Maryland Associate Athletics Director Michael Lipitz began working with a committee of students to consider rules of conduct. The committee ultimately recommended that the university promote voluntary compliance, although rules and formal punishment remain a "last resort" if a proposed standing monitoring committee determines that voluntary compliance is ineffective. Other schools, such as Western Michigan University, currently have, or are studying the need for, similar codes to restrict profanity and other abusive language. And the approach of a new academic year may bring new incidents and new university attempts at regulating fan expression.

4   One can envision guidelines restricting profanity and epithets in signs and chants, as well as imposing a general requirement that students keep things stylish, clever, clean, and classy. Presumably, the sanction would be removal from the arena. The ostensible purpose behind such guidelines is to enable the majority of fans to enjoy the game unburdened by objectionable or offensive signs, messages, and chants. But any such policy enacted and enforced at a public university such as Maryland should not and perhaps will not survive First Amendment scrutiny. On the other hand, a private college, not bound by the strictures of the First Amendment, obviously remains free to impose such restrictions.

5   The speech at issue is expression by fans related to a sporting event, to all aspects of the game and all the participants in the game—what we can call "cheering speech." Cheering speech can be directed at players, coaches, officials, executives, administrators, or other fans. It can be in support of one's own players and team, against the opposing players and team or even critical of one's own players and team. It can be about events on the field or it can target broader social and political issues surrounding the game, the players or sport in general.

6   In advising the university that it could regulate cheering speech, Anderson insisted that fans at sporting events, particularly children, are "captive auditors." They are captives in the arena or stadium; the only way to avoid being offended by the chants or sings is to leave the arena or stop coming to games. This captive status, Anderson argued, alters the ordinary First Amendment burden. Rather than requiring objecting listeners to "avert their eyes" (or ears) to avoid objectionable speech, the university can force speakers, especially students, to alter their manner of communicating to protect the sensibilities of these captive fans.

7   In reality, the captive-audience doctrine is far more limited than Anderson suggests. Courts have found listeners to be captives in only four places: their own homes, the workplace, public elementary and secondary schools, and inside and around abortion clinics. And even in those places, captive-audience status permits government to limit oral expression but not the same message in written form on pickets, signs, or clothing. One certainly could avert one's eyes to avoid viewing the message written on a sign or on the body of a student at a basketball game.

> "One certainly could avert one's eyes to avoid viewing the message written on a sign or on the body of a student at a basketball game."

8   Of course, one problem with cheering speech is that much of it is oral. Fans have complained not only about signs and T-shirts, but also about chants and taunts targeting players, coaches and officials, which other fans may be unable to avoid no matter where in the arena they sit. Objectors must perform the more difficult task of averting their ears to avoid offensive cheers, something that children may be even less able to do. It is true that courts have upheld content-neutral regulations on sound and noise levels to protect captive audiences, beginning with the Supreme Court case *Kovacs v. Cooper* in 1949. But government never has been permitted to protect captive auditors by singling out particular profane or offensive oral messages for selective restriction while leaving related messages on the same subject, uttered at the same volume, undisturbed.

9   More important, the captive-audience doctrine never has been applied to listeners in public places of recreation and entertainment, places to which people voluntarily go for the particular purpose of engaging in expressive activity, in this case cheering on their favorite college team. Fans who pay to attend a college basketball game at an on-campus arena are not captive auditors there, any more than an individual walking on a city street who stumbles across an objectionable political rally or an individual whose office sits above the route of an objectionable parade.

10   The Hobson's choice that Anderson believes this creates for fans—leave the arena and stop attending games or tolerate offensive cheers—is precisely the choice people make in any public place at which expression occurs. It is the same choice that people in the California courthouse had to make when confronted with a jacket emblazoned with the message "F - - - the Draft," a message and manner of expression that the Supreme Court found to be protected from prosecution under a disturbing-the-peace statute in the 1971 landmark case *Cohen v. California.* In fact, leaving was even less of an option there for an objecting auditor whose job required her to remain in the courthouse or an objector conducting business before the court and likely required to be there on pain of contempt or default. It is difficult to reconcile that "F - - - the Draft" is a protected message in a courthouse, but "F - - - Duke" is unprotected amid the cacophony of 20,000 screaming basketball fans. It is even less comprehensible that Paul Cohen's intellectual heir could be prohibited from wearing his jacket (for example, to protest the so-called "backdoor draft"[1] created by extending reservists' service) at a university sports arena governed by a fan speech code.

11   The real import of *Cohen* is the principle that a speaker's choice of words and manner of communication are essential elements of the overall message expressed and government cannot prohibit certain words or manner without also suppressing certain messages in the process. A cheering fan's point of view is bound up in the decision to formulate a particular message by telling an opponent that he "sucks" or by targeting more personal issues. Fans have created controversy by targeting a player whose girlfriend had posed in *Playboy,* chanting "rapist" at a player who had pled guilty to sexual assault and waving fake joints at a player with a history of use. "Fear the Turtle," "We Hate Duke" and "Duke Sucks" are three ways of cheering for the Maryland Terrapins, as well as cheering against Duke. But each conveys a distinct message and point of view and each has ample grounds for constitutional protection within the expressive milieu of a college sports stadium.

12   Because word choice and communicative manner are essential components of free-speech protection, it becomes impossible to enforce any fan-conduct policy in a uniform, non-arbitrary way. The state cannot neutrally define what words or manner are offensive or establish any meaningful standard to measure offensiveness. Justice John Marshall Harlan's memorable phrase in *Cohen* was that "one man's vulgarity is another's lyric," and government's inability to make principled distinctions means "the Constitution leaves matters of taste and style so largely to the individual."

---

[1]Some say that extending the hours of duty of National Guard and reservist troops beyond their expected length of time amounts to a form of conscription.

13   Under current doctrine, offensiveness cannot be measured from the standpoint of the most sensitive person in the crowd; the level of permissible expression cannot be reduced to what the least-tolerant listener will accept. Nor should it be measured from the standpoint of children in the crowd, because, as the Court long has insisted, the level of discourse for an adult audience cannot be reduced to what is fit or proper for children. The university sports arena exemplifies the problem of the mixed audience—how can government regulate speech in the interest of protecting children when the speech occurs before a mixed audience of children and adults? The pithy answer may be that it simply cannot do so. There is no, and can be no,

> "The university sports arena exemplifies the problem of the mixed audience."

baseline for oral speech before a mixed audience; either children unavoidably hear some "adult" expression or we reduce the level of speech to what is suitable for a sandbox.

14   In seeking to control abusive cheering speech, universities apparently do not distinguish among expressive forms. On one hand is blatant use of profanity; on the other hand are epithets or chants that do not employ any of the seven dirty words, but that target opposing teams, players, coaches or officials, perhaps with references to personal life or criminal difficulties. The presumption apparent in Anderson's recommendation to the University of Maryland was that a public university could serve the same interest in protecting children through a single conduct policy that banned both "F - - - Duke" chants and signs and chants and signs targeting a player accused of sexual assault. One can imagine attempts to require students to keep things "polite" or "positive"—cheer for your team and your players, but do not jeer or criticize the opponent (or, for that matter, your own team). Even conceding a government interest in protecting sensitive and juvenile ears from the seven dirty words in public spaces, government goes a step beyond when it begins to restrict particular nonprofane messages that bear on the game played on the field or on the participants in that game.

15   Moreover, the sexual-assault example presents an additional wrinkle. Taunting a player who has been accused of sexual assault may be, at least in part, a social or political statement, protesting or drawing attention to the problem of athlete misbehavior or to the fact that this player continues to be allowed to play for the school despite his off-court misconduct.

16   Perhaps the level of protection turns on the subtlety of the chants. Students are obvious in their attempts to offend when they use profanity, chant "rapist," or wave fake joints. But what if Maryland students chant or wear T-shirts bearing the slogan "Duck Fuke"? This is an obvious play on the profanity that created controversy at Maryland, but it does not use (as opposed to hinting at) dirty words. Should hinting at profanity be enough to justify a restriction on protected manner of expression?

17   Or what if the offensiveness is lost on those who might otherwise be offended? Students at Allen Field House at the University of Kansas were praised for their cleverness during the 2004 season when they chanted "salad tosser" at Texas Tech basketball coach Bob Knight. On the surface, the taunt was a reference to Knight's

infamous verbal altercation several days earlier with the Texas Tech chancellor at a salad bar in Lubbock. But the phrase also is a slang reference to a particular sexual act, a double entendre the students surely knew when they began the chant, but many listeners likely did not.

18   Dissenting in *Cohen*, Justice Harry Blackmun derided Paul Cohen's jacket as "an absurd and immature antic." By contrast, Justice Harlan insisted that the expression at issue was, in fact, of "no small constitutional consequence." Free speech scholars laud *Cohen* for recognizing that government must leave matters of expressive taste and style to the individual. One could dismiss offensive signs, T-shirts and taunts at college basketball games as similarly absurd and immature antics. However, as in *Cohen*, skirmishes over what fan expression will be permitted at public university sporting events are of no small constitutional consequence.

19   College sport has become, for better or for worse, a central part of college life and culture. The prevailing belief among university administrators and most commentators is that successful athletic teams, particularly in high-profile football and men's basketball, can be a source of university pride, publicity, media attention, revenue and increased donations. The non-athlete students who pack the stadium provide an essential ingredient of that overall culture. Students are encouraged to attend games and make noise, to be excited and passionate about their school, to cheer for their team and players (and against the opposing team and players), and to create a playing environment that will be intimidating or distracting to the opponent and will give their team a home-court advantage. Indeed, it is somewhat ironic that Duke players were at the receiving end of the taunts that prompted Maryland to consider an arena speech code. Duke students have attained wide notoriety for their sometimes-clever, sometimes-offensive cheering speech and the headaches they cause opposing teams and players.

20   The grandstand at the arena or stadium has become the central public forum for cheering speech. Fans are invited to the arena and encouraged to speak, loudly and in however vivid or stark terms, to support, oppose, cheer, jeer, criticize and even taunt teams, players, coaches, and officials in that game. Having created this forum for students to express themselves, a public university has ceded control over the manner in which students do so, at least within the parameters of protected speech. Fans must remain free to jeer as well as cheer players and teams and in as blatant or profane a manner as they wish.

> "The grandstand at the arena or stadium has become the central public forum for cheering speech."

21   Perhaps one may not particularly enjoy sitting, or having one's children sit, in an arena where students are shouting expletives throughout the game. But commitment to a neutral free-speech principle means tolerating a great deal of speech that one personally does not like or does not wish to hear. And there is nothing wrong with hortatory efforts by the university, coaches and, most important, other students to encourage fans, especially student fans, to keep their cheering stylish, clean, classy, and creative. The "voluntary compliance" policies recommended in June by the student committee at the University of Maryland included a program under which students could exchange profane T-shirts for noncontroversial ones, contests

that would encourage appropriate signs and banners, having coaches address students about the need for good sportsmanship and fan behavior and distributing newspapers at games with "creative witty cheers" for students to use.

22   The point is that a state university may not formally punish—even via noncriminal sanction such as removal from the arena—those students who depart [from] generally accepted norms by loudly wielding a particular loaded word to inform officials or opposing players that they are not very good at what they do.

READING CLOSELY AND THINKING CRITICALLY

1.   In your own words, state the thesis of "Fan Profanity." Be sure to indicate the issue and assertion.
2.   John K. Anderson bases his support of a speech code for fans, in part, on the captive-audience doctrine. What is that doctrine? Does Wasserman think the captive-audience doctrine applies to speech at sporting events? Explain.
3.   According to Wasserman, how is *Cohen v. California* relevant to fan profanity issues?
4.   Do you think the expression "Duck Fuke" should qualify as profanity? Why or why not?
5.   Why do you think some university officials are concerned about fan profanity?
6.   How successful do you think the University of Maryland's voluntary policing policy will be? Explain your view.

EXAMINING STRUCTURE AND STRATEGY

1.   What strategy does Wasserman use in the first two paragraphs?
2.   Paragraph 3 has an important function in the essay. What is that function?
3.   Which paragraphs raise and counter objections?
4.   The topic sentence of paragraph 16 (the last sentence) is a question, as is the topic sentence of paragraph 17 (the first sentence). What does the author achieve by framing these topic sentences as questions?

NOTING COMBINED PATTERNS

1.   Comparison is an important pattern in "Fan Profanity." How does Wasserman use comparison to help build his argument?
2.   How does Wasserman use exemplification?
3.   How does Wasserman use cause-and-effect analysis to help achieve his persuasive purpose?
4.   What elements of definition appear in the essay?

CONSIDERING LANGUAGE AND STYLE

1. What characteristics of the essay reflect the fact that Wasserman is an attorney writing about a legal issue?

2. Consult a dictionary if you are unsure of the meaning of any of these words: *epithets* (paragraphs 2, 4, 14), *Hobson's choice* (paragraph 10), *cacophony* (paragraph 10), *milieu* (paragraph 11), *pithy* (paragraph 13), *double entendre* (paragraph 17), *hortatory* (paragraph 21).

For discussion and writing assignments based on "Fan Profanity," see page 650.

BACKGROUND: Former law clerk to Supreme Court Justice William J. Brennan, Jr., Robert O'Neil was president of the University of Wisconsin system and the University of Virginia, where he also taught in the law school, specializing in constitutional law and free speech and the Internet. The founding director of the Thomas Jefferson Center for the Protection of Free Expression and the first president of Virginia's Coalition for Open Government, O'Neil has testified before congressional committees on how proposed legislation will affect the First Amendment. He has written several books, including *Free Speech: Responsible Communication under Law, The Rights of Public Employees* (1993), *Free Speech in the College Community* (1997), and *How a Sea Change in Civil Liability Threatens to Drown the First Amendment* (2001)."What Limits Should Campus Networks Place on Pornography?" first appeared in 2003 in the *Chronicle of Higher Education,* a publication for college faculty and administrators.

THE PATTERN AND ITS PURPOSES: As a former college president and as an attorney specializing in constitutional issues, Robert O'Neil is uniquely qualified to **inform** readers of the issues surrounding censorship of pornography on the Internet, which he does with the help of *cause-and-effect analysis.* He also **argues** for a compromise solution to the conflict between free-speech advocates who oppose censorship and those who want to restrict pornography to avoid offending those who are troubled by the material.

What Limits Should Campus Networks Place on Pornography?

BY ROBERT O'NEIL

What if you were about to present a PowerPoint lecture to a large undergraduate class, but found instead on your computer a series of sexually explicit ads and material from pornographic Web sites? That's essentially what happened recently to Mary Pedersen, a nutrition-science professor at California Polytechnic State University at San Luis Obispo. That incident and the increasing presence of such imagery at Cal Poly have led to a novel, although undoubtedly predictable, struggle over computer content—one that is quite likely to be replicated at countless campuses in the coming months.

2   A concerned faculty group at Cal Poly has announced its intention to bring before the Academic Senate, sometime this spring, a "Resolution to Enhance Civility and Promote a Diversity-Friendly Campus Climate." Specifically, the measure would prohibit using the university's computers or network to access or download digital material generally described as "pornography." The resolution would also forbid the "transmission" of hate literature and obscenity on the Cal Poly network.

As you read
Evaluate how
convincingly
O'Neil argues
his thesis.

3   The sponsoring faculty members have offered several reasons for proposing such drastic action. First and foremost, they contend that the ready availability of

Copyright © 2002 by Mike Keefe. *The Denver Post,* April 21, 2002. Reprinted with permission.

sexually explicit imagery can create occasional but deeply disturbing encounters like Pedersen's discovery of unwelcome and unexpected material on her classroom computer. The pervasive presence of such images, proponents of the resolution argue, is inherently demeaning to female faculty members, administrators, and students.

4   Indeed, they suggest that the university might even be legally liable for creating and maintaining a "hostile workplace environment" if it fails to take steps to check the spread of such offensive material. That concern has been heightened by a putative link to a growing number of sexual assaults in the environs of the university.

5   Those who call for tighter regulation cite several other factors to support antipornography measures. In their view, a college or university must maintain the highest of standards, not only in regard to the integrity of scholarship and relations between teachers and students, but also in the range of material to which it provides electronic access. The clear implication is that the ready availability of sexually explicit and deeply offensive imagery falls below "the ethical standards that the university claims to uphold."

6   Critics of easy access to such material also claim that it can divert time, talent, and resources from the university's primary mission. Kimberly Daniels, a local lawyer who is advising the resolution's sponsors, told the student newspaper that "it is offensive that Cal Poly is taking the position that it is acceptable for professors to view pornography during work hours in their work office." That risk is not entirely conjectural. In fact, one professor left the institution last year after being convicted on misdemeanor charges for misusing a state-owned computer, specifically for the

purpose of downloading in his office thousands of sexually explicit images. Local newspapers have also reported that the FBI is investigating another former Cal Poly professor who allegedly used a campus computer to view child pornography.

7 Finally, the concerned faculty group insists that the free flow of pornographic materials may expose the Cal Poly computer network to a greater risk of virus infection. They cite a student's recent experience in opening a salacious virus-bearing attachment that the student mistakenly believed had been sent by one of his professors.

8 The proposed Academic Senate resolution has touched off an intense debate. The university's existing computer-use policy presumes that access and choice of material are broadly protected, although it adds that "in exceptional cases, the university may decide that such material directed at individuals presents such a hostile environment under the law that certain restrictive actions are warranted." The new proposal would focus more sharply on sexually explicit imagery, and would require those who wish to view such material through the campus network to obtain the express permission of the university's president.

9 Defenders of the current approach, including the senior staff of the university's office of information technology, insist that a public university may not banish from its system material that is offensive, but legal, without violating First Amendment rights. Those familiar with the operations of such systems also cite practical difficulties in the enforcement of any such restrictions, given the immense volume of digital communications that circulate around the clock at such a complex institution.

10 The debate at Cal Poly echoes what occurred some six years ago in Virginia. The General Assembly enacted what remains as the nation's only ban on public employees' use of state-owned or state-leased computers to access sexually explicit material—at least without express permission of a "superior" for a "bona fide research purpose." Six state university professors immediately challenged the law on First Amendment grounds. A district judge struck down the statute, but the U.S. Court of Appeals for the Fourth Circuit reversed that ruling. The law had been modified before that judgment, and many Virginia professors have since received exemptions or dispensations, but the precedent created by the appeals-court decision remains troubling for advocates of free and open electronic communications.

11 The Virginia ruling complicates the Cal Poly situation. The First Amendment challenge of those who oppose the Academic Senate resolution is less clear than it might at first appear. Two premises underlying that resolution—the need to protect government-owned hardware and the imperative to combat sexual hostility in the public workplace—contributed both to the passage of the Virginia ban, and to its eventual success in the federal courts. What's more, the U.S. Equal Employment Opportunity Commission some months ago gave its blessing to a hostile-workplace complaint filed by Minneapolis Public Library staff members who were offended by persistent display of graphic sexual images on reading-room terminals.

12 Thus, there is more than a superficial basis for the claims of CalPoly's porn-banishers that (in the words of one faculty member) "the First Amendment doesn't protect . . . subjecting others to inappropriate material in the workplace." Even the information-technology consultant who has championed the current computer-use policy at the university has conceded that access to controversial material is fully protected only "as long as it isn't offending others."

13 Although the desire to reduce the potential for offense and affront to other users of a campus computer network seems unobjectionable, its implications deserve careful scrutiny. In the analogous situation of public terminals in a library reading room, it is one thing to ask a patron who wishes to access and display sexually explicit material—or racially hateful material, for that matter—to use a terminal facing away from other users and staff members. It is quite another matter to deny access to such material altogether on the plausible premise that, if it can be obtained at all, there is a palpable risk that its visible display will offend others. To invoke an analogy that is now before the U.S. Supreme Court in a challenge to the Children's Internet Protection Act: It is one thing for a library to provide—even be compelled to provide—filtered access for parents who wish it for their children, but quite another to deny all adult patrons any unfiltered access.

14 What Cal Poly should seek to do, without impairing free expression, is to protect people from being gratuitously assaulted by digital material that may be deeply offensive, without unduly restricting access of those who, for whatever reason, may wish to access and view such material without bothering others. The proposal in the resolution that permission may be obtained from the university's president, for bonafide research purposes, is far too narrow. Among other flaws, such a precondition might well deter sensitive or conscientious scholars, whether faculty members or students, who are understandably reluctant to reveal publicly their reasons for wishing to access sexually explicit images or hate literature.

15 A responsible university, seeking to balance contending interests of a high order, might first revisit and make more explicit its policies that govern acceptable computer use and access, by which all campus users are presumably bound. Such policies could condemn the flaunting of thoughtless dissemination of sexually explicit material and digital hate literature, expressing institutional abhorrence of such postings, without seeking to ban either type of material. The computer network might also establish a better warning system through which to alert sensitive users to the occasional and inevitable presence of material that may offend. Finally, a broader disclaimer might be in order, recognizing the limited practical capacity of a university server to control (or even enable users to avoid) troubling material.

16 What is needed is a reasonable balance that avoids, as Justice William O. Douglas warned a half-century ago, "burning down the house to roast the pig." That aphorism has special felicity here; in the offensive flaunting of sexually explicit imagery, there is a "pig" that doubtless deserves to be roasted. But there is also a house of intellect that must remain free and open, even to those with aberrant tastes and interests.

READING CLOSELY AND THINKING CRITICALLY

1. What reasons do the Cal Poly concerned faculty give for supporting a resolution to restrict access to Internet pornography and hate materials?

2. What are the reasons to oppose the resolution?

3. What conflicting principles are inherent in any move to restrict Internet content?

Combining Patterns of Development

A patchwork quilt, like the one on the facing page, is made by sewing together fabric in patterns of different shapes, sizes, and colors to create a single work of art. Although made of many different patterns, the quilt does not seem like a hodgepodge. In fact, it is attractive and has a distinct unity. What makes the quilt attractive, and what gives it a distinct unity?

PATTERNS FOR A PURPOSE

An important focus of this book is to demonstrate how you can use the patterns of development to achieve your purpose for writing. In fact, this focus is so important that it gives this book its title, *Patterns for a Purpose*.

In addition to demonstrating how individual patterns of development can help you achieve your writing purpose, *Patterns for a Purpose* has shown how you can *combine* two or more patterns to achieve your purpose. Chapters on individual patterns have included readings that combine the individual pattern with other patterns. To emphasize the usefulness of combining patterns, this chapter focuses on explaining and illustrating how to combine patterns to achieve a range of writing purposes.

USING THE PATTERNS OF DEVELOPMENT FOR A PURPOSE

As you've seen throughout this book, sometimes you can achieve your writing purpose using a single pattern of development, and other times you need to combine two or more patterns. For example, assume you are the editor of a company newsletter and must write an article to inform new employees about vacation and sick leave policies. For this target audience, a single pattern—process analysis—may be sufficient to explain how the policies work. However, if your audience is long-term employees and your purpose is to inform them of changes in vacation and sick leave policies, you may need two patterns—process analysis to explain how the new policies work and comparison-contrast to make sure employees understand how the new policies differ from the old. If, in another article, your purpose is to profile the employee of the month to inspire other employees, you might use exemplification to show the employee's accomplishments, narration to tell about a time the employee did something extraordinary, and cause-and-effect analysis to explain how the employee's work helps the company.

When you combine patterns to achieve your writing purpose, you will often have a primary pattern, on which you draw more heavily, and secondary patterns. For example, to convince readers to practice meditation, you might use exemplification as a primary pattern to illustrate the benefits of meditation and process analysis and classification as secondary patterns to explain how meditation works and what kinds of meditation there are, to help readers decide which kind is best for them. In as essay to inform readers about meditation, you might give more equal weight to each of these patterns.

PROCESS GUIDELINES: STRATEGIES FOR COMBINING PATTERNS

1. **Selecting a topic.** If your topic has been assigned, look for combinations of patterns suggested by that topic. For example, the essay topic "What is media bias and how common is it?" suggests that you will combine a definition of media bias with examples of its occurrence. If you are trying to develop you own topic, thinking about the patterns can also help you. Thus, for media bias, you might think of exemplification and focus on examples of media bias. Similarly, thinking about cause-and-effect analysis could lead you to focus on the reasons for and consequences of media bias; classification could lead you to a focus on types of media bias; and definition could lead you to a focus on the meaning of media bias. Often, looking at your topic through the lens of patterns, you will decide to develop your topic in a way that combines patterns of development.

2. **Achieving your purpose and assessing your audience.** Ask yourself how multiple patterns can help you achieve your purpose with your target audience.

3. **Generating ideas.** Just as patterns can help you select a topic, so they help you generate ideas by looking at your topic from different angles. To generate ideas for a newsletter article about the employee of the month, for instance, consider each pattern and the detail it can

Using Transitions and Other Coherence Devices

If you have trouble signaling the relationships among the ideas you express with combined patterns, consult the transition chart beginning on page 67. The transitions in this chart, along with the other coherence devices explained on pages 67–69, can also help you move smoothly from pattern to pattern.

provide. Ask "What can I describe?" and you might answer "the employee's desk—for humor." Ask "What can I narrate?" and you might answer "the time the employee administered CPR to another worker."

4. **Organizing details.** Consider whether your pattern combination suggests combining certain organizational schemes. For example, if you combine process analysis and cause-and-effect analysis, you may need to order your details with a combination of chronological and progressive orders.

5. **Revising.** For help revising an essay with multiple patterns, you can consult the general checklist on page 76 and the revising checklists in Chapters 5–12 that are relevant to the particular patterns of development you use.

---

www.mhhe.com/clousepatterns6   Blended Essay

For more help with combining patterns, click on

Writing > Writing Tutor: Blended Essay

Annotated Student Essay

In the following essay, student-writer Eve Pugh combines definition, cause-and-effect analysis, contrast, and exemplification to inform about the nature of knowledge and to argue that people should not consider street smarts better than book smarts. After you read, you will have an opportunity to evaluate the essay.

Taking Book Smarts to the Street
Eve Pugh

Paragraph 1
This introduction gives background information. It also indicates that the writer will discuss the nature of knowledge to show that the book smarts of college and the street smarts of everyday life should not be falsely contrasted.

People often distinguish between "street smarts" and "book smarts." 1 In fact, some even assert what they believe to be their superiority over others by emphasizing their "real-world" (street-smart) experience over the academic (book-smart) experience of their peers. "Poor you," they say. "I've been backpacking across Europe while you've been stuck at your desk," Such an assertion creates a false contrast between college and everyday life. To understand the limitations of this argument, one must first consider knowledge—what it really is and how it really works.

Paragraph 2
To fulfill the informational purpose, this paragraph defines knowledge and contrasts what people believe about academic learning with what it actually is. Notice the examples.

The myth that everyday experience somehow supersedes aca- 2 demic endeavors relies on a misconception of knowledge. It is not merely an accumulation of data and information. Instead, it is the result of a process of discovery and critical thinking that alters one's outlook on life. The everyday-experience-is-better argument implies that knowledge acquired through study applies only to very specific, academic contexts that are divorced from the "real world." When people claim that college exists outside of the "real world," they suggest that the knowledge learned in school has little or no value in one's day-to-day life. They concede that learning to write well in English classes has practical value, as does studying how to compute interest in math classes. However, they see no practical purpose for studying the Napoleonic Wars in history classes, existentialism in philosophy classes, or Maslow's hierarchy of needs in psychology classes. "What good is it?" they demand to know. Their simplistic argument equates knowledge with facts and information that can be put to use in day-to-day living, failing to account for the invaluable experience of obtaining deeper, richer ways of thinking about oneself and of approaching the world that a college education can provide.

Paragraph 3
This paragraph advances the persuasive purpose by raising and countering an objection. It also uses cause-and-effect analysis to explain the positive effects of academic learning.

Of course, pursuing a particular course of study offers a certain 3 skill set and knowledge base that can often prepare students for particular professions, and those who value street smarts appreciate the practicality of career education. They do not, however, see the value of courses not directly related to the skills and information necessary for performing a particular job. They argue that a computer programmer does not need sociology classes, and a dental hygienist does not need political science courses. This argument against a broad-based education fails to acknowledge that the process of working toward an academic degree by taking a variety of courses in different fields—including all the frustrations and successes that process involves—has great value because it instills a sense of curiosity and wonder that transcends easily forgettable facts and figures. Taking a variety of courses helps people better understand the larger world, not just the narrow area defined by their jobs. And most important, this scholarly stance is vital in an uncertain economy in which the more creative and resourceful job applicants have a clear advantage over their peers. In this sense, knowledge can be measured by how well a person is able to adapt to unpredictable situations, to adjust to sudden changes in career and personal life, and to achieve a better quality of life. Now, that's "practical."

Consider what some think is the least practical of all majors — 4 philosophy. Philosophy majors learn how to read, think, question, and debate critically, which gives them the ability to approach the world from an intellectual perspective. They learn how to solve problems, write and speak clearly in many contexts, analyze situations and respond, and persuade. They also learn to make ethical choices in a world that is becoming more ethically compromised. In other words, the process of getting a degree in philosophy helps students learn how to be successful human beings and understand the world around them. Ironically, more employers are recognizing how "practical" these abilities are, so philosophy majors are more employable than ever.

The claim that "street smarts" are better than "book smarts" rules 5 out the possibility that both kinds of knowledge complement one another. In fact, this claim creates a false division between ways of acquiring knowledge that go hand in hand. To have worldly knowledge means to be able to navigate through everyday life with a grace and dexterity that

Paragraph 4
This paragraph includes cause-and-effect analysis and exemplification to show the benefits of academic learning and thereby advance the persuasive purpose.

Paragraph 5
With definition and cause-and-effect analysis, this paragraph explains that street smarts and book smarts work together.

come from understanding one's relationship to others. Such an under-standing takes time and effort to develop, and the intellectual training that comes from a college education fosters this understanding in students both in and out of school.

Paragraph 6
This conclusion includes definition and leaves the reader with a final impression.

Knowledge is more than the ability to recite facts, figures, dates, 6 theories, and formulas. It is an intellectual stance, a critical perspective that reveals a world of experiences, situations, and relationships. It is an intersection between quiet study and lively engagement with people and experiences. So, the next time someone says to get out in the world, hit the books.

PEER REVIEW

Responding to "Taking Book Smarts to the Street"

Analyze and assess "Taking Book Smarts to the Street" by responding to these questions:

1. Does the essay hold your interest? Why or why not?
2. Does the author achieve her informative and persuasive purposes? Explain.
3. Could the author have achieved her purpose if she used only one pattern? Explain.
4. Are all the author's points adequately supported? Explain.
5. What do you like best about the essay? Why?
6. What change do you think would improve the essay? Why?

EXAMINING VISUALS · Combining Patterns on a Web Site

As the following screenshot illustrates, images—like text—often combine patterns.

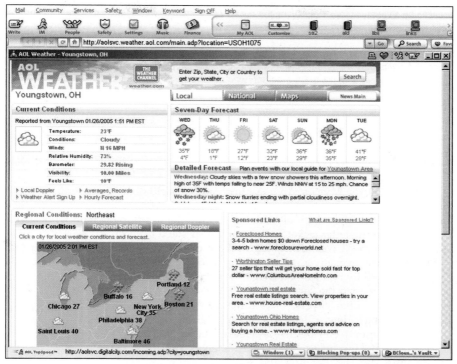

The AOL.com triangle logo and AOL are registered trademarks of America Online, Inc. The AOL.com screenshot is © 2005 by America Online, Inc. The America Online content, name, icons, and trademarks are used with permission.

- What element of description appears on this Web site reproduction?
- What element of division?
- What element of contrast?
- How do all these patterns help the Web site achieve its informational purpose?

BACKGROUND: Freelance writer Elizabeth Svoboda has been a contributing editor for *Popular Science* and is currently a contributing writer for *Fast Company* magazine. She has written for a number of publications, including *Discover, Psychology Today,* and *Salon.* The winner of the Evert Clark/Seth Payne Award for young science journalists, Svoboda's science articles have focused on a variety of topics, including the connection between water slides and chaos theory, fuel cells, asteroid hunters, and scents. "Closet Cases" was first published in *Psychology Today* in 2009.

COMBINED PATTERNS AND THEIR PURPOSE: Elizabeth Svoboda combines *definition, cause-and-effect analysis, comparison-contrast,* and *process analysis* to **inform** readers about what it is like to be a person who cannot throw anything away.

CLOSET CASES

BY ELIZABETH SVOBODA

FOR MORE THAN 30 years, Ange Aguirre rarely got rid of anything. From elementary school on, she squirreled away her possessions in boxes and corners, and when she married at 19, she took it all with her — from the third-grade math work sheets to the letter jacket to the teddy bear she'd been given the day she was born. "I was on my high school drill team, and I had every gift that was ever given to me during a football game," says Aguirre, now 39 and living near San Diego. "I had notes people had written to me when I was in the seventh grade."

As you read Think about the complicated relationships people have with their possessions.

2 Like layers of sediment, Aguirre's belongings piled higher and higher over time, teetering in unwieldy stacks and choking off access to closet shelves. But it wasn't until she and her husband were preparing to move across the country to California that she admitted her tendency to hoard was affecting her life. "We have eight children, and things were getting crowded with their toys and belongings," she says. "I had to do something about it." But when she resolved to tackle the mountain of stuff, her attachment to cherished items got

"Why is it that some people feel such a strong urge to hold onto things, while others shred, dump, and recycle with ease?"

in the way of her judgment, making it almost physically painful to trash them. "They were something to hold on to when the days got tough, to bring me back to a good time in my life."

3 It's the most extreme sufferers of pack-rat-itis who make headlines—like Patrice Moore, who was buried alive in his New York City apartment in 2003 when his stacks of paper and magazines collapsed on top of him. (He survived after a stint in the intensive-care unit.)

4 But far more common is a less severe tendency to keep too much stuff around—not so much that your *National Geographics* reach to the ceiling but enough that you put off hosting a dinner party because you can't find the top of your dining-room table. "Hoarding runs all the way from very mild to very extreme," says Randy Frost, a psychologist at Smith College and author of *Stuff.* "The key is

JUNK BONDS: For decades, Ange Aguirre had trouble letting go of stuff.

whether it interferes with your life." It's an inclination that can be set in motion by the kind of economic uncertainty now convulsing the country.[1]

5   Why is it that some people feel such a strong urge to hold onto things, while others shred, dump, and recycle with ease? Packratting may have some genetic basis: Children and other close relatives of hoarders are more likely to be hoarders themselves. Hoarding may be linked to a sequence of genes on chromosome 14 that's also found in families with obsessive-compulsive disorder—not surprising, since a large number of OCD patients feel the urge to hoard and save. While hoarding can be a symptom of OCD, "there are a lot of people who don't have any other OCD symptoms; they're just hoarders," Frost says.

_____
[1]At the time the essay was written, the United States was experiencing an economic recession.

6   Many hoarders suffer from depression and anxiety disorders, he adds—and, feeling down can worsen a tendency to accumulate too many things. "With depression, you often see people who have clutter problems, because they don't have the energy to get rid of stuff."

7   Extreme pack rats also show different brain activation patterns than non-pack rats. A UCLA study showed that hoarders had lower-than-normal baseline levels of activity in an area of the limbic system called the cingulate gyrus, suggesting a deficit in emotional self-control. Researchers believe this may help explain the decision-making, attentional, and other cognitive problems of compulsive hoarders, accounting for the problems they have in deciding what to keep and what to throw away.

8   What really distinguishes pack rats from minimalists, though, is their tendency to develop emotionally fraught relationships with the things they own.

9   While hoarding is related to compulsive shopping, an addiction to acquiring things, hoarders are distinct from mall rats in that they bond so strongly to their existing possessions. "We often see an attachment to possessions that is quite remarkable," says Frost. But this attachment isn't just a materialistic obsession with stuff for stuff's sake. "Sometimes the objects are reminders of a significant event, and contribute to the person's sense of identity."

10   "If a person thinks, 'Having cookbooks makes me a cook,' then getting rid of one of those cookbooks gets in the way of their definition of who they are," explains Frost. A recent study indicated that people with hoarding problems were also more likely to report feeling distanced from their parents growing up. This may explain why some people develop "possession fever" and others don't: Things can stand in for the love they lacked early in life.

11   Hoarded objects can also become totems that testify to the existence of a treasured relationship. Jeanne Olson, a 42-year-old blogger, found exactly that when sorting through boxes of her mother's old belongings. "There's a certain amount of, if you don't keep that tea cozy, are you rejecting her? How do you separate the person from the stuff?"

12   Squirreling things away may also be symptomatic of a high level of generalized anxiety about the world—a fundamental insecurity that can be triggered by events that spin us out of control, such as an illness or job loss. "We see the objects in our home as symbols of safety and comfort," Frost says. "This tendency seems to be exaggerated in people who hoard, because they think everything they own has this power."

13   Conquering a hoarding problem is possible, but it's important to start slow. Many pack rats equate their possessions with everything that's good in life, says Dena Rabinowitz, a Manhattan psychologist. Going cold turkey—emptying your shelves directly into the dumpster—is bound to lead to regret, so set concrete boundaries for yourself that will allow you to de-clutter while still honoring your attachments to a limited extent.

14   Instead of keeping an entire box of old college essays, choose one or two that you're most proud of and throw out the rest; rather than saving a month's worth of newspapers, clip the articles that resonate with you and put them in a folder. "People say, 'Can't I have any nostalgic objects?' Well, of course you can," says Rabinowitz. "Moderation is healthy. Excess is not. If you have a shelf of mementos, that's great, but if you have a house full of them, that's excessive. And when you

have excess, each item loses its meaning." When you're truly torn about whether to keep something, Frost and Rabinowitz recommend putting it in a sealed box for six months to a year. If you don't use it during that time, you can pitch it with little regret.

15 After procrastinating half a lifetime on purging her excess stuff, Aguirre finally reached her breaking point last fall. She told her family to leave the house for one day and began excavating her closet. "I'd been preparing for it for a week, and I stuck to it—I reduced the number of boxes I had in there by half," she says.

16 "I had to completely shut off my emotions and just start tossing. There were boxes I wouldn't even let myself look inside." While the initial weed-out was painful, Aguirre says the benefits of taking the minimalist plunge are becoming more evident with time—she's got extra closet space, for one—and she doesn't miss her sloughed-off possessions. "There's not a single thing I look back on now and say, 'Oh, shoot, I needed that.'"

READING CLOSELY AND THINKING CRITICALLY

1. In paragraph 3, Svoboda mentions the coined term "pack-rat-itis." Based on the information in the essay, how would you define that term?
2. Why are the behaviors of the pack rat and the minimalist so different?
3. What are some factors that may cause people to become pack rats?
4. What enabled Ange Aguirre finally to get rid of some of her belongings after years of being unable to do so? Do you think other pack rats can do what she did?

EXAMINING STRUCTURE AND STRATEGY

1. The thesis of "Closet Cases" is implied rather than stated. In your own words, write out that thesis.
2. Why does Svoboda open with the example of Ange Aguirre?
3. Why does Svoboda close with the example of Ange Aguirre?
4. How does the author achieve transition from her general discussion of hoarding to her discussion of the causes of hoarding?

NOTING COMBINED PATTERNS

1. Svoboda uses a number of patterns in "Closet Cases." Which one is the primary pattern?
2. In addition to the example of Ange Aguirre that opens and closes the essay, the author uses examples in paragraphs 3, 10, and 11. How do those examples help the author achieve her informational purpose? How does comparison-contrast in paragraphs 8 and 9 help the author achieve her purpose?
3. How does the author use definition? How does the definition help the author achieve her writing purpose?

1. Svoboda uses language related to the natural world, such as "squirreled away" in paragraph 1. Cite other examples of this kind of language. What is the effect of the references to the natural world?

2. Consult a dictionary if you are unsure of the meaning of these words: *totem* (paragraph 11), *tea cozy* (paragraph 11).

FOR DISCUSSION IN CLASS OR ONLINE

The essay focuses more on the causes of hoarding than on the effects. What are some of the effects? What problems do you think hoarding creates for the hoarder and the hoarder's family?

WRITING ASSIGNMENTS

1. **Writing in your journal.** How important are your possessions to you? In a page or so, describe your degree of attachment to one or more of your possessions, or to your possessions generally, and why you feel the way you do.

2. **Combining patterns for a purpose.** The purposes given here are possibilities. You may establish whatever purpose you like, within your instructor's guidelines.

   • **Definition and exemplification.** In paragraph 9, Svoboda refers to a "mall rat." To inform and perhaps entertain, explain what a mall rat is, and use examples to illustrate aspects of that definition.

   • **Definition and description.** In paragraph 8, Svoboda refers to "minimalists." To inform, explain what a minimalist is and describe the appearance of a minimalist's dwelling.

   • **Classification and exemplification.** In paragraph 11, Svoboda says, "Hoarded objects can also become totems that testify to the existence of a treasured relationship." Classify ways people can "testify to the existence" of their important relationships.

   • **Cause-and-effect analysis and exemplification.** Hoarding is an example of excessive behavior, usually associated with the home. However, the classroom, too, can be a setting for excessive or inappropriate behavior—for example, if students monopolize time, cheat, or disrupt class. Illustrate one kind of excessive or inappropriate student behavior, and discuss its causes and/or effects.

3. **Analyzing and assessing.** Svoboda's purpose is informational. Take a close look at her essay, and assess whether it is likely to be sufficiently informational for the average college student who is not a psychology major.

4. **Connecting and synthesizing the readings.** Defining normal behavior may be impossible because of the wide area covered by "normal." Even Svoboda acknowledges that hoarding to some extent is common (paragraph 4). Nonetheless, in a society, we define normal by making assumptions about what is normal. What is considered normal in our society? What price do individuals pay if they diverge from that definition? Do we as a society pay a price for having the definition? In addition to your own experience and observation, you can draw on "The Poncho Bearer" (page 212), "Ring Leader" (page 217), and "Caring for Your Introvert" (page 541) for ideas.

5. **Drawing on sources.** Svoboda discusses some possible causes of hoarding. Learn more about the causes and write a summary of them, being sure to note what researchers think the most likely causes are. For information, type "causes of hoarding" into googlescholar.com, or use *PsycInfo* in your campus library reference room.

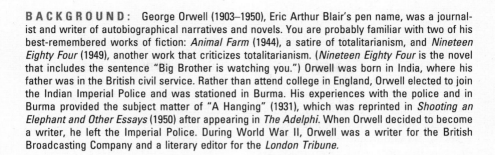

BACKGROUND: George Orwell (1903–1950), Eric Arthur Blair's pen name, was a journalist and writer of autobiographical narratives and novels. You are probably familiar with two of his best-remembered works of fiction: *Animal Farm* (1944), a satire of totalitarianism, and *Nineteen Eighty Four* (1949), another work that criticizes totalitarianism. (*Nineteen Eighty Four* is the novel that includes the sentence "Big Brother is watching you.") Orwell was born in India, where his father was in the British civil service. Rather than attend college in England, Orwell elected to join the Indian Imperial Police and was stationed in Burma. His experiences with the police and in Burma provided the subject matter of "A Hanging" (1931), which was reprinted in *Shooting an Elephant and Other Essays* (1950) after appearing in *The Adelphi*. When Orwell decided to become a writer, he left the Imperial Police. During World War II, Orwell was a writer for the British Broadcasting Company and a literary editor for the *London Tribune*.

www.mhhe.com/clousepatterns6   George Orwell

For more information on this author, go to

More resources > Chapter 14 > George Orwell

COMBINED PATTERNS AND THEIR PURPOSES: George Orwell was strongly influenced by the British colonial rule in India. Although Orwell was English, as a democratic socialist, he came to reject British imperialism, partly as a result of his experiences in Burma and with the Imperial Police, including the one narrated in "A Hanging." Orwell combines *narration* and *description* in "A Hanging" to **relate his experience** and **express his feelings** about the hanging of a prisoner. Orwell also works to **inform** his readers of the horrors of capital punishment and to **persuade** them that it is wrong.

A HANGING

BY GEORGE ORWELL

IT WAS IN BURMA, a sodden morning of the rains. A sickly light, like yellow tinfoil, was slanting over the high walls into the jail yard. We were waiting outside the condemned cells, a row of sheds fronted with double bars, like small animal cages. Each cell measured about ten feet by ten and was quite bare within except for a plank bed and a pot for drinking water. In some of them brown, silent men were squatting at the inner bars, with their blankets draped round them. These were the condemned men, due to be hanged within the next week or two.

As you read
Try to identify the point Orwell is making with his narration.

2   One prisoner had been brought out of his cell. He was a Hindu, a puny wisp of a man, with a shaven head and vague liquid eyes. He had a thick, sprouting mustache, absurdly too big for his body, rather like the mustache of a comic man on the films. Six tall Indian warders were guarding him and getting him ready for the gallows. Two of them stood by with rifles and fixed bayonets, while the others handcuffed him, passed a chain through his handcuffs and fixed it to their belts, and lashed his arms tight to his sides. They crowded very close about him, with their hands always on him in a careful, caressing grip, as though all the while feeling him to make sure he was there. It was like men handling a fish which is still alive and may jump back into the water. But he stood quite

unresisting, yielding his arms limply to the ropes, as though he hardly noticed what was happening.

3   Eight o'clock struck and a bugle call, desolately thin in the wet air, floated from the distant barracks. The superintendent of the jail, who was standing apart from the rest of us, moodily prodding the gravel with his stick, raised his head at the sound. He was an army doctor, with a gray toothbrush mustache and a gruff voice. "For God's sake, hurry up, Francis," he said irritably. "The man ought to have been dead by this time. Aren't you ready yet?"

> "'The man ought to have been dead by this time. Aren't you ready yet?'"

4   Francis, the head jailer, a fat Dravidian[1] in a white drill suit and gold spectacles, waved his black hand. "Yes sir, yes sir," he bubbled. "All is satisfactorily prepared. The hangman is waiting. We shall proceed."

5   "Well, quick march, then. The prisoners can't get their breakfast until this job's over."

6   We set out for the gallows. Two warders marched on either side of the prisoner, with their rifles at the slope; two others marched close against him, gripping him by the arm and shoulder, as though at once pushing and supporting him. The rest of us, magistrates and the like, followed behind. Suddenly, when we had gone ten yards, the procession stopped short without any order or warning. A dreadful thing had happened—a dog, come goodness knows whence, had appeared in the yard. It came bounding among us with a loud volley of barks and leapt round us wagging its whole body, wild with glee at finding so many human beings together. It was a large woolly dog, half Airedale, half pariah. For a moment it pranced around us, and then, before anyone could stop it, it had made a dash for the prisoner, and jumping up tried to lick his face. Everybody stood aghast, too taken aback even to grab the dog.

7   "Who let that bloody brute in here?" said the superintendent angrily. "Catch it, someone!"

8   A warder detached from the escort, charged clumsily after the dog, but it danced and gamboled just out of his reach, taking everything as part of the game. A young Eurasian jailer picked up a handful of gravel and tried to stone the dog away, but it dodged the stones and came after us again. Its yaps echoed from the jail walls. The prisoner, in the grasp of the two warders, looked on incuriously, as though this was another formality of the hanging. It was several minutes before someone managed to catch the dog. Then we put my handkerchief through its collar and moved off once more, with the dog still straining and whimpering.

9   It was about forty yards to the gallows. I watched the bare brown back of the prisoner marching in front of me. He walked clumsily with his bound arms, but quite steadily, with that bobbing gait of the Indian who never straightens his knees. At each step his muscles slid neatly into place, the lock of hair on his scalp danced up and down, his feet printed themselves on the wet gravel. And once, in spite of the men who gripped him by each shoulder, he stepped lightly aside to avoid a puddle on the path.

---

[1] A native speaker of one of the southern Indian languages.

10   It is curious; but till that moment I had never realized what it means to destroy a healthy, conscious man. When I saw the prisoner step aside to avoid the puddle, I saw the mystery, the unspeakable wrongness, of cutting a life short when it is in full tide. This man was not dying, he was alive just as we are alive. All the organs of his body were working—bowels digesting food, skin renewing itself, nails growing, tissues forming—all toiling away in solemn foolery. His nails would still be growing when he stood on the drop, when he was falling through the air with a tenth-of-a-second to live. His eyes saw the yellow gravel and the gray walls, and his brain still remembered, foresaw, reasoned—even about puddles. He and we were a party of men walking together, seeing, hearing, feeling, understanding the same world; and in two minutes, with a sudden snap, one of us would be gone—one mind less, one world less.

> "This man was not dying, he was alive just as we are alive."

11   The gallows stood in a small yard, separate from the main grounds of the prison, and overgrown with tall prickly weeds. It was a brick erection like three sides of a shed, with planking on top, and above that two beams and a crossbar with the rope dangling. The hangman, a gray-haired convict in the white uniform of the prison, was waiting beside his machine. He greeted us with a servile crouch as we entered. At a word from Francis the two warders, gripping the prisoner more closely than ever, half led, half pushed him to the gallows and helped him clumsily up the ladder. Then the hangman climbed up and fixed the rope round the prisoner's neck.

12   We stood waiting, five yards away. The warders had formed in a rough circle round the gallows. And then, when the noose was fixed, the prisoner began crying out to his god. It was a high, reiterated cry of "Ram! Ram! Ram! Ram!"[2] not urgent and fearful like a prayer or cry for help, but steady, rhythmical, almost like the tolling of a bell. The dog answered the sound with a whine. The hangman, still standing on the gallows, produced a small cotton bag like a flour bag and drew it down over the prisoner's face. But the sound, muffled by the cloth, still persisted, over and over again: "Ram! Ram! Ram! Ram! Ram!"

13   The hangman climbed down and stood ready, holding the lever. Minutes seemed to pass. The steady, muffled crying from the prisoner went on and on, "Ram! Ram! Ram!" never faltering for an instant. The superintendent, his head on his chest, was slowly poking the ground with his stick; perhaps he was counting the cries, allowing the prisoner a fixed number—fifty, perhaps, or a hundred. Everyone had changed color. The Indians had gone gray like bad coffee, and one or two of the bayonets were wavering. We looked at the lashed, hooded man on the drop, and listened to his cries—each cry another second of life; the same thought was in all our minds; oh, kill him quickly, get it over, stop that abominable noise!

14   Suddenly the superintendent made up his mind. Throwing up his head he made a swift motion with his stick. "Chalo!"[3] he shouted almost fiercely.

---

[2]The prisoner calls upon Rama, Hindu god who sustains and preserves.
[3](Hindi) "Hurry up!"

15   There was a clanking noise, and then dead silence. The prisoner had vanished, and the rope was twisting on itself. I let go of the dog, and it galloped immediately to the back of the gallows; but when it got there it stopped short, barked, and then retreated into a corner of the yard, where it stood among the weeds, looking timorously out at us. We went round the gallows to inspect the prisoner's body. He was dangling with his toes pointed straight downwards, very slowly revolving, as dead as a stone.

16   The superintendent reached out with his stick and poked the bare brown body; it oscillated slightly. "*He's* all right," said the superintendent. He backed out from under the gallows, and blew out a deep breath. The moody look had gone out of his face quite suddenly. He glanced at his wrist watch. "Eight minutes past eight. Well, that's all for this morning, thank God."

17   The warders unfixed bayonets and marched away. The dog, sobered and conscious of having misbehaved itself, slipped after them. We walked out of the gallows yard, past the condemned cells with their waiting prisoners, into the big central yard of the prison. The convicts, under the command of warders armed with lathis,[4] were already receiving their breakfast. They squatted in long rows, each man holding a tin pannikin,[5] while two warders with buckets marched around ladling out rice; it seemed quite a homely, jolly scene, after the hanging. An enormous relief had come upon us now that the job was done. One felt an impulse to sing, to break into a run, to snigger. All at once everyone began chattering gaily.

18   The Eurasian boy walking beside me nodded toward the way we had come, with a knowing smile: "Do you know, sir, our friend" (he meant the dead man) "when he heard his appeal had been dismissed, he pissed on the floor of his cell. From fright. Kindly take one of my cigarettes, sir. Do you not admire my new silver case, sir? From the boxwallah, two rupees eight annas. Classy European style."

19   Several people laughed—at what, nobody seemed certain.

20   Francis was walking by the superintendent, talking garrulously; "Well, sir, all has passed off with the utmost satisfactoriness. It was all finished—flick! Like that. It is not always so—oah, no! I have known cases where the doctor was obliged to go beneath the gallows and pull the prisoner's legs to ensure decease. Most disagreeable!"

> "Several people laughed—at what, nobody seemed certain."

21   "Wriggling about, eh? That's bad," said the superintendent.

22   "Ach, sir, it is worse when they become refractory! One man, I recall, clung to the bars of his cage when we went to take him out. You will scarcely credit, sir, that it took six warders to dislodge him, three pulling at each leg. We reasoned with him, 'My dear fellow,' we said, 'think of all the pain and trouble you are causing to us!' But no, he would not listen! Ach, he was very troublesome!"

23   I found that I was laughing quite loudly. Everyone was laughing. Even the superintendent grinned in a tolerant way. "You'd better all come out and have a

---

[4]Policemen's wooden clubs.

[5]Small pan.

drink," he said quite genially. "I've got a bottle of whiskey in the car. We could do
with it."

24 We went through the big double gates of the prison into the road. "Pulling at
his legs!" exclaimed a Burmese magistrate suddenly, and burst into a loud chuck-
ling. We all began laughing again. At that moment Francis' anecdote seemed
extraordinarily funny. We all had a drink together, native and European alike, quite
amicably. The dead man was a hundred yards away.

READING CLOSELY AND THINKING CRITICALLY

1. What is Orwell's attitude toward capital punishment? What is his attitude toward the
   condemned prisoners? How can you tell what these attitudes are?

2. Why does the superintendent say that he wants Francis and the other guards to hurry
   and get the prisoner to the gallows? Do you think the reason he gives is the real
   one? Explain.

3. Why do you think Orwell calls the entrance of the dog "a dreadful thing"?
4. What is the significance of the condemned man stepping aside "to avoid the puddle" (paragraph 9)?
5. Why are the spectators so unnerved by the prisoner's repeated calls to his God?
6. How would you describe the superintendent's attitude toward the prisoner and the execution?
7. Of what significance is the fact that "native and European alike" had a drink together after the hanging (paragraph 24)?

EXAMINING STRUCTURE AND STRATEGY

1. Orwell often uses dialogue in the essay. How does the dialogue help him achieve his purpose?
2. What is the effect of the last two sentences of the essay? Do you think they help Orwell achieve his persuasive purpose? Explain.
3. Would the narration have been more effective—that is, would Orwell have better achieved his persuasive purpose—if he had said what crime the prisoner committed? Explain.

NOTING COMBINED PATTERNS

1. Orwell uses a considerable amount of description in the essay. Cite an example and explain how it helps Orwell achieve his purpose. Is the description a primary or secondary pattern?
2. What is the point of the narration?
3. Where does Orwell pause the narration to comment on events? How does that commentary help him achieve his purpose?

CONSIDERING LANGUAGE AND STYLE

1. Paragraph 1 includes two similes. (See page 128 on similes.) What are they and what do they contribute?
2. What is the tone of "A Hanging"? (See page 69 on tone.) Give examples of words and phrases that help convey that tone.
3. Consult a dictionary if you are unsure of the meaning of any of these words: *sodden* (paragraph 1), *pariah* (paragraph 6), *gamboled* (paragraph 8), *incuriously* (paragraph 8), *timorously* (paragraph 15), *oscillated* (paragraph 16), *garrulously* (paragraph 20), *refractory* (paragraph 22).

FOR DISCUSSION IN CLASS OR ONLINE

How does "A Hanging" present an argument against capital punishment? Cite the specific strategies that help Orwell make his case, and then go on to explain what kind of readers are likely to respond to those strategies.

1. **Writing in your journal.** Do you believe in the death penalty? Explain why or why not. As an alternative, explain whether your opinion about the death penalty has changed as a result of reading "A Hanging."

2. **Combining patterns for a purpose.** The purposes in the assignments are possibilities. You may establish whatever purpose you like, within your instructor's guidelines.

   - **Narration and cause-and-effect analysis.** During the course of the events in "A Hanging," Orwell decides that capital punishment is wrong. To relate your experience and express your feelings, narrate an account of a time you realized something important. Explain how you were affected by the realization.

   - **Process analysis and comparison-contrast.** Orwell tells about something he thinks is wrong: capital punishment. Explain a process you think is wrong, such as hazing, Little League tryouts, spelling bees, or financial aid. To convince your reader that there is a better way, contrast that process with one you think would be better.

   - **Narration and description.** The men who witnessed and supervised the hanging were clearly uncomfortable, which helps to explain their behavior before, during, and after the execution. Tell a story about an event to which witnesses had a strong reaction, such as an accident, a death, an embarrassing moment, or an argument. Describe the reaction. Your purpose can be to inform.

   - **Definition and exemplification.** Orwell's narration tells of oppression. To inform, define *oppression* or *discrimination*, and give examples that illustrate that definition.

3. **Analyzing and assessing.** Identify the strategies Orwell uses to move readers' emotions and assess how the emotional appeal affects readers. Be sure to cite the text to support your points.

4. **Connecting and synthesizing the readings.** How do you think we should punish people for committing the most serious crimes? To answer this question, you can draw on your own ideas and one or more of these readings: "A Hanging," "The Lottery" (page 199), and "Adult Crime, Adult Time" (page 608).

5. **Drawing on sources.** Orwell's essay titled "Shooting an Elephant" also draws on his experiences as a police officer in Burma. You can find it in your campus library as part of *Shooting an Elephant and Other Essays* or on the Internet at http://www. george-orwell.org/Shooting_an_Elephant/0.html. Read that essay and then explain what "A Hanging" and "Shooting an Elephant" reveal about Orwell's view of government. Be sure to back up your assertions with specific references to the essays.

BACKGROUND: Born in 1944 in San Francisco, Richard Rodriguez is a first-generation Mexican American who spoke only Spanish until he was six years old. He is an editor at Pacific News Service and a contributing editor for *Harper's Magazine, U.S. News & World Report,* and the Sunday "Opinion" section of the *Los Angeles Times.* A prolific author who frequently writes of his heritage, Rodriguez has published numerous articles in the *New York Times,* the *Wall Street Journal,* the *American Scholar, Time, Mother Jones,* and the *New Republic,* as well as other publications. His three autobiographical books are *Hunger of Memory* (1981), from which "Complexion" is taken; *Days of Obligation: An Argument with My Mexican Father* (1992); and *Brown: The Last Discovery of America* (2002). In 1997, Rodriguez earned the prestigious George Foster Peabody Award for his essays on American life for the PBS series *The News Hour with Jim Lehrer.* He has also received the Frankel Medal from the National Endowment for the Humanities and the International Journalism Award from the World Affairs Council of California.

www.mhhe.com/clousepatterns6	Richard Rodriguez

For more information on this author, go to

More resources > Chapter 14 > Richard Rodriguez

COMBINED PATTERNS AND THEIR PURPOSES: In "Complexion," Richard Rodriguez **expresses his feelings** and **relates his experience** by combining *contrast, narration,* and *description* with his discussion of the *effects* his skin color had on his self-concept. In doing so, he also **informs** his audience about the Mexican American experience and reminds the reader of the adolescent struggle to feel at ease with one's physical appearance.

Complexion

BY RICHARD RODRIGUEZ

Complexion. My first conscious experience of sexual excitement concerns my complexion. One summer weekend, when I was around seven years old, I was at a public swimming pool with the whole family. I remember sitting on the damp pavement next to the pool and seeing my mother, in the spectator's bleachers, holding my younger sister on her lap. My mother, I noticed, was watching my father as he stood on a diving board, waving to her. I watched her wave back. Then I saw her radiant, bashful, astonishing smile. In that second I sensed that my mother and father had a relationship I knew nothing about. A nervous excitement encircled my stomach as I saw my mother's eyes follow my father's figure curving into the water. A second or two later, he emerged. I heard him call out. Smiling, his voice sounded buoyant, calling me to swim to him. But turning to see him, I caught my mother's eye. I heard her shout over to me. In Spanish she called through the crowd: "Put a towel on over your shoulders." In public, she didn't want to say why. I knew.

2 That incident anticipates the shame and sexual inferiority I was to feel in later years because of my dark complexion. I was to grow up an ugly child. Or one who

As you read Consider how the author defines masculinity.

thought himself ugly. (*Feo.*) One night when I was eleven or twelve years old, I locked myself in the bathroom and carefully regarded my reflection in the mirror over the sink. Without any pleasure I studied my skin. I turned on the faucet. (In my mind I heard the swirling voices of aunts, and even my mother's voice, whispering, whispering incessantly about lemon juice solutions and dark, *feo* children.) With a bar of soap, I fashioned a thick ball of lather. I began soaping my arms. I took my father's straight razor out of the medicine cabinet. Slowly, with steady deliberateness, I put the blade against my flesh, pressed it as close as I could without cutting, and moved it up and down across my skin to see if I could get out, somehow lessen, the dark. All I succeeded in doing, however, was in shaving my arms bare of their hair. For as I noted with disappointment, the dark would not come out. It remained. Trapped. Deep in the cells of my skin.

3   Throughout adolescence, I felt myself mysteriously marked. Nothing else about my appearance would concern me so much as the fact that my complexion was dark. My mother would say how sorry she was that there was not money enough to get braces to straighten my teeth. But I never bothered about my teeth. In three-way mirrors at department stores, I'd see my profile dramatically defined by a long nose, but it was really only the color of my skin that caught my attention.

4   I wasn't afraid that I would become a menial laborer because of my skin. Nor did my complexion make me feel especially vulnerable to racial abuse. (I didn't really consider my dark skin to be a racial characteristic. I would have been only too happy to look as Mexican as my light-skinned older brother.) Simply, I judged myself ugly. And, since the women in my family had been the ones who discussed it in such worried tones, I felt my dark skin made me unattractive to women.

5   Thirteen years old. Fourteen. In a grammar school art class, when the assignment was to draw a self-portrait, I tried but could not bring myself to shade in the face on the paper to anything like my actual tone. With disgust then I would come face to face with myself in mirrors. With disappointment I located myself in class photographs—my dark face undefined by the camera which had clearly described the white faces of classmates. Or I'd see my dark wrist against my long-sleeved white shirt.

6   I grew divorced from my body. Insecure, overweight, listless. On hot summer days when my rubber-soled shoes soaked up the heat from the sidewalk, I kept my head down. Or walked in the shade. My mother didn't need anymore to tell me to watch out for the sun. I denied myself a sensational life. The normal, extraordinary, animal excitement of feeling my body alive—riding shirtless on a bicycle in the warm wind created by furious self-propelled motion—the sensations that first had excited in me a sense of my maleness, I denied. I was too ashamed of my body. I wanted to forget that I had a body because I had a brown body. I was grateful that none of my classmates ever mentioned the fact.

7   I continued to see the *braceros*,[1] those men I resembled in one way and, in another way, didn't resemble at all. On the watery horizon of a Valley afternoon, I'd see them. And though I feared looking like them, it was with silent envy that I

---

[1]Mexican laborers admitted into the country temporarily to do seasonal work, such as harvesting crops.

regarded them still. I envied them their physical lives, their freedom to violate the taboo of the sun. Closer to home I would notice the shirtless construction workers, the roofers, the sweating men tarring the street in front of the house. And I'd see the Mexican gardeners. I was unwilling to admit the attraction of their lives. I tried to deny it by looking away. But what was denied became strongly desired.

8   In high school physical education classes, I withdrew, in the regular company of five or six classmates, to a distant corner of a football field where we smoked and talked. Our company was composed of bodies too short or too tall, all graceless and all—except mine—pale. Our conversation was usually witty. (In fact we were intelligent.) If we referred to the athletic contests around us, it was with sarcasm. With savage scorn I'd refer to the "animals" playing football or baseball. It would have been important for me to have joined them. Or for me to have taken off my shirt, to have let the sun burn dark on my skin, and to have run barefoot on the warm wet grass. It would have been very important. Too important. It would have been too telling a gesture—to admit the desire for sensation, the body, my body.

9   Fifteen, sixteen. I was a teenager shy in the presence of girls. Never dated. Barely could talk to a girl without stammering. In high school I went to several dances, but I never managed to ask a girl to dance. So I stopped going. I cannot remember high school years now with the parade of typical images: bright drive-ins or gliding blue shadows of a Junior Prom. At home most weekend nights, I would pass evenings reading. Like those hidden, precocious adolescents who have no real-life sexual experiences, I read a great deal of romantic fiction. "You won't find it in your books," my brother would playfully taunt me as he prepared to go to a party by freezing the crest of the wave in his hair with sticky pomade. Through my reading, however, I developed a fabulous and sophisticated sexual imagination. At seventeen, I may not have known how to engage a girl in small talk, but I had read *Lady Chatterley's Lover.*

10   It annoyed me to hear my father's teasing: that I would never know what "real work" is: that my hands were so soft. I think I knew it was his way of admitting pleasure and pride in my academic success. But I didn't smile. My mother said she was glad her children were getting their educations and would not be pushed around like *los pobres.*[2] I heard the remark ironically as a reminder of my separation from *los braceros.* At such times I suspected that education was making me effeminate. The odd thing, however, was that I did not judge my classmates so harshly. Nor did I consider my male teachers in high school effeminate. It was only myself I judged against some shadowy, mythical Mexican laborer—dark like me, yet very different.

---

[2]The poor ones.

READING CLOSELY AND THINKING CRITICALLY

1.   What effects did the color of Rodriguez's complexion have on him?

2.   In what ways did the women in Rodriguez's family make him feel self-conscious and inferior?

3. Why do you think that Rodriguez was so attracted to the lives of the Mexican gardeners and construction workers?

4. Using the information in the essay for clues, explain the author's idea of masculinity.

5. Why did Rodriguez read so much? Why do you think he was afraid that reading and education would make him effeminate?

6. "Complexion" came from Rodriguez's autobiographical *Hunger of Memory*. What kind of reader do you think would enjoy reading about Rodriguez's life?

EXAMINING STRUCTURE AND STRATEGY

1. In which paragraph does Rodriguez indicate what is *not* an effect of his reaction to his complexion?

2. In what order are the effects of Rodriguez's skin color arranged? What are the clues to this arrangement?

3. If the first paragraph omitted the initial fragment "Complexion" and began instead with the sentence that follows—"My first conscious experience of sexual excitement concerns my complexion"—how would the emphasis shift?

NOTING COMBINED PATTERNS

1. What is Rodriguez's primary pattern of development? How does he use that pattern?

2. In which paragraph does Rodriguez use narration to help develop the cause-and-effect relationship?

3. With what people does Rodriguez contrast himself? How does that element of contrast help the author achieve his purpose?

4. Cite an example of descriptive language, and explain how the description helps the author achieve his purpose.

CONSIDERING LANGUAGE AND STYLE

1. Rodriguez uses sentence fragments intentionally in paragraphs 1, 2, 5, 6, 8, and 9. Ordinarily, sentence fragments are an editing error. Here, the fragments serve a purpose. What is that purpose?

2. Rodriguez uses three Spanish words: *feo, braceros,* and *los pobres.* What does this use of Spanish contribute to his essay? Explain.

3. Consult a dictionary if you are unsure of the meaning of any of these words: *buoyant* (paragraph 1), *menial* (paragraph 4), *listless* (paragraph 6), *taboo* (paragraph 7), *precocious* (paragraph 9), *pomade* (paragraph 9).

FOR DISCUSSION IN CLASS OR ONLINE

With some classmates, consider the factors that shape a person's self-concept. Discuss the influence of family, friends, teachers, coaches, television, advertisements, and anything else you can think of.

1. **Writing in your journal.** Rodriguez tells about feeling self-conscious because of his skin color. Write about some aspect of your physical appearance that made you self-conscious as an adolescent, and explain the reason for your feeling. As an alternative, write about some feature of your appearance that made you proud.

2. **Combining patterns for a purpose.** The purposes in the assignments are possibilities. You may establish whatever purpose you like, within your instructor's guidelines.

   • **Description and cause-and-effect analysis.** Pick one aspect of your physical appearance, such as your height, weight, nose, or skin color. To relate experience, express feelings, and inform, describe that feature of your appearance and explain the effect it has had on you. (The previous journal writing may give you some ideas.)

   • **Classification and exemplification.** Rodriguez says that he was shy as an adolescent and that he withdrew from the company of family and friends because of his insecurity. To inform, classify the kinds of behaviors adolescents exhibit in response to how they feel about their looks. Give examples for each category in your classification. Then, use your classification as a basis for arguing whether schools should institute courses to help students feel comfortable with their looks or improve their looks.

   • **Definition and classification.** To inform, write an extended definition of *body image* and classify the most common kinds.

   • **Narration and comparison-contrast.** In paragraph 1, Rodriguez tells about his realization that his parents had a sexual relationship. Tell about a time when you came to understand something about one or both or your parents or other caregiver. To relate experience and express feelings, contrast your feelings and understanding before and after the realization. If you prefer, write about another adult in your life, such as a coach, clergy member, teacher, or grandparent.

3. **Analyzing and assessing.** Is "Complexion" a good essay to include in a high school literature course? Analyze both the content and the author's technique to make your assessment.

4. **Connecting and synthesizing the readings.** School has a significant impact on the self-concepts of young people. Explain school's potential to affect the way we view ourselves. The ideas in "Complexion" and "The Poncho Bearer" (page 212) may give you some ideas.

5. **Drawing on sources.** Ask 10 men and 10 women this question: "If you could get free plastic surgery on one part of your body, what would you change and why?" Report your findings and discuss any conclusions you can draw from them.

BACKGROUND: Award-winning journalist, short story writer, biographer, and novelist Pagan Kennedy helped pioneer the 'zine movement. She is a frequent contributor to the *Boston Globe* and *New York Times.* Kennedy's writing topics are diverse and include alternative fuel, rock musicians, Boston hoodlums, and roommates, as well as profiles of a teenage female weightlifter, an Islam mystic, and an auto mechanic. A fan of alternative fiction, Kennedy published the 'zine *Pagan's Head* for six years. Kennedy's books include *Black Livingstone: A True Tale of Adventure in Nineteenth Century Congo* (2002), which is the biography of an early black American missionary to Africa, William Sheppard; *Exes* (1998), which is about the 'zine she published; and *Pagan Kennedy's Living: A Handbook for Maturing Hipsters* (1997), which is a nonfiction collection she characterizes as "a Martha Stewart for people who sleep on stained futons and have seven housemates." Her most recent books are *The First Man-Made Man: The Story of Two Sex Changes, One Love Affair, and a Twentieth-Century Medical Revolution* (2006), and *Confessions of a Memory Eater* (2006). "One Room, 3,000 Brains" first appeared in the *Boston Globe Magazine* in June 2004.

COMBINED PATTERNS AND THEIR PURPOSES: In "One Room, 3,000 Brains," Pagan Kennedy combines *cause-and-effect analysis, description, narration,* and *process analysis* to achieve several purposes. Most apparently, she **informs** readers about the Harvard Brain Tissue Resource Center and the work done there. More subtly, she **informs** about the changing understanding of mental illness, and she aims to **persuade** readers to donate their brains to science. In addition, the story of one researcher's medical history **relates an experience** and **expresses feelings.**

ONE ROOM, 3,000 BRAINS

BY PAGAN KENNEDY

WHEN I PEER DOWN into one of the buckets in a sink, I see my first human brain. It's actually half a brain, trailing some stem, and the noodlelike folds are pearly in color, rather than the gray you'd expect. "We don't want the smell to be too strong," says George Tejada, explaining the need to soak the half-brain in water. It has been preserved in formaldehyde, which gives off a powerful stench.

As you read
Give some thought to how society treats people who have a mental illness.

2   We're standing in the dissection room of the Harvard Brain Tissue Resource Center, a.k.a. the Brain Bank, which is housed on the McLean Hospital campus in Belmont. A few minutes ago, Tejada peeled off a latex glove so we could shake hands. "Don't worry, my hands are clean," he assured me. I did not doubt him. Tejada, the assistant director of tissue processing at the Brain Bank, could pass for the headmaster of a prep school, with his crisp buttondown shirt and pressed khakis. The dissection room itself, where human brains arrive and get sliced up at a rate of about one per day, also appears to be disappointing spick-and-span. Aside from the buckets in the sink—and the map of the brain regions taped up above the counter—it would be hard to guess what goes on here.

3   The institution collects brains from donors and distributes tissue to researchers around the world. The Brain Bank stocks "normal" brains as well as those donated by people who had schizophrenia, bipolar disorder, Huntington's disease, and Parkinson's disease. In part, it is because of the Brain Bank—and other such repositories—that neuroscientists are finally beginning to zero in on the

genes involved in such mental disabilities, a crucial step needed to speed the development of lifesaving drugs.

4   Thirty years ago, there were no brain banks in the United States—at least not officially. Now, more than 100 such repositories exist. Over the past few decades, psychiatry has gone through a monumental transition, away from talk therapy and toward drug therapy. So scientists are sorting, storing, and examining human brains as never before, peering through microscopes at tiny slices of tissue for clues about why we go mad. This is all happening at a time when the proportion of mentally ill people worldwide who receive treatment is "woefully inadequate," according to an unprecedented new study by a World Health Organization consortium and published this month in the *Journal of the American Medical Association.*

5   Just this year, McLean researchers announced that they had pinpointed what they called energy deficiencies in the brain cells of people with bipolar disorder, an important insight that could contribute to the development of specific drugs to help the 2.3 million Americans the illness afflicts. It is this type of brain work that marks a profound shift in the way we think about our own thoughts.

> "It is this type of brain work that marks a profound shift in the way we think about our own thoughts."

6   Dr. Francine M. Benes, director of the Brain Bank, explains just how powerful this kind of analysis has proved to be. She says, "We're on the threshold of finding the markers for schizophrenia," that is, the genes that contribute to a person's susceptibility to the disease.

7   And to boost genetic research at other institutions, the Brain Bank has put a database online. It is open to researchers and the general public (it can be found on the Web at http://national_databank.mclean.harvard.edu). Benes's hope is that scientists who receive tissue from the Brain Bank will submit the results of their research to the database, helping to create a superstorehouse of brain data for the field.

8   It all sounds very worthy and hygienic, but I must admit that I had come to the Brain Bank hoping to be grossed out, at least just a little. My ideas about what might go on at a facility that houses more than 3,000 human brains had been inflamed by an episode of the original *Star Trek* in which DayGlo-colored brains order slaves to fight battles for their amusement. And then there is an old sci-fi movie called *They Saved Hitler's Brain,* in which the Fuhrer's cut-off head, kept alive inside a glass jar, commands what's left of the Nazi empire. Something about iced brains captures the imagination—after all, no one would bother to make a movie called *They Saved Hitler's Liver.* The brain seems to contain the essence of the self. Yet, unlike so many other dear and familiar body parts—our eyes, our arms, our toes—it exists under wraps. Even as I write that sentence, I'm aware of my own brain dwelling in the loft apartment of my skull, doing who-knows-what up there. It is me, and it is also eerily remote.

9   "This is a problem that's not going to go away soon," says Benes about the complex feelings people have about their brains and, therefore, about donating that particular organ to science. "It's believed by many that the soul of their loved one resides in the brain, or they see the brain as what gives one a special connectedness

in the spiritual." For years, when people donated their bodies to organ banks, brains were not part of the deal. Now, the taboo against collecting brains has begun to relax. The New England Organ Bank and the New England Eye & Tissue Transplant Bank, for instance, have quietly begun to include brains in the roster of donations they collect. The brain is on its way to becoming just another body part.

> "For years, when people donated their bodies to organ banks, brains were not part of the deal."

10   While this is a great boon to the Brain Bank, in terms of recruiting donors, outreach is only one small part of what goes on here. Most of the work happens after the donor dies, at which time the cells in his or her brain immediately begin to deteriorate. Within hours of getting a call from the donor's family, the Brain Bankers must find a pathologist in the appropriate region of the country, arrange for that pathologist to extract the brain and put it in a special container, and fly the brain to McLean by same-day shipping. After that, the brain will be assigned a number, sliced up and photographed, frozen, preserved in formaldehyde, examined, entered into a database, and distributed to worthy investigators.

11   The brain in the bucket, in fact, turns out to be the only one I come across here that looks remotely brainlike. Every other piece of tissue has been so carefully preserved and processed that you'd be hard-pressed to say what it is. Tejada shows me into a room full of freezers, and opens a door to reveal plastic bags, each of which holds a brain hemisphere cut into 16 sections. Mist rolls out into the room—the freezer is kept at 80 below zero. The bags themselves appear to contain flash-frozen shrimp.

12   When a brain arrives here, usually half of it gets frozen while the other half ends up in formaldehyde—a system designed to give researchers as many options as possible. In the "Tupperware room," slices of brain tissue marinate in chemicals; each half-brain is stored in the kind of plastic container you might use to microwave leftover pasta. From the looks of the original labels, which still cling to some of the containers, the Brain Bank chose an off-brand rather than genuine Tupperware.

13   Tejada leads me back to his office and shows me a photo of one of the brains. Such mug shots are made available to researchers, along with other information, in order to help them select which tissue sample they would like to order. The brain in the photo, freshly cut out of the donor's head, gleams with blood. Unlike the brains in sci-fi movies, this one does not look up to the task of issuing commands to Nazi followers. It's just a piece of meat. I'm reminded of what William James said: "The brain itself is an excessively vascular organ, a sponge full of blood." This photo is a powerful argument for using a biological model to understand what goes on in the mind.

14   "I was part of the shift" toward seeing mental illness as an organic problem, says Benes, who is trim and wears a starched lab coat. We're sitting in her office, and she's holding research on her lap—a sheaf of papers covered with numbers that represent the gene profiles of schizophrenic, bipolar, and control-group brains.

15   In 1973, Francine Benes attended a neuroscience meeting at a ski resort in Colorado. Then a cell biologist, she had no particular expertise in mental illness. Nonetheless, she found herself in a talk on schizophrenia, delivered by Dr. Janice

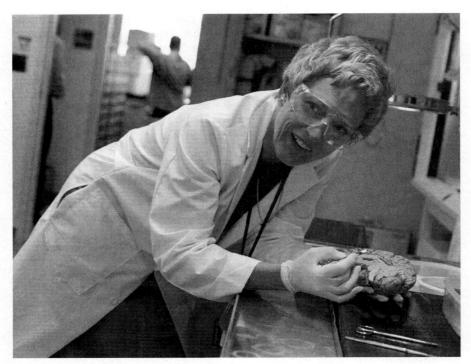
Dr. Francine Benes Holding a Human Brain

R. Stevens. "I was standing in the back of the room, and it blew me away," Benes says. Stevens proposed that schizophrenia was due to a dopamine disturbance in a part of the brain called the nucleus accumbens—a radical theory back when psychiatrists were still blaming mothers, who were presumed to have driven their children mad with Joan Crawford–like behavior. Stevens's paper helped to erase that stigma. The illness became a matter of bad wiring rather than bad mothering. "Schizophrenia could now be visualized in terms of the circuitries in the brain," Benes says.

16   The revelation changed the direction of Benes's life. She returned to medical school to get her MD, and, in 1982, established the Laboratory for Structural Neuroscience at McLean. Early on, "there was me and maybe two other people who were doing postmortem schizophrenia research," she says. By the late 1980s, however, researchers were routinely examining postmortem brain tissue in order to search for the causes of Alzheimer's and Huntington's disease. Using the same methods to investigate mental illness no longer seemed so strange. These days, Benes says, "the stigma is gone, and you have the excitement of getting inside the cells," chasing after the genes that lead to mental dysfunction.

17   Most exciting, brain scientists have begun to borrow ideas from the colleagues who study problems that affect other parts of the body. "At this juncture, we're starting to move into alignment with cancer research and hematology research," Benes says. "That is going to prove to be the most historic step in this field." Treating the brain as just another part of the body—vulnerable to high cholesterol, secondhand smoke, and bad genes—may lead to breakthroughs that were not possible back when the brain seemed to be something special and separate.

> "Most exciting, brain scientists have begun to borrow ideas from the colleagues who study problems that affect other parts of the body."

18   "I am a Brain Banker, asking for a deposit from you," Jill Bolte Taylor sings to me over the phone from her home in Bloomington, Indiana. She's sitting with a guitar in her lap and a phone receiver lying on the floor before her, strumming like a cowboy. "Find the key to unlock this thing we call insanity," she warbles. "Just dial 1-800-BRAIN-BANK for information, please." And then she ends with a whoop worthy of Hank Williams.

19   Taylor, the Brain Bank's spokeswoman for psychiatric disorders, tours the country, exhorting the public and especially those with mental illnesses to donate their brains to science. In just about every talk she gives, "there's this wonderful moment when the audience realizes, 'Oh, my gosh, she wants my brain,'" Taylor says. "The tension in the room gets really thick. Everyone's looking down like we're all in the first grade—'Don't call on me, don't call on me.' So I'll pull out my guitar and sing the Brain Bank jingle. It lightens everything up. It's been a wonderful marketing tool."

20   Taylor hooked up with the Brain Bank in 1993, a postdoc working in Benes's lab, researching the organic causes of schizophrenia. She was determined to prove they existed. Her brother had schizophrenia.

21   "The thinking in the professional community for decades was that it was a character flaw caused in part by the schizophrenogenic mother—they blamed the family," she says. Taylor fought against that stigma on two fronts: as a Harvard researcher and as a board member of the National Alliance for the Mentally Ill, a group that pioneered the effort to understand mental illness as a biological problem rather than a failure of the will. "It's only been 10 years really that it has been put out that severe mental illness, schizophrenia in particular, is a biologically based brain disorder," Taylor says. In the mid-1990s, Taylor worked in the lab from Monday through Friday, and then would often hop on a plane over the weekend to deliver lectures around the country, spreading the word about brain donation. "When I first started, we were receiving fewer than five psychiatric brains a year," she says. Now that figure has jumped to 25.

22   Taylor admits that, back then, she was something of an overachiever. "I had been driven toward excellence by very powerful anger," she says. "And that anger was related to growing up with a sibling who was not normal. You're constantly on guard. You trust him, and then he hurts you emotionally."

23   On December 10, 1996, Taylor, then 37 years old, woke up to find she had a brain disorder of her own. "Inside four hours, I watched my mind deteriorate in its ability to process incoming information," she says. A fist-sized hemorrhage had formed in the left hemisphere of her brain, between the two centers that process

language. Because the hemorrhage had also knocked out the portion of the brain that creates fear, she felt only curiosity as her mental functions shut down. "I learned as much about my brain in those four hours as I had in my whole academic career," she says. "Eventually, my right arm went completely paralyzed, and that's when my brain said, 'Oh, my gosh, I'm having a stroke. I'm having a stroke? I'm a very busy woman. Well, I can't stop this from happening, so I'll do this for a week, learn what I can learn from it, and then I'll get back to work.'"

24   In fact, recovery took years. "I was an infant in a woman's body," she says. She was unable to wiggle her toes or roll over in bed. "I couldn't understand when I heard other people making language at me. I lost my ability to read and write." It was two years before she could cook and talk on the phone at the same time, and many more before she could hop from rock to rock without planning exactly where to put her feet.

25   Last summer, year seven of her recovery, Taylor slipped into water skis for the first time since her stroke. As a girl, she'd been a slalomer, so comfortable on the water that her skis felt like part of her feet. Now, as the boat pulled away, she found her balance and began cutting through the glassy water. "All of a sudden, there was this moment when my body took its position, and every cell remembered that it was powerful. Off I went. It was pure bliss. I had recovered who I was before that hemorrhage."

"Last summer, Taylor slipped into water skis for the first time since her stroke."

26   No longer a workaholic, she enjoys a laid-back life in Indiana. She continues to spread the word about brain donations, and she also makes brains—out of stained glass. Taylor's creations are suitable for hanging against a big sunny window, where you can watch the world through the yellow and blue and green pieces of glass that represent the nuclei and gyri and limbic system.

27   Right now, in one window of my computer, I'm donating my brain to science, typing information into an online form at *www.brainbank.mclean.org/questionnaire.htm*. It's no more difficult than ordering a book from Amazon.com. You give your name, address, next of kin, and use a pull-down menu to let the Brain Bank know what kind you've got. For a moment, I linger over that list, deciding how to classify myself: normal control, schizophrenia, bipolar disorder, Parkinson's disease, Huntington's disease. I click on "normal control," knowing that designation could change. That bloodsoaked sponge in my head, so soft, so frangible, could be destroyed by any of a number of diseases. I have seen them up close on a computer screen at McLean. There, a helpful man in a lab coat showed me slides of brain tissue that had been eaten away by abnormalities, from the tangles of Alzheimer's to the bloom of melanoma cells.

28   We hope, of course, that all of this study of brain tissue will lead to the discovery of new pills and treatments. But along the way, perhaps it will offer another benefit, too. The more we know about the neurological disorders, the more likely we are to feel compassion for the people who have those disorders. I'm remembering something that Jill Taylor said about the moment when her brother was diagnosed with schizophrenia: "It was a relief. Finally, I could separate him from the disease. I could forgive him. I could love him again as my big brother."

READING CLOSELY AND THINKING CRITICALLY

1. Something about the Brain Bank disappoints the author. What is it?
2. What is the purpose of the Brain Bank?
3. Why have people been reluctant to donate their brains to science even when they are willing to donate other body parts?
4. What is the stigma associated with mental illness? Why does this stigma exist?
5. In paragraph 5, Kennedy says that brain research "marks a profound shift in the way we think about our own thoughts." What does she mean?

EXAMINING STRUCTURE AND STRATEGY

1. "One Room, 3,000 Brains" originally appeared in the *Boston Globe Magazine*. Are the title and first sentence likely to engage the interest of readers of a large metropolitan daily newspaper? Explain.
2. Part of the article is written in the present tense; see, for example, paragraphs 2, 6, and 11. Why is the present tense used?
3. How does Kennedy make a scientific subject accessible to readers of the *Boston Globe*?

NOTING COMBINED PATTERNS

1. What is the purpose of the description in paragraph 1? How does the description in paragraphs 2, 11, and 13 help Kennedy achieve her purpose?
2. What is the purpose of the process analysis in paragraphs 10 and 12? How does the process analysis in paragraph 27 help Kennedy achieve her purpose?
3. What is the purpose of the narration in paragraphs 15–16? What is the purpose of the narration in paragraphs 23–26?
4. What is the purpose of the cause-and-effect analysis in paragraphs 4–5? In paragraphs 8–9? In paragraph 22?

CONSIDERING LANGUAGE AND STYLE

1. Kennedy uses language not commonly associated with writing about scientific topics. For example, in paragraph 8, she refers to the location of the brain as being in a loft apartment, and in paragraph 12, she refers to tissue samples as being in off-brand Tupperware. Cite another example of such unusual word choice. What effect does this word choice have? Why does Kennedy use such word choice?
2. Kennedy uses simple, specific words. For example, in paragraph 2, she says the researcher "peeled off a latex glove." Give two other examples of simple, specific word choice. What effect does this word choice have?
3. Consult a dictionary if you do not know the meaning of these words: *repositories* (paragraphs 3, 4), *dopamine* (paragraph 15), *postmortem* (paragraph 16), *hematology* (paragraph 17), *exhorting* (paragraph 19), *slalomer* (paragraph 25).

Is there still a stigma associated with mental illness? Explain why or why not.

WRITING ASSIGNMENTS

1. **Writing in your journal.** Are you willing to donate your brain to science? What about other body parts, such as your heart, corneas, skin, or liver? In a page or two, explain how you feel and why.

2. **Combining patterns for a purpose.** The purposes in the assignments are possibilities. You may establish whatever purpose you like, within your instructor's guidelines.

    *   **Description and process analysis.** Describe a body part, and explain its function in a way that gives your reader a fresh appreciation for something that is familiar.
    *   **Narration and cause-and-effect analysis.** To relate an experience and express feelings, tell about a time you or someone you know was ill or incapacitated. In addition, explain the effect of the illness or incapacitation.
    *   **Cause-and-effect analysis and narration.** The director of the Brain Bank made a career change as a result of a conference she attended. To relate your experience and perhaps express your feelings, narrate an account of what caused you to make an important decision about your life, career, or schooling. How has the decision worked out?
    *   **Process analysis and exemplification.** To inform your reader, explain a process you know well for someone who knows little about that process. For example, you could explain how to surf, how to train a dog, how an automobile hybrid engine works, or how cells divide. To convince your reader of the importance of the process, give examples of ways the process is useful, interesting, or significant.

3. **Analyzing and assessing.** Analyze the detail and word choice in the essay, and explain how they help the author achieve her persuasive and informational purposes with her intended audience, the readers of the *Boston Globe*. Your responses to number 3 of "Examining Structure and Strategy" and number 2 of "Considering Language and Style" may help you.

4. **Connecting and synthesizing the readings.** Research is showing us that schizophrenia, bipolar disorder, and other forms of mental illness are brain disorders. Unfortunately, they can lead the afflicted to commit violent acts. Knowing that, do you think we need to make any changes in our criminal justice system? In addition to your own ideas, you can use the ideas in any of the following selections: "One Room, 3,000 Brains," "A Hanging" (page 665), and "Young Voices from the Cell" (page 613).

5. **Drawing on sources.** Write an article for your campus newspaper that explains brain donation to the campus community. Visit www.brainbank.mclean.org and click on these links: "How to Make a Donation" and "Types of Tissue Collected." Summarize the main points to help people make up their minds. As an alternative, visit the National Alliance for the Mentally Ill site at www.nami.org, and summarize the information about one mental illness discussed there.

BACKGROUND: A professor at the Missouri School of Journalism and associate dean of graduate studies, Esther Thorson is the third woman to win the Distinguished Advertising Educator Award. Thorson has researched how people process information in television ads, how community news affects citizens, how people respond to television, and how health campaigns affect people. Her publications include hundreds of academic journal articles and book chapters. "Dissect an Ad," first written in 1996, is now part of the Public Broadcasting System's "By the People" Web site, which covers various aspects of the 2004 presidential election campaign.

COMBINED PATTERNS AND THEIR PURPOSE: Using *division, cause-and-effect analysis,* and *exemplification,* Esther Thorson identifies the components of political advertisements to **inform** readers about how the ads persuade people by appealing to their emotions.

DISSECT AN AD

BY ESTHER THORSON

BOTH PUNDITS AND CITIZENS spend a lot of time making fun of political commercials. They're short, simple-minded, and as election day approaches, they become more obnoxiously frequent. There seems good reason to ridicule the idea that they affect how people vote and how they think about government and politicians.

As you read
Determine why it's important to examine political ads carefully.

2   But a large body of studies carried out in the last 15 years shows quite clearly that political commercials have major effects on people. In Presidential elections, television commercials consume most of the money spent by candidates in their attempts to get elected. This is also true of state-level elections.

3   The bottom line, then, is that it's important for citizens to look carefully at political ads. Certainly the truth or falsity and, regardless of "truth," the deceptiveness of ad content is important to examine. Many newspapers and television analysis programs provide the citizen a good opportunity to learn more about the quality of the verbal content of political commercials. Although a majority of Americans are not aware of this, government closely controls the truth value of national product advertising on television. But because of the principle of free speech, a principle protected by the U.S. Constitution, there is no control whatsoever on the content of a political commercial. Basically, a politician can say anything she or he wishes in a political ad. The only "control" over content in a political ad is media and public response to that content.

> "Basically, a politician can say anything she or he wishes in a political ad."

4   But ads communicate more than their verbal content. Like any persuasive message developed by a professional communicator, every aspect of their few-seconds duration is carefully designed to influence. Aspects of ads beyond their verbal content are called structural features.

5   This guide describes ten of the structural features that political ads use most commonly. Recognizing a persuasive tool for what it is helps people understand the true impact of ads on themselves and others. Regardless of what verbal content

an ad uses, it will employ one or many of these persuasive tools. Recognizing them and figuring out what their intended meaning is can provide important new insight into a political ad.

CANDIDATE MYTHOLOGIES

6   When people think about a political office-holder like the President, Vice President, Governor, or Senator, they often, unbeknownst to themselves, attribute mythological features to that person. Common mythologies about the U.S. President represent him as:

a.   War hero
b.   Man of the people
c.   Father
d.   Savior
e.   Friend

7   These perceptions are "myths" in that they carry a lot of cultural baggage with them, but they are never true features of a president. They're used, however, to create emotion in viewers. If that face up on the screen asking for your vote is your "friend," you feel differently about him. If he's a "hero," he may make you feel proud or safe. If he's your "father," you may feel you can trust him.

8   Myths like these are generally not spoken, but represented in images. A candidate shown with people trying to touch him, shake his hand, or clapping for him is being represented as a hero. Shown with his family, he's obviously a father, but he's also a father when shown kissing babies or supporting laws that aid children. Probably the most common spoken myth is "friend." "Friend of the people," "the working man's friend," are popular ad phrases. Clasping a voter around the shoulders or a warm handshake visually represents "friend."

> "A candidate shown with people trying to touch him, shake his hand, or clapping for him, is being represented as a hero."

BACKGROUND LOCATIONS

9   Where the candidate is when he is shown, or where the opponent is shown to be in an attack ad, is critically important to what is being communicated. Kennedy was shown walking along the beach. Perot was almost always in a paneled den or office. Clinton was most frequently surrounded by people. Each of the backgrounds is used to communicate a variety of things about the candidate.

PROPS

10   Props are objects shown in the scenes. The most common prop is the American flag. Desks are important props. Headlines in newspapers are props used to verify statistical and factual claims. ("If the newspaper said it, it must be true.") A podium is a prop and sometimes other people can serve as props. Once, a U.S. Senate candidate in Wisconsin even used a cardboard standup of Elvis as a prop.

EMOTION-COMMUNICATING FACES

11   While any scene, any piece of music, any statement can induce emotion, the most common emotional device is the human face: the fear and anger in the face of [the] teen druggie, the admiration and enthusiasm in crowd faces, babies' faces crying, fierce, uncaring expressions on the faces of opponents. All of these faces and their expressions are carefully planted in ads. A most common approach is to take the face of an opponent at its most unattractive and show that face as background for words written on the screen to indicate what awful things he has done. Faces are probably a candidate's most direct conduit to creating feelings in viewers.

APPEALS

12   Every ad, political or otherwise, has at its center an appeal. This is the main message of the ad and it is designed to speak to a viewer's emotions: insurance ads appeal to fears of disasters; cosmetics ads appeal to personal ego; many high-ticket products appeal to greed. Political ads are no different. Ads for candidates can appeal to positive feelings such as patriotism or pride, but they can also elicit fears, especially if they are attack ads. These fears include things like war, crime, job loss or poor education. They may even imply that their opponent is untrustworthy or that he will take health benefits away from your parents or even that he will lead the country into war. Consultants are always looking for "hot button" issues—issues that will be effective with a large percentage of voters. Once found, they will include these issues in the major appeal of the ad and sometimes in several minor appeals as well.

MUSIC AND BACKGROUND SOUNDS

13   Almost all political ads use music. It's usually orchestral, stately, designed to sound inspiring to a broad spectrum of listeners. Volume of music is very important. A common approach is have a crescendo of sound at the end of an ad. Background music is borrowed from horror movies when the ad attacks an opponent. Music is often fiercely patriotic-sounding.

14   Background noises are important and seldom consciously noticed by viewers. Sirens, traffic noise, [and] drumbeats are commonly employed. A good way to pick up use of music and background sounds, of course, is to look away from the screen during the ad. You'll find a lot going on there that you'd otherwise be unlikely to notice.

> "Background music is borrowed from horror movies when the ad attacks an opponent."

FILM EDITING AND CAMERA USE

15   Slow-motion is commonly used to increase the salience of an image. Extreme close-ups increase our perceptions of importance. They're also used to emphasize emotion, evil, and truthfulness. Often the camera comes in closer to the candidate as he begins his pledge to us voters—whatever that pledge may be. Jump-cuts occur when scenes are edited together and the central figure moves suddenly from

one location to another. Shooting from above the candidate when he's greeting a crowd provides an impression of warmth and bonding. Black and white pictures usually mean the topic is serious and, most likely, negative.

CLOTHING

16 What a candidate is wearing is carefully chosen to show the viewer something "important" about him. An expensive suit shows power, taste, authority. Shirt sleeves show hard work and empathy with ordinary people. Jacket over the shoulder shows ease, warmth, confidence. A loosened tie usually indicates the same characteristics.

DEPICTED ACTIONS

17 What the candidate is doing in a support ad and what the opponent is doing in an attack ad are important. Getting off a plane shows characteristics like international expertise and concern, familiarity and caring about the whole country, or just plain old power. Interacting with the family shows caring. Holding hands with a spouse does the same. Signing papers shows ability to get important things done. Greeting ordinary people shows popularity and caring. Speaking from a podium emphasizes power and good ideas.

18 In the opponent, the activity is sometimes representing as "silly" or weak. A good example is the 1988 ad which featured Dukakis's helmeted head popping out of the top of an army tank. The opponent is sometimes shown with an incriminating "other." Candidates are usually doing things in color. Opponents are usually doing things in black and white.

SUPERS AND CODE WORDS

19 Supers are words printed in large letters on the screen. They appear over a background that is supposed to exemplify whatever is being said by the super. A super says, "Pay attention to this factoid or claim." It is often a phrase that communicates outrage at something the opponent has said or done such as, "RAISED TAXES THREE TIMES IN THREE YEARS." A super can also emphasize the larger appeal being made in the ad such as, "WRONG FOR YESTERDAY. WRONG FOR TOMORROW." Supers can use code words, which are words that sound simple but carry significant unconscious meaning for viewers. For example, when the word "values" is used in ads, it makes the candidate sound upright and moral, but often the exact values represented by the candidate are not made clear. The implication of the ad is that the candidate featured has values, but his or her opponent does not. Many argue that "crime" and "welfare" are code words that encourage viewers to look at these issues through a racial lens. Even a seemingly innocuous word like "yesterday" can be a code word if the meaning is implied to be that someone or something is too old and no longer relevant, rather than meaning it just occurred in the past.

> "The implication of the ad is that the candidate featured has values, but his or her opponent does not."

READING CLOSELY AND THINKING CRITICALLY

1. Why is it important to examine televised political advertisements critically?
2. In paragraph 9, Thorson states that background locations "communicate a variety of things about the candidate." What do you think they communicate?
3. The components of televised political ads are calculated to appeal to emotions, not reason. Why?
4. Do you think televised political advertisements are deceptive? Explain.

EXAMINING STRUCTURE AND STRATEGY

1. What is the purpose of "Dissect an Ad"? Where is the purpose stated? Do you think the purpose is an important one? Why or why not?
2. Why does Thorson include the information in paragraphs 1 and 2? Why didn't she just begin with the information in paragraph 3?
3. Is the supporting detail adequate? Explain.

NOTING COMBINED PATTERNS

1. Most of the essay is developed with division and cause-and-effect analysis, the dominant patterns of development. Explain why these patterns are used and how they help Thorson achieve her writing purpose.
2. How does Thorson use exemplification? How important is that exemplification?

CONSIDERING LANGUAGE AND STYLE

1. Paragraph 6 explains that political advertisements can attribute "mythological features" to a candidate. What is a mythological feature?
2. Consult a dictionary if you do not know the meaning of any of these words: *pundits* (paragraph 1), *conduit* (paragraph 11), *salience* (paragraph 15), *innocuous* (paragraph 19).

FOR DISCUSSION IN CLASS OR ONLINE

How do you decide which political candidates you favor? Where do you get most of your information about political candidates—from TV ads, from newspapers, from Internet news? How reliable are these sources?

WRITING ASSIGNMENTS

1. **Writing in your journal.** What did you learn as a result of reading "Dissect an Ad"? Can you apply what you learned to nonpolitical advertisements? Explain.
2. **Combining patterns for a purpose.** The purposes in the assignments are possibilities. You may establish whatever purpose you like, within your instructor's guidelines.

- **Description, exemplification, and cause-and-effect analysis.** With your eyes closed, listen to several television advertisements. Describe what you hear and draw conclusions about how sound is used in advertisements, using three or more ads as examples. Now repeat the exercise and watch some ads with the sound off. What is missed? Your purpose is to inform readers about how sound is used to influence people to buy products.

- **Division and exemplification.** Study magazine advertisements for either cosmetics or some personal hygiene product, such as shampoo, mouthwash, or soap. Inform readers by dividing the ads into their components so consumers understand how the ads work. Use the components of the ads you study as examples of persuasive strategies.

- **Description, exemplification, and cause-and-effect analysis.** Paragraph 16 notes that clothing communicates certain characteristics of political candidates. In high school, too, clothing often communicates a great deal. Students often make judgments about each other based on what they wear, and sometimes they become very competitive about clothing. To persuade your reader, argue that high school students in public schools should or should not have to wear uniforms.

- **Classification and exemplification.** Political figures are not the only people with mythological features. Movie, television, and sports stars also have mythological features attributed to them. Classify these mythological features, and give examples of movie, television, and sports stars to whom these features are attributed.

3. **Analyzing and assessing.** Explain how the information in the essay can be applied to other, nonpolitical advertisements on television. Be sure to illustrate your points with examples of ads.

4. **Connecting and synthesizing the readings.** Are political advertisements a form of lying? To support your assertion, you can draw on ideas in "Dissect an Ad," "Lifosuction" (page 250), and "White Lies" (page 488).

5. **Drawing on sources.** Visit the Public Broadcasting System site called "The 30 Second Candidate" at www.pbs.org/30secondcandidate/front.html. Click on "tricks of the trade." There you can manipulate a political ad to make it favorable to a candidate and then unfavorable to the candidate. Compare and contrast the two ads you create, and give the conclusions you form as a result of the experience.

BACKGROUND: A superb essayist whose literary accomplishments won him the Presidential Medal of Freedom in 1963, Elwyn Brooks White (1899–1985) was a reporter for the *Seattle Times* before moving to New York to become an advertising copywriter. He went on to write for the *New Yorker* for 50 years and helped establish its reputation for excellence with his "Talk of the Town" column. He soon became known for his prose style and his personal essays, which often display an ironic view of the world. White also wrote the "One Man's Meat" column for *Harper's,* where "Once More to the Lake" first appeared in 1941. You may know White as the author of the popular children's book *Charlotte's Web* (1952) or as the author, with William Strunk, Jr., of the popular and enduring writer's guide *The Elements of Style* (1959), a reference often checked by students and professional writers alike.

COMBINED PATTERNS AND THEIR PURPOSES: In "Once More to the Lake," E. B. White uses *description* to **relate the experience** of his visits to a family vacation spot in Maine, visits he made both as a child and as an adult. Using *narration,* White recounts a visit that he made with his son. Using *comparison-contrast,* he reveals that the spot is, at once, the same and different after the passing of years. Be sure to notice that White's description allows him to **express his feelings** about the vacation spot. Notice, too, how it leads the author to an unnerving conclusion.

ONCE MORE TO THE LAKE
BY E. B. WHITE

ONE SUMMER, along about 1904, my father rented a camp on a lake in Maine and took us all there for the month of August. We all got ringworm from some kittens and had to rub Pond's Extract on our arms and legs night and morning, and my father rolled over in a canoe with all his clothes on; but outside of that the vacation was a success and from then on none of us ever thought there was any place in the world like that lake in Maine. We returned summer after summer—always on August 1 for one month. I have since become a salt-water man, but sometimes in summer there are days when the restlessness of the tides and the fearful cold of the sea water and the incessant wind that blows across the afternoon and into the evening make me wish for the placidity of a lake in the woods. A few weeks ago this feeling got so strong I bought myself a couple of bass hooks and a spinner and returned to the lake where we used to go, for a week's fishing and to revisit old haunts.

As you read Notice how the essay makes you feel. Do you find the essay upbeat or depressing?

2   I took along my son, who had never had any fresh water up his nose and who had seen lily pads only from train windows. On the journey over to the lake I began to wonder what it would be like. I wondered how time would have marred this unique, this holy spot—the coves and streams, the hills that the sun set behind, the camps and the paths behind the camps. I was sure that the tarred road would have found it out, and I wondered in what other ways it would be desolated. It is strange how much you can remember about places like that once you allow your mind to return into the

"I took along my son, who had never had any fresh water up his nose and who had seen lily pads only from train windows."

grooves that lead back. You remember one thing, and that suddenly reminds you of another thing. I guess I remembered clearest of all the early mornings, when the lake was cool and motionless, remembered how the bedroom smelled of the lumber it was made of and of the wet woods whose scent entered through the screen. The partitions in the camp were thin and did not extend clear to the top of the rooms, and as I was always the first up I would dress softly so as not to wake the others, and sneak out into the sweet outdoors and start out in the canoe, keeping close along the shore in the long shadows of the pines. I remembered being very careful never to rub my paddle against the gunwale for fear of disturbing the stillness of the cathedral.

3   The lake had never been what you would call a wild lake. There were cottages sprinkled around the shores, and it was in farming country although the shores of the lake were quite heavily wooded. Some of the cottages were owned by nearby farmers, and you would live at the shore and eat your meals at the farmhouse. That's what our family did. But although it wasn't wild, it was a fairly large and undisturbed lake and there were places in it that, to a child at least, seemed infinitely remote and primeval.

4   I was right about the tar: It led to within half a mile of the shore. But when I got back there, with my boy, and we settled into a camp near a farmhouse and into the kind of summertime I had known, I could tell that it was going to be pretty much the same as it had been before—I knew it, lying in bed the first morning smelling the bedroom and hearing the boy sneak quietly out and go off along the shore in a boat. I began to sustain the illusion that he was I, and therefore, by simple transposition, that I was my father. This sensation persisted, kept cropping up all the time we were there. It was not an entirely new feeling, but in this setting it grew much stronger. I seemed to be living a dual existence. I would be in the middle of some simple act, I would be picking up a bait box or laying down a table fork, or I would be saying something and suddenly it would be not I but my father who was saying the words or making the gesture. It gave me a creepy sensation.

"I seemed to be living a dual existence."

5   We went fishing the first morning. I felt the same damp moss covering the worms in the bait can, and saw the dragonfly alight on the tip of my rod as it hovered a few inches from the surface of the water. It was the arrival of this fly that convinced me beyond any doubt that everything was as it always had been, that the years were a mirage and that there had been no years. The small waves were the same, chucking the rowboat under the chin as we fished at anchor, and the boat was the same boat, the same color green and the ribs broken in the same places, and under the floorboards the same fresh water leavings and debris—the dead hellgrammite, the wisps of moss, the rusty discarded fishhook, the dried blood from yesterday's catch. We stared silently at the tips of our rods, at the dragonflies that came and went. I lowered the tip of mine into the water, tentatively, pensively dislodging the fly, which darted two feet away, poised, darted two feet back, and came to rest again a little farther up the rod. There had been no years between the ducking of this dragonfly and the other one—the one that was part of memory. I

looked at the boy, who was silently watching his fly, and it was my hands that held his rod, my eyes watching. I felt dizzy and didn't know which rod I was at the end of.

6　　We caught two bass, hauling them in briskly as though they were mackerel, pulling them over the side of the boat in a businesslike manner without any landing net, and stunning them with a blow on the back of the head. When we got back for a swim before lunch, the lake was exactly where we had left it, the same number of inches from the dock, and there was only the merest suggestion of a breeze. This seemed an utterly enchanted sea, this lake you could leave to its own devices for a few hours and come back to, and find that it had not stirred, this constant and trustworthy body of water. In the shallows, the dark, water-soaked sticks and twigs, smooth and old, were undulating in clusters on the bottom against the clean ribbed sand, and the track of the mussel was plain. A school of minnows swam by, each minnow with its small individual shadow, doubling the attendance, so clear and sharp in the sunlight. Some of the other campers were in swimming, along the shore, one of them with a cake of soap, and the water felt thin and clear and unsubstantial. Over the years there had been this person with the cake of soap, this cultist, and here he was. There had been no years.

7　　Up to the farmhouse to dinner through the teeming dusty field, the road under our sneakers was only a two-track road. The middle track was missing, the one with the marks of the hooves and the splotches of dried, flaky manure. There had always been three tracks to choose from in choosing which track to walk in; now the choice was narrowed down to two. For a moment I missed terribly the middle alternative. But the way led past the tennis court, and something about the way it lay there in the sun reassured me; the tape had loosened along the backline, the alleys were green with plantains and other weeds, and the net (installed in June and removed in September) sagged in the dry noon, and the whole place steamed with midday heat and hunger and emptiness. There was a choice of pie for dessert, and one was blueberry and one was apple, and the waitresses were the same country girls, there having been no passage of time, only the illusion of it as in a dropped curtain—the waitresses were still fifteen; their hair had been washed, that was the only difference—they had been to the movies and seen the pretty girls with the clean hair.

> "There had always been three tracks to choose from in choosing which track to walk in; now the choice was narrowed down to two."

8　　Summertime, oh, summertime, pattern of life indelible with fadeproof lake, the wood unshatterable, the pasture with the sweetfern and the juniper forever and ever, summer without end; this was the background, and the life along the shore was the design, the cottages with their innocent and tranquil design, their tiny docks with the flagpole and the American flag floating against the white clouds in the blue sky, the little paths over the roots of the trees leading from camp to camp and the paths leading back to the outhouses and the can of lime for sprinkling, and at the souvenir counters at the store the miniature birchbark canoes and the postcards that showed things looking a little better than they looked. This was the

American family at play, escaping the city heat, wondering whether the newcomers in the camp at the head of the cove were "common" or "nice," wondering whether it was true that the people who drove up for Sunday dinner at the farmhouse were turned away because there wasn't enough chicken.

9   It seemed to me, as I kept remembering all this, that those times and those summers had been infinitely precious and worth saving. There had been jollity and peace and goodness. The arriving (at the beginning of August) had been so big a business in itself, at the railway station the farm wagon drawn up, the first smell of the pine-laden air, the first glimpse of the smiling farmer, and the great importance of the trunks and your father's enormous authority in such matters, and the feel of the wagon under you for the long ten-mile haul, and at the top of the last long hill catching the first view of the lake after eleven months of not seeing this cherished body of water. The shouts and cries of the other campers when they saw you, and the trunks to be unpacked, to give up their rich burden. (Arriving was less exciting nowadays, when you sneaked up in your car and parked it under a tree near the camp and took out the bags and in five minutes it was all over, no fuss, no loud wonderful fuss about trunks.)

10   Peace and goodness and jollity. The only thing that was wrong now, really, was the sound of the place, an unfamiliar nervous sound of the outboard motors. This was the note that jarred, the one thing that would sometimes break the illusion and set the years moving. In those other summertimes all motors were inboard; and when they were at a little distance, the noise they made was a sedative, an ingredient of summer sleep. They were one-cylinder and two-cylinder engines, and some were make-and-break and some were jump-spark, but they all made a sleepy sound across the lake. The one-lungers throbbed and fluttered, and the twin-cylinder ones purred and purred, and that was a quiet sound, too. But now the campers all had outboards. In the daytime, in the hot mornings, these motors made a petulant, irritable sound; at night in the still evening when the afterglow lit the water, they whined about one's ears like mosquitoes. My boy loved our rented outboard, and his great desire was to achieve single-handed mastery over it, and authority, and he soon learned the trick of choking it a little (but not too much), and the adjustment of the needle valve. Watching him I would remember the things you could do with the old one-cylinder engine with the heavy flywheel, how you could have it eating out of your hand if you got really close to it spiritually. Motorboats in those days didn't have clutches, and you would make a landing by shutting off the motor at the proper time and coasting in with a dead rudder. But there was a way of reversing them, if you learned the trick, by cutting the switch and putting it on again exactly on the final dying revolution of the flywheel, so that it would kick back against compression and begin reversing. Approaching a dock in a strong following breeze, it was difficult to slow up sufficiently by the ordinary coasting method, and if a boy felt he had complete mastery over his motor, he was tempted to keep it running beyond its time and then reverse it a few feet from the dock. It took a cool nerve, because if you threw the switch a twentieth of a second too soon you would catch the flywheel when it still had speed

> "The only thing that was wrong now, really, was the sound of the place."

enough to go up past center, and the boat would leap ahead, charging bull-fashion at the dock.

11   We had a good week at the camp. The bass were biting well and the sun shone endlessly, day after day. We would be tired at night and lie down in the accumulated heat of the little bedrooms after the long hot day and the breeze would stir almost imperceptibly outside and the smell of the swamp drift in through the rusty screens. Sleep would come easily and in the morning the red squirrel would be on the roof, tapping out his gay routine. I kept remembering everything, lying in bed in the mornings—the small steamboat that had a long rounded stern like the lip of a Ubangi, and how quietly she ran on the moonlight sails, when the older boys played their mandolins and the girls sang and we ate doughnuts dipped in sugar, and how sweet the music was on the water in the shining night, and what it had felt like to think about girls then. After breakfast we would go up to the store and the things were in the same place—the minnows in a bottle, the plugs and spinners disarranged and pawed over by the youngsters from the boys' camp, the Fig Newtons and the Beeman's gum. Outside, the road was tarred and cars stood in front of the

store. Inside, all was just as it had always been, except there was more Coca-Cola and not so much Moxie and root beer and birch beer and sarsaparilla. We would walk out with the bottle of pop apiece and sometimes the pop would backfire up our noses and hurt. We explored the streams, quietly, where the turtles slid off the sunny logs and dug their way into the soft bottom; and we lay on the town wharf and fed worms to the tame bass. Everywhere we went I had trouble making out which was I, the one walking at my side, the one walking in my pants.

> "We would walk out with the bottle of pop apiece and sometimes the pop would backfire up our noses and hurt."

12   One afternoon while we were at that lake a thunderstorm came up. It was like the revival of an old melodrama that I had seen long ago with childish awe. The second-act climax of the drama of the electrical disturbance over a lake in America had not changed in any important respect. This was the big scene, still the big scene. The whole thing was so familiar, the first feeling of oppression and heat and a general air around camp of not wanting to go very far away. In midafternoon (it was all the same) a curious darkening of the sky, and a lull in everything that had made life tick; and then the way the boats suddenly swung the other way at their moorings with the coming of a breeze out of the new quarter, and the premonitory rumble. Then the kettle drum, then the snare, then the bass drum and cymbals, then crackling light against the dark, and the gods grinning and licking their chops in the hills. Afterward the calm, the rain steadily rustling in the calm lake, the return of light and hope and spirits, and the campers running out in joy and relief to go swimming in the rain, their bright cries perpetuating the deathless joke about how they were getting simply drenched, and the children screaming with delight at the new sensation of bathing in the rain, and the joke about getting drenched linking the generations in a strong indestructible chain. And the comedian who waded in carrying an umbrella.

13   When the others went swimming my son said he was going in, too. He pulled his dripping trunks from the line where they had hung all through the shower and wrung them out. Languidly, and with no thought of going in, I watched him, his hard little body, skinny and bare, saw him wince slightly as he pulled up around his vitals the small, soggy, icy garment. As he buckled the swollen belt, suddenly my groin felt the chill of death.

READING CLOSELY AND THINKING CRITICALLY

1. Why does White return to the lake after an absence of 40 years? Do you think the reasons the author gives are the only ones? Explain.

2. What do you think White's dominant impression of the lake is as an adult?

3. What conclusion does White draw about the passage of time? Where is that conclusion best expressed?

4. White mentions several times that he has trouble distinguishing himself from his son and that he has trouble distinguishing the present from the past. Why do you think he experiences this blurring of identities and time?

5. White believes that his past summers at the lake were "infinitely precious and worth saving" (paragraph 9). Why?

6. If White had visited the lake more regularly over the past 40 years, do you think the visit narrated and described in the essay would have prompted the same feelings and realizations? Explain.

7. Is "Once More to the Lake" upbeat or depressing? Explain.

EXAMINING STRUCTURE AND STRATEGY

1. To make the essay vivid, White appeals to the senses of smell, touch, and sound in addition to the sense of sight. Mention one example each of a description that appeals to smell, touch, and sound. Underline the specific words that appeal to the senses.

2. Cite two other descriptions that you find particularly appealing. Underline the specific words.

3. White does not refer to his son by name, nor does he describe the boy very much. Why does he not give his son more identifying characteristics?

NOTING COMBINED PATTERNS

1. Without White's vivid description, much of the essay's joy would be lost. What else would be lost? Is description a primary or secondary pattern?

2. What narration does White include? How does the narration help him achieve his purpose for writing? Is narration a primary or secondary pattern?

3. In what way does White compare and contrast? How does the comparison-contrast help White achieve his purpose for writing? Is comparison-contrast a primary or secondary pattern?

CONSIDERING LANGUAGE AND STYLE

1. Look up the meaning of *paean* in a dictionary; then read paragraph 8 aloud. How is that paragraph similar to a paean?

2. What metaphor (see page 128) does White include in paragraph 2? In paragraph 12? What do these metaphors contribute?

3. Consult a dictionary if you are unsure of the meaning of any of these words: *incessant* (paragraph 1), *gunwale* (paragraph 2), *primeval* (paragraph 3), *helgrammite* (paragraph 5), *pensively* (paragraph 5), *indelible* (paragraph 8), *petulant* (paragraph 10), *Ubangi* (paragraph 11), *premonitory* (paragraph 12), *languidly* (paragraph 13).

FOR DISCUSSION IN CLASS OR ONLINE

"Once More to the Lake" deals with issues of youth and age. With your classmates, discuss the extent to which we are concerned with issues of youth and age in our culture. Cite specific examples to support your ideas.

1. **Writing in your journal.** In paragraph 12, when he writes of the thunderstorm, White notes that "the joke about getting drenched [links] the generations in a strong indestructible chain." What events, experiences, and circumstances link the generations in your family or in your locale? Explain in a page or two.

2. **Combining the patterns for a purpose.** The purposes in the assignments are possibilities. You may establish whatever purpose you like, within your instructor's guidelines.

   • **Description and process analysis.** Paragraph 12 describes a thunderstorm. To entertain and inform your reader, write your own description of a thunderstorm or other weather event as it develops, peaks, and wanes.

   • **Description and comparison-contrast.** If you have ever returned to a place after being gone for a while, compare and contrast by describing how the place was when you returned and how it was at the earlier time. For example, you could describe your first trip home after being away at school for several months or your elementary school after seeing it for the first time as an adult. Your purpose is to relate your experience and express your feelings.

   • **Narration and description.** Narrate a story about a place that holds special significance for you, and describe that place to help readers understand why the place is important to you. Your purpose is to express your feelings and perhaps relate experience.

   • **Narration and cause-and-effect analysis.** In the essay, White recognizes his own mortality. Tell about an event that caused you to recognize your mortality—or at least your inability to control something. To relate experience and express feelings, narrate what happened and use cause-and-effect to explain how you were affected.

3. **Analyzing and assessing.** "Once More to the Lake" is considered by many English instructors to be a classic essay worthy of inclusion in any anthology of essays (like this one). Analyze the essay and assess what makes it a classic piece. Alternatively, argue that the essay should not be considered a classic.

4. **Connecting and synthesizing the readings.** In "Once More to the Lake," "The Homestead on Rainy Creek" (page 140), and "In the Kitchen" (page 317), the authors tell about childhood places that hold special meaning to them as adults. Discuss one or more of the ways that places from our childhood can influence us as both children and adults.

5. **Drawing on sources.** Advertisers are often accused of targeting youthful populations at the expense of older ones. Decide for yourself whether this allegation is true. Watch television commercials for at least three popular programs and review recent magazine advertisements from at least three mainstream publications—*Time, Newsweek, TV Guide,* or *People,* for example. Then write an essay arguing that advertisers either do or do not target younger consumers and neglect older ones. Back up your points with descriptions of specific commercials and advertisements.

"Really? Someone told me it's
not plagiarism if they're dead."

Copyright © Marc Tyler Nobleman/www.mtncartoons.com. Reprinted with permission.

Locating, Evaluating, and Drawing on Sources

CONSIDER THE PATTERN

As the cartoon on the facing page suggests, students do not always understand what constitutes plagiarism. How do you define plagiarism? Why do you think there is confusion about plagiarism?

USING SOURCES

Especially in academic settings, writers frequently draw on the work of other writers. For example, you may use an idea from an essay in this book to back up one of your points, or another writer's idea may prompt you to write an essay of your own. One of the exciting aspects of writing is that writers engage in ongoing conversations by responding to each other's ideas and using them for support or departure points. In addition, when they take in-depth looks at subjects, writers often produce research papers, in which they mention and discuss the work of other writers on the subject. To be part of the ongoing conversation and to produce credible research papers, you must learn how to locate relevant, reliable sources and to draw on them fairly and responsibly. In Chapter 4, on writing in academic settings, you saw how to paraphrase, summarize, and quote in a fair and responsible way. In Chapter 4 and throughout the book, you have also seen how to avoid plagiarism in using sources. Here we look at the process of locating and evaluating sources and at documenting those sources.

LOCATING SOURCES

With today's information explosion, the amount of material available to researchers is both thrilling and daunting. To locate the source material that is best for your purpose, you need efficient strategies, such as those explained next.

www.mhhe.com/clousepatterns6　　　　　　　　　Library

For more help with locating sources, click on

Research > Using the Library

1. Tour your campus library to learn about what resources it offers, where they are located, and how to use them. You may be tempted to rely solely on Internet research, but your campus library houses a considerable amount of information unavailable on the Internet. Many libraries offer self-guided tours that you can take at your convenience; others have regularly scheduled tours or workshops given by staff.

2. Decide on the kind of information you need. Perhaps you are in the earliest stages of a writing project and need an overview of a subject such as gun control in order to narrow your topic. Or perhaps you already have your narrow topic and need a sense of the most compelling arguments for and against a ban on assault weapons. Or you may need a single piece of specific information, such as the number of registered handguns in the country. Knowing your needs makes your research go more efficiently.

3. Consult your librarian. He or she can direct you to print and electronic resources that will save you time. Also, if you need materials unavailable in your library, the librarian can assist you in obtaining them through interlibrary loan.

4. Use reference works. Reference books are in a specific area of the library and cannot be checked out. Many reference works are available electronically from your library, in some cases as online databases linked through your library's Web page. Reference works include the following:

- General encyclopedias, such as *World Book*, which offer an overview of a broad spectrum of topics
- Specialty encyclopedias, like *Encyclopedia of Education* and *Encyclopedia of Crime and Justice*, which give more in-depth information in a specific subject area
- Discipline or genre-specific works, such as *The Oxford Companion to Art*, *A Political Handbook of the World*, and *The Oxford Companion to American Literature*
- Biographical dictionaries, such as *Who's Who in America* and *International Who's Who*, which give sketches of the lives and accomplishments of famous people

- Almanacs and yearbooks, such as *World Almanac, Information Please Almanac,* and *Facts on File,* which provide statistics and information on current events.

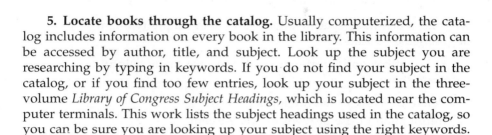

www.mhhe.com/clousepatterns6   Resources

For more help with locating sources, click on

Research > Discipline Specific Resources

5. Locate books through the catalog. Usually computerized, the catalog includes information on every book in the library. This information can be accessed by author, title, and subject. Look up the subject you are researching by typing in keywords. If you do not find your subject in the catalog, or if you find too few entries, look up your subject in the three-volume *Library of Congress Subject Headings,* which is located near the computer terminals. This work lists the subject headings used in the catalog, so you can be sure you are looking up your subject using the right keywords.

6. Locate magazines, journals, and newspapers with indexes. Periodicals (magazines, journals, and newspapers) can be a good source of up-to-date information. To discover useful periodicals, look up your subject in a print or electronic index, such as one of the following:

Business Periodicals Index
Current Index to Journals in Education
Government Publications Indexes
Humanities Index
InfoTrac
New York Times Index
ProQuest
Reader's Guide to Periodical Literature
Resources in Education
ScienceSource
Social Sciences Index

7. Use Internet search engines. By using more than one search engine, you can get a broader range of results, but remember that search engines do not tell you which sites are reliable. You must use your judgment, and if you are unsure, ask your instructor or a librarian. Here is a list of some useful search engines:

AltaVista at www.altavista.com
Bing at www.bing.com
Dogpile at www.dogpile.com
Excite at www.excite.com
Google at www.google.com

Metacrawler at www.metacrawler.com

Yahoo at www.yahoo.com

For a more academically focused search, try Google scholar at http://scholar.google.com.

With a keyword-based search engine, using Boolean commands such as AND, OR, and NOT can help you search more efficiently by helping the search engine refine the results it delivers. For example, this Boolean search

"bilingual education" AND "Hispanic children"

will find much more specific information than simply typing in "bilingual" or "bilingual education."

8. Use other online references. Among the many helpful online references are these:

Reference Desk at www.refdesk.com

Information Please at www.infoplease.com

Biography.com at www.biography.com

Online Newspapers at www.onlinenewspapers.com

Internet Public Library at www.ipl.org

World Wide Web Virtual Library at www.vlib.org

In addition, check the online resources your library subscribes to. They are listed on your library home page and often are available via your campus network or in computer labs.

EVALUATING PRINT AND INTERNET SOURCES

When you locate sources, you must evaluate their quality and their suitability for your purpose. The questions here can help you evaluate your sources. Keep in mind that it is particularly important to carefully evaluate Internet sources, as they are far more wide-ranging in quality than are print sources.

Questions about Quality

For All Sources

- **Is the author reliable?** Check the source for information on the author's credentials, or type the author's name into a search engine. What are the author's publications, degrees, and professional affiliations? What is the author's professional experience? What professional acknowledgment has the author received?
- **Is the author and/or publisher associated with a particular point of view?** For example, if you come across a piece published by the National Rifle Association, you can assume a pro-gun stance. You can, of course, use the piece, but with the bias in mind.

- **Who is sponsoring the Web site?** A Web site connected with, for example, a university or major news organization can be assumed to be reliable. If a Web site is connected with an organization you are unfamiliar with, look on the Web site and elsewhere for information about the organization.
- **Does the page look professional?** Is it free of grammatical and spelling errors?
- **Does the site include links to other credible sites?** Credible sites often link to other sites that have reliable sponsors. A site that links to sites that seem suspect is itself likely to be suspect.
- **Can the information be verified elsewhere?** Check other sites, reference works, books, or periodicals to be sure any surprising or questionable information can be corroborated. Consult with your instructor if you cannot verify information and are unsure about a site.

Questions about Suitability

For Print and Internet Sources

- **Is the source recent enough?** Your topic will determine how current the information needs to be. Battlefield strategies of the Civil War is a far less time-sensitive topic than new treatments for AIDS. For Internet sources, look to see when the site was last updated.
- **Can you understand the material?** If the material is too technical or specialized, it will not be helpful to you.
- **Is the source at the right level?** Assess whether the material is written for elementary, high school, or college students; the general public; or professionals. Avoid material that is too simplistic, and based on your purpose, decide whether you want to use sources that are aimed at general audiences and/or sources aimed at professionals.

---

www.mhhe.com/clousepatterns6   Source

For more help with evaluating sources, click on
Research > CARS Source Evaluation Tutor

DRAWING ON SOURCES:
PARAPHRASING, SUMMARIZING, AND QUOTING

To incorporate source material into your writing, you can write a paraphrase, a summary, or a direct quotation. When you **paraphrase,** you restate the ideas in a source using your own words and style; when you **summarize,** you condense all or a large part of a source by giving its main ideas in your own words and style; and when you **quote,** you restate the exact words in a source. The specific conventions you must follow when you paraphrase, summarize, or quote are explained in detail in Chapter 4, which also shows you the best ways to integrate paraphrases, summaries, and quotations into your paper. Be sure to check pages 106 and 108 when you incorporate sources using one of these strategies. You must also document your paraphrases, summaries, and quotations, as described in the next section.

DOCUMENTING SOURCES (MLA STYLE)

For proper **documentation,** you must show your reader the source of your paraphrases, summaries, and quotations. The documentation conventions given in this book are those of the *MLA Handbook for Writers of Research Papers* (7th ed., 2009), published by the Modern Language Association (MLA). These conventions are often called "MLA style." Although MLA style is commonly used in college writing in the humanities, some disciplines and some instructors favor writing in other conventions. In the social sciences, for example, the conventions of the American Psychological Association (APA) are often preferred. When in doubt, check with your instructor to find out which documentation conventions you should follow.

---

www.mhhe.com/clousepatterns6   Bibliomaker

For more help with documenting sources, click on

Research > Avoiding Plagiarism > Using Copyrighted Materials
Research > Bibliomaker
Research > Links to Documentation Sites

To document according to MLA conventions, you will include in-text citations and a Works Cited page. Together, these tell readers exactly where the material that you drew on came from.

In-Text Citations

When you refer to sources in your text, use in-text citations. At the point in your paper where your paraphrase, summary, or quotation occurs, include the author and the page number in the source where the material comes from. Several important rules for in-text citations are given below. For additional rules, consult a handbook or research paper guide.

- **For first use of a source, include the author's full name. (The title can also be included.)**

    > In "Fan Profanity," Howard M. Wasserman explains that "many free-speech controversies, especially on college campuses, are grounded in concerns for civility, politeness, and good taste" (639).

- **On subsequent uses, the author's last name is sufficient.**

    Wasserman goes on to explain that when governments regulate speech, "courts strike down the regulations as violating the First Amendment" (639).

- **Follow the paraphrase, summary, or quotation with a parenthetical text citation giving the page number the borrowed material is from.** If the sentence does not include the author's name, the parenthetical citation should include it. Otherwise, only the page number is given.

    Steinberg believes that of all the problems facing a society, the problem of "serious juvenile crime" is among the most difficult to grapple with (602).

    One psychologist believes that of all the problems facing a society, the problem of "serious juvenile crime" is among the most difficult to grapple with (Steinberg 602).

- **For online sources that do not have page numbers, include only the author's name.** If the author's name is not given, use the title.

    Linaman says that boys living with their mothers experience more hostility than girls do, both immediately after the divorce and far beyond (Linaman).

- **If you quote or paraphrase a quotation that is cited in a second source, note the secondhand nature of the borrowing with *qtd. in* (meaning "quoted in") in the parenthetical citation.**

    Justice John Marshall Harlan best described the relative nature of profanity when he said, "'One man's vulgarity is another's lyric'" (qtd. in Wasserman 641).

The Works Cited Page

A Works Cited page is a listing of your sources alphabetized by author. (For an example of a Works Cited page, see page 716.) It includes full bibliographic information on each source from which you quoted, summarized, or paraphrased.

For correct MLA documentation, the entries on your Works Cited page should follow the models given below. If you use sources that do not fit these models, consult a handbook or a research paper guide.

---

www.mhhe.com/clousepatterns6 Bibliomaker

For more help with MLA documentation, click on

Research > Bibliomaker
Research > Links to Documentation Sites
Research > Sample Research Paper > Sample Paper in MLA Style

Books

Book by One Author

> Gladwell, Malcolm. *Blink: The Power of Thinking without Thinking.* New York:
> Little, Brown, 2005. Print.

Book by Two or Three Authors

> Hallowell, Edward M., and John J. Ratey. *Delivered from Distraction: Getting the Most*
> *Out of Life with Attention Deficit Disorder.* New York: Ballantine, 2004. Print.

Book by More Than Three Authors

> Davidson, James West, et al. *Nation of Nations: A Concise Narrative of the*
> *American Republic.* 4th ed. New York: McGraw, 2006. Print.

Revised Edition of a Book

> Miller, Casey, and Kate Swift. *The Handbook of Nonsexist Writing.* 2nd ed. New
> York: Harper, 1988. Print.

A Book with an Editor

> Marshall, Sam A., ed. *1990 Photographer's Market.* Cincinnati: Writer's Digest, 1989. Print.

A Book by an Author with an Editor

> Arnold, Matthew. *Culture and Anarchy.* Ed. J. Dover Wilson. Cambridge: Cam-
> bridge UK, 1961. Print.

Encyclopedia Article

> "Terrorism." *Encyclopaedia Britannica*, 2001 ed. Print.

More Than One Book by the Same Author

> Tannen, Deborah. *I Only Say This Because I Love You: How the Way We Talk*
> *Can Make or Break Family Relationships throughout Our Lives.* New York:
> Random House, 2006. Print.
>
> - - -. *You Just Don't Understand: Women and Men in Conversation.* New York:
> Ballantine, 1990. Print.

Selection from an Anthology

> Baker, Russell. "The Plot against People." *Patterns for a Purpose: A Rhetorical Reader.*
> Ed. Barbara Fine Clouse. 3rd ed. New York: McGraw, 2003. 474–75. Print.

Periodicals

Article from a Weekly or Biweekly Magazine

> Klein, Joe. "The Trouble with Polls and Focus Groups." *Time* 4 Oct. 2004: 29. Print.
>
> "Advice for the Asking." *Newsweek* 27 Sept. 2004: 60. Print.

Article from a Monthly or Bimonthly Magazine

Rauch, Jonathan. "Divided We Stand." *The Atlantic Monthly* Oct. 2004: 39–40. Print.

Newspaper Article

Oppenheimer, Andres. "Don't Ignore Corporate Corruption." *The Vindicator* [Youngstown, Ohio] 13 Oct. 2004: A10. Print.

Article from a Scholarly Journal

Knipe, Penley. "Paper Profiles: American Portrait Silhouettes." *Journal of the American Institute for Conservation* 41 (2002): 203–23. Print.

Pierrous, Palmyre. "Communicating in Art Museums: Language and Concepts in Art Education." *Journal of Museum Education* 28.1 (2003): 3–7. Print.

Portable Databases on Storage Media Such as CD-ROMs

If the portable database is a periodical that is also published in print, follow the conventions for periodicals and provide the title of the electronic source, the medium ("Diskette" or "CD-ROM," for example), the distributor's name, and the date of electronic publication. If the periodical is published as a portable database only, omit the publication information for the print version.

"Real Facts about the Sun." *The Dynamic Sun.* Washington, D.C.: NASA, 2000. CD-ROM.

Online Sources

In general, your citation should include the author's name, the title of the work, the title of the online site, the date of electronic publication, and the date you accessed the source. (The date of access is the second date in the following examples.) Include the URL, in angle brackets, only when the source would be difficult to locate using a search engine or a search box at the site. For an example of an entry with angle brackets, see the "Online Source That Is Difficult to Find" example below.

Article from a Scholarly Web site

Ahmed, Aziza. "Victorian Women Travelers in the 19th Century." *Postcolonial Studies.* Ed. Deepika Bahri. Emory, Fall 1998. Web. 1 Dec. 2009.

Work Cited Only on the Web

"Bisphenol A in Your Body: How It Got There and How to Minimize Your Exposure." *Enviroblog.* Environmental Working Group, 26 Sept. 2007. Web. 1 Dec. 2009.

Article in an Online Newspaper

Tyson, Ann Scott. "Off Welfare, Yes. But No Job." *The Christian Science Monitor.* The First Church of Christ, Scientist, 9 Apr. 1998. Web. 24 April 1998.

Article in an Online Magazine

Fromartz, Samuel. "Groovin' with Scofield, Medeski, Martin, and Wood." *All about Jazz.* All About Jazz, 3 April 1998. Web. 10 April 2004.

Article in an Online Journal

Woodruff, Eliot Ghofur. "Metrical Phase Shifts in Stravinsky's *The Rite of Spring.*" *Music Theory Online* 12.1 (2006): n. pag. Web. 3 Apr. 2006.

Journal Article from an Online Database

Harker, Brian. "Louis Armstrong and the Clarinet." *American Music* 21.2 (2003): 137–58. *Academic Search Premier.* Web. 17 Nov. 2008.

Newspaper Article from an Online Database

Jervis, Rick. "General Sees Rift in Iraq Enemy." *USA Today* 26 Jan. 2006: A1. *Academic Search Premier.* Web. 8 June 2006.

Blog Posting

Gladwell, Malcolm. "NBA Heuristics." Gladwell.com. 10 Mar. 2006. Web. 21 May 2006.

Online Posting to a Listserv or Newsgroup

Taylor, Richard. "Meat Eaters Are More Likely to Have B12 Deficiencies." Vegetarians. Google Groups, 22 Aug. 2002. Web. 1 Dec. 2008.

Online Source That Is Difficult to Find (URL Included)

Archives of African American Music and Culture. Indiana U, 21 Dec. 2007. Web. 21 Nov. 2008. <http://www.indiana.edu/~aamc/>.

Other Sources

Radio or Television Program

Moyers, Bill, and Robert Bly. *A Gathering of Men.* PBS. WNET, New York, 8 Jan. 1990. Television.

Personal Interview

DeSalvo, Joy. Personal interview. 30 Sept. 2006.

Recording

Brooks, Mel, comp. *The Producers.* Orch. Doug Besterman. Perf. Nathan Lane, Matthew Broderick, and Gary Beach. Sony Classical, 2001. CD.

Film or Video

The Matrix. Dir. Andy Wachowski and Larry Wachowski. Perf. Keanu Reeves, Laurence Fishburne, and Carrie-Anne Moss. Warner Bros., 1999. DVD.

Image of a Painting, Photograph, or Other Artwork from a Print Source

> Remington, Frederic. *A Dash for the Timber, 1889.* Amon Carter Museum, Fort
>
> Worth. *American Art: History and Culture.* Ed. Wayne Craven. New York:
>
> McGraw, 1994. 387. Print.

Note: Provide the institution or owner and the city, as well as publication information for the source in which the painting or photograph appears.

Image of a Painting, Photograph, or Other Artwork from an
Electronic Source

> Cézanne, Paul. *The Bather.* 1885. Museum of Modern Art, New York. MOMA.org.
>
> Web. 14 June 2004.

AVOIDING PLAGIARISM

Plagiarism occurs if you use another person's ideas, words, manner of expression, or research without properly crediting the source. Plagiarism in academic writing is a serious offense. Because avoiding plagiarism is such an important issue, it is discussed throughout this book: See Chapter 4, (page 112), the "Using Sources for a Purpose" sections in Chapters 5–13, and Appendix C.

To avoid plagiarism, remember the following:

- Follow all of the conventions for handling paraphrases, summaries, and quotations, as discussed in Chapter 4.
- Provide in-text parenthetical citations for each of your paraphrases, summaries, and quotations, as discussed in this chapter.
- Provide a Works Cited page with correct, compete bibliographic information for every source from which you paraphrased, summarized, or quoted, as discussed in this chapter.
- Never turn in someone else's writing as your own.
- Do not download material from the Internet or copy material from a print source without following all the documentation conventions.
- Use the plagiarism checklist in Appendix C to be sure you are handling source material responsibly.
- If you are unsure about what to document or how to document, talk with your instructor, see a writing center tutor, or consult a handbook or research paper guide. Online, you can go to owl.english.purdue.edu.

www.mhhe.com/clousepatterns6

Avoiding Plagiarism

For more help with avoiding plagiarism, click on
Research > Avoiding Plagiarism

Annotated Student Essay

The following student paper was written after the author read "Immigrants" on page 566 and did some research on the experience of international students in the United States. It illustrates how writers can combine their own ideas with research material in an essay. The notations in the margin call your attention to some of the essay's features, including its use of MLA conventions. (For two other examples of student essays that incorporate sources, see pages 362 and 589.)

Rebecca Hollingsworth

Professor Howell

English 551

8 February 2010

The Struggle to Belong

Paragraph 1
This introduction uses a quotation from "Immigrants" to synthesize a theme in the poem with a situation faced by foreign students. The thesis is the last sentence.

Pat Mora's poem "Immigrants" explores the desires and fears of foreigners as they attempt to assimilate into American culture. The poem contrasts symbols of America, such as the flag and apple pie, with the accents of immigrants as they talk to their children, to highlight the tension between American and non-American, nativeness and foreignness. At the same time, the poem depicts the hopes and struggles that define the immigrant experience. "Immigrants" reveals the particular challenges that foreigners face in the United States, giving a voice to the emotional and psychological implications of trying to blend in. Mora's poem ends with the profound, poignant anxiety shared by immigrant parents: "'Will they like/our boy, our girl, our fine american/boy, our fine american girl?'" (lines 12–14). Although all immigrants experience uncertainty as they transition into a new culture, foreign students—immigrants or otherwise—face an additional challenge. For these students, the struggle to belong socially is complicated by the drive to succeed academically.

Paragraph 2
This paragraph uses a statistic about the increased number of foreign students to emphasize the need to help these students. Notice that the information on the source is in a parenthetical citation.

Recent data indicate that more and more international students are attending college in the United States. According to a 2009 press release, enrollments of foreign students increased by 8% in the 2008–09 academic year, bringing the total number of international students at American colleges and universities to a record-breaking 671,616 (Institute of International Education). Now more than ever, international students are benefiting from a college education in the United States, so the need to address the challenges these students face is increasingly real and pressing.

Researchers have acknowledged that international students have **3** problems. As Jenny J. Lee and Charles Rice assert, "Enrolling large numbers of international students does not necessarily equate with a positive experience once they are admitted" (405). Differences in cultural background, tradition, religion, language, social behavior, and academic expectations can all contribute to a sense of alienation for foreign students. According to Debra A. McLachlan and Jessica Justice, poor English skills can be especially detrimental to international students' attempts to assimilate (28). Yet, as McLachlan and Justice report in their study, international students are less likely than their native peers to find the resources and services they need to cope with these challenges effectively, so that "it is common for international students to suffer quietly and not seek assistance" (30). In fact, a crisis has developed at colleges and universities throughout the United States, where foreign students are finding it harder to transition into college life and yet are trying to deal with their problems on their own. The anxiety expressed by the parents in Mora's poem seems justified in this case, for foreign students do not seem to be fitting in.

Who is to blame for the isolation that many international students **4** feel while studying and living abroad? Whereas McLachlan and Justice focus on the personal causes of such alienation, Lee and Rice argue that broader, societal issues are at work. According to Lee and Rice, some international students, especially those from non-Western countries, experience a particular kind of discrimination, which they call "neo-racism":

> This framework [the theory of neo-racism] helps to identify direct and indirect undermining of international students' capacity to become fully participating members of their host community, disadvantaging institutional policies, hostility towards cultural attributes (e.g., language barriers and foreign accents), and the negative stereotyping of whole nations or cultures, all of which hinder intercultural diplomacy and friendship and obstruct intellectual growth, which should be the outcome of exchange. (405)

Paragraph 3
This paragraph synthesizes quotations and paraphrases from two sources to describe the problems foreign students face that make it hard for them to fit in. Notice that for each paraphrase and quote, the source is made clear by the sentence and parenthetical citation. Also notice the reference to the poem to connect the body to the introduction.

Paragraph 4
The topic sentence (sentence 1) indicates that this paragraph will discuss the reason for the problem explained in the previous paragraphs. The topic sentence is supported with source material. Notice how the long quotation is handled.

Lee and Rice suggest that international students are excluded, both explicitly and subtly, from fully participating in college life. Cultural assimilation, then, becomes an impossible goal. Lee and Rice ask the academic community to recognize the discrimination that some foreign students experience and to increase efforts on campus to cultivate international students' well-being, making them feel more at home (406).

What, then, can be done to help international students assimilate? 5 The most obvious answer is to address the isolation so many international students face. To deal with the self-imposed isolation that prevents so many foreign students from seeking help, colleges should structure programs for international students. These programs should include American student mentors who have been trained to help international students make friends and who are able to direct them to campus services that will help them solve any problems that arise. Interacting with their mentors, international students would also improve their English skills, which will further facilitate their assimilation. Additionally, programs for international students should be designed to meet the criteria described by two researchers who have studied the problems foreign students encounter. That is, programs should help students establish "a series of achievement outcomes, such as completing school work, planning for the future, achieving an individual career vision, pursuing success in academic studies, seeking a development of professional knowledge, experiencing a different world, and increasing knowledge about the world" (Tseng and Newton). In other words, colleges can help students structure their academic lives by helping them set goals that guide their activities, thereby giving them a shared purpose that fosters a greater sense of belonging. Their student mentors could help them assess whether they are meeting their goals and get them help if they are not.

A more difficult but perhaps more important solution asks colleges 6 to address the neo-racism that Lee and Rice mention. Fostering a climate of inclusion, tolerance, and understanding of all cultures and

Paragraph 5
The topic sentence idea (in the first two sentences) indicates that a solution to the problem explained in the earlier paragraphs will be given. The paragraph synthesizes the author's ideas with source material. Notice that the parenthetical citation does not include a page number since the source is unpaginated.

Paragraph 6
This paragraph includes the writer's ideas about how to solve the problem explained in earlier paragraphs.

individual differences will benefit everyone—international and American students alike. A good way to begin is to charge classroom teachers with working to involve international students in discussions and in making them feel welcome and valued. Also helpful would be campus-wide lectures and symposia that feature international speakers and that focus on breaking down stereotypes. In the future, changes in American elementary and high school curriculums—for more emphasis on foreign languages and on foreign cultures—might make students more welcoming to international students that they meet when they go to college.

The process of assimilating into a new culture takes time and 7 inevitably involves some degree of struggle. For international students, the challenges associated with being the cultural other are exacerbated by the demands of college life. With help from the campus community, however, the alienation depicted in Mora's poem "Immigrants" can be mitigated for international students.

Paragraph 7
This paragraph is the conclusion. It provides closure by restating the thesis idea and mentioning the poem.

Works Cited

Institute of International Education. *Record Numbers of International Students in U.S. Higher Education.* New York: IIE, 16 Nov. 2009. Print.

Lee, Jenny J., and Charles Rice. "Welcome to America? International Student Perceptions of Discrimination." *Higher Education* 53.3 (2007): 381–409. *Academic Search Elite.* Web. 5 Feb. 2010.

McLachlan, Debra A., and Jessica Justice. "A Grounded Theory of International Student Well-Being." *The Journal of Theory Construction & Testing* 13.1 (2009): 27–32. Print.

Mora, Pat. "Immigrants." *Patterns for a Purpose: A Rhetorical Reader.* Ed. Barbara Fine Clouse. 6th ed. New York: McGraw-Hill, 2011. 566 Print.

Tseng, Wen-Chih, and Fred B. Newton. "International Students' Strategies for Well-Being." *College Student Journal* 36.4 (2002): n. pag. *Academic Search Elite.* Web. 5 Feb. 2010.

Works Cited
Begin the works cited entries on a new page.

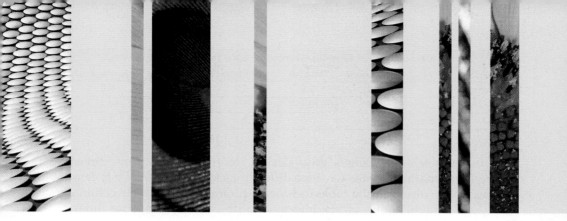

Appendix A
Document Design

You would never turn in a paper typed in an impossibly small font and with no margins. Whatever kind of document you are producing, following principles of document design will help you achieve your writing purpose.

VISUALS FOR ESSAYS

Often, you will want to supplement the content of your essays with visuals. Visuals such as tables, charts, and graphs can present large amounts of information clearly and concisely. They can also serve to reinforce points graphically. For instance, if you are writing a comparison–contrast essay examining two plans for your school's recycling program, you might use a bar graph to show how one plan will reduce significantly more waste per month than the other.

All the visuals you include in your essays should be easily comprehensible and should help you achieve your purpose — do not add visuals just to make your paper look more interesting or to meet a length requirement. Also, keep in mind that different types of visuals are better suited to presenting different types of information, as the next sections explain.

Tables

A *table*, which presents information in columns and rows, is best used to organize data for readers so they can scan and understand the information quickly. Tables function less to show relationships and more to make large amounts of data clear. For instance, consider this table showing response times by a university's security patrol for various locations around campus.

Campus Patrol Response Time, Fall 2009 (in minutes)					
Location	September	October	November	December	Average
Morrison Hall	6.2	5.8	5.2	6.8	**6.0**
Hassenger Stadium	9.8	10.1	9.4	11.3	**10.2**
Snyder Auditorium	3.4	3.8	2.9	4.2	**3.6**

Note that this table contains a great deal of information—response times during four separate months for three different locations. Yet all of it is easy to grasp. Note also that the table includes a prominent title, clear column labels, and a highlighting of key information (the average response time). These are all elements of a well-executed table.

Pie Charts

To illustrate graphically how something is divided—the various parts of a whole, in other words—you may want to use a *pie chart*. Pie charts give visual emphasis to how much the various elements make up of a total—the amount of time per day spent on different activities, for instance, or the amount of pollution that comes from various sources. An effective pie chart has only a few divisions with some clear contrasts between them. A pie chart divided into 30 almost identical slices does not communicate much. Combine categories in your pie chart to highlight key differences, as the student who made the pie chart below does. By limiting the pie chart to only four categories, the student makes the relationships among the various spending categories clear and striking.

University Spending on Campus Staff, 2009

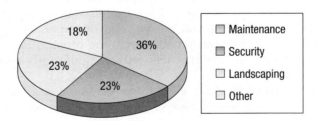

Bar and Line Graphs

Bar graphs and *line graphs* are most effective in showing comparisons between two or more variables, especially over time. Consider the following bar graph, which compares the number of university employees in landscaping and security over four years.

The bar graph clearly shows for a four-year period a decline in security personnel and a rise in employees working in landscaping. A table could present this same information, but the effect would not be as striking. The bars give the numbers a visual impact.

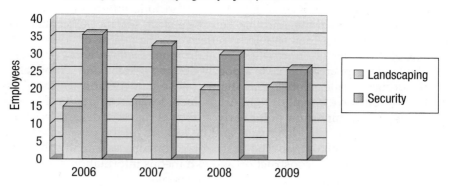

Security and Landscaping Employees, 2006–2009

The information might be even more strongly communicated in a line graph. While bar graphs are useful in showing and comparing total amounts, line graphs are more effective in showing trends over time. Notice that, when we present the data in a line graph, the rise in the number of landscaping employees and the fall in the number of security employees receives greater emphasis than in the bar graph.

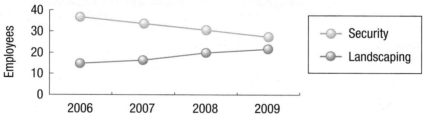

Security and Landscaping Employees, 2006–2009

With both bar graphs and line graphs, be sure to include a prominent title and to label your *x*- and *y*-axes. If you include a key, as in the bar and line graphs above, make sure it is straightforward and gives all the information a reader will need to interpret the graph.

E-MAIL DESIGN

You probably don't think of an e-mail as something you "design." E-mails are often written quickly and without much attention to spelling or grammar, much less to their overall appearance. Still, at times in your academic or professional career, you will need to communicate significant information via e-mail. You'll want to organize your e-mail so that it is easy to understand. Keep in mind that most people read e-mails the way they write them— quickly and imprecisely. Just because you are writing an important e-mail does not mean the recipients will read it that way. So you'll want to ensure that key points jump out at the reader, that the most important information comes first, that you are concise and do not include information irrelevant to your reason for writing, and that you use a clear, specific subject line. The significance of your e-mail should be reflected in the quality of your writing: Follow all the rules of punctuation, capitalization, spelling, and grammar.

Following are an example of a poorly designed e-mail and a more effectively designed one. Notice that the second e-mail demonstrates all the features of effective e-mail design: Adam includes a specific subject line; he places his most important point early and puts his key ideas in boldface; he uses concise, focused language; and he follows all the rules of spelling, grammar, and punctuation. The first e-mail contains essentially the same content, but its sloppy construction and extraneous information make it less likely to elicit an immediate or relevant response.

From: az99@nku.edu

To: rj88@nku.edu; sp36@nku.edu

Subject: Work

hey guys — how was your weekend? i have been feeling sick all morning. anyway. i was thinking we shld get going on our group project. email me and we can set something up. how's everyone's thursday? maybe we can do it on the new student union, since that is something we're all interested in. Oh, also, I ran into Prof. Caldwell & he said we need to have an outline done by next class. So def. email me.

–Adam

Poorly Designed E-mail

From: az99@nku.edu

To: rj88@nku.edu; sp36@nku.edu

Subject: ENG 111 Group Presentation - Meet on Thursday?

Hi Sol and Roger,

I'm emailing because we need to start working on our **group project for English 111.** I ran into Professor Caldwell, and he reminded me that we need our outline done by next class. Can we plan to **meet Thursday, around noon?** Please email me back to let me know.

Thanks,

Adam

Effectively Designed E-mail

POWERPOINT SLIDES

One of the most popular tools for creating visual supplements, especially for oral presentations, is *PowerPoint.* This software lets you design a slide show featuring text, graphics, and animations to support a classroom or workplace presentation. Because PowerPoint slides are often viewed from a distance (from the back of a classroom, for example), be sure the text on your slides is large and legible. Don't crowd your slides with too much clip art or other graphics—use images only when they support your discussion or contribute to your message. In general, with PowerPoint, less is more: Keep your text and images to a minimum. Remember, the slides are the *support* for your presentation. Keep them general and brief, and give the specifics yourself.

Following are two examples of effectively designed PowerPoint slides. Note that both slides have large type and lots of white space and that the only image included is an important one. They offer the highlights of a discussion clearly and cleanly, and do not overwhelm the viewer with excessive information.

Campus Security Issues	Making Fullard Hall Safer
<ul><li>Too many unlit pathways</li><li>Campus security is slow to respond to complaints</li><li>No late-night shuttle bus from fraternity row back to campus</li><li>Chancellor Street security booth is often unattended</li></ul>	<ul><li>Keep the skyway open after midnight</li><li>Add keycard access to the dining hall</li><li>Have all non-student guests sign in with security</li></ul> 

WEB SITE DESIGN

If you decide to create a Web site, whether for personal use or as part of a business endeavor, you want to be sure it represents you well.

Reprinted with permission from PoeMuseum.org.

One of the keys to building an impressive, easy-to-use Web site is navigation. Every page on your site should include a list of links to the major parts of your site. This way, no matter where a user is on the site, he or she can get to other parts without repeated clicking and searching. Another key is to limit the number of graphics you use. Web sites with numerous pictures on every page do not look sophisticated or high-tech—they look crowded, and they often load slowly. Build your site around a few high-impact images, and group any other images you want to include under a *Pictures* link. Finally, be aware of your audience. What will they be looking for when they visit your site? Make the answer to this question the centerpiece of your design.

Consider the Web site on the last page. It is the home page of the Edgar Allan Poe Museum in Richmond, Virginia. The design of this page is simple and effective. It is immediately clear what the site offers. The single, central picture of Poe draws the viewer's interest. And the navigation bar across the top of the screen provides access to all the major sections of the site.

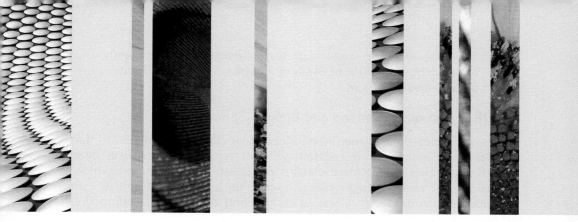

Appendix B
A Guide to Common Errors

To be efficient, edit to find and correct grammar and usage mistakes *after* you revise your essay. That way, you will not spend time correcting errors in sentences that you ultimately change or delete. As a reference to common errors, this appendix can help you edit. However, if you make mistakes often, you should use a handbook and consult a tutor at your campus writing center.

ERROR 1: Sentence Fragments

A *sentence fragment* lacks something required for full sentence status: a subject, all or part of a verb, or a completed idea. To solve the problem, add the missing element. With incomplete-idea fragments, you can often join the fragment to an existing sentence to supply what is missing.

fragment (missing subject) A hundred students protested the choice of commencement speaker. But relented when the administration threatened disciplinary action.

sentence (subject added) A hundred students protested the choice of commencement speaker. But they relented when the administration threatened disciplinary action.

fragment (missing verb part) Several job applicants failed to make a good impression. They chewing gum during their interviews.

sentence (missing verb part added) Several job applicants failed to make a good impression. They were chewing gum during their interviews.

fragment (incomplete idea) Because so many students are in debt. The Office of Student Affairs is offering a credit-management seminar.

sentence (fragment joined to another sentence)   Because so many students are in debt, the Office of Student Affairs is offering a credit-management seminar.

ERROR 2: Run-on Sentences and Comma Splices

A *run-on sentence* occurs when two independent clauses (word groups that can stand as sentences) are written without separation. A *comma splice* occurs when two independent clauses are separated with nothing more than a comma. To solve the problem, separate the independent clauses with a period and capital letter or with a comma and coordinating conjunction (*and, but, or, nor, for, so, yet*) or with a semicolon.

run-on sentence	Hybrid cars are becoming popular they are still expensive.
comma splice	Hybrid cars are becoming popular, they are still expensive.
correct sentence	Hybrid cars are becoming popular. They are still expensive.
correct sentence	Hybrid cars are becoming popular, but they are still expensive.
correct sentence	Hybrid cars are becoming popular; they are still expensive.

ERROR 3: Verb and Pronoun Agreement Errors with Compounds

A *compound* occurs when two or more words or phrases are joined by *and, or, nor, either . . . or,* or *neither . . . nor.*

A. When the parts of the compound are linked by *and,* use a plural verb or pronoun.

plural verb	The small print and fancy font make the document difficult to read.
plural pronoun	Carlotta and Josef spend all their money at the mall.

B. When the parts of the compound begin with *each* or *every,* use a singular verb or pronoun.

singular verb	Each assembly-line worker and each shift manager expects to increase productivity.
singular pronoun	Every bulb and every seedling bloomed in its pot.

C. When plural words are joined by *or, nor, either . . . or,* or *neither . . . nor,* use a plural verb or pronoun.

plural verb	Neither the students nor their teachers enjoy exam week.
plural pronoun	The football players or the basketball players will volunteer their time at the youth center.

D. When plural and singular words are joined by *nor, either . . . or,* or *neither . . . nor,* make the verb or pronoun agree with the nearer word.

singular verb and pronoun	Neither the apples nor the juice <u>tastes</u> as fresh as <u>it</u> should.
plural verb and pronoun	Neither the juice nor the apples <u>taste</u> as fresh as <u>they</u> should.

ERROR 4: Verb and Pronoun Agreement Errors with Indefinite Pronouns

Indefinite pronouns refer in general to a member or members of a group, without specifying particular people, places, items, or ideas.

A. These indefinite pronouns are always singular, so they are used with singular verbs and pronouns:

anybody	everyone	nothing
anyone	everything	one
anything	neither	somebody
each	nobody	someone
either	none	something
everybody	no one	

singular verb	Everybody <u>hates</u> getting stuck in traffic.
singular pronoun	Each boy selected <u>his</u> favorite bat.

B. These indefinite pronouns are plural, so they are used with plural verbs and pronouns:

both   few   many   several

plural verb	Both <u>were</u> uncertain about whether to turn right or left.
plural pronoun	Few of the students remembered <u>their</u> homework.

C. These indefinite pronouns can be either singular or plural, depending on how they are used in the sentence:

all	some	most
any	more	

singular verb and pronoun	Most of the manuscript <u>is</u> still in <u>its</u> binder.
plural verb and pronoun	Most of the potatoes <u>are</u> rotting in <u>their</u> storage bin.

ERROR 5: Verb and Pronoun Agreement Errors with Intervening Words

Words that come between the subject and verb or between the pronoun and its *antecedent* (the word the pronoun substitutes for) do not affect agreement rules.

words between subject and verb   A <u>box</u> of books <u>is</u> on the floor.

words between pronoun and antecedent   The <u>chest</u> of drawers fell on <u>its</u> side.

ERROR 6: Person Shifts

If you use *I, we,* or a noun, do not shift to *you*—unless you mean to address the reader—or you will have a problem called *person shift*.

person shift   People shouldn't crash-diet. <u>You</u> must eat sensibly all the time to lose weight and stay thin.

correct sentence   People shouldn't crash-diet. <u>They</u> must eat sensibly all the time to lose weight and stay thin.

ERROR 7: Unstated Antecedent

The problem of an *unstated* antecedent occurs when the noun to which a pronoun refers (the *antecedent*) is not written. To solve the problem, substitute a noun for the pronoun.

unstated antecedent   When I called the customer service department, <u>they</u> said I would get a refund. (They *has no stated antecedent.*)

correct sentence   When I called the customer service department, the representative said I would get a refund.

unstated antecedent   Stevie is very impulsive. <u>It</u> will get him in trouble one day. (It *has no stated antecedent.*)

correct sentence   Stevie is very impulsive. His impulsiveness will get him in trouble one day.

ERROR 8: Dangling Modifiers

A *dangling modifier* occurs when an opening modifier (a descriptive word or phrase) has no sensible subject to describe. To solve the problem, either rewrite the sentence, adding a subject for the modifier to describe, or rewrite the modifier.

dangling modifier   While checking on the baby, the toast burned. (*Did the toast check on the baby?*)

correct sentence   While checking on the baby, I burned the toast.

correct sentence   While I was checking on the baby, the toast burned.

ERROR 9: Incorrect Apostrophes for Possession

Use apostrophes with nouns and certain indefinite pronouns to show possession according to the following rules.

A. If the noun or indefinite pronoun does not end in *s*, add an apostrophe and an *s*: *the boy's hat; somebody's seat; Clare's question.*

B. If a *singular* noun ends in *s*, add an apostrophe and an *s*: *Carlos's understanding; the business's stock.*

C. If a *plural* noun ends in *s*, add an apostrophe only: *the five governors' summit.*

D. To show joint ownership, use the apostrophe with the last noun: *Michael and Ray's decision.*

E. To show individual ownership, use an apostrophe with every noun: *Michael's and Ray's decisions.*

F. If the word is hyphenated, use an apostrophe with the last element of the word: *my mother-in-law's new job.*

G. Do not use an apostrophe with possessive pronouns (*its, hers, his, ours, yours, theirs, whose*).

incorrect	The glass bowl fell from <u>it's</u> shelf and broke.
correct	The glass bowl fell from <u>its</u> shelf and broke.

ERROR 10: Incorrect Commas

Many rules govern the use of commas; these are some of the most important ones.

A. Use commas before a *coordinating conjunction* (*and, but, or, nor, for, so, yet*) when these words separate *independent clauses* (word groups that can stand as sentences):

> The umpire called a strike, but the coach protested the call.

Do not use a comma when a coordinating conjunction does not separate *two* independent clauses. Here, there is only one independent clause:

> The coach berated the team and ended the practice.

B. Place a comma after an introductory element. An *introductory element* is a word, phrase, or clause that comes before the sentence subject.

introductory word	<u>Sadly</u>, the concert was cancelled.
introductory phrase	<u>In the bright morning sun</u>, I couldn't see the ball.
introductory clause	<u>Before you leave for class</u>, we should talk.

C. Use commas to set off nonessential elements. A *nonessential element* is a word, phrase, or clause that adds meaning but is not necessary for identifying what it refers to.

nonessential   Officer Ellington, who saved the child, is being honored.

essential   The police officer who saved the child is being honored.

ERROR 11: Incorrect Semicolons

A. Use a semicolon to separate *independent clauses* (word groups that can be sentences) *not* joined by a *coordinating conjunction* (*and, but, or, nor, for, so, yet*).

correct   The storm passed; it moved east toward the coast.

incorrect   The storm passed; and it moved east toward the coast.

incorrect   The storm passed; and moved east toward the coast.

B. Use a semicolon before a *conjunctive adverb* (words such as *therefore, furthermore, consequently, however, thus, nonetheless,* and *meanwhile*) that joins independent clauses. Also, place a comma after the conjunctive adverb.

correct   The city council offered businesses tax incentives; therefore, the company decided to relocate downtown.

incorrect   The city council offered businesses tax incentives, therefore, the company decided to relocate downtown.

Do not use a semicolon if the conjunctive adverb does not separate independent clauses.

correct   City council, therefore, offered the business tax incentives.

ERROR 12: Errors with *Who* and *Whom*

Use *who* as a subject. Use *whom* as the object of a verb or as the object of a preposition.

who as subject   Cassie is the only one who understands Vince. (Who is *the subject of the verb* understands.)

whom as object of a verb   The actor, whom the critics adore, won the Oscar for Best Actor. (Whom is *the object of the verb* adore.)

whom as object of a preposition   At whom are you leveling that criticism? (Whom is *the object of the preposition* at.)

ERROR 13: Errors with *Its* and *It's*

Its is a possessive pronoun, so use it to show ownership. *It's* is a contraction meaning *it is* or *it has*.

possessive pronoun   The sandwich slid off its plate.

contraction   It's not too late to enter the contest.

contraction   It's been a year since I quit smoking.

Appendix C
Understanding Plagiarism

Plagiarism occurs if you use another person's ideas, words, manner of expression, or research as if they were your own. There are two kinds of plagiarism: intentional and unintentional.

Intentional plagiarism occurs if you knowingly cheat by turning in someone else's paper, perhaps one purchased on the Internet or "borrowed" from a friend as your own work; it also occurs if you deliberately copy one or more passages from a source and present them as your own work. Because intentional plagiarism is deliberately dishonest—and in some cases illegal—it is a very serious offense with serious consequences, which may include academic suspension. Plagiarizing copyrighted material can lead to legal prosecution.

Unintentional plagiarism occurs if you do not paraphrase, summarize, or quote correctly, or if you fail to provide parenthetical text citations and works cited entries, as explained in Chapters 4 and 15. Even if unintentional, plagiarism is a serious offense. After all, other authors work hard to research, write, and publish their material, and you must treat their work with respect and acknowledge when you are using it in your own paper.

AVOIDING INTENTIONAL PLAGIARISM

Sometimes students think they can plagiarize and escape detection, but the odds of that are slim. Almost always, instructors can detect plagiarism because they know you, they know your writing style and ability, and they understand research. Remember, avoiding intentional plagiarism is easy:

- Do not turn in someone else's paper as your own.
- Never copy or paste material into your paper without following all the conventions for handling source material.

AVOIDING UNINTENTIONAL PLAGIARISM

To avoid unintentional plagiarism, do the following:

- Introduce the source material with the name of the author and/or source. (See pages 706–707.)
- Provide an in-text text citation for the source material. (See page 706.)
- Provide a Works Cited page. (See page 716.)
- When you research, take notes carefully, distinguishing between your ideas and the words and ideas from sources by placing exact words in quotation marks and marking each paraphrase or summary. As part of these notes, write out all the information you will need for your parenthetical citations and works cited entries.

Including Points of Common Knowledge

You do not have to document information that is common knowledge. *Common knowledge* includes well-known facts, undisputed historical events, common sayings, and generally agreed upon information. Here are some examples of common knowledge—information that does *not* require documentation:

- Abraham Lincoln was assassinated by John Wilkes Booth.
- Plants bend toward the sun.
- It's always darkest before the dawn.
- In general, the National Rifle Association opposes gun control legislation.

If you are unsure whether to document a point, err on the side of caution. It is better to document too much than to document too little and unintentionally plagiarize as a result. Of course, your instructor can advise you when you are unsure.

Avoiding Plagiarism with Paraphrases

In Chapter 4, you learned that to **paraphrase,** you rewrite an author's ideas in your own words and style. To avoid plagiarism when you paraphrase, remember the following points, explained in detail in Chapter 4:

- Change the expression and wording of the source material so it is in your style.
- Do not add ideas not in the source or change the author's meaning.
- If you use the author's distinctive phrasing, put the words in quotation marks.

To illustrate these points, here are examples of acceptable and unacceptable paraphrases.

source	An economic system does not exist in a vacuum. Someone or some group makes important decisions about how to use resources and how to allocate goods, whether it be a tribal chief or a parliament or a dictator. A cultural universal common to all economic systems, then, is the exercise of power and authority.

–Richard T. Shaefer, *Sociology*, p. 423

acceptable paraphrase	One sociologist has noted that in every economy, one or more persons determine the use and distribution of resources and goods. Thus, economic systems do not function without the use of power (Shaefer 423).

The paraphrase is acceptable for the following reasons:

- The wording and style are changed.
- The meaning has not been added or altered.

unacceptable paraphrase	One sociologist has noted that an economic system does not exist alone. Anyone can make decisions about how to use and distribute resources and allocate goods. Thus, power and authority are a cultural universal in all economies. This fact holds true regardless of whether the power or authority is benign or cruel (Shaefer 423).

The paraphrase is unacceptable for the following reasons:

- The writing style is too similar to that of the writer in the source.
- The second sentence alters the meaning of the source material, and the last sentence includes an idea that does not directly appear in the source.

Avoiding Plagiarism with Quotations

In Chapter 4, you learned that **quotations** reproduce the exact words from a source. To avoid plagiarism when you quote, remember the following points, explained in detail in Chapter 4:

- Use quotation marks when you include exact words from a source.
- Quote accurately, using ellipses for omissions and brackets for additions.
- Use single quotation marks for quotation marks that appear within a quotation.
- Set off long quotations.

Compare the following acceptable and unacceptable quotations from the Shaefer source above.

acceptable quotation	According to Shaefer, "Someone or some group makes important decisions about how to use resources and how to allocate goods. . . . A cultural universal common to all economic systems, then, is the exercise of power and authority" (423).

The quotation is acceptable for the following reasons:

- It has an introduction and parenthetical citation.
- The quote is accurate.
- Exact words appear in quotation marks.
- Ellipses appear to mark words left out.

unacceptable quotation	According to Shaefer, "Someone makes important decisions about using resources and how to allocate goods. A cultural universal common to all economic systems is the exercise of power and authority" (423).

The quotation is unacceptable for the following reasons:

- The quote is not accurate.
- Words have been left out and changed without using ellipses and brackets.

You can use the following checklist to be sure you have avoided unintentional plagiarism. If you need help, refer to the pages in parentheses.

Plagiarism Checklist

1. _____ You have documented all ideas and opinions that are not yours and all facts and statistics that are not common knowledge. (page 706)

2. _____ You have an in-text citation for each paraphrase, summary, and quotation. (page 706)

3. _____ You have a Works Cited page at the end of your paper that lists every source from which you paraphrased, summarized, or quoted. Each entry is in the correct form. (page 707)

4. _____ You have used quotation marks around exact words taken from sources. (page 108)

5. _____ You have quoted accurately, using ellipses if you omitted words and brackets if you added them. (page 108)

6. _____ You have paraphrased and summarized accurately, without adding or altering meaning. (page 106)

7. _____ Your paraphrases and summaries are written in your own wording and style. (page 106)

TEXT CREDITS

Chapter 1 p. 5 From William G Nickels, James McHugh, and Susan McHugh, in *Understanding Business*, 7th ed., p. 19. Copyright © 2004 by The McGraw-Hill Companies. Reprinted with permission of The McGraw-Hill Companies. **pp. 13–15** Rose del Castillo Guibault, "Americanization is Tough on 'Macho'." Copyright © 1996 by Rose del Castillo Guibault. Reprinted by permission of the author. **p. 18 graph** From Thomas Patterson, *We the People*, 8th ed., Fig. 6.1. Copyright © 2009 by The McGraw-Hill Companies, Inc. Reprinted with permission of The McGraw-Hill Companies. **pp. 23–27** Mortimer Adler, "How to Mark a Book" was originally published in the *Saturday Review*, 1940. Reprinted by permission of the Estate of Mortimer Adler.

Chapter 2 pp. 55–57 Gail Godwin, "The Watcher at the Gates" in *The New York Times*, January 9, 1997. Reprinted by permission of the author.

Chapter 3 pp. 87–88 Christopher Buckley, "College Essay" in *The New Yorker*, November 28, 2005. Reprinted by permission of the author.

Chapter 4 pp. 115–116 Alan Brinkley, "The Mall" from *American History: A Survey*, 13th ed., Vol. II, pp. 876–877. Copyright © 2009 by The McGraw-Hill Companies, Inc. Reprinted with permission of The McGraw-Hill Companies.

Chapter 5 pp. 140–142 N. Scott Momaday, "The Homestead on Rainy Mountain Creek" from *The Man Made of Words*. Copyright © 1997 by N. Scott Momaday. Reprinted by permission of the author. **pp. 145–147** "World at Dawn: The Pleasure of Life Rekindled" from *Dawn Light: Dancing with Cranes and Other Ways to Start the Day* by Diane Ackerman. Copyright © 2009 by Diane Ackerman. Used by permission of W.W. Norton & Company, Inc. **pp. 150–153** "The Deer of Providencia" from *Teaching a Stone to Talk: Expeditions and Encounters* by Annie Dillard. Copyright © 1982 by Annie Dillard. Reprinted by permission of HarperCollins Publishers. **pp. 156–161** "Struck by Lightning," Chapter 1 and Chapter 2 from *A Match To The Heart* by Gretel Ehrlich. Copyright © 1994 by Gretel Ehrlich. Used by permission of Viking Penguin, a division of Penguin Group (USA) Inc. **pp. 164–172** Barry Corbet, "Embedded." Copyright © 2007 Estate of Barry Corbet. Originally published in *AARP The Magazine*,

January/February 2007. Reprinted by permission of the Estate of Barry Corbet. **p. 176** "The Vietnam Wall" from *The Lime Orchard Woman* by Alberto Riós. Copyright © 1988 by Alberto Riós. Published by The Sheep Meadow Press. Reprinted by permission of the author.

Chapter 6 pp. 199–200 Chris Abani, "The Lottery" in *The New York Times Magazine*, February 1, 2004. Copyright © 2004 by Chris Abani. Reprinted by permission of the author. **pp. 203–204** "Salvation" from *The Big Sea* by Langston Hughes. Copyright © 1940 by Langston Hughes, renewed 1968 by Arna Bontemps and George Houston Bass. Reprinted by permission of Hill and Wang, a division of Farrar, Straus & Giroux, LLC **pp. 207–209** Shawn Macomber, "Stripping Away Free Expression" in *Reason* magazine, July, 2009. Reprinted with permission from *Reason* magazine and Reason.com. **pp. 212–214** John Schwartz, "The Poncho Bearer" in *The New York Times*, January 7, 2007. Copyright © 2007 by The New York Times. All rights reserved. Used by permission. **pp. 217–220** Natalie Kusz, "Ring Leader." Originally published in *Allure*, February 1996. All rights reserved. Copyright © 1996 by Natalie Kusz. Reprinted by permission of Brandt & Hochman Literary Agents, Inc. **pp. 223–228** "The View of Me from Mars" from *Dreams of Distant Lives* by Lee K. Abbott. Copyright © 1987 by Lee K. Abbott. Reprinted by permission of the author.

Chapter 7 pp. 250–253 Cullen Murphy, "Lifosuction" in *The Atlantic Monthly*, February 2002. Copyright © 2002 Cullen Murphy. Reprinted by permission of the author. **pp. 255–259** Jennifer Saranow, "The Snoop Next Door" in *The Wall Street Journal*, January 12, 2007, p. W1. Copyright © 2007 by Dow Jones & Company, Inc. Reproduced with permission of Dow Jones & Company, Inc. in the format textbook via Copyright Clearance Center. **pp. 262–267** "On Being the Target of Discrimination" by Ralph Ellison. Copyright © 1989 by Ralph Ellison from *The Collected Essays of Ralph Ellison* by Ralph Ellison, edited by John F. Callahan. Used by permission of Modern Library, a division of Random House, Inc. **pp. 270–272** Jeffrey Kluger, "The Art of Simplexity" in *Time* magazine, June 12, 2008. Copyright © 2008 Time Inc. All rights reserved. Reprinted by permission. **pp. 275–281** "Untouchables" from *Rachel and Her Children: Homeless Families in America* by Jonathan Kozol. Copyright © 1988

TEXT CREDITS

by Jonathan Kozol. Used by permission of Crown Publishers, a division of Random House, Inc. **pp. 284–286** "Reunion" from *The Stories of John Cheever* by John Cheever. Copyright © 1978 by John Cheever. Used by permission of Alfred A. Knopf, a division of Random House, Inc.

Chapter 8 pp. 307–309 "Science: It's Just Not Fair" from "Weird Science" in *Dave Barry is Not Taking this Sitting Down!* by Dave Barry. Copyright © 2000 by Dave Barry. Used by permission of Crown Publishers, a division of Random House, Inc. **pp. 311–315** Diana Cole, "Don't Just Stand There" in *The New York Times*, April 16, 1989. Reprinted by permission of the author. **pp. 317–322** "In the Kitchen" from *Colored People: A Memoir* by Henry Louis Gates, Jr. Copyright © 1994 by Henry Louis Gates, Jr. Used by permission of Alfred A. Knopf, a division of Random House, Inc. **pp. 325–330** Timothy Harper, "Shoot to Kill" was first published in *The Atlantic Monthly*. Copyright © 2000 by Timothy Harper. Reprinted by permission of the author. **pp. 333–339** "Behind the Form-aldehyde Curtain" from *The American Way of Death* by Jessica Mitford. Reprinted by permission of the Estate of Jessica Mitford. Copyright © 1963, 1978 by Jessica Mitford. All rights reserved. **p. 342** "The Traveling Onion" from *Yellow Gloves* by Naomi Shihab Nye. Copyright © 1986 by Naomi Shihab Nye. Reprinted by permission of the author.

Chapter 9 p. 364 Mental transformation line art: From *Persepolis 2: The Story of a Return* by Marjane Satrapi, translated by Anjali Singh. Translation copyright © 2004 by Anjali Singh. Used by permission of Pantheon Books, a division of Random House, Inc. **pp. 367–370** Bruce Catton, "Grant and Lee: A Study in Contrasts" from *The American Story*. Copyright © 1956 by the U.S. Capitol Historical Society. All rights reserved. Reprinted with permission. **pp. 373–376** "Never Do that to a Book" from *Ex Libris: Confessions of a Common Reader* by Anne Fadiman. Copyright © 1998 by Anne Fadiman. Reprinted by permission of Farrar, Straus & Giroux, LLC. **pp. 379–382** "Am I Blue?" from *Living by the Word: Selected Writings 1973–1987* by Alice Walker. Copyright © 1986 by Alice Walker. Reprinted by permission of Houghton Mifflin Harcourt Publishing Company. **pp. 385–390** Deborah Siegel, "The New Trophy Wife" in *Psychology Today*, January 1, 2004. Reprinted with permission from *Psychology Today* magazine.

Copyright © 2004 Sussex Publishers LLC. **pp. 393–399** Deborah Tannen, "Squeaky Wheels and Protruding Nails: Direct and Indirect Speech" from "Indirectness at Work" in *The New York Times Magazine*, August 28, 1994. Copyright © 1994 Deborah Tannen. Reprinted by permission of the author. This article is adapted in part from the author's book, *Talking from 9 to 5* (Quill, 1994). **pp. 402–405** Arthur Campa, "Anglo vs. Chicano: Why?" in *Western Review*, Vol. IX, Spring 1972. Reprinted by permission of *Western Review: A Journal of the Humanities*, Western New Mexico University, Silver City, NM. **p. 408** "Fire and Ice" from *The Poetry of Robert Frost*, edited by Edward Connery Lathem. Copyright © 1923, 1969 by Henry Holt and Company. Copyright 1951 by Robert Frost. Reprinted by permission of Henry Holt and Company, LLC.

Chapter 10 pp. 428–429 Andrew Sullivan, "Why the M Word Matters to Me" in *Time*, February 8, 2004. Copyright © 2004, Time, Inc. All rights reserved. Reprinted by permission. **pp. 432–434** Brad Stone, "Web of Risks" in *Newsweek* August 21, 2006. Magazine issue. Copyright © 2006 News-week, Inc. All rights reserved. Reprinted by permission. **pp. 437–439** James Surowiecki, "Paying to Play" in *The New Yorker*, July 12 & 19, 2004. Copyright © 2004 by James Surowiecki. Reprinted by permission of the author. **pp. 442–445** Carlin Flora, "The Beguiling Truth About Beauty" in *Psychology Today*, May 1, 2006. Reprinted with permission from *Psychology Today* magazine. Copyright © 2006 Sussex Publishers LLC. **pp. 448–451** Brent Staples, "Just Walk On By: A Black Man Ponders His Power to Alter Public Space." Copyright © 1986 by Brent Staples. Reprinted by permission of the author. Brent Staples writes for *The New York Times* and is author of the memoir *Parallel Time: Growing Up in Black and White*. **pp. 454–459** Dorothy Siegel, "What is Behind the Growth of Violence on College Campuses?" Reprinted with permission. **pp. 461–467** "Lullaby" from *Storyteller* by Leslie Marmon Silko. Copyright © 1981 by Leslie Marmon Silko. Published by Seaver Books, New York, NY. Reprinted by special arrangement with Skyhorse Publishing.

Chapter 11 pp. 488–490 "White Lies" from *Lying: Moral Choice in Public and Private Life* by Sissela Bok. Copyright © 1978 by Sissela Bok. Used by permission of Pantheon Books, a division of Random House, Inc. **pp. 492–494** Martin Luther King, Jr., "The Ways of Meeting Oppression" from *Stride Toward Freedom* by Martin Luther King, Jr. Copyright ©1991 Martin Luther King, Jr., copyright renewed 1963 Coretta Scott King. Reprinted by arrangement with The Heirs to the Estate of Martin Luther King, Jr., c/o Writer's House as agent for the proprietor, New York NY. **pp. 497–501** Bill Bunn, "What's Really In Your Shampoo?" first appeared in Salon.com, at http://www.Salon.com, August 13, 2009. An online version remains in the Salon archives. Reprinted with permission. **pp. 504–506** "Globalization: The Super-Story" from "Prologue: The Super-Story" in *Longitudes and Attitudes: Exploring the World After September 11* by Thomas L. Friedman. Copyright © 2002 by Thomas L. Friedman. Reprinted by permission of Farrar, Straus & Giroux, LLC. **pp. 509–515** William K. Zinsser, "College Pressures" in *Blair & Ketchum's Country Journal*, April 1979. Copyright © 1979 by William K. Zinsser. Reprinted by permission of the author. **p. 518** "Do Not Go Gentle into That Good Night" by Dylan Thomas from *The Poems of Dylan Thomas.* Copyright © 1952 by Dylan Thomas. Reprinted by permission of New Directions Publishing Corporation.

Chapter 12 pp. 536–539 Stanley Fish, "Conspiracy Theories 101" in the Opinion/Editorial page of *The New York Times*, July 23, 2006. Copyright © 2006 by The New York Times. All rights reserved. Used by permission. **pp. 541–543** Jonathan Rauch, "Caring For Your Introvert." Copyright © 2003 by Jonathan Rauch. First published in *The Atlantic Monthly,* March 2003. Reprinted by permission of the author. **pp. 546–549** Jo Goodwin Parker, "What is Poverty?" from *America's Other Children: Public Schools Outside Suburbia* by George Henderson. Copyright © 1971 University of Oklahoma Press, Norman. Reprinted with permission of the publisher. All rights reserved. **pp. 551–559** Malcolm Gladwell, "The Art of Failure" in *The New Yorker,* August 21–28, 2001. Copyright © 2001 by Malcolm Gladwell. Reprinted by permission of the author. Malcolm Gladwell is a staff writer for *The New Yorker* magazine. **pp. 562–563** "I Remember Masa" from *Weedee Peepo* by Jose Antonio Burciaga. Reprinted with permission from the publisher, UT-Pan American Press, The University of Texas-Pan American. **p. 566** "Immigrants" is reprinted with permission from the publisher of *Borders* by Pat Mora. Copyright © 1986 Arte Publico Press, University of Houston.

Chapter 13 pp. 592–593 "Financial Incentives for Organ Donation," National Kidney Foundation Position Paper. Reprinted with permission from The National Kidney Foundation. **pp. 595–597** Sally Satel, "The Case for Paying Organ Donors" in *The Wall Street Journal,* October 18, 2009. Reprinted by permission of the author, Sally Satel, Resident Scholar, American Enterprise Institute. **pp. 599–601** "Little Adult Criminals" in the Editorial Page of *The New York Times,* May 23, 2001. Copyright © 2001 by The New York Times Company. All rights reserved. Used by permission. **pp. 602–606** Laurence Steinberg, "Should Juvenile Offenders Be Tried as Adults?" in *USA Today Magazine,* January 2001. Copyright © 2001 by The Society for the Advancement of Education. Reprinted with permission. **pp. 608–611** Linda Collier, "Adult Crime, Adult Time: Outdated Juvenile Laws Thwart Justice." Copyright © 1988 by Linda J. Collier. Reprinted by permission of the author. **pp. 613–619** Timothy Roche and Amanda Bower, "Young Voices from the Cell" in *Time,* May 20, 2001. Copyright © 2001, Time Inc. All rights reserved. Reprinted by permission. **pp. 622–625** Cinnamon Stillwell, "Mob Rule on College Campuses" in *San Francisco Chronicle* on SFGate.com. Copyright © 2007 by San Francisco Chronicle. Reproduced with permission of San Francisco Chronicle in the format textbook via Copyright Clearance Center. **pp. 627–630** Charles R. Lawrence III, "The Debate Over Placing Limits on Racist Speech Must Not Ignore the Damage it Does to Victims" in *The Chronicle of Higher Education,* October 25, 1989. Copyright © 1989 by Charles R. Lawrence, III. Reprinted by permission of the author. **pp. 632–637** Harvey A. Silverglate and Greg Lukianoff, "Speech Codes: Alive and Well at Colleges" in *The Chronicle of Higher Education,* 2003. Reprinted by permission of the authors. **pp. 639–644** Howard Wasserman, "Fan Profanity," September 25, 2004. Appeared on First Amendment Center Online, http://www.firstamendmentcenter.org. Reprinted by permission of the author. **pp. 646–649** Robert M. O'Neil, "What Limits Should Campus Networks Place on Pornography?" in *The Chronicle of Higher Education,* 2003. Reprinted by permission of the author.

Chapter 14 pp. 660–663 Elizabeth Svoboda, "Field Guide to the Pack Rat: Closet Cases" in *Psychology Today,* January 1, 2009. Reprinted with permission from *Psychology Today* magazine. Copyright © 2009 Sussex Publishers LLC. **pp. 665–669** "A Hanging" from *Shooting an Elephant and Other Essays* by George Orwell. Copyright © 1931 by George Orwell, 1950 by Sonia Brownell Orwell and renewed 1978 by Sonia Pitt-Rivers. Reprinted by permission of Houghton Mifflin Harcourt Publishing Company. **pp. 672–674** "Complexion" from *Hunger of Memory* by Richard Rodriguez. Copyright © 1982 by Richard Rodriguez. Reprinted by permission of Georges Borchardt, Inc. on behalf of the author. **pp. 677–682** Pagan Kennedy, "One Room, 3000 Brains" in *The Boston Globe,* June 2004. Reprinted by permission of the author. **pp. 685–688** Esther Thorson, "Dissect an Ad." Copyright © 1996 by Esther Thorson. Reprinted by permission of the author. **pp. 691–696** "Once More to the Lake" from *One Man's Meat* by E.B. White. Text copyright © 1941 by E.B. White. Copyright renewed. Reprinted by permission of Tilbury House Publishers, Gardiner, Maine.

Photo Credits:

Chapter 1 p. 2 © Superstock; **p. 19** Lewis Hine, Courtesy of the U.S. National Archives and Records Administration; **p. 21** Doug Menuez @ Radical Media, Courtesy State Farm Insurance.

Chapter 2 p. 28 Creatas/JupiterImages.

Chapter 3 p. 58 First draft of *All the President's Men* from The Watergate Papers of Woodward & Bernstein collection at the Harry Ransom Humanities Research Center, The University of Texas at Austin. Used with permission; **p. 84** Eon/Danjaq/Sony/The Kobal Collection/Jay Maidment.

Chapter 4 p. 90 © Image Source/Corbis.

Chapter 5 p. 118 © F. Subiros/photocusine/Corbis; **p. 145** © Derek Crow/Bridgeman Art Library/Getty Images; **p. 172** Courtesy of Muffy Moore; **p. 175** © Danita Delimont/Alamy.

Chapter 6 p. 180 © AP Photo/Tsugufumi Matsumoto; **p. 208** © AP Photo/Keith Srakocic; **p. 214** © The New York Times/Redux Pictures; **p. 230** © Royalty-Free/Corbis.

Chapter 7 p. 232 © Siri Stafford/Lifesize/Getty Images; **p. 252** © Greg Clarke; **p. 256** © Ann Johansson; **p. 289** © Elliott Erwitt/Magnum Photos.

Chapter 8 p. 306 © Bo Bridges Photography; **p. 326** © AP Photo/Ed Andrieski; **p. 346** Courtesy Lexmark International.

Chapter 9 p. 348 © Nation Wong/zefa/Corbis; **p. 366** Marvel/Sony Pictures/The Kobal Collection/Melissa Moseley; **p. 369L** © NARA; **p. 368R** Courtesy of the Library of Congress, LC-USZ61–903; **p. 411L** © Corbis; **p. 411R** © Fred Mullane/New-Sport/Corbis.

Chapter 10 p. 412 TM and Copyright © 20th Century Fox Film Corp. All rights reserved./Courtesy Everett Collection; **p. 427** Used with permission. © 2004 Mothers Against Drunk Driving. All rights reserved. www.madd.org; **p. 470** © H. Armstrong Roberts/Corbis.

Chapter 11 p. 487 Deborah Samuel Photography; **p. 498** © Nigel Reed QEDimages/Alamy.

Chapter 12 p. 535 © Jack Hollingsworth/Getty Images; **p. 537** © mirko ilic corp; **p. 569** © The McGraw-Hill Companies, Inc./John Flournoy, photographer.

Chapter 13 p. 600 © AP Photo/Gary I. Rothstein; **p. 610** © Don Murray/ZUMA; **p. 616** © AP Photo/Don Gill.

Chapter 14 p. 652 Historic Costume and Textile Museum, Department of Apparel, Textiles, and Interior Design, Kansas State University, Object #1987.825.1; **p. 661** © VEER Rogovin/Getty Images; **p. 669** © Esbin-Anderson/The Image Works; **p. 680** Rose Lincoln, Harvard News Office; **p. 695** Reso-Diaphor Images/Index Stock Imagery, Inc.

This glossary provides definitions of the terms set in boldface throughout the text and gives the pages where the terms are first used. Words in small capital letters are defined elsewhere in the glossary.

alternating pattern   In COMPARISON-CONTRAST, the arrangement of detail whereby a point is made for one subject and then for the other subject until all points have been made for both subjects.   page 305 (See also BLOCK PATTERN.)

analogy   A comparison of two elements from different categories in order to shed light on one or both elements. For example, comparing marriage to roller-coaster ride is an analogy, as is comparing divorce to a medieval seige.   page 354

anecdote   A brief NARRATION often used as an example.   page 183

argumentation   The use of reason and logic to persuade a reader to agree with an assertion. Argumentation employs compelling evidence and counters significant objections to the writer's assertion to earn the reader's agreement.   page 357 (See also PERSUASION.)

audience   The readers for a particular piece of writing. For example, the audience for your campus newspaper is the students, faculty, staff, and administration of your college. Different audiences have different characteristics, and writers must be aware of those characteristics to meet the needs of their readers.   page 31

block pattern   In COMPARISON-CONTRAST, the arrangement of detail by first presenting all the points about one subject and then all the points about the second subject.   page 355 (See also ALTERNATING PATTERN.)

body paragraph   A paragraph composed of a TOPIC SENTENCE that gives a main idea and SUPPORTING DETAILS that develop that idea. A body paragraph helps support the THESIS.   page 62

causal chain   In CAUSE-AND-EFFECT ANALYSIS, a sequence that occurs when a cause leads to an effect, and that effect becomes a cause leading to another effect, and so on.   page 417

cause-and-effect analysis   A PATTERN OF DEVELOPMENT that examines the reasons for an event (causes), the results of an event (effects), or both.   page 413

chronological order   The arrangement of details in an essay according to a time sequence, usually beginning with the first event and proceeding to the second and subsequent events.   page 47 (See also FLASHBACK.)

classification   A PATTERN OF DEVELOPMENT that groups items into related categories according to a specific principle. In classification, items that share characteristics are grouped together.   page 473 (See also DIVISION.)

cliché   An overused expression, such as "dumb as dirt."   page 128

coherence   The smooth connection of SUPPORTING DETAILS and BODY PARAGRAPHS in a clear, understandable way. To achieve coherence, writers use transitions, logical ordering of ideas, and repetition of keywords and ideas to show how ideas relate to each other.   page 65

comparison-contrast   A PATTERN OF DEVELOPMENT that notes the similarities and/or differences between two subjects. Comparison notes similarities, and contrast notes differences.   page 349

conclusion The final sentences or paragraph of an essay, meant to provide resolution and closure. An effective conclusion creates a satisfying ending and does not close abruptly.   page 70

context See WRITING CONTEXT.

critical-analysis A type of writing that gives one or more conclusions drawn about a text after analyzing and assessing it during CRITICAL READING.   page 97

critical reading Analyzing and assessing written text to draw conclusions about its significance, meaning, implications, reliability, and connections to other ideas.   page 4

deduction A form of reasoning that moves from the general to the specific, from a GENERALIZATION (the major premise) to a specific case (the minor premise) to a conclusion.   page 582 (See also INDUCTION.)

definition A PATTERN OF DEVELOPMENT that gives the meaning of a term.   page 523   (See also EXTENDED DEFINITION, FORMAL DEFINITION, and STIPULATIVE DEFINITION.)

description A PATTERN OF DEVELOPMENT that uses words to create mental images for the reader.   page 120 (See also EXPRESSIVE DETAILS and OBJECTIVE DETAILS.)

direct quotation The reproduction of exact spoken or written words.   pages 108 and 186

directional process analysis A form of PROCESS ANALYSIS that gives the steps in a procedure so the reader can perform it.   page 291 (See also EXPLANATORY PROCESS ANALYSIS.)

division A PATTERN OF DEVELOPMENT that breaks an entity down into its parts.   page 473 (See also CLASSIFICATION.)

documentation The formal crediting of borrowed material (PARAPHRASE and DIRECT QUOTATION) by noting the source of the borrowing according to conventions of a particular discipline. Papers written in a literature or composition class are often documented according to the conventions of the Modern Language Association (MLA).   page 706

dominant impression In DESCRIPTION, the quality the descriptive details are meant to convey.   page 124

editing The process of finding and correcting errors in grammar, usage, punctuation, capitalization, and spelling.   page 81

errors in logic See LOGIC, ERRORS IN.

ethos One of three elements of a successful argument. (The other two elements are LOGOS and PATHOS.) Ethos refers to establishing the reliability and trustworthiness of the writer of an argument.   page 577

euphemism A polite or indirect substitute for an unpleasant expression. For example, "pass away" is a euphemism for "die."   page 340

exemplification A PATTERN OF DEVELOPMENT that uses specific instances (examples) to clarify a point, add interest, or persuade.   page 234 (See also HYPOTHETICAL EXAMPLE.)

explanatory process analysis A form of PROCESS ANALYSIS that explains how something works, how it is made, or how it is done. The procedure explained is not meant to be carried out by the reader.   page 292 (See also DIRECTIONAL PROCESS ANALYSIS.)

expressive details   In DESCRIPTION, points that give a subjective or emotional view of what is being described.   page 124 (See also OBJECTIVE DETAILS.)

extended definition   A form of DEFINITION in which the writer goes beyond the literal meaning of a word to give the significance, private meanings, and personal experiences associated with that word.   page 524 (See also FORMAL DEFINITION and STIPULATIVE DEFINITION.)

fact   A statement that can be proven or that has been proven. For example, it is a fact that plants manufacture oxygen from carbon dioxide.   page 4 (See also OPINION.)

first draft   A writer's initial effort to get ideas down in essay form. A first draft is usually very rough and in need of REVISION.   page 59

flashback   A form of CHRONOLOGICAL ORDER that involves moving from one point in time to a more distant point in the past and back again.   page 188

formal definition   A definition that states the term to be defined, its class, and how it differs from other members of the class—for example, "an antibiotic is a type of drug that attacks bacteria."   page 523 (See also DEFINITION, EXTENDED DEFINITION, and STIPULATIVE DEFINITION.)

generalization   A broad statement that asserts that something is true in most cases or in every case.   page 63 (See also DEDUCTION.)

hypothetical example   An illustration based on something that *could* happen.   page 238 (See also EXEMPLIFICATION.)

induction   A form of reasoning that moves from specific evidence to a general conclusion.   page 581 (See also DEDUCTION and INFERENCE.)

inference   A conclusion drawn on the basis of what a speaker or writer suggests, rather than what is specifically stated. In INDUCTION, an inference is the conclusion drawn; it is usually not certain beyond a doubt.   pages 5 and 582

intentional plagiarism   Knowingly submitting someone else's work as one's own.   page 729 (See also PLAGIARISM.)

introduction   One or more paragraphs that open an essay. The introduction is meant to engage a reader's interest; many times the introduction also presents the THESIS.   page 60

irony   See SITUATIONAL IRONY and VERBAL IRONY.

journalist's questions   Who? What? When? Where? Why? How? In NARRATION, the answers form much of the supporting detail.   page 185

learning log   A journal used by students to reflect on the content of their courses, record questions, and note how information relates to other courses.   page 113

logic, errors in   Forms of faulty reasoning that lead a person to a false conclusion.   page 7

logos   One of the three elements of a successful argument. (The other elements are ETHOS and PATHOS.) Logos refers to sound reasoning, facts, evidence, statistics, and authoritative statements used to back up an assertion.   page 575 (See also LOGIC, ERRORS IN.)

metaphor   An implied comparison made without using the words *like* or *as*—for example, "the play's opening act was a train wreck."   page 129

narration   A PATTERN OF DEVELOPMENT that involves telling a story.   page 181

objective details   In DESCRIPTION, points that give a factual, unemotional picture of what is described.   page 124 (See also EXPRESSIVE DETAILS.)

opinion   A statement of a person's judgment, interpretation, or belief. Unlike a FACT, an opinion cannot be proven. For example, it is an opinion that the current movie rating system is inadequate.   page 4

paraphrase   The restatement of an author's written ideas in one's own words and style. Paraphrases are used in essays and research papers that draw on sources.   pages 106 and 705

pathos   One of the three elements of a successful argument. (The other elements are LOGOS and ETHOS.) Pathos refers to the appeal to emotions, attitudes, beliefs, and values.   page 577

patterns of development   Ways to think and write about a topic. The patterns of development include DESCRIPTION, NARRATION, EXEMPLIFICATION, PROCESS ANALYSIS, COMPARISON-CONTRAST, CAUSE-AND-EFFECT ANALYSIS, CLASSIFICATION-DIVISION, and DEFINITION.   page 52

persuasion   Uses appeals to emotions, values, and beliefs to convince a reader to act a particular way.   page 571 (See also ARGUMENTATION.)

plagiarism   A form of academic dishonesty that occurs when a person submits another's words, ideas, or work as his or her own, or when a person fails to provide DOCUMENTATION of borrowed material.   pages 112 and 729 (See also INTENTIONAL PLAGIARISM and UNINTENTIONAL PLAGIARISM.)

process analysis   A PATTERN OF DEVELOPMENT that explains how something is made, how something is done, or how something works.   page 291 (See also DIRECTIONAL PROCESS ANALYSIS and EXPLANATORY PROCESS ANALYSIS.)

progressive order   The arrangement of details from the least important or compelling points to the most important or compelling points.   page 47

purpose   The reason a person writes, the goal the writer hopes to achieve. A writer's purpose can be to entertain, to express feelings or relate experience, to inform, and/or to persuade.   page 30

quotation   See DIRECT QUOTATION.

revising   The process of evaluating and making changes in a draft's content, organization, and expression of ideas in order to improve it. The revision process can involve writing multiple drafts.   page 75

role   The way the writer presents himself or herself. For example, a writer can assume the role of a student, parent, average reader, concerned citizen, voter, and so forth.   page 33

sensory detail   DESCRIPTION that appeals to any of the five senses (sight, sound, taste, smell, touch).   page 125 (See also EXPRESSIVE DETAILS and OBJECTIVE DETAILS.)

simile   A comparison made using the word *like* or the word *as*—for example, "the overheated radiator spewed water like a geyser."   page 128

situational irony   When something happens that runs counter to what is expected to happen—for example, a person swerving to avoid hitting a car only to hit a track.   page 205 (See also VERBAL IRONY.)

spatial order   The arrangement of details across space—for example from top to bottom, near to far, front to back, or left to right.   page 47

stipulative definition   Explains a special or unexpected way a term is used—for example: "By spouse, I do not refer merely to the legally married partner. I also refer to a same-sex partner in a committed relationship."   page 523 (See also DEFINITION, EXTENDED DEFINITION, and FORMAL DEFINITION.)

summary   The brief restatement of the main points of a piece of writing in one's own words and style, given without adding or altering meaning.   pages 108 and 705

supporting details   In a BODY PARAGRAPH, all the points made to prove or explain the TOPIC SENTENCE.   page 62

synthesis   The process whereby a person relates new information to previously learned information. Also, the bringing together of material from two or more sources.   pages 6 and 101

thesis   The central point or controlling idea of an essay; the idea that everything else in the essay relates to and that the BODY PARAGRAPHS support.   page 42

tone   The writer's attitude or feeling about the reader or about the subject of the writing. Tone can be neutral, angry, sympathetic, annoyed, and so on. page 69

topic sentence   In a BODY PARAGRAPH, the sentence that expresses the main idea. A topic sentence can be stated or implied.   page 62

unintentional plagiarism   Paraphrasing, quoting, or summarizing incorrectly, or otherwise using source material without correct DOCUMENTATION.   page 729 (See also PLAGIARISM.)

verbal irony   When an author says one thing but really means the opposite. An example of verbal irony is saying "Oh, that's *great!*" (Your tone indicates that something is not great at all.)   page 340 (See also SITUATIONAL IRONY.)

writing context   The combination of the writer's PURPOSE, AUDIENCE, and ROLE. The writing context creates the situation within which a person writes.   page 30

THE PATTERNS

The following patterns of development help writers develop a thesis, support their points, and achieve their purpose for writing:

- **Description** uses words to convey the way something looks, sounds, feels, tastes, and/or smells, so the reader can form a mental picture of what is being described. A travel brochure may describe a Florida beach for a prospective traveler. (See Chapter 5.)

- **Narration** tells a story, including what happened, how it happened, why it happened, where it happened, when it happened, and/or who was involved, in order to make a point. A newspaper article may narrate the account of a bank robbery. (See Chapter 6.)

- **Exemplification** gives one or more examples to clarify or prove the thesis. A magazine article contending that television commercials insult men might include examples of insulting commercials. (See Chapter 7.)

- **Process analysis** explains how something is made or done by presenting the steps in a procedure. A biology textbook's explanation of how plants make oxygen is a process analysis. (See Chapter 8.)

- **Comparison** shows how two things are alike; **contrast** shows how two things are different; comparison–contrast shows both similarities and differences. A history textbook might compare two Civil War generals; a newspaper editorial might contrast two political candidates; a company e-mail might compare and contrast two phone systems under consideration. (See Chapter 9.)

- **Cause-and-effect analysis** explains the causes of an event, the effects of an event, or both the causes and effects of an event. A gardening book might explain the cause of poor yield in a vegetable garden; an economics textbook might explain the effects of inflation; a magazine article might explain the causes and effects of stress. (See Chapter 10.)

- **Classification** groups three or more things into categories according to the items' characteristics. **Division** breaks something down into its parts. An advertising agency's report might classify television viewers according to their viewing habits, or it might analyze the characteristics of a typical viewer. (See Chapter 11.)

- **Definition** explains the meaning of something that is confusing, misunderstood, or unappreciated. A political columnist might define electoral math in a column about who is likely to win a presidential election. (See Chapter 12.)